Lecture Notes in Artificial Intelligence   2417

Subseries of Lecture Notes in Computer Science
Edited by J. G. Carbonell and J. Siekmann

Lecture Notes in Computer Science

Edited by G. Goos, J. Hartmanis, and J. van Leeuwen

T0190056

Springer
Berlin
Heidelberg
New York
Barcelona
Hong Kong
London
Milan
Paris
Tokyo

Mitsuru Ishizuka   Abdul Sattar (Eds.)

PRICAI 2002:
Trends in
Artificial Intelligence

7th Pacific Rim International Conference on Artificial Intelligence
Tokyo, Japan, August 18-22, 2002
Proceedings

 Springer

Series Editors

Jaime G. Carbonell, Carnegie Mellon University, Pittsburgh, PA, USA
Jörg Siekmann, University of Saarland, Saarbrücken, Germany

Volume Editors

Mitsuru Ishizuka
University of Tokyo, School of Information Science and Technology
Department of Information and Communication Engineering
7-3-1 Hongo, Bunkyo-ku, Tokyo 113-8656, Japan
E-mail: ishizuka@miv.t.u-tokyo.ac.jp

Abdul Sattar
Griffith University, School of Information Technology
Knowledge Representation and Reasoning Unit (KRRU)
Faculty of Engineering and Information Technology
PMB 50 Gold Coast Mail Centre
Queensland 9726 Australia
E-mail: a.sattar@gu.edu.au

Cataloging-in-Publication Data applied for

Die Deutsche Bibliothek - CIP-Einheitsaufnahme

Trends in artificial intelligence : proceedings / PRICAI 2002, 7th Pacific
Rim International Conference on Artificial Intelligence, Tokyo, Japan,
August 18 - 22, 2002. Mitsuru Ishizuka ; Abdul Sattar (ed.). - Berlin ;
Heidelberg ; New York ; Barcelona ; Hong Kong ; London ; Milan ; Paris ;
Tokyo : Springer, 2002
  (Lecture notes in computer science ; Vol. 2417 : Lecture notes in
artificial intelligence)
  ISBN 3-540-44038-0

CR Subject Classification (1998): I.2

ISSN 0302-9743
ISBN 3-540-44038-0 Springer-Verlag Berlin Heidelberg New York

Springer-Verlag Berlin Heidelberg New York,
a member of BertelsmannSpringer Science+Business Media GmbH

http://www.springer.de

© Springer-Verlag Berlin Heidelberg 2002
Printed in Germany

Typesetting: Camera-ready by author, data conversion by PTP-Berlin, Stefan Sossna e.K.
Printed on acid-free paper   SPIN: 10873772   06/3142   5 4 3 2 1 0

Preface

The Pacific Rim International Conferences on Artificial Intelligence (PRICAI) are biennial international events. The PRICAI series aims at stimulating research by promoting exchange and cross-fertilization of ideas among different branches of Artificial Intelligence. It also provides a common forum for researchers and practitioners in various fields of AI to exchange new ideas and share their experience.

This volume contains the proceedings of the 7th Pacific Rim International Conference on Artificial Intelligence (PRICAI 2002) held in Tokyo, Japan. PRICAI 2002 received 161 submissions from 25 countries. From these, 57 papers (35%) were accepted for presentation and are included in this volume. Over 30 papers were accepted for poster presentations, and a 1-page abstract for each poster is included in this volume. All submitted papers were refereed by two or more reviewers selected by the Program Committee members. The reviewers' comments were carefully examined and discussed by the members of the Program Committee to ensure fairness and consistency in the selection process.

The papers in this volume give an indication of new trends in Artificial Intelligence. The topics covered include AI Foundations, Knowledge Representation and Reasoning, Constraint Satisfaction, Machine Learning, Knowledge Acquisition and Management, Agents and Their Applications, Neural Networks, Document Analysis and Categorization, Internet/Web Intelligence, Multimedia and Emotion, Intelligent Robots, and Machine Perception.

The technical program comprised two days of workshops and tutorials, followed by paper sessions, invited talks, and special sessions. The invited speakers, Prof. Norman Foo (Univ. New South Wales), Prof. Eduard Hovy (USC/ISI), Prof. Micheal Pazzani (UC Irvine/Adaptiveinfo), Dr. Thomas Rist (DFKI), and Prof. Ryohei Nakatsu (ATR/Kwansei-Gakuin Univ.), are internationally distinguished researchers. We thank them for also preparing papers on their talks. These papers are included in these proceedings.

The success of a conference depends on support and cooperation from many individuals and organizations; PRICAI 2002 was no exception. The PRICAI 2002 conference was sponsored by the Japanese Society for Artificial Intelligence (JSAI), in cooperation with 12 other academic institutes. Support from the National Institute of Informatics (NII), Japan, is also gratefully acknowledged.

We would like to take this opportunity to thank the authors, Program Committee members, reviewers and fellow members of the Conference Committee for their time and effort spent on making PRICAI 2002 a successful and enjoyable conference. Thanks also go to Maurice Pagnucco for coordinating workshops and organizing a special session on workshop summaries, and to Koichi Hori for coordinating tutorials. We also thank the PRICAI steering committee for giving us an opportunity to organize the program of PRICAI 2002.

Finally, we thank Springer-Verlag and its Computer Science Editor, Alfred Hofmann, Erika Siebert-Cole, and Anna Kramer, for efficient assistance in publishing these proceedings of PRICAI 2002 as a volume in its Lecture Notes in Artificial Intelligence series. Also, Junichiro Mori of the University of Tokyo helped us in preparing the files for this volume.

August 2002   Mitsuru Ishizuka
                                                     Abdul Sattar

Organization

PRICAI 2002 was organized by the Japanese Society for Artificial Intelligence (JSAI), and held at the National Center of Science in Tokyo, Japan, August 18–22, 2002. Six workshops also took place jointly with the main PRICAI conference.

Conference Committee

General Chair:
Hozumi Tanaka
(Tokyo Inst. of Tech, Japan)

Organizing Chair:
Takao Terano
(Tsukuba Univ., Japan)

Program Co-chairs:
Mitsuru Ishizuka
(Univ. of Tokyo, Japan)
Abdul Sattar
(Griffith Univ., Australia)

Workshop Chair:
Maurice Pagnucco
(Univ. of New South Wales, Australia)

Tutorial Chair:
Koichi Hori
(Univ. of Tokyo, Japan)

Finance Co-Chairs:
Masaaki Okochi
(IBM Japan)
Fumihiro Maruyama
(Fujitsu Laboratories, Japan)

Publicity Co-chairs:
Hideki Asoh
(AIST, Japan)
Hideaki Takeda
(National Institute of Informatics, Japan)

Local Arrangement Co-chairs:
Katsumi Nitta
(Tokyo Inst. of Tech., Japan)
Hideaki Takeda
(National Institute of Informatics, Japan)

Secretariat:
Procom International, Japan

Program Committee

Hideki Asoh
Keith C.C. Chan
Joongmin Choi
Jim Delgrande
David Dowe
George Ferguson
Scott Goodwin
Hans Guesgen
Shun-Chin Hsu
M. Ishizuka (*Co-chair*)
Boonserm Kijsirikul
Alfred Kobsa
Dekang Lin
Chunnian Liu
John Lloyd
Chee-Kit Looi
Dickson Lukose
Abhaya Nayak
Masayuki Numao

Helmut Prendinger
M. Sasikumar
A. Sattar (*Co-chair*)
Arul Siromoney
Von-Wun Soo
Yasuyuki Sumi
Hideaki Takeda
Takao Terano
Takenobu Tokunaga
Sveta Venkatesh
Wayne Wobcke
Hyun S. Yang
Roland Yap
Wai-Kiang Yeap
Suk I. Yoo
Zaharin Yusoff
Chengqi Zhang
Ming Zhou

Referees

Shotaro Akaho
Takeuchi Akira
James Allen
Azat Arslanov
S. Arunkumar
Hideki Asoh
Mike Bain
Seungryang Bang
Mike Barley
Nadia Bianchi-Berthouze
Adrian Bickerstaffe
Katalin Bimbo
Michael Blumenstein
Pierre Boulos
John Bui
Hyeran Byun
Jiannong Cao
Longbing Cao

Yllias Chali
Cherry Chan
Luca Chittaro
Sung-Bae Cho
P. Chongstitvatana
Greg Collie
Nigel Collier
Joshua Comley
Jirapun Daengdej
James Delgrande
Guozhu Dong
David Dowe
Myrosia Dzikovska
George Ferguson
Leigh Fitzgibbon
Norman Foo
Ada Fu
Li-Chen Fu

Jianfeng Gao
C. U. Garcia
N. Gautham
Patrick Gebhard
Aditya Ghose
Ranadhir Ghosh
Scott Goodwin
Rajeev Gore
Hans Guesgen
Jens Happe
Yoichi Hayashi
Martin Henz
Shoji Hirano
Cheng-Seen Ho
Kahlil Hodgson
Shinichi Honiden
Lucas Hope
Maw-Kae Hor

Chun-Nan Hsu
Shun-Chin Hsu
Joshua Huang
Eva Hudlicka
Aaron Hunter
Kentaro Inui
Kevin Irwig
Takashi Ishikawa
Mitsuru Ishizuka
Takayuki Ito
Koji Iwanuma
Makoto Iwayama
Kiyoshi Izumi
Noriaki Izumi
Margaret Jefferies
Dong Hong Ji
Jesse Jin
Li Jinyan
Murray Jorgensen
A. Kannan
B.C.M. Kao
Harish Karnick
Nobuo Kawaguchi
Shinjiro Kawato
Ed Kazmierczak
Boonserm Kijsirikul
Byungkook Kim
Hojoon Kim
Incheol Kim
Jeonghoon Kim
Jonghwan Kim
Juntae Kim
Minkoo Kim
Svetlana Kiritchenko
Yasuhiko Kitamura
Dong-il Ko
Ming-Tat Ko
Alfred Kobsa
Tang Enya Kong
Sang Hoe Koo
Hyung Joon Kook
Stefan Kopp
Kevin Korb
Olena Kravchuk
Rob Kremer

Yau-Hwang Kuo
Rex Kwok
Peng Lam
Bogju Lee
Eun-seok Lee
Geunbae Lee
Hahn-Ming Lee
Jaeho Lee
Lyndon Lee
Lee Minho
Soowon Lee
Wei Li
Yuefeng Li
Marc Light
Ardissono Liliana
Chih-Jen Lin
Dekang Lin
Feng-Tse Lin
Shun-Shii Lin
Cheng-Yuan Liou
Huan Liu
Jiming Liu
Jyi-shane Liu
Rey-Long Liu
John Lloyd
Ute Loerch
Chee-Kit Looi
Robert Luk
Dickson Lukose
V. Uma Maheswari
Enes Makalic
Hitoshi Matsubara
Shigeo Matsubara
Tomoko Matsui
Yoshio Matsumoto
Yutaka Matsuo
Eric McCreath
K.M. Mehata
Robert Mercer
Alessandro Micarelli
Kyonho Min
David Mitchell
Pabitra Mitra
Satoru Miyano
Takahiro Miyashita

Kavitha Mohanraj
Jun Morimoto
Yoichi Motomura
Noboru Murata
Shiv Nagarajan
Kumiyo Nakakoji
Abhaya Nayak
Eric Neufeld
Jianyun Nie
Kazushi Nishimoto
Kyung-Whan Oh
Sangrok Oh
Hayato Ohwada
Osamu Okada
Takashi Okada
Manabu Okumura
Shigeru Omatsu
Cheng Soon Ong
Mehmet Orgun
Maurice Pagnucco
Wanlin Pang
Patrick Pantel
Jong C. Park
Young-Taek Park
B.V. Pawar
Adrian Pearce
Catherine Pelachaud
Du Peng
Pushkar Piggott
Marie Piron
Yusuf Pisan
Ravi Prakash
Helmut Prendinger
Jefferson Provost
Wayne Pullan
Pat Riddle
Malcolm Ryan
Walid Saba
Santi Saeyor
Sunita Sarawagi
Ichiro Sato
Ken Satoh
Abdul Sattar
Matthias Scheutz
Oliver Schulte

Bart Selman
Kiyoaki Shirai
Arul Siromoney
John Slaney
Tony Smith
Von-Wun Soo
Prem Sreenivasan
Uma Srinivasan
D.K. Subrahmanian
R.K. Subramanian
Masanori Sugimoto
Chuen-Tsai Sun
Einoshin Suzuki
Joe Suzuki
Kazuya Takabatake
Toru Takahashi
Yasufumi Takama
Shiro Takata
Yoshiaki Takata
Hideaki Takeda
Peter Tan
Chularat Tanprasert
Ahmed Tawfik
Kazunori Terada
Takao Terano

Joel Tetreault
T. Theeramunkong
Sylvie Thiebaux
John Thornton
Nuttakorn Thubthong
Kai Ming Ting
Paul Treffner
Andre Trudel
Kwok Ching Tsui
Anthony Tung
Charles Twardy
Akira Utsumi
Al Valdes
Svetha Venkatesh
Brijesh Verma
Bao Vo
Toby Walsh
Huaiqing Wang
Xiaofeng Wang
Ying-Hong Wang
Takashi Washio
Ian Watson
Lu Si Wei
Geoff West
Kay Wiese

Michael Winikoff
Wayne Wobcke
Andrew Wong
Lung-Hsiang Wong
Samuel Wong
Kenji Yamanishi
Hyunseung Yang
Yiyu Yao
Roland Yap
Wai Yeap
Kazutaka Yokota
Ken-ichi Yoshida
Masaharu Yoshioka
Soe-Tsyr Yuan
Zarin Yusof
Byoung-Tak Zhang
Chengqi Zhang
Dongmo Zhang
Xiaolong Zhang
Yan Zhang
Zili Zhang
Jun Zhao
Ning Zhong
Lingzhong Zhou
Ingrid Zukerman

Organizing Committee

Hozumi Tanaka (Tokyo Inst. of Tech)
Takao Terano (Tsukuba Univ.)
Mitsuru Ishizuka (Univ. of Tokyo)
Koichi Hori (Univ. of Tokyo)
Naomichi Sueda (Toshiba)
Masaaki Okochi (IBM Japan)
Norihiro Hagita (NTT)
Hideki Asoh (AIST)
Atsushi Nagasaka (Oki)
Kazunori Ueda (Waseda Univ.)
Katsumi Nitta (Tokyo Inst. of Tech.)
Masayuki Numao (Tokyo Inst. of Tech.)
Hideaki Takeda (National Inst. of Informatics)
Shinichi Honiden (National Inst. of Informatics)
Fumihiro Maruyama (Fujitsu Laboratories)
Kazuhide Iwata (JSAI)

Sponsor

The Japanese Society for Artificial Intelligence (JSAI)

Cooperating Institutes

The Institute of Electronics, Information and Communication Engineers (IEICE)
Information Processing Society of Japan (IPSJ)
The Institute of Electrical Engineers of Japan (IEEJ)
The Society of Instrument and Control Engineers (SICE)
The Association for Natural Language Processing (NLP)
Japanese Neural Network Society (JNNS)
Japan Society for Fuzzy Theory and Systems (SOFT)
The Operations Research Society of Japan (ORSJ)
The Virtual Reality Society of Japan (VRSJ)
Japan Society for Software Science and Technology (JSSST)
The Robotics Society of Japan (RSJ)
The Japanese Cognitive Science Society (JCSS)

Supporting Institute

National Institute of Informatics (NII)

Table of Contents

Invited Talks

Commercial Applications of Machine Learning for Personalized
Wireless Portals 1
  Michael J. Pazzani

Learning, Collecting, and Using Ontological Knowledge for NLP 6
  Eduard Hovy

Hidden Variables in Knowledge Representation 7
  Norman Y. Foo

Intellimedia Systems: Research and Applications at the
Intersection of Multimedia and Artificial Intelligence 9
  Thomas Rist

Integration of Multimedia and Art for New Human-Computer
Communications 19
  Ryohei Nakatsu

Logic and AI Foundation

R-UNSEARCHMO: A Refinement on UNSEARCHMO 29
  Yuyan Chao, Norimitsu Kawana, Lifeng He, Tsuyoshi Nakamura,
  Hidenori Itoh

Deontic Relevant Logic: A Strong Relevant Logic Approach to
Removing Paradoxes from Deontic Logic 39
  Takahiro Tagawa, Jingde Cheng

Solving the Ramification Problem: Causal Propagation in an
Argumentation-Theoretic Approach 49
  Quoc Bao Vo, Norman Y. Foo

Representation and Reasoning of Actions

Representing Actions over Dynamic Domains 60
  Yan Zhang, Norman Y. Foo

Consistency of Action Descriptions 70
  Dongmo Zhang, Samir Chopra, Norman Y. Foo

Solving Factored MDPs with Large Action Space Using Algebraic
Decision Diagrams 80
    Kee-Eung Kim, Thomas Dean

Dynamic Fuzziness 90
    Andrzej Buller

Constraint Satisfaction

Distributed Reinforcement of Arc-Consistency 97
    Ahlem Ben Hassine, Khaled Ghédira

Parallel Execution of Stochastic Search Procedures on Reduced SAT
Instances 108
    Wenhui Zhang, Zhuo Huang, Jian Zhang

Two Transformations of Clauses into Constraints and Their
Properties for Cost-Based Hypothetical Reasoning 118
    Yutaka Matsuo, Mitsuru Ishizuka

Foundations for Agents

Hidden Markov Modeling for Multi-agent Systems 128
    Noda Itsuki

Modelling PRS-Like Agents' Mental States 138
    Wayne Wobcke

Genetic Algorithm and Social Simulation 148
    Pinata Winoto

Foundations for Learning

Adaptive Directed Acyclic Graphs for Multiclass Classification 158
    Boonserm Kijsirikul, Nitiwut Ussivakul, Surapant Meknavin

Network Optimization through Learning and Pruning in Neuromanifold .. 169
    Hyunjin Lee, Hyeyoung Park, Yillbyung Lee

DIC: A Novel Discrete Incremental Clustering Technique for the
Derivation of Fuzzy Membership Functions 178
    W.L. Tung, C. Quek

Reinforcement Learning

Application of Episodic Q-Learning to a Multi-agent Cooperative Task ... 188
    Akira Ito

LC-Learning: Phased Method for Average Reward Reinforcement
Learning – Analysis of Optimal Criteria – 198
 Taro Konda, Tomohiro Yamaguchi

LC-Learning: Phased Method for Average Reward Reinforcement
Learning – Preliminary Results – 208
 Taro Konda, Shinjiro Tensyo, Tomohiro Yamaguchi

Knowledge Acquisition and Management

Extension of the RDR Method That Can Adapt to Environmental
Changes and Acquire Knowledge from Both Experts and Data 218
 Takuya Wada, Tetsuya Yoshida, Hiroshi Motoda, Takashi Washio

Case Generation Method for Constructing an RDR Knowledge Base...... 228
 Keisei Fujiwara, Tetsuya Yoshida, Hiroshi Motoda, Takashi Washio

Data Mining and Knowledge Discovery

Association Rules Using Rough Set and Association Rule Methods 238
 Defit Sarjon, Noor Md Sap Mohd

Change-Point Estimation Using New Minimum Message Length
Approximations... 244
 Leigh J. Fitzgibbon, David L. Dowe, Lloyd Allison

Knowledge Discovery from Structured Data by Beam-Wise Graph-Based
Induction 255
 Takashi Matsuda, Hiroshi Motoda, Tetsuya Yoshida, Takashi Washio

Neural Network Learning

BackPOLE: Back Propagation Based on Objective Learning Errors....... 265
 W.L. Tung, C. Quek

A Method on Improvement of the Online Mode Error Backpropagation
Algorithm for Pattern Recognition 275
 Tae-Seung Lee, Ho-Jin Choi, Young-Kil Kwag, Byong-Won Hwang

Optimizing a Multiple Classifier System 285
 Hirotaka Inoue, Hiroyuki Narihisa

Learning for Robots

Generalization of Iterative Learning Control for Multiple
Desired Trajectories in Robotic Systems 295
 M. Arif, T. Ishihara, H. Inooka

Learning Topological Maps from Sequential Observation and Action
Data under Partially Observable Environment 305
    Takehisa Yairi, Masahito Togami, Koichi Hori

A Saliency Map Model for Active Perception Using Color
Information and Local Competitive Mechanism 315
    Kyungjoo Cheoi, Yillbyung Lee

Generation of Optimal Biped Walking for Humanoid Robot by
Co-evolving Morphology and Controller 325
    Ken Endo, Funinori Yamasaki, Takashi Maeno, Hiroaki Kitano

Multi-agent Applications

Multi-agent Coordination in Planning 335
    Jeroen Valk, Cees Witteveen

A Multi-agent Based Approach to the Inventory Routing Problem 345
    Yizhi Lao, Hon Wai Leong

An Agent-Based Hybrid Intelligent System for Financial Investment
Planning 355
    Zili Zhang, Chengqi Zhang

Socially Intelligent Aerial Combat Simulator 365
    Henry Hexmoor, Xin Zhang

Bayesian Network

Construction of Large-Scale Bayesian Networks by Local to Global
Search 375
    Kyu-Baek Hwang, Jae Won Lee, Seung-Woo Chung, Byoung-Tak Zhang

Using Bayesian Networks with Hidden Nodes to Recognise Neural
Cell Morphology 385
    Jung-Wook Bang, Duncan Gillies

Recognizing 100 Speakers Using Homologous Naive Bayes 395
    Hung-Ju Huang, Chun-Nan Hsu

Document Analysis and Categorization

An Approach to Microscopic Clustering of Terms and Documents 404
    Akiko Aizawa

Effective Methods for Improving Naive Bayes Text Classifiers 414
    Sang-Bum Kim, Hae-Chang Rim, DongSuk Yook, Heui-Seok Lim

Efficiently Clustering Documents with Committees 424
    Patrick Pantel, Dekang Lin

Topic Extraction from Text Documents Using Multiple-Cause
Networks 434
    Jeong-Ho Chang, Jae Won Lee, Yuseop Kim, Byoung-Tak Zhang

A Comparative Study on Statistical Machine Learning Algorithms
and Thresholding Strategies for Automatic Text Categorization 444
    Kang Hyuk Lee, Judy Kay, Byeong Ho Kang, Uwe Rosebrock

PATI: An Approach for Identifying and Resolving Ambiguities 454
    Jae Won Lee, Sung-Dong Kim

Internet/Web Intelligence and Bioinformatics

Extracting User Profiles from E-mails Using the Set-Oriented
Classifier 463
    Sebon Ku, Bogju Lee, Eunyong Ha

Wrapper Generation by Using XML-Based Domain Knowledge
for Intelligent Information Extraction 472
    Jaeyoung Yang, Jungsun Kim, Kyoung-Goo Doh, Joongmin Choi

Modified PrefixSpan Method for Motif Discovery in Sequence
Databases 482
    Hajime Kitakami, Tomoki Kanbara, Yasuma Mori, Susumu Kuroki,
    Yukiko Yamazaki

A Multi-agent Bioinformatics Integration System with Adjustable
Autonomy 492
    Konstantinos Karasavvas, Albert Burger, Richard Baldock

Intelligent Learning Environments

Using Case-Based Reasoning Approach in Planning Instructional
Activities 502
    Rhodora L. Reyes, Raymund C. Sison

Feature Construction for Student Group Forming Based on Their
Browsing Behaviors in an E-learning System 512
    Tiffany Y. Tang, Keith C. Chan

Web-Based Tutoring System for Computer Security 522
    Chong-woo Woo, Jin-woo Choi

Face Recognition

A Simple Illumination Normalization Algorithm for Face Recognition 532
    Jaepil Ko, Eunju Kim, Hyeran Byun

A Self-Adaptive Architecture and Its Application to Robust Face
Identification 542
  Paul Robertson, Robert Laddaga

Multimedia and Emotion

Realizing Audio-Visually Triggered ELIZA-Like Non-verbal Behaviors 552
  Hiroshi G. Okuno, Kazuhiro Nakadai, Hiroaki Kitano

Audio-to-Visual Conversion Using Hidden Markov Models............... 563
  Soonkyu Lee, DongSuk Yook

Scripting the Bodies and Minds of Life-Like Characters 571
  Helmut Prendinger, Sylvain Descamps, Mitsuru Ishizuka

An Affective Decision Making Agent Architecture Using Emotion
Appraisals 581
  Penny Baillie, Dickson Lukose

Poster Papers

Logic Programming for Agents 591
  Hisashi Hayashi, Kenta Cho, Akihiko Ohsuga

Evolutionary Multi-agents System for Prediction of Social
Behavior in Large Cities 592
  Marie Piron, Alain Cardon, Christophe Cambier

Agent-Based Cooperative Distributed Tutoring Systems 594
  Elhadi Shakshuki, Trang Dang

A Computational Model of Reasoning as Socially-Constructed Process.... 595
  Ruediger Oehlmann

Managing Information Complexity of Supply Chains via Agent-Based
Genetic Programming 596
  Ken Taniguchi, Setsuya Kurahashi, Takao Terano

Semantic Integration of E-business Models Based on Multi-layered
Repository 597
  Noriaki Izumi, Takahira Yamaguchi

Randomization and Uncertain Inference............................... 598
  Henry E. Kyburg, Choh Man Teng

Checkers Strategy Evolution with Speciated Neural Networks............ 599
  Kyung-Joong Kim, Sung-Bae Cho

Generation and Optimization of Fuzzy Neural Network Structure 600
  Zbigniew Świątnicki, Vladimír Olej

FuzzyDrive: A Fuzzy Rule-Based Auto Pilot System 601
    W.L. Tung, C. Quek

Implementing NRDR Using OO Database Management System
(OODBMS) 602
    Ghassan Beydoun, Lina Al-Jadir

Using Ripple Down Rules for Actions and Planning 604
    Rex B.H. Kwok

A Generative Dependency Grammar 605
    Stefan Diaconescu

Indonesian Morphological Parser with Minimum Connectivity Cost to
Solve Ambiguities 606
    Mohammad Teduh Uliniansyah, Shun Ishizaki, Kiyoko Uchiyama

Target Word Selection Using WordNet and Data-Driven Models in
Machine Translation 607
    Yuseop Kim, Jeong-Ho Chang, Byoung-Tak Zhang

A Study on Using Natural Language as a Computer Communication
Protocol 608
    *Ichiro Kobayashi, Michiaki Iwazume, Shino Iwashita, Toru Sugimoto,
    Michio Sugeno*

Automatic Indexing Based on Term Activities 609
    Naohiro Matsumura, Yukio Ohsawa, Mitsuru Ishizuka

Answer Extraction by Flexible Matching, Filtering, and Interpretation 610
    Kyung-Soon Lee, Jae-Ho Kim, Key-Sun Choi

A Statistical Identification and Verification Method for Biometrics 611
    Kwanyong Lee, Hyeyoung Park

Proposal of a Multimodal Dialogue Description Language 612
    *Masahiro Araki, Kiyoshi Ueda, Masashi Akita, Takuya Nishimoto,
    Yasuhisa Niimi*

Image Classification by Web Images 613
    Keiji Yanai

Real-Time Face Detection and Tracking Using PCA and NN 615
    Chang-Woo Lee, Yeon-Chul Lee, Sang-Yong Bak, Hang-Joon Kim

A Wrapper-Based Approach to Robot Learning Concepts from Images 616
    Nicolas Bredeche, Jean-Daniel Zucker, Yann Chevaleyre

An Effective HMM-Based Intrusion Detection System with Privilege
Change Event Modeling 617
    Hyuk-Jang Park, Sung-Bae Cho

A Method on Improving of Enrolling Speed for the MLP-Based
Speaker Verification System through Reducing Learning Data 619
    Tae-Seung Lee, Ho-Jin Choi, Seung-Hoe Choi, Byong-Won Hwang

Syntactic Representations of Semantic Merging Operations 620
    Thomas Meyer, Aditya Ghose, Samir Chopra

Author Index 621

Commercial Applications of Machine Learning for Personalized Wireless Portals

Michael J. Pazzani

111 Innovation Drive, Suite 200
Irvine, CA 92612
USA
pazzani@adaptiveinfo.com

Abstract. Consumers and businesses have access to vast stores of information on the Internet, ranging from newspapers, shopping catalogs, restaurant guides, classified ads, jobs listings, dating services to discussion groups and e-mail. All this information is typically accessible only while users are in front of a computer at home or in an office. Wireless devices allow unprecedented access to information from any location at any time. The presentation of this information must be tailored to the constraints of mobile devices. Small screens, slower connections, high latency and limited input capabilities present new challenges. Agents that learn user's preferences and select information for the user are a convenience when displaying information on a 19-inch desktop monitor accessed over a broadband connection; they are essential on a handheld wireless device. This paper summarizes commercially deployed systems using machine learning methods for personalizing mobile information delivery.

1 The Need for Adaptive Personalization

Many wireless data services cope with small screens and limited capabilities of wireless devices by reducing the amount of information available to users. One news site makes four business articles available to mobile users and one wireless carrier limits the user to less than ten wireless games to download. This is equivalent to a newspaper having only the front page of each section available or an electronic game store having a single shelf of products.

However, it is rarely the case that a small offering can satisfy the needs of a diverse group of consumers. Here, we describe the experience that AdaptiveInfo has had with personalizing delivery of wireless news and downloadable content such as Java applications for mobile phones. The experience with wireless readers of the Los Angeles Times wireless web site is that users read much more than what appears on the front page of the print edition – only 31.6% of the content read wirelessly is among the top five stories in each section on the regular web site, showing that mobile users want more content than a one-size-fits-all approach can deliver. Similarly, in an analysis of downloadable content for mobile personal digital assistants, we found that the top 10 items account for less than 40% of the sales for games and less than 30% of the sales for utilities. While a limited one-size-fits-all approach is easy to use, if a mobile

M. Ishizuka and A. Sattar (Eds.): PRICAI 2002, LNAI 2417, pp. 1-5, 2002.
© Springer-Verlag Berlin Heidelberg 2002

wireless experience is to meet the demands of consumers, it cannot limit its offerings to a small number of options.

Many wireless carriers offer a limited degree of customization, where users fill out forms with check boxes to select items of particular interest. Most carriers report that only 2–5% of users customize their experience. Three factors contribute to the limited usage of such approaches. First, it is often complicated to create an account on the web and associate that account with a wireless device, limiting the audience to the technically sophisticated and to those who plan ahead of time. Second, the options tend to be very coarse-grained, allowing users to select from general categories such as "Business News" rather than specific topics such as "Inflation." Third, topic profiles require maintenance to be useful. For example, many people don't regularly follow politics but gain interest during elections. Others closely follow particular sports teams but change their reading habits during the Olympics. Few users are willing to continually maintain their customized profile on a regular web site for an optimal wireless web experience.

Explicit customization approaches, such as web-based questionnaires, place the burden of personalization on the user. We advocate adaptive personalization, an automated approach that uses machine learning techniques to construct a model of each user's interests. It is important that adaptive systems learn from a few examples so that the benefits of personalization are available to new users. It is equally important that the personalization system adapt quickly to changing user interests so that they don't frustrate long-term customers by preventing them from finding novel items. To be truly useful in a mobile context, user's interests must be inferred implicitly from actions and not obtained exclusively from explicit content ratings provided by the user.

2 Machine Learning of User Models

We have pursued a hybrid approach to user modeling [1,2] that combines similarity-based machine learning algorithms [3], Bayesian algorithms [4] and community-based algorithms [5]. We uniquely (but anonymously) identify each user and keep a history of the items presented and how the user interacts with them. Simple rules use this implicit feedback on items to create positive and negative training examples passed to each machine learning algorithm. The similarity-based learning methods are particularly useful in identifying new trends while the Bayesian methods are useful for identifying general themes of interest. The hybrid approach combining recommendations from the above approaches achieves a balance of learning and adapting quickly to changing interests while avoiding brittleness. An additional use of the similarity-based component is to make sure that each screen does not contain too many similar items. Finally, in many domains, we also try to leverage existing efforts to define a baseline or default order to use in the absence of personalized information. For example, we take editorial input into account in ordering news stories by boosting the priority of lead stories. The effect of this boosting is that first-time users of the wireless news site see articles in the same order as on the unpersonalized wired web site and that all users always see the lead story in each section. This also allows the adaptive personalization engine to learn more about each user. Users who elect not to receive personalized content for privacy reasons obtain this same default order.

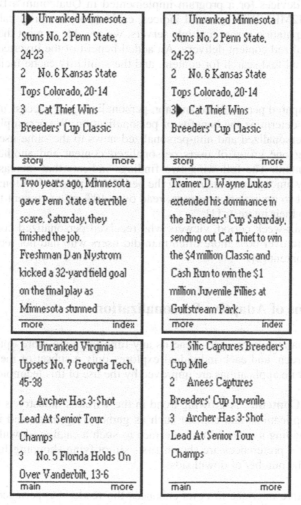

Fig. 1. (Left) Trace of a first-time user interested in football. After reading a football article, the user asks for the next set of headlines and is sent additional football headlines. (Right) Trace of a first-time user interested in horse racing.

Figure 1 shows an example of two different consumers using the same mobile news site for the first time. Both users are presented with the same initial set of articles. One user selects a college football story, and then when that user requests additional sports news, other college football stories are shown. In contrast, another user selects a horse racing story and receives additional horse racing headlines on the third screen. Note that both users are also shown a headline of a golf story to make sure that a variety of content is shown.

Scalability of the machine learning algorithms is a key concern. Because our target mobile devices have limited processing power and memory and slow network access (cf. [4]), our personalization technology resides on a server that interacts with a browser on the devices (or a program implemented in Qualcomm's BREW or Sun Microsystem's J2ME). With inverted indices, caching of similarity calculations and distributing computation across multiple servers, we are able to meet the performance needs of personalized content delivery. An added benefit of the inverted index is that it does support full text search for content, and the similarity cache facilitates finding related content.

We have compared personalized and non-personalized news access under a variety of conditions to determine the benefits of personalization. We accomplish this either by alternating personalized and non-personalized news to the same user on different days, or sending one group of users personalized content and another group non-personalized content. The following two findings indicate that increased usage and increased loyalty among users are among the benefits of personalization:
1. In a visit to a wireless site, users read over 40% more content that is person-alized to their interests [1].
2. Over a six-week period, viewers who received personalized content returned to the site over 60% more often than did users who had not received person-alized content [2].

3 Applications of Adaptive Personalization

Adaptive personalization provides benefits any time there are more options than eas-ily fit on the screen, and each individual explores only a subset of the available op-tions. Many mobile applications are improved by the use of this technology.

Downloadable Content. A growing trend in the wireless industry is to allow users to download applications and content such as games, ring tones and images to cell phones. By providing a personalized interface to such a catalog, downloadable items that meet a user's preferences are shown first- simplifying shopping for applications and increasing the number of downloads.

News. An adaptive interface to news enhances the reader's experience. It makes it easy to follow news stories that unfold across several days. When the user is reading letters to the editor or opinion pages, items related to articles read in the past are dis-played. By ensuring that a variety of articles of potential interest are displayed to the user, including breaking news and lead stories, users stay informed of important events while pursuing their particular interests.

Classified Ads. Wireless classified ads benefit considerably from adaptive personal-ization. It is difficult to page through long lists on most mobile devices. Therefore, it is critical to get the most personally relevant information to the user on the initial screens. Personalization also saves users from filling out many forms to specify their interests precisely. Instead, the user typically enters a more general specification and the adaptive interface learns about the user's precise requirements. Other applications related to classified ads include online dating services and online employment listings.

Restaurants and Entertainment Listings. Adaptive personalization automatically learns customers' tastes in restaurants, nightclubs, etc. Positive feedback is indicated by actions such as calling the restaurant or looking for directions. Many restaurant listing services simply list restaurants by distance from the customer. In contrast, an adaptive interface uses distance as one factor, but orders the nearby restaurants according to the customer's preferences. Furthermore, diversity is factored into the listings so that many restaurants of the same chain are not included in the same display.

4 Conclusion

False starts in the wireless industry have shown that a literal translation of wired web sites to mobile web sites results in service that is not usable. Merely squeezing data onto small screens detracts from the user experience on mobile devices. By adaptively learning users' preferences, all users can have easy access to information that is personally relevant while allowing a mobile operator to provide a large offering to meet a diverse set of needs.

References

1. Billsus, D. & Pazzani, M. (2000). User Modeling for Adaptive News Access, *User Modeling and User-Adapted Interaction*, 10(2/3): 147-180.
2. Billsus, D., Brunk, C., Evans, C., Gladish., B. & Pazzani, M.. (2002) . *Adaptive Interfaces for Ubiquitous Web Access*. Commun. ACM 45, 5.
3. Cover, T. & Hart, P. (1967). Nearest Neighbor pattern classification, IEEE Transactions on Information Theory, 13, pp. 21-27.
4. Duda, R. & Hart, P. (1973). Pattern Classification and Scene Analysis. New York, NY: Wiley and Sons.
5. Pazzani, M. (1999). A Framework for Collaborative, Content-Based and Demographic Filtering. Artificial Intelligence Review 13(5-6): 393-408

Learning, Collecting, and Using Ontological Knowledge for NLP

Eduard Hovy

Information Sciences Institute
of the University of Southern California
4676 Admiralty Way
Marina del Rey, CA 90292-6695, U.S.A. hovy@isi.edu
http://www.isi.edu/natural-language/nlp-at-isi.html

Abstract. Research on Natural Language Processing (NLP) has produced a number of applications. Despite often being used in the real world, quality ceilings stubbornly persist, including for machine translation (around 70(around 45to 25text summarization (around 50Various approaches can be taken to overcome these ceilings, including especially statistical methods that learn transformations. Still, however, NLP systems operate at the word level, without knowledge of the content of their material. In order to operate with meaning rather than form, NLP systems need to use a level of representation deeper than words or syntax. Shallow semantics has long been a candidate, but no-one has yet built a true large-scale semantic knowledge repository for use in NLP applications. Attempts to use WordNet, the major contender, have shown that it requires more detailed content to realize its full potential, while efforts to use CYC show how hard it is to build general-purpose ontologies with enough internal consistent to support NLP applications. In this talk I outline recent statistical efforts to automatically acquire knowledge, from text and dictionaries, that may be placed into terminological ontologies and used by NLP systems.

M. Ishizuka and A. Sattar (Eds.): PRICAI 2002, LNAI 2417, p. 6, 2002.

Hidden Variables in Knowledge Representation

Norman Y. Foo

Artificial Intelligence Laboratory, School of Computer Science and Engineering,
University of New South Wales, Sydney NSW 2052;
http://www.cse.unsw.edu.au/~norman

Abstract. It is a truism that knowledge representation is about choosing the right level of granularity. Granularity is intimately connected with abstraction, component interaction, historical dependency, and similar systems-theoretic properties. As every choice must elide something, unless the purpose to which a representation is carefully restricted, there will be predictive, explanatory and similar inadequacies. In order to understand and analyze such inadequacies a useful approach is to examine the role of what might be collectively called "hidden variables", the entities that are elided. These can range from properties omitted from a representation to those which have been aggregated into an abstract property. The conflation of finite-memory dependencies into Markov processes is another example. This talk will survey the effects of hidden variables in knowledge representation and indicate techniques for reasoning about them.

1 Extended Summary

This is an extended summary of the talk, the details of which are accessible from the author's web-site. The talk is divided into five parts as indicated by the subsections below.

1.1 What Is a Representation?

A systems-theoretic framework is presented for fixing the concepts addressed in the talk. This framework is an adaptation of Zeigler's work in modeling and simulation. It serves to make explicit many ideas that may otherwise be confusing simply because of lack of precision. In this framework there are three components: the "real system", a "base system" determined by all admissible experiments, and a "representation" which attempts to capture the properties of the base system. It is powerful enough to model the activities favored by AI scientists who use formal representations (not necessarily logical).

1.2 Philosophical Precedents

Hidden variables were known as *theoretical terms* in the philosophy of science. The positivist stance attempted to abolish these in favor of entirely *observational*

M. Ishizuka and A. Sattar (Eds.): PRICAI 2002, LNAI 2417, pp. 7–8, 2002.

terms. Ramsey introduced a scheme, inspired by Russell's theory of definite descriptions, whereby a formal language containing theoretical terms could in principle eliminate them. Craig proved that in principle purely observational terms sufficed to recursively axiomatize a theory. Both these approaches faced severe criticism, not the least from practising scientists for whom theoretical terms were at least pragmatically efficacious. Later we will show that from the modern perspective of knowledge representation theoretical terms are in fact necessary.

1.3   Model Theory

The development of model theory has provided useful approaches to reasoning about hidden variables. For instance, theorems due to Robinson and Lyndon, coupled with belief revision ideas and formalizations of *experiments*, serve to show when a knowledge representation system has hidden predicates. These will be illustrated by appeal to highly intuitive examples. Both theorems give conditions on when the union $T_1 \cup T_2$ of two theories are inconsistent. Our examples will identify inconsistency in an experimental setting as nondeterminism in observations. In that way a formal account can be given for (originally) hidden variables like "genes".

1.4   Succinctness and Coherence

The Craig theorem mentioned above suffers from "verbosity". Practical knowledge representation systems have to be relatively succinct. Advances in reasoning about change, for instance, indicate that *causal rules* derive their intuitive power because they are succinct. If one is saddled with a verbose representation, it is often the case that by discovering hidden variables that a new representation can be obtained which "compresses" the verbose one. How far can this compression be taken will impinge on the active field of descriptive complexity. One reason the compression works is that hidden variables can render a new theory more *coherent*, a concept that has been quantified. Indeed, the underlying philosophy of inductive learning and data mining is related to both succinctness and coherence.

1.5   Nondeterminism

Engineers are familiar with the practice of handling incompletely specified transition systems by appeal to probabilistic representations. Physicists know that probabilistic phenomena may be unavoidable in microscopic dimensions. Probability should not be conflated with nondeterminism, although both may indicate the presence of hidden variables. It is important to understand to what extent hidden variables can account for both. This understanding is a step toward the removal (reduction) of apparent nondeterminism by making hidden variables (more) explicit.

Intellimedia Systems: Research and Applications at the Intersection of Multimedia and Artificial Intelligence

Thomas Rist

German Research Center for Artificial Intelligence
Stuhlsatzenhausweg 3
66123 Saarbrücken , Germany
rist@dfki.de
http://www.dfki.de/~rist/

Abstract. Solutions to challenging applications often emerge from a fruitful combination of knowledge, methods, and techniques from different disciplines. This talk introduces Intellimedia, a promising research field located at the intersection of research on Multimedia Systems and Artificial Intelligence. In essence, Intellimedia research aims at the innovative and intelligent usage of multiple media to improve human-machine interfaces as well as computer-mediated human-human communication. Hereby the attribute "intelligent" eventually refers to the deployment of AI techniques, such as knowledge representation, planning, rule-based reasoning, constraint satisfaction, and machine learning. The broad variety of potential Intellimedia application fields will be illustrated by a number of selected scenarios taken from ongoing projects. Among these scenarios are: electronic show rooms in which life-like characters convey product information to the user in the form of possibly interactive performances, mobile access to multimedia content on the web, and personalized in-car entertainment services.

1 Introduction

Around one and a half decade ago a number of researchers from different AI-related areas including natural language processing, knowledge representation, expert system research but also other disciplines, notably computer graphics, started work towards intelligent, multimodal and multimedia user interfaces [1]. One of the driving rationales behind this initiative has been the wish to take full advantage of the new emerging media formats for the purpose of more expressive, more effective and more efficient human machine interaction. Since then, considerable progress has been made with regards to systems that can accept multimodal input from the user, e.g., speech in combination with pointing gestures, and intelligent presentation systems that automatically chose or generate suitable media combinations for conveying information to their users. However, at the same time, new visions for future services and products have emerged creating new challenges for research on human-machine interfaces. The advent of the web, the overwhelming success of mobile communication and computing

M. Ishizuka and A. Sattar (Eds.): PRICAI 2002, LNAI 2417, pp. 9-18, 2002.

devices, and the upcoming trend towards embedded intelligence everywhere may be mentioned here. Right from its opening back in 1988, DFKI's department on Intelligent User Interfaces has been contributing to work on human-machine interface research aiming at an innovative and intelligent usage of multiple media to improve human-machine interfaces as well as computer-mediated human-human communication. The term Intellimedia has been coined in order to emphasize the fruitful combination of methods and knowledge from Multimedia Systems' research on the one hand, and Artificial Intelligence research on the other hand. In this contribution we present a number of selected projects that illustrate the deployment of AI techniques in multimedia user interfaces.

2   Presenting Information through Life-Like Characters

The last decade has seen a general trend in HCI to make human-computer dialogue more like human-human dialogue. Computers are ever less viewed as tools and ever more as partners or assistants to whom tasks may be delegated. Trying to imitate the skills of human presenters, some R&D projects have begun to deploy animated agents (or characters) in wide range of different application areas including e-Commerce, entertainment, personal assistants, training / electronic learning environments. Based either on cartoon drawings, recorded video images of persons, or 3D body models, such agents provide a promising option for interface development as they allow us to draw on communication and interaction styles humans are well familiar with.

DFKI has contributed to this area of research by introducing a plan-based approach to automate the process of writing scripts that control and constrain the behaviour of presentation agents. This approach has been successfully applied to build a number of applications in which information is conveyed either by a single presenter or by a team of presentation agents. Looking at past and current projects conducted at DFKI we observe an ongoing evolution of character-based presentation systems. As depicted in Figure 1, this evolution starts from systems in which a character presents information content in the style of a TV-presenter.

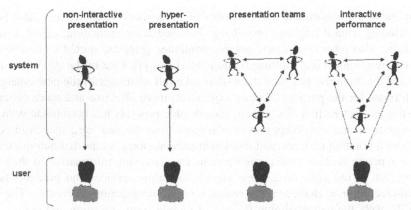

Fig. 1. Ongoing evolution of presentation systems deploying life-like characters

The evolution moves on with the introduction of presentation teams that convey information to the user by performing role plays. In order to explore new forms of active user involvement during a presentation, the next step may lead to systems that convey information in the style of interactive performances. From a technical point of view, this evolution is mirrored in different approaches to determine the behavior of the employed characters.

2.1 Animated Presenters

In our earlier work, we have conducted two projects to develop systems that fall into this category: the PPP (Personalized Plan-Based Presenter) project [2, 3] and the AiA (Adaptive Communication Assistant for Effective Infobahn Access) project [4]. In PPP we addressed the automated generation of instructions for the operation of technical devices which were delivered to the user by an animated agent, the so-called PPP-Persona. For instance, to explain how to switch on a device, PPP-Persona showed the user a picture of the device, pointed to the on-off switch while instructing him or her verbally how to manipulate the switch (cf. Figure 2).

Fig. 2. Shots taken from the PPP Persona system. The character explains an electrical device.

Both PPP and AiA rely on our earlier work on presentation design. Action sequences for composing multimedia material and designing scripts for presenting this material to the user are formalized as operators of a planning system. The effect of a planning operator refers to a complex communicative goal (e.g. to describe a technical device in PPP or a hotel with vacancies in AiA) whereas the expressions in the body of the operator indicate which acts have to be executed in order to achieve this goal (e.g. to show an illustration of a certain object and to describe it). In addition, the plan operators allows us to specify spatial and temporal layout constraints for the presentation segments corresponding to the single acts. The input of the presentation planner is a complex presentation goal. To accomplish this goal, the planner looks for operators whose headers subsume it. If such an operator is found, all expressions in the body of the operator will be set up as new subgoals. The planning process terminates if all subgoals have been expanded to elementary production/retrieval or presentation tasks (for details see [4]).

2.2 Employing Multiple Agents in Presentation Tasks

Most systems that use presentation agents rely on settings in which the agent addresses the user directly as if it were a face-to-face conversation between human beings. Such a setting seems quite appropriate for a number of applications that draw on a distinguished agent-user relationship, e.g., when an agent serves as a personal guide or assistant in information spaces like the www (as the PPP Persona and its siblings). However, there are also situations in which the emulation of a direct agent-to-user communication is not necessarily the most effective way to present information. Empirical evidence suggests that, at least in some situations, indirect interaction can have a positive effect on the user's performance. At DFKI we have built a number of systems with multiple presenters to explore their usage in several application domains including:

- *Inhabited Market Place I* (IMP I); a virtual place in which seller agents provide product information to potential buyer agents [5, 6]. Featuring a car-sales scenario the user will acquire information about cars by observing the simulated sales dialogues (for an impression of the scenario including seller and buyer agents see Figure 2).
- *Kaufmann & Schrauber*; a system similar to the previous one but this time for the presentation of complex software products. In the generated dialogues Kaufmann is particularly interested in the software's added value for the customer while Schrauber represents technical competence.
- *Gerd & Matze*; an automated live report system that generates commentaries for the simulator league of Robot World-Cup Soccer. The user is assumed to sit behind the two soccer fans Gerd and Matze all watching a RoboCup soccer game on screen. In addition to the visual input, the user receives verbal comments on the game delivered by Gerd and Matze [5, 6].
- *Magic Monitor*; a system to illustrate and replay message exchanges in a multi-user communication system. Cartoon-style characters represent different conversation partners which may be humans or virtual conversational characters [6].
- *Avatar Arena*; a testbed for the simulation of negotiation dialogues between affective characters embedded in a social context [7].

The above mentioned systems have in common that the behavior of all involved characters is scripted by a single script writing component prior to the performance. Such an approach bears the advantage that it enables the generation of coherent dialogues. It requires, however, that all the knowledge to be communicated to the audience is known in advance. Consequently, it is less suitable in situations where the characters have to immediately respond to events at presentation runtime, such as user interactions. Our current research focus is on highly interactive systems that allow users to intervene and to take part in a multi character conversation at any time. Work in this direction includes the development of:

- *Puppet*; an interactive 3D learning environment for young children. Adopting a dramaturgic model for improvisational theatre, a child takes on an active role in the development of a farmyard-story [6, 8].
- *Inhabited Market Place II*; an interactive follow-up version of IMP I allowing the user to participate in a car-sales dialogue via a text input widget. Figure 3. shows a screenshot of this system. The user is visually represented by the avatar in the center. In order to provide the user with a convincing experience, the characters have to react immediately to queries and comments made by the user [6].
- *CrossTalk;* an interactive installation that explores a switch between theatre and meta-theatre as a new variant to present information in a public space, e.g., at a booth of a trade faire. In addition, CrossTalk agents live on two separated screens which are spatially arranged as to form a triangle with the user to stimulate a spatially extended interaction experience.
- *Smartakus;* an interactive helper agent that responds to multimodal user input (voice, gesture, and facial expressions). Smartakus is developed as part of the large-scale SmartKom project [9] on multimodal interaction funded by the German Ministry of Education and Research.

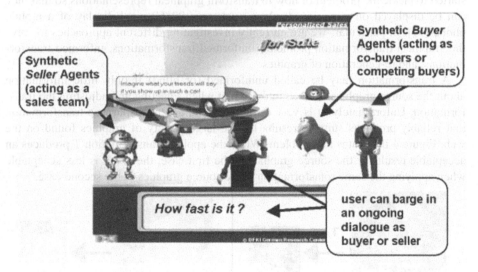

Fig. 3. The Inhabited Market Place II. User participates in a multi-agent sales dialogue.

3 Intellimedia for Mobile Users

A second strand of DFKI's research on intelligent user interfaces addresses information delivery to mobile users [10]. In the following subsections we present two projects that again have a focus on information presentation.

3.1 Customizing Graphics for Tiny Displays of Mobile Devices

Recently, we have seen a variety of mobile appliances such as mobile phones, micro PDA's, and also first working prototypes of wrist watches and jewellery that - in addition to their original functionality and purpose - provide wireless access to the Internet and the World-Wide-Web. While it is debatable whether web-browsing is amongst the most useful applications for the users of such mobile devices, there is no doubt that these appliances provide a high potential for a broad range of new information services that can accommodate for the specific needs of mobile users. For example, think of the commuter who wishes to get the latest travel info, whereas the financial analyst would like to inspect the development of shares and initiate transactions while being on the move.

Compared to the PC-world, however, mobile access is still quite restricted especially with regard to the display of graphical representations, such as images, drawings, diagrams, maps, and logos. Since graphical representations are increasingly used in the world-wide-web for the purpose of information presentation the adaptation of graphics for tiny displays is a challenge that should not be neglected. At DFKI we started to tackle the problem of how to transform graphical representations so that they can be displayed on very tiny displays, such as a 90*60 pixel display of a mobile phone [11]. In particular, we are currently investigating different approaches to solve the graphical transformation problem: uniformed transformations, informed transformations, and re-generation of graphics.

A transformation may be called uninformed (or blind) if only little information about the source graphics is taken into account when selecting and adjusting the transformation. Unfortunately, it is very difficult to find a general-purpose transformation that reliably produces suitable results for the large variety of graphics found on the web. Figure 4 illustrates the problem. While the applied transformation T produces an acceptable result for the source graphics in the first case, the result is less acceptable when applying the same transformation to the source graphics in the second case.

Fig. 4. Applying the same transformation T to two different source pictures in order to obtain a small black and white target picture that can be displayed on a mobile device.

A more promising approach starts with an analysis of the source graphics in order to inform the selection and adjustment of transformation parameters. Basically the analysis phase performs a classification of the source amongst syntactic or even semantic features. For instance, in our current work, the set of implemented semantic

classifiers comprises classifiers that distinguish between portrait and non-portrait images, outdoor versus indoor images, outdoor images that show a scene with blue sky,
clouds, sunset, water, forest or meadows, and snow-covered landscapes. In the ideal
case, each image class can be associated with a certain transformation that produces
acceptable results for the vast majority of instances of that class.

However, it is still difficult to correlate recognized features of an image on the one
hand with available transformations and their parameter adjustments on the other
hand. We are currently investigating in how far this problem can be solved by deploying machine learning techniques. A screenshot of our trainable image transformation system is shown in Figure 5.

Fig. 5. A screenshot of the image transformation system used for testing a machine-learning
approach. After the training phase, the system selects and recommends one of eight transformations for yet unseen source images.

In the training phase, a graphics design expert manually assigns transformations to
source images and thereby allows the system to recognize and generalize correspondences between image features and transformation parameters.

When loading a source image into the system, the image gets displayed in the left
part of the frame and an analysis is carried out to construct a feature vector that can be
used to classify images. In our current test setting we use some 430 features that result
from regional color distributions of an image. In contrast, our repertoire of transformations comprises eight different transformations and is yet quite small. The result of
applying each of the eight available transformations to a source image is displayed on
the right-hand side of the screenshot in Figure 5.

In our ongoing research we also address the use of multiple modalities to access and interact with information services via mobile devices. Especially the combination of voice input together with graphical selections as well as the combined display of graphical and audio output is very likely to become a predominant interaction paradigm for users of tiny mobile devices – eventually enabled by the upcoming 3G telecommunication infrastructure and mobile devices.

3.2 Media and Content Management in an Intelligent Driver Support System

An interesting domain for further Intellimedia research concerns next-generation in-car information and entertainment systems [12]. In applications like car navigation or intelligent driver assistance, computers are increasingly used to actively assist users in task performance. An important form of assistance is the "just-in-time" provision of information on what to do next, and under certain circumstances, how to do it. Information delivery can take advantage of multiple presentation modalities and media, such as verbal utterances, acoustic markers, static and dynamic graphical displays. Content, form, and timing of the information delivery should be chosen so that the user can perform his/her task without disruption or delays. The assistance system must carefully monitor progression of the task performance by the user. Therefore, it must be able to adapt information delivery to the particular needs of the user, and as much as possible contribute to the overall well-being of the user. Three basic research challenges need to be addressed in this application domain: (a) the need for fusion of multiple modalities and multiple sensors to infer intent and driver state, (b) the need to explicitly model cognitive / affective / physiological states and processes as a basis for the formulation of selection rules for content, media and modalities, (c) the need to model user engagement in concurrent tasks and activities, some of which are continuous in nature and must not be suspended like the driving task.

However, with regards to driver entertainment, it is less clear what the system's support should look like since the user does not perform tasks in the classical sense, i.e., tasks that can be captured and formally (or at least semi-formally) represented by task-models. In one of our current research scenarios we aim at an automated compilation of a personalized and situated entertainment program (i.e., "the private DJ in the trunk"). The implementation of such a functionality requires appropriate criteria for the selection of program contributions, such as music titles. Our current prototype relies on two basic working assumptions:

– Playing a certain piece of music elicits emotional responses and that this impact can be anticipated to a certain extent.
– A "good" music program, i.e., one that would be highly appreciated by the user, is more than the sum of its individual pieces. Hence, knowledge about the user's preferences for single titles is not sufficient for automated compilation of an entertainment program. Rather, program compilation must take into account various contextual factors, including among many other potentially relevant factors: the anticipated length of the total program (i.e., is the driver on a short trip or on a

longer journey), the play history, changes in the driver's affective state, and the current driving situation.

A rough architecture for an automated music program composer is illustrated in Figure 6. At the heart of this system lies a rule-based title selector that takes as primary input a repository of available music titles (which are either stored on-board, e.g., on CDROMs, or which can be downloaded via TCP/IP from a server on request). Program composition and title selection is informed by a number of dynamically updated knowledge sources including a general context model, a driver's preference model, and a model that captures some aspects of the driver's physiological, and cognitive / affective state.

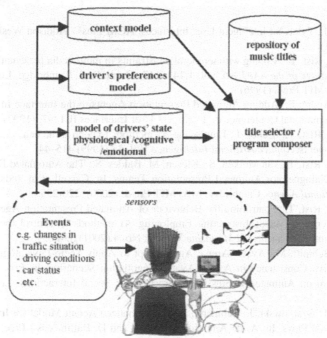

Fig. 6. Sketch of an in-car entertainment system that compiles personalized music programs

The models are updated taking into account various available information sources. Among these sources are data obtained by sensors built into the car in order to observe: the external environment (e.g., road, traffic, and weather conditions), car status information (e.g., speed), the internal environment (e.g., noise in the cockpit), and possibly the driver (e.g., finger temperature measured at the steering wheel). A further important source of information is given by the user's feedback on a suggested music program. For instance, the user may skip a proposed title, and/or express constraints on the search space for the next title to be played (e.g., by restricting the selection to a specific genre, interpret, album, or title). As pointed out before, a list of the top most-liked titles won't be sufficient for the purpose of composing an entertainment program. Rather, the goal is to learn about the most appropriate and most appreciated sequences of music titles for a certain driving session. An analysis of the issue revealed much similarity with the analysis of shopping baskets as it is conducted in retail and e-Commerce applications by means of data mining techniques. That is, the music program may be compared with a shopping basket of selected titles, while a shopping event has its counterpart in a driving session. However, since the in-car scenario provides a much richer set of information that can be co-related with music programs, a much more fine-grained preference model of the user (driver) can be obtained in this scenario as compared to the classical shopping scenario.

References

1. Sullivan, J., Tyler, S.: Intelligent User Interfaces. ACM Press / Addison Wesley, Reading, MA (1991).
2. André, E., Rist, T. : Coping with temporal constraints in multimedia presentation planning. In *Proceedings of the AAAI '96*, vol. 1:142–147. Menlo Park, Cambridge, London: AAAI Press/The MIT Press (1996).
3. Rist, T., André, E.: Adding Animated Presentation Agents to the Interface In *Proceedings of the* International Conference on Intelligent User Interfaces IUI '97, (1997) 79-86.
4. André, E., Rist, T., Müller, J.: Employing AI methods to control the behavior of animated interface agents. *Applied Artificial Intelligence* Vol. 13 (1999) 415–448.
5. André, E., Rist, T., van Mulken, S., Klesen, M. Baldes, S.: The Automated Design of Believable Dialogues for Animated Presentation Teams. In: Cassell et al. (eds.): *Embodied Conversational Agents*, Cambridge, MA: MIT Press. (2000) 220-255.
6. André, E., Rist, T.: Controlling the Behaviour of Animated Presentation Agents in the Interface: Scripting versus Instructing Employing AI methods to control the behavior of animated interface agents. *AI Magazine* Vol. 22, No. 4 (2001) 53-66.
7. Rist, T., Schmitt, M.: Avatar Arena: An Attempt to Apply Socio-Physiological Concepts of Cognitive Consistency in Avatar-Avatar Negotiation Scenarios. In *Proc. of* AISB'02 Symposium on Animated Expressive Characters for Social Interactions, London (2002) 79-84.
8. Klesen, M., Szatkowski, J., Lehmann, N.: A Dramatized Actant Model for Interactive Improvisational Plays. In: A. de Antonio, R. Aylett, and D. Ballin (eds.) Proc. of the Third International Workshop on Intelligent Virtual Agents. Lecture Notes in Artificial Intelligence 2190. Heidelberg: Springer Verlag (2001).
9. Wahlster, W., Reithinger, N., Blocher, A.: SmartKom: Multimodal Communication with a Life-Like Character. Smartkom Report No. 5, DFKI, Saarbrücken, Germany (2001).
10. Rist, T., Brandmeier, P., Herzog, G., André, E.: Getting the Mobile Users in: Three Systems that Support Collaboration in an Environment with Heterogeneous Communication Devices. In Proc. of *Advanced Visual Interfaces 2000*, (2000) 250-254.
11. Rist, T., Brandmeier, P.: Customising Graphics for Tiny Displays of Mobile Devices. In Proc. of the Third International Workshop on Human Computer Interaction with Mobile Devices, Lille, France (2001) 47-52.
12. Rist, T., Booth, S.: Adaptation of Information Delivery to Support Task-Level Connuity. In C. Stephanidis (ed.) Universal Access (Proc. of UAHCI-01) Lawrence Erlbaum, London (2001) 421-425.

Integration of Multimedia and Art for New Human-Computer Communications

Ryohei Nakatsu

ATR/Kwansei Gakuin University*

2-2-2, Hikaridai, Seika-cho, Soraku-gun, Kyoto, 619-0288 Japan

nakatsu@atr.co.jp

1. Introduction

Recently, the word *Kansei* has come to be used quite frequently, especially in the case of communications. The communications of today's young people via mobile telephones is sometimes called "*Kansei*-transmitting communications." In this case, they express *Kansei* by adding emotions and sensitivity to their voice. This is a typical method of *Kansei* expression. At the same time, the use of the body such as facial expressions and body motions is an important and essential means of expressing *Kansei* information in daily life. This is why face-to-face communications is the ultimate form of communications, and so far, no tele-communication means has been able to replace it.

These facts show that the means of expressing non-logical information such as *Kansei* is the basis of our communications and, therefore, technologies that support people in expressing and transmitting their *Kansei* will be essential factors for future communications.

For *Kansei* communications, there are several important issues to be considered. First, as we express our *Kansei* by using multiple modalities, the usage of multimedia is essential. Second, it is important to investigate why *Kansei* is essential for human communications. This will lead to the notion that even in the case of human computer communications the treatment of *Kansei* is indispensable. Third, as the treatment of *Kansei* is very difficult based on engineering approach alone, it is necessary for us to adopt new approach.

In this paper, first we will observe the trend of several media and it will be stated that in the future the integration of various media would occur. Also, investigation is made into the meaning that *Kansei* has in communications. It will be revealed that *Kansei* expression/transmission is the basis of our communications. Then as an approach to treat *Kansei*, a methodology called Art & Technology will be proposed. Based on the above discussion, two examples of research activities are described that were conducted in ATR Media Integration & Communications Research Laboratories with the aim of developing technologies that support communications based on *Kansei* expression.

M. Ishizuka and A. Sattar (Eds.): PRICAI 2002, LNAI 2417, pp. 19-28, 2002.
© Springer-Verlag Berlin Heidelberg 2002

2. Trends of Communication Media

2.1 Multimedia and Future Communication Media

What will be the future form of communications?   We proposed "hyper-communications" as a new communications concept in the future[1]. This was first based on the viewpoint that the boundary of communications media and other media would become ambiguous in the multimedia era and network era. Actually, such a movement is being caused by the various media (including communications). For example, a place for a new means of communications, the Internet, is being caused by the world of communications. It is thought that the Internet is a huge cyberspace that joins the whole world. People communicate with other people in that space and also shop.

In addition, looking at the movie industry, recent movies have been introducing digital techniques and computer graphics techniques and have been moving over to movies of a new generation. These techniques have given the ability to create very realistic worlds, i.e., cyberspaces, in which expression had been difficult in conventional movies. Also, video games, especially role playing games (RPGs), have made it possible for people to enjoy a story by becoming the main characters in a cyberspace. From these trends, it can be predicted for "communications in a cyberspace" to become one keyword for the new communications (Fig. 1).

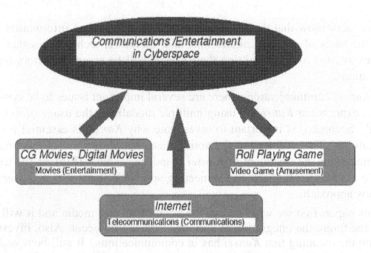

Fig. 1. New Trends in Various Kinds of Media.

2.2 Nonverbal Aspect of Communications

Next, our attention is to focus on the information exchanged in communications. Figure 2 shows a model of communications for human(2). In the surface layer, a layer exists that manages communications based on the use of languages. It is possible to say that research on communications and information processing has come to deal with the mechanisms in this layer. For example, objects that have come to be treated in speech recognition are the logic information included in sounds.

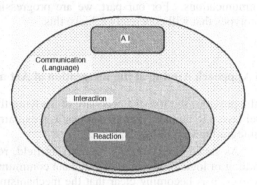

Fig. 2. Communication Model.

The logic information, however, is only a part of the information composing the sounds. Other rich information contained in the sounds include emotion information and "kansei" information. It is considered that such information is generated by a layer in a deeper level, i.e., the interaction layer in Fig. 2 or the reaction layer.

The interaction layer manages acts such as the changes in the speaking turns, for the rhythm and production of the utterances, to maintain the communication channels. This layer plays an important role for smoothly carrying out communications for humans. Below the interaction layer is the reaction layer. This layer manages the more basic operations of humans. For example, this layer has functions such as to turn the face to the location from which a sound had come or to close the eyes at the sudden appearance of light.

In this way, it can be considered that human communications plays a role with important functions of a deeper layer (in addition to logical acts and the treatment of information), and that non-logical types of information like emotions and *Kansei* are generated and solved through the movements of the above layers.

Conventional communications have come to apply logical communications, but in the future, other types of communications will become important. This, for instance, can be understood by observing the interest taken by young people in talking with portable telephones. In this case, it is possible to say that this phenomenon involves confirming sense-specific and emotions-specific relationships with partners and not the exchange of information with logical meanings. Consequently, the transmission of non-logical information will become another keyword of the new type of communications.

From the above considerations, communications to transmit non-logical information by using a cyberspace can be expected to be the form of the new means of communications. For our part, we are progressing with research on concepts and prototypes that will concretely achieve this.

2.3 Approach Aiming at the Integration of Art and Technology

In the previous section, the necessity of studying the action mechanisms of the deeper level layers in human communications was explained. This section proposes the idea of integrating technology and art[2].

As stated before, in the engineering field, research is being done targeting the handling of logical information in human communications. As the research advances, however, it is becoming clear that the mechanisms of deeper level communications, like communications based on emotions or senses do play an essential role in our daily communications. It is, therefore, inevitable to be able to handle information on emotions and senses, which had not been handled in the engineering field up to now. On the other hand, artists have long handled human emotions and senses. Therefore, further development is expected by having engineers collaborate with artists.

Art too has seen a notable movement recently. This is due to the emergence of a field called Interactive Art. The important function of art is to have an artist transfer his/her concepts or messages to an audience by touching their emotions or senses. In the long history of art, this means of communications has been refined and made sophisticated. However, it cannot be denied that in traditional art, the flow of information in communications has been one-way, that is, information is transferred from the artist to a passive audience.

With Interactive Art, the audience can change expressions in art works by inter-

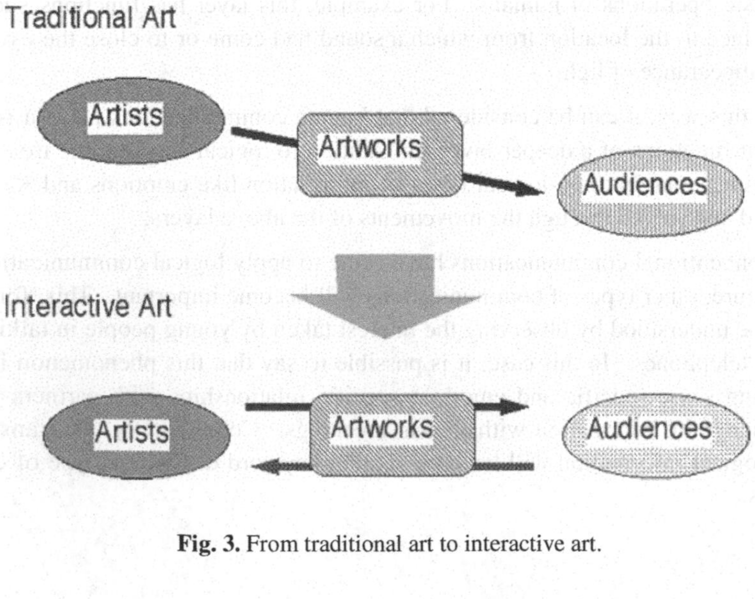

Fig. 3. From traditional art to interactive art.

acting with them.   That is, the audience provides feedback to the various art works and this consequently enables information to flow from the audience to the artist. Therefore, in Interactive Art, information flow is both ways, that is, true communications is achieved. A comparison of information flows between traditional art and Interactive Art is illustrated in Fig. 3.

At the same time it should be pointed out that this Interactive Art is still developing and that interactions remain at the primitive level, like causing a change by pushing a button.   Therefore, it is necessary for Interactive Art to adopt image/speech processing technologies to raise primitive interactions to the communications level.

For this aim, from an engineering viewpoint, collaboration with art is required to give computers human-like communications functions. From the art side, adopting new technologies is necessary to improve the current Interactive Art, from the level of interactions to that of communications.   As both approaches share the same target, the time is ripe for collaboration between art and technology to progress.

In the following chapters, two examples of research activities being conducted at ATR Media Integration & Communications Research Laboratorics based on the previous considerations will be btitly.

3. MIDAS: Mic Intreractive Dance System

3.1 Overview

Our research purpose is to establish a framework of non-verbal multimedia communication technologies by which we can express our emotional images directly.   Art is an adequate reference for our research, because artists express their emotion by creating artwork. Dance is a form of art, and human motion is important in non-verbal communication.   Therefore, it can be said that human motion analysis is important for our research purpose.

For this purpose we have developed an emotion extraction method for human body motion. This method can be applied to multimedia communication systems. MIDAS (MIC Interactive Dance System) is one of the applications. In this system, a performer can express his or her emotions by utilizing video and sound and can dance freely without any restrictions. MIDAS is unique as an emotional interaction system.

3.2 Overview of MIDAS

Choreographers have long been studying human motion in order to characterize it. A famous Austrian choreographer, Rudolf Laban (1879-1958), proposed The Effort-Shape description[3] for human motion : The Effort-Shape description can describe human motion in terms of its quality and expression.

The Effort-Shape description is adequate for categorizing human motion with emotional features. In this description, there are four parameters: space, weight, time and flow.

In addition, another study has shown that dance motion patterns can be categorized into seven typical motives[4]. The seven motives represent the emotions of happy, solemn, lonely, natural, sharp, dynamic and flowing.

The Effort-Shape description and the seven motives provide background knowledge for our research. We expect that Time-Space-Energy parameters can be obtained by image processing, and that the seven motives can be analyzed in subjective assessment experiments

3.3 Method of Extracting Emotion from Human Body Motion

A professional dancer's scene captured by a camera was used for the emotion analysis. The dancer performed in accordance with the seven motives. Simple image processing was used to extract physical features from the dancer's sequences. To translate the physical features into emotional information, we applied a multiple regression method. Finally, we obtained a set of linear functions representing the relationship between the physical features and emotional information contained in human motion.

The extracted emotional information is sent to a multimedia controller. The multimedia controller manages a video switcher, real-time disc system, and sound system. The multimedia controller interprets the received emotional information and selects adequate video and sound clips. The video clips are displayed on a 120-inch projection monitor. The sound clips are played simultaneously. Fig.4 shows a schematic of MIDAS[5].

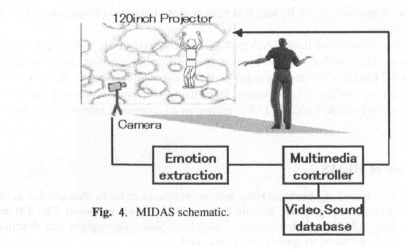

Fig. 4. MIDAS schematic.

3.4 Future Work

MIDAS has many aspects in addition to a dancing system. Some people say that this system can be used for psychotherapy. Educational applications can be considered too. Of course, MIDAS can be changed to an interactive multimedia game by replacing the video and sound content. We are planning to develop an application for amusement. Figure 5 shows an example of its content, where a performer can control the avatar motion.

Fig. 5. Apperance of MIDAS

This means that several performers will be able to use MIDAS. In the current MIDAS, only one performer can use it, because it may be impossible to represent the emotions of plural performers by using a set of video and sound. In addition, we can extend MIDAS to a telecommunications system where performers can dance over a network.

4. Costune

4.1 Overview

Music plays an essential role as a communications medium. For example, the members of a jazz band communicate with each other by performing music, and the band conveys a certain impression to the audience by their music. Thus, music is essentially a powerful communications medium as well as a universal language.

Several wearable musical instruments have been developed, e.g., YAMAHA MIBURI™ and BODYCODER[6], However, the authors see them as a simple extension of ordinary musical instruments; sound is still the only vehicle for communications and the aspect of a communications tool is not apparent in its design.

We designed "CosTune" to be a communications tool rather than a simple musical instrument. The most significant feature of CosTunes is that they are equipped with wireless network functions. This allows users to communicate with anyone, anytime, and anywhere by means of music in an ad hoc manner without scattering sound. We think that this feature makes CosTune a supporting tool for forming communities in the real world.

4.2 System Design and Prototype

The CosTune consists of a wearable input device and a portable control unit (Figure 6). The wearable input device is a cloth on which a number of tactile sensors that correspond to, for instance, the keys of a piano are

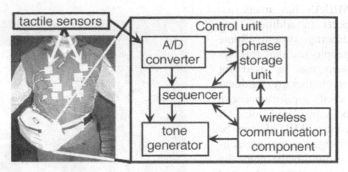

Fig. 6. Components of the Costune

mounted. By ma-nipulating the sensors, the user can play music. The portable control unit is equipped with an A/D converter, a tone generator, a wireless communications component, a phrase storage unit and a sequencer.

The output signals from the sensors on the wearable input device are input to the A/D converter that converts input analog signals into MIDI data..

The wireless communications component transmits as well as receives "phrase packets" to and from other CosTunes and servers. The phrase data, as MIDI data, that are obtained from the received phrase packets are also input to the tone generator.

In order to preliminarily evaluate whether we

(a) Jacket type CosTune

Fig. 7. Prototype Costune.

can actually perform songs while walking and whether we can form a session with a number of players using a wireless network, we created and tested a prototype system and obtained a promising result (Figure 7).

4.3 Discussion

CosTune as communityware in the real world There are several systems and projects that allow people to perform remote sessions by exchanging performance data in MIDI format over the Internet. CosTune is similar to these attempts in terms of phrase exchange through a network. However, as for musical performances, we regard communications in the real world as the most important while communications using systems are done in virtual worlds. Therefore, we insisted on a wireless communications component with a comparatively narrow communications area. Additionally, we insisted on a wireless ad hoc networking function that always automatically looks for other users who have similar musical tastes. These allow people to meet in the real world and to have jam sessions in a face-to-face manner; an essential joy of musical performances.

Moreover, we are interested in the characteristics of the "areas" of cities, towns and so on. Specific kinds of people tend to gather in specific kinds of areas. They generate the "atmosphere of the area" and the atmosphere of the area attracts those who like it. As a result, areas acquire unique characteristics, e.g., SoHo in N.Y. and Harajuku in Tokyo. We think that the music that is performed in an area must reflect the characteristics of the area. Conversely, the jam sessions and composed musical pieces must become different depending on the areas where a CosTune user visits. Therefore, we think people who want to enjoy the music of a specific area should actually visit the area and meet the people of the area.

5. Conclusion

In this paper, we described communication for exchanging *Kansei* information and introduced several systems that support people in expressing their *Kansei*. First we investigated communication and pointed out that *Kansei* communication will become essential for future communications and telecommunications. As a result, we made it clear that the technologies that support *Kansei* expression are key factors for future communications. Also we proposed a new approach, called Art & Technology, to develop technologies *for Kansei* communications.

Then we introduced two systems that are being studied by the authors and that are good examples of such technologies. First we described an interactive dance system called MIDAS. In this system, the dance movement of a user is analyzed and classified into one of seven typical dance motives. According to the result the system can generate music and images that fit the motion of the user. Then we described the design and applications of CosTune, a music-mediated communications tool. CosTune is equipped with several sensors mounted on clothes as well as ad hoc networking functions to exchange phrase data and user profile information with other CosTunes and servers that are located around town. CosTune will allow a user to hold an ad hoc session on a street corner with other users who share similar musical tastes even if they just happen to meet there and do not know each other.

Although the study of technologies that support *Kansei* expression is in its initial stage, the prototypes we have developed show good performance and we believe that this area will become one of the central areas for the communications research.

References

[1] Nakatsu, R. (1998). Toward the Creation of a New Medium for the Multimedia Era, *Proceedings of the IEEE*, Vol. 86, No. 5, pp.825-836.
[2] Nakatsu, R. (1997). Image/Speech Processing that Adopts an Artistic Approach -Integrating Art and Technology-, *Proceedings of ICASSP1997*, pp.207-210.
[3] Hutchinson, A. (1996) Labanotation. In: *Dance Books*.
[4] Matsumoto, C. (1987). Dance Research : Problem Situation and Learning of Problem Solving II – Qualities of Movements and Feeling Values, *Proc. Japanese Association of Physical Education and Sports for Girls and Women*, pp. 53-89, 1987 (in Japanese)
[5] Iwadate, Y. (1999). Study on Image Expression, *IEICE HCS99-53*, pp.87-94 (in Japanese).
[6] Bromwich, M. A. and Wilson, J. A. (1998). BODYCODER: A Sensor Suit and Vocal Performance Mechanism for Real-time Performance, *Proc. International Computer Music Conference 1998*, pp. 292-295.

R-UNSEARCHMO: A Refinement on UNSEARCHMO*

Yuyan Chao[1], Norimitsu Kawana[1], Lifeng He[2], Tsuyoshi Nakamura[1], and
Hidenori Itoh[1]

[1] Department of Artificial Intelligence and Computer Science
Nagoya Institute of Technology, Nagoya, 466-8555 Japan
[2] Faculty of Information Science and Technology
Aichi Prefectural University, Aichi, 480-1198 Japan

Abstract. By not utilizing the reasoning results derivable whenever
refutations are found at nodes in proof trees, UNSEARCHMO might
repeat some reasoning that has been made before. Addressing this problem, this paper presents a refinement on UNSEARCHMO, called R-
UNSEARCHMO, by summarizing the derived refutations as lemmas and
utilizing them in the further reasoning. In this way, R-UNSEARCHMO
can avoid repeated reasoning and always search a subspace of that UN-
SEARCHMO does. Somewhat surprisingly, our refinement almost takes
no additional cost. We describe the refinement, present the implementation and provide examples to demonstrate the power of our refinement.

1 Introduction

Simple in principle and easy to implement in Prolog, SATCHMO (SATisfiability
CHecking by MOdel generation) 12) has attracted much attention in automated
reasoning field 11), 9), 6), 1), 5), 10).

The basic idea of SATCHMO is to use forward chaining to build a model
for a given clause set: if it turns out that all possible interpretations fail to be
models, the given clause set is unsatisfiable. The major weakness of SATCHMO
is that it might perform many forward chaining reasoning steps that are needed
to generate all candidate models, but not to find a refutation.

UNSEARCHMO 4), an improvement of I-SATCHMO 5), eliminates redundant search space by intelligent backtracking 2), 13). The principle is very simple: a violated clause used for forward chaining is irrelevant if one of its consequent atoms is unnecessary for the reasoning. Whenever a clause is found to
be irrelevant, UNSEARCHMO prunes away the branches corresponding to the
unprocessed atoms in the consequence of the clause.

Since UNSEARCHMO does not utilize the reasoning results derivable whenever refutations are found at nodes in proof trees, it might repeat some reasoning that has been made before. In other words, the same subtree might be
constructed at different nodes in a proof tree.

* This work is partially supported by the Japan Society for the Promotion of Science
and the Artificial Intelligence Research Promotion Foundation of Japan.

M. Ishizuka and A. Sattar (Eds.): PRICAI 2002, LNAI 2417, pp. 29–38, 2002.

Addressing this problem, our extension, called R-UNSEARCHMO, summarizes the refutations derived in the reasoning as lemmas and utilizes them to avoid repeated reasoning 8), 7), 15). Somewhat surprisingly, according to the experimental results, our refinement almost takes no additional cost.

The rest of the paper is organized as follows. In the next section, we give the outline of SATCHMO and UNSEARCHMO. Section 3 presents our refinement on UNSEARCHMO. We list the implementation of R-UNSEARCHMO in Prolog in section 4. Section 5 presents experimental results to demonstrate the power of our refinement.

2   SATCHMO and UNSEARCHMO

In this paper, a problem for checking unsatisfiability is represented by means of *positive implicational clauses*, each of which has the form $A_1, \ldots, A_n \rightarrow C_1; \ldots; C_m$ $(n, m \geq 0)$. We refer to the implicit conjunction $A_1, \ldots, A_n$ as the *antecedent* of the clause, with each A_i being an *antecedent atom*. The implicit disjunction $C_1; \ldots; C_m$ is referred to as the *consequence* of the clause, and each C_j a *consequent atom*. A clause with an empty consequence, i.e., $m = 0$, is called a *negative clause* and is written as $A_1, \ldots, A_n \rightarrow \perp$, where $\perp$ denotes *false*. On the other hand, for a clause with an empty antecedent, i.e., $n = 0$, the antecedent atom *true* is added.

A given clause set S is divided into two subsets[1]: (1) $\mathcal{NC}$, the negative clause set that consists of all negative clauses in S; (2) $\mathcal{FC}$, the Forward Chaining component that consists of all the remaining clauses. Moreover, as in SATCHMO and I-SATCHMO, we assume that all of clauses in our case satisfies the so-called *range-restricted property*, where a clause is range-restricted iff every variable in its consequent also occurs in its antecedent.

Suppose that $\mathcal{M}$ be a set of ground atoms, then a conjunction (disjunction) of ground atoms is *satisfiable* in $\mathcal{M}$ if all (some) of its members belong to $\mathcal{M}$, and otherwise is *unsatisfiable*. A ground clause $\mathcal{A} \rightarrow \mathcal{C}$ is said to be *satisfiable* in $\mathcal{M}$, if $\mathcal{C}$ is satisfiable or $\mathcal{A}$ is unsatisfiable in $\mathcal{M}$, and else *violated*. If every clause in a clause set S is satisfiable in $\mathcal{M}$, then $\mathcal{M}$ is said to be a *model* of S.

It is well-known that a clause set S is satisfiable if and only if we can find at least a model for S. Accordingly, to check whether a given clause set S is satisfiable, SATCHMO goes to construct a model for the clause set. From an empty model candidate $\mathcal{M}$, it satisfies each violated clause in $\mathcal{M}$ by asserting one of the consequent atoms of the clause into the model candidate $\mathcal{M}$ (in this way, the violated clause becomes satisfiable in $\mathcal{M}$) in turn. If it succeeds with no violated clause in $\mathcal{M}$ anymore, $\mathcal{M}$ is a model of S. Then, the given clause set is proved satisfiable. Otherwise, if no model can be established anyway, the given clause set is proved unsatisfiable.

---

[1] Although any decidable Horn clause set that consists of all negative clauses can be used as the backward chaining component 9), 5), 10), in this paper, for convenience of presentation, all Horn clauses are used as forward chaining clauses.

Given a clause set $\mathcal{S}=\mathcal{NC} \cup \mathcal{FC}$, the reasoning procedure of SATCHMO can be graphically illustrated by constructing a *proof tree* described as follows.

Definition 1. (SATCHMO) For the current node D (initially the root node Φ, an empty set), and the *corresponding ground consequent atom set* $\mathcal{I}_D$ (initially empty):

1. If $\mathcal{NC} \cup \mathcal{I}_D \vdash \perp$, then $\mathcal{NC} \cup \mathcal{FC} \cup \mathcal{I}_D$ is unsatisfiable. Create a leaf node $\perp$ below node D. The branch terminates there.
2. If $\mathcal{NC} \cup \mathcal{I}_D \nvdash \perp$, select a clause from $\mathcal{FC}$ that is violated in $\mathcal{I}_D$. If no such clause exists, $\mathcal{I}_D$ is a model of $\mathcal{NC} \cup \mathcal{FC}$, the process ceases to construct the proof tree and reports that $\mathcal{S}$ is satisfiable.
4. For the selected violated clause $A_1, \ldots, A_n \to C_1; \ldots; C_m$, create a child node for each consequent atom C_i $(1 \le i \le m)$ below the current node D. Taking node C_i as the new current node, call this procedure recursively in the depth-first strategy with the augmented ground consequent atom set $\mathcal{I}_{C_i}$, where $\mathcal{I}_{C_i} = \mathcal{I}_D \cup \{C_i\}$. If $\mathcal{NC} \cup \mathcal{FC} \cup \mathcal{I}_{C_i}$ is unsatisfiable for every C_i, then, $\mathcal{NC} \cup \mathcal{FC} \cup \mathcal{I}_D$ is unsatisfiable.

For node D, the corresponding consequent atom set, $\mathcal{I}_D$, the set of atoms occurring in the branch from the root node to node D, is a *partial interpretation* of $\mathcal{S}$. If all of the branches below node D terminate in a leaf node $\perp$, it means that $\mathcal{I}_D$ cannot be extended to a model of $\mathcal{S}$, i.e., $\mathcal{S} \cup \mathcal{I}_D$ is unsatisfiable. In such cases, we say that node D is proved *unsatisfiable* or a *refutation* is derived at node D. When the root node Φ is proved unsatisfiable, no model can be generated for $\mathcal{S}$, $\mathcal{S}$ is unsatisfiable.

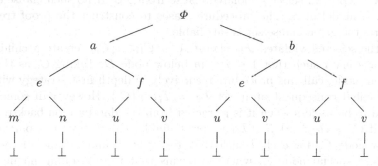

Fig. 1. The proof tree constructed by SATCHMO in Example 1

Example 1. Consider the following clause set.

$\mathcal{NC} : m \to \perp. \ n \to \perp. \ u \to \perp. \ v \to \perp.$
$\mathcal{FC} : true \to a; b. \ true \to e; f. \ e \to m; n. \ true \to u; v.$

The proof tree generated by SATCHMO is shown in Figure 1.

SATCHMO is potentially inefficient for theorem proving. In order to construct a model for a given clause set, SATCHMO has to satisfy every violated clause. However, some of violated clauses might be irrelevant to find a refutation. When irrelevant non-Horn clauses are invoked by forward chaining, the search space will be expanded exponentially. Let us see the use of the clause $true \rightarrow a; b$ in Example 1. Since neither a nor b contributes to the further reasoning, satisfying this violated clause does not help us find a refutation or anything else but doubles the search space.

An idea to eliminate redundant search space is incorporating intelligent backtracking 2), 13) into SATCHMO. I-SATCHMO 5) and UNSEARCHMO 4) are such approaches. Their principle for finding irrelevant clauses is very simple: a violated clause used for forward chaining is *irrelevant* if one of its consequent atoms is useless for the further reasoning. When an $\mathcal{FC}$ clause being processed is known to be irrelevant, the branches corresponding to the unprocessed consequent atoms of the clause are pruned away.

The algorithm of UNSEARCHMO can be described as follows.

Definition 2. (UNSEARCHMO) For the current node D (initially the root node Φ) and its corresponding consequent atom set $\mathcal{I}_D$ (initially empty):

1. If $\mathcal{NC} \cup \mathcal{I}_D \vdash \bot$, $\mathcal{S} \cup \mathcal{I}_D$ is unsatisfiable. Create a leaf node $\bot$ below node D. The branch terminates there. The useful consequent atom set for the refutation at node D, $\mathcal{U}_D$, consists of all atoms in $\mathcal{A}$, where $\mathcal{A}$ is the antecedent of a negative clause such that $\mathcal{I}_D \vdash \mathcal{A}$.

2. If $\mathcal{NC} \cup \mathcal{I}_D \not\vdash \bot$, select a violated clause from $\mathcal{FC}$. If no such clause exists, $\mathcal{I}_D$ is a model of $\mathcal{S}$. The procedure ceases to construct the proof tree and reports the given clause set is satisfiable.

3. For the selected violated $\mathcal{FC}$ clause $\mathcal{A} \rightarrow C_1; \ldots; C_m$, create a child node C_i for every i such that $1 \leq i \leq m$ below node D. Taking C_i as the new current node, call this procedure recursively in depth-first strategy with the augmented consequent atom set $\mathcal{I}_{C_i} = \mathcal{I}_D \cup \{C_i\}$. However, if some C_i is found to be useless when it is retracted from the database on backtracking, i.e., if $C_i \notin \mathcal{U}_{C_i}$: (a) $\mathcal{S} \cup \mathcal{I}_D$ is unsatisfiable; (b) remove the partial tree below node C_j for each j such that $1 \leq j < i$, and instead of each C_j, create a special node $\otimes$, where $\otimes$ means that the reasoning having been made there is not necessary; (c) instead of node C_k for each k such that $i < k \leq m$, create a special node $\times$, where $\times$ means that the branch is pruned away from there; (d) the useful consequent atom set for node D, $\mathcal{U}_D$, is established just the same as $\mathcal{U}_{C_i}$. On the other hand, if all of the node C_i are proved unsatisfiable with all of C_i found to be useful, then: (a) $\mathcal{S} \cup \mathcal{I}_D$ is unsatisfiable; (b) the useful consequent atom set for node D $\mathcal{U}_D = \{\mathcal{U}_{C_1} - \{C_1\}\} \cup \cdots \cup \{\mathcal{U}_{C_m} - \{C_m\}\} \cup \mathcal{A}$.

The given clause set is unsatisfiable if and only if the root node is proved unsatisfiable, i.e., all branches of the proof tree terminate in a leaf $\bot$, $\otimes$ or $\times$.

Example 2. Consider the clause set given in Example 1. The proof tree constructed by UNSEARCHMO is shown in Figure 2.

Since f is not useful for the refutation at nodes f, the reasoning made at node e is unnecessary. Moreover, since a is not useful, the reasoning from node b is pruned away.

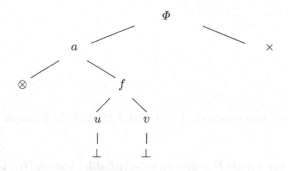

Fig. 2. The proof tree constructed by UNSEARCHMO in Example 2

3   R-UNSEARCHMO: A Refinement on UNSEARCHMO

However, not untilizing the reasoning results during the reasoning, UN-SEARCHMO might repeat some reasoning. In other words, the same subproof tree might be constructed at different nodes in a proof tree. Let us see the following example.

Example 3. Consider the following clause set $\mathcal{S}$.

$\mathcal{NC} : e, s \rightarrow \perp.\ u, f \rightarrow \perp.\ t \rightarrow \perp.\ w, v \rightarrow \perp.$
$\mathcal{FC} : true \rightarrow u;\ w.\ u \rightarrow s;\ t.\ true \rightarrow u;\ v.\ true \rightarrow e;\ f.$

The proof tree constructed by UNSEARCHMO is shown in Figure 3.

The subtrees below the two nodes u are the same. The computation for constructing the subtree below node u on the right is redundant.

Generally, such redundant computation can be avoided by untilizing the reasoning results derived during previous reasoning 8), 7). In our case, for a given clause set $\mathcal{S}$ when some node D is proven unsatisfiable, the useful consequent atom set for the refutation, $\mathcal{U}_D$ can be derived. According to the soundness of UNSEARCHMO, $\mathcal{S} \cup \mathcal{U}_D$ is unsatisfiable. In other words, whenever $\mathcal{U}_D$ can be satisfied in the database, the same subtree below node D can be constructed in exactly the same way. Therefore, $\mathcal{U}_D$ can be used as a *lemma*. We use $lemma(\mathcal{U}_D)$ to denote such a lemma in this paper.

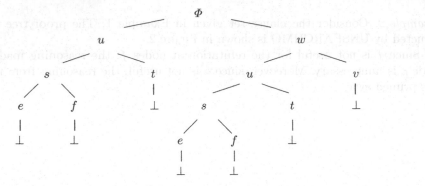

Fig. 3. The proof tree constructed by UNSEARCHMO in Example 3

In this way, whenever a node D is proven unsatisfiable, $lemma(\mathcal{U}_D)$ is asserted into the database, where $\mathcal{U}_D$ is the useful consequent atom set for the refutation at node D, and whenever a lemma can be satisfied at a node, the node is proven unsatisfiable. Moreover, when a new lemma $\mathcal{U}$ is derived, all lemmas $\mathcal{V}$ in the database such that $\mathcal{V} \in \mathcal{U}$ can be removed from the database.

Summarizing the above discussion, the algorithm of UNSEARCHMO for constructing a proof tree for a given clause set $S = \mathcal{NC} \cup \mathcal{FC}$, as presented earlier, can be modified as follows.

Definition 3. (R-UNSEARCHMO) For the current node D (initially the root node Φ) and its corresponding consequent atom set $\mathcal{I}_D$ (initially empty):

1. If there exists a lemma $lemma(\mathcal{L})$ in the database such that $\mathcal{I}_D \vdash \mathcal{L}$, $S \cup \mathcal{I}_D$ is unsatisfiable. Create a node $\oslash$ below node D. The branch terminates there. The useful consequent atom set for the refutation at node D, $\mathcal{U}_D$, consists of all atoms in $\mathcal{L}$.
2. If $\mathcal{NC} \cup \mathcal{I}_D \vdash \bot$, $S \cup \mathcal{I}_D$ is unsatisfiable. Create a leaf node $\bot$ below node D. The branch terminates there. The useful consequent atom set for the refutation at node D, $\mathcal{U}_D$, consists of all atoms in $\mathcal{A}$, where $\mathcal{A}$ is the antecedent of a negative clause such that $\mathcal{I}_D \vdash \mathcal{A}$.
3. If $\mathcal{NC} \cup \mathcal{I}_D \not\vdash \bot$, select a violated clause from $\mathcal{FC}$. If no such clause exists, $\mathcal{I}_D$ is a model of S. The procedure ceases to construct the proof tree and reports the given clause set is satisfiable.
4. For the selected violated $\mathcal{FC}$ clause $\mathcal{A} \rightarrow C_1; \dots; C_m$, create a child node C_i for every i such that $1 \leq i \leq m$ below node D. Taking C_i as the new current node, call this procedure recursively in depth-first strategy with the augmented consequent atom set $\mathcal{I}_{C_i} = \mathcal{I}_D \cup \{C_i\}$. However, if some C_i is found to be useless when it is retracted from the database on backtracking, i.e., if $C_i \notin \mathcal{U}_{C_i}$: (a) $S \cup \mathcal{I}_D$ is unsatisfiable; (b) remove the partial tree below node C_j for each j such that $1 \leq j < i$, and instead of each C_j, create a special node $\otimes$; (c) instead of node C_k for each k such that $i <$

$k \leq m$, create a special node $\times$; (d) the useful consequent atom set for node D, $\mathcal{U}_D$, is established just the same as $\mathcal{U}_{C_i}$. On the other hand, if all of node C_i are proved unsatisfiable with all of C_i are found to be useful, then: (a) $\mathcal{S} \cup \mathcal{I}_D$ is unsatisfiable; (b) the useful consequent atom set for node D $\mathcal{U}_D = \{\mathcal{U}_{C_1} - \{C_1\}\} \cup \cdots \cup \{\mathcal{U}_{C_m} - \{C_m\}\} \cup \mathcal{A}$; (c) $lemma(\mathcal{U}_D)$ is added to the database and all of $lemma(\mathcal{H})$ such that $\mathcal{H} \vdash \mathcal{U}_D$ are retracted from the database.

The given clause set is unsatisfiable if and only if the root node is proved unsatisfiable, i.e., every branch of the proof tree terminates in a leaf $\perp$, $\oslash$, $\otimes$ or $\times$, where $\otimes$ and $\times$ have the same meanings as in the algorithm of UNSEARCHMO.

The correctness of our refinement is quite straightforward. According to the soundness of UNSEARCHMO, for any node D in the proof tree for a given clause set $\mathcal{S}$ such that is proved unsatisfiable, $\mathcal{S} \cup \mathcal{U}_D$ is unsatisfiable, where $\mathcal{U}_D$ is the useful consequent atom set for the refutation at node D derived by UNSEARCHMO. The further details are omitted.

Example 4. Consider the clause set given in Example 3.

The proof tree constructed by UNSEARCHMO is shown in Figure 4.

When the refutation at node s on the left side of the proof tree is derived, the corresponding useful consequent set $\mathcal{U}_s$ derived there is $\{u, s\}$, and $lemma(u, s)$ is asserted into the database. Then, when node u on the left side is proved unsatisfiable, where the corresponding useful consequent set $\mathcal{U}_u$ derived there is $\{u\}$, $lemma(u, s)$ is removed from the database and $lemma(u)$ is asserted into the database.

At node u on the right side of the proof tree, where the consequent atom set is $\mathcal{I}_u = \{w, u\}$, we have $\mathcal{I}_u \vdash u$, i.e., $lemma(u)$ can be satisfied there. Therefore, node u is proved unsatisfiable by a lemma.

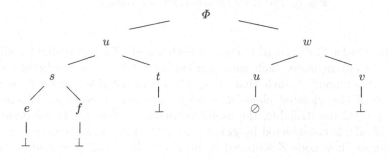

Fig. 4. The proof tree constructed by UNSEARCHMO in Example 4

4 Implementation

The Prolog code in Prolog for R-UNSEARCHMO is shown in Figure 5. The unsatisfiability of a given clause set is checked by running unsatisfiable(*top*, *root*), where *root* denotes the root Φ of a proof tree, and *top* is a virtual node to denote the parent node of node *root*.

```
?- op(1200, xfx, '--->').

    unsatisfiable(P,Z):-                    toList(A,L,F):-
      lemma(L),                               (A=..[F,X,Y],!,
      is_provable(L),                           L=[X|Lo],
      asserta(u_a_set(L,P,Z))).                 toList(Y,Lo,F));
                                              L=[A].
    unsatisfiable(P,Z):-
      A ---> bottom,                        is_violated(A,C):-
      A, toList(A, L),                        Ao ---> Co,
      asserta(u_a_set(L,P,Z))).               Ao, not Co,
                                              toList(Ao,A,','),toList(Co,C,';').
    unsatisfiable(P,Z):-
      !,is_violated(A,C),                  get_u_a_set(U,A,Z,X,0):-
      !,each_unsatisfiable(Z,C),             u_a_set(U,Z,X),
      (retract(is_useless(X)),F=0; F=1),     (retract(u_a_set(_,Z,_)),fail; true).
      get_u_a_set(U,A,Z,X,F),              get_u_a_set(U,A,Z,X,1):-
      asserta(u_a_set(U,P,Z)),               combine_u_a_set(So,B,Z),
      (F==0; assert_lemma(U)).               list_to_set(So, S).

    each_unsatisfiable(_,[]).
    each_unsatisfiable(Z,[X|C]):-          combine_u_a_set([So|S],B,Z):-
      asserta(X),                            retract(u_a_set(Sx,Z,Y)),
      !,unsatisfiable(Z,X),                  delete(X,Sx,So),
      retract(X),                            combine_u_a_set(U,B,Z).
      u_a_set(U,Z,X),                      combine_u_a_set(B,B,_).
      (member(X,U),!,each_unsatisfiable(Z,C);
       asserta(is_useless(X))).            assert_lemma(U):-
                                             lemma(E), subset(U,E),
    is_provable([]).                         retract(lemma(E)), fail.
    is_provable([X|A]):-                   assert_lemma(U):-
      X,is_provable(A).                      asserta(lemma(U)).
```

Fig. 5. The R-UNSEARCHMO's program

unsatisfiable(P, Z) is used to check whether node Z is unsatisfiable, where P is node Z's parent node. each_unsatisfiable(Z, C), to check whether each child node X of node Z such that $X \in C$ is unsatisfiable, where C is the consequence of the violated clause A ---> C selected at node Z. Whenever node Z is proved unsatisfiable, the useful consequent atom set U for node Z, u_a_set(U, P, Z), is constructed by get_u_a_set(U, A, Z, X, F), where F is the flag that denotes how node Z is proved unsatisfiable. If node Z is proved unsatisfiable such that some $X \in C$ is found to be useless (at that time, is_useless(X) is asserted into the database), F is set to 0. Otherwise, i.e., node Z is proved unsatisfiable such that each $X \in C$ is found to be useful for the refutation at node X, the flag F is set to 1. Moreover, when F is 1, i.e., assert_lemma(U) is executed, which makes the process for asserting the new lemma lemma(U).

5   Experimental Results

In this section, we give examples to show the power of R-UNSEARCHMO, in comparison to SATCHMO and UNSEARCHMO. All experimental results are made under SWI-Prolog on an Intel PentiumIII/500MHZ workstation with the running time given in seconds.

All problems are selected from the TPTP problem library 14) and the experimental results are given in Table 1, where — means that no answer can be obtained, $> 1h$, the running time is over one hour, and S, U and R mean SATCHMO, UNSEARCHMO and R-UNSEARCHMO, while S_L, U_L and R_L, their level-saturation versions, respectively. The problems from 1 to 14 are unsatisfiable, in which the problems from 11 to 14 contain recursive clauses (therefore, only level-saturation versions are available). The problems 15 and 16 are satisfiable. We can find that the performance of R-UNSEARCHMO is better than that of UNSEARCHMO in almost all cases. This does not only mean that R-UNSEARCHMO is efficient, but also means that our refinement almost takes no additional cost.

In this paper, for convenience of presentation, we have not distinguished Horn clauses and non-Horn clauses. If we use, as did in SATCHMORE and $\mathcal{A}$-SATCHMORE, Prolog for reasoning on a selected decidable Horn clause set, the performance of R-UNSEARCHMO can be further improved.

Table 1. The experiment results for SATCHMO, UNSEARCHMO and R-UNSEARCHMO

		S	U	R	S_L	U_L	R_L
1	PUZ010-1	50.25	34.48	28.76	$>1h$	2572.21	42.72
2	PUZ023-1	0.04	0.03	0.02	$>1h$	307.42	209.18
3	PUZ024-1	0.04	0.02	0.03	118.36	0.05	0.01
4	PUZ025-1	0.05	0.04	0.05	$>1h$	$>1h$	$>1h$
5	PUZ026-1	0.04	0.06	0.04	19.67	0.03	0.04
6	PUZ030-1	0.03	0.08	0.08	16.83	0.60	0.30
7	SWV009-1	18.57	0.05	0.04			
8	SYN443-1	$>1h$	$>1h$	14.97	$>1h$	$>1h$	475.89
9	SYN447-1	$>1h$	$>1h$	$>1h$	$>1h$	$>1h$	173.40
10	SYN511-1	$>1h$	$>1h$	15.22	$>1h$	$>1h$	61.97
11	SWV002-1	—	—	—	$>1h$	$>1h$	2877.93
12	PUZ001-2	—	—	—	900.78	0.22	0.17
13	PUZ005-1	—	—	—	$>1h$	0.18	0.10
14	MSC007-2.005	—	—	—	35.79	17.45	5.74
15	PUZ018-2	$>1h$	2947.17	3.73	$>1h$	$>1h$	85.57
16	SYN437-1	$>1h$	$>1h$	300.79	$>1h$	$>1h$	$>1h$

6   Conclusion

In this paper, we have proposed a refinement on UNSEARCHMO. By our R-UNSEARCHMO, the repeated reasoning can be avoided. Some experimental results have shown that our method is powerful for theorem proving.

Our refinement, although we did not discuss in this paper, can be easily incorporated into SATCHMORE and $\mathcal{A}$-SATCHMORE to improve their performances.

References

1. F. Bry, and A. Yahya, 'Positive Unit Hyperresolution Tableaux and Their Application to Minimal Model Generation', *J. of Automated Reasoning*, 25:35-82, 2000.
2. P.T. Cox, 'Finding backtrack points for intelligent backtracking', *Implementations of Prolog*, Campbell, J.A. (ed.). pp.216-233, Ellis Horwood, 1984.
3. R. Demolombe, 'An Efficient Strategy for Non-Horn Deductive Databases', *Theoretical Computer Science*, **78** pp.245-249, 1991.
4. L. He, 'UNSEARCHMO: Eliminating Redundant Search Space on Backtracking for Forward Chaining Theorem Proving', *Proceedings of the Seventeenth Intl. Joint Conf. on Artificial Intelligence*, Seatle, U.S.A, 2001.
5. H. Lifeng, 'I-SATCHMO: an Improvement of SATCHMO', *J. of Automated Reasoning*, **27**: pp.313-322, 2001.
6. L. He, Y. Chao, Y. Simajiri, H. Seki and H. Itoh, '$\mathcal{A}$-SATCHMORE: SATCHMORE with Availability Checking', *New Generation Computing*, 16:55-74, 1998.
7. R. Letz, K. Mayr and C. Goller, 'Controlled Integration of the Cut Rule into Connection Tableau Calculi', *J. of Automated Reasoning*, **13**: pp.297-337, 1994.
8. D.W. Loveland, 'A Simplified Format for the Model Elimination Theorem-Proving Procedure', *J. of the ACM 16*, pp.349-363, 1969.
9. D.W. Loveland, D.W. Reed and D.S. Wilson, 'SATCHMORE: SATCHMO with RElevancy', *J. of Automated Reasoning*, **14**: pp.325-351, 1995.
10. D.W. Loveland and A.H. Yahya, 'SATCHMOREBID: SATCHMO(RE) with BIDirectional Relevancy', *New Generation Computing*. To appear.
11. D.W. Ramsay, 'Generating Relevant Models', *J. of Automated Reasoning*, **7**: pp.359-368, 1991.
12. R. Manthey and F. Bry, 'SATCHMO: a theorem prover implemented in Prolog', *Proceedings of 9th intl. Conf. on Automated Deduction*, 1988.
13. F. Oppacher and E. Suen, 'HAPR: A Tableau-Based Theorem Prover', *J. of Automated Reasoning*, **4**: pp.69-100, 1988.
14. G. Sutcliffe and C. Suttner, http://www.cs.jcu.edu.au/~tptp/
15. R.M. Stallman and G.J. Sussman, 'Forward Reasoning and Dependecy-Derected Backtracking in a System for Computer-Aided Circuit Analysis', *Artificial Intelligence*, Vol. 9, pp.135-1196, 1977.

Deontic Relevant Logic: A Strong Relevant Logic Approach to Removing Paradoxes from Deontic Logic

Takahiro Tagawa[1] and Jingde Cheng[2]

[1] Computing and Communications Center, Kyushu University
Fukuoka, Fukuoka 812-8581, Japan
tagawat@ec.kyushu-u.ac.jp
[2] Department of Information and Computer Sciences, Saitama University
Saitama, Saitama 338-8570, Japan
cheng@ics.saitama-u.ac.jp

Abstract. In this paper, we propose a strong relevant logic approach to solve the problems of deontic logic paradoxes. Since the paradoxes in deontic logic have the same form as the paradoxes in traditional (weak) relevant logic, which have been rejected by our strong relevant logic, we show that a new family of logic, named deontic relevant logics, can be established by introducing deontic operators and relative axioms and inference rules into strong relevant logics such that those deontic logic paradoxes are rejected by deontic relevant logics.

1 Introduction

Deontic logic is the logic that deals with actual and ideal states or behavior of agents, and expected to be applied to wide areas such as legal reasoning, validation, specification, and so on. However, there are problems called the "deontic logic paradoxes" in deontic logic, and it is necessary for practical applications of deontic logic to remove those paradoxes from deontic logic in some way.

In this paper, we propose a strong relevant logic approach to solve the problems of deontic logic paradoxes. Since the paradoxes in deontic logic have the same form as the paradoxes in traditional (weak) relevant logic, which have been rejected by our strong relevant logic, we show that a new family of logic, named deontic relevant logics, can be established by introducing deontic operators and relative axioms and inference rules into strong relevant logics such that those deontic logic paradoxes are rejected by deontic relevant logics.

Section 2 is the introduction to the deontic logic and its paradoxes. Section 3 is about the relevant logics, paradoxes in relevant logics, and the strong relevant logics which exclude paradoxes from relevant logics. In Section 4 we propose deontic relevant logics and discuss how the deontic logic paradoxes are rejected in these logics. The rest of the paper are the comparison with related works of others and conclusion.

M. Ishizuka and A. Sattar (Eds.): PRICAI 2002, LNAI 2417, pp. 39–48, 2002.
© Springer-Verlag Berlin Heidelberg 2002

2   Paradoxes in Deontic Logic

Deontic logic is the logic that deals with actual and ideal states or behavior of agents. Traditionally the deontic logic has been used to analyze the normative sentences by philosophers who studies law, moral, and ethics. In 1980s, it was discovered by computer scientists and AI researchers that there are wide areas of applications of the deontic logic such as legal reasoning, specification, validation, and the deontic logic have been studied by them actively since then. The application first come to mind and most expected to deontic logics is the legal expert systems. In the systems, the laws and/or rules in some domain are represented by deontic formulas, and the system derives the legal consequence of given real or hypothetical state of affairs represented by the set of sentences, by reasoning based on the deontic logic. This can be used to give advice to the users what rights and obligations they have in their situation.

The most well-known deontic logic is so-called the standard deontic logic(**SDL** for short), which was first formalized by von Wright [1,2,3]. **SDL** has all tautologies of the classical mathematical logic(**CML** for short) and $O(A \rightarrow B) \rightarrow (OA \rightarrow OB)$, and $\neg(OA \wedge O\neg A)$ as axioms, and "From A and $A \rightarrow B$ to infer B (Modus Ponens)", "if A is a logical theorem of **SDL**, the OA is so (O-necessitation)" as inference rules. In **SDL**, a modal operator O is used to represent the obligation. For a sentence A, OA can be read as saying that "A should be done" or "It is obligatory that A". According to this interpretation, $O\neg A$ represents the forbiddance "It is forbidden that A" or "It is forbidden to do A". Similarly, $\neg O\neg A$ represents the permission "It is permitted that A" or "You may do A".

There are well-known problems called "the deontic logic paradoxes" in **SDL**. Those problems are called "paradoxes" because some sentences, which are logically valid in **SDL** or conclusions of valid reasonings based on **SDL**, have readings in natural language which are contrary to human intuition. Much discussion have been done about these problems, and numbers of systems of deontic logics have been proposed and studied to solve these problems.

Due to the deontic logic paradoxes, for some given promises, a legal expert system based on **SDL** cannot necessarily derive legal consequence which are naturally consistent with our common-sense. It is necessary for the practical applications of deontic logic to solve or avoid the problems of deontic logic paradoxes.

Here we show main important deontic logic paradoxes.

a) **Paradox of derived obligation.** In **SDL**, $OA \rightarrow O(\neg A \rightarrow B)$ is a logical theorem. This formula means that, "If it is obligatory that A, then, it is obligatory, that 'if A does not hold, then (arbitrary) B hold' ", in other words, "Arbitrary B is obligated if the obligation A cannot be fulfilled". Of course this is not valid in human thinking[3].

b) **Alf Ross's paradox.** A formula $OA \rightarrow O(A \vee B)$ is a logical theorem of **SDL**. This formula means that, " If it is obligatory that A, then it is obligatory that A or B." for any sentences A and B. We must regard this as valid if we accept **SDL**. However, statements in this form such as " If you ought to post the letter, then you ought to post the letter or burn the letter." cannot be considered as valid in human thinking. Adding an arbitrary proposition as a disjunct of the obligation seems to be unreasonable and therefore this formula is unacceptable[2, 3,6].

c) **Paradox of Good Samaritan.** Suppose that there is a sentence saying that "You ought to help someone who has been robbed." If we read p as "You help someone" and q as "Someone has been robbed", then the sentence can be represented by the **SDL** formula $O(p \wedge q)$. On the other hand, $O(A \wedge B) \to OB$ is a logical theorem of **SDL**, so here the formula Oq can be derived. This formula can be read as "Someone ought to have been robbed." Of course such reasoning is strange and not valid in human thinking, while we must regard it as valid when we accept **SDL** [3,4,5,6]. Moreover, $O\neg q \to O\neg(p \wedge q)$ is a logical theorem of **SDL** . This sentence can be read as "If anyone should not be robbed, then you should not help someone who has been robbed." But this reading is contrary to our intuition about obligation and forbiddance.

d) **Ceteris paribus problem.** $(A \to OB) \to (A \wedge C \to OB)$ and $O(A \to B) \to O(A \wedge C \to B)$ are the logical theorems of **SDL**. They mean that, the obligation in some condition never can be withdrawn or changed even if some condition is added to premises[4,5]. However, it is usual that the obligation at one time (*prima facie* duty) is withdrawn and overruled by new and stronger obligation (*actual obligation*) when some new conditions are added, in our everyday life. So we cannot accept these sentences, $(A \to OB) \to (A \wedge C \to OB)$ and $O(A \to B) \to O(A \wedge C \to B)$, as the representations of our thought about the obligation. The concept of " *ceteris paribus*", i.e. "other things being equal", is an implicit presumption for any reasoning. Almost all entailment relations in human knowledge have the form "from some constant condition, to derive some constant result" and do not insist the validity under the condition with some new and additional premises. In other words, we do not necessarily derive the same conclusion when new other conditions are added to the premise. This problem is not peculiar to the deontic logic, however, especially serious in context which concerns to the obligations and rights, because the withdrawal of a duty urged by new conditions or reasons is usual in our life, and the analysis of whether one thing is obligated or is not is the most important issue of the laws and other rules on which our society is founded.

e) **Contrary-to-duty obligation paradox.** Suppose that there is a set of **SDL** formulas to represent some situation, $\{ Op, O(p \to q), \neg p \to O\neg q, \neg p \}$. Contradictictory sentences $Op \wedge O\neg p$ and $\neg(Op \wedge O\neg p)$ (this is a logical theorem of **SDL**) can be derived based on **SDL** from this set. The situation represented by above set is ordinary, not uncommon. So we must say that there is an inadequacy in **SDL** to represent some situation by a set of sentences and to reason some obligations from it. The most known example of this paradox is the Chisolm's paradox, where p above is read as " You go to the assistance of your neighbors" and q as "You tell them(neighbors) that you will come." Here, You must tell them because you must go. On the other hand, You must not tell them because you don't go –while you must go. Sentences to represent each obligation are contradictory each other here[2,4,5,6].

3   Strong Relevant Logic

Relevant logics are construed during the 1950s–1970s in order to find a satisfactory way of grasping the notion of entailment[8,9,10,11]. **T**, **E**, and **R** are well-known among relevant logic systems. The most important feature of the relevant logics is that they have a primitive intensional logical connective "$\Rightarrow$" as a natural representation of the notion of entailment.

The basic idea of the relevant logics is that, for the truth of $A \Rightarrow B$, it is necessary that there should be something in common to both A and B. This is called the "relevance" in an entailment relation. Anderson and Belnap proposed a necessary condition for the relevance between A and B in $A \Rightarrow B$ that A and B must share a variable. This property is called "the relevance principle". All logical theorems of relevant logics in the form $A \Rightarrow B$ satisfy the condition of the relevance principle[8,9].

As the logical basis of knowledge-based systems, relevant logics are better than **CML**[12,14]. (1) The conclusion of a reasoning based on relevant logics is necessarily relevant to the premises and vice versa, while this is not necessarily true in **CML**. (2) The logical theorems of relevant logics do not include so-called material-implicational paradoxes in **CML**, such as $A \to (B \to A)$, $B \to (\neg A \vee A)$, $(\neg A \wedge A) \to B$ and so on. (3) Relevant logics are paraconsistent, i.e., the inference from A and $\neg A$ to B (where A and B can be any two formulas) is not valid in the logics, and therefore they can underlie reasoning under inconsistency. On the other hand, **CML** is explosive and reasoning under inconsistency falls into nonsense.

Cheng pointed out that, though the traditional relevant logics have rejected the material-implicational paradoxes, there still are some logical axioms and theorems which are not natural in the sense of entailment[12,13,14]. For instance, in these logic, $A \wedge B \Rightarrow A$, $A \wedge B \Rightarrow B$, $(A \Rightarrow B) \Rightarrow (A \wedge C \Rightarrow B)$, $A \Rightarrow A \vee B$, $B \Rightarrow A \vee B$, $(A \Rightarrow B) \Rightarrow (A \Rightarrow B \vee C)$ and so on, are logical axioms or theorems. Cheng named these logical axioms and logical theorems "conjunction-implicational paradoxes" and "disjunction-implicational paradoxes". As an example, let us see $A \wedge B \Rightarrow A$, which is a logical axiom or theorem of almost all relevant logics. B, as a conjunct of the antecedent of $A \wedge B \Rightarrow A$, is irrelevant to the truth of the entailment, because B may irrelevant to A, or B may be the negation of A. However, propositions in this form such as "if snow is white and 1+1=2, then 1+1=2", "if snow is white and 1+1=3, then snow is white", "if snow is white snow is not white, then snow is white" and so on, cannot be considered as valid in human logical thinking, of course. Moreover, $(A \Rightarrow B) \Rightarrow (A \wedge C \Rightarrow B)$ is a logical theorem of almost relevant logics and is valid in the logics. Therefore, from any given entailment formula $A \Rightarrow B$ and the logical theorem, we can infer $A \wedge C \Rightarrow B$ by using Modus Ponens with the entailment. However, from the viewpoint of human logical thinking, this reasoning is not necessarily considered as valid in the sense of entailment, because there may be no necessarily relevant relation between C and B and we cannot say "if A and C, then B" if we do not investigate the content of $A \wedge C \Rightarrow B$. These are the conjunction-implicational paradoxes. Similar argument holds for disjunction-implicational paradoxes, for example, $A \Rightarrow A \vee B$ and $(A \Rightarrow B) \Rightarrow (A \Rightarrow B \vee C)$.

The "antecedent part" and the "consequent part" of a formula or a subformula A are defined inductively, as follows[8,9,11]:

1. A is a consequent part of A itself.
2. If $\neg B$ is a consequent {antecedent} part of A, then B is an antecedent {consequent} part of A.
3. If $B \Rightarrow C$ is a consequent{antecedent} part of A, then B is an antecedent {consequent} part of A and C is a consequent {antecedent} part of A.
4. If $B \wedge C$ or $B \wedge C$ is an antecedent {consequent} part of A, then both B and C are antecedent {consequent} part of A.

These designation "antecedent part" and "consequent part" comes from the Gentzen sequent style formulation of relevant logic. The ultimate premises of sequent style calculus proof of logical theorem A are axioms "$p \vdash p$", and the left p appears in A as an antecedent part and the right p appears in A as a consequent part[8,9].

Based upon definition of "antecedent part" and "consequent part" above, we have proposed the strong relevance principle, saying that, for relevant logics to be free of not only material-implicational but also conjunction-implicational and disjunction-implicational paradoxes, it is a necessary condition that, in all axioms and logical theorems, every variable occurring in the formula should occur at least once as an antecedent part and at least once as a consequent part. By using this necessary condition in addition to the "relevance principle", we can exclude not only material-implicational paradoxes but also conjunction-implicational and disjunction-implicational paradoxes from logic systems[15].

Relevant logics **Rc**, **Ec**, and **Tc** are proposed in order to construct paradox-free relevant logics[13,14]. Axioms and logical theorems of these relevant logics satisfy the condition of relevance principle and the strong relevant principle, so we can say that **Rc**, **Ec** and **Tc** are not only material-implicational paradox-free, but also conjunction-implicational and disjunction-implicational paradox-free relevant logics[15]. We call these logics as "strong relevant logics."

4   Deontic Relevant Logic

Here we propose the deontic relevant logics **DTc**, **DEc** and **DRc**, by introducing deontic modal operators and relative axioms and inference rules into the strong relevant logics **Tc**, **Ec**, and **Rc** respectively.

The logical connectives, deontic operators, axiom schemata, and inference rules of our deontic relevant logics are as follows:

Primitive logical connectives:
$\Rightarrow$: entailment
$\neg$: negation
$\wedge$: extensional conjunction

Defined logical connectives:

$\vee$: extensional disjunction, $A \vee B \stackrel{\text{def}}{=} \neg(\neg A \wedge \neg B)$

$\rightarrow$: material implication, $A \rightarrow B \stackrel{\text{def}}{=} \neg(A \wedge \neg B)$ or $\neg A \vee B$

Deontic operators and intended informal meaning:

O: obligation, OA means "It is obligatory that A"

P: permission, $PA \stackrel{\text{def}}{=} \neg O \neg A$, PA means "It is permitted that A"

Axiom schemata:

E1 $A \Rightarrow A$
E2 $(A \Rightarrow B) \Rightarrow ((C \Rightarrow A) \Rightarrow (C \Rightarrow B))$
E2' $(A \Rightarrow B) \Rightarrow ((B \Rightarrow C) \Rightarrow (A \Rightarrow C))$
E3 $(A \Rightarrow (A \Rightarrow B)) \Rightarrow (A \Rightarrow B)$
E3' $(A \Rightarrow (B \Rightarrow C)) \Rightarrow ((A \Rightarrow B) \Rightarrow (A \Rightarrow C))$
E3" $(A \Rightarrow B) \Rightarrow ((A \Rightarrow (B \Rightarrow C)) \Rightarrow (A \Rightarrow C))$
E4 $(A \Rightarrow ((B \Rightarrow C) \Rightarrow D)) \Rightarrow ((B \Rightarrow C) \Rightarrow (A \Rightarrow D))$
E4' $(A \Rightarrow B) \Rightarrow (((A \Rightarrow B) \Rightarrow C) \Rightarrow C)$
E4" $((A \Rightarrow A) \Rightarrow B) \Rightarrow B$
E4"' $(A \Rightarrow B) \Rightarrow ((B \Rightarrow C) \Rightarrow (((A \Rightarrow C) \Rightarrow D) \Rightarrow D))$
E5 $(A \Rightarrow (B \Rightarrow C)) \Rightarrow (B \Rightarrow (A \Rightarrow C))$
E5' $A \Rightarrow ((A \Rightarrow B) \Rightarrow B)$

N1 $(A \Rightarrow (\neg A)) \Rightarrow (\neg A)$
N2 $(A \Rightarrow (\neg B)) \Rightarrow (B \Rightarrow (\neg A))$
N3 $(\neg(\neg A)) \Rightarrow A$

C1 $A \wedge B \Rightarrow A$
C2 $A \wedge B \Rightarrow B$
C3 $(A \Rightarrow B) \wedge (A \Rightarrow C) \Rightarrow (A \Rightarrow B \wedge C)$
C4 $(LA \wedge LB) \Rightarrow L(A \wedge B)$ where $LA \stackrel{\text{def}}{=} (A \Rightarrow A) \Rightarrow A$

D1 $A \Rightarrow A \vee B$
D2 $B \Rightarrow A \vee B$
D3 $(A \Rightarrow C) \wedge (B \Rightarrow C) \Rightarrow (A \vee B \Rightarrow C)$
DCD $A \wedge (B \vee C) \Rightarrow (A \wedge B) \vee C$

C5 $A \wedge A \Rightarrow A$
C6 $A \wedge B \Rightarrow B \wedge A$
C7 $(A \Rightarrow B) \wedge (B \Rightarrow C) \Rightarrow (A \Rightarrow C)$
C8 $A \wedge (A \Rightarrow B) \Rightarrow B$
C9 $\neg(A \wedge \neg A)$
C10 $A \Rightarrow (B \Rightarrow (A \wedge B))$

DR1 $O(A \Rightarrow B) \Rightarrow (OA \Rightarrow OB)$
DR2 $OA \Rightarrow PA$
DR3 $\neg(OA \wedge O \neg A)$
DR4 $O(A \wedge B) \Rightarrow OA \wedge OB$
DR5 $P(A \wedge B) \Rightarrow PA \wedge PB$

Inference rules:
$\Rightarrow E$:   "from A and $A \Rightarrow B$ to infer B"(Modus Ponens)
$\wedge I$:   "from A and B to infer $A \wedge B$"(Adjunction)
O-necessitation: "if A is a logical theorem, then OA is so."

Our deontic relevant logic systems may be defined as follows, where we use "$A|B$" to denote any choice of one from two axiom schemata A and B.

$\mathbf{T}_\Rightarrow = \{E1,\ E2,\ E2',\ E3|E3''\}+\Rightarrow E$
$\mathbf{E}_\Rightarrow = \{E1,\ E2|E2',\ E3|E3',\ E4|E4'\}+\Rightarrow E$
$\mathbf{R}_\Rightarrow = \{E1,\ E2|E2',\ E3|E3',\ E5|E5'\}+\Rightarrow E$
$\mathbf{T}_{\Rightarrow\neg} = \mathbf{T}_\Rightarrow + \{N1,\ N2,\ N3\}$
$\mathbf{E}_{\Rightarrow\neg} = \mathbf{E}_\Rightarrow + \{N1,\ N2,\ N3\}$
$\mathbf{R}_{\Rightarrow\neg} = \mathbf{R}_\Rightarrow + \{N2,\ N3\}$
$\mathbf{T} = \mathbf{T}_{\Rightarrow\neg} + \{C1-C3,\ D1-D3,\ DCD\}+\wedge I$
$\mathbf{E} = \mathbf{E}_{\Rightarrow\neg} + \{C1-C4,\ D1-D3,\ DCD\}+\wedge I$
$\mathbf{R} = \mathbf{R}_{\Rightarrow\neg} + \{C1-C3,\ D1-D3,\ DCD\}+\wedge I$
$\mathbf{Tc} = \mathbf{T}_{\Rightarrow\neg} + \{C3,\ C5-C10\}+\wedge I$
$\mathbf{Ec} = \mathbf{E}_{\Rightarrow\neg} + \{C3-C10\}+\wedge I$
$\mathbf{Rc} = \mathbf{R}_{\Rightarrow\neg} + \{C3,\ C5-C10\}+\wedge I$
$\mathbf{DTc} = \mathbf{Tc} + \{DR1-DR5\}+O$-necessitation
$\mathbf{DEc} = \mathbf{Ec} + \{DR1-DR5\}+O$-necessitation
$\mathbf{DRc} = \mathbf{Rc} + \{DR1-DR5\}+O$-necessitation

As to these deontic relevant logics, we have the following fact.

$Th(\mathbf{SDL}) \supset Th(\mathbf{DTc/DEc/DRc})$, where $Th(L)$ is the set of all of logical theorems of logic L.

As conservative extensions of the strong relevant logics, these deontic relevant logics are paraconsistent, and free of not only material-implicational paradoxes but also conjunction-implicational paradoxes and disjunction-implicational paradoxes.

We discuss about the characteristics of the deontic logic paradoxes in reference to the relevant logics. Because of some formal characteristics and properties of strong relevant logics, our deontic relevant logics can solve or avoid the problems of deontic logic paradoxes referred in previous section.

a) **Paradox of derived obligation.** The corresponding formula of the paradox of derived obligation, $OA \Rightarrow O(\neg A \Rightarrow B)$, cannot be derived as a logical theorem of our deontic relevant logics. So the paradox of derived obligation will not arise in these logics.

b) **Alf Ross's paradox.** $OA \to O(A \vee B)$ can be derived as a logical theorem of **SDL** and this logical theorem is called Alf Ross's paradox. We can regard this Alf Ross's paradox as a kind of disjunction-implicational paradoxes referred in previous section, happened in connection with deontic modality. In deontic relevant logics, corresponding formula $OA \Rightarrow O(A \vee B)$ cannot be derived as a logical theorem. So Alf Ross's paradox will not arise in our deontic relevant logics.

c) **Paradox of Good Samaritan**. We can regard this paradox as a kind of conjunction-implicational paradoxes happened in connection with deontic modality, just like Alf Ross's paradox as disjunction-implicational paradoxes. $O(A \wedge B) \Rightarrow OB$ is not a logical theorem of our deontic relevant logics. So Oq cannot be derived as a conclusion of reasoning with premise $O(p \wedge q)$. Furthermore, $O\neg A \Rightarrow O\neg(A \wedge B)$ also cannot be derived as a logical theorem of our deontic relevant logics. So the paradox of Good Samaritan will not arise in our deontic relevant logics.

d) **Ceteris paribus problem**. The logical theorem of **CML**, $(A \rightarrow B) \rightarrow (A \wedge C \rightarrow B)$, and the logical theorems of **SDL**, $(A \rightarrow OB) \rightarrow (A \wedge C \rightarrow OB)$ and $O(A \rightarrow B) \rightarrow O(A \wedge C \rightarrow B)$ are problems because they mean that, the conclusion (and/or obligation) in some condition never can be withdrawn or changed even if some condition is added to premises, and this contradicts the ceteris paribus condition. On the other hand, as shown in previous section, $(A \Rightarrow B) \Rightarrow (A \wedge C \Rightarrow B)$ is a conjunction-implicational paradox, and it has been rejected from strong relevant logics. Our deontic relevant logics are the conservative extensions of those strong relevant logics, and neither $(A \Rightarrow OB) \Rightarrow (A \wedge C \Rightarrow OB)$ nor $O(A \Rightarrow B) \Rightarrow O(A \wedge C \Rightarrow B)$ can be derived from these logics. Here, the condition of "ceteris paribus" is satisfied naturally.

e) **Contrary-to-duty obligation paradox**. The representation of contrary-to-duty obligation situation based on **SDL** is called a paradox, because the set to represent the situation gives rise to the contradiction. The problem of contradiction here is that, if the set of sentences includes contradiction, then any sentence can be derived from such set and such set falls into nonsense, because the representation and reasoning here are based on **SDL**, the conservative extension of **CML**. In other words, the explosiveness of the **CML** and **SDL** is very the reason why contradictions should be avoided here. On the other hand, as referred in previous section, the relevant logics are paraconsistent, i.e., the set of sentences will make sense and be of use even if there are contradictory sentences in the set. So contradiction in the set of sentences to represent contrary-to-duty obligation situation is not a critical trouble to whole set, if representation and reasoning of sentences are based on our deontic relevant logics, the conservative extension of strong relevant logics. The choice which to take as actual obligation among two derived obligations must be made on some ground, however, the existence of contradiction in the set is allowable here, as a representation of some state. Adopting our deontic relevant logics can be said at least as a avoidance or detoxification of the problem of the contrary-to-duty obligation paradox, even if it may not be a complete solution.

5   Comparison with Related Works

Stelzner's "relevant deontic logic" gives the new definition of the relevance in entailment relation to avoid the some of deontic logic paradoxes, and shows the relevant entailment relation which should hold between obligations[7]. As a result, Stelzner's logic excludes Ross's paradox. The paradox of Good Samaritan is partly excluded. $O\neg A \Rightarrow O\neg(A \wedge B)$ is rejected, while $O(A \wedge B) \Rightarrow OB$ is regarded as sound entailment in this logic.

Dyadic deontic logic and deontic tense logic are proposed in order to solve the problem of contrary-to-duty obligation paradox[2,3,4,5,6]. In these logics, obligations are defined to be relative to the context or time point in which they hold. As a result, two derived obligations who were contradictory each other in contrary-to-duty obligation situation in **SDL**, are not contradictory in these logics, because these obligations do not hold at same time. In other words, the contradiction in contrary-to-duty obligation situation is avoided there, while the contradiction is regarded as harmless in itself there in our deontic relevant logics.

6   Conclusion

We have proposed the deontic relevant logics, by introducing deontic modal operators and relative axioms and inference rules into the strong relevant logics. These logics have solved, or avoided, the problems of deontic logic paradoxes naturally. No new paradoxes unknown to **SDL** will arise in these deontic relevant logics, because all of logical theorems of these deontic relevant logics are also the logical theorems of **SDL**.

These deontic relevant logics would be able to be applied to the legal expert systems, because such systems based on these logics can derive valid legal consequence of given states of affairs represented by the set of sentences and laws or rules represented by the set of formulas of the logics, while the systems based on **SDL** cannot do.

There is a problem, the choice of *prima facie* duty and *actual obligation* in contrary-to-duty obligation situation to be solved. The existence of contradictory obligations is moderately allowable here, however, the legal expert system would be of no use if the system tells you that you have two contradictory duties at the same time. There should be a decision about which is to be taken as actual obligation among two derived obligations, and such decision should be based on some rational frameworks or models.

A future work, which is important to deontic relevant logic as well as strong relevant logic, is to find some elegant semantic structure for them.

References

[1] G.H.von Wright, "Deontic Logic," Mind, Vol.60, pp.1–15, 1951.
[2] G.H.von Wright, "An Essay in Deontic Logic and the General Theory of Action," Acta Philosophica Fennica, Vol.21, 1968.
[3] G.H.von Wright, "On the Logic of Norms and Actions," in Risto Hilpinen (ed.) , "New studies in Deontic Logic : Norms, Actions, and the Foundations of Ethics," pp.3–35, D. Reidel, 1981.
[4] L. Åqvist, "Introduction to Deontic Logic and the Theory of Normative Systems," Bibliopolis, 1987.
[5] L. Åqvist, "Deontic Logic, " in D. Gabbay and F. Guenthner (eds.), "Handbook of Philosophical Logic," Vol.2, pp.605-714, Kluwer Academic Publishers, 1984.
[6] H. Castañeda, "The Paradoxes of Deontic Logic: The Simplest Solution to All of Them in One Fell Swoop," in Risto Hilpinen (ed.) , "New studies in Deontic Logic: Norms, Actions, and the Foundations of Ethics," pp.37–85, D. Reidel, 1981.

[7] W.Stelzner, "Relevant Deontic Logic," Journal of Philosophical Logic, Vol.21, pp.193–216,1992.

[8] A.R.Anderson and N.D.Belnap Jr., "Entailment: The Logic of Relevance and Necessity," Vol.1, Princeton University Press, 1975.

[9] A.R.Anderson, N.D.Belnap Jr., and J.M.Dunn, "Entailment: The Logic of Relevance and Necessity," Vol.2, Princeton University Press, 1992.

[10] J.M.Dunn, "Relevance Logic and Entailment," in D.Gabbay and F.Guenthner (eds.), "Handbook of Philosophical Logic," Vol.3, pp.117–224, D.Reidel, 1986.

[11] S.Read, "Relevant Logic: A Philosophical Examination of Inference," Basil Blackwell, 1988.

[12] J.Cheng, "Logical Tool of Knowledge Engineering: Using Entailment Logic rather than Mathematical Logic," Proc. ACM 19th Annual Computer Science Conference, pp.218-238, 1991.

[13] J.Cheng, " Rc – A Relevant Logic for Conditional Relation Representation and Reasoning," Proc. 1st Singapore International Conference on Intelligent Systems, pp.171-176, 1992.

[14] J.Cheng, "The Fundamental Role of Entailment in Knowledge Representation and Reasoning," Journal of Computing and Information, Vol.2, No.1, pp.853–873, 1996.

[15] T.Tagawa, J.Ohori, J.Cheng, and K.Ushijima, "On the Strong Relevance Principle in Relevant Logics," Journal of Japanese Society for Artificial Intelligence, Vol. 13, No. 3, pp. 387-394, 1998 (in Japanese).

Solving the Ramification Problem: Causal Propagation in an Argumentation-Theoretic Approach*

Quoc Bao Vo[1] and Norman Y. Foo[2]

[1] Dept. of Computer Science, University of Saarland, Germany,
bao@ags.uni-sb.de
[2] Knowledge Systems Group - School of Computer Science and Engineering
University of New South Wales - Sydney NSW2052 Australia
norman@cse.unsw.edu.au

Abstract. In this paper, we further develop a framework for reasoning about action. We show how the proposed formalism copes with complex action domains in the presence of indirect effects. Furthermore, we also introduce an alternative representation of dynamic systems that enables the proposed formalism to deal with sophisticated problems. We consider this to be the intermediate level between common-sense knowledge and scientific knowledge.

1 Introduction and Motivation

In [9], a formalism for reasoning about action underlied by an assumption-based nonmonotonic reasoning mechanism was introduced. The framework presented in that paper introduces a solution for the frame and the qualification problem but without indirect effects. The present paper attempts to address the open issues with the proposed formalism by lifting the above mentioned restrictions.

While there have been several formalisms dealing with the ramification problem (see e.g. [3], [4], [7]), there are still several issues that need a more careful consideration. We consider three examples to motivate our discussion.

Example 1 Consider Thielscher's (1997) circuit in Figure 1. This example is interesting because it gives a coun-
terexample for the minimalistic ap-
proaches e.g. [4]. In the state given
in Fig. 1, after performing the action of closing switch sw_1, two next
states are equally possible: one in
which *detect* is on, and another it is
off. Only the latter is sanctioned in
a minimalistic account. Through this

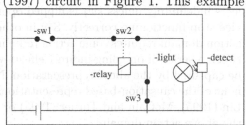

Fig. 1: Thielscher's circuit

example, Thielscher pointed out the need of keeping track of the chains of applications of indirect effects.

---

* This work was performed while the first author was at the School of Computer Science and Engineering, University of New South Wales.

M. Ishizuka and A. Sattar (Eds.): PRICAI 2002, LNAI 2417, pp. 49–59, 2002.
© Springer-Verlag Berlin Heidelberg 2002

Thielscher proposes a way to remedy this problem by keeping track of the applications of the domain constraints which are re-expressed in terms of causal relationships. Thus, given the above example, his formalism is able to arrive at a next state in which the *detect* is on. Following such chains of causal relationships, the dynamic system undergoes several intermediate states before arriving at the next state.

In this paper, we proceed one step further from Thielscher's position by formally representing the intermediate states as possible states of the world.[1] Observe that given an observation, there may be several chains of causal relationships that bring about that observation.[2] Unless intermediate states are explicitly represented and reasoned about, there is no way can an agent has a full insight to the system in hand and certain information would be missing.

Example 2 Consider Lin's (1995) spring-loaded suitcase with two latches. Let's assume that the latches can be toggled if the suitcase is closed. The following state constraint is supposed to apply in this domain: $up(Latch_1) \wedge up(Latch_2) \supset open(Suitcase)$. The question is: *how does a robot close the above suitcase back after opening it?* McCain and Turner [5] also consider this problem and their answer is:

> In general, when both latches are up, it is impossible to perform *only* the action of closing the suitcase; one must also concurrently toggle at least one of the latches.

(McCain and Turner, 1997, p. 464, *italic is original.*)

The problem now is how to represent the action of holding the suitcase closed such that it would overcome the above indirect effect caused by the loaded spring.

Example 3 Consider the circuit shown in Figure 2. In this circuit, it is quite obvious that after performing the action $flip_1$ whose direct effect is having sw_1 closed, the following circular sequence of indirect effects will take place: $\{relay_1, \neg relay_2\} \rightarrow \neg sw_2 \rightarrow \{\neg relay_1, relay_2\} \rightarrow$ $sw_2 \rightarrow \{relay_1, \neg relay_2\}$. This sequence of course would potentially carry on the above sequence of indirect effects indefinitely unless sw_1 is flipped open or some device stop functioning correctly. Say in other words, this action domain requires some action to be inserted in between a series of on going indirect effects which can not be captured by the above representation. Note also that

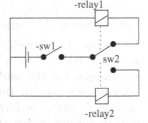

none of the causation-based representations proposed by **Fig. 2:** Another circuit Lin (1995), McCain and Turner (1995) or Thielscher (1997) is able to deal with the above action domain.

---

[1] Note that this point of view also corresponds to the traditional definition of states as snapshots of the world.

[2] For example, given *detect* is not on in the next state, it can be that either the *light* has never been bright or the *light* may have been bright but the *detect* is not sufficiently sensitive to detect its momentary brightness.

To summarise, in this paper we introduce an expressive representation scheme in order to cope with indirect effects in sophisticated action domains. Due to the space limitation, we make several simplifications in domain representation and defer the comprehensive version of this formalism to the full paper. This also shows one advantage of our solution: a simple representation can be achieved by simply removing the involved assumptions.

2 Preliminaries and Background

For the representational framework, we extend Drakengren and Bjäreland's [2] language which is in turn based on the formalism proposed by Sandewall ([6]).

2.1 Syntax and Semantics

Following Sandewall ([6]), the underlying representation of time is a (*discrete*) *time structure* $\mathbf{T} = \langle \mathcal{T}, <, \Theta, N \rangle$ consisting of
- a *time domain* $\mathcal{T}$ whose members are called *timepoints*;
- $< \subseteq \mathcal{T} \times \mathcal{T}$, the *precedes relation* which is a total order;
- $\Theta \in \mathcal{T}$, the *origo* satisfying $\Theta < t$ for all t;
- $N : \mathcal{T} \to \mathcal{T}$, the *successor function*.

Given a time structure $\mathbf{T} = \langle \mathcal{T}, <, \Theta, N \rangle$, a *signature* with respect to $\mathbf{T}$ is a tuple $\sigma = \langle T, \mathcal{F}, \mathcal{A} \rangle$, where T is a set of *timepoint variables*, $\mathcal{F}$ is a set of *propositional fluent names*, and $\mathcal{A}$ is a set of *action names*. We assume that all sets in σ are countable. We denote $\overline{\mathcal{F}} = \{\neg f \mid f \in \mathcal{F}\}$. A member of $\mathcal{F}^* = \mathcal{F} \cup \overline{\mathcal{F}}$ is a *fluent literal*.

For each fluent literal $\varphi \in \mathcal{F}^*$, we introduce the following two propositions: RQ_φ, and FA_φ. RQ_φ is associated with the assumed qualifications upon the preconditions in an ramification description regarding the literal φ. FA_φ is associated with the frame assumptions regarding φ. Given a set of fluent literals $\Gamma \subseteq \mathcal{F}^*$, we denote $FA_\Gamma \overset{def}{=} \{FA_\varphi \mid \varphi \in \Gamma\}$ and $RQ_\Gamma \overset{def}{=} \{RQ_\varphi \mid \varphi \in \Gamma\}$.

A *timepoint expression* is one of the following:
- a member of $\mathcal{T}$,
- a timepoint variable in T,
- an expression formed from timepoint expressions using N. For readability, we will write τ^+ instead of $N(\tau)$. For k applications of N to a timepoint expression τ, we write $N^k(\tau)$.

We denote the set of timepoint expressions by $\mathcal{TE}$.

Definition 1 Let $\sigma = \langle T, \mathcal{F}, \mathcal{A} \rangle$ be a signature and $\tau, \upsilon \in \mathcal{TE}$, $f \in \mathcal{F}$, $A \in \mathcal{A}$, $R \in \{=, <\}$, $\otimes \in \{\wedge, \vee, \to, \leftrightarrow\}$. Define the *basic (domain description) language* Λ over σ by: $\Lambda ::= \mathbf{T} \mid \mathbf{F} \mid f \mid [\tau, \upsilon]A \mid \tau R \upsilon \mid \neg\Lambda \mid \Lambda_1 \otimes \Lambda_2 \mid [\tau]\Lambda$,
and the *assumption base* $\mathcal{AB}$ by:

$\mathcal{AB} = \mathcal{AB}_{RQ} \cup \mathcal{AB}_{FA}$, where $\mathcal{AB}_{RQ} = \{[\tau]RQ_\varphi \mid \tau \in \mathcal{TE}$ and $\varphi \in \mathcal{F}^*\}$ and $\mathcal{AB}_{FA} = \{[\tau]FA_\varphi \mid \tau \in \mathcal{TE}$ and $\varphi \in \mathcal{F}^*\}$.. Given a set of assumptions Δ, we denote $\Delta_{FA} = \Delta \cap \mathcal{AB}_{FA}$ and $\Delta_{RQ} = \Delta \cap \mathcal{AB}_{RQ}$.

The *domain description language* $\mathcal{L}$ (over σ) is defined: $\mathcal{L} = \Lambda \cup \mathcal{AB}$.

$[\tau, \upsilon]A$ means the action A is performed during the time interval $[\tau, \upsilon]$. $[\tau]RQ_\varphi$ means the fluent literal φ is assumed to be qualified to hold by the end of the interval $[\tau, \tau^+]$. $[\tau]FA_\varphi$ means the fluent literal φ is assumed by default to persist from the time point τ to the next, i.e. the *principle of inertia*.

The semantics of $\mathcal{L}$ is defined in [9] following the semantics of propositional logic.

Definition 2 Let $\sigma = \langle T, \mathcal{F}, \mathcal{A} \rangle$ be a signature. A *state* over σ is a function from $\mathcal{F}$ to the set $\{T, F\}$ of truth values. A *history* over σ is a function h from T to the set of states. A *valuation* is a function ϕ from $T\mathcal{E}$ to T. A *narrative assignment* is a function η from $T \times \mathcal{A} \times T$ to the set $\{T, F\}$. In addition, we define $\varepsilon_r : T \times RQ_{\mathcal{F}^*} \to \{T, F\}$ and $\varepsilon_f : T \times FA_{\mathcal{F}^*} \to \{T, F\}$. An interpretation over σ is a tuple $\langle h, \phi, \eta, \varepsilon_r, \varepsilon_f \rangle$ where h is a history, ϕ is a valuation, η is a narrative assignment and $\varepsilon_r, \varepsilon_f$ are defined as above.

Definition 3 Let $\gamma, \delta \in \Lambda$ and $I = \langle h, \phi, \eta, \varepsilon_r, \varepsilon_f \rangle$ an interpretation. Assume $\tau, \upsilon \in T\mathcal{E}$, $f \in \mathcal{F}$, $A \in \mathcal{A}$, $R \in \{=, <\}$, $\varphi \in \mathcal{F}^*$, $\otimes \in \{\wedge, \vee, \to, \leftrightarrow\}$, and $\chi \in \{T, F\}$. Define the truth value of γ in I for a timepoint $t \in T$, denoted $I(\gamma, t)$ as follows:

$$I(\chi, t) = \chi, \qquad\qquad\qquad I(f, t) = h(t)(f),$$
$$I([\tau, \upsilon]A, t) = \eta(\tau, A, \upsilon), \qquad I([\tau]RQ_\varphi, t) = \varepsilon_r(\tau, RQ_\varphi, \upsilon),$$
$$I([\tau]FA_\varphi, t) = \varepsilon_f(\tau, FA_\varphi), \qquad I(\tau R\upsilon, t) = \phi(\tau)R\phi(\upsilon),$$
$$I(\neg\gamma, t) = \neg I(\gamma, t), \qquad\qquad I(\gamma \otimes \delta, t) = I(\gamma, t) \otimes I(\delta, t),$$
$$I([\tau]\gamma, t) = I(\gamma, \phi(\alpha)).$$

Two formulas γ and δ are equivalent iff $I(\gamma, t) = I(\delta, t)$ for all I and t. An interpretation I is a *model* of a set $\Gamma \subseteq \Lambda$ of formulas, denoted $I \models \Gamma$, iff $I(\gamma, t) = T$ for every $t \in T$ and $\gamma \in \Gamma$. A formula $\gamma \in \Lambda$ is *entailed* by a set $\Gamma \subseteq \Lambda$ of formulas, denoted $\Gamma \models \gamma$, iff γ is true in all models of Γ.

2.2   Background

We reproduce the relevant definitions from Bondarenko *et al.*'s [1] and Vo and Foo's [9] works for completeness.

While part of the domain knowledge, e.g. the dynamics of the domain, certain common sense laws, is encoded in $\mathcal{R}$ as inference rules, the reasoners usually requires further input: (i) a theory $T(\subseteq \mathcal{L})$ consisting of the agent's belief, e.g. her observations; and (ii) an *assumption base* $Ab(\subseteq \mathcal{L})$ consisting of the plausible assumptions the agent is ready to make in order to build his arguments. It is these assumptions that the reasoner uses to conjecture plausible conclusions. The reasoner needs to deliberate over the assumptions to avoid over-assuming the implausibles. The pair $\langle T, Ab \rangle$ is the special case of the so-called assumption-based framework defined by Bondarenko *et al.*'s (1997).

Let a deductive system $\langle \mathcal{L}, \mathcal{R} \rangle$ and a theory T and an assumption base Ab be given, we define:[3]

---

[3] see [9] for a more detailed account of these descriptions.

- $\Delta \subseteq Ab$ *attacks* an assumption $\alpha \in Ab$ iff $T \cup \Delta \vdash_{\mathcal{R}} \neg\alpha$.
- $\Delta \subseteq Ab$ attacks a set of assumptions $\Delta' \subseteq Ab$ iff Δ attacks some assumption $\alpha \in \Delta'$.
- $\Delta \subseteq Ab$ *rejects* an assumption $\alpha \in Ab$ iff (i) Δ does not attack itself, and (ii) $\Delta \cup \{\alpha\}$ attacks itself.
- $\Delta \subseteq Ab$ *leniently rejects* an assumption $\alpha \in Ab$ iff (i) Δ reject α, and (ii) Δ does not attack α.
- $Lr(\Delta) \overset{def}{=} \{\alpha \in Ab \mid \alpha$ is leniently rejected by $\Delta\}$. For readability, we will write $Lr_P(\Delta)$ instead of $(Lr(\Delta))_P$ for $P \in \{FA, RQ\}$.
- $\Delta \subseteq Ab$ is *presumable* iff (a) $\Delta = \{\alpha \in Ab \mid T \cup \Delta \vdash_{\mathcal{R}} \alpha\}$, (b) Δ does not attack itself, and (c) for each assumption $\alpha \notin \Delta$, α is rejected by Δ.

Definition 4 Let a deductive system $\langle \mathcal{L}, \mathcal{R} \rangle$ and a theory T and an assumption base Ab be given. A set of assumptions $\Delta \subseteq Ab$ is *F-plausible* iff

1. Δ is plausible;
2. $Lr_{FA}(\Delta)$ is minimal (with respect to set inclusion); and
3. Δ_{FA} is maximal relative to the above two conditions.

3   Technical Framework

First, we observe that the ordering in which domain constraints are applied plays an essential role in a technically sound framework. Moreover, it's no longer guaranteed that domain constraints would be strictly satisfied at every time point.[4] To help the reader better understand this technical subtlety, it's useful to think that changes are attributable to events. However, events are further divided into two categories: external and internal. Basically, external events correspond to the direct effects of actions performed by some agents (including the reasoner.) On the other hand, internal events correspond to the indirect effects when certain conditions about the world are met and can be attributed to the Nature.

Like external events, internal events also happen in certain orders. Although it's not straightforward to observe these orders[5], it's important that a reasoner is able to reason about them. From the above discussion, we propose to add one more dimension into the set of assumptions of a given domain description. The new dimension consists of RQ-assumptions.

Definition 5 Let $\sigma = \langle T, \mathcal{F}, \mathcal{A} \rangle$ be a signature. Assume $\tau, \upsilon \in \mathcal{TE}$, $A \in \mathcal{A}$, $R \in \{=, <\}$, $\Phi \subseteq \Lambda$, and $\varphi \in \mathcal{F}^*$. A *domain description* D is defined to be a tuple $\langle \mathcal{L}, \mathcal{R}, AB, \Gamma \rangle$, where:

---

[4] Of course, it's not necessary that the state of the world at every time point is observable to a reasoner. However, it is important that she be aware of such states and able to reason about them.

[5] Unless indirect effects are somehow delayed and become observable to the reasoner, they usually take place immediately after direct effects.

1. $\mathcal{L}$ is the domain description language and $\mathcal{AB}$ an assumption base over σ;
2. $\mathcal{R} = \mathcal{R}_C \cup \mathcal{R}_F \cup \mathcal{R}_A \cup \mathcal{R}_Q \cup \mathcal{R}_R$ is the set of inference rules of the assumption-based framework. $\mathcal{R}_C$ is the set of inference rules of (classical) propositional logic. The inference rules in $\mathcal{R}_F$ and $\mathcal{R}_Q$, are called *frame-based* and *qualification-based*, respectively. $\mathcal{R}_A$ is the set of *action descriptions*.[6] In addition, we have a set of *ramification-based inference rules* $\mathcal{R}_R$ of the form: $\frac{\Phi, [\tau]RQ_\varphi}{[\tau^+]\varphi \wedge \neg[\tau]FA_{\neg\varphi}}$.
3. The theory $\Gamma \subseteq \Lambda$.

Given a set of assumptions Δ, we denote $\Delta_{FA} = \Delta \cap \mathcal{AB}_{FA}$ and $\Delta_{RQ} = \Delta \cap \mathcal{AB}_{RQ}$.

Definition 6 Let $\sigma = \langle T, \mathcal{F}, \mathcal{A} \rangle$ be a signature and $D = \langle \mathcal{L}, \mathcal{R}, \mathcal{AB}, \Gamma \rangle$ a domain description over σ. An interpretation $I = \langle h, \phi, \eta, \varepsilon_r, \varepsilon_f \rangle$ is a *model* of D iff
 (a) I is a model of Γ; and
 (b) for each $r \in \mathcal{R}$, if $I \models prem(r)$ then $I \models cons(r)$.

Now, regarding the ramification problem, the basic idea is that the state obtained by updating the previous state may not necessarily be stable due to the presence of indirect effects. By representing indirect effects as causal rules (using inference rules in our framework) we can reason about which causal rules have fired and (relatively) when. Moreover, since these causal rules don't take the same amount of time to fire, we should be able to reason about different possible orders in which they fire. This will be achieved by a distinction between stable and unstable states.

Definition 7 A timepoint expression $\tau \in \mathcal{TE}$ is *stable* wrt a given domain description $D = \langle \mathcal{L}, \mathcal{R}, \mathcal{AB}, \Gamma \rangle$ and $\Delta \subseteq \mathcal{AB}$ iff there does not exist any ramification-based inference rule $r \in \mathcal{R}_R$ such that (a) $r = \frac{\Phi, [\tau]RQ_\varphi}{[\tau^+]\varphi \wedge \neg[\tau]FA_{\neg\varphi}}$ and $\Gamma \cup \Delta \vdash_\mathcal{R} \Phi, [\tau]RQ_\varphi$, and (b) $\Gamma \cup \Delta \not\vdash_\mathcal{R} [\tau]\varphi$.

Definition 8 Let $D = \langle \mathcal{L}, \mathcal{R}, \mathcal{AB}, \Gamma \rangle$ be a domain description. A set of assumptions Δ is said to be *ramification-compliant* iff
(a) there doesn't exist any $\delta \in \mathcal{AB}_{RQ}$ such that $Th_\mathcal{R}(\Delta \cup \{\delta\}) \neq Th_\mathcal{R}(\Delta) \cup \{\delta\}$,
(b) there doesn't exists any unstable timepoint expression $\tau \in \mathcal{TE}$ such that $[\tau]FA_\varphi \in \Delta$ for every $\varphi \in \mathcal{F}^*$.

Observe that by using unstable time points, we have conceptually isolated the ramification problem from the task of reasoning about the (explicit) actions.

Definition 9 Let $D = \langle \mathcal{L}, \mathcal{R}, \mathcal{AB}, \Gamma \rangle$ be a domain description. A set of assumptions Δ is *generally plausible for action domains*, or simply *AD-plausible*, iff
 - Δ is ramification-compliant, and
 - Δ is F-plausible relative to the above condition.

---

[6] The reader is referred to [9] for a detailed description of these inference rules.

Remark:

(1) From the above definition, it can be seen that a solution for the ramification is (in a sense) independent from the frame and the qualification problems regarding action occurrences.

(2) Given the above temporal ontology, it's worth noting that the traditional notion of state constraints may no longer hold in this representation regarding time points. More precisely, only states associated with stable time points are subject to these constraints.

3.1   Connection to Thielscher's (1997) Causal Representation

The question is, of course, whether the above computational mechanism gives satisfactory conclusions for problems in reasoning about action. While many formalisms have been proposed, a general criterion for reasoning about action formalisms still seems to be missing. One of the recent frameworks which has shown its potential in satisfactorily solving (to some extent) the ramification problem is Thielscher's causal theory [7]. In the following, we will show that the above notion of AD-plausible sets of assumptions captures the essence of Thielscher's solution to the ramification problem.

Since Thielscher's system is unable to deal with (potentially) infinite sequences of indirect effects e.g. the situation in example 3, we need some restrictions on the domain descriptions expressible in fluent calculus.

Definition 10 A domain description $D = \langle \mathcal{L}, \mathcal{R}, \mathcal{AB}, \Gamma \rangle$ is *non-stratified* iff there exist two sets $\Phi \subseteq \Lambda$ and $\{\varphi_1, \ldots, \varphi_n\} \subseteq \mathcal{F}^*$ such that

(a) for each $1 \leq i \leq n$, $\Phi \cup \{[\tau]\varphi_i\}$ is consistent, for every $\tau \in \mathcal{TE}$; and

(b) for each $1 \leq i \leq n$, if $k = (i \bmod n) + 1$, then there exists a set $\Psi^k \subseteq \Lambda$ such that $\Phi \cup \{[\tau]\varphi_i\} \vdash_{\mathcal{R}} \Psi^k$, and $\dfrac{\Psi^k, [\tau]RQ_{\varphi_k}}{[\tau^+]\varphi_k \wedge \neg[\tau]FA_{\neg\varphi_k}} \in \mathcal{R}_R$.

Given a domain description $D = \langle \mathcal{L}, \mathcal{R}, \mathcal{AB}, \Gamma \rangle$, we'll denote $E_D(\Delta) \overset{def}{=} Th_{\mathcal{R}}(\Gamma \cup \Delta)$, the extension of an action theory D according to Δ.

Definition 11 Let $\sigma = \langle T, \mathcal{F}, \mathcal{A} \rangle$ be a signature.

1. A set $S \subseteq \mathcal{F}^*$ is an *instantwise state* iff for every $\varphi \in \mathcal{F}^*$, either $\varphi \in S$ or $\neg\varphi \in S$. IS will be used to denote the set of instantwise states of Λ,

2. Let $D = \langle \mathcal{L}, \mathcal{R}, \mathcal{AB}, \Gamma \rangle$ be a domain description. D is *simplistic* iff (a) for each $r \in \mathcal{R}_A$, r is of the form $\dfrac{[\tau]\Psi, [\tau,v]A}{[v]\varphi \wedge \neg[\tau]FA_{\neg\varphi}}$ and for each $r \in \mathcal{R}_R$, r is of the form $\dfrac{[\tau]\Psi, [\tau]RQ_\varphi}{[\tau^+]\varphi \wedge \neg[\tau]FA_{\neg\varphi}}$, where $\Psi \subseteq \mathcal{F}^*$; and (b) $\Gamma = \emptyset$.

Let $\Omega \subseteq \mathcal{R}_R$, we denote $CONS_R(\Omega) = \{\varphi \in \mathcal{F}^* \mid \dfrac{[\tau]\Psi, [\tau]RQ_\varphi}{[\tau^+]\varphi \wedge \neg[\tau]FA_{\neg\varphi}} \in \Omega\}$.
Similarly, let $\Omega \subseteq \mathcal{R}_A$, we denote $CONS_A(\Omega) = \{\varphi \in \mathcal{F}^* \mid \dfrac{[\tau]\Psi, [\tau,v]A}{[v]\varphi \wedge \neg[\tau]FA_{\neg\varphi}} \in \Omega\}$.
In the following, we abbreviate simplistic and stratified domain descriptions as *SSDs*.

Following Thielscher [7] and McCain and Turner [4], for a given domain description D, we formalise the relations $Res_D \subseteq IS \times \mathcal{A} \times IS$ and $Causes_D \subseteq IS \times IS$ so that Res_D represents the direct effects of actions from $\mathcal{A}$ on a state-based basis and $Causes_D$ represents state-based causal relations accoring to the ramification-based inference rules in D. The formal definitions for Res_D and $Causes_D$ are provided in [8].

Given a domain description D, a state $S \in IS$ is *stable* regarding D iff there does not exists any $S' \in IS$ such that $Causes_D(S, S')$.

Definition 12 Let $\sigma = \langle T, \mathcal{F}, \mathcal{A} \rangle$ be a signature and D a SSD. Suppose $w \in IS$ and $\alpha \in \mathcal{A}$. The *state transition* from w in D according to α, denoted $Trans_D^\alpha(w)$, is defined to be the transitive closure of $Causes_D$ regarding the state $\omega_1 \in IS$ satisfying $(w, \alpha, \omega_1) \in Res_D$. Formally, $Trans_D^\alpha(w) = \{\varpi \in IS \mid$ there exists a sequence $\omega_1, \ldots, \omega_n \in IS$ such that $(w, \alpha, \omega_1) \in Res_D$ and $\varpi = \omega_n$ and $(\omega_i, \omega_{i+1}) \in Causes_D$ for each $1 \leq i < n$ and ϖ is stable regarding $D\}$.

Let I be an interpretation for $\mathcal{L}$ and $t \in \mathcal{T}$,

• we use $[I]^t$ to denote the instantwise state specified by I at timepoint t: $[I]^t \stackrel{def}{=} \{\varphi \in \mathcal{F}^* \mid I(\varphi, t) = \mathrm{T}\}$. If $[I]^t$ is stable then t is said to be a *stable timepoint* in I.

• we use N_I to denote a function that maps a timepoint $t \in \mathcal{T}$ to the next stable timepoint in I: $N_I(t) \in \mathcal{T}$ such that $[I]^{N_I(t)}$ is stable and for every $u \in \mathcal{T}$, if $t < u < N_I(t)$ then $[I]^u$ is not stable.

Theorem 1 Let $\sigma = \langle T, \mathcal{F}, \mathcal{A} \rangle$ be a signature and $D_0 = \langle \mathcal{L}, \mathcal{R}, \mathcal{AB}, \emptyset \rangle$ a SSD and $\alpha \in \mathcal{A}$. Suppose that $w \in IS$. Define a domain description $D = \langle \mathcal{L}, \mathcal{R}, \mathcal{AB}, \Gamma \rangle$, where $\Gamma = \{[\Theta]\varphi \mid \varphi \in w\} \cup \{[\Theta, \Theta^+]\alpha\}$. A set Δ of assumptions in D is AD-plausible iff for each model M of $E_D(\Delta)$, $[M]^{N_M(\Theta)} \in Trans_D^\alpha([M]^\Theta)$, i.e. $[M]^{N_M(\Theta)}$ belongs to the state transition from $[M]^\Theta$ in D according to α.

4 Running Examples

Example 1 (*continued.*) We re-formulate the action theory for this example in terms of our formalism:

$$\frac{[\tau]sw_1, [\tau]sw_2, [\tau]RQ_{light}}{[\tau^+]light \wedge \neg[\tau]FA_{\neg light}}, \qquad \frac{[\tau]sw_1, [\tau]sw_3, [\tau]RQ_{relay}}{[\tau^+]relay \wedge \neg[\tau]FA_{\neg relay}},$$

$$\frac{\neg[\tau]sw_i, [\tau]RQ_{\neg light}}{\neg[\tau^+]light \wedge \neg[\tau]FA_{light}}(i = 1, 2), \qquad \frac{\neg[\tau]sw_i, [\tau]RQ_{\neg relay}}{\neg[\tau^+]relay \wedge \neg[\tau]FA_{relay}}(i = 1, 3),$$

$$\frac{[\tau]relay, [\tau]RQ_{\neg sw_2}}{\neg[\tau^+]sw_2 \wedge \neg[\tau]FA_{sw_2}}, \qquad \frac{[\tau]light, [\tau]RQ_{detect}}{[\tau^+]detect \wedge \neg[\tau]FA_{\neg detect}},$$

$$\frac{\neg[\tau]sw_i, [\tau, v]toggle_i}{[v]sw_i \wedge \neg[\tau]FA_{\neg sw_i}}(i = 1, 2, 3), \qquad \frac{[\tau]sw_i, [\tau, v]toggle_i}{\neg[v]sw_i \wedge \neg[\tau]FA_{sw_i}}(i = 1, 2, 3),$$

$$\frac{[\tau]\zeta, [\tau]FA_\zeta}{[\tau^+]\zeta}, \text{ where } \zeta \in \mathcal{F}^*.$$

$\Gamma = \{\neg[\Theta]sw_1, [\Theta]sw_2, [\Theta]sw_3, \neg[\Theta]relay, \neg[\Theta]light, \neg[\Theta]detect\} \cup \{[\Theta, N(\Theta)]$ $flip_1\}$.

Consider Δ such that $\Delta_{RQ} = \mathcal{AB}_{RQ} \setminus \{[N^2(\Theta)]RQ_{detect}, [N^3(\Theta)]RQ_{detect}\}$ and $\Delta_{FA} = \mathcal{AB}_{FA} \setminus \{[N(\Theta)]FA_{\neg light}, [N(\Theta)]FA_{\neg relay}, [N^2(\Theta)]FA_{sw_2}, [N^3(\Theta)]$ $FA_{light}\}$.

Δ is AD-plausible resulting to the next stable state is $\omega = \{sw_1, \neg sw_2, sw_3,$ $relay, \neg light, \neg detect\}$ at $[N^4(\Theta)]$.

However, the set $\Delta' \subseteq \mathcal{AB}$, where $\Delta'_{RQ} = \mathcal{AB}_{RQ} \setminus \{[N^2(\Theta)]RQ_{detect}\}$ and $\Delta'_{FA} = \mathcal{AB}_{FA} \setminus \{[N(\Theta)]FA_{\neg light}, [N(\Theta)]FA_{\neg relay}, [N^2(\Theta)]FA_{sw_2}, [N^3(\Theta)]$ $FA_{light}, [N^3(\Theta)]FA_{\neg detect}\}$, is also AD-plausible which results to the next stable state $\omega' = \{sw_1, \neg sw_2, sw_3, relay, \neg light, detect\}$ at $[N^4(\Theta)]$.

Moreover, the set $\Delta'' \subseteq \mathcal{AB}$, where $\Delta''_{RQ} = \mathcal{AB}_{RQ}$ and $\Delta''_{FA} = \mathcal{AB}_{FA} \setminus$ $\{[N(\Theta)]FA_{\neg light}, [N(\Theta)]FA_{\neg relay}, [N^2(\Theta)]FA_{sw_2}, [N^2(\Theta)]FA_{\neg detect}, [N^3(\Theta)]$ $FA_{light}\}$, is AD-plausible which also results to the next stable state ω' at $[N^4(\Theta)]$.

Example 2 (*continued.*) We re-formulate the action theory for this example in terms of our formalism:

$$\frac{[\tau]upL_1, [\tau]upL_2, [\tau]RQ_{open}}{[\tau^+]open \wedge \neg[\tau]FA_{\neg open}}, \qquad \frac{[\tau, v]flip_i, [\tau]upL_i}{\neg[v]upL_i \wedge \neg[\tau]FA_{upL_i}}(i = 1, 2),$$

$$\frac{[\tau, v]flip_i, \neg[\tau]upL_i}{[v]upL_i \wedge \neg[\tau]FA_{\neg upL_i}}(i = 1, 2), \qquad \frac{[\tau, v]close, [\tau]upL_1, [\tau]upL_2}{\neg[v]open \wedge \neg[\tau]FA_{open}},$$

$$\frac{[\tau_1, \tau_2]held\_closed, \neg[\tau_1]open, \tau_1 \leq \tau \leq \tau_2}{[\tau]held\_closed \wedge \neg[\tau]FA_{\neg held\_closed}}, \qquad \frac{[\tau]held\_closed}{\neg[\tau]RQ_{open}},$$

$$\frac{[\tau]\zeta, [\tau]FA_\zeta}{[\tau^+]\zeta}, \text{ where } \zeta \in \mathcal{F}^*.$$

The theory is described as follows:
$\Gamma = \{[\Theta]upL_1, [\Theta]upL_2, [\Theta]open, [\Theta]\neg held\_closed\} \cup$
$\{[c_1, c_2]close, [c_2, c_3]hold\_closed, [c_4, c_5]flip_1\} \cup$
$\{\Theta \leq c_1 < c_2 \leq c_4 < c_5 \leq c_3\}$

Consider $\Delta \subseteq \mathcal{AB}$ such that $\Delta_{RQ} = \mathcal{AB}_{RQ} \setminus \{[c]RQ_{open} \mid c_2 \leq c \leq c_3\}$ and $\Delta_{FA} = \mathcal{AB}_{FA} \setminus (\{[c_1]FA_{open}\} \cup \{[c]FA_{\neg held\_closed} \mid c_2 \leq c \leq c_3\} \cup \{[c_4]FA_{upL_1}\})$.

Δ is AD-plausible resulting to the following:
$[c_1]\{upL_1, upL_2, open, \neg held\_closed\}, \qquad [c_2]\{upL_1, upL_2, \neg open, held\_closed\},$
$[c_4]\{upL_1, upL_2, \neg open, held\_closed\}, \qquad [c_5]\{\neg upL_1, upL_2, \neg open, held\_closed\},$
$[c_3]\{\neg upL_1, upL_2, \neg open, held\_closed\}.$

Example 3 (*continued.*) The domain description:

$$\frac{[\tau]sw_1, [\tau]sw_2, [\tau]RQ_{relay_1}}{[\tau^+]relay_1 \wedge \neg[\tau]FA_{\neg relay_1}}, \qquad \frac{[\tau]sw_1, \neg[\tau]sw_2, [\tau]RQ_{relay_2}}{[\tau^+]relay_2 \wedge \neg[\tau]FA_{\neg relay_2}},$$

$$\frac{[\tau]relay_1, [\tau]RQ_{\neg sw_2}}{\neg[\tau^+]sw_2 \wedge \neg[\tau]FA_{sw_2}}, \qquad \frac{[\tau]relay_2, [\tau]RQ_{sw_2}}{[\tau^+]sw_2 \wedge \neg[\tau]FA_{\neg sw_2}},$$

$$\frac{\neg[\tau]sw_i, [\tau, v]toggle_i}{[v]sw_i \wedge \neg[\tau]FA_{\neg sw_i}}(i = 1, 2), \qquad \frac{[\tau]sw_i, [\tau, v]toggle_i}{\neg[v]sw_i \wedge \neg[\tau]FA_{sw_i}}(i = 1, 2),$$

$$\frac{[\tau]\zeta, [\tau]FA_\zeta}{[\tau^+]\zeta}, \text{ where } \zeta \in \mathcal{F}^*.$$

The state of the circuit in Fig. 2 is captured by the following action theory:
$\Gamma = \{\neg[\Theta]sw_1, [\Theta]sw_2, \neg[\Theta]relay_1, \neg[\Theta]relay_2\} \cup \{[c_1, c_2]toggle_1, [c_3, c_4]toggle_1\}$
$\cup \{\Theta \leq c_1 < c_2 < c_3 < c_4\}$.

Consider $\Delta \subseteq \mathcal{AB}$ such that $\Delta_{RQ} = \mathcal{AB}_{RQ}$ and
$\Delta_{FA} = \mathcal{AB}_{FA} \setminus (\{[c_1]FA_{\neg sw_1}\} \cup \{[c_3]FA_{sw_1}\} \cup$
$\{[c]FA_{\neg relay_1} \mid c_2 \leq c \leq c_3 \text{ and } c = N^k(c_2) \text{ where } k = 4i \text{ and } i = 0, 1, 2, \ldots\} \cup$
$\{[c]FA_{sw_2}, [c]FA_{relay_1} \mid c_2 \leq c \leq c_3 \text{ and } c = N^k(c_2) \text{ where } k = 4i + 1 \text{ and }$
$i = 0, 1, 2, \ldots\} \cup$
$\{[c]FA_{\neg relay_2} \mid c_2 \leq c \leq c_3 \text{ and } c = N^k(c_2) \text{ where } k = 4i+2 \text{ and } i = 0, 1, 2, \ldots\} \cup$
$\{[c]FA_{\neg sw_2}, [c]FA_{relay_2} \mid c_2 \leq c \leq c_3 \text{ and } c = N^k(c_2) \text{ where } k = 4i + 3 \text{ and }$
$i = 0, 1, 2, \ldots\})$.

Δ is AD-plausible resulting to several possible models for this domain depending on when switch sw_1 is toggled to be off:
$[c_1]\{\neg sw_1, sw_2, \neg relay_1, \neg relay_2\}, \qquad [c_2]\{sw_1, sw_2, \neg relay_1, \neg relay_2\},$
$[c_3]\{sw_1, \pm sw_2, \mp relay_1, \pm relay_2\}, \qquad [c_4]\{\neg sw_1, \pm sw_2, \mp relay_1, \pm relay_2\}.$

5 Conclusion

In this paper, we explore a new abstraction level which we believe to be an intermediate layer between the common sense knowledge and the scientific knowledge. Sophisticated domain knowledge as well as representation are, we argue, required to achieve an adequate underlying representation and reasoning process. Among the merits of this approach, we emphasize the following:

• Nonmonotonicity is handled by assumptions and argumentation-theoretic approach.

• The flexibility of working with different kinds of information representation since there is no restriction on the syntax of the system.

• Expressivity: temporal information is explicitly represented. Thus the system is capable of capturing many important features of temporal reasoning.

References

1. A. Bondarenko, Phan M. Dung, Robert A. Kowalski, and Francesca Toni. An abstract, argumentation-theoretic approach to default reasoning. *AIJ*, 93:63–101, 1997.
2. T. Drakengren and M. Bjäreland. Reasoning about action in polynomial time. *AIJ*, 115:1–24, 1999.
3. Fangzhen Lin. Embracing causality in specifying the indirect effects of actions. In *International Joint Conference on Artificial Intelligence*, 1995.
4. Norman McCain and Hudson Turner. A causal theory of ramifications and qualifications. In *International Joint Conference on Artificial Intelligence*, 1995.

5. Norman McCain and Hudson Turner. Causal theories of action and change. In *National Conference on Artificial Intelligence*, pages 460–465, 1997.
6. Eric Sandewall. *Features and Fluents*. Oxford University Press, Oxford, 1994.
7. Michael Thielscher. Ramification and causality. *AIJ*, 89:317–364, 1997.
8. Quoc Bao Vo. *Meta-Constructs and Their Roles in Common Sense Reasoning*. PhD thesis, School of Computer Science and Engineering, University of New South Wales, Sydney, Australia, 2001. Submitted.
9. Quoc Bao Vo and Norman Y. Foo. Solving the qualification problem (in the presence of the frame problem). In *Australian Joint Conference on Artificial Intelligence*, pages 519–531, 2001.

Representing Actions over Dynamic Domains

Yan Zhang[1] and Norman Y. Foo[2]

[1] School of Computing and Information Technology
University of Western Sydney
Penrith South DC, NSW 1797, Australia
yan@cit.uws.edu.au
[2] School of Computer Science and Engineering
University of New South Wales
NSW 2052, Australia
norman@cse.unsw.edu.au

Abstract. Current action theories are usually based on static domains in the sense that objects in the domain are fixed and actions only change properties or relationships related to these objects, but cannot create new objects or destroy current objects in the domain. In this paper, we propose a new action language called $\mathcal{D}$ which handles *dynamic domains*. In the context of $\mathcal{D}$ actions may not only have normal effects as in other action theories, but also have effects of creating or destroying things in the domain. $\mathcal{D}$ has a similar syntax of $\mathcal{A}$ family languages but with a different model theoretic semantics in which a term is allowed to be *undefined* in the domain at some states. We also investigate the semantic properties of $\mathcal{D}$ in detail and illustrate how our approach overcomes the difficulty in representing actions over dynamic domains.

1 Introduction

Given a dynamic system, state change occurs over the domain of the system if some actions are executed. Conventionally, the domain of a system may be viewed as a collection of objects dealt with in the system activities. For example, in the blocks world, its domain could include a number of blocks and a table, and the effects of actions related to this world may change positions or colors of these blocks. By examining current action theories, e.g. [2,7], it is clear that these approaches only consider *static domains* in reasoning about change where objects in the domain are usually fixed from the beginning and actions may just change objects' properties (e.g. paint block a to red color) or relationships among different objects (e.g. move block a onto b). However, in many situations, the domain we deal with is *dynamic*. For instance, a tower may be built from three individual blocks. But before the proper action/actions of building a tower is/are performed, there is no such object called *tower* consisting of these three blocks in the domain. Also, after burning a letter, this letter then no longer exists in the domain.

In this paper, we propose a new action language called $\mathcal{D}$ which handles *dynamic domains*. In the context of $\mathcal{D}$ actions may not only have normal effects

M. Ishizuka and A. Sattar (Eds.): PRICAI 2002, LNAI 2417, pp. 60–69, 2002.
© Springer-Verlag Berlin Heidelberg 2002

as in other action theories, but also have effects of creating or destroying things in the domain. $\mathcal{D}$ has a similar syntax to $\mathcal{A}$ family languages but with a different model theoretic semantics in which a term of $\mathcal{D}$ is allowed to be undefined in the domain at some states. We also investigate the semantic properties of $\mathcal{D}$ in detail and illustrate how our approach overcomes the difficulty in representing actions over dynamic domains. The paper is organized as follows. Section 2 describes the syntax of $\mathcal{D}$, and Section 3 proposes a model theoretic semantics for $\mathcal{D}$. Section 4 investigates the semantic properties of $\mathcal{D}$ in detail. Finally, Section 5 concludes the paper with some discussions.

2 Syntax of $\mathcal{D}$

$\mathcal{D}$ is based on an arbitrary first order language with an extra nonempty set of symbols that are called *action constructors* or *actions*. An action constructor may take variables to denote a generic action while by substituting these variables with ground terms, it forms a specific action. For example, we can view $Move(x, y)$ to be a generic action of moving x onto y, while $Move(a, b)$ is considered as an instance of $Move(x, y)$ where a and b are constants.

A *formula* of $\mathcal{D}$ is any first order formula in the language without occurrence of any action constructors. There are different types of *propositions* in $\mathcal{D}$ as defined below.

A *value proposition* is an expression with one of the following two forms:

$$C \textbf{ after } \overline{A}, \tag{1}$$

$$\textbf{destroyed } P_1, \cdots, P_k \textbf{ after } \overline{A}, \tag{2}$$

where C is a formula, $P_1, \cdots, P_k$ are atoms, and $\overline{A}$ is a string of actions. (1) states that C holds after the sequence of actions $\overline{A}$ is executed in the initial state. For instance,

$$On(x, y) \textbf{ after } Move(x, y)$$

is a value proposition, where $On(x, y)$ is a formula and $Move(x, y)$ is an action. As a special case, if $\overline{A}$ is an empty string, we rewrite (1) as the form

$$\textbf{initially } C, \tag{3}$$

which we also call the *initial value proposition*. In this case, we restrict C to be a sentence (i.e. no free variable occurrence).

Proposition (2), on the other hand, represents the fact that after performing $\overline{A}$ in the initial state, the objects characterized in atoms $P_1, \cdots, P_k$ are destroyed (see next for more detail).

Note that a value proposition of the form (1), (2) or (3) may include free variables. In this case, it actually represents a scheme of specifying a class of specific propositions if we substitute these free variables with ground terms in the language. For example, from the scheme $On(x, y)$ **after** $Move(x, y)$ we may obtain a specific value proposition $On(a, b)$ **after** $Move(a, b)$ by substituting x and y with a and b respectively. We call a value proposition without free variables *closed*. In the rest of the paper, without declaring explicitly a value proposition is usually referred to its closed form.

An *action proposition with normal effect* is an expression of the form

$$A \textbf{ causes } C \textbf{ if } P, \tag{4}$$

where A is an action, and C and P are formulas. This proposition states that if in a state where precondition P is satisfied, then after A is executed, C should be satisfied in the resulting state. For instance,

$$Move(x, y) \textbf{ causes } On(x, y) \wedge \neg Clear(y) \textbf{ if } Clear(y)$$

is an action proposition with normal effect.

An *action proposition with creating effect* is an expression of the form

$$A \textbf{ creates } C \textbf{ if } P, \tag{5}$$

where A is an action, and C and P are formulas. (5) represents the effect of a special action which *creates* something. Intuitively, (5) asserts that if P is satisfied in a state, then after performing action A, C should be true in the resulting state. It is important to note that in any previous state where action A has not been performed, we cannot assume that C is false in that state. In fact, since the object that has property C is created by A, before A is performed, the object with property C does not exist. Consider the following proposition

$$MakeFile(a) \textbf{ creates } File(a)$$

which expresses that action $MakeFile(a)$ makes a file that has a name a. Clearly, before this action is executed, constant a does not denote to any specific object in our domain.

An *action proposition with destroying effect* is an expression of the form

$$A \textbf{ destroys } P_1, \cdots, P_k \textbf{ if } P, \tag{6}$$

where A is an action, $P_1, \cdots, P_k$ are atoms and P is formula. Similarly, this proposition represents the effect of a special action which *destroys* something. For instance, a proposition

$$DeleteFile(a) \textbf{ destroys } File(a) \textbf{ if } File(a)$$

expresses the effect of action deleting a file. From our intuition, after deleting the file a, the file should not exist any more in our domain. In other words, after performing this action, the constant a in the language should no longer denote to any specific object in our domain. As a result of this action, we may represent a value proposition as follows:

$$\textbf{destroyed } File(a) \textbf{ after } DeleteFile(a).$$

To generalize our presentation on action effects, we specify a *generalized action proposition* as the form

$$A \textbf{ causes } C_1 \textbf{ creates } C_2 \textbf{ destroys } P_1, \cdots, P_k \textbf{ if } P. \tag{7}$$

Note that if no C_2 and $P_1, \cdots, P_k$ occur, (7) reduces to proposition (4). Similarly, if no C_1 and $P_1, \cdots, P_k$ occurs, it then reduces (5) and reduces to (6) if no C_1 and C_2 occurs. Generally, we will allow an action to have different types of effects. For example, when an action creates something, it may also destroys some other thing at the same time, or it may also produce some normal effects. This will be illustrated in next section. Without confusion, in our context, we will simply call (4) - (7) *action propositions*. According to our previous discussion, an action proposition with free variable occurrences is viewed as an action scheme, from which we can obtain a class of *ground action propositions* by substituting these free variables with ground terms.

Finally, a *constraint* is an expression of the form

$$\textbf{always } C, \tag{8}$$

where C is a sentence. As the usual function of domain constraints, (8) simply states that C should be satisfied in all possible states.

Now we specify a *domain description* Σ of $\mathcal{D}$ to be a finite set of initial value propositions, action propositions and constraints.

3   Semantics of $\mathcal{D}$

In this section, we define a formal semantics for language $\mathcal{D}$. The basic idea is as follows. We first propose a new structure for an arbitrary first order language $\mathcal{L}$ in which we allow a syntactic term of the language to be undefined in the domain of qualification. Within this structure, a truth value function is defined on any formula of $\mathcal{L}$ that may include those undefined terms in the domain. Then we extend this truth value function to $\mathcal{D}$ by specifying proper truth conditions on value propositions and constraints. Finally, we define a state transition function on this type of structures.

3.1 d-Structures

Let $\mathcal{L}$ be an arbitrary first order language. A d-structure of $\mathcal{L}$ is defined as follows.

Definition 1. *A d-structure M of $\mathcal{L}$ is any ordered pair $(D, \mathcal{F})$, where D is a set of objects (to be called the* domain*) and $\mathcal{F}$ is a unary function such that:*

(i) $\mathcal{F}$ is total to assign every n-placed predicate symbol P a set of ordered n-placed tuples of elements of D;

(ii) $\mathcal{F}$ is partial to assign every defined ground term an element of D.

Note that a d-structure M is usually associated with a set of ground terms of $\mathcal{L}$ where each term in the set is defined in M (i.e. mapped to some object in the domain of M) and all other ground terms of $\mathcal{L}$ are then undefined in M. Clearly, if the set of defined ground terms is identical to the set of all ground terms of $\mathcal{L}$, a d-structure is reduced to a classical first order structure of $\mathcal{L}$.

Definition 2. *Given a d-structure $M = (D, \mathcal{F})$, a primary assignment α_M in M is a partial unary function from the set of sentences of $\mathcal{L}$ to $\{T, \; F\}$ such that*

(i)   *if φ is of the form $P(a_1, \cdots, a_n)$ and $\mathcal{F}(a_i)$ is defined for every i $(1 \le i \le n)$, then $\alpha_M(\varphi) = T$ if $(\mathcal{F}(a_1), \cdots, \mathcal{F}(a_n)) \in \mathcal{F}(P)$, and otherwise $\alpha_M(\varphi) = F$;*
(ii) *(a) if φ is of the form $a = b$ and both $\mathcal{F}(a)$ and $\mathcal{F}(b)$ are defined, then $\alpha_M(\varphi) = T$ if $\mathcal{F}(a) = \mathcal{F}(b)$, and otherwise $\alpha_M(\varphi) = F$; (b) if φ is of the form $a = b$ and exactly one of $\mathcal{F}(a)$ and $\mathcal{F}(b)$ is defined, then $\alpha_M(\varphi) = F$;*
(iii) *for any other φ, $\alpha_M(\varphi)$ is not defined.*

Definition 3. *Given a d-structure $M = (D, \mathcal{F})$, a completion of M is a d-structure $M' = (D', \mathcal{F}')$ such that*

(i) $D \subseteq D'$;
(ii) *for any predicate symbol P, $\mathcal{F}(P) \subseteq \mathcal{F}'(P)$;*
(iii) *for every individual ground term a, $\mathcal{F}'(a)$ is defined and $\mathcal{F}'(a) = \mathcal{F}(a)$ if $\mathcal{F}(a)$ is also defined.*

Intuitively, a completion M' of M is a classical structure in which every ground term is defined, and for a term that is defined in M, its interpretation in M' is consistent to that in M. For a given d-structure M, M may have many different completions. We denote the set of all completions of M as $Comp(M)$.

Definition 4. *Let $M = (D, \mathcal{F})$ be a d-structure, $M' = (D', \mathcal{F}')$ a completion of M. A supplementary assignment $\alpha_{M,M'}$ in M with respect to completion M' is a total unary function from the set of sentences of $\mathcal{L}$ to $\{T, F\}$ such that*

(i)   *if φ is atomic and $\alpha_M(\varphi)$ is defined, then $\alpha_{M,M'}(\varphi) = \alpha_M(\varphi)$;*
(ii) *if φ is atomic and $\alpha_M(\varphi)$ is not defined, then $\alpha_{M,M'}(\varphi) = \alpha_{M'}(\varphi)$;*
(iii) *if φ is of the form $\neg\psi$, then $\alpha_{M,M'}(\varphi) = T$ iff $\alpha_{M,M'}(\psi) = F$, and otherwise $\alpha_{M,M'}(\varphi) = F$;*
(iv) *if φ is of the form $\psi \wedge \upsilon$, then $\alpha_{M,M'}(\varphi) = T$ iff $\alpha_{M,M'}(\psi) = \alpha_{M,M'}(\upsilon) = T$, and otherwise $\alpha_{M,M'}(\varphi) = F$;*
(v)   *if φ is of the form $\forall x\psi$ then $\alpha_{M,M'}(\varphi) = T$ iff $\alpha_{M,M'}(\psi_x[a]) = T$ for every individual ground term a such that $\mathcal{F}(a)$ is defined, and otherwise $\alpha_{M,M'}(\varphi) = F$.*

Definition 5. *Let $M = (D, \mathcal{F})$ be a d-structure, and $Comp(M)$ the set of all completions of M. The assignment α_M^* in M is a partial unary function from the set of sentences of $\mathcal{L}$ to $\{T, F\}$ such that*

(i) $\alpha_M^*(\varphi) = T$ *iff $\alpha_{M,M'}(\varphi) = T$ for every completion M' of M in $Comp(M)$;*
(ii) $\alpha_M^*(\varphi) = F$ *iff $\alpha_{M,M'}(\varphi) = F$ for every completion M' of M in $Comp(M)$;*
(iii) $\alpha_M^*(\varphi)$ *is not defined in all other cases.*

Definition 6. *A sentence φ is d-satisfiable iff there exists some d-structure M such that $\alpha_M^*(\varphi) = \text{T}$. φ is d-invalid iff there exists some d-structure M, either $\alpha_M^*(\varphi) = \text{F}$ or $\alpha_M^*(\varphi)$ is not defined. φ is d-valid, denoted as $\models_d \varphi$, iff φ is not d-invalid.*

3.2   Transition Function, Models, and Entailment

Consider two d-structures $M_1 = (D_1, \mathcal{F}_1)$ and $M_2 = (D_2, \mathcal{F}_2)$ which are associated with two sets of ground terms of $\mathcal{L}$, named $\mathcal{C}^{M_1}$ and $\mathcal{C}^{M_2}$ respectively, where only terms in $\mathcal{C}^{M_1}$ and $\mathcal{C}^{M_2}$ are defined in M_1 and M_2 respectively. We say that M_1 and M_2 are *comparable* if for every ground term $a \in \mathcal{C}^{M_1} \cap \mathcal{C}^{M_2}$, $\mathcal{F}_1(a) = \mathcal{F}_2(a)$. Let M_1 and M_2 be two comparable d-structures associated with two set of ground terms $\mathcal{C}^{M_1}$ and $\mathcal{C}^{M_2}$ respectively. We define the *difference* between M_1 and M_2, denoted as $Diff^d(M_1, M_2)$, to be the set of ground atoms as follows:

$$Diff^d(M_1, M_2) = \{P(a_1, \cdots, a_n) \mid \text{ for any } a_1, \cdots, a_n \in \mathcal{C}^{M_1} \cap \mathcal{C}^{M_2},$$
$$\alpha_{M_1}^*(P(a_1, \cdots, a_n)) \neq \alpha_{M_1}^*(P(a_1, \cdots, a_n))\}. \qquad (9)$$

To simplify our following presentation, we consider each action proposition in a generalized form (7):

$$A \textbf{ causes } C_1 \textbf{ creates } C_2 \textbf{ destroys } P_1, \cdots, P_k \textbf{ if } P.$$

Definition 7. *A transition function Res maps a d-structure to another d-structure according to a ground action proposition, where $Res(A, M)$ is defined as follows.*

(i)   If $\alpha_M^*(P) = \text{T}$[1], then $Res(A, M) = M'$, where M' is a d-structure such that M and M' are comparable, in which
$$\mathcal{C}^{M'} = \mathcal{C}^M \cup \{a_1, \cdots, a_n \mid a_1, \cdots, a_n \text{ occur in } C_2\}$$
$$- \{a_1', \cdots, a_m' \mid P'(\cdots, a_i', \cdots) \text{ is one of}$$
$$P_1, \cdots, P_k \ (1 \leq i \leq m)\},$$
and $\alpha_{M'}^*(C_1 \wedge C_2) = \text{T}$;

(ii) If $\alpha_M^*(P) = \text{F}$ or undefined, or $\alpha_M^*(P) = \text{T}$ but there is no M' satisfies the above condition, then $Res(A, M) = M$.

Res is called a minimal transition function if $Diff^d(M, Res(A, M))$ is minimal with respect to the set inclusion for any A and M.

The meaning of a transition function defined above is quite intuitive. If the precondition of A is true in M, then A changes M to a comparable M' in which the defined terms are those defined terms in M together with adding some new defined terms if A creates new objects and eliminating some defined terms from M if A destroys some things.

---

[1] That is, the precondition of A is d-satisfied in M.

We can extend the transition function to the case of a sequence of ground actions $\overline{A}$. $Res(\overline{A}, M)$ is defined as follows. If $\overline{A} = \epsilon$, i.e. empty string, then $Res(\overline{A}, M) = M$, otherwise, $Res(\overline{A}, M) = Res(A, Res(\overline{A'}, M))$, where $\overline{A} = \overline{A'}A$. A sequence of actions $\overline{A}$ is called a *subsequence* of $\overline{A'}$ if the relation holds: $\overline{A'} = A_1 A_2 \cdots A_k \cdots A_n$ and $\overline{A} = A_1 A_2 \cdots A_k$. We say that action A is *executable* in M if $\alpha_M^*(P) = \text{T}$ (note that P is the precondition of A). A sequence of two actions $A_1 A_2$ is executable in M if A_1 is executable in M and there exists some M' in which A_2 is executable while $M' = Res(A_1, M)$. Generally, a sequence of actions $\overline{A}$ is *executable* in M if any of its subsequences is executable in M. Now we are in a position to provide a formal semantics for value propositions and constraints in $\mathcal{D}$.

Definition 8. *Given a d-structure M and a transition function Res, a pair $\Psi = (M, Res)$ is a signature of $\mathcal{D}$ with respect to M and Res. The satisfaction of ground value propositions and constraints in Ψ is defined as follows.*

(i) *A value proposition of the form C **after** $\overline{A}$ is d-satisfied in Ψ if $\alpha_{M'}^*(C) = \text{T}$ where $Res(\overline{A}, M) = M'$;*

(ii) *A value proposition of the form **destroyed** $P_1, \cdots, P_k$ **after** $\overline{A}$ is d-satisfied in Ψ if there exists a subsequence $\overline{A'}$ of $\overline{A}$ such that $\overline{A'}$ is executable in M and contains actions $A_1, \cdots, A_l$ with destroying effects including $P_1, \cdots, P_k$;*

(iii) *A constraint of the form **always** C is d-satisfied in Ψ if $\alpha_M^*(C) = \text{T}$ and $\alpha_{M'}^*(C) = \text{T}$ where $Res(\overline{A}, M) = M'$ and $\overline{A}$ is any action sequence.*

Proposition 1. *Let $\Psi = (M, Res)$ be a signature of $\mathcal{D}$. If a value proposition **destroyed** $P_1, \cdots, P_k$ **after** $\overline{A}$ is d-satisfied in Ψ, then $\alpha_{M'}^*(P_i)$ is not defined for $i = 1, \cdots, k$, where $M' = Res(M, \overline{A})$.*

Definition 9. *Given a domain description Σ. A signature $\Psi = (M, Res)$ of $\mathcal{D}$ is a model of Σ if (i) the set $\mathcal{C}^M$ of defined terms in M is formed by including all ground terms occurring the initial value propositions and constraints of Σ, (ii) every initial value proposition and constraint of Σ are d-satisfied in Ψ, and (iii) Res is minimal. A ground value proposition or constraint θ is d-entailed by Σ, denoted as $\Sigma \models_d \theta$, if θ is d-satisfied in every model of Σ.*

Example 1. **Burning a Letter.** Consider a scenario where a robot needs to destroy a letter. If two actions, for example, striking a match and burning something with the lighted match, are available for the robot, then the robot may need to perform these two action sequentially in order to burn the letter. This domain can be easily formalized within our action language $\mathcal{D}$. Firstly, we have the following initial value propositions:

$$\text{initially } Match(a), \tag{10}$$

$$\text{initially } Letter(b), \tag{11}$$

which express that a is a match and b is a letter. We also specify two action propositions:

$$Strike(x) \textbf{ causes } Lighted(x) \textbf{ if } Match(x), \tag{12}$$

$$Burn(x, y) \textbf{ destroyed } Letter(y)$$
$$\textbf{if } Match(x) \wedge Lighted(x) \wedge Letter(y). \tag{13}$$

The first action proposition (12) says that if x is a match, then striking x causes that x is lighted, while (13) represents the action of burning a letter y with the lighted match x. Now a domain description Σ^L consists of propositions (10) -(13). Then without much difficulty, we can derive the following desired results:

$$\Sigma^L \models_d Lighted(a) \textbf{ after } Strike(a),$$
$$\Sigma^L \models_d \textbf{destroyed } Letter(b) \textbf{ after } Strike(a); Burn(a, b).$$

4   Semantic Properties of Domain Descriptions

In this section, we further investigate some semantic properties of domain descriptions. Firstly, we show that if no function symbols occur in language $\mathcal{D}$ and a domain description Σ does not include action propositions with creating or destroying effects, then there exists a corresponding action language $\mathcal{D}'$ where Σ can be characterized by the language $\mathcal{A}$-like model theoretic semantics [2] on $\mathcal{D}'$.

Formally, let $\mathcal{D}$ be an action language without function symbols and Σ a domain description on $\mathcal{D}$ that does not include action propositions with creating and destroying effects. We specify an action language $\mathcal{D}'$ which is obtained from $\mathcal{D}$ by restricting all constants in $\mathcal{D}'$ to be those occurring in the initial value propositions and constraints in Σ. Then for any signature $\Psi = (M, Res)$ of $\mathcal{D}$, we can specify a *reduced signature* $\Psi' = (M', Res')$ of $\mathcal{D}'$ as follows:

(i) M' is a classical first order structure on $\mathcal{D}'$ obtained from M by setting $\mathcal{C}^{M'}$ to be the set of all constants of $\mathcal{D}'$ (see Definitions 1 and 2).

(ii)   The truth value of a first order sentence φ in M' is then defined as the usual way in the first order logic. For example, φ is satisfied in M', denoted as $M' \models \varphi$, iff φ is true in M'.

(iii) Let M_1 and M_2 be two structures on $\mathcal{D}'$. $Diff(M_1, M_2)$ denotes the set of all ground atoms that have different truth values in M_1 and M_2 respectively.

(iv)   For an action proposition of the form A **causes** C **if** P, the transition function Res' is defined as $Res'(A, M_1) = M_2$ where $M_2 \models C$ if $M_1 \models P$, otherwise $Res'(A, M_1) = M_1$[2]. Res' is *minimal* if $Diff(M_1, Res'(A, M_1))$ is minimal for any A and M_1.

(v)   The satisfaction of ground value propositions and constraints in $\Psi' = (M', Res')$ is defined as in Definition 8 by replacing $\alpha^*_M(C) = \text{T}$ with $M \models C$ and without considering actions with destroying effects (i.e. condition (ii) in Definition 8).

Then we say that a reduced signature $\Psi' = (M', Res')$ is a *reduced model* of Σ on $\mathcal{D}'$ if Ψ' is generated from the above procedure such that every initial value proposition and constraint of Σ are satisfied in Ψ' and Res' is minimal. It can

---

[2] Note that here both M_1 and M_2 are structures on $\mathcal{D}'$.

be verifed that the above semantics for Σ on $\mathcal{D}'$ is coincident with the one for $\mathcal{A}$ language proposed by Gelfond and Lifschitz in [2].

Given a value proposition or constraint θ, θ is *entailed* by Σ, denoted as $\Sigma \models \theta$, if θ is satisfied in every reduced model of Σ. Then we have the following result.

Theorem 1. *(Reduction Theorem) Let $\mathcal{D}$ be an action language without function symbols, Σ a domain description on $\mathcal{D}$ that does not include action propositions with creating and destroying effects, and $\mathcal{D}'$ is a language obtained from $\mathcal{D}$ by restricting all constants in $\mathcal{D}'$ to be those occurring in initial value propositions and constraints of Σ. Then for any value proposition or constraint θ on $\mathcal{D}'$, $\Sigma \models_d \theta$ iff $\Sigma \models \theta$.*

Theorem 2. *(Creating Effect Theorem) Given a domain description Σ, suppose $\Sigma \models_d C(t)$ **after** $\overline{A}$ where t is a ground term occurring in C. If there is a subsequence $\overline{A'}$ of $\overline{A}$ such that t does not occur in any C' such that $\Sigma \models_d C'$ **after** $\overline{A'}$, then an action with the form A **creates** $C''(t)$ if P must be in $\overline{A}$ after $\overline{A'}$, i.e. $\overline{A} = \overline{A'} \cdots A \cdots$.*

Theorem 2 states that if an object is in the domain after executing a sequence of actions, but it is not in the domain sometime earlier, then this object must be created by an action sometime later. Similarly, the following theorem says that if an object is destroyed from the domain after performing a sequence of actions, and it is in the domain sometime before, then this object must be destroyed by an action sometime later.

Theorem 3. *(Destroying Effect Theorem) Given a domain description Σ, suppose $\Sigma \models_d$ **destroyed** $P_1(t)$ **after** $\overline{A}$ where t is a ground term occuring in predicate P_1. If there is a a subsequence $\overline{A'}$ of $\overline{A}$ such that $\Sigma \models_d C(t)$ **after** $\overline{A'}$, then an action with the form A **destroys** $P_1(t), \cdots$ if P must be in $\overline{A}$ after $\overline{A'}$, i.e. $\overline{A} = \overline{A'} \cdots A \cdots$.*

Now we investigate the monotonicity properties of domain descriptions. It is well known that monotonicity is an important property for knowledge representation and reasoning that can be used to simplify a reasoning procedure. However, like most of other systems of reasoning about change, our action formulation based on language $\mathcal{D}$ is *nonmonotonic*: by adding more action propositions or constraints into a domain description, the set of value propositions entailed by the expanded domain description may shrink. Instead, our domain descriptions indeed satisfy a kind of *restricted monotonicity* which characterizes an important feature for the underlying reasoning principle. Given a domain description Σ, an action sequence $\overline{A}$ is *executable* in Σ if for each model $\Psi = (M, Res)$ of Σ, $\overline{A}$ is executable in M. Then we have the following result.

Theorem 4. *(Restricted Monotonicity) Let Σ be a domain description on $\mathcal{D}$. Σ' is a domain description obtained from Σ by adding more initial value propositions. Then for any value proposition θ with the form C **after** $\overline{A}$ or* **destroyed** $P_1, \cdots, P_k$ **after** $\overline{A}$ *where $\overline{A}$ is executable in Σ, $\Sigma \models_d \theta$ implies $\Sigma' \models_d \theta$.*

5   Further Discussions

In this paper, we propose a new action language $\mathcal{D}$ which can represent actions with creating or destroying effects over dynamic domains. Although $\mathcal{D}$ shares the syntactic feature of $\mathcal{A}$ family languages, it has a significantly different model theoretic semantics compared to previous action theories. This new semantics also provides a foundation to handle dynamic domains in reasoning about change.

People may argue that within the classic logic framework, there may have other alternatives to represent actions with creating or destroying effects. For instance, using the $\mathcal{A}$ language, it seems feasible to represent action of burning a letter as the following proposition:

$Burn(x,y)$ **causes** $\neg Letter(y)$
if $Match(x) \land Lighted(x) \land Letter(y)$.

However, in general, this is not correct if we want to add a constraint to characterize all objects in the domain that we want to deal with: **always** $\forall x(Match(x) \lor Letter(x))$. This constraint intuitively says that all objects to be dealt with in the domain are either matches or letters. Considering that after burining y, $\neg Letter(y)$ is held, then the domain constraint becomes invalid.

On the other hand, *Free logic* has been studied in philosophical logics [1] in which terms can denote somethings that are not in the universe. Nevertheless, to the best of our knowledge, there is no detailed study on how free logic can be applied in reasoning about action and change, it is not clear to us yet whether we can directly use free logic to achieve our purpose addressed in this paper. In this sense, it appears that our work here presents an original contribution to handle dynamic domains in reasoning about action and change. Furthermore, our results also show that the complexity of reasoning within the $\mathcal{D}$ lanuage is not harder than that in the original $\mathcal{A}$ language [5,8].

References

1. E. Bencivenga, Free logic. *Handbook of Philosophical Logic*, Vol. III, pp373-426, 1986.
2. M. Gelfond and V. Lifschitz, Representing action and change by logic programs. *Journal of Logic Programming*, **17**: 301-322 (1993).
3. E. Giunchiglia and V. Lifschitz, An action language based on causal explanation: preliminary report. In *Proceedings of AAAI-98*, pp 623-630, 1998.
4. G.N. Kartha and V. Lifschitz, Actions with indirect effects (Preliminary report). In *Proceedings of Kr'94*. 1994.
5. P. Liberatore, The complexity if the language $\mathcal{A}$. *Electronic Transactions on Artificial Intelligence*, Vol. 1 (1997) 13-38.
6. V. Lifschitz, Two components of an action language. *Annals of Mathematics and Artificial Intelligence*, **21** (1997), pp. 305-320.
7. M. Winslett. Reasoning about action using a possible models approach. In *Proceedings of AAAI-88*, pages 89-93, 1988.
8. Y. Zhang and N.Y. Foo The language $\mathcal{D}$ - An action language over dynamic domains. Manuscript, January 2002.

Consistency of Action Descriptions

Dongmo Zhang[1], Samir Chopra[2], and Norman Y. Foo[2]

[1] School of Computing and Information Technology
University of Western Sydney, Australia
[2] Knowledge Systems Group
School of Computer Science and Engineering
The University of New South Wales, Australia

Abstract. As a contribution to the metatheory of reasoning about actions, we present some characteristics of the consistency of action theories. Three levels of consistency are investigated for the evaluation of action descriptions: uniform consistency, consistency of formulas and regional consistency. The first two provide an intuitive resolution of problems of explanation conflicts and fluent dependency. The concept of regional consistency provides for a measure of ramification. A highly expressive form of action descriptions, the normal form, is introduced to facilitate this analysis. The relative satisfiability of the situation calculus is generalized to accommodate non-deterministic effects and ramifications.

1 Introduction

The metatheory of logical frameworks for reasoning about actions has received justified attention in recent times [12,15,10,21,18].. These studies have helped to establish a systematic methodology for the evaluation of the various frameworks proposed for reasoning about action. An important baseline property for all formal systems is *consistency*. In reasoning about actions, an accurate and consistent action description is crucial since problems in the action description infect all further reasoning about the dynamic domain it describes. We show that the issues raised in the consistency analysis of action descriptions are significant and interesting. The consistency of both the logical system itself *and* the action description of the dynamic domain needs to be evaluated. Incorrect, incomplete and inconsistent action descriptions can be detected and rectified, leading to a better understanding of the dynamic domain and a better formalization of the problem.

Since consistency of a formal system is defined in terms of the associated deductive system and its properties require semantic consideration, a sound and complete logic of action would be most helpful in consistency analysis. With this in mind, we exploit an extended propositional dynamic logic, $EPDL$ [24]. This system offers a unified treatment of reasoning about direct and indirect effects of actions, thus enabling a representation of action effects and causal ramifications. We introduce techniques for consistency analysis of action descriptions in $EPDL$ frameworks. Three different levels of consistency are provided: *uniform consistency* of action descriptions, Σ-*consistency* of formulas and *regional consistency* of action descriptions. Uniform consistency conveys information about what kinds of action descriptions guarantee proper runs of a dynamic system. Σ-consistency of formulas informs us of which situations a dynamic system can start up

M. Ishizuka and A. Sattar (Eds.): PRICAI 2002, LNAI 2417, pp. 70–79, 2002.
© Springer-Verlag Berlin Heidelberg 2002

from and run properly. It also serves as a tool with which to detect incorrect and inadequate action descriptions. The concept of regional consistency provides for a measure of ramification. Addressing the issue of consistency of action descriptions provides an alternative approach to thinking about classical problems in reasoning about action.[1]

2   EPDL Preliminaries

We summarize some basic facts of the extended propositional dynamic logic ($EPDL$) (see [24] for more details). In propositional dynamic logic (PDL), a causal relation between an action α (primitive or compound) and a property A is expressed by the modal formula: $[\alpha]A$, meaning "α (always) causes A if α is feasible". For example, $[Turn\_off]\neg light$ says that "turning off the switch causes the light to be off". The dual operator $\langle\alpha\rangle A$, reads "α is feasible and may (or possibly) cause(s) A to be true". For instance, $\langle Spin\rangle \neg loaded$ says that "spinning a gun barrel may cause it to be unloaded". $\langle\alpha\rangle\top$ means "α is feasible or executable". In $EPDL$, propositions are allowed as modalities. The formula $[\varphi]A$, termed *propositional causation*, represents a cause-effect relationship between the proposition φ and the formula A and is read as "φ **causes** A". For example, $[short\ -circuit]damaged$ says that "short-circuits cause the circuit to be damaged".

A language $\mathcal{L}_{EPDL}$ of $EPDL$ consists of a set **Flu** of fluent symbols and a set **Act**$_P$ of primitive action symbols. Propositions ($\varphi \in$ **Pro**), formulas ($A \in$ **Fma**) and actions ($\alpha \in$ **Act**) are defined by the following BNF rules:

$$\varphi ::= f \mid \neg\varphi \mid \varphi_1 \to \varphi_2$$
$$A ::= f \mid \neg A \mid A_1 \to A_2 \mid [\alpha]A \mid [\varphi]A$$
$$\alpha ::= a \mid \alpha_1;\alpha_2 \mid \alpha_1 \cup \alpha_2 \mid \alpha^* \mid A?$$

where $f \in$ **Flu** and $a \in$ **Act**$_P$.

The definitions of $\top$(**true**), $\bot$(**false**), $\vee$, $\wedge$, $\leftrightarrow$ are as usual. A literal is a fluent or its negation. The set of all the literals is denoted by **Flu$_L$**. We introduce the following notation:

$\langle[\alpha]\rangle A =_{def} \langle\alpha\rangle\top \wedge [\alpha]A$, meaning "$\alpha$ *must cause* A";

$\prec \alpha \succ A =_{def} \langle\alpha\rangle\top \to \langle\alpha\rangle A$, meaning "if α *is feasible*, α *may cause* A".[2]

The semantics for $\mathcal{L}_{EPDL}$ is similar to PDL. Since the propositional modality $[\varphi]$ is treated as a normal modal operator, the semantic conditions for propositional modalities are exactly the same as action modalities except for the following extra conditions:

1. If $M \models_w \varphi$, then $(w, w) \in R_\varphi$.
2. If $\models \varphi \leftrightarrow \psi$, then $R_\varphi = R_\psi$.

The axiom system for $EPDL$ extends PDL [8] by one axiom:

CW axiom: $[\varphi]A \to (\varphi \to A)$

and one inference rule:

CE: From $\varphi \leftrightarrow \psi$ infer $[\psi]A \leftrightarrow [\varphi]A$

---

[1] Due to space limitation, we omitted proofs of Theorems. See "http://www.cit.uws.edu.au/~dongmo/PRICAI02_full.pdf" for a full version of the paper.

[2] Note that these two operators are dual, i.e., $\prec \alpha \succ A = \neg\langle[\alpha]\rangle\neg A$.

The classical K axiom and inference rule N (necessitation) are respectively extended to accommodate propositional modalities:

EK axiom: $[\gamma](A \to B) \to ([\gamma]A \to [\gamma]B)$

EN: *From A infer* $[\gamma]A$.

where $\varphi, \psi \in$ **Pro**, $A \in$ **Fma** and $\gamma \in$ **Pro** $\cup$ **Act**.

A formula A is *provable* from a set Γ of formulas, denoted by $\Gamma \vdash A$, if there exist $A_1, \cdots, A_n \in \Gamma$ such that $\vdash (A_1 \wedge \cdots \wedge A_n) \to A$. Γ is *consistent* in $EPDL$ if $\Gamma \not\vdash \bot$.

3   Action Descriptions and Their Normal Forms

$EPDL$ provides a formal language via *action descriptions* to describe the behavior and internal relationships of a dynamic system. These specify the effects and feasibility of actions, causal ramifications and other domain constraints.

Example 1. Consider the Yale Shooting Problem [9]. Let **Flu** $= \{alive, loaded, walking\}$ and **Act$_P$** $= \{Load, Shoot, Wait\}$. This problem can be specified by the following action description:

$$\Sigma = \left\{ \begin{array}{l} \neg loaded \to [Load]loaded \\ loaded \to [Shoot]\neg alive \\ loaded \to [Shoot]\neg loaded \\ [\neg alive]\neg walking \\ \langle Load \rangle \top, \langle Wait \rangle \top, \langle Shoot \rangle \top \end{array} \right\}$$

Formulas in an action description are significantly different from ordinary formulas. For instance, the sentence "*loaded* $\to$ [*Shoot*]$\neg alive$" says that whenever *loaded* is true, *Shoot* causes $\neg alive$. In the language of situation calculus, this is written as $\forall s(loaded(s) \to \neg alive(do(Shoot, s)))$. Indeed, we need to view the action description of a dynamic domain as a set of extra axioms (domain axioms in the situation calculus [20]) rather than an ordinary set of formulas in reasoning about the domain.

Definition 1. [24] *Let* Σ *be an action description. A formula A is Σ-provable, written as* $\vdash^\Sigma A$, *if it belongs to the least set of formulas which contains all the theorems of EPDL, all elements of* Σ, *and is closed under Modus Ponens and EN.*

If Γ is a set of formulas, then $\Gamma \vdash^\Sigma A$ means there exists $A_1, \cdots, A_n \in \Gamma$ such that $\vdash^\Sigma (A_1 \wedge \cdots \wedge A_n) \to A$.

Example 2. Consider the action description in Example 1. We can easily prove that

1. $\neg loaded \vdash^\Sigma [Load; Shoot]\neg alive$
2. $\neg loaded \vdash^\Sigma [Load; Shoot]\neg walking$
3. $\vdash^\Sigma \langle [Load; Wait; \textbf{if } \neg loaded? \textbf{ do } Load \textbf{ endif}; Shoot] \rangle \neg alive$

Note that the action description in Example 1 does not completely specify the domain since it does not include information about *unaffected* fluents. Without frame axioms we can neither prove nor refute the very intuitive relation:

$\neg loaded \vdash^\Sigma [Load; Wait; Shoot]\neg alive$.

A solution to the frame problem then, is necessary for reasoning with such incomplete action descriptions.

Let Σ be an action description. A model M of $EPDL$ is a Σ-model if $M \models B$ for any $B \in \Sigma$. It can be proved that if Σ is finite, then A *is Σ-provable iff A is valid in every Σ-model* [24].

3.1 Normal Action Descriptions

An action description can be any set of formulas in the $EPDL$ language. However, in most cases we prefer the simple normal form in order to obtain better properties and more convenient treatment. The following kinds of formulas are said to be in *normal form*:

- $[\varphi]L$ (causal law)
- $\varphi \to [a]L$ (deterministic action law)
- $\varphi \to\prec a \succ L$ (non-deterministic action law)
- $\varphi \to \langle a \rangle \top$ (qualification law).

where φ is a propositional formula, L is a literal and a is a primitive action.

An action description Σ is *normal* if each formula in Σ is in normal form. It is easy to see that the action descriptions in Example 1, 3, 5 and 7 are normal. Action description Σ_1 in Example 6 is normal but Σ_2 is not.

Although the normal form is restricted, it is quite expressive. It can express *direct* or *indirect, deterministic* or *non-deterministic* effects of actions, and *qualifications* of actions. Most normal forms in other action theories can be transformed into $EPDL$ normal form (propositional case only). For instance, action descriptions written in the form of pre-condition axioms and successor state axioms in the *propositional* situation calculus language (i.e., there are no sorts *object* and function symbols in the language [20]) can be translated into the $EPDL$ normal form by the following procedure:

1. For each pre-condition axiom $Poss(a, s) \equiv \varphi(s)$, the associated laws are:
$\varphi \to \langle a \rangle \top, \neg\varphi \to [a]f, \neg\varphi \to [a]\neg f$
where f can be any fluent symbol (choosing one).

2. For each successor state axiom $f(do(\pi, s)) \equiv \varphi(\pi, s)$, where π is an action variable, the associated laws are:
$\varphi \to [a]f, \neg\varphi \to [a]\neg f$
where π is instantiated by each primitive action a.

Most components of action languages [6] can also be expressed by $EPDL$ normal form. For example, "a **causes** L **if** φ" in the action language $\mathcal{A}$ can be translated to "$\varphi \to [a]L$"; a static law "**caused** L **if** φ" in the language $\mathcal{C}$ is translated to "$[\varphi]L$"; and an expression "a **may cause** L **if** φ" in $\mathcal{C}$ is translated to "$\varphi \to\prec a \succ L$". The same translation procedure will work for action descriptions in STRIPS [3].

4   Consistency of Action Descriptions

As noted above, an action description acts as an axiomatic specification of a dynamic system highlighting the importance of consistency. We now consider three different levels of consistency: *consistency of formulas, consistency of action descriptions* and *consistency of formulas with action descriptions*. Each of these conveys different information about the dynamic system under consideration.

4.1   Uniform Consistency of Action Descriptions

As defined above, a set Γ of formulas is consistent if $\Gamma \not\vdash \bot$. Semantically, it means that there is a model in which Γ is satisfied in *some* world. As far as the consistency of an action description is concerned, however, ordinary consistency is not enough to guarantee that a dynamic system runs properly. As a set of domain axioms, an action description should be consistent with *any possible evolution of the dynamic system under any combination of actions*. With this in mind, we define the consistency of action descriptions as follows:

Definition 2. Let Σ be a set of formulas. Σ is *uniformly consistent* if $\nvdash^{\Sigma} \perp$.

By the soundness and completeness of Σ-provability [24], we have

Theorem 1. Σ *is uniformly consistent if and only if there exists a Σ-model.*

Obviously, uniform consistency implies ordinary consistency. The following highlights the difference between the two.

Example 3. Let $\mathbf{Flu} = \{f_1, f_2, f_3\}$ and $\mathbf{Act} = \{a\}$. $\Sigma = \{\langle a \rangle \top, [a]f_1, [a]f_2, f_1 \rightarrow [a]f_3, f_2 \rightarrow [a]\neg f_3\}$. Then Σ is consistent but not uniformly so.

By the finite model property of $EPDL$, the uniform consistency of an action description is decidable. However, satisfiability in $EPDL$ is $EXPTIME$-hard. So deciding the consistency of action descriptions is, in general, intractable. Can we put any syntactical restrictions on action descriptions, say normal form, to make it easier? Is any action description in normal form uniformly consistent? Unfortunately, Example 3 shows that this is not true. Further assumptions are necessary.

Let Σ be a normal action description. For any fluent f and any primitive action a, if we merge the action laws about a and $f(\neg f)$ in each form together, there are at most five laws about a and f in Σ:

$$\varphi \rightarrow \langle a \rangle \top$$
$$\varphi_{1,1} \rightarrow [a]f, \varphi_{1,2} \rightarrow [a]\neg f$$
$$\varphi_{2,1} \rightarrow \prec a \succ \neg f, \varphi_{2,2} \rightarrow \prec a \succ f$$

If φ, $\varphi_{1,1}$ and $\varphi_{1,2}$ are true simultaneously, then the action description will contain a contradiction. Similarly for φ, $\varphi_{1,j}$ and $\varphi_{2,j}$ ($j = 1$ or $j = 2$). For simplicity, we make the following assumption.

Assumption 1: $\vdash \neg\varphi \vee \neg\varphi_{1,1} \vee \neg\varphi_{1,2}$ *and* $\vdash \neg\varphi \vee \neg\varphi_{1,j} \vee \neg\varphi_{2,j}$ $(j = 1, 2)$.

If some law is absent, say $\varphi_{1,1} \rightarrow [a]f$, we use $\perp \rightarrow [a]f$ instead. Note that if φ is a proposition, then $\vdash \varphi$ in $EPDL$ if and only if φ is a tautology in the classical propositional logic.

The assumption 1 only acts on action laws. Similar assumptions could be also made about causal laws. An effect of an action can be either a direct effect (caused by an action) or an indirect effect (caused by other propositions). In most cases (but not all), we can separate the indirectly affected fluents from the directly affected ones [11].

Assumption 2: *There is a partition* $\{\mathbf{Flu}_d, \mathbf{Flu}_i\}$ *of* $\mathbf{Flu}$ *such that* $\mathbf{Flu} = \mathbf{Flu}_d \cup \mathbf{Flu}_i$ *and*

1. for each $f \in \mathbf{Flu}_i$, *if both* $[\varphi_1]f$ *and* $[\varphi_2]\neg f$ *are in* Σ, *then* $\vdash \neg\varphi_1 \vee \neg\varphi_2$.

2. for each causal law $[\varphi]L$, *all the fluents in* φ *are from* $\mathbf{Flu}_d$ *and* L *is a literal in* $\mathbf{Flu}_i$;

The first condition of the assumption is similar to the assumption 1. The second condition is intended to avoid recursive indirect effects of actions. For the sake of simplicity, we only allow two layers of causal propagation (as in [11]). More complicated cases can be investigated by using the approach in [2].

Definition 3. A normal action description is *safe* if it is satisfies the Assumptions 1 and 2.

It is easy to see that the action descriptions in Example 1 and 5 are safe but 3 and 7 are not. An interesting observation is any action description which is translated from an action description in the propositional situation calculus is *innately* safe.

Proposition 1. *If Σ is an action description generated by the procedure in Section 3.1 from a set of precondition axioms and successor state axioms in the propositional situation calculus, then Σ is safe.*

The following theorem is one of the main results in the paper.

Theorem 2. *Let Σ be a normal action description. If it is safe then is uniformly consistent.*

This theorem gives us a sufficient condition to check the consistency of an action description by using only propositional logic and the syntax of the action description. Therefore if an action description is written in normal form the consistency checking of the action description becomes a co-NP problem. Specially, as a corollary of the theorem and Proposition 1, an action description is innately uniformly consistent if it is written as a set of precondition axioms and successor state axioms. Note that pre-condition axioms and successor state axioms in propositional situation calculus language are much less expressive than normal form.

4.2 Σ-Consistency of Formulas

As defined, a set of formulas is consistent if a contradiction cannot be derived from it. More precisely, its consistency means that it is consistent with the basic axioms and inference rules of $EPDL$, which does not guarantee that it is consistent with arbitrary action descriptions.

Let Σ be an action description. A set Γ of formulas is *Σ-consistent* if $\Gamma \not\vdash^{\Sigma} \bot$. It is easy to see that Σ-consistency of Γ requires the consistency of Γ, the uniform consistency of Σ, and even more. For example, $\{loaded, \neg alive, walking\}$ is consistent, but not Σ-consistent, where Σ is the action description in Example 1, which is uniformly consistent. Σ-consistency of a set of formulas conveys the information that a dynamic system can properly run from an initial situation as specified by the formulas. More interestingly, we notice that in classical logic, a set's inconsistency is due to the set itself if the deductive system of the logic is consistent. Σ-inconsistency of a set, is however, due to both the set *and* the action description. If the set consists of observed facts, the inconsistency must lie in the action description. This provides us with a formal tool to detect incorrect or inadequate action descriptions.

Example 4. Consider the Yale shooting scenario with a new action *Entice* and add the following action law and qualification law (c.f. [23]):

$\neg walking \rightarrow [Entice]walking$
$\neg alive \rightarrow [Entice]\neg alive$
$\langle Entice \rangle \top$

Putting these together with the action description in Example 1 generates a new action description Σ'. Then Σ' is still safe and so uniformly consistent. Note that the set $\{\neg alive, \neg walking\}$ is Σ'-inconsistent.

We can easily see that there is no any problem with the set $\{\neg alive, \neg walking\}$ (these can be observed facts). The problem here can only lie in the action description and specifically, in the newly introduced action laws. Indeed, the qualification law $\langle Entice\rangle\top$ is problematic. A correct description of the qualification of $Entice$ would be: $alive \rightarrow \langle Entice\rangle\top$. We might be tempted to think that this consistency check provides a solution to the qualification problem: we can automatically generate qualification laws from a given action description by default reasoning instead of explicitly listing them in the action description. Unfortunately, this does not always work.

Example 5. Consider the following circuit introduced by [23] and its action description:

$$\Sigma = \left\{ \begin{array}{l} [sw_1 \wedge sw_2]\, light \\ [\neg sw_1 \vee \neg sw_2]\, \neg light \\ \neg sw_i \rightarrow [Toggle_i]sw_i \\ sw_i \rightarrow [Toggle_i]\neg sw_i \\ \langle Toggle_i\rangle\top \\ i = 1, 2 \end{array} \right\}$$

The first sentence says that switch 1 and switch 2 being closed causes the light to be on. The second says that one of the switches being open causes the light to be off. $\neg sw_i \rightarrow [Toggle_i]sw_i$ means that if switch i is open, then toggling switch i causes it to be on. Suppose now that we have an action Hit_the_Bulb. The action laws about the action are:

$light \rightarrow [Hit\_the\_Bulb]\neg light$

$\langle Hit\_the\_Bulb\rangle\top$

Adding these as well as the frame axioms $sw_1 \rightarrow [Hit\_the\_Bulb]sw_1$ and $sw_2 \rightarrow [Hit\_the\_Bulb]sw_2$ to Σ, results in an action description, Σ', which is uniformly consistent. Notice that $\{sw_1, sw_2, light\}$ is Σ'-inconsistent, which is obviously unacceptable. In this case, it is not reasonable to change the qualification law $\langle Hit\_the\_Bulb\rangle\top$ into $\neg sw_1 \vee \neg sw_2 \rightarrow \langle Hit\_the\_Bulb\rangle\top$. The problem is now in the causal law $[sw_1 \wedge sw_2]light$. We term this the *qualification problem of effect propagation* (for a similar discussion see [14]). The examples above have shown that consistency checks can help us detect incorrect action descriptions. The Stolen Car Problem [22] shows that Σ-inconsistency can be due to the *inadequacy* of the action description.

Example 6. Consider the following action description:

$$\Sigma_1 = \left\{ \begin{array}{l} in\_park \rightarrow [Wait]in\_park \\ \neg in\_park \rightarrow [Wait]\neg in\_park \\ \langle Wait\rangle\top \end{array} \right\}$$

Σ_1 says that waiting does not affect the state of a parked car. It is easy to see that $\{in\_park, [Wait]\neg in\_park\}$ is Σ_1-inconsistent. However, the observed facts are exactly that originally the car was parked (in_park) and that it is not there after a period of time ($[Wait]\neg in\_park$).

The problem here is that the agent with this action description has no idea about car's theft: presumably, it should realize that leaving a car alone might cause it to be stolen ($\prec Wait \succ stolen$). A car's theft means that it had been parked somewhere, but disappeared after a period of time. $(in\_park \rightarrow [Wait] (\neg in\_park \leftrightarrow stolen))$. So the correct action description should be:

$$\Sigma_2 = \left\{ \begin{array}{l} \prec Wait \succ stolen \\ in\_park \rightarrow [Wait](\neg inpark \leftrightarrow stolen) \\ \langle Wait \rangle \top \end{array} \right\}$$

where $stolen$ is a fluent. Then we have an explanation for the observed facts: $\{in\_park, [Wait]\neg in\_park\} \vdash^{\Sigma_2} [Wait]stolen$.

We would like to remark that consistency checking can help us detect the incorrectness and inadequacy of an action description but it can not remedy the action description because they are actually two types of problems.

The following theorem is quite useful in the diagnosis of Σ-consistency:

Theorem 3. *Let Σ be a normal and safe action description. Let $D(\Sigma) = \{\varphi \rightarrow L : [\varphi]L \in \Sigma\}$. For any set Γ of propositional formulas, if $\Gamma \cup D(\Sigma)$ is consistent, then Γ is Σ-consistent.*

Therefore, we can check the Σ-consistency of a set of propositional formulas using propositional logic (the complexity of which is in **NP** $\cup$ **co-NP**).

Let us compare the result above with a similar meta-theorem in the situation calculus [18]. Suppose that Σ consists of pre-condition axioms and successor state axioms, and Γ consists of initial state axioms as in the situation calculus. According to Theorem 3 and Proposition 1, Γ is Σ-consistent if and only if Γ is consistent in propositional logic (note that $D(\Sigma)$ is empty here). This coincides with the *Relative Satisfiability* theorem (Theorem 1 in [18]), which says that an action theory $\mathcal{D}$ is satisfiable iff the initial state axioms and unique name axioms are satisfiable. In other words, the foundational axioms, pre-condition axioms and successor state axioms cannot introduce inconsistency. Since the situation calculus in [18] applies to only domains without non-deterministic actions and ramifications, Theorem 3 can be viewed as a generalization of the *Relative Satisfiability* theorem[3].

4.3   Regional Consistency of Action Descriptions

Ramification in dynamic systems arises as a consequence of fluent dependencies. The following notion of consistency provides for a means of assessing the fluent dependencies present in a system.

Definition 4. *Let Σ be an action description and U be a subset of* **Flu**. *Σ is regionally consistent over U if any interpretation I of U is Σ-consistent[4]. Σ is universally consistent if it is regionally consistent over* **Flu**.

Regional consistency of action descriptions reflects local independence of fluents. In other words, if Σ is regionally consistent over U, any change of truth-value of fluents in U does not affect each other (but does affect the fluents outside U). This information is computationally important because once the value of a fluent in U is changed, only the fluents outside U need to be revaluated (see [7]).

---

[3] There are extended versions of situation calculus in the literature [16,13] which can deal with non-deterministic or indirect effects of actions expressed by successor state axioms. However, Relative Satisfiability is not necessarily true in the extended frameworks without introducing extra restrictions on action descriptions.

[4] An interpretation I of U means a maximal consistent set of literals over U

Example 7. Consider the circuit introduced by [23] and described with the following simplified action description

$$\Sigma = \left\{ \begin{array}{l} \neg sw_i \to [Toggle_i] sw_i \\ sw_i \to [Toggle_i] \neg sw_i \\ [sw_1 \land sw_2] light \\ [\neg sw_1 \lor \neg sw_2] \neg light \\ [sw_1 \land sw_3] \neg sw_2 \\ \langle Toggle_i \rangle \top \\ i = 1, 2, 3 \end{array} \right\}$$

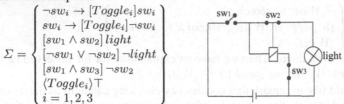

Then Σ is regionally consistent over $\{sw_1, sw_3\}$, but not over $\{sw_1, sw_2, sw_3\}$ or any supersets. This implies Switch 1 and Switch 3 can be controlled independently, but Switch 2 cannot. So if we take an action $toggle_1$, only those facts which are relevant to the direct effect (sw_1) and the indirect effects (sw_2 and $light$) need to be revaluated (sw_3 can be ignored).

Regional consistency acts also as a *measure* of ramification. The larger the consistent area of an action description, the less ramification it has. If an action description is universally consistent, there is *no* ramification between fluents.

Proposition 2. *Let Σ be a normal and safe action description. $\{\mathbf{Flu}_d, \mathbf{Flu}_i\}$ is a partition of $\mathbf{Flu}$ which satisfies Assumption 2 of safety. Then Σ is reginally consistent over $\mathbf{Flu}_d$. If there are no causal laws in Σ, then Σ is universally consistent.*

As noted previously, any action description which is translated from a set of pre-condition axioms and successor state axioms in the propositional situation calculus is universally consistent. This explains why the solution for the frame problem in [20] applies only to actions without ramifications.

The idea of regional consistency is close to the one of *frames in the space of situations*[11]. A frame is a set of fluents which are directly affected by actions. With the concept, the values of the frame fluents can be specified by effect axioms and the law of inertia while the values of non-frame fluents are determined by domain constraints or causal laws. It has been remarked in [11] that a frame be neither too large nor too small. However, it is not clear that what kind of sets of fluents are qualified to be a frame. For the case of normal and safe action descriptions, it is obvious that $\mathbf{Flu}_d$ is a "qualified" frame. For the general case, it is still an open problem. We believe that regional consistency is helpful towards a solution to the problem.

5   Conclusion

In this study we have investigated the characteristics of the consistency of action theory. Three levels of consistency were introduced for the evaluation of action descriptions. These provide an intuitive resolution of problems of explanation conflicts, fluent dependency and a measure of ramification. The highly expressive normal form of action descriptions greatly facilitates such an analysis. Several meta-theorems on the consistency of normal action descriptions have been given which show how to generate a consistent action description and how to check the consistency of normal action descriptions. Our results generalize the Relative Satisfiability Theorem in the situation calculus to allow non-deterministic effects of actions and ramifications. Although our approach is based on the extended propositional dynamic logic (for its unified expression of direct and indirect effects of actions and its sound and complete deductive system), all the results on the consistency of action descriptions are applicable to other formalisms of actions since the expressions of action descriptions are often intertranslatable. The application of these techniques also leads to new insights on classical problems in reasoning about actions.

References

1. M. A. Castilho, O. Gasquet, and A. Herzig, Formalizing action and change in modal logic i: the frame problem. *Journal of Logic and Computations*, 9:701-735, 1999.
2. M. Denecker, D. T. Dupré, and K. Van Belleghem, An inductive definition approach to ramifications, *Electronic Transactions on Artificial Intelligence, vol 2*, 1998.
3. R. Fikes and N. Nilsson, Strips: a new approach to the application of theorem proving to problem solving. In *Proceedings of the 2nd International Joint Conference on Artificial Intelligence*, 608-620. William Kaufmann, 1971.
4. N. Foo and D. Zhang, Dealing with the ramification problem in the extended propositional dynamic logic. in F. Wolter, H. Wansing, M. de Rijke, and M. Zakharyaschev eds, *Advances in Modal Logic, Volume 3*, CSLI Publications, 2001.
5. N. Foo and D. Zhang, Lazy-formalization to the frame problem, *manuscript*.
6. M. Gelfond and V. Lifschitz, Action language. *Electronic Transactions on AI*, 16(3), 1998.
7. M. L. Ginsberg and D. E. Smith, Reasoning about action I: a possible worlds approach, in: *Artificial Intelligence*, 35(1988), 165-195.
8. R. Goldblatt, *Logics of Time and Computation*. Stanford University Press, 1987.
9. S. Hanks and D. McDermott, Nonmonotonic logic and temporal projection. *Artificial Intelligence*, 33(3):379-412, 1987.
10. G. N. Kartha, Soundness and completeness theories for three formalizations of action. In: *IJCAI'93*, 724-729, 1993.
11. V. Lifschitz, Frames in the space of situations. *Artificial Intelligence*, 46:365-376, 1990.
12. V. Lifschitz, Towards a metatheory of action. In: *KR'91*, 376-386, 1991.
13. V. Lifschitz, Situation calculus and causal logic. In: *KR-98*, 536-546, 1998.
14. F. Lin and R. Reiter, State constraints revisited. *Journal of Logic and Computation*, 4(5):655–677, 1994.
15. F. Lin and Y. Shoham, Provably correct theories of action, *J. ACM* 42(2):293-320, 1995.
16. F. Lin, Embracing causality in specifying the indirect effects of actions. In: *IJCAI-95*, 1985-1991, 1995.
17. J. McCarthy and P. J. Hayes, Some philosophical problems from the standpoint of artificial intelligence, in: B. Meltzer and D. Michie, eds., *Machine Intelligence 4*, Edingburgh University Press, Edinburgh, 463-502, 1969.
18. F. Pirri and R. Reiter, Some contributions to the metatheory of the situation calculus. *Journal of ACM*, 3(46):325–361, 1999.
19. H. Prendinger and G. Schurz, Reasoning about action and change: A dynamic logic approach. *Journal of Logic, Language, and Information*, 5:209–245, 1996.
20. R. Reiter, The frame problem in the situation calculus: a simple solution (sometimes) and a completeness result for goal regression. In V. Lifschit, editor, *Artificial Intelligence and the Mathematical Theory of Computation*, Academic Press, 359–380, 1991.
21. E. Sandewall, *Features and Fluents*. Oxford University Press, 1994.
22. Murray Shanahan, *Solving the Frame Problem: a mathematical investigation of the common sense law of inertia*. MIT Press, 1997.
23. M. Thielscher, Ramification and causality, *Artificial Intelligence*, 89:317–364, 1997.
24. D. Zhang and N. Foo, EPDL: a logic for causal reasoning, *Proceedings of IJCAI-01*, 131-136, 2001.

Solving Factored MDPs with Large Action Space Using Algebraic Decision Diagrams

Kee-Eung Kim[1] and Thomas Dean[2]

[1] Center for Advanced Software Engineering
Samsung SDS
159-9 Gumi-Dong Bundang-Gu Seongnam-Si, Gyeonggi-Do 463-810
Korea
kekim@samsung.co.kr
[2] Department of Computer Science
Brown University
Providence, RI 02912-1910
U.S.A.
tld@cs.brown.edu

Abstract. We describe an algorithm for solving MDPs with large state and action spaces, represented as factored MDPs with factored action spaces. Classical algorithms for solving MDPs are not effective since they require enumerating all the states and actions. As such, model minimization techniques have been proposed, and specifically, we extend the previous work on model minimization algorithm for MDPs with factored state and action spaces. Using algebraic decision diagrams, we compactly represent blocks of states and actions that can be regarded equivalent. We describe the model minimization algorithm that uses algebraic decision diagrams, and show that this new algorithm can handle MDPs with millions of states and actions.

1 Introduction

Markov Decision Processes (MDPs) employing representations that factor states, associated transition and reward functions in terms of component functions of state variables (fluents) have been widely adopted as a framework for decision theoretic planning under uncertainty (Boutilier *et al.* [2]). Since the number of states in these Factored MDPs (FMDPs) is exponential in the number of fluents, traditional iterative methods that require enumerating states are typically not practical. As such, using model minimization algorithm to reduce the number of states of a given FMDP has been proposed (Dean and Givan [4], Givan *et al.* [6]).

In this paper, we extend the previous work on model minimization algorithm for MDPs with factored state *and* action spaces (Dean *et al.* [5]). The model minimization algorithm reformulates the FMDP with factored action space as an explicitly represented MDP with reduced state and action spaces, allowing us to solve the original problem using classical MDP algorithms. Each state and action in such a minimized MDP represent a large number of states and

M. Ishizuka and A. Sattar (Eds.): PRICAI 2002, LNAI 2417, pp. 80–89, 2002.

actions in the original model. To compactly represent the states and actions, we use Algebraic Decision Diagrams (ADDs) as opposed to the previous algorithm using decision trees. The result is that we can now handle MDPs to the sizes intractable for the previous algorithm. We describe how the core operators in the FA-FMDP minimization algorithm are implemented in terms of ADDs and show the results of experiments on some interesting problem domains.

2   FMDPs with Factored Action Spaces (FA-FMDPs)

Dean *et al.* [5] presented the model minimization algorithm to FMDPs with factored action spaces, which we call FA-FMDP hereafter. Formally, the FA-FMDP is defined as follows:

Definition 1 (FA-FMDP) *An FA-FMDP is defined as a tuple* $M = \{\boldsymbol{X}, \boldsymbol{A}, T, R\}$ *where*

- $\boldsymbol{X} = [X_1, \ldots, X_n]$ *is a vector of state fluents which collectively define the state. We use* Ω_{X_i} *to denote the set of values for* X_i. Ω_{X_i} *is the sample space of* X_i *when* X_i *is considered as a random variable. Thus, the state space for* M *is* $\Omega_{\boldsymbol{X}} = \prod_i \Omega_{X_i}$. *We use lower case letters* $\boldsymbol{x} = [x_1, \ldots, x_n]$ *to denote a particular instantiation of the state fluents, and* $X_{i,t}$ *and* $x_{i,t}$ *denote, respectively, a state fluent and its value at a particular time* t.
- $\boldsymbol{A} = [A_1, \ldots, A_m]$ *is a vector of action fluents which collectively define the action. Similar to the state fluents, the action space for* M *is* $\Omega_{\boldsymbol{A}} = \prod_i \Omega_{A_i}$, *and* $\boldsymbol{a} = [a_1, \ldots, a_n]$ *denotes a particular instantiation of action fluents.*
- T *is the set of transition probabilities, represented as the set of conditional probability distributions, one for each action and fluent:*

$$T(\boldsymbol{X}_t, \boldsymbol{A}_t, \boldsymbol{X}_{t+1}) = \prod_{i=1}^{n} P(X_{i,t+1}|\mathrm{pa}(X_{i,t+1}))$$

  where $\mathrm{pa}(X_{i,t+1})$ *denotes the set of parents of* $X_{i,t+1}$ *in the graphical model (see below). Note that* $\forall i, \mathrm{pa}(X_{i,t+1}) \subseteq \{X_{1,t}, \ldots, X_{n,t}, A_{1,t}, \ldots, A_{m,t}\}$.
- $R : \Omega_{\boldsymbol{X}} \times \Omega_{\boldsymbol{A}} \to \Re$ *is the reward function.*

Figure 1 presents an example of the graphical model for a FA-FMDP. Note that the conditional probability for each fluent is stored as a decision tree rather than a table for the economy of representation, which we call Conditional Probability Tree (CPT) (Boutilier *et al.* [2]).

Having a factored action space allows us to compactly model domains with a large number of actions, such as controlling multiple effectors on a robot or allocating a set of resources. To prevent us from facing the combinatorial explosion, we are interested in exploiting the regularity in state space *and* action space. For example, a robot traversing a darkened room can adjust its camera in a variety of ways, but only the sonar and infrared sensors will have any impact on the robot's success in navigating the room. If we model this example as a

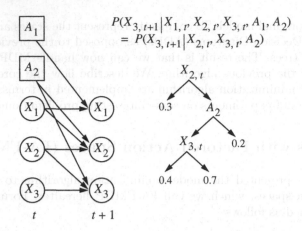

Fig. 1. Graphical representation of a FA-FMDP and the Conditional Probability Tree (CPT) of fluent X_3. CPT stores conditional probabilities, *e.g.*, $P(X_{3,t+1}|X_{2,t}) = 0.3$.

FA-FMDP, there are three action fluents, and only two of them are relevant to an optimal policy, namely sonar and infrared, when the state fluent indicating the luminosity of the room is set to "dark". This is the idea behind the model minimization algorithm for FA-FMDPs — the algorithm abstracts out useless actions from consideration in appropriate sets of states.

3   Model Minimization Algorithm for FA-FMDPs

Let us make following definitions regarding FA-FMDPs for use with the model minimization algorithm (more detailed discussion can be found in Dean *et al.* [5]):

Definition 2 *Given a FA-FMDP $M = \{X, A, T, R\}$, a partition P of the space $\Omega_X \times \Omega_A$ (which is a refinement of the reward partition), we make the following definitions:*

- **Projection** : *The projection $P|_X$ of P onto X is the partition of Ω_X such that two states x and x' are in the same block if and only if for every action a in A, the pairs (x, a) and (x', a) are in the same block of P. Likewise, the projection $P|_A$ of P onto A is the partition of Ω_A such that two actions a and a' are in the same block if and only if for every state x in X, the pairs (x, a) and (x, a') are in the same block of P.*
- **Stability** : *A block C of a partition P is called stable with respect to a block B of $P|_X$ if and only if every two pairs (x, a) and (x', a') in block C satisfy $T(x, a, B) = T(x', a', B)$. A block C is said to be stable if C is stable with respect to every block of $P|_X$.*
- **Homogeneity** : *P is homogeneous if and only if every block is stable.*
- **Quotient MDP** : *When P is homogeneous, the Quotient MDP is defined to be the explicit MDP $M_P = \{P|_X, P|_A, T_P, R_P\}$ where T_P is defined as*

---

1. Input: FA-FMDP $M = \{\boldsymbol{X}, \boldsymbol{A}, T, R\}$ and partition P induced by the reward function R.
2. Compute $P' = \text{BACKUP}(P)$.
3. If $|P'| < |P|$, set $P = P'$ and go to step 2.
4. Set $P = P'$ and output the quotient MDP $M_P = \{P|_{\boldsymbol{X}}, P|_{\boldsymbol{A}}, T, R\}$.

Fig. 2. The FA-FMDP minimization algorithm using BACKUP operator.

the transition probabilities between the blocks of P, and R_P is defined as the reward function on the blocks of P.

It follows that the optimal value function V^* and the optimal policy π^* of the quotient MDP obtained by the minimization algorithm is also the optimal value function and the optimal policy for the original FA-FMDP.

The goal of the minimization algorithm is to compute the *coarsest homogeneous partition* — a homogeneous partition with the smallest number of blocks. Define $P' = \text{BACKUP}(P)$ which produces a refined partition P' of P, with the property that every block in P' is stable with respect to every block in P. $\text{BACKUP}(P)$ uses partition P_X for each state space fluent X, the partition induced by the values of conditional probabilities for fluent X. In other words, each block of P_X corresponds to a leaf in the CPT for fluent X. For example, P_{X_3} in Figure 1 is given by $\{X_2, \overline{X_2} \wedge A_2 \wedge X_3, \overline{X_2} \wedge A_2 \wedge \overline{X_3}, \overline{X_2} \wedge \overline{A_2}\}$. Let $\boldsymbol{X}_P$ be the set of all state space fluents which are mentioned in any formula in the representation of the current partition P. First, construct the intersection I_P of partition P and all partitions P_X with fluent X being in $\boldsymbol{X}_P$:

$$I_P \equiv P \cap \bigcap_{X \in \boldsymbol{X}_P} P_X$$

I_P makes all the distinctions needed within $\boldsymbol{X} \times \boldsymbol{A}$ so that within each block of I_P, the block transition probability to each block of $P|_{\boldsymbol{X}}$ is the same, which implies that blocks in I_P are stable with respect to the blocks in P. Note, however, that I_P may make distinctions that do not need to be made, thus lead to a non-minimal partition. As such, it is necessary to define $\text{BACKUP}(P)$ as the *clustering* of the partition I_P in which blocks of I_P are merged if they have identical block transition probabilities to the blocks of $P|_{\boldsymbol{X}}$. We merge two blocks taking the disjunction of the block formulas for those blocks. Figure 2 shows the pseudo-code of the minimization algorithm using the BACKUP operator.

4 Using Algebraic Decision Diagrams (ADDs)

The minimization algorithm uses Algebraic Decision Diagrams (ADDs) to represent the partitions. The ADD is a generalization of the Boolean Decision Diagram (BDD), in which the terminal nodes can have an arbitrary value instead of a Boolean value in $\{0, 1\}$ (Bryant [3], Bahar *et al.* [1]). An ADD represents a function $f : \{0, 1\}^n \to \Re$ with a set of non-terminal nodes and terminal nodes. The function that an ADD represents is defined as follows (Figure 3):

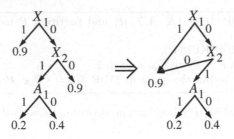

Fig. 3. An example of a decision tree and an equivalent ADD.

– The function of a terminal node is a constant function of the value stored in the terminal node.
– The function of a non-terminal node labeled with fluent X is defined as $X \cdot f_1 + \overline{X} \cdot f_0$, where f_1 is the function of the child node connected by the edge labeled 1, and f_0 is the function of the other child node.
– The function f of an ADD is the function of the start node.

To use ADDs, we first obtain ADD representations for the transition probabilities and the reward. This procedure is done in the same manner as Hoey *et al.* [8]. In the case of transition probabilities, we view the CPT for fluent X_i as function

$$
\begin{aligned}
T_{X_{i,t+1}}&(X_{1,t}, \ldots, X_{n,t}, A_{1,t}, \ldots, A_{m,t}) \\
&\equiv X_{i,t+1} \cdot P(X_{i,t+1}|X_{1,t}, \ldots, X_{n,t}, A_{1,t}, \ldots, A_{m,t}) \qquad (1) \\
&+ \overline{X_{i,t+1}} \cdot \left(1 - P(X_{i,t+1}|X_{1,t}, \ldots, X_{n,t}, A_{1,t}, \ldots, A_{m,t})\right),
\end{aligned}
$$

and hence, the transition probability is

$$
\begin{aligned}
T(X_{1,t}, &\ldots, X_{n,t}, A_{1,t}, \ldots, A_{m,t}, X_{1,t+1}, \ldots, X_{n,t+1}) \\
&= \prod_{i=1}^{n} T_{X_{i,t+1}}(X_{1,t}, \ldots, X_{n,t}, A_{1,t}, \ldots, A_{m,t}).
\end{aligned}
$$

After we obtain ADD representations of $T_{X_{i,t+1}}$ for all i, we can construct the ADD for the transition probability through the ADD multiplication operator. Constructing ADD representations of $T_{X_{i,t+1}}$ (Equation 1) is done through traversing the CPT of X_i representing $P(X_{i,t+1}|X_{1,t}, \ldots, A_{1,t}, \ldots)$. When we encounter non-terminal node X_i during the traversal, we first calculate the ADD representation for left subtree and right subtree, which we respectively call f_0 and f_1, and then replace the node by the ADD representation $X_i f_1 + \overline{X_i} f_0$. The reward function given as a decision tree is converted in the same manner.

Once we construct the ADD representations of the transition probability and the reward function, we can implement the core parts of the minimization algorithm in terms of ADD operators. *The ADDs in this paper represent partitions by assigning unique block numbers to the terminal nodes.* First, we describe the projection of partition P onto the state space, which we denote $P|_{\mathbf{X}}$. The projection is done by summing over all possible values taken by the action fluent,

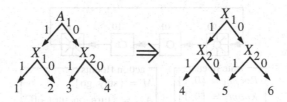

Fig. 4. A bad case of existential abstraction. When we sum over action fluent A_1, two blocks merge since the additions of the block numbers are the same.

---

1. Input: Partition P of $\Omega_X \times \Omega_A$, in ADD representation.
2. For each action fluent A_i,
   a) Let $f = A_i \cdot |P| + \overline{A_i}$.
   b) Do existential abstraction (see the text) of $f \cdot P$ over A_i and store the result as P.
   c) Normalize terminal nodes in P so that they are numbered from 0 to $|P| - 1$.
3. Output P.

Fig. 5. The algorithm for projecting ADD representation of a partition onto the state space.

---

1. Input: Partition P of $\Omega_X \times \Omega_A$ and transition probabilities T, all in ADD representation.
2. Calculate projection of P onto the state space and call it $P|_X$.
3. For each block $B \in P|_X$,
   a) Construct ADD for representing block B so that the ADD returns 1 if the assignment of the state fluents belongs to B, and returns 0 otherwise. Call it P_B and mark the fluents to be at time step $t + 1$.
   b) Perform ADD matrix-vector multiplication of T and P_B by summing over all the variables at time step $t + 1$. Let the result be P'_B.
   c) Normalize terminal nodes in P'_B so that they are numbered from 0 to $|P'_B| - 1$.
   d) Calculate $P = P \cdot |P'_B| + P'_B$.
   e) Normalize terminal nodes in P so that they are numbered from 0 to $|P| - 1$.
4. Output P.

Fig. 6. The algorithm for the BACKUP operator on ADD representation of a partition.

through the ADD operator *existential abstraction*. Note that we can accidentally merge two blocks during the existential abstraction. As an example shown in Figure 4, when we sum over action fluent A_1, two blocks $X_1 \wedge \overline{X_2}$ and $\overline{X_1} \wedge X_2$ merge although they should not. This behavior can be simply avoided by rescaling the block numbers so that the blocks with A_1 being true are multiplied by the size of the partition. The overall algorithm of $P|_X$ is shown in Figure 5. $P|_A$ is computed in the same manner, except that we sum over all state fluents.

The pseudo-code for the BACKUP operator is shown in Figure 6. To merge stable blocks that have the same transition probabilities with respect to the

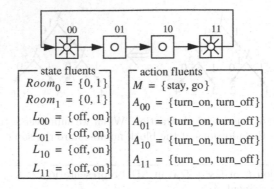

Fig. 7. An example of ROBOT-k domain with 4 rooms.

blocks in $P|_{\mathbf{X}}$, we compute the projection $P|_{\mathbf{X}}$ in step 2. We obtain stable blocks with respect to each block B in $P|_{\mathbf{X}}$, as shown in step 3 (b).

5   Experiments

In this section, we present results from experiments regarding two versions of the FA-FMDP minimization algorithms, one using decision trees and the other using ADDs. A preliminary result from the decision tree version of the minimization algorithm appeared in Dean *et al.* [5]. The ADD version of the minimization algorithm uses C++ implementation of Colorado University Decision Diagram (CUDD) package (Somenzi [9]) for manipulating ADDs.

Robot navigation in dark rooms (ROBOT-k). Consider a robot navigating in a simple collection of rooms (Figure 7). Suppose that there are k rooms connected in circular chain and each room has a light which is either on or off. The robot is in exactly one of the k rooms and so there are $k2^k$ states. At each stage, the robot can choose to go forward or stay in the current room and choose to turn on or off any of the k lights, so there are 2^{k+1} actions. The fluents $Room_b$ encode the b-th bit for the binary representations of the room numbers. The fluents L represent the status of the lights in the rooms. The robot receives a reward of 1 for being in the room k and otherwise receives no reward. If the light is on in the room where the robot is currently located and the robot chooses to go, then it will end up in the next room with probability 1 at the next time step. If the light is off and it chooses to go, it will remain in the current room with probability 1. If the robot chooses to stay, then it will remain in the current room with probability 1.

Jobshop scheduling (JOBSHOP-k-l). Consider a machine shop that needs to allocate k machines to l tasks (Figure 8). The tasks are partially ordered, meaning that some tasks have pre-requisite tasks. Each task requires one or more specific machines to be allocated. Each machine is capable of working on only one task at each time step. Once a task succeeds in occupying the required set of machines, the task gets accomplished at the next time step with some probability. Thus, there are $task_1, \ldots, task_l$ state fluents holding the value

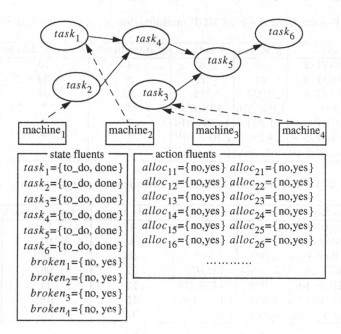

Fig. 8. An example of JOBSHOP-k-l domain with 4 machines and 6 tasks. The solid arrows between tasks specify dependencies as pre-requisites. The dashed arrows between machines and tasks specify allocations.

either "to_do" or "done". All the machines become available at the next time step whether the assigned task gets accomplished or not. As action fluents, if $alloc_{ij}$ is set "yes", task j succeeds in occupying machine i between the current time step and the next time step. The constraint that there is only one task allocated to each machine is implemented by adding state fluents $broken_1, \ldots, broken_k$. $broken_i$ represents whether the machine i is broken, and this fluent becomes "yes" whenever $alloc_{ij}$ and $alloc_{ij'}$ for different j and j' are set "yes", which means we tried to allocate the machine to two different tasks at the same time. Once $broken_i$ is set "yes", it never becomes "false". When a specified final task is done, the reward of 1 is given, but if any of $broken_i$ is set "yes", then reward of -10 is given.

Results. Table 1 shows experimental results from the minimization algorithm using decision trees. We show as well as the running time of the algorithm, the number of states and actions of the unminimized MDP, and the number of state and action blocks of the minimized MDP. The JOBSHOP domains were randomly generated by assigning random numbers to the success probabilities. In summary, the algorithm with decision trees suffered from generating large intermediate partitions for the BACKUP operator in domains such as ROBOT-16 and JOBSHOPs.

The total number of action blocks is the sum of the number of action blocks obtained through projection constrained to each state block. If we project the homogeneous partition onto the action space, we lose the information that there

Table 1. Results from the FA-FMDP minimization algorithm using decision trees.

Domain	# states	# actions	# state blocks	# action blocks	Time
ROBOT-2	8	8	4	16	0.01 s
ROBOT-4	64	32	8	32	0.03 s
ROBOT-8	2,024	512	16	64	1.9 s
ROBOT-16	1,048,576	131,072	*	*	*
JOBSHOP-4-6	1,024	16,777,216	*	*	*
JOBSHOP-5-8	8,192	1.10×10^{12}	*	*	*
JOBSHOP-6-10	65,536	1.15×10^{18}	*	*	*

Table 2. Results from the FA-FMDP minimization algorithm using ADDs.

Domain	# states	# actions	# state blocks	# action blocks	Time
ROBOT-2	8	8	4	12	0.15 s
ROBOT-4	64	32	8	24	0.18 s
ROBOT-8	2,024	512	16	48	1.02 s
ROBOT-16	1,048,576	131,072	32	96	2.49 s
JOBSHOP-4-6	1,024	16,777,216	13	44	3.03 s
JOBSHOP-5-8	8,192	1.10×10^{12}	45	109	6.20 s
JOBSHOP-6-10	65,536	1.15×10^{18}	57	143	13.68 s

is a limited number of action fluents pertinent to each state block and end up with a large number of actions. Note that this deviates from the original definition of a quotient MDP, but this is necessary to obtain a meaningful minimization.

Table 2 shows the results from experiments using the algorithm with ADDs. The algorithm can minimize the domains that the decision tree version cannot. Note also the difference in the numbers of actions blocks due to limited expressiveness of decision trees. Figure 9 shows the algorithm for the projection of the homogeneous partition onto the action space constrained to each state block.

All the experiments were run on a Sun Ultra 10 with 256MB main memory.

6   Discussion and Related Work

We have presented an FA-FMDP minimization algorithm that uses ADDs to compactly represent the partitions of the state and action space. The expressiveness in the representation of ADDs allows us to handle MDPs with large state and action spaces that are daunting problems for decision trees. We also provided a new projection method to obtain action blocks, which preserves information on irrelevant action fluents for each state blocks. This method results in typically smaller models than the original approach in Dean et al. [5]. Future work includes implementing ϵ-approximate model reduction (Givan et al. [6]).

The FA-FMDP minimization algorithm draws from the work of finding the regularities in finite state automata (Hartmanis and Stearns [7]). The preliminary implementation of the FA-FMDP minimization algorithm by Dean et al. [5] used decision trees for representing the partitions. ADDs are used in other MDP

1. Input: Partition P of $\Omega_X \times \Omega_A$, and $P|_X$, all in ADD representation.
2. For each block $B \in P|_X$,
   a) Construct ADD for representing block B so that the ADD returns 1 if the assignment of the state fluents belongs to B, and returns 0 otherwise. Call it P_B.
   b) Calculate $P'_B = P_B \cdot P$.
   c) Normalize the terminal nodes in P'_B so that they are numbered from 1 to $|P'_B|$.
   d) For each state fluent X_i,
      i. Let $f = X_i \cdot (|P'_B| + 1) + \overline{X_i}$.
      ii. Do existential abstraction of $f \cdot P'_B$ over X_i and store the result as P'_B.
      iii. Normalize the terminal nodes in P'_B so that they are numbered from 1 to $|P'_B|$.
3. Output P'_B for all B.

Fig. 9. The algorithm for projecting the ADD representation of a homogeneous partition onto the action space.

algorithms as well. Hoey et al. [8] uses ADDs to compactly represent value functions in FMDPs. Subsequent work by St-Aubin et al. [10] provides an algorithm for approximate representation of value functions to reduce the size of ADDs.

References

1. R. Iris Bahar, Erica Frohm, Charles Gaona, Gary Hachtel, Enrico Macii, Abelardo Pardo, and Fabio Somenzi. Algebraic decision diagrams and their applications. In *Proceedings of the International Conference on Computer-Aided Design*, 1993.
2. Craig Boutilier, Thomas Dean, and Steve Hanks. Decision-theoretic planning: Structural assumptions and computational leverage. *Journal of Artificial Intelligence Research*, 11, 1999.
3. Randal E. Bryant. Graph-based algorithms for boolean function manipulation. *IEEE Transactions on Computers*, C-35(8):677–691, 1986.
4. Thomas Dean and Robert Givan. Model minimization in Markov decision processes. In *Proceedings AAAI-97*, 1997.
5. Thomas Dean, Robert Givan, and Kee-Eung Kim. Solving planning problems with large state and action spaces. In *Proceedings AIPS-98*, 1998.
6. Robert Givan, Sonia Leach, and Thomas Dean. Bounded-parameter Markov decision processes. *Artificial Intelligence*, 122:71–109, 2000.
7. Juris Hartmanis and R.E. Stearns. *Algebraic Structure Theory of Sequential Machines*. Prentice-Hall, 1966.
8. Jesse Hoey, Robert St-Aubin, Alan Hu, and Craig Boutilier. SPUDD: Stochastic planning using decision diagrams. In *Proceedings UAI-99*, 1999.
9. Fabio Somenzi. *CUDD: CU Decision Diagram Package Release 2.3.0*. Department of Electrical and Computer Engineering, University of Colorado at Boulder, 1998.
10. Robert St-Aubin, Jesse Hoey, and Craig Boutilier. APRICODD: Approximate policy construction using decision diagrams. In *Proceedings NIPS-2000*, 2000.

Dynamic Fuzziness

Andrzej Buller

ATR Human Information Science Laboratories
2-2-2 Hikaridai, Seika-cho, Soraku-gun, Kyoto 619-0288 Japan
buller@atr.co.jp

Abstract. The paper proposes a generalization of the notion of the fuzzy set, intended to make it useful in the modeling of mental mechanisms of intelligent autonomous agents. In order to better represent the intrinsic dynamics of mental processes, the traditional membership value from the range [0, 1] is replaced with a function mapping time onto the range [0, 1]. Psychological justification of the development of a Dynamic Fuzzy Set theory, a method of Dynamic Fuzzy Calculus (DFC), as well as a computational example are provided.

1 Introduction

The fuzzy sets introduced in the 60's [10] reflect the way humans categorize, which in the 70's was confirmed experimentally by cognitive psychologists [9]. The key observation was that when people were asked to press a button to indicate true or false in response to a statement of the form "An [example] is a [category]", reaction times depended on the representativeness of the given example as a member of a given category. The average time of hesitation as to which button to press can be represented as a function of the value of the membership of the example to a fuzzy set representing the category. Nevertheless, the nature of the hesitation itself, or the reasons of the commonly known evidence that "..in a number of circumstances hate changes into love and love into hate" [6] has not attracted cognitive scientists.

The development of social cognition caused in the 90's an increasing interest in the intrinsic dynamics of human categorization. Experiments confirmed that when judging a perceived person or social situation people sometimes oscillate from highly positive feelings to highly negative ones even in the absence of new data about the object of interest [8]. Similar oscillations were demonstrated by computational models of human working memory that treated the mental process as a "debate" in a "society of memes" in a cellular working memory [5]. The idea of *Dynamic Fuzzy Calculus* (DFC) emerged from the research on these models [2].

DFC is not to be confused with applications of fuzzy calculus to the control of dynamic systems. DFC, being developed as a synthesis of Dynamic Logic (see [7]) and classic fuzzy sets theory (see [10]), handles sets that are themselves dynamic, replacing the traditional membership value from the range [0, 1] with a function mapping time onto the range. Is such generalization necessary? The answer to this question de-

M. Ishizuka and A. Sattar (Eds.): PRICAI 2002, LNAI 2417, pp. 90-96, 2002.
© Springer-Verlag Berlin Heidelberg 2002

pends on the complexity of behavior we want to analyze in an investigated system or to see demonstrated by a constructed system. The modeling of mental processes of intelligent autonomous agents seems to be hard task when based on concepts offered by Fuzzy Set Theory. Dynamic fuzziness is intended to be a useful extension to the theory.

Let us therefore consider the working definition:

Dynamic Fuzzy Set (**DFS**) *is a fuzzy set such that an element belongs to the set with a membership value that changes in time.*

A calculation of the dynamic fuzzy membership value for a given time, called is itself a dynamic process (Figure 1). Where can DFS be applied?

Let us consider a situation wherein two subjects $S1$ and $S2$ on January 1 are victims of the same assault by the same perpetrator P. Among a number of possible plots of the victims' feelings towards the perpetrator, let us consider the possibility that: the feelings of $S1$ start from extreme hatred on January 1 and then a linear decay of the hatred takes place towards indifference on January 31, while $S2$ feels constant and extreme hatred that on January 24 turns suddenly into perverse love. A model based on classic fuzzy sets can provide information on the victims' feelings in a particular moment in time or an average value for a given period. Let us consider fuzzy sets H1, H2, L1, and L2, which contain people hated by $S1$, people hated by $S2$, people loved by $S1$, and people loved by $S2$, respectively. When taking into account January 31, the membership values can be provided as, say: $\mu_{H_1}(P)=0$, $\mu_{H_2}(P)=0$, $\mu_{L_1}(P)=0$, $\mu_{L_2}(P)=1$. Such figures do not look too informative. The same applies to the average value for all of January, which could be: $\mu_{H_1}(P)=0.5$, $\mu_{H_2}(P)=0.67$, $\mu_{L_1}(P)=0$, $\mu_{L_2}(P)=0.33$. In both cases the most essential information is lost. Hence the necessity of a replacement of membership values with membership functions of time. Dynamic Fuzzy Set theory replaces $\mu_{H_1}(P)$, $\mu_{H_2}(P)$, ... with $\mu_t(H1, P)$, $\mu_t(H1, P)$, ..., respectively and offers an extraordinary way of calculating such memberships.

$$\mu_t(D_1, e_1), \; \mu_t(D_1, e_2), \; ...$$
$$\mu_t(D_2, e_1), \; \mu_t(D_2, e_2), \; ...$$
$$...$$
$$\mu_t(D_j, e_1), \; \mu_t(D_j, e_2), \; ...$$

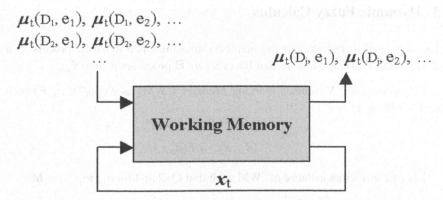

Fig. 1. Dynamic Fuzzy Calculus (DFC). $\mu_t(D_j, e_i)$ – membership of e_i to dynamic fuzzy set D_j, x_t – vector of Working Memory state variables.

The basic tool for Dynamic Fuzzy Calculus (DFC) is Working Memory, which is understood as a theater in which populations of *memes* fight for domination (cf. [1]). Every meme points to two objects, in which one is a set while the second one is an element belonging to the set. The memes may exchange parts of their informational content, or, when contradictory, eliminate each other. Particular memberships are calculated every time-clock based on the number of copies of a given meme versus the number of copies of contradictory memes.

2 Dynamic Fuzzy Sets

Let us introduce some auxiliary notions:

   $\neg$ – operator of negation, such that for any literal e we assume $\neg(\neg e) = e$;

   T – a period of interest, i.e., a finite set of integers representing moments in *time*.

   Let $\mathbf{E} = \{\theta, e_1, \neg e_1, e_2, \neg e_2, ...\}$ be a universe of discourse, where θ denotes an *object of interest*, while $e_1, \neg e_1, e_2, \neg e_2, ...$ denote other objects or sets of objects.

   Let $\mathbf{M} = \mathbf{E}^2$ be the space of ordered pairs of objects. We will call the pairs *memes* and denote them $\langle ele' \rangle$. The meme $\langle \theta | \theta \rangle$ will be denoted θ and called an *empty meme*.

   Let $\mathbf{A}$ be a space of functions such that $\forall_{\mu \in \mathbf{A}} \mu : \mathbf{M} \to [0; 1]^Q$, where Q is a positive integer. Let us also consider the space $\mathbf{B}$ such that $\forall_{d \in \mathbf{B}} d : \mathbf{T} \to \mathbf{A}$. Any element of $\mathbf{B}$ may be considered as a system of relationships between objects. Each of the relationships applies to a given meme and expresses itself as a vector $(\mu_{1,t}(m), \mu_{2,t}(m), ..., \mu_{Q,t}(m))$, where $\forall_{q,t,m \in 1..Q \times \mathbf{T} \times \mathbf{M}} 0 \le \mu_{q,t}(m) \le 1$.

We will call $\mu_{q,t}(\langle ele' \rangle)$ a value of qth-order membership of e' to a *dynamic fuzzy set* e. When $\mu_{1,t}(\langle ele' \rangle)$ remains constant or almost constant for every $t \in \mathbf{T}$, $\mu_{1,t}(\langle ele' \rangle)$ becomes $\mu_e(e')$, i.e., the traditionally understood membership of e' to a fuzzy set e.

3 Dynamic Fuzzy Calculus

The source of inconstancy of the membership values is a dynamic process in a machine called Working Memory that for every $d \in \mathbf{B}$ processes d_t onto d_{t+1}.

   Let us consider *N-channel Working Memory* (^{N}WM) as a couple $\langle x, F \rangle$ such that $x : \mathbf{T} \to \mathbf{M}^N$ and

$$F : \mathbf{A} \times \mathbf{M}^N \to \mathbf{A} \times \mathbf{M}^N,$$

$$(d_{t+1}, x_{t+1}) = F(d_t, x_t).$$

Let us consider an instance of ^{N}WM such that Q=2 and for $m_0, m_1, ... \in \mathbf{M}$

$$d_t = ((\mu_{1,t}(m_0), \mu_{2,t}(m_0)), (\mu_{1,t}(m_1), \mu_{2,t}(m_1)), ...),$$

$$x_t = (x_{0,t}, x_{1,t}, ..., x_{N-1,t}), \text{ N mod 3 = 0},$$

where function F works in such a way that for every $m \in \mathbf{M}$

$$\mu_{q,t}(m) = g_q(m, x_t),$$

$$x_{i,t+1} = \begin{cases} u_{i,t+1} & \text{if } f_i(x_t) = \theta \text{ and } i \in \mathbf{u} \\ f_i(x_t) & \text{otherwise,} \end{cases}$$

where $u_{i,t}$ is a meme coming in t-th clock to i-th channel of $^N WM$ from an external source, $\mathbf{u}$ is a set of input channels, and, assuming $P(event)$ as probability of *event*:

$$P(u_{i,t} = m) = \mu_{1,t}(m)\mu_{2,t}(m) / \sum_{m' \in M} \mu_{1,t}(m') \, \mu_{2,t}(m').$$

Several definitions of functions f and g has been investigated. In the computational example provided below the definitions described in **Appendix** were used.

4 Computational Example

Let us consider a subject that would like to have a date with somebody who is nice and rich. Once somebody proposes the subject of a date, however, the date proponent is neither a hundred per cent nice nor a hundred per cent rich. Let us assume that the subject judges the date proponent's nicety and richness at 75% and 25%, respectively and the judgment remain constant within the period of interest **T**. Assuming that the subject's mind works based on a function similar to F defined above, we can simulate the subject's feelings about the proposal.

Let **A** be the dynamic fuzzy set of persons with whom the subject could have a date. Let θ be the object of interest, i.e. the date proponent. Let **N** and **R** represent θ's 'nicety' and 'richness', respectively. Hence, the universe of discourse becomes

$$\mathbf{E} = \{\,\theta, \mathbf{N}, \neg\mathbf{N}, \mathbf{R}, \neg\mathbf{R}, \mathbf{A}, \neg\mathbf{A}\,\},$$

while $\mu_{1,t}(\langle\mathbf{N}|\theta\rangle)=.75$, $\mu_{1,t}(\langle\mathbf{R}|\theta\rangle)=.25$ for every $t \in \mathbf{T}$.

Let meme supply to the Working Memory be such that for every $t \in \mathbf{T}^*$:

$$\mu_{1,t}(\langle\mathbf{A}|\mathbf{N}\rangle)=\mu_{1,t}(\langle\mathbf{A}|\mathbf{R}\rangle) = 1.0, \; \mu_{2,t}(\langle\mathbf{N}|\theta\rangle) = \mu_{2,t}(\langle\mathbf{R}|\theta\rangle) = .01,$$

$$\mu_{2,t}(\langle\mathbf{A}|\mathbf{N}\rangle)=\mu_{2,t}(\langle\mathbf{A}|\mathbf{R}\rangle) = .075, \text{ and } \forall_{e \in \mathbf{E}, \; q \in 1..Q} \; \mu_{i,t}(\langle\neg e|\theta\rangle) = 1 - \mu_{q,t}(\langle e|\theta\rangle).$$

What is to be calculated is $\mu_{1,t}(\langle\mathbf{A}|\theta\rangle)$, i.e., the value of membership of the date proponent to the dynamic fuzzy set of acceptable candidates. When $\forall_{i \in 1..N} \; x_{0,t} = \theta$, and $\mathbf{u} = \{60, 61, 179, 180, 298, 299\}$, for f and g defined as in **Appendix**, function F returned $\mu_{1,t}(\langle\mathbf{A}|\theta\rangle)$, such as in Figure 2.

Similar results have been obtained for non-randomized meme supply to Working Memory [3]. Preliminary results of applying of DFC to simple pattern recognition have also been reported [4].

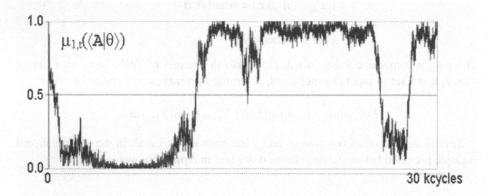

Fig. 2. Oscillating feelings of a simulated subject represented as a first-degree membership $\mu_{1,t}$ of an object of interest (θ) to a dynamic fuzzy set **A**. The plot seem to feet well to the Freudian statement that "..in a number of circumstances hate changes into love and love into hate".

5   Conclusions

Experimentally confirmed psychological evidence (about subjects' oscillations from highly positive feelings to highly negative ones and back even when the knowledge about an object of interest remains constant) provides justification for cognitive modeling based on Dynamic Fuzzy Sets (DFS) with membership values changing over time. Dynamic Fuzzy Calculus (DFC), based on meme interaction in Working Memory implemented as a discrete dynamic system, provides comparable oscillations that can be interpreted in terms of the memory states tending to a 2-state limit-cycle attractor. There is a good chance that the emerging Dynamic Fuzzy Set Theory, when more developed, will provide a computational tool facilitating investigations in psychodynamics, social cognition, memetics, and advanced robotics.

Acknowledgement. This research was conducted as a part of the *Research on Human Communication* supported by the Telecommunications Advancement Organization of Japan.

References

1.   Buller, A.: Fizzy-Fuzzy Inferencing, In: Furuhashi, T., Uchikawa, Y. (Eds.) Fuzzy Logic, Neural Networks, and Evolutionary Computation, Springer-Verlag, Berlin/Heidelberg/ New York... (1996) 172-187
2.   Buller, A.: Dynamic Fuzzy Sets for Cognitive Modeling. Proceedings of The Sixth International Symposium on Artificial Life and Robotics (AROB 6th '01), January 15-17 (2001), Tokyo, Japan, 150-151

3. Buller, A., Kaiser, L., Shimohara, K.: Para-evolutionary Paradigm of Reasoning, In: Baba,
    N., Jain, L.C., Howlett, R.J. (Eds.) Knowledge-Based Intelligent Information Engineering
    Systems & Allied Technologies (KES'2001). IOS Press, Amsterdam (2001) 127-131.
4. Buller, A., Kaiser, L., Shimohara, K.: MemeStorms: A Cellular Automaton for Pattern
    Recognition and Dynamic Fuzzy Calculus, The Seventh International Symposium on Arti-
    ficial Life and Robotics (AROB 7th '02), January 16-18 (2002), Beppu, Japan, 528-531.
5. Buller, A., Shimohara, K.: Decision Making as a Debate in the Society of Memes in Neu-
    ral Working Memory. The Journal of 3D Images, 13 (3) (1999) 77-82
6. Freud S.: The Ego and the Id. W.W.Norton, New York (1923/1990)
7. Harel, D., Kozen, D., Tiuryn J.: Dynamical Logic. MIT Press, Cambridge MA (2000)
8. Nowak, A., Vallacher R.A.: Dynamical Social Psychology. Guilford Press, New York
    (1998)
9. Rosh, E.: Principles of categorization. In: Rosch, E., Lloyd, B.B. (Eds.) Cognition and
    Categorization. Erlbaum, Hillsdale NJ (1978) 27-48
10. Zadeh, L.: Fuzzy Sets. Information and Control, 8 (1965)

Appendix: Functions Defining Working Memory

Primary interaction function α: $\mathbf{M}^2 \to \mathbf{M}$ works as shown in Table 1.

Secondary interaction function ψ: $\mathbf{M}^3 \to \mathbf{M}$ works as shown in Table 2.

Tertiary interaction function y : $\mathbf{M}^3 \to \mathbf{M}^3$ works such that

$$y_0(m_0, m_1, m_2) = \psi(m_1, m_2, m_0),$$
$$y_1(m_0, m_1, m_2) = \psi(m_0, m_1, m_2),$$
$$y_2(m_0, m_1, m_2) = \psi(m_2, m_0, m_1).$$

Interconnection function p: $0..N\text{-}1 \times 0..2 \to 0..N\text{-}1$ defines the Working Memory
channel network, i.e., $p(i,0)$, $p(i,1)$, and $p(i,2)$ to determine the channels that provide
the three memes that, interacting, produce a resulting meme to be put into channel i.
Let us take K, L $\in$ 1.. N such that K×L=N, K mod 2 = 0.
For $p(i,j) = 3(\varphi_{i,q} + K\lambda_i) - j + 2$, where

$$\varphi_{i,q} = (k_i + K + j - 1) \ mod \ K,$$

$$\lambda_i = \begin{cases} l_i & \text{iff } k_i \ mod \ 2 \neq 0 \text{ and } j \neq 1 \\ (l_i + 1) \ mod \ L & \text{otherwise,} \end{cases}$$

where $k_i = \lfloor i/3 \rfloor \ mod \ K$, $l_i = \lfloor \lfloor i/3 \rfloor / K \rfloor$ In such a case the channels of Working Memory form a regular grid of the size K×L with 3-input-3-output nodes. If the nodes take
the geometrical form of hexagonal tiles, the Working Memory will appear as a planar
surface inhabited by continuously migrating and interacting memes.

Main interaction functions f : $1..N \times \mathbf{M}^N \to \mathbf{M}$ and g : $1..K \times \mathbf{M} \times \mathbf{M}^N \to [0; 1]$ work
such that for any $X = \{x_0, x_1, ..., x_N\} \in \mathbf{M}^N$,

$$f_i(m_0, m_1, \ldots, m_{N-1}) = y_{i \bmod 3}(m_{p(i,0)}, m_{p(i,1)}, m_{p(i,2)}),$$

$$g_1(\langle e|\theta\rangle, X) = N_{\langle e|\theta\rangle}(X) / (N_{\langle e|\theta\rangle}(X) + N_{\langle -e|\theta\rangle}(X)),$$

where $N : \mathbf{M} \times \mathbf{M}^N \rightarrow \mathbf{Z}$ is a function that returns a number of copies of a given h $\in \mathbf{M}$ in $X = (x_1, x_2, \ldots, x_N) \in \mathbf{M}^N$; formally, $N_h(X) = C_N$, $C_0 = 0$, $C_{i+1} = C_i + \beta(x_i = h)$, where $\mathbf{Z}$ is the space of integers, while β is a one-argument function that for a given statement returns 1 when the statement is true, while otherwise it returns 0, e.g. $\beta(1=2) = 0$; $\beta(\neg s \vee s) = 1$ for any s.

A sensible plot of $g_1(m, X)$ for m other than $\langle e|\theta\rangle$, as well as of g_q for $q>1$, is subject to further investigation.

Table 1. Primary interaction function. It is assumed that: $e \neq \theta$, $e' \neq \theta$, $e \neq e'$, $\varepsilon \neq \theta$, and $e \neq -e'$.

m_0	m_1	$\alpha(m_0, m_1)$
$\langle e|e'\rangle$	$\langle e|\theta\rangle$	$\langle e|\theta\rangle$
$\langle e|\theta\rangle$	$\langle e|e'\rangle$	θ
$\langle e|e'\rangle$	$\langle -e|\theta\rangle$	$\langle -e|\theta\rangle$
$\langle -e|\theta\rangle$	$\langle e|e'\rangle$	θ
$\langle e|\theta\rangle$	$\langle -e|\theta\rangle$	θ
$\langle e|e''\rangle$	$\langle \varepsilon|\varepsilon''\rangle$	$\langle e|e''\rangle$
$\langle \varepsilon|\varepsilon''\rangle$	$\langle e|e''\rangle$	$\langle \varepsilon|\varepsilon''\rangle$
$\langle e|e''\rangle$	θ	$\langle e|e''\rangle$
θ	$\langle e|e''\rangle$	θ

Table 2. Secondary interaction function (β– a one-argument function that for a given statement returns 1 when the statement is true, while otherwise it returns 0.

$\beta(m_0 \neq \theta)$	$\beta(m_1 \neq \theta)$	$\beta(m_2 \neq \theta)$	$\psi(m_0, m_1, m_2)$
1	1	1	m_1
1	1	0	$\alpha(m_0, m_1)$
1	0	1	θ
0	1	1	$\alpha(m_2, m_1)$
1	0	0	θ
0	1	0	m_1
0	0	1	θ
0	0	0	θ

Distributed Reinforcement of Arc-Consistency

Ahlem Ben Hassine and Khaled Ghédira

Laboratoire URIASIS, Institut Supérieur de Gestion de Tunis-Tunisie
{Ahlem.BenHassine, Khaled.Ghedira}@isg.rnu.tn

Abstract. Arc-consistency caught many researchs' attention, involving the discovery of a large number of algorithms in the Constraint Satisfaction Problems (CSP) literature. These algorithms can be applied within or before the search of solutions, in order to eliminate inconsistencies and consequently to prune the search space. In this paper, we adopt a distributed approach due to the omnipresence of naturally distributed CSP real applications. So, a new distributed arc-consistency approach is proposed, discussed and illustrated through an example. Correctness, termination properties, complexity computing as well as experimental results are also given.

Keywords: Constraint Satisfaction Problems (CSP), Multi-Agent System, Arc-Consistency.

1. Introduction

Arc consistency techniques have shown a great interest in CSPs which are known to be NP-Complete. They reduce the complexity by eliminating domain inconsistencies and consequently pruning the search space. Informally, a binary CSP [9] is composed of a finite set of n variables $X=\{X_1, ..., X_n\}$, each of which is taking values in an associated finite domain $D=\{D_1, ..., D_n\}$ and a set of e constraints between these variables $C=\{C_{ij}, ...\}$, C_{ij} being a binary constraint between X_i and X_j. The constraints restrict the values the variable can simultaneously take. $R=\{R_{ij}, ...\}$ is the set of e relations, where R_{ij} is the set of allowed pairs of values for the corresponding C_{ij}. Solving a CSP consists in finding one or all-complete assignments of values to variables satisfying all the constraints. A value a, from D_i, is supported by a value b, from D_j, along C_{ij} *iff* (a, b) satisfies C_{ij} (i.e. (a, b) belongs to the relation R_{ij} associated to C_{ij}), b is called a *support* for a along C_{ij}, we note that $S_{ij}(a, b)$. A value a from D_i is *viable iff* $\forall X_k$ such that $\exists C_{ik} \in C$, $k = 1 ...n$, there exist a support b for a in D_k. A CSP is arc-consistent or 2-consistent if and only if for each variable $X_i \in X$ ($i = 1..n$), and for each value $a \in D_i$, a is viable. So arc-consistency achievement consists in transforming a CSP P (X, D, C, R) into another equivalent and more simple CSP P' (X, D', C, R), where $D'_i \subseteq D_i \in D$. This is obtained by removing all and only arc inconsistent values in order not to affect the set of satisfiable assignments of the CSP. A CSP is consistent if it has at least one solution, otherwise, it is inconsistent. There are two approaches to achieve arc-consistency: the centralized and distributed ones. Among the former, we quote arc-consistency applied to vision problems [12], AC-1, AC-2 and AC-3 algorithms[8], AC-4[10], AC-5[4], AC-6[1], AC-Inference and AC-7[2], and AC2000 and AC2001[3].

M. Ishizuka and A. Sattar (Eds.): PRICAI 2002, LNAI 2417, pp. 97-107, 2002.
© Springer-Verlag Berlin Heidelberg 2002

In this paper, we are interested in the distributed approaches due to the natural distribution of many real CSP applications, and the advents of both distributed computing and networking technologies. The most recent research proceeds by adapting classical arc-consistency techniques to the distributed framework: DisAC4[11], DisAC6 and DisAC9 [6]. DisAC4 is a coarse-grained parallel algorithm designed on the basis of AC-4 and the DisCSP formalism [13], which defines an agent as responsible of a subset of variables. DisAC4 is used for a distributed memory computer using asynchronous message passing communication. Unfortunately, it has been restricted to diffusion Networks (*Ethernet*), which leads to an underlying synchronism between processes. The theoretical complexity is $O(\frac{n^2 d^2}{k})$, where n is the number of variables, d is the size of the largest domain and k is the number of the processors. With regards to DisAC6, it is based on AC-6 and DisCSP. The basic idea of this algorithm is to scatter the problem among autonomous processes and make them asynchronously interact by point-to-point messages containing useful information (in order to perform the global arc-consistency). The worst time complexity is $O(n^2 d^3)$ and the space complexity is $O(n^2 d)$ with $O(nd)$ the amount of message operations. DisAC9 is an improvement of DisAC6. It is an optimal algorithm in the number of message passing operations. It exploits the bidirectionality property of constraint relations, which allows agents to induce acquaintances relations. The worst time complexity of this algorithm is $O(n^2 d^3)$ with nd messages and with a total amount of space in $O(n^2 d)$.

In a different way:
- Our approach (that we call DRAC for *Distributed Reinforcement of Arc Consistency*) does not rely on any existing centralized algorithm.
- It is based on a Multi-Agent system associating an agent per constraint.
- It uses dual constraint-graphs to represent CSPs. A binary CSP can be associated to a constraint-graph the nodes of which (respectively arcs) represent variables (respectively constraints). As for high-order constraints, they can be represented according to primal constraint-graph or dual constraint-graph [5]. The primal constraint-graph represents variables by nodes and associates an arc with any two nodes residing in the same constraint. A dual constraint-graph represents each constraint by a node and associates a labeled arc with any two nodes that share at least a variable. The arcs are labeled with the shared variables.
- It directly addresses generalized CSPs without transforming the initial problem into a binary one. It is known that the transformation procedures increase both the temporal and spatial complexity. So, we expect that the use of the dual graph associated to both the "agent ⟺ constraint" assignment and the point-to-point asynchronous message passing protocol, would be very appropriate in order to directly achieve arc-consistency for generalized CSPs.

Note that the goal of DisAC9 is essentially to reduce the total amount of messages by doing more local computations, because of the high cost of messages passing in a distributed multiprocessor architecture. As we intend to use a mono-processor machine, we ignore the cost of messages passing, and rather focus on reducing the local agent computation. So, our objective is different: the full global arc-consistency is obtained as a result of the interactions between the Constraint Agents by exchanging inconsistent values. In other words, the full global arc-consistency is obtained as a side effect of the agent interactions between reactive agents; each having a local goal. As a starting point of our whole research, we focus on binary CSPs.

This paper is organized as follows. First we present the Multi-Agent architecture and its global dynamic. Second we discuss and illustrate the proposed approach through an example. Then, we prove the correctness, the termination properties and the complexity computing. Finally, we exhibit the experimental results.

2. DRAC Architecture

This approach involves two kinds of agents (Constraint agents and Interface agent) communicating by asynchronous point-to-point messages. The last agent has been added in order to detect whether the full global arc-consistency has been achieved and, especially, to inform the user of the result. Each agent has a simple structure: acquaintances (the agents that it knows), a local memory composed of its static and dynamic knowledge, a *mailBox* where it stores the received messages and a behavior. In the proposed model, agents communicate by sending messages. An agent can send a message to another one only if it knows it (it belongs to its acquaintances). For the transmission between agents, we assume that messages are received in the order they are sent. The delay in delivering messages is finite.

- **Constraint Agents :** Each agent has its own* variables, its acquaintances consist of both all the agents with which it shares a variable (denoted by Γ_s), and the Interface agent. Its acquaintances and its associated relation define its static knowledge, while its dynamic knowledge concerns its internal state, the domains of its own variables and a parameter called *EndBehavior* which specifies whether its behavior is completed or not.

- **Interface Agent :** The Interface agent has as acquaintances all the Constraint agents of the system, denoted by Γ, which represent its static knowledge. Its dynamic knowledge consists of the internal state of all its constraints.

3. DRAC Dynamic

The objective of this paper is to transform a CSP P (X, D, C, R) into another equivalent CSP P'(X, D', C, R) via the interactions between the Constraint agents, which are trying to reduce their domains. Before detailing these interactions and the underlying global dynamic, we present the communication protocol, the data structures and the basic primitives relative to an agent C_{ij}.

3.1 Communication Protocol

The communication protocol is based on the two following message passing primitives.

- *SendMsg(Sender, Receiver, " Message")* where *Receiver* can be more than one.
- *GetMsg()* extracts the first message from the *mailBox0*.

---

* The variables implied in this constraint.

As far as the exchanged messages are concerned, the Multi-Agent dynamic involves three types (without considering the messages relative to the detection of the equilibrium state) namely:

- *"Start"* message, sent by the interface to all the agents in order to activate them,
- *"ReduceDomains"* message, sent by a Constraint agent to its acquaintances in order to propagate its deleted values.
- *"StopBehavior"* message sent by a Constraint agent, which has a domain wipe-out, to the interface.
- *"StopLocalBehavior"* message sent by the interface to all the agents of the system to make them stop their local behavior.

3.2 Data Structures

- *Acquaintances*$_{Xi}$ (resp. *Acquaintances*$_{Xj}$) = the set of Constraint agents sharing the variable X_i (resp. X_j) with C_{ij}.
- $D_i^{c_{ij}}$ and $D_j^{c_{ij}}$ represent the local view of respectively D_i and D_j. Both are supposed to be totally ordered. $D_i^{c_{ij}}$ (resp. $D_j^{c_{ij}}$) is called the occurrence of D_i (resp. D_j).

Note that some occurrences of a given D_i may be different, but all occurrences of D_i $\forall i \in \{1..n\}$ must be identical when the full global arc-consistency is reached (this property is proven in the subsection 5.1). At this stage, let us refer to the final obtained domain $D_i^{c_{ij}}$ (resp. $D_j^{c_{ij}}$) by $f\ D_i^{c_{ij}}$ (resp. $f\ D_j^{c_{ij}}$).

- $SPx_ix_j = \{(a\ b\ y)$ such that $a \in D_i^{c_{ij}}$, $b \in D_j^{c_{ij}}$ and $y \in \{0, 1\}$ | if $y = 0$, b is the first support of a. Otherwise b is one support of $a\}$.
- *TestedVal*$_{X_i}$ (resp. *TestedVal*$_{X_j}$): the set of the current viable values of X_i (resp. X_j).
- *InconsistentValue*$_{X_i}$ (resp. *InconsistentValue*$_{X_j}$) the set of the current non-viable values of X_i (resp. X_j)..
- *EndBehavior* : a Boolean parameter that indicates whether the agent behavior is finished or not.

3.3 Basic Primitives

- *addTo*(SPx_ix_j, $(a\ b\ y)$) : insert $(a\ b\ y)$ in the set SPx_ix_j,
- *First*($D_i^{c_{ij}}$) : returns the first value in $D_i^{c_{ij}}$ if $D_i^{c_{ij}} \neq \varnothing$, else returns *nil*,
- *Last*($D_i^{c_{ij}}$) : returns the greatest value in $D_i^{c_{ij}}$ if $D_i^{c_{ij}} \neq \varnothing$, else returns *nil*,
- *Next*(a, $D_i^{c_{ij}}$) : returns the first viable value occurring after a in $D_i^{c_{ij}}$ if $a \neq$ *Last*($D_i^{c_{ij}}$), else returns *nil*,
- *FirstSupport*(a, $D_j^{c_{ij}}$, h) : returns the first support of a value a in $D_j^{c_{ij}}$ greater or equal to h accordingly to C_{ij}, if it exists, else returns *nil*.

3.4 Global Dynamic

At the initial state, the Interface agent creates all the Constraint agents and activates them (Fig 1.). Each agent C_{ij} reduces the domains ($D_i^{c_{ij}}$ and $D_j^{c_{ij}}$) of its own variables X_i and X_j, by computing local viable values (see §1). To achieve this, C_{ij} looks for one support (the first one) for each value of its variables. When the first support $b \in D_j^{c_{ij}}$

of a value $a \in D_i^{C_{ij}}$ relatively to C_{ij} is found, then $(a\ b\ 0)$ is added to the list of supports $SPx_i x_j$ (Fig1.line6.) and respectively when the first support $c \in D_i^{C_{ij}}$ of a value $b \in D_j^{C_{ij}}$ is found then $(c\ b\ 1)$ is added to the list of supports $SPx_j x_i$ (Fig2.line15.), i.e. b could not be the first support of c. A value a is deleted from $D_i^{C_{ij}}$ if and only if a has no support in $D_j^{C_{ij}}$. Each agent uses the bidirectionality property of constraints relations: $a \in D_i^{C_{ij}}$ supports $b \in D_j^{C_{ij}}$ ($S_{ij}(b, a)$) if and only if $b \in D_j^{C_{ij}}$ supports $a \in D_i^{C_{ij}}$ ($S_{ij}(a, b)$). This property, already used by AC-7, allows us to avoid checking for $S_{ji}(b, a)$ if $S_{ij}(a, b)$ has already been successfully checked, i.e. a is also a support for b. At the end of this computation, deleted values are announced to related acquaintances (Fig1.line 18. and 20.). Each agent that has received this message starts processing it. It first updates the domains of its variables by deleting non viable received values (Fig2.line3.). Afterwards, it updates computed support information (Fig2. line5.). In the case where b is a non-viable value, and if the value of y is 0, the agent looks for another support for a in $D_i^{C_{ij}}$ greater than b (as AC-6). Otherwise it looks for a support from scratch i.e. the first value in $D_i^{C_{ij}}$. This can lead to a new deletion of values (Fig2. line13.) and by consequence to new outgoing messages.

```
0Begin

1.SPx_ix_j← ∅; EndBehavior ← False; InconsistentValue_Xi ← D_i^{Cij};

2. InconsistentValue_Xj ← D_j^{Cij}; TestedVal_Xi ← ∅; TestedVal_Xj ← ∅;

3.For each (a, b)∈ R_ij do
4.   If ((a ∈ D_i^{Cij}) AND (b ∈ D_j^{Cij}))

5.   Then If (a ∉ TestedVal_Xi)

6.        Then addTo (SPx_ix_j, (a  b  0)); TestedVal_Xi ← TestedVal_Xi ∪ {a};

7.             InconsistentValue_Xi ← InconsistentValue_Xi /{a};

8.             If (b ∉ TestedVal_Xj)

9.             Then InconsistentValue_Xj ← InconsistentValue_Xj /{b};

10.                 TestedVal_Xj ← TestedVal_Xj ∪ {b};

11.        Else If (b ∉ TestedVal_Xj)

12.             Then addTo(SPx_ix_j,(a b 1)); TestedVal_Xj ← TestedVal_Xj ∪ {b};

13.                  InconsistentValue_Xj ← InconsistentValue_Xj /{b};

14. D_i^{Cij} ← TestedVal_Xi ; D_j^{Cij} ← TestedVal_Xj ;

15. If D_i^{Cij} = ∅ OR D_j^{Cij} = ∅

16. Then SendMsg(C_ij,Interface,"StopBehavior"); EndBehavior ← True;

17. Else For each C_ik ∈ Acquaintances_Xi do
18.      SendMsg(C_ij,C_ik,"ReduceDomains:InconsistentValue_Xi of:X_i");

19.      For each C_jk ∈ Acquaintances_Xj do
20.      SendMsg(C_ij,C_jk,"ReduceDomains:InconsistentValue_Xj of:X_j");

End
```

Fig. 1. *"Start"* message (Executed by each Constraint agent (C_{ij}))

An agent is satisfied when it has no more reduction to do on its variable domains or when one of its reduced domain wipe-out (Fig1. line15. and Fig2. line16.). But it is clear that this satisfaction state is not definitive. Indeed, if there exists at least one unsatisfied Agent, it may cause the unsatisfaction of other Constraint agents and this is due to the propagation of constraints. So, interactions and especially reductions must carry on. So reducing domains on an agent may, consequently, cause an eventual domain reductions on another agent. Therefore, these interactions must carry on until the stable equilibrium state, where all the agents are definitely satisfied and consequently no more reduction is possible. Note that this dynamic allows a premature detection of failure: absence of solutions. Thus, in the case of failure, the "*StopBehavior*" message is sent by the constraint (which has detected this failure) to the interface in order to stop the whole process. In this case, the Interface agent in turn sends a "*StopLocalBehavior*" message to each constraint to make them stop their local activity (their attribute *EndBehavior* is set to *true*) and informs the user of the absence of solutions. The maximal reinforcement of global arc-consistency is obtained as a side effect from the interactions described above.

2ReduceDomains: **DelVal** *of:X_i*

3Begin

1. *InconsistentValue$_{xi}$* ← ∅;

2.**For each** $(a \in DelVal)$ **AND** $(a \in D_i^{Cij})$ **do**

3. $D_i^{Cij} ← D_i^{Cij} / \{a\}$;

4. $S →$ the set of all values b in $SP_{x_ix_j}$ having a as a support;

5. Delete from $SP_{x_ix_j}$ all tuples $(a \ b \ y)$;

6. **For each** $b \in S$ **do**

7.   **If** b has not another support in $SP_{x_ix_j}$

8.   **Then If** a is the first support of b $(y = 0)$

9.   **Then** $h ← Next(a, D_i^{Cij})$;

10.   **Else** $h ← First (D_i^{Cij})$;

11. $c ← FirstSupport (b, D_i^{Cij}, h)$;

12.   **If** $c = $ nil

13.   **Then** *InconsistentValue$_{x_j}$* ← *InconsistentValue$_{x_j}$* ∪ $\{b\}$;

14. $D_j^{Cij} ← D_j^{Cij} / \{b\}$;

15.   **Else** $addTo (SP_{x_jx_i},(c \ b \ 1))$;

16. **If** $D_i^{Cij} = ∅$ **OR** $D_j^{Cij} = ∅$

17. **Then** $SendMsg(C_{ij},$Interface,"*StopBehavior*"); *EndBehavior* ←True;

18. **Else For each** $C_{jk} \in$ Acquaintances $_{x_j}$ **do**

19. $SendMsg(C_{ij},C_{jk},$"*ReduceDomains:InconsistentValue$_{x_j}$ of:X_j*");

End

Fig. 2. "*ReduceDomains*"message (Executed by each Constraint agent (C_{ij}))

3.5 Agent Behaviors

Constraint Agent Behavior. A Constraint agent is satisfied:
- When one of its domains is empty. In this case it asks the interface to stop the whole process and to communicate the failure result to the user.
- When all possible local reductions are done to take into account the just received messages containing the values deleted by the other Constraint acquaintances. In this case, it updates its internal state.

Otherwise, i.e. in the case of unsatisfaction behavior, it sends a message containing inconsistent values to the concerned acquaintances: $SendMsg$(self, Γ_s, "$ReduceDomains\ of$").

Interface Agent Behavior. When all the agents are satisfied or when it has received a failure message, the Interface agent is satisfied and in this case it makes all the agents, stop their local behavior: $SendMsg$(self, Γ, "$StopLocalBehavior$"), and communicates the obtained result to the user. Otherwise, in the case of unsatisfaction behavior, it checks the system state, using the algorithm described in [7].

4 Example

Let us consider the binary CSP P (X, D, C, R) : X = $\{X_1, X_2, X_3, X_4, X_5\}$, D = $\{D_1, D_2, D_3, D_4, D_5\}$ with $D_1 = D_2 = D_3 = D_4 = D_5 = \{1\ 2\ 3\ 4\ 5\}$; C=$\{C_{15}, C_{34}, C_{35}, C_{45}\}$; R=$\{R_{15}, R_{34}, R_{35}, R_{45}\}$ with R_{15} =$\{(1\ 3)\ (2\ 2)\ (2\ 4)\ (2\ 5)\ (3\ 4)\ (5\ 3)\}$, R_{34} =$\{(1\ 1)\ (1\ 2)\ (2\ 1)\ (2\ 4)\ (3\ 3)\ (4\ 4)\}$, R_{35} =$\{(1\ 1)\ (2\ 1)\ (2\ 4)\ (3\ 5)\ (5\ 1)\}$, R_{45} =$\{(1\ 2)\ (1\ 3)\ (2\ 3)\ (2\ 5)\ (3\ 3)\ (3\ 5)\ (4\ 1)\ (4\ 5)\}$.

The associated Multi-Agent system involves the Constraint agents C_{15}, C_{34}, C_{35} and C_{45}, and the Interface agent. As mentioned before, the Interface agent activates the Constraint ones. Each one performs, first, all the necessary reductions on its variable domains by computing the first viable support for each value of its variables, and then generates the sets of inconsistent values ($InconsistentValue_{x_i}$) (Fig3.) and transmits them to its concerned acquaintances.

Agents	Dynamic Knowledge
C_{15}	$SP_{X_1X_5}$= $\{(1\ 3\ 0)\ (2\ 2\ 0)\ (2\ 4\ 1)\ (2\ 5\ 1)\ (3\ 4\ 0)\ (5\ 3\ 0)\}$ $D^{C_{15}}_{1}$ =$\{1\ 2\ 3\ 5\}$; $InconsistentValue_x$ = $\{4\}$; $D^{C_{15}}_{5}$ =$\{2\ 3\ 4\ 5\}$; $InconsistentValue_x$ = $\{1\}$
C_{34}	$SP_{X_3X_4}$= $\{(1\ 1\ 0)\ (1\ 2\ 1)\ (2\ 1\ 0)\ (2\ 4\ 1)\ (3\ 3\ 0)\ (4\ 4\ 0)\}$ $D^{C_{34}}_{3}$ = $\{1\ 2\ 3\ 4\}$; $InconsistentValue_x$ = $\{5\}$; $D^{C_{34}}_{4}$ = $\{1\ 2\ 3\ 4\}$; $InconsistentValue_x$ = $\{5\}$
C_{35}	$SP_{X_3X_5}$= $\{(1\ 1\ 0)\ (2\ 1\ 0)\ (2\ 4\ 1)\ (3\ 5\ 0)\ (5\ 1\ 0)\}$ $D^{C_{35}}_{3}$ = $\{1\ 2\ 3\ 5\}$; $InconsistentValue_x$ = $\{4\}$; $D^{C_{35}}_{5}$ = $\{1\ 4\ 5\}$; $InconsistentVal_{uxx}$ = $\{2\ 3\}$
C_{45}	$SP_{X_4X_5}$= $\{(1\ 2\ 0)\ (1\ 3\ 1)\ (2\ 3\ 0)\ (2\ 5\ 1)\ (3\ 3\ 0)\ (4\ 1\ 0)\}$ $D^{C_{45}}_{4}$ = $\{1\ 2\ 3\ 4\}$; $InconsistentVauel_x$ = $\{5\}$; $D^{C_{45}}_{5}$ = $\{1\ 2\ 3\ 5\}$; $InconsistentValue_x$ = $\{4\}$

Fig. 3.

After receiving this message, each agent performs all the necessary reductions on its variable domains. To illustrate this, let us consider the agent C_{35}, which receives three messages from its acquaintances ($InconsistentValue_{X3}$ = {5}, $InconsistentValue_{X5}$ = {1}, $InconsistentValue_{X5}$ = {4}). First, it updates its variables domains ($D_3^{C_{35}}$ = {1 2 3} and $D_5^{C_{35}}$={5}) and its support sets (SPx_5x_5= {(3 5 0)}) and then it looks for another support in $D_5^{C_{35}}$ for X_3={1, 2}. But these values have not a viable support, so they must be deleted from the domain of X_3 and this deletion must be propagated to the concerned acquaintances. The same dynamic resumes as before until all the agents are satisfied. The final obtained problem P (X, fD, C, R) is then globally arc-consistent with: fD_1 = {2}, fD_2= {1 2 3 4 5}, fD_3 = {3}, fD_4 = { 3 }, fD_5= {5}.

5 Discussions

The objective of this sub-section is to show that our approach leads to the full global arc-consistency. For this, we have to prove the following assertions :

- $\forall i \in \{1..n\}, \forall j \neq k, fD_i^{C_{ij}} = fD_i^{C_{ik}}$.
- $\forall i \in \{1..n\}, \forall C_{ij} \in C, \forall val \in fD_{C_{ij}}^{C_{ij}}$ (resp. $fD_j^{C_{ij}}$); val is viable.
- $\forall i \in \{1..n\}, \forall C_{ij} \in C, \forall val \in D_i$ (resp. D_j), if val is viable then $val \in fD_i^{C_{ij}}$ (resp. $val \in fD_j^{C_{ij}}$).

In fact, the first assertion concerns the process of deleted values propagation. Since $C_{ik} \in Acquaintances_{Xi}$ of C_{ij} (and conversely) and since all the messages are received in a finite period of time and in the same order in which they are sent, C_{ij} (resp. C_{ik}) has to be informed by each deleted value[2]. Then the equality between $fD_i^{C_{ij}}$ and $fD_i^{C_{ik}}$ is guaranteed.

The second assertion concerns the correctness of the *ReduceDomains* procedure. Each time the deletion of a value (from $D_j^{C_{ij}}$) leads to a non-viable value in the domain of a variable X_i. The agent C_{ij} send a message to all the concerned acquaintances C_{ik} in order to update their X_i domain. So, all the non-viable values are deleted from the domain of all the agents.

For the third assertion, there are two cases where a value a is deleted from the domain of a variable X_i, the first is that the agent C_{ij} has detected that a has no support in $D_j^{C_{ij}}$ according to R_{ij}. Therefore a is a non-viable value and must be discarded. The second case is when the agent C_{ij} has received a message to update the domain of X_i by deleting the value a. Thus this value has been detected as non-viable by the agent which sends the message. Consequently, only non-viable value will be deleted.

With regards to termination, the dynamic of DRAC approach stops when the system reaches its stable equilibrium state. At this state, all the agents are satisfied. An agent is satisfied when it has no more reductions to do on its variable domains or when one of its related new reduced domains is wipe-out. The detection of the stable equilibrium state is achieved by using the well known algorithm of [7], a state where all agents are waiting for a message and there is no message in the transmission channels. If all the agent of the system are in the state of waiting, and there exists only one

---

[2] Let us recall that the deleted values must be immediately transmitted to the concerned acquaintances.

agent C_{ij} which has deleted one value a from the domain of one of its variables (X_i or X_j). We assume that this agent shared this altered variable with another agent C_{ik}. The latter must be informed of the loss of the value a in order to propagate the constraints. Hence, there is a message in transit for it, which invalidates our transmission hypothesis.

As far as complexity is concerned, let us consider a CSP P having n for the total number of variables, d for the size of the variable domains and e for the total number of constraints. The number of Agents is e. If we consider a fully connected constraint network, we will have $e-1$ acquaintances for each Constraint agent. Each agent C_{ij} maintains a list SPx_ix_j of supports, with the size of $2d-1$ in the worst case. Since there are e agents, the total amount of space is $(2d-1)e$ (for a fully connected graph e will be set to $n(n-1)/2$, in the worst case). So the space needed is $(n(n-1)/2)*(2d-1) \approx O(n^2d)$. This space is the same as that of AC-7.

The worst case in the execution time of a distributed algorithm occurs when it proceeds with a sequential behavior. For our model, this occurs when only one value is deleted at a time. This leads to nd successive deletions. Our approach is composed of two steps; the first one is the initializing step, where each agent performs d^2 operations to generate the support sets. For each deleted value, the agent will perform $O(d^2)$ operations to search another support for this value. So, each agent performs $O(d^2)$ operations. Thus the total time complexity of DRAC (with e agents and nd successive deletions), in the worst case, is $O(end^3)$. This complexity is equal to that of DisAC-9 down to the number of variables.

6 Experimentation

The implementation was developed with Actalk, an object based on concurrent programming language with Smalltalk-80 environment. In this language framework, an agent is implemented as an actor having the Smalltalk object structure enriched by an ability to send/receive messages to/from its acquaintances, buffering the received messages in its own mailbox. The DRAC efficiency is assessed through a comparison with AC-7 [2] (Table1.) on the basis of randomly generated samples which belong to the transition phase, which consists of both arc-consistent problems and arc inconsistent problems. Each sample is designed on the base of the following parameters: $n=20$, $d=10$, $<p/q>$ where p (resp. q) represents the density (resp. the tightness). The table 1. shows that AC-7 performs more constraint checks than DRAC, especially for the problems where arc-consistency establishing often succeed (for example $<0,4/0,4>$ and $<0,9/0,5>$). Despite the use of the bidirectionality by both AC-7 and DRAC, DRAC requires less constraint checks than AC-7. This advantage is due to the fact that the main operation of AC-7 consists in seeking a support, for each value. Thus, a constraint check is needed for each value except for the case where the bidirectionality property can be applied, whilst the DRAC init step (Fig1.) consists in exploring the relation of each constraint only once in order to generate the SPx_ix_j sets. Note that this advantage is due to the fact that the relations are expressed in extension, i.e. by authorized couples of values, which can be examined without any additional computations. Therefore, DRAC is more appropriate than AC-7 in this case of relations. Otherwise, the experimental results would be expected to be similar.

Table1. DRAC vs. AC-7 Results in mean number of Constraint Checks on a Pentium III, 800Mhz (10 instances are generated for each set of <p/q> parameters)

	<0,2/0,3>	<0,3/0,3>	<0,4/0,4>	<0,5/0,4>	<0,6/0,4>	<0,7/0,4>	<0,8/0,4>	<0,9/0,5>
AC7	1981,1	2107,9	2937,5	3879,4	4909,1	5416,3	5797,6	5626,2
DRAC	461,5	1343,2	287,7	661,4	2006,6	2991,4	3579,9	321,8

7 Conclusion

The objective of this paper is to present a new model able to achieve full global arc-consistency in a totally distributed way without any help from centralized algorithms. A Multi-Agent approach, that we have called DRAC, has been proposed. Its correctness and termination have been proved. The spatial complexity is similar to AC7's and the temporal complexity is equal to DisAC-9's, down to the number of variables. Our approach consists of Constraint agents, which exchange their local inconsistent values in order to help themselves reduce the domains of the variables that they involve. This process is performed until an equilibrium state is reached, and corresponds to a failure relative to an absence of solutions or to a full global arc-consistency. Thus, this state is obtained as a side effect of the interactions between the Constraint agents whose behaviors are simple and reactive. As we associate an agent per Constraint, the dual constraint-graph is proved to be well appropriate to represent the agent network. Consequently, any generalized CSP can be naturally and directly (without any non-binary ⇒ binary transformation) handled by DRAC. This will be the main object of our perspectives.

References

1. Bessière, C. *Arc consistency and arc consistency again.* Artificial Intelligence 65, 1994.
2. Bessière, C.; Freuder, E. and Régin, J-C. *Using constraint Metaknowledge to Reduce Arc Consistency Computation.* Artificial Intelligence, Vol. 107, 1999, p125-148.
3. Bessière, C.; Régin, J-C. *Refining the Basic Constraint Propagation Algorithm.* In Proceedings   IJCAI-01.
4. Deville, Y. and Hentenryck, P. V. *En efficient arc consistency algorithm for a class of CSP problems.* In Proceedings of IJCAI'91, Australia.
5. Dechter, R. and Pearl, J. *Tree-Clustering Schemes for Constraint-Processing.* In AAAI-88.
6. Hamadi, Y. *Optimal Distributed Arc-Consistency.* CP'99, p. 219-233.
7. Lamport, L. and Chandy, K. M. *Distributed snapshots: Determining global states of distributed systems.* TOCS, 3(1) : 63-75, Feb 85.
8. Mackworth, A. K. *Consistency in networks of relations.* Artificial Intelligence, 8, 1977.
9. Montanari, U. *NetWorks of Constraints: Fundamental properties and applications to picture processing.* Information Sciences, 7, 1974. P.95-132.

10. Mohr, R. and Henderson, T. C. *Arc and path consistency revisited*. Artificial Intelligence, 28, 1986 p225-233.
11. Nguyen, T. and Deville, Y. *A Distributed Arc-Consistency Algorithm*. In : First Int. Workshop on Concurrent Constraint Satisfaction, 1995.
12. Waltz, D. L. *Understanding Line Drawings of Scenes with Shadows*. in: the Psychology of Computer Vision, McGraw Hill, 1975 (first published in:Tech.Rep. AI271, MIT MA, 1972).
13. Yokoo, M.; Ishida, T. and Kuwabara, K. *Distributed Constraint Satisfaction for DAI Problems*. In the 10th International Workshop on Distributed Artificial Intelligence, 1990.

Parallel Execution of Stochastic Search Procedures on Reduced SAT Instances*

Wenhui Zhang, Zhuo Huang, and Jian Zhang

Key Laboratory of Computer Science
Institute of Software, Chinese Academy of Sciences
P.O.Box 8718, Beijing, China
{zwh,hz,zj}@ios.ac.cn

Abstract. We present a technique for checking instances of the satisfiability (SAT) problem based on a combination of the Davis-Putnam (DP) procedure and stochastic methods. We first use the DP procedure to some extent, so as to partition and reduce the search space. If the reduction does not lead to an answer, a stochastic algorithm is then used to search each subspace. This approach is proven to be efficient for several types of SAT instances. A parallel implementation of the method is described and some experimental results are reported.

1 Introduction

The Satisfiability (SAT) problem in the propositional logic is very well known. It is a key problem in computer science. It also plays an important role in real world applications such as planning, hardware verification and testing.

Since SAT is an NP-complete problem, we do not expect that there is an efficient algorithm which can determine the satisfiability of every instance of the problem. But it is still worthwhile to do research on practical techniques which can solve many SAT instances efficiently.

We may distinguish between two types of SAT algorithms: complete search and incomplete search. A complete search algorithm gives an answer to a SAT instance no matter it is satisfiable or not. An incomplete search algorithm may give an answer only when the SAT instance is satisfiable.

One of the most efficient complete search algorithm for SAT is the Davis-Putnam (DP) procedure. Many systems based on this procedure have been implemented (such as [6,9]) and many interesting problems have been solved by these tools. A major problem with DP is that it may have to go through a very large search space.

A typical incomplete search algorithm for SAT combines local search and random walks [5,2]. The WSAT tool [7] is based on such a method, and is claimed to be more efficient than DP-based tools on some SAT instances.

* This work was supported by the National Science Fund for Distinguished Young Scholars (No. 60125207) and the "973" project (No. G1998030600).

M. Ishizuka and A. Sattar (Eds.): PRICAI 2002, LNAI 2417, pp. 108–117, 2002.

However, WSAT may come into difficulties on big SAT instances with many variables. The main purpose of our work is to improve the efficiency by combining the DP procedure and incomplete SAT algorithms. In order to utilize computational resources distributed in networked workstations, we have also implemented our approach as a distributed system.

2   The Basic Approach

We first briefly describe the DP procedure. Let S be a set of clauses and a be a literal occurring in S. Let $S|a$ be the result of removing clauses containing a and removing $\neg a$ from the rest of the clauses. The principle of the DP-procedure is as follows.

- S is satisfiable if S is empty.
- $S \cup \{a\}$ is unsatisfiable if $\neg a \in S$ is a unit clause.
- if $S = S' \cup \{a\}$, checking the satisfiability of S is reduced to checking the satisfiability of $S'|a$.
- if none of the above rule is applicable, select a literal a, check the satisfiability of $S|a$ and the satisfiability of $S|\neg a$. If either of them is satisfiable, S is satisfiable.

The last rule is called the branching rule and the strategy for selecting a literal is referred to as the branching strategy. We adopt the following strategy in our implementation of DP. To select a literal for branching, we use the look ahead strategy on the 5 best and the 5 worst propositional variables based on the weight of variables appearing in shortest clauses. (The definition of weights is omitted due to the limited space of this paper.) In addition, we require that both of the positive and negative literals must appear in the clauses, in order for a variable to be selected.

In the hybrid approach, we first use the DP procedure partially, and produce some subproblems. Then the subproblems are given to WSAT. There are two parameters for controlling the number of subproblems. One is the maximum depth to be searched by DP, denoted by $MaxDep$; the other is the maximum number of subproblems, denoted by $MaxSubP$. Each of them determines the other. For instance, if the depth is 4, the number is 16; if the number is 16, the depth for each subproblem is 4; if the number is 15, the depth for the first 14 subproblems is 4 and the depth for the last subproblem is 3.

If a subproblem is proven to be satisfiable within the given depth, the satisfiability checking is finished. If all subproblems are proven to be unsatisfiable within the depth, the satisfiability checking is also finished. Otherwise, the subproblems which have not yet been proven to be unsatisfiable are recorded in files. (The number of such problems may be less than $MaxSubP$.) In each subproblem, the propositional variables are renumbered consecutively from 1 to the number of remaining variables. These subproblems are given to WSAT in a loop until a solution is found or the maximum number of repetitions is reached. In the current implementation, the information of renumbering is not saved. This information could be important for producing a model of the original problem.

The following picture illustrates our approach. Here $MaxDep = 2$. Applying the DP procedure to the original problem P, we get two subproblems P_0 and P_1. Applying DP again to them, we get the subproblems P_{00}, P_{01}, P_{10} and P_{11}. Suppose that P_{10} is found to be unsatisfiable. Then we shall apply WSAT to the remaining three subproblems, i.e. P_{00}, P_{01} and P_{11}.

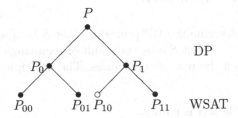

Experimental Results

We have applied our approach to the following test suites[1] and achieved good results. (We can only choose satisfiable problem instances since WSAT does not give meaningful results on unsatisfiable instances.)

- SAT encoding of logistics planning problem [5,4] referred to as LOGISTICS instances. There are four instances in this test suite. These instances are relatively easy for WSAT. Our approach is better for the most difficult one of these problems (i.e. *logistics.d.cnf*).
- SAT encoding of the All-Interval Series problem [2] referred to as AIS instances. There are also four instances in this test suite. The first three instances can be solved by WSAT within a few seconds. The last one is harder.
- SAT encoding of the quasigroup problem instances referred to as QG instances. There are 22 instances in the package and 10 of them are satisfiable. Instead of using the downloaded QG instances, we use the more compact instances generated by SATO [9].

The left part of Table 1 shows the sizes of the SAT instances.

Test 1: For each of the instances described in Table 1, 12 tests were carried out. Each test was carried out on a SUN BLADE 1000 with 750 MHz and 512 MB. The maximum number of subproblems ($MaxSubP$) was set to 15.

The right part of Table 1 shows the sizes of the subproblems produced by the DP-procedure. The ratio between the subproblem size and the problem size varies a lot. The ratio is small for QG instances and big for the LOGISTICS instances. The instances *qg1-07.cnf*, *qg2-07.cnf*, *qg6-09.cnf*, and *qg7-09.cnf* were solved by the DP-procedure and the columns for the subproblem sizes are irrelevant to these instances. We will not consider these problem instances later.

---

[1] See *http://www.intellektik.informatik.tu-darmstadt.de/SATLIB/benchm.html*

Table 1. Description of SAT Instances

Problem Instance	NumOf Variables	NumOf Clauses	NumOfCls in Subproblems		
			Average	Smallest	Biggest
logistics.a	828	6,718	6,562	6,550	6,596
logistics.b	843	7,301	7,117	7,115	7,137
logistics.c	1,141	10,719	10,508	10,505	10,539
logistics.d	4,713	21,991	20,945	20,007	21,472
ais6	61	581	440	396	537
ais8	113	1,520	1,209	1,058	1,454
ais10	181	3,151	2,595	2,265	3,061
ais12	265	5,666	4,792	4,212	5,552
qg1-07	343	8,578	-	-	-
qg1-08	512	23,106	9,074	6,030	12,064
qg2-07	343	11,254	-	-	-
qg2-08	512	28,945	8,442	6,244	9,735
qg3-08	512	17,689	3,670	3,269	4,506
qg4-09	729	28,751	6,947	4,117	8,976
qg5-11	1,331	64,377	14,797	7,482	20,249
qg6-09	729	28,463	-	-	-
qg7-09	729	28,751	-	-	-
qg7-13	2,197	125,923	31,353	21,285	45,452

We applied WSAT to each problem instance, with the maximum number of trials set to 3000. The maximum number of trials for each of the subproblems was set to 200. The shortest time, the longest time and the average time for finding a solution were calculated. The time for using the DP-procedure was calculated separately. These calculated values are presented in Table 2.

Table 2. Result of Test 1

Problem Instance	NumOf Subprobs	hybrid SAT					WSAT			
		DP	H-Avg	H-Min	H-Max	F	W-Avg	W-Min	W-Max	F
logistics.a	15	1.5	1.2	0.2	3.0		1.1	0.2	3.6	
logistics.b	15	1.6	0.7	0.1	1.5		0.6	0.1	1.0	
logistics.c	15	2.0	3.4	0.3	12.8		5.8	1.4	15.5	
logistics.d	15	3.3	9.4	0.7	28.4		14.6	0.9	50.1	
ais6	15	0.3	1.1	1.0	1.3		0.0	0.0	0.0	
ais8	15	0.4	0.2	0.0	0.4		0.3	0.0	0.6	
ais10	15	0.5	3.6	0.2	7.7		1.6	0.1	3.6	
ais12	15	1.0	18.7	9.6	34.6		121.5	23.3	227.4	
qg1-08	15	2.1	936.6	146.8	2201.2		3637.7	148.0	7270.0	5
qg2-08	15	2.0	1571.0	231.2	4004.6	1	5831.0	828.3	8749.3	9
qg3-08	10	0.6	4.5	4.0	5.0		27.9	1.7	81.7	
qg4-09	15	1.6	9.8	4.4	16.5		386.9	6.8	856.2	
qg5-11	3	1.7	45.6	0.9	100.3		9460.1	9455.7	9465.1	12
qg7-13	13	5.2	5298.5	5290.1	5310.5	12	15261.1	15208.2	15273.0	12

Table 2 shows the following information (with running times measured in seconds):

- the number of subproblems (with $MaxSubP = 15$);
- the performance of the hybrid approach:
  - the running time of the DP-procedure,
  - H-Avg: the average running time of WSAT on the subproblems,
  - H-Min: the minimum running time of WSAT on the subproblems,
  - H-Max: the maximum running time of WSAT on the subproblems;
  - the number of failures (i.e. when no solution is found);
- the performance of WSAT without DP-reduction (i.e., applying WSAT directly on the original problem instance):
  - W-Avg: the average running time,
  - W-Min: the minimum running time,
  - W-Max: the maximum running time;
  - the number of failures (i.e. when no solution is found).

Based on the experimental results, we compare our approach with the original WSAT procedure as follows:

- For the SAT instances that can be solved with WSAT within a few seconds, our approach does not have much advantage, since we have to add the time usage of the DP-procedure to that of WSAT.
- For the medium hard instances (e.g. with time usage between 10 and 1000 seconds in W-Avg), the advantage of our approach is obvious.
- For many of the hardest instances, we may achieve much better results. The instances *qg4-09.cnf* and *qg5-11.cnf* are witness to such a good result.
- Generally, the advantages of partitioning a problem into subproblems compared to using WSAT alone is that each subproblem is much smaller than the original problem. A consequence of this is that the time needed for each trial of such a subproblem with WSAT is much shorter. For instance, 10 trials for the quasigroup instance *qg7-13.cnf* on our computer need 31.0 seconds. After partitioning the problem into 13 subproblems (3 subproblems are proved to be unsatisfiable within depth 4), the times for 10 trials for each of the subproblems range from 7.9 to 14.6 seconds. Another advantage is that a solution of such a subproblem is expected to be found with much less time, if this subproblem indeed has a solution, as demonstrated by the above experimental results.

3   The Parallel Approach

We have implemented the approach as a distributed system for checking different subproblems in parallel. The system (called PSAT) consists of one master and a number of slaves. The pseudo-code of PSAT is as follows:

```
PSAT(args,input-file)
{
    master: {
        arguments-split();            /* split args into args-1 and args-2 */
        broadcast(args-2);            /* broadcast args-2 to all slaves */
        DP(args-1,input-file);              /* apply the DP procedure */
        get-all-subproblems();
        while (1) {
            listen-to-slaves();
            if (slave-report()) {
                if (success) abort-all;
                else if (found-unfinished-subproblems()) send-new-work();
                else send-stop();
                if (all-finished()) exit;
            }
        }
    }
    slave: {
        receive(args-2);
        while (unfinished) {
            receive-new-work();
            if (have-new-work) {
                WSAT(args-2,new-work);  /* apply WSAT to new-work */
                report-to-master();
            }
            else exit;
        }
    }
}
```

The task of the master is as follows:

1. Apply the DP-procedure.
   If a model is obtained within the depth, the instance is satisfiable (and the
   program is terminated). Otherwise we check whether there are subproblems.
   If there is no subproblem, the instance is unsatisfiable (and the program is
   terminated).
2. Establish connection with the slaves and distribute the subproblems to them.
   In our system, the files containing subproblems do not need to be communicated to different computers. They are stored in one place which can be
   read by different computers via NFS file-system. The only information to be
   passed to the slaves is the identification of the subproblems. In this way, we
   have avoided heavy communication of the clauses of the subproblems.
3. Get the results from the slaves.

The task of a slave is to use the tool WSAT on the received subproblem,
trying to find a model for this subproblem. In the pseudo-code, args-1 refers

to the arguments needed by DP ($MaxDep$ and $MaxSubP$), while args-2 refers to the arguments of WSAT (e.g., the number of trials). The input file contains the SAT instance and DP is the procedure for partitioning and reducing the instance. The subproblems are identified by the parameter *new-work* and are to be solved by WSAT on different workstations. The tool PSAT is implemented by using *Message Passing Interface (MPI)* which is the de facto standard of parallel programming.

Test 2: We use the same test suites for the testing of our distributed system. The experiments were carried out on a Linux cluster which consists of 8 nodes connected by Fast Ethernet Switch (D-Link DES1008). Each node has two 1GHz Pentium III processors with 2048 MB memory. A problem is partitioned in such a way that the number of subproblems is the same as the number of slaves. Since there is one master process, we can have 15 slave processes. Thus we set $MaxSubP$ to be 15.

For each of the instances, 12 tests were carried out. For each of the tests:

- WSAT was applied to the instance with a given new seed. The maximum number of trials was 2000 (the number was reduced from 3000 to 2000 in order to reduce the testing time, and this has increased the percentage of failed tests for the hard instances).
- PSAT was applied to the same instance with the same seed for all WSAT applications within PSAT. The maximum number of trials for each subproblem was 200.

Table 3. Result of Test 2

Problem Instance	NumOf Jobs	PSAT					WSAT			
		DP	P-Avg	P-Min	P-Max	F	W-Avg	W-Min	W-Max	F
logistics.a	15	0.5	0.3	0.2	0.4		1.1	0.2	1.9	
logistics.b	15	0.5	0.1	0.4	0.6		0.7	0.2	1.4	
logistics.c	15	0.7	0.9	0.4	1.6		3.6	0.2	9.5	
logistics.d	15	1.5	1.2	0.7	1.6		23.7	8.4	54.2	
ais6	15	0.0	0.0	0.0	0.0		0.0	0.0	0.0	
ais8	15	0.1	0.1	0.0	0.1		0.1	0.0	0.5	
ais10	15	0.2	0.4	0.2	1.0		1.6	0.3	3.4	
ais12	15	0.3	2.5	0.2	7.4		74.9	2.4	178.2	
qg1-08	15	0.9	55.2	1.2	103.4		1620.8	135.9	2785.4	4
qg2-08	15	0.9	89.9	4.0	293.4		4320.2	2211.6	4773.7	11
qg3-08	15	0.3	0.3	0.2	0.9		27.2	2.0	75.8	
qg4-09	15	0.6	1.3	0.6	2.4		107.8	6.3	322.9	
qg5-11	3	1.1	7.7	1.2	18.5		8210.6	7166.4	8825.0	12
qg7-13	13	3.2	720.9	713.9	724.6	12	10732.2	9233.6	10941.7	12

Table 3 shows the same types of information as Table 2. With respect to the approach presented in section 2, we had expected that we might get a speed up by a factor of around 15, since we have 15 slaves. However the situation is more complicated.

The processors used in this test are different from that used in the previous tests, and the result is not directly comparable. We have compared the ratio between the time usage with DP reduction (only counting the time usage of WSAT in the approach) and the time usage without DP reduction of this table and that of Table 2. For the easy SAT instances, the speed up was much lower than expected. On the other hand, the speed up was better for many of the other instances, such as qg1-08 and qg2-08.

Apparently there is no fixed factor for the speed up with the parallel approach due to the nature of the randomness of WSAT. However the conclusion is clear and we may say that the parallel approach is much better than the sequential approach with respect to the time usage and our approach is appropriate for utilizing parallel computing power and unused networked workstations for checking the satisfiability of SAT instances.

Test 3: To investigate how the number of subproblems affects the satisfiability test, we solved several hardest instances with different values for $MaxSubP$. The experiments were carried out on a Dawning 2000-II supercomputer with 82 nodes (80 nodes for computing and 2 nodes as the server). Each node has two 333MHz PowerPC CPU. The results are summarized in Table 4. As previously, the running times are given in seconds.

Table 4. Result of Test 3

Problem Instance	Max Depth	NumOf Jobs	Init Time	DP Time	Wsat Time
Logistics.d	2	4	0.0440	4.2341	12.1859
Logistics.d	3	8	0.4691	8.5456	6.2693
Logistics.d	4	16	0.8818	14.2175	10.3217
Logistics.d	5	32	0.5465	26.1273	12.9071
Ais12.cnf	2	4	0.2080	1.5362	2.2571
Ais12.cnf	3	8	0.2173	2.5335	1.9988
Ais12.cnf	4	16	0.9606	5.1357	1.8886
Ais12.cnf	5	32	1.3835	10.1181	1.9326
Qg511.cnf	2	4	0.1216	4.7137	86.5016
Qg511.cnf	3	4	0.1232	7.0734	29.0169
Qg511.cnf	4	3	0.3157	6.8622	29.6516
Qg511.cnf	5	3	0.3937	11.4745	41.5507
Qg511.cnf	6	2	0.2204	10.6388	23.1538

Here, column 2 gives the value of $MaxDep$ (i.e., depth of the DP search tree), and column 3 gives the number of subproblems that have not been finished by DP. The other columns show the running times of PSAT at various stages.

It can be seen that, on the AIS problem and the quasigroup problem, there is a notable reduction of stochastic search time as $MaxDep$ is increased to a certain value. On the LOGISTICS problem, the timing difference is not significant. Note also that the time for DP increases as $MaxDep$ becomes larger. This is due to the fact that the subproblems have to be written into files.

4   Related Works

There exist several parallel and networked implementations of reasoning algorithms. For instance, efficient parallel and networked DP provers are reported in [1,10]. The purposes of these implementations are to divide and distribute a SAT instance in order to utilize the parallel computing power and networked workstations. Appropriate search space partitioning and workload balancing are the essential aspects in such implementations. The purpose of our implementation is different. We try to improve stochastic SAT solvers by first using an implementation of the DP procedure to partition and reduce SAT instances. We may achieve speed up by a factor much higher than the number of available networked workstations. This has been illustrated by the experimental results.

Other ways of combining complete and incomplete search have been proposed in the literature [3,8]. For example, one may use incomplete methods first and then use complete search [11]. This can be considered as an improvement of the backtracking procedure, while our approach is essentially an enhancement of stochastic search. We do not know of any parallel implementations of other hybrid methods. It is natural to parallelize our method because, after the first stage of (backtracking) search, we obtain some subproblems whose search spaces are disjoint.

5   Conclusion

We have combined the DP-procedure with WSAT for the satisfiability test. This approach is more efficient than using WSAT alone. We have also implemented the approach as a distributed system and have achieved additional efficiency by utilizing parallel computing power and unused networked workstations. As the instances of the test suites are concerned, the speed up factor of the sequential approach is significant for medium hard instances and is higher for the more difficult instances. Additional speed-up has been achieved by using the parallel approach. Generally, the speed up depends on the maximum number of subproblems and the number of available workstations.

The advantages of partitioning a problem into subproblems compared to using WSAT alone is that each subproblem is much smaller than the original problem. The implications of this are that the time needed for each trial of such a subproblem with WSAT is much shorter; and a solution of such a subproblem is expected to be found with much less time, if this subproblem indeed has a solution. For hard SAT instances, the speed up with our approaches is significant. Our approach is therefore an important step forward in SAT research and has scaled up the applicability of SAT tools.

As our approach is an enhancement of incomplete search, in this paper, we are mainly concerned with the performance gains over the sequential WSAT. In the future, we plan to compare our tool with DP provers. It is also necessary to improve our current implementation, to carry out more experiments and to further investigate several issues (e.g., the impact of the number of subproblems).

Acknowledgements. We would like to thank the anonymous reviewers for helpful comments. The Dawning supercomputer was made available to us through the Computer Network Information Center, Chinese Academy of Sciences. Yunquan Zhang also helped us with some of our experiments.

References

1. Max Böhm and Ewald Speckenmeyer. A fast parallel SAT-solver - efficient workload balancing. Annals of Mathematics and Artificial Intelligence 17(3-4):381–400. 1996.
2. Holger H. Hoos. Stochastic Local Search - Methods, Models, Applications. PhD thesis, CS Department, TU Darmstadt, 1998.
3. N. Jussien and O. Lhomme. Local search with constraint propagation and conflict-based heuristics. Proc. of the 17th National Conf. on Artificial Intelligence (AAAI), 169–174, 2000.
4. Henry Kautz, David McAllester and Bart Selman. Encoding Plans in Propositional Logic. Proc. KR'96, 374–384. 1996.
5. Henry Kautz and Bart Selman. Pushing the Envelope: Planning, Propositional Logic, and Stochastic Search. Proc. of the 13th National Conference on Artificial Intelligence (AAAI'96), 1194–1201, 1996.
6. Chu Min Li and Anbulagan. Heuristics Based on Unit Propagation for Satisfiability Problems. Proc. of the 15th Int'l Joint Conf. on Artificial Intelligence (IJCAI-97), 366–371, 1997.
7. Bart Selman, Henry A. Kautz and Bram Cohen. Noise Strategies for Improving Local Search. Proc. of the 12th National Conf. on Artificial Intelligence (AAAI), Vol.1, 337–343, 1994.
8. A. Schaerf, Combining local search and look-ahead for scheduling and constraint satisfaction problems, *Proc. Int'l Joint Conf. on Artificial Intelligence (IJCAI-97)*, Vol.2, 1254–1259, 1997.
9. Hantao Zhang and Mark E. Stickel. Implementing the Davis-Putnam Method. Journal of Automated Reasoning 24(1/2):277–296 (2000).
10. Hantao Zhang, Maria Paola Bonacina and Jieh Hsiang. PSATO: a distributed propositional prover and its application to quasigroup problems. J. of Symbolic Computation 21(4):543–560. 1996.
11. Jian Zhang and Hantao Zhang. Combining Local Search and Backtracking Techniques for Constraint Satisfaction, Proc. of the 13th National Conference on Artificial Intelligence (AAAI-96), Vol.1, 369–374, 1996.

Two Transformations of Clauses into Constraints and Their Properties for Cost-Based Hypothetical Reasoning

Yutaka Matsuo and Mitsuru Ishizuka

University of Tokyo, Hongo 7-3-1, Tokyo 113-8656, Japan
matsuo@miv.t.u-tokyo.ac.jp,
http://www.miv.t.u-tokyo.ac.jp/~matsuo

Abstract. This paper describes two ways to transform propositional clauses into mathematical constraints, and gives an overview of mathematical optimization approaches to inference. The first transformation, which translates constraints into linear inequalities, has been applied to cost-based abduction in the past and showed good performance. The second one, which produces nonlinear equalities, is commonly used in other representations, such as SAT. We clarify their differences and advantages, and show the radical performance transition of linear inequalities. We are mainly targeting at cost-based hypothetical reasoning (or abduction), but through preprocessing, the discussion has generality.

1 Introduction

Hypothetical reasoning (or 'abduction') is a useful framework for knowledge-based systems that allows to find explanations for observations [1,2]. In *cost-based abduction* [3,4], hypotheses have associated costs, and the cost of a proof is simply the sum of the costs of the hypotheses required to complete that proof. It has been shown in [3] that belief revision in Bayesian networks can be accurately modeled by cost-based abduction. Unfortunately, the computational complexity of computing the minimal cost explanation is NP-hard, even for very basic forms of propositional abduction [5].

Though it is more natural to describe systems in a more expressive language such as first-order logic, propositional logic is still of importance. Prendinger and Ishizuka compile a first-order system description of cost-based abduction to a propositional representation, mainly focusing on model-based diagnosis [6]. An efficient engine for propositional cost-based abduction plays an crucial role in such systems.

Recently, significant progress towards highly efficient inference mechanisms can be seen for propositional cost-based abduction [4,7,8]. These methods employ search mechanisms borrowed from mathematical programming, a programming paradigm that may exploit the continuous rather than the discrete value domain. The main idea is to transform Horn clauses into linear constraints and seek the optimal point using linear programming techniques, e.g., the simplex method.

Besides cost-based abduction, several efficient mechanisms have also been developed for other kinds of propositional reasoning, such as satisfiability problems (SAT) or constraint satisfaction problems (CSP). In the SAT case, starting from GSAT [9], a set of powerful new local search heuristics has been developed [10,11,12]. Especially,

M. Ishizuka and A. Sattar (Eds.): PRICAI 2002, LNAI 2417, pp. 118–127, 2002.

DLM-2000 (discrete Lagrangian method) [13] can solve some of the hardest satisfiability problems of DIMACS benchmark problems.

In this paper, we will describe two types of transformation from propositional clauses to mathematical constraints. The first one, called *transformation* **L**, has been used widely in the context of cost-based abduction, which transforms clauses into linear inequalities. The second one, called *transformation* **NL**, translates clauses into nonlinear equalities, which can be considered as underlying some algorithms for SAT. These two transformations have different characteristics; transformation **L** is likely to find a low-cost solution, while transformation **NL** efficiently searches for a feasible solution. We will show an example in which transformation **L** performs well, but by adding clauses, the performance deteriorates. We also show that transformation **NL** doesn't cause such a radical transition.

The rest of the paper is organized as follows. In the following section, we first briefly describe the preprocessing of a hypothetical reasoning problem in order to obtain a knowledge base with a small number of clauses. Then we explain two transformations of clauses into constraints. Section 3 is devoted to a detailed discussion of the characteristics and the differences of two transformations, including the performance transition of transformation **L**. Finally, we discuss future works and conclude this paper.

2 How to Make Constraints?

A *hypothetical reasoning problem* (HRP) is characterized by a set $\mathcal{G}$ of goals (e.g., observations) to be explained, given background knowledge Σ, e.g., the behavioral model of some device. A *solution* to a HRP is a set of hypotheses $H \subseteq \mathcal{H}$ which, if assumed, would explain the observations.

Definition 1. *A* hypothetical reasoning problem *(HRP) is a quadruple* $HRP = \langle T, I, \mathcal{H}, \mathcal{G} \rangle$, *such that*

(i) T *is a propositional Horn theory, i.e., a set of clauses* t *of the form* "$q \leftarrow p_1 \wedge \ldots \wedge p_n$" *where* $q, p_1, \ldots, p_n$ *are atomic formulas. If* $n > 0$ *then* C *is called a* rule *(or* non-unit clause*), else* $(n = 0)$ C *is called a* fact *(or* unit clause*). The atom* q *is called the* head *of the clause, the conjunction* $p_1 \wedge \ldots \wedge p_n$ *is called the* body *of the clause.*

(ii) I *is a set of* inconsistency constraints, *i.e., a set of Horn clauses of the form* "$inc \leftarrow h_1 \wedge \ldots \wedge h_n$" *where each* $h_i (1 \leq i \leq n)$ *denotes a hypothesis, and the symbol* inc *denotes the logical constant* falsum.

(iii) $\mathcal{H}$ *is a set of atoms that denote element hypotheses ('assumable' states).*

(iv) $\mathcal{G}$ *is a set of goal atoms denoting, e.g., observations.*

Definition 2. *Let* $HRP = \langle T, I, \mathcal{H}, \mathcal{G} \rangle$ *be a hypothetical reasoning problem. A set* $H \subseteq \mathcal{H}$ *is a* solution hypotheses set *(or* solution*) for HRP iff (i) for each* $g \in \mathcal{G}$: $T \cup H \vdash g$, *(ii)* $I \cup H \not\vdash inc$.

Cost-based hypothetical reasoning employs the *minimum cost solution* criterion. It assumes that a numerical weight (or cost) $c(h)$ is assigned to each element hypothesis $h \in \mathcal{H}$ (c is a function from $\mathcal{H}$ to the natural numbers). Then the cost of a solution, $C(H)$, can be defined as

$$C(H) = \sum_{h \in H} c(h). \tag{1}$$

2.1 Preprocessing

Before applying the transformation, we first compile the HRP, including goal atoms, to a small set of conjunctive normal form (CNF) formulas. The following steps are executed sequentially.

Relevance reasoning. Construct the *query-tree* [14] in a top-down (from a goal to leaves) fashion and get T, I, and $\mathcal{H}$ reduced.

Completion. Apply completion for each rule $t \in T$ and get augmented T in order to make backward inference possible. We change "$q \leftarrow p$" to "$q \leftarrow p$" and "$p \leftarrow q$," and refer the original rule as a *top-down* rule and the added rule as a *bottom-up* rule, following [3].

Eliminating top-down rules. Eliminate top-down rules and get reduced T. This is possible because in case of cost-based abduction, an optimal solution for *semi-induced problems*, which consist of bottom-up rules without top-down rules, can be transformed into the best explanation for the original problem in the linear order of steps with respect to the number of rules under a weak assumption [4]. Thus the original rules in theory T are only utilized in the form of bottom-up rules.

Merging goal atoms and eliminating unit clauses. Assign $g \in \mathcal{G}$ true, eliminate unit clauses and get reduced T and $\mathcal{H}$. If we assign goal atoms true, some clauses in T may turn to be unit. We assign the atom true in a unit clause $t \in T$ and eliminate t from T. This process is repeated until no unit clauses are detected in T, or inconsistency detected. This is a simple version of eliminating one-literal clauses in the Davis-Putnam procedure [15].

We now have a new propositional theory T' and a new set of inconsistency constraints I'. We create a new knowledge base KB' of the CNF formulas, consisting of $t \in T'$ and $ic \in I'$. In order to find the (minimum cost) solution to a HRP, we should find the (minimum cost) satisfying assignment to KB'. The set of atoms in KB' is denoted as N. Note that the clauses in KB' are not necessarily Horn.

In [3,4], *WAODAGs* (or, weighted AND/OR directed acyclic graphs) are used to represent cost-based abduction. However, we allow clauses in KB' to be any CNF formulas, thus the following discussion can be applied also to SAT problems under minimum cost solution criterion.

2.2 Transformation into Linear Constraints

First we associate the variable x_p with $p \in N$. We use $x_p = 1$ for "p is true," and $x_p = 0$ for "p is false."

Assume KB' has the clause,

$$p_1 \vee \neg p_2 \vee \neg p_3. \tag{2}$$

In order for formula (2) to be true, at least one of the literals p_1, $\neg p_2$, and $\neg p_3$ has to be true, equivalently, the mathematical constraint $x_{p1} + (1 - x_{p2}) + (1 - x_{p3}) \geq 1$ has to be satisfied. We define *transformation* L as follows.

Definition 3. Transformation L *is a transformation from a clause to a linear inequality constraint, constructed as follows:*
(i) replace the literals p and $\neg p$ by x_p and $(1 - x_p)$, respectively,
(ii) generate the LHS (left-hand side) of an inequality by replacing disjunction $(\vee)$ by the arithmetic operation "$+$,"
(iii) generate the inequality "$LHS \geq 1$."

Together with the cost function (1) and 0-1 relaxation, transformation L defines *problem L.*

Definition 4. Problem L *is a continuous linear programming problem, where (i) the objective function to be minimized is defined by (1), and (ii) subject to the constraints derived from transformation L for each clause $c \in KB'$, and (iii) relaxed 0-1 constraints $0 \leq x_p \leq 1$ for each atom $p \in N$.*

Problem L can be applied to other representations than cost-based abduction, such as SAT. However, as Selman describes [16], in most formulations the solution to the linear relaxation of any SAT problem simply sets all the variables to the value "1/2," thus yielding no guidance at all.

But still solving *problem L* is useful in the case of cost-based abduction. Santos, Jr. revealed that 97% of the randomly generated WAODAGs were solved using only linear programming without supplementary branch-and-bound [4]. Although randomly generated problems have some pitfalls [17], we discuss later that there is a region where transformation L does work well.

2.3   Transformation into Nonlinear Constraints

Consider (2) again. It is logically equivalent to $\neg(\neg p_1 \wedge p_2 \wedge p_3)$, which means $\neg p_1 \wedge p_2 \wedge p_3$ should be false, thus at least one of $\neg p_1, p_2$, and p_3 should be false, so that the formula is true. Equivalently we can write down a constraint as $(1 - x_{p1})x_{p2}x_{p3} = 0$. We define *transformation* NL as follows.

Definition 5. Transformation NL *is a transformation from a clause to a nonlinear equality constraint, constructed as follows:*
(i) negate the clause,
(ii) replace the literals p and $\neg p$ by x_p and $(1 - x_p)$, respectively,
(iii) make the LHS of an equality replacing conjunction $(\wedge)$ by the arithmetic operation "$\times$,"
(iv) make the equality "$LHS = 0$."

Combining the cost function (1) and 0-1 relaxation, we obtain *problem NL.*

Definition 6. Problem NL *is a continuous nonlinear programming problem, where (i) the objective function to be minimized is defined by (1), and (ii) subject to the constraints derived from transformation NL for each clause $c \in KB'$, and (iii) relaxed 0-1 constraint $0 \leq x_p \leq 1$ for each atom $p \in N$.*

Problem NL is one of the most simple form of transformations, and it can be considered as underlying some algorithms. For example, Gu has developed a SAT problem model, called *UniSAT*, which transforms a SAT problem into an unconstrained optimization problem on real space [10,18]. UniSAT7 transforms a CNF $(x_1 \vee \neg x_2) \wedge (\neg x_1 \vee x_2 \vee x_3)$ into $f = (x_1 - T)^p (x_2 + F)^p + (x_1 + F)^p (x_2 - T)^p (x_3 - T)^p$, where T, F, and p are constants. This method in the case of $T = 1$ and $F = 0$ is nothing but the p-norm penalty method [19] to solve *problem NL*.

In DLM, or discrete Lagrangian method [20], a SAT problem (with n variables and m clauses) is formulated as a discrete constrained optimization problem; Minimize$_{x \in \{0,1\}^n} \sum_{i=1}^{m} U_i(x)$, subject to $U_i(x) = 0 \quad \forall i \in \{1, 2, \ldots, m\}$, where $U_i = 0$ if clause i is satisfied, and $U_i = 1$ if clause i is not satisfied. We can easily see that the constraint constructed by transformation **NL** satisfies the requirements of U_i. Thus, applying continuous Lagrangian methods to *problem NL*, similar method to DLM can be derived (though some devices are needed e.g., to force the updated value of x should be 0 or 1 in each iteration). The overview of such subgradient algorithms are seen in [21].

In summary, transformation **L** is efficiently used in the context of cost-based abduction, while transformation **NL** underlies some SAT algorithms to solve highly constrained problems. The approach here follows the treatment of pseudo-boolean optimization problems [22].

3   Discussion of Two Transformations

3.1   Difference of Two Transformations

One major difference between transformation **L** and transformation **NL** is that transformation **L** gives a necessary condition for variables to be a satisfying assignment, whereas transformation **NL** gives a necessary and sufficient condition.

Given a truth assignment to atoms, obviously we can satisfy constraints of either transformation **L** or transformation **NL** by substituting 1/0 to the corresponding variables according to the truth value. Conversely, given values of variables which satisfy constraints of transformation **NL**, we can construct a truth assignment as follows.

Theorem 1. *Given a set of clauses KB' and a set of atoms N, if the variables x_p $(p \in N)$ satisfy constraints derived from transformation **NL** of the clauses $c \in KB'$, we can construct a truth assignment satisfying the clauses $c \in KB'$ as follows. For all the atoms $p \in N$, (i) if $x_p = 1$, then set p* true, *(ii) if $x_p = 0$, then set p* false, *(iii) otherwise, set p arbitrarily* true *or* false.

Proof. The proof is obvious by Definition 5   □.

On the other hand, this is not the case for transformation **L**, even if we round variables, e.g., if $x_p \geq 0.5$ then set p true, otherwise set p false. Despite of this disadvantage, *problem L* has some merits. The most important one is that it may produce the optimal solution quite rapidly, only by simplex method. Besides, (i) it may provide the guidance for the 0-1 optimal solution, (ii) it provides the lower bound of cost of the 0-1 optimal solution, and (iii) it shows the unsatisfiability of KB' if *problem L* is infeasible. The

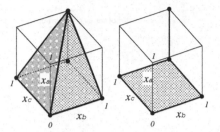

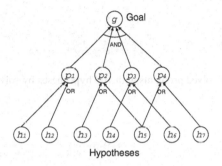

Transformation L   **Transformation NL**

Fig. 1. Feasible region of "$(\neg a \vee b) \wedge (\neg a \vee c)$."

Fig. 2. Set covering problem.

feasible region of transformation **L** is a convex polygon as shown in Fig. 1, thus the search point proceeds easily toward the gradient direction of the objective function. However, transformation **NL** produces the tightly constrained feasible region, thus to proceed toward the direction to decrease the objective function (not Lagrangian function) is harder than transformation **L**.

3.2 Performance Transition of Transformation L

It has been believed that *problem L* works well on HRPs, however, the performance depends considerably on the 'hardness' of the problem. Here we pick up a very simple but sufficiently suggestive example to show the transition of performance by transformation **L**.

Fig. 2 is a set covering problem represented by a HRP. A solution for the HRP is a set of hypotheses which covers all the intermediate propositions. For example, $\{h_2, h_5, h_6\}$ is a solution to prove the goal. Here, the cost of each hypothesis is set to be 1, and each intermediate proposition has two OR children randomly chosen. If we add intermediate propositions while keeping the number of hypotheses constant, then the number of solutions decreases, i.e., the problem gets harder. For example, if we add a new intermediate proposition p_5, such that "$p_5 \leftarrow h_4 \vee h_7$" and "$g \leftarrow p_1 \wedge \ldots \wedge p_4 \wedge p_5$," then $\{h_2, h_5, h_6\}$ is not a solution anymore. Yet this problem has always at least one solution, to set all hypotheses true. In this manner, we get series of problems gradually getting more tightly constrained.

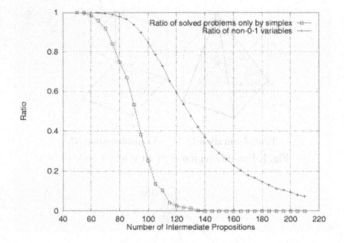

Fig. 3. Ratio of solved problems with 100 hypotheses by solving *problem L.*

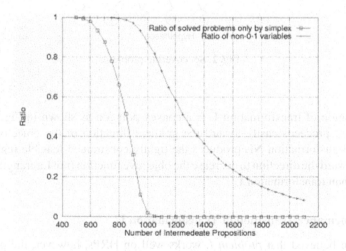

Fig. 4. Ratio of solved problems with 1000 hypotheses by solving *problem L.*

In the experiment, starting from 100 hypotheses and 50 intermediate propositions, we gradually add the intermediate propositions. Fig. 3 shows the ratio of solved problems only by solving *problem L* (using simplex method). One dot represents the average of 500 instances. Almost all the problems can be solved only by simplex method when the number of intermediate propositions m is less than 60, however few problems can be solved when m exceeds 140. At $m = 140$, 63% of the variables are set to 1/2, and provide no guidance at all. In the case of 1000 hypotheses starting from 500 intermediate propositions, the drop is even steeper as shown in Fig. 4.

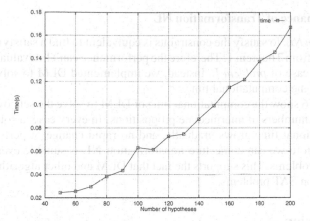

Fig. 5. Computational time to solve problems **NL** with 100 hypotheses by DLM.

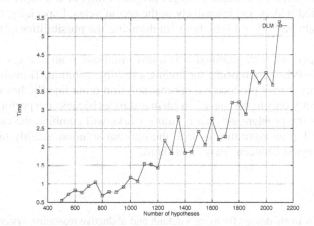

Fig. 6. Computational time to solve problems **NL** with 1000 hypotheses by DLM.

Not only for this set covering problem but also for other problem instances, such as shortest path problem and assignment problem, we have found the same phenomenon. By adding clauses, HRPs are less likely to be solved only by solving *problem L*.

Lastly, the curves in Fig. 3 and 4 remind us of the *phase transition* phenomenon [23, 24]. For example, in the case of random 3-SAT instances with 50 variables, if the ratio of clauses-to-variables is less than 3.5, the formula is almost certainly satisfiable, while if the ratio is over 5.2, almost all formulas are unsatisfiable. This phase transition focuses on the likelihood of satisfiability, however, ours focuses on the likelihood of solvability by solving *problem L*. We expect our performance transition has some correspondence with the phase transition of satisfiability, but further study is needed to derive some conclusions.

3.3   Performance of Transformation NL

As for *problem NL*, to satisfy the constraints is equivalent to find a satisfying assignment of the clauses from Theorem 1. Therefore the performance can't be evaluated in the same way as in the case of *problem L*. Instead, we implemented DLM to solve *problem NL* and measured the computational time.

Fig. 5 and 6 show the computational time of DLM to solve the set covering problem with different numbers of intermediate propositions. In every case, a solution is found. The computational time grows gradually, and no rapid change of performance is observed. Therefore we can conjecture transformation **NL** is suitable even for seriously constrained problems. This supports the fact that DLM and other algorithms show good performance on SAT problems.

4   Conclusion

The relation between logic and 0-1 integer programming, or OR (operations research), has been studied widely and intensively in the recent years. Especially, the latest good overviews might be [25] and [26], both emphasizing the possibilities of the integration of AI and OR.

In this paper, we have clarified two transformations from clauses to constraints. Transformation **NL** is appropriate for finding a feasible solution. Transformation **L** has the merit in that it may produce the optimal solution quite rapidly, however, it can be applied efficiently only to the "easy" problem instances because the performance rapidly deteriorates as the problem gets hard. Future works will combine the two transformations and develop an algorithm to seek the optimal solution, mainly targeting on an intermediate region between "easy" and "hard."

References

1. Poole, D.: A methodology for using a default and abductive reasoning system. International Journal of Intelligent Systems **5** (1990) 521–548
2. Kakas, A., Kowalski, R., Toni, F.: The role of abduction in logic programming. In: Handbook of Logic in Artificial Intelligence and Logic Programming. Oxford University Press (1995)
3. Charniak, E., Shimony, S.E.: Cost-based abduction and MAP explanation. Artificial Intelligence **66** (1994) 345–374
4. Santos, Jr., E.: A linear constraint satisfaction approach to cost-based abduction. Artificial Intelligence **65** (1994) 1–27
5. Eiter, T., Gottlob, G.: The complexity of logic-based abduction. Journal of the Association for Computing Machinary **42** (1995) 3–42
6. Prendinger, H., Ishizuka, M.: Qualifying the expressivity / efficiency tradeoff: Reformation-based diagnosis. In: Proceedings 16th National Conference on Artificial Intelligence (AAAI–99). (1999) 416–421
7. Ohsawa, Y., Ishizuka, M.: Networked bubble propagation: A polynomial-time hypothetical reasoning method for computing near-optimal solutions. Artificial Intelligence **91** (1997) 131–154
8. Ishizuka, M., Matsuo, Y.: SL method for computing a near-optimal solution using linear and non-linear programming in cost-based hypothetical reasoning. In: Proceedings 5th Pacific Rim Conference on Artificial Intelligence (PRICAI-98). (1998) 611–625

9. Selman, B., Levesque, H., McAllester, D.: A new method for solving hard satisfiability problems. In: Proceedings 9th National Conference on Artificial Intelligence (AAAI-92). (1992) 440–446

10. Gu, J.: Local search for satisfiability (SAT) problem. IEEE Transactions on Systems, Man, and Cybernetics **23** (1993) 1108–1129

11. Selman, B., Kautz, H., Cohen, B.: Noise strategies for improving local search. In: Proceedings 11th National Conference on Artificial Intelligence (AAAI-94). (1994) 337–343

12. Frank, J.: Learning short-term weights for GSAT. In: Proceedings 15th International Joint Conference on Artificial Intelligence (IJCAI-97). (1997) 384–391

13. Wu, Z., Wah, B.W.: An efficient global-search strategy in discrete Lagrangian methods for solving hard satisfiability problems. In: Proceedings 17th National Conference on Artificial Intelligence (AAAI-2000). (2000) 310–315

14. Levy, A.Y., Fikes, R.E., Sagiv, Y.: Speeding up inferences using relevance reasoning: a formalism and algorithms. Artificial Intelligence **97** (1997) 83–136

15. Davis, M., Putnam, H.: A computing procedure for quantification theory. Journal of the Association for Computing Machinary **7** (1960) 201–215

16. Selman, B., Kautz, H., McAllester, D.: Ten challenges in propositional reasoning and search. In: Proceedings 15th International Joint Conference on Artificial Intelligence (IJCAI-97). (1997) 50–54

17. Mitchell, D., Levesque, H.: Some pitfalls for experimenters with random SAT. Artificial Intelligence **81** (1996) 111–125

18. Gu, J.: Global optimization for satisfiability problem. IEEE Transactions on Knowledge and Data Engineering **6** (1994) 361–381

19. Nemhauser, G.L., Kan, A.H.G.R., Todd, M.J., eds.: Optimization: Handbooks in Operations Research and Management Science, Volume 1. North-Holland, Amsterdam (1989)

20. Shang, Y., Wah, B.W.: A discrete Lagrangian-based global-search method for solving satisfiability problems. Journal of Global Optimization **12** (1998)

21. Schuurmans, D., Southey, F., Holte, R.C.: The exponentiated subgradient algorithm for heuristic boolean programming. In: Proceedings 17th International Joint Conference on Artificial Intelligence (IJCAI-01). (2001) 334–341

22. Hammer, P., Simeone, B.: Quadratic functions of binary variables. In: Combinatorial Optimization, Lecture Notes in Mathematics. Volume 1403. (1989)

23. Selman, B., Mitchell, D., Levesque, H.: Generating hard satisfiability problems. Artificial Intelligence **81** (1996) 17–29

24. Gomes, C., Selman, B., Crato, N.: Heavy-tailed phenomena in satisfiability and constraint satisfaction problems. Journal of Automated Reasoning **24** (2000) 67–100

25. Gomes, C.: Structure, duality, and randomization: Common theme in AI and OR. In: Proceedings 17th National Conference on Artificial Intelligence (AAAI-2000). (2000) 1152–1158

26. Hooker, J.N.: Logic, optimization, and constraint programming. (INFORMS journal on Computing) To appear.

Hidden Markov Modeling for Multi-agent Systems

Noda Itsuki[1,2]

[1] Cyber Assist Research Center National Institute of Advanced Industrial Science and Technology

[2] PRESTO, Japan Science and Technology Corporation (JST)

Abstract. A formalization of multi-agent systems (MAS) as hidden Markov models (HMM) is proposed and investigated from a view point of interaction among agents and environments. Conventional formalizations of agents as HMM do not take changes of environments in account, so that it is hard to analyze behaviors of agents that act in dynamic environments. The proposed formalization enables HMM to handles changes of environment and interaction among agents via environment directly inside of state-transitions. I first investigate HMM that represents changes of the environment in the same state-transitions of agent itself. Then I derive a structured model in which environment, agent, and another agent are treated as separated state-transitions and coupled with each other. For this model, in order to reduce the number of parameters, I introduce "symmetricity" among agents. Moreover, I discuss relation between reducing dependency in transitions and assumption of cooperative behaviors in MAS.

1 Introduction

Hidden Markov models (HMM) and other probabilistic methods become to be used in order to analyze behaviors of an agent or a team of agents [8,2]. Because the behaviors of intelligent agents are complicated and structured, however, we should apply HMM carefully. Especially in the case that agents interact with each other via environments, it is necessary to assume a kind of structure of states in HMM. Because it is difficult to acquire such structure through learning, it is better to use HMM in which states are structured suitably. In this case, we must pay attention the learning performance and reasonabilities of the structure.

In this article, I propose a formalization of multi-agent systems (MAS) as HMM that can handle interaction between agents effectively through learning. In the following sections, I introduce an integrated HMM of agents and environment in Section 2. Then I extend the model to represent interaction among agents in Section 3, and discuss the relation between assumptions on MAS and complexity of HMM in Section 4.

M. Ishizuka and A. Sattar (Eds.): PRICAI 2002, LNAI 2417, pp. 128–137, 2002.

2 HMM for Agents with Dynamic Environment

2.1 Agent Model with Environment

In general, an autonomous agent is modeled as a Mealy-type HMM (shown in Figure 1(a)), that is, the agent's behaviors are decided by the following manner:

- The agent has finite internal states.
- The internal state changes in a discrete time step.
- The next state $(s^{\langle t+1 \rangle})$ is determined only by the previous state $(s^{\langle t \rangle})$.
- The agent' action $(a^{\langle t+1 \rangle})$ is selected by the current state-transition $(s^{\langle t \rangle} \rightarrow s^{\langle t+1 \rangle})$.

This formalization lacks the effect of interaction between the agent and the environment. So, we introduce the following assumption:

- The internal state and the environment have a probabilistic relation.

This means that the environment $(e^{\langle t \rangle})$ can be determined by the internal state $(s^{\langle t \rangle})$ under the probabilistic relation $(Pr(e^{\langle t \rangle}|s^{\langle t \rangle}))$. In other words, the changes of the environment can be treated as a Moore-type HMM (Figure 1(b)).

In summary, an agent and its environment can be defined as a following Moore-Mealy-type HMM (MM-HMM).

$$\text{Agent} = \langle S, A, E, P, Q, R, \pi \rangle,$$

where $S = \{s_i\}$ is a set of internal states, $A = \{a_i\}$ is a set of action symbols, $E = \{e_i\}$ is a set of environment symbols, $P = \{p_{ij} = Pr(j^{\langle t+1 \rangle}|i^{\langle t \rangle})|i, j \in S, \forall t\}$ is a probability matrix of state-transitions, $Q = \{q_{ij}(a) = Pr(a^{\langle t+1 \rangle}|i^{\langle t \rangle}, j^{\langle t+1 \rangle})|i, j \in S, a \in A, \forall t\}$ is a probability tensor of actions for each transition, $R = \{r_i(e) = Pr(e^{\langle t \rangle}|i^{\langle t \rangle})|i \in S, e \in E, \forall t\}$ is a probability vector of environment for each state, $\pi = \{\pi_i = Pr(i^{\langle 0 \rangle})\}$ is a probability vector of initial states, and $\langle t \rangle$ on the right shoulder of a variable indicates time t.

2.2 Environment as Output

The above formalization looks little bit strange because it represents environment as output from states rather than as input to state-transitions. Input-output HMMs, in which the environment is treated as input to state-transitions [1,6], can be another candidate to model relations between agents and environments. There are the following different points between these two formalizations:

- When we represent the environment as output, we can apply the HMM for planning. Suppose that initial and goal situations of environment $(e^{\langle 0 \rangle}$ and $e^{\langle T \rangle})$ are given. Then, the planning can be formalized as follows:
  To get the most likely path of state-transitions that maximize the probability $Pr(e^{\langle 0 \rangle}, e^{\langle T \rangle}|\text{Agent})$.

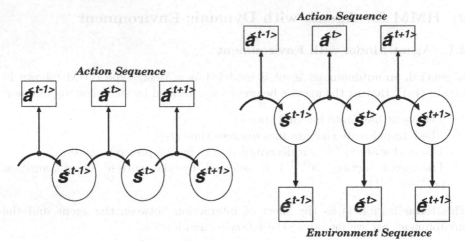

(a) Agent Model by Mealy-type HMM. (b) Agent Model by Moore-Mealy-type HMM.

Fig. 1. Agent HMM.

Because the environment is treated as output in the proposed method, we can seek the most likely path simply using well-known algorithm like Viterbi's one. On the other hand, we need additional simulator or inverse model of environment when the environment is handled as input.

- In the case that we use continuous value for input of HMM, we need to use iterative methods of gradient ascent to learn the parameters in a cycle, which requires more computation power. On the other hand, in the proposed method, we can apply usual adaptation algorithm for HMM.

Representing environment in states, of course, increases complexity of state-transitions, so that the formalization has poor scalability. In the next section, I show a way to overcome this problem.

3   Symmetrically Coupled HMM

3.1   Symmetricity Assumption

In Section 2, we represent changes of environment and agent's intention by a single HMM. However, the number of states increases exponentially when the agent has more complex intentions or behaves in richer environments. This is significant when HMM handles interactions among agents. In this case, we will face *generalization performance problem*: As the number of states or learning parameters increase, the huge number of examples are required to guarantee the generalization performance. In order to avoid this problem, I introduce *symmetricity assumption* among agents as follows:

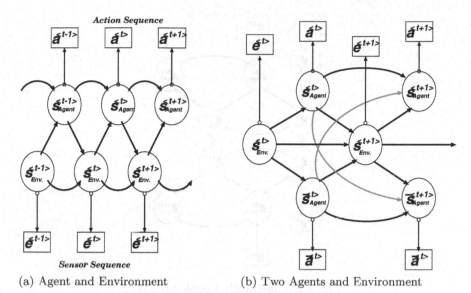

(a) Agent and Environment   (b) Two Agents and Environment

Fig. 2. Coupled HMMs of Agents and Environment.

symmetricity assumption

Every agent has the same rules of behavior. In other words, every agent
shares the same state-transition rules with each other.

To reflect the above assumption in HMM, first, I divide the internal state into
two states, environment state s_e and agent state s_a, and form a coupled HMM as
shown in Figure 2-(a). In this model, sensor data $e^{\langle t \rangle}$ and action command $a^{\langle t \rangle}$
are determined by environment state $s_e^{\langle t \rangle}$ and agent state $s_a^{\langle t \rangle}$ respectively. Transitions of both states are determined as follows: The next environment state $s_e^{\langle t+1 \rangle}$
is determined according to the current environment and agent states $\{s_e^{\langle t \rangle}, s_a^{\langle t \rangle}\}$.
The next agent state $s_a^{\langle t+1 \rangle}$ is determined according to the current agent state
and the new environment $\{s_a^{\langle t \rangle}, s_e^{\langle t+1 \rangle}\}$.

In the second step, I introduce the second agent who cooperates with the
first agent as shown in Figure 2-(b). In this coupling, both state-transitions are
affected by the second agent state $\bar{s}_a^{\langle t \rangle}$. This is summarized as the following
probabilities of state-transitions:

$$Pr(s_e^{\langle t+1 \rangle}|*) = Pr(s_e^{\langle t+1 \rangle}|s_e^{\langle t \rangle}, s_a^{\langle t \rangle}, \bar{s}_a^{\langle t \rangle})$$
$$Pr(s_a^{\langle t+1 \rangle}|*) = Pr(s_a^{\langle t+1 \rangle}|s_a^{\langle t \rangle}, \bar{s}_a^{\langle t \rangle}, s_e^{\langle t+1 \rangle})$$

In order to complete the state-transition for Figure 2-(b), we must consider about
transitions of the second agent state $\bar{s}_a$. Here, I apply *symmetricity assumption*
for the second state-transition, that is, the probabilities of state-transitions of
the second agent are determined by the same one of the first agent. The most
naive implementation of this assumption can be represented by the following the
probabilities:

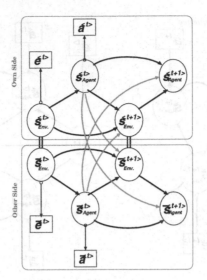

Fig. 3. Symmetrically Coupled HMM.

$$Pr(\bar{s}_{a}^{\langle t+1\rangle}|*) = Pr(\bar{s}_{a}^{\langle t+1\rangle}|\bar{s}_{a}^{\langle t\rangle}, s_{a}^{\langle t\rangle}, s_{e}^{\langle t+1\rangle})$$
$$= Pr(s_{a}^{\langle t+1\rangle} = \bar{s}_{a}^{\langle t+1\rangle}|s_{a}^{\langle t\rangle} = \bar{s}_{a}^{\langle t\rangle}, \bar{s}_{a}^{\langle t\rangle} = s_{a}^{\langle t\rangle}, s_{e}^{\langle t+1\rangle})$$

This formulation is valid when both agents share the same environment state. In general, however, two agents may have different environment states inside of them, because the environment state in this formalization is a kind of internal world state that each agent has independently. Such a situation is not avoidable especially when the sensor data $e^{\langle t\rangle}$ is represented from the viewpoint of each agent. In order to overcome this problem, I propose a *symmetrically coupled HMM* (sCHMM) shown in Figure 3. In this model, the second agent has its own environment state $\bar{s}_{e}^{\langle t\rangle}$. Using this, the transition of $\bar{s}_{a}^{\langle t\rangle}$ are represented as follows:

$$Pr(\bar{s}_{a}^{\langle t+1\rangle}|*) = Pr(s_{a}^{\langle t+1\rangle} = \bar{s}_{a}^{\langle t+1\rangle}|s_{a}^{\langle t\rangle} = \bar{s}_{a}^{\langle t\rangle}, \bar{s}_{a}^{\langle t\rangle} = s_{a}^{\langle t\rangle}, s_{e}^{\langle t+1\rangle} = \bar{s}_{e}^{\langle t+1\rangle}),$$

where the transition of the second environment state $\bar{s}_{e}^{\langle t\rangle}$ follows:

$$Pr(\bar{s}_{e}^{\langle t+1\rangle}|*) = Pr(s_{e}^{\langle t+1\rangle} = \bar{s}_{e}^{\langle t+1\rangle}|s_{e}^{\langle t\rangle} = \bar{s}_{e}^{\langle t\rangle}, s_{a}^{\langle t\rangle} = \bar{s}_{a}^{\langle t\rangle}, \bar{s}_{a}^{\langle t\rangle} = s_{a}^{\langle t\rangle})$$

3.2   Formalization and Learning Procedure

The sCHMM agent described in the previous section can be summarized as the following tuple:

$$\text{Agent} = \langle S_{e}, S_{a}, E, A, P_{e}, P_{a}, Q_{e}, Q_{a}, \pi_{e}, \pi_{a}\rangle,$$

where $S_a = \{s_{ai}\}$ and $S_e = \{s_{ei}\}$ are sets of states for agent and environment respectively, $E = \{e_i\}$ is a set of sensed environment symbols, and $A = \{a_i\}$ is a set of agent action symbols. $P_e = \{p_{eijkl} | i \in S_{env}, j, k \in S_{agt}, \forall t\}$ and $P_a = \{p_{ajklm} | j, k \in S_{agt}, m \in S_{env}, \forall t\}$ are probability tensors of state-transitions of environment and agent respectively, $Q_e = \{q_{ei}(e) | i \in S_e, e \in E, \forall t\}$ and $Q_a = \{q_{aj}(a) | j \in S_a, a \in A, \forall t\}$ are probability tensors of is observed symbols of environment and actions respectively, and $\pi_e = \{\pi_{ei} = Pr(s_e^{\langle 0 \rangle} = i) | i \in S_e\}$ and $\pi_a = \{\pi_{aj} = Pr(s_a^{\langle 0 \rangle} = j) | j \in S_a\}$ are probability vectors of initial states of environment and agent respectively. Each element of P_e, P_a, Q_e, and Q_a represents the following probability.

$$p_{eijkl} = Pr(s_e^{\langle t \rangle} = l \mid s_e^{\langle t-1 \rangle} = i, s_a^{\langle t-1 \rangle} = j, \bar{s}_a^{\langle t-1 \rangle} = k)$$

$$p_{ajklm} = Pr(s_a^{\langle t \rangle} = m \mid s_a^{\langle t-1 \rangle} = j, \bar{s}_a^{\langle t-1 \rangle} = k, s_e^{\langle t \rangle} = l)$$

$$q_{ei}(e) = Pr(e^{\langle t \rangle} = e \mid s_e^{\langle t \rangle} = i)$$

$$q_{aj}(a) = Pr(a^{\langle t \rangle} = a \mid s_a^{\langle t \rangle} = i)$$

We can derive a learning procedure for sCHMM as shown below. Suppose that sequences of sensor information $\{e^{\langle t \rangle}\}$, agent's own actions $\{a^{\langle t \rangle}\}$, and other's actions $\{\bar{a}^{\langle t \rangle}\}$ are observed $(0 \le t < T)$. We can calculate agent's own forward and backward probabilities, $\alpha_{lmn}^{\langle t \rangle}$ and $\beta_{ijk}^{\langle t \rangle}$ respectively, as follows:

$$\alpha_{lmn}^{\langle t \rangle} = \begin{cases} \pi_{el}\pi_{am}\pi_{an}Q_{(lmn)}(W^{\langle 0 \rangle}) & ; t = 0 \\ \displaystyle\sum_{(ijk)} \alpha_{ijk}^{\langle t-1 \rangle} P_{(ijk)(lmn)}Q_{(lmn)}(W^{\langle t \rangle}) & ; otherwise \end{cases}$$

$$\beta_{ijk}^{\langle t \rangle} = \begin{cases} 1 & ; t = T - 1 \\ \displaystyle\sum_{(lmn)} P_{(ijk)(lmn)}Q_{(lmn)}(W^{\langle t+1 \rangle})\beta_{lmn}^{\langle t+1 \rangle} & ; otherwise \end{cases},$$

where

$$P_{(ijk)(lmn)} = p_{eijkl} \cdot p_{ajklm} \cdot p_{akjln}$$

$$Q_{(ijk)}(W^{\langle t \rangle}) = Q_{(ijk)}(e^{\langle t \rangle}, a^{\langle t \rangle}, \bar{a}^{\langle t \rangle})$$

$$= q_{ei}(e^{\langle t \rangle}) \cdot q_{aj}(a^{\langle t \rangle}) \cdot q_{ak}(\bar{a}^{\langle t \rangle})$$

In the same way, forward and backward probabilities of the second agent, $\bar{\alpha}_{lmn}^{\langle t \rangle}$ and $\bar{\beta}_{ijk}^{\langle t \rangle}$, can be calculated as follows:

$$\bar{\alpha}_{lnm}^{\langle t \rangle} = \begin{cases} \pi_{el}\pi_{am}\pi_{an}Q_{(lnm)}(\bar{W}^{\langle 0 \rangle}) & ; t = 0 \\ \displaystyle\sum_{(ikj)} \bar{\alpha}_{ikj}^{\langle t-1 \rangle} P_{(ikj)(lnm)}Q_{(lnm)}(\bar{W}^{\langle t \rangle}) & ; otherwise \end{cases}$$

$$\bar{\beta}_{ikj}^{\langle t \rangle} = \begin{cases} 1 & ; t = T - 1 \\ \displaystyle\sum_{(lnm)} P_{(ikj)(lnm)}Q_{(lnm)}(\bar{W}^{\langle t+1 \rangle})\beta_{lnm}^{\langle t+1 \rangle} & ; otherwise \end{cases},$$

where $\bar{W}^{\langle=\rangle}\{\bar{e}^{\langle t\rangle}, \bar{a}^{\langle t\rangle}, a^{\langle t\rangle}\}$ and $\bar{e}^{\langle t\rangle}$ is the sensor information received by the second agent. Using these probabilities, we can adapt transition and output probabilities $p_{eijkl}, p_{ajklm}, q_{ei}, q_{ej}$ as follows:

$$p_{eijkl} \leftarrow \sum_m \sum_n \hat{P}_{(ijk)(lmn)}$$

$$p_{ajklm} \leftarrow \frac{\sum_i \sum_n \hat{P}_{(ijk)(lmn)}}{\sum_i p_{eijkl}}$$

$$q_{ei}(e) \leftarrow \sum_j \sum_k \sum_a \sum_{\bar{a}} \hat{Q}_{(ijk)}(e, a, \bar{a})$$

$$q_{aj}(a) \leftarrow \sum_i \sum_k \sum_e \sum_{\bar{a}} \hat{Q}_{(ijk)}(e, a, \bar{a}),$$

where

$$\hat{P}_{(ijk)(lmn)} = \frac{\sum_t \xi_{(ijk)(lmn)}^{\langle t\rangle} + \sum_t \bar{\xi}_{(ikj)(lnm)}^{\langle t\rangle}}{\sum_t \gamma_{ijk}^{\langle t-1\rangle} + \sum_t \bar{\gamma}_{ikj}^{\langle t-1\rangle}} \tag{1}$$

$$\hat{Q}_{(ijk)}(W) = \frac{\sum_{t, W^{\langle t\rangle}=W} \gamma(ijk)^{\langle t\rangle} + \sum_{t, W^{\langle t\rangle}=W} \bar{\gamma}_{ikj}^{\langle t\rangle}}{\sum_t \gamma(ijk)^{\langle t\rangle} + \sum_t \bar{\gamma}_{ikj}^{\langle t\rangle}} \tag{2}$$

$$\xi_{(ijk)(lmn)}^{\langle t\rangle} = \alpha_{(ijk)}^{\langle t-1\rangle} P_{(ijk)(lmn)} Q_{(lmn)}(W^{\langle t\rangle}) \beta_{(lmn)}^{\langle t\rangle}$$

$$\bar{\xi}_{(ikj)(lnm)}^{\langle t\rangle} = \bar{\alpha}_{(ikj)}^{\langle t-1\rangle} P_{(ikj)(lnm)} Q_{(lnm)}(\bar{W}^{\langle t\rangle}) \bar{\beta}_{(lnm)}^{\langle t\rangle}$$

$$\gamma_{(lmn)}^{\langle t\rangle} = \alpha_{(lmn)}^{\langle t\rangle} \beta_{(lmn)}^{\langle t\rangle}$$

$$\bar{\gamma}_{(lnm)}^{\langle t\rangle} = \bar{\alpha}_{(lnm)}^{\langle t\rangle} \bar{\beta}_{(lnm)}^{\langle t\rangle}$$

4   Discussion: The Number of Parameters in the Model

As mentioned before, the number of parameters in HMM is an important factor for generalization performance of learning. In the case of coupled HMM, especially, the number of parameters increase exponentially. Actually, if we use the model shown in Figure 2-(b) without symmetricity assumption, the number of parameters in the state-transition is

$$|S_e|^2 |S_a|^N + N |S_e| |S_a|^{N+1}$$

where N is the number of agents. This is already reduced from the number of parameters $(|S_e||S_a|^N)^2$ in the case we represent the same model using single HMM. Compared with this, symmetrically coupled HMM has fewer parameters as follows:

$$|S_e|^2 |S_a|^N + |S_e| |S_a|^{N+1}$$

In addition to it, the symmetricity assumption increases the virtual number of examples. Eq. 1 and Eq. 2 mean that the same HMM can be trained by using both pairs of $\{e^{\langle t \rangle}, a^{\langle t \rangle}\}$ and $\{\bar{e}^{\langle t \rangle}, \bar{a}^{\langle t \rangle}\}$ for a given observation $\{e^{\langle t \rangle}, a^{\langle t \rangle}, \bar{a}^{\langle t \rangle}\}$. As a result, the generalization performance of learning is improved by the virtually doubled examples.

It is, however, true that an sCHMM still has too many parameters for real applications. Therefore, it is meaningful to introduce additional assumptions to reduce the number of parameter. Fortunately, in the case of cooperative interaction in the multi-agent systems, we can pick-up reasonable assumptions as follows:

– *"no explicit communication"* assumption: In the formalization of sCHMM, the transition of the agent state is affected by the previous states of other agents. This means that agents use explicit communication with each other. In the case of human cooperative behaviors like real soccer, on the other hand, we do not use so much explicit communication, but guess others' intentions via sensor information instead. In such case, the transition of the agent state can be represented as follows:

$$Pr(s_a^{\langle t+1 \rangle}|*) = Pr(s_a^{\langle t+1 \rangle}|s_a^{\langle t \rangle}, s_e^{\langle t+1 \rangle})$$

In this case, the total number of the parameters is reduced to:

$$|S_e|^2 |S_a|^N + |S_e| |S_a|^2$$

– *"filtering"* assumption: Usually, when we write a code of agent behavior, we classify states systematically. For example, in the code shown in Section 1 states are grouped by agent's roles (agent states) first then branched by world status (environment states) second. This can be represented by the following manner in the transition of HMM:

$$Pr(s_a^{\langle t+1 \rangle}|*) = Pr(s_a^{\langle t+1 \rangle}|s_e^{\langle t+1 \rangle}) \cdot Pr(s_a^{\langle t+1 \rangle}|s_a^{\langle t \rangle})$$

In this case, the number of parameters are reduced to:

$$|S_e|^2 |S_a|^N + |S_e| |S_a| + |S_a|^{N+1}$$

– *"shared joint intention"* assumption: During a cooperation of multiple agents each agent believes that all agents share the joint intention. This means that each agent believes that other agents will behave as it wants. In this case, the transition of environment states can be represented as follows:

$$Pr(s_e^{\langle t+1 \rangle}|*) = Pr(s_e^{\langle t+1 \rangle}|s_e^{\langle t \rangle}, s_a^{\langle t \rangle})$$

This will reduce the number of parameters to:

$$|S_e|^2 |S_a| + |S_e| |S_a|^{N+1}$$

Note that this assumption can not be applied with the *"no explicit communication"* assumption, because the sCHMM is reduced into a simple CHMM like Figure 2-(a) that does not reflect cooperation among agents.

5 Related Works

Brand et al. [2,4] proposed coupled HMM and its learning method, in which several HMMs are coupled via inter-HMM dependencies. Jordan et al. [7,3, 5] proposed factorial HMM and hidden Markov decision trees. Both of works mainly focused on reducing the complexity in EM processes. Even using these HMMs, the complexity of calculation of a naive implementation increase exponentially, so that it is hard to handle the large number of states. They use mean field approximation or N-heads dynamic programming to reduce the cost of the approximation of posterior probabilities. However, they does not focused on symmetricity in agent-interactions and generalization performance problem.

These methods can be applicable to our model. Actually, a naive implementation of learning method derived in the previous section costs $O(TN^4M^2)$, which is too huge for dynamical application like soccer. Above methods will reduce the cost into $O(TN^2M)$, which is reasonable cost for real application.

6 Concluding Remarks

In this article, we proposed a formalization of MAS as HMM to represent interaction among agents and environments. In order to avoid the explosion of the number of parameters, I introduced *symmetricity assumptions* among agents, and propose *symmetrically coupled HMM* (sCHMM) and its learning procedure. I also investigated various assumption of MAS, by which the number of parameters in HMM is reduced effectively.

There are the following open issues on the proposed method:

- The cost of calculation increases exponentially when structures of agents and environments become complicated. In order to reduce the complexity, several techniques like mean field approximation and N-head dynamic programming should be applied to these models.
- The incremental learning will suit to acquire high-level cooperative behaviors. We may be able to realize the step-by-step learning using dependency of the initial parameters.

References

1. Yoshua Bengio and Paolo Frasconi. An input output hmm architecuture. In G. Tesauro, D. Touretzky, and T. Leen, editors, *Advances in Neural Information Processing Systems*, pages 427–434. The MIT Press, 1995.
2. Matthew Brand. Coupled hideen markov models for modeling interacting processes. Perceptual Computing/Learning and Common Sense Technical Report 405, MIT Lab, jun 1997.
3. Zoubin Ghahramani and Michael I. Jordan. Factorial hidden markov models. *Machine Learning*, 29:245–275, 1997.
4. Coupled hidden Markov models for complex action recognition. Matthew brand and nuria oliver and alex pentland. Perceptual Computing/Learning and Common Sense Technical Report 407, MIT Media Lab, 20 1996.

5. Michael I. Jordan, Zoubin Ghahramani, Tommi Jaakkola, and Lawrence K. Saul. An introduction to variational methods for graphical models. *Machine Learning*, 37(2):183–233, 1999.
6. Michael I. Jordan, Zoubin Ghahramani, and Lawrence K. Saul. Hidden markov decision trees. In Michael C. Mozer, Michael I. Jordan, and Thomas Petsche, editors, *Advances in Neural Information Processing Systems*, volume 9, page 501. The MIT Press, 1997.
7. Michael I. Jordan, Zoubin Ghahramani, and Lawrence K. Saul. Hidden markov decision trees. In Michael C. Mozer, Michael I. Jordan, and Thomas Petsche, editors, *Advances in Neural Information Processing Systems 9*, page 501. The MIT Press, 1997.
8. Nuria M. Oliver, Barbara Rosario, and Alex Pentland. A bayesian computer vision system for modeling human interactions. *IEEE Transactions on Pattern Analysis and Machine Intelligence*, 22(8):831–843, 2000.

Modelling PRS-Like Agents' Mental States

Wayne Wobcke

School of Computer Science and Engineering
University of New South Wales
Sydney NSW 2052, Australia
wobcke@cse.unsw.edu.au

Abstract. In recent years, there have been increased efforts towards defining rigorous operational semantics for a range of agent programming languages. At the same time, there have been increased efforts to develop logical frameworks for modelling belief, desire and intention (and related notions) that make closer connections to the workings of particular architectures, thus aiming to provide some computational interpretation of these abstract models. However, there remains a substantial gap between the more abstract logical approaches and the more computationally oriented operational approaches. In this paper, we present a modelling of the mental states of PRS-like agents developed using a combination of dynamic logic and BDI logic that allows a mapping between the operational semantics and the model-theoretic semantics, considering the statics, though not the dynamics, of mental states. This represents a first step towards bridging the gap between theory and practice for an agent programming language that includes a simple notion of intention.

1   Introduction

As more agent programming languages are designed and more implementations of existing languages developed, there is an increased need to provide such languages with precise definitions. For agent languages and systems, two types of semantic definition have been the focus of much research: operational semantics, usually in Plotkin-style transition systems, and "denotational" semantics, usually based on modal logic with Kripke-style possible worlds semantics, including such descendants as temporal logic and dynamic logic. However, especially for languages based on a BDI (Belief, Desire, Intention) agent architecture, there remains a substantial gap between the two levels of semantic description. This gap means that "cognitive" properties of agents, such as rationality and commitment, that are typically modelled at the higher "denotational" level of abstraction, are not systematically connected to the properties of implemented agents as described at the operational level.

In recent years, there have been increased efforts towards defining rigorous operational semantics for a range of agent programming languages. In this paper, we focus on languages based on the BDI architecture as embodied in PRS and its variants, Georgeff and Lansky [8], Georgeff and Ingrand [7], Lee *et al.* [12], and the abstract architecture of Rao and Georgeff [15]. However, precisely because operational definitions typically dispense with "cognitive" concepts such

M. Ishizuka and A. Sattar (Eds.): PRICAI 2002, LNAI 2417, pp. 138–147, 2002.
© Springer-Verlag Berlin Heidelberg 2002

as rationality, commitment and goal-directedness, in favour of notions such as process, concurrency and (computational) environment and state, an operational semantics provides only limited assistance to developers of agent programs in reasoning about these higher-level properties. A contributing factor is that, whereas for the case of knowledge, there is a standard way of *ascribing* knowledge to an agent derived from the computational interpretation of its program, as in the approach of Fagin *et al.* [6], the notions of belief, desire and intention do not enjoy this property – at least not for the specific notions employed in PRS style languages.[1]

On the other hand, starting with the work of Cohen and Levesque [3], there has been a strand of research aiming to formalize the logical properties of intention – both as understood by Bratman [1] and as instantiated in various BDI agent architectures, e.g. Rao and Georgeff [14], Konolige and Pollack [11], Wooldridge [18]. One major problem with such semantic modelling from the point of view of agent programming is that there is no clear way of mapping the abstract BDI models onto the computational states of an implemented agent (i.e. the converse problem to that described above), although the work of Singh [17] on strategies, and of Cavedon and Rao [2] on plans is a step in this direction. The consequence is that any properties of an agent's mental states that are shown to hold in virtue of some semantic modelling do not necessarily apply to the implemented agent being modelled, potentially making the higher-level analysis irrelevant for practical considerations.

In this paper, we provide a modelling for the semantics of PRS-like agents' mental states, focusing on the statics of such states (we do not consider belief revision or intention update in this paper). We present a logical modelling of PRS-like agent programs based on a new logic which we call Agent Dynamic Logic (ADL), that combines elements from Emerson and Clarke's Computation Tree Logic [5], Pratt's Propositional Dynamic Logic [13] and Rao and Georgeff's BDI Logic [14].

We begin with brief summaries of Computation Tree Logic and BDI Logic.

2   Computation Tree Logic

In Computation Tree Logic (CTL), Emerson and Clarke [5], the basic idea is that temporal logic formulae are evaluated over a tree-like branching time structure whose states correspond to the internal states of a computation, and whose branches represent possible computation sequences. A distinction is made between *path* formulae and *state* formulae: path formulae are evaluated with respect to paths, i.e. single branches in the time tree (so refer to the properties of a single possible computation sequence), while state formulae are evaluated with respect to states (so refer to properties of the set of possible computation sequences emanating from a state).

---

[1] *ConGolog*, de Giacomo *et al.* [4], is exceptional in having both an operational semantics and a semantics based on the situation calculus; however, this higher-level semantics does not capture a notion of intention.

Definition 1. *The* CTL *path formulae are defined as follows. If* α *and* β *are state formulae, then* $\Box\alpha$ *(henceforth* α *holds),* $\Diamond\alpha$ *(eventually* α *holds),* $\bigcirc\alpha$ *(* α *holds in the next state) and* $\alpha\mathcal{U}\beta$ *(eventually* β *holds and* α *holds until* β *holds) are path formulae.*

Definition 2. *The* CTL *state formulae are defined as follows. First, any formula of the base propositional language* $\mathcal{L}$ *is a state formula. Second, if* α *is a path formula, then* $\mathsf{A}\alpha$ *(* α *holds on all paths) and* $\mathsf{E}\alpha$ *(* α *holds on some path) are state formulae.*

Definition 3. *A* CTL *time tree* $\langle \mathcal{T}, \prec \rangle$ *is a nonempty set of time points* $\mathcal{T}$ *and a binary relation* $\prec$ *on* $\mathcal{T}$ *that is irreflexive, transitive, discrete, serial, backwards linear and rooted.*

Definition 4. *A path in a* CTL *time tree* $\langle \mathcal{T}, \prec \rangle$ *is a maximal subset* $\mathcal{T}'$ *of* $\mathcal{T}$ *for which* $\prec$ *restricted to* $\mathcal{T}'$ *is connected (for all* $t, u \in \mathcal{T}'$, $t \prec u$, $u \prec t$ *or* $t = u$).

Definition 5. *A subtree of a* CTL *time tree* $\langle \mathcal{T}, \prec \rangle$ *is a time tree* $\langle \mathcal{T}', \prec' \rangle$ *where* $\mathcal{T}' \subseteq \mathcal{T}$, $\prec' \subseteq \prec$ *is* $\prec$ *restricted to the elements of* $\mathcal{T}'$ *and the following condition is satisfied.*

   path complete   *for all* $t, u \in \mathcal{T}'$, $v \in \mathcal{T}$, *if* $t \prec v \prec u$ *then* $v \in \mathcal{T}'$

The following definition of a "world" is from Rao and Georgeff [14].

Definition 6. *Let* $\mathcal{S}$ *be a nonempty set of states. A world* w *over a* CTL *time tree* $\langle \mathcal{T}, \prec \rangle$ *based on* $\mathcal{S}$ *is a function on* $\mathcal{T}$ *giving a state* $w_t \in \mathcal{S}$ *for each time point* $t \in \mathcal{T}$ *(in the context of a particular world* w, w_t *is called a* situation*). For convenience, say that time points and paths in* $\mathcal{T}$ *are also time points and paths in* w.

Finally, the semantics of CTL state and path formulae can be defined with respect to (time points and paths in) worlds using the following definitions. The properties of trees ensure that the first two auxiliary definitions are well defined.

Definition 7. *For any point* t *in a* CTL *time tree* $\langle \mathcal{T}, \prec \rangle$, *the subtree of* $\langle \mathcal{T}, \prec \rangle$ *generated from* t, *denoted* $\langle \mathcal{T}_t, \prec_t \rangle$, *is defined to be that subtree of* $\langle \mathcal{T}, \prec \rangle$ *consisting of the set of points* $\mathcal{T}_t = \{u \in \mathcal{T} : t \preceq u\}$, *where* $\prec_t$ *is defined as* $\prec$ *restricted to* $\mathcal{T}_t$.

Definition 8. *Let* $\langle \mathcal{T}, \prec \rangle$ *be a* CTL *time tree, let* p *be a path in* $\mathcal{T}$ *and let* t *be a time point in* p. *The successor* $s_p(t)$ *of* t *in* p *is that state* $u \in p$ *for which* $t \prec u$ *but there is no* $v \in p$ *with* $t \prec v \prec u$.

Definition 9. *Let* $\mathcal{S}$ *be a set of states and let* $\mathcal{L}$ *be a language for expressing time-independent properties of states (we assume there is a satisfaction relation* $\models$ *between states and formulae of* $\mathcal{L}$*). Let* w *be a world over a* CTL *time tree* $\langle \mathcal{T}, \prec \rangle$ *based on* $\mathcal{S}$. *Then* w *satisfies a* CTL *formula at a time point* t *in* $\mathcal{T}$ *as follows.*

$$w \models_t \alpha \qquad\quad \textit{if } w_t \models \alpha, \textit{ for } \alpha \textit{ a formula of } \mathcal{L}$$
$$w \models_t \mathsf{A}\alpha \qquad\quad \textit{if } w \models_p \alpha \textit{ for every path } p \textit{ in } \langle \mathcal{T}_t, \prec_t \rangle$$
$$w \models_t \mathsf{E}\alpha \qquad\quad \textit{if } w \models_p \alpha \textit{ for some path } p \textit{ in } \langle \mathcal{T}_t, \prec_t \rangle$$

$$w \models_p \square\alpha \qquad\quad \textit{if } w \models_u \alpha \textit{ for every } u \in p$$
$$w \models_p \Diamond\alpha \qquad\quad \textit{if } w \models_u \alpha \textit{ for some } u \in p$$
$$w \models_p \bigcirc\alpha \qquad\quad \textit{if } w \models_{s_p(t)} \alpha$$
$$w \models_p \alpha\mathcal{U}\beta \qquad\; \textit{if there is } u \in p \textit{ with } w \models_u \beta, \textit{ and } w \models_v \alpha \textit{ for every}$$
$$v \in p \textit{ with } v \prec u$$

3   BDI Logic

To enable Computation Tree Logic to be used for modelling rational agents, Rao and Georgeff [14] extended CTL with modal operators for modelling beliefs, desires (goals) and intentions. In this section, we give a reconstruction of this framework more suited to modelling PRS-like agents. The basic notion is a BDI interpretation, which in Rao and Georgeff's framework, is a set of worlds over the subtrees of a single time tree, where this time tree is a branching time structure as described above, and each "world" consists of an assignment of a state to each time point in the tree over which it is based. The semantics is augmented to include (accessibility) relations on situations corresponding to each modality, see also Wooldridge [18].

The following definition is a simplification of Rao and Georgeff's in that only the propositional version is given, and also a slight modification, in that the set of states $\mathcal{S}$ is made explicit. However, in our version of the logic, which we call BDI-CTL, we introduce a modification to the language that makes it more suitable for reasoning about PRS-like agents. In particular, the language BDI-CTL includes three modal operators, B (belief), G (goal) and I (intention), but the operators G and I are defined in terms of other primitives that are based on elements of dynamic logic.

The formal definitions of the accessibility relations in Rao and Georgeff's framework rely on the notion of a subworld of a world. A subworld of a world w contains, for each time point t, a subset of the possible futures of t that w admits, according to whether or not the corresponding path is contained in the subtree from which the subworld is derived.

Definition 10. *A* subworld *of a world w over a time tree $\langle \mathcal{T}, \prec \rangle$ based on a set of states $\mathcal{S}$ is the world w restricted to a subtree of $\langle \mathcal{T}, \prec \rangle$ whose root is the root of w.*

Definition 11. *A* BDI interpretation *is a tuple $\langle \mathcal{T}, \prec, \mathcal{S}, \mathcal{W}, \mathcal{B}, \mathcal{I} \rangle$ where $\langle \mathcal{T}, \prec \rangle$ is a time tree, $\mathcal{S}$ is a nonempty set of states, $\mathcal{W}$ is a nonempty set of worlds based on $\mathcal{S}$ with each world over a subtree of $\langle \mathcal{T}, \prec \rangle$, $\mathcal{B}$ is a subset of $\mathcal{W} \times \mathcal{T} \times \mathcal{W}$ defined only for tuples (w, t, w') for which t is a time point in w and w', and $\mathcal{I}$ is a function $\mathcal{W} \times \mathcal{T} \to \mathcal{W}$ mapping each time point t in a world w to a subworld of w whose root is t.*

Any particular world $w \in \mathcal{W}$ defines a set of futures the agent considers possible starting from the initial situation in that world. Since each world is based on a branching time structure, the actions are modelled as being non-deterministic. However, since the agent has only partial information about its environment, it may be ignorant of exactly which situation it is embedded in; the agent considers only that it is embedded in a situation in which its current beliefs are true. This ignorance is captured using the relation $\mathcal{B}$. More formally, the beliefs of the agent in some situation w_t (at a time point t in a world w) are precisely those propositions holding at all epistemic alternatives w', i.e. in those situations w'_t such that $\mathcal{B}(w, t, w')$. The relation on situations is assumed to be symmetric, transitive and Euclidean, and moreover, the relations $\mathcal{B}$ and $\mathcal{I}$ are assumed to satisfy the condition that $\mathcal{B}(w, t, w')$ iff $\mathcal{B}(\mathcal{I}(w), t, \mathcal{I}(w'))$, i.e. the epistemic alternatives of $\mathcal{I}(w)$ at t are the intended subworlds of the epistemic alternatives of w at t.

The intentions of the agent are those actions the agent considers that eventually it will successfully perform, according its current view of the world, i.e. not taking into account the potential for the world to change so as to force the agent to revise or abandon its intentions. Intentions are modelled using the function $\mathcal{I}$, which defines, for any particular world, which futures in that world are intended by the agent: in the "intended" futures, all the agent's actions are performed successfully. More formally, the intentions of an agent with respect to a world w are those action formulae π for which on all possible futures in $\mathcal{I}(w)$, the agent does π, i.e. the intentions of an agent are represented by formulae of the form $\mathsf{BA}\Diamond do(\pi)$, and this is the basis of the definition below. For the purposes of exposition, in this section, we will simply assume that each formula $do(\pi)$ is an atomic propositional formula satisfiable at a situation. Finally, the goals of the agent are simply those formulae α such that the agent intends to perform the action $achieve\ \gamma$.

Definition 12. *Let $\langle \mathcal{T}, \prec, \mathcal{S}, \mathcal{W}, \mathcal{B}, \mathcal{I} \rangle$ be a BDI interpretation. Then a world $w \in \mathcal{W}$ satisfies a BDI logic formula at a time point t in w as follows.*

$$w \models_t \mathsf{B}\alpha \quad \textit{if } w' \models_t \alpha \textit{ whenever } \mathcal{B}(w, t, w')$$
$$w \models_t \mathsf{I}\pi \quad \textit{if } \mathcal{I}(w) \models_t \mathsf{BA}\Diamond do(\pi)$$
$$w \models_t \mathsf{G}\gamma \quad \textit{if } w \models_t \mathsf{I}(\text{achieve } \gamma)$$

4   Agent Dynamic Logic

In this section, we adapt BDI logic to include a modelling of PRS-like agent programs using dynamic logic. In Propositional Dynamic Logic (PDL), Pratt [13], see also Goldblatt [9], the execution of a standard computer program is modelled using transition functions over internal machine states. For such programs, execution is assumed always to be successful (though not necessarily terminating) and machine states are assumed to change only as the result of program execution. However, in modelling agent programs, both these assumptions need to be relaxed: success is not always guaranteed and the environment is subject to change due to forces external to the agent. Moreover, though this is not considered in this paper, the agent's mental states (beliefs, goals and intentions) also change through time.

Analogous to PDL, the language ADL (Agent Dynamic Logic) includes modal operators corresponding to each program (concrete hierarchical plan) ϕ, and the semantics is based on computation trees, as in the approach of Harel [10]. However, the semantics is much more closely aligned to the behaviour of the PRS-like interpreter than more general earlier frameworks for modelling action, e.g. Segerberg [16], Singh [17] and Cavedon and Rao [2]. In particular, we aim, following Cavedon and Rao's work, to make explicit reference to the dynamic logic of action in modelling the agent's intentions.

The original semantics of PDL was defined in terms of a family of binary state transition relations $\mathcal{R}_\pi$, one for each program π. The relation $\mathcal{R}_\pi$ is intended to capture the possible input-output pairs corresponding to π: more precisely, $\langle s, t \rangle \in \mathcal{R}_\pi$ iff t is a state that can be reached through executing π starting at the initial state s. In ADL, an interpretation consists of a family of BDI interpretations (sets of worlds) $\mathcal{R}_\pi$, one for each (agent) program, with the important modification that the worlds may be over trees with finite branches. This derives from the semantics of PDL based on computation trees developed by Harel [10].

The reason for using BDI interpretations to capture the meaning of programs, rather than just worlds (or computation trees in Harel's sense), is that the meaning of the test statement in the PRS-like language must be defined with respect to the agent's belief states, not with respect to world states. In our semantics, *states* are understood as world states external to the agent, not machine states internal to the agent. Now consider the conditional and iterative constructs. In standard PDL, the *if-then-else* and *while* statements are defined in terms of the sequencing, union, iteration and test primitives as follows.

$$\textbf{if } \alpha \textbf{ then } \pi \textbf{ else } \chi \equiv (\alpha?; \pi) \cup (\neg\alpha?; \chi)$$
$$\textbf{while } \alpha \textbf{ do } \pi \equiv (\alpha?; \pi)^*; \neg\alpha?$$

But the conditional and iterative constructs in PRS agent programs behave very differently: the tests in the PRS statements are tests, not on the state of the world, but on the agent's belief state (a distinction not needed for standard PDL). Thus the set of possible worlds that realize an execution of a PRS-like agent's program must ultimately be defined with respect to the agent's beliefs (at execution time).

Definition 13. *A PRS interpretation is a pair $\langle \mathcal{S}, \mathcal{R} \rangle$, where $\mathcal{S}$ is a set of states and $\mathcal{R}$ is a family of sets of BDI interpretations $\mathcal{R}_\pi$ based on $\mathcal{S}$, one such BDI interpretation for each program π.*

Definition 14. *Let $\langle \mathcal{S}, \mathcal{R} \rangle$ be a PRS interpretation and $\langle \mathcal{T}, \prec, \mathcal{S}, \mathcal{W}, \mathcal{B}, \mathcal{I} \rangle$ be a BDI interpretation. Then a world $w \in \mathcal{W}$ satisfies the formula $do(\pi)$ at a time point t in w as follows.*

$w \models_t do(\pi)$ *if some subworld of w is the prefix of a world in $\mathcal{R}_\pi$*

Definition 15. *A subworld w is a prefix of a world w' if for each end node n of w, there is a world w_n such that replacing each n in w by w_n results in the world w'.*

Each primitive action π (except for the special action *achieve* γ – see below), is assumed to be modelled by a set of worlds each over a computation tree of depth 1, one world for each possible initial state $s \in \mathcal{S}$: call such a world a π-world. Each π-world with root s has one child state for each possible outcome of executing the action π in s. In addition, a subworld of each π-world is assumed to define the successful executions of π (note that this makes the notion of success state dependent). This definition is meant to capture both the nondeterminism inherent in action execution, a feature of standard programs that can also be modelled in PDL, and also the notion of intended successful execution of an action. Now each BDI interpretation contains a set of worlds, with the situations in those worlds possibly related under the epistemic alternative and intended future relations $\mathcal{B}$ and $\mathcal{I}$. The meaning of each $\mathcal{R}_\pi$ is a set of BDI interpretations where the initial situations of all the worlds in the interpretation form a single equivalence class of epistemic alternatives, and where the relation $\mathcal{I}$ is defined by inheriting this relation from each world (this makes the notion of success independent of the agent's beliefs).

We need to define operations on sets of BDI interpretations that correspond to the program construction operators, in particular for sequencing, alternation and iteration, which, in standard PDL, are expressed using composition, set union and reflexive, transitive closure (of binary state transitions relations). The operation for sequencing is a kind of "concatenation" of worlds, analogous to concatenation of computation sequences. Let w_1 and w_2 be worlds over time trees $\mathcal{T}_1$ and $\mathcal{T}_2$, let s be an end point of $\mathcal{T}_1$ and let r be the root of $\mathcal{T}_2$. Say w_2 *extends* w_1 at s if the state associated with s, $w_1(s)$, equals that associated with r in $\mathcal{T}_2$, $w_2(r)$, and the set of states associated with the epistemic alternatives of $w_1(s)$ is the same as that associated with the epistemic alternatives of $w_2(r)$. Then the concatenation of w_1 and w_2, denoted $w_1 \oplus w_2$, is a world over a time tree in which, intuitively, each state at each end point s of $\mathcal{T}_1$ is replaced by a copy of the world w_2 whenever w_2 extends w_1 at s. The definition of $w_1 \oplus w_2$ can be made more precise as follows.

Definition 16. *Let w_1 and w_2 be worlds (in BDI interpretations) over time trees $\langle \mathcal{T}_1, \prec_1 \rangle$ and $\langle \mathcal{T}_2, \prec_2 \rangle$. Let S be the set of end points of $\mathcal{T}_1$, and let S' be the subset of S for which $w_1(s) = w_2(r_2)$ where r_2 is the root of $\mathcal{T}_2$, and $\{root(w) : \mathcal{B}(w_1, s, w)\} = \{root(w) : \mathcal{B}(w_2, r, w)\}$, where $root(w)$ is the state associated with the root of w. For each element s of S', let w_2^s be a world over a tree $\mathcal{T}_2^s$ structurally isomorphic to $\mathcal{T}_2$, whose valuation, precedence and accessibility relations are the same as w_2 on corresponding elements. Then the concatenation of w_1 and w_2, denoted $w_1 \oplus w_2$ is defined over a tree consisting of $\mathcal{T}_1 - S'$ and all the sets $\mathcal{T}_2^s$ with a precedence ordering $\prec$ extending $\prec_1$ and all the $\prec_2^s$ by also defining $t_1 \prec t_2$ if $t_1 \in \mathcal{T}_1 - S'$, $t_1 \prec_1 s$ and $t_2 \in \mathcal{T}_2^s$.*

If W_1 and W_2 are sets of worlds, $W_1 \oplus W_2$ is the set of worlds formed by simultaneously concatenating, for each end point s of each world w_1 in W_1, w_1

and a world w_2 in W_2 that extends w_1 at s (if one exists). We assume that for each distinct state, there is only one world in W_2 whose root is associated with that state, hence there is at most one world in W_2 that extends w_1 at s, for any given end point s of w_1.

For alternation, we utilize an operation that merges two worlds if they have identical initial states. Let w_1 and w_2 be worlds over time trees $\mathcal{T}_1$ and $\mathcal{T}_2$ with roots r_1 and r_2, and suppose that $w_1(r_1) = w_2(r_2)$ and the set of states associated with the epistemic alternatives of both situations are the same. Then the merger of w_1 and w_2, denoted $w_1 \uplus w_2$, is that world formed by identifying the two roots and joining together w_1 and w_2 at this situation.

Definition 17. *Let w_1 and w_2 be worlds (in BDI interpretations) over time trees $\langle \mathcal{T}_1, \prec_1 \rangle$ and $\langle \mathcal{T}_2, \prec_2 \rangle$ with roots r_1 and r_2, such that $w_1(r_1) = w_2(r_2)$ and $\{root(w) : \mathcal{B}(w_1, r_1, w)\} = \{root(w) : \mathcal{B}(w_2, r_2, w)\}$, where $root(w)$ is the state associated with the root of w. Let the tree $\mathcal{T}$ be defined as the set of time points $\mathcal{T}_1 \cup \mathcal{T}_2$ in which r_1 (and its epistemic alternatives) and r_2 (and its corresponding epistemic alternatives) are identified, and with $\prec$ defined as $\prec_1 \cup \prec_2$] (so that the identified r_1 and r_2 is the root of $\mathcal{T}$, and the children of this node are the children of r_1 from $\mathcal{T}_1$ and of r_2 from $\mathcal{T}_2$). Then the merger of w_1 and w_2, denoted $w_1 \uplus w_2$, is the world defined over the tree $\langle \mathcal{T}, \prec \rangle$ that is inherited from w_1 and w_2, i.e. $(w_1 \uplus w_2)(t)$ is $w_1(t)$ if $t \in \mathcal{T}_1$ and is $w_2(t)$ if $t \in \mathcal{T}_2$.*

If W_1 and W_2 are sets of worlds (each set containing at most one world with any given initial state), $W_1 \uplus W_2$ is the set of worlds formed by merging all pairs of worlds w_1 and w_2 in $W_1 \cup W_2$ whose roots have identical states and equivalent sets of epistemic alternatives.

We can finally give the constraints on the sets of computation trees $\mathcal{R}_\pi$ that ensure that each respects the operational semantics of the program construction operators.

$$\mathcal{R}_{\pi;\chi} = \mathcal{R}_\pi \oplus \mathcal{R}_\chi$$
$$\mathcal{R}_{\pi \cup \chi} = \mathcal{R}_\pi \uplus \mathcal{R}_\chi$$
$$\mathcal{R}_{\pi^*} = \mathcal{R}_\pi^* \text{ (the reflexive, transitive closure of } \mathcal{R}_\pi \text{ under } \oplus)$$
$$\mathcal{R}_{\alpha?} = \wp(\{\langle s, s \rangle : s \in \mathcal{S}, s \models \alpha\}) - \emptyset$$

In the definition for the test statement $\alpha?$, $\langle s, s \rangle$ denotes a tree with two elements, a root node and a child node, both with the associated state s, and $\wp$ denotes the powerset constructor, assuming all initial situations of the trees in any element of the powerset are belief equivalent (so such situations satisfy $B\alpha$).

The family of relations $\mathcal{R}_\pi$ must be extended from programs to (concrete hierarchical) plans. Let $\mathcal{W}$ denote the set of all possible worlds, B_0 the set of BDI interpretations all of whose worlds are of depth 0, and define $b \models \alpha$ for a BDI interpretation with set of worlds $\mathcal{W}$ if for each world $w \in \mathcal{W}$, $w \models_t \alpha$ where t is the root of w. Then the family of relations R_π must be extended to sets of concrete hierarchical plans. The definition below is based on the definition of concurrency as sequence interleaving. The operator $|$ is used to denote list concatenation, i.e. $[\pi | P]$ denotes a plan whose highest level program is π and which has a suffix P.

Definition 18. *The relations $\mathcal{R}_\pi$ for the empty program Λ and for programs* achieve γ *corresponding to a subgoal γ are defined as follows.*

$$\mathcal{R}_\Lambda = B_0$$
$$\mathcal{R}_{\text{achieve } \gamma} = \biguplus \{\mathcal{R}_\pi \cap \{b : b \models pre(\pi) \wedge context(\pi)\} : \pi \in L, post(\pi) \vdash \gamma\}$$

Here $pre(\pi)$, $post(\pi)$ and $context(\pi)$ are the precondition, postcondition and context of a plan π in the plan library L. Thus Λ is executable in every situation in every world, and leaves the state unchanged, while achieve γ is modelled as a set of PRS interpretations in which γ is achieved by the successful execution of a (hierarchical) plan built from plans in the plan library. Note carefully that this condition is actually a set of recursive definitions of $\mathcal{R}_{\text{achieve } \gamma}$ for all formulae γ at once; it is recursive because the plans π may include subgoals of the form achieve δ (and here, of course, δ may be γ). Thus the meaning of achieve γ involves a least fixpoint construction.

Definition 19. *Let P be a concrete hierarchical plan. Then the relation $\mathcal{R}_P$ is defined as follows.*

- $\mathcal{R}_{[\pi]} = \mathcal{R}_\pi$
- *if π is* achieve $\gamma; \chi$ *then* $\mathcal{R}_{[\pi|P]} = \mathcal{R}_P \oplus \mathcal{R}_\chi$, *otherwise* $\mathcal{R}_{[\pi|P]} = \mathcal{R}_P \oplus \mathcal{R}_\pi$

Definition 20. *Let I be a set of concrete hierarchical plans. Then the set of worlds R_I corresponding to I is defined as $\mathcal{R}_I = \bigotimes_{P \in I} \mathcal{R}_P$, where $\bigotimes$ denotes interleaving of a set of worlds indexed by a set $\mathbb{I}$: $\bigotimes_{i \in \mathbb{I}} W_i$ is the smallest set of worlds satisfying the following condition.*

$$\bigotimes_{i \in \mathbb{I}} W_i = \{head(W_i) \oplus W_i' : i \in \mathbb{I} \text{ and } W_i' \in \bigotimes_{i \in \mathbb{I}} \{W - W_i \cup tails(W_i)\}\}$$

Here, $head(w)$ is the subworld of w derived from the subtree of depth 1 starting at the root of w, and $tails(w)$ is the set of worlds that are derived from those subtrees of w whose root nodes are the children of the root node of w.

5   Conclusion

We presented a formal modelling of the mental states of PRS-like agents based on a combination of Computation Tree Logic, Propositional Dynamic Logic and BDI Logic called Agent Dynamic Logic. This provides a modelling much more closely aligned to the operational semantics of PRS-like agents than in previous work, and to some extent explains how the notions of belief, desire and intention are employed in PRS-like architectures. The formalism also enables a rigorous semantic definition of subgoals achieve γ as corresponding to plans which, when successfully executed within the PRS-like architecture, actually will achieve the subgoal γ provided that no contingency arises during execution that forces the plan's abandonment. One limitation of the present work is that only the statics of mental states has been modelled – the temporal structures used in the modelling capture the "future directedness" of the agent's intentions as viewed from a single point in time, but not the changes in the agent's mental state as time progresses; a more complete model would include such mental state dynamics.

References

1. Bratman, M.E. (1987) *Intention, Plans and Practical Reason.* Harvard University Press, Cambridge, MA.
2. Cavedon, L. & Rao, A.S. (1996) 'Bringing About Rationality: Incorporating Plans Into a BDI Agent Architecture.' in Foo, N.Y. & Goebel, R.G. (Eds) *PRICAI'96: Topics in Artificial Intelligence.* Springer-Verlag, Berlin.
3. Cohen, P.R. & Levesque, H.J. (1990) 'Intention is Choice with Commitment.' *Artificial Intelligence*, **42**, 213–261.
4. De Giacomo, G., Lespérance, Y. & Levesque, H.J. (2000) '*ConGolog*, a Concurrent Programming Language Based on the Situation Calculus.' *Artificial Intelligence*, **121**, 109–169.
5. Emerson, E.A. & Clarke, E.M. (1982) 'Using Branching Time Temporal Logic to Synthesize Synchronization Skeletons.' *Science of Computer Programming*, **2**, 241–266.
6. Fagin, R., Halpern, J.Y., Moses, Y. & Vardi, M.Y. (1995) *Reasoning About Knowledge.* MIT Press, Cambridge, MA.
7. Georgeff, M.P. & Ingrand, F.F. (1989) 'Decision-Making in an Embedded Reasoning System.' *Proceedings of the Eleventh International Joint Conference on Artificial Intelligence*, 972–978.
8. Georgeff, M.P. & Lansky, A.L. (1987) 'Reactive Reasoning and Planning.' *Proceedings of the Sixth National Conference on Artificial Intelligence (AAAI-87)*, 677–682.
9. Goldblatt, R. (1992) *Logics of Time and Computation. Second Edition.* Center for the Study of Language and Information, Stanford, CA.
10. Harel, D. (1979) *First-Order Dynamic Logic.* Springer-Verlag, Berlin.
11. Konolige, K. & Pollack, M.E. (1993) 'A Representationalist Theory of Intention.' *Proceedings of the Thirteenth International Joint Conference on Artificial Intelligence*, 390–395.
12. Lee, J., Huber, M.J., Kenny, P.G. & Durfee, E.H. (1994) 'UM-PRS: An Implementation of the Procedural Reasoning System for Multirobot Applications.' *Conference on Intelligent Robotics in Field, Factory, Service, and Space*, 842–849.
13. Pratt, V.R. (1976) 'Semantical Considerations on Floyd-Hoare Logic.' *Proceedings of the Seventeenth IEEE Symposium on Foundations of Computer Science*, 109–121.
14. Rao, A.S. & Georgeff, M.P. (1991) 'Modeling Rational Agents within a BDI-Architecture.' *Proceedings of the Second International Conference on Principles of Knowledge Representation and Reasoning (KR'91)*, 473–484.
15. Rao, A.S. & Georgeff, M.P. (1992) 'An Abstract Architecture for Rational Agents.' *Proceedings of the Third International Conference on Principles of Knowledge Representation and Reasoning (KR'92)*, 439–449.
16. Segerberg, K. (1989) 'Bringing It About.' *Journal of Philosophical Logic*, **18**, 327–347.
17. Singh, M.P. (1994) *Multiagent Systems.* Springer-Verlag, Berlin.
18. Wooldridge, M.J. (2000) *Reasoning About Rational Agents.* MIT Press, Cambridge, MA.

Genetic Algorithm and Social Simulation

Pinata Winoto

Department of Computer Science, University of Saskatchewan
Saskatoon, S7N 5A9, Canada
piw410@mail.usask.ca

Abstract. Artificial agents have been deployed in simulating social or economic phenomena in order to find optimal policy to govern agents' society. However, with an increase of the complexity of agents' internal behaviors as well as their social interactions, modeling social behaviors and tracking down optimal policies in mathematical form become intractable. In this paper, genetic algorithm is used to find optimal solutions to deter criminals in order to reduce the social cost caused by the crimes in the artificial society. The society is characterized by multiple-equilibria and noisy parameters. Sampling evaluation is used to evaluate every candidate. The results of experiments show that genetic algorithms can quickly find the optimal solutions.

1   Introduction

Many works had been done in simulating social or economic phenomena by using artificial agents in computer simulations, for example in [1]-[6]. One of the simulation's purposes is to find optimal policy in governing a society. Since the society could be open and contain many heterogeneous agents, who are able to learn from and adapt to their environment, the impact of public policy on social welfare is no longer deterministic. With an increase of the complexity of agent's internal behavior and its social interactions, modeling the social behavior in mathematical form becomes intractable. Consequently, traditional optimization techniques cannot be used in finding optimal public policy(-ies). Generally, multiple equilibria and noises characterize most social simulations. Some equilibria may be unstable or non-stationary, and the movement from one equilibrium point to others is very slow. Therefore, most simulations are time consuming and repeated sampling becomes very costly. The minimum number of sampling in evaluating a policy may spreads from few times until hundreds times. Too little sampling could mislead the interpretation of the result [7].

This paper reports an ongoing project in optimizing agent society through public policy. The search space is finite, but exhaustively evaluating all points is extremely costly. A similar work in searching optimal policy could be found in Takadama *et al.* [8], where they used evolutionary approach to find optimal policy in the simulation of city planning. Other similar works in optimizing stochastic simulation are [9] and [10]. In [9] Bingül *et al.* used GA to find optimal solutions of a stochastic simulation of military operations, a black box THUNDER software. In [10] Stroud used Kalman-

M. Ishizuka and A. Sattar (Eds.): PRICAI 2002, LNAI 2417, pp. 148-157, 2002.
© Springer-Verlag Berlin Heidelberg 2002

Extended GA to simulate atmosphere phenomena, which is characterized by many non-stationary outcomes.

Here, a repeated evaluation method is used in the evaluation of fitness value as studied in [11]-[14]. Under some assumptions, such as identical and independent distribution of noises along searching point, the optimal sampling could be derived [12][13]. Nissen and Propach [14] relax this assumption and show that increasing sampling number will effectively increase the accuracy of the results. But they did not derive the optimal sampling and its relation to population size. Some refinement to reduce computation cost by inheriting fitness value was proposed in [15][16].

Since there are various settings of GA, such as population size, selection mechanism, crossover mechanism, probability of crossover and mutation, etc., an appropriate setting is needed for the optimization problem described in this paper. In the next part, the algorithm used and the preliminary test using simple stochastic polynomial function is described. After that, a description of the social simulation and how to apply GA in finding optimal solution are given. Then, the analysis of experimental result is provided, which then followed by some conclusions.

2   Repeated-Evaluation Genetic Algorithm

GA is a population-based algorithm that consists of iterated cycles of *evaluation, selection, reproduction,* and *mutation.* Each cycle is called a generation. During each generation, a set of genetic operators will be applied to the existing chromosomes to create a new population, which is more adaptive than previous one. In the simulation described later, the selected GA properties are as follow:

- Fitness value: the *evaluation* is repeated n times and their *mean* value is returned.
- *Selection*: the fittest chromosomes are chosen to generate offspring. A linear ranking is used, and depends on n we choose 10%, 20% or half of the best populations as the parents.
- *Reproduction/crossover*: the *crossover rate* is set to 0.6. And each gene/bit of parents is considered independently. In our simulation, the chromosome length is 10 bit.
- *Mutation*: the *mutation rate* is set to 0.05.

In solving stochastic optimization problem in this paper, two type algorithms are considered, repeated-evaluation GA and sub-population-based GA. The repeated-evaluation GA follows typical GA except that it repeats the calculation of fitness value n times:

1. (Initialization) Randomly generate a population of N chromosomes.
2. Evaluate the fitness $f(x)$ of each chromosome n times, and return its average value.
3. Sort the population according to their average fitness value and replicate $m\%$ of the best chromosomes, and repeat the following steps until N chromosomes (offspring) have been created:
    a. randomly select a pair of parent chromosomes from the population;
    b. with the crossover probability 0.6, cross each parent gene;
    c. mutate the resulting offspring with the mutation probability 0.05, and insert it in the new population;
4. The new population replaces the current population.

5. Repeat step 2 to 4 as many as r times.
6. (Terminate) Return the best chromosome.

In the sub-population-based GA, after initialization (step 1) the chromosome is evaluated once (i.e., $n = 1$). But the whole population is duplicated n times and every chromosome is evaluated independently. After all chromosomes are evaluated, $1/n$ best population is selected from each sub-population to form a mating pool. Finally, classical operators are applied to this mating pool to generate new generation, and the process is repeated. Generally, there is no big difference between repeated-evaluation and sub-population-based GA. For instance, by modifying the repeated-evaluation GA such that it uses the whole sampling value rather than their mean value in its selection mechanism, then the repeated-evaluation GA becomes a sub-population-based GA. Conversely, if the selection criteria in a sub-population-based GA is based on the average performance of the corresponding sub-population, then it becomes a repeated-evaluation GA. Definitely, many other criteria can be used besides mean and sampling value, such as mean-variance, maximum or minimum value, etc. Some experiments are needed in order to choose one of them. As a preliminary test before they are used in social simulation, they are tested using a stochastic polynomial function:

$$y = -(x - 500)^2 + 100000 + [25000 + 2(x - 500)^2]\,\varepsilon \qquad (1)$$

where $\varepsilon \in [-0.5, 0.5]$. The best x is 500, as shown in middle of solid line in figure 1.

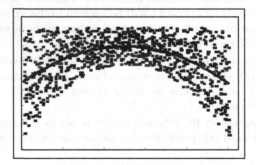

Fig. 1. The stochastic testing function y(x) and its noise distribution

We test our algorithms by repeating every setting 100 times. The settings are as follows:
1. generations $r = \{1, 2, 5, 10, 20, 40, 80, 160\}$
2. sampling $n = \{5, 10\}$
3. population size $N = \{100, 200, 500, 1000\}$

The effects of them are shown in figure 2, 3, and 4. Figure 2 and 3 show the effect of the number of generations to the best result. Both are run for population size = 100. In figure 2, the repetition of evaluation = 5 for repeated-evaluation-based GA, and replication = 5 for sub-population based GA. In figure 3, the repetition and replication = 10. It is shown from the lower part graphs that increasing the number of iterations/generations will reduce the variance of the results (decreasing pattern of standard deviations). It is also shown from the upper graphs that by increasing the number of generations, both algorithms eventually move to a stable local optimum (approx. 510). This optimum point is not the best (=500), but increasing the population size can increase the chance of finding better solutions (figure 4). However, it is very costly to find better solutions. For example, when the number of population increase from 100 to 1000, the gain of accuracy is < 40% (stable local optimum = 506.9). It is also shown from the numerical data (not shown here) that increasing the number of evaluation (repetition and replication) does not affect the result significantly.

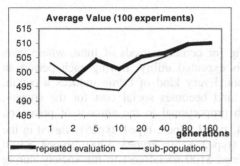
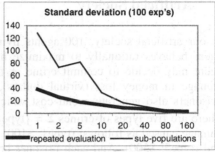

Fig. 2. The effect of the number of generations (5 times samplings or 5 times replications)

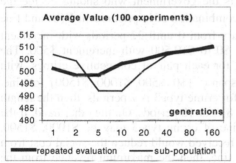
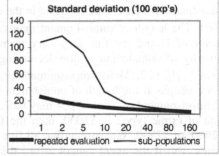

Fig. 3. The effect of the number of generations (10 times samplings or 10 times replications)

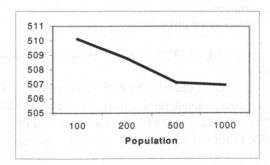

Fig. 4. The effect of population size to the accuracy of solution

The main difference observed from our first experiment is that sub-population-based GA is more volatile in the smaller number of generation (higher standard deviation), while repeated-evaluation GA is more stable. Besides, sub-population-based GA is more time consuming. Considering the cost-performance value, we choose repeated-evaluation GA in optimizing our social simulation, which is explained in the next section.

3   Artificial Society

In our artificial society, 100 agents living for certain periods of time, where each agent behaves rationally to maximize his expected utility. During each period an agent may decide to commit crime or not. Every kind of crime induces a certain damage in money loss (virtual dollars), and becomes social cost for the society. Prisoners also generate social cost which proportional to the amount of prisoners. There are five types of crimes $\Sigma = \{$type1, type2, type3, type4, type5$\}$, varied in the damage caused as follows: (type1: $100), (type2: $150), (type3: $200), (type4: $300) and (type5: $500). And each prisoner brings $100 social cost to the society during each period.

The probability of conviction is set to be 0.2 for each type of crime, and cost the society $36,000 for each period. And it is the government who should decide the punishment for each type of crime in the combination of imprisonment $Y(\sigma)$ and fine $F(\sigma)$. The length of imprisonment may vary from 0 until 21 periods with increment factor of 1, and the fine may vary from $0 to $10,500 with increment $500. The severity of punishment is non-decreasing for each pair of consecutive crimes, with span $\in \{0, 1, 2, 3\}$ for imprisonment or span $\in \{\$0, \$500, \$1000, \$1500\}$ for fine. For example, if the length of punishment for crime type3 is 7 periods, then the length of imprisonment of crime type4 may be 7, 8, 9 or 10 periods. On the other hand, if the fine of crime type2 is $1000, then the fine of crime type3 may be $1000, $1500, $2000, or $2500. We assume that all fine received would reduce the social cost from crime. But if the agent cannot afford the fine, then the maximum revenue from the fine is the agent's current wealth. Moreover, each agent who does not commit crime may contribute to the society $100 in each period. A minimum social cost is the main objective of the government.

Each agent has the following properties:

- agent.Lifespan $\in \{30, 31, 32, ..., 50\}$, represents his lifespan determined by uniform distribution.
- agent.Age $\in \{0, 1, 2, ..., $ agent.Lifespan$\}$, represents his age.
- agent.Status $\in \{$clear, wanted, imprisoned$\}$, represents his status.
- agent.Wealth $\in (0, 1, 2, ..., 10000\}$, represents his wealth.
- agent.CrimeExperience $\in \{0, 20, 40, ..., 1000\}$, represents his experiences in crimes.
- agent.HighestCrime $\in \{0, 1, 2, 3, 4, 5\}$, represents the most severe crime he has committed if any.
- agent.Imprison: represents how many periods left in prison if under custody.

In each period an agent may decide whether to commit crime or not, depending on his expected benefits from committing crime. The expected benefit depends on the *perceived* disutility from imprisonment and fine, the expected payoff from crime, and the probability of apprehension. We adopt perceived value rather than real value since the former is more realistic [22]. We divide the disutility from imprisonment into three main categories, i.e., linear function (proportional), convex function, and concave function. This categorization follows the analysis by [21]. The following functions are used:

$$DU(Y) = \alpha\, Y + F' \qquad \text{(linear)}$$
$$DU(Y) = \alpha\, Y^{\beta} + F' \qquad \text{(convex)}$$
$$DU(Y) = \alpha\, Y^{\gamma} + F' \qquad \text{(concave)}$$

where $\alpha \in [300, 700)$, $\beta \in [0.5, 0.8)$, $\gamma \in [1.1, 1.4)$, $Y = Y(\sigma)$ is the length of imprisonment, and

$$F' = F(\sigma) \qquad \text{if agent.Wealth} > F(\sigma)$$
or $\quad F' = \text{agent.Wealth} \qquad \text{otherwise}$

Obviously, $DU(Y) = DU(Y(\sigma)) \propto DU(\sigma)$, i.e., disutility depends on the type of crime. The expected payoffs from crime $X(\sigma)$ are determined stochastically by uniform distribution as integer value: (type1; [$90, $110]), (type2; [$140, $160]), (type3; [$190, $210]), (type4; [$290, $310]), and (type5; [$490, $510]), where the value inside the square bracket represents the minimum and maximum payoffs respectively. Furthermore, the expected benefit $EB(\sigma)$ for each type of crime follows the von Neumann-Morgenstern expected utility with the assumption that the agent is risk neutral, i.e.,

$$EB = (1-p_c)X + p_c\, DU \qquad \text{if agent.Status} = \text{clear}$$
or $\quad EB = (1-p_c)X \qquad \text{if agent.Status} = \text{criminal},$

where $p_c(\sigma)$ refers to the perceived value of the probability of conviction which equals to the conviction rate in the last period rather than 0.2 as our setting. There are many explanations for the formulae used above [18]-[20]. Different formulae could be applied with regards to the assumption considered. Since this part is not our main concern, we adopt the most commonly used.

The expected return from working (not commit crime) is a fixed $50. We also assume that each agent with experiences in crime type T would only consider committing the same type of crime or more severe crime. Each agent chooses by comparing the benefit from all available options. And in order to take the wealth effect into the decision process, "clear" agent with wealth equals to W has probability $W/10000$ not to commit crime. Each agent accumulates wealth from either work or crime.

After all agents decide whether to commit crime or not and act in accordance, police will start to arrest them. Each criminal has the chance of 0.2 being convicted for his most severe crime. If an agent dies, then a new agent will be born to replace him. The simulation runs for 100 periods, and the data from the last 10 periods are recorded for analysis. Because in these periods we would encounter agents from 2-nd, 3-th, and 4-th generations with various age and experiences which are enough for our analysis.

3.1   Chromosome Representation

Recall that our main purpose is to find the optimal punishment for each type of crime such that the social cost would be minimized as much as possible. Therefore, the control variables are the severity of punishment for each type of crime. Since we only have 5 types of crime and 2 types of punishment, i.e., imprisonment and fine, we only need chromosomes with length equals to 10, and it is not binary but integer value in each bit of the chromosome. The first gene represents the length of sentence for the crime type1, which varies from 0 to 10. The second until fifth genes represent the increment of length of imprisonment compared to its previous type, which varies from 0, 1, 2 and 3. The sixth gene represents the fine for crime type1 also varies from $0 to $5000 with an increment factor $500. And the seventh until tenth genes also represent the increment of fine compared to its previous type, which also varies from 0, 1, 2 and 3 x $500. Overall, there are 6553600 different combinations. For example, **2 0 0 1 1 4 3 3 1 1** represents that the punishment of crime type1 is 2 years and 4 x $500 = $2000; type2 is 2+0 = 2 years and (4+3) x $500 = $3500; type3 is 2+0+0 = 2 years and (4+3+3) x $500 = $5000; type4 is 2+0+0+1 = 3 years and (4+3+3+1) x $500 = $5500; and type5 is 4 years and $6000. This encoding method will simplify the crossover and mutation. Each individual (chromosome) runs the simulation 5, 10 or 20 times and takes the average value of its social cost (repeated evaluation). The selection we used is to choose the half-best population and then replicate it once for each. And the crossover is to cross each gene of parents by the probability of 0.6. The fitness value is the average social cost.

3.2   Experimentation and Results

The values of parameters we choose are population = 50, probability of crossover = 0.6, probability of mutation = 0.05, and generation = 40. The convergence of the simulation is shown in table 1, and table 2. Y1, Y2, Y3, Y4, and Y5 represent the length of imprisonment for crime type1, type2, type3, type4 and type5 respectively. F(1), F(2), F(3), F(4), and F(5) represent the fines imposed for crime type1, type2, type3, type4 and type5 respectively. Table 1 shows the dispersed deterrence patterns from the first 5 individuals in the fifth generation taken from one of the experiment. And table 2 shows the corresponding patterns in the 21-st generation where the deterrence patterns are converging and lower social costs are attained. Table 3 shows the standard deviations for each parameter in the 1st, 5th, 10th and 21st generations. Obviously, the standard deviations decrease as generations increase. Therefore we can conclude that the solutions converge. Moreover, the minimal social cost also decrease as generations increase, which means that better solutions are reached as generation increases (see figure 5).

Table 4 shows the effect of sampling in evaluation (5, 10, and 20 times). It is shown from the social cost that the number of sample has no big impact when the sample is 5, 10 or 20. But it does not means that the most optimal result is reached. Because in the previous work with this simulation [7], it showed that a slight differences of policies may not impact the whole performances. In some cases, only after hundreds of repetitions, it can be concluded that which policies are better. Or in other words, in few repetitions the optimal policy does not fall in a point, but a thick line or region. However, from the social cost perspective, it can be concluded that GA is robust in searching "good" policy (-ies).

In order to test the optimal deterrence patterns from GA, several solutions are run for 30 times. And some arbitrary deterrence patterns are also tested as comparisons. One of the results is shown in table 5, in which the patterns of deterrence for each crime with their associated pairs of (length of imprisonment; fine) are as follows:

T1: 1(1,$2500); 2(1,$2500);3(1,$3500); 4(1,$4500); 5(2,$4500)

T2: 1(1,$500); 2(1,$1000); 3(1,$2000); 4(1,$2500); 5(2,$2500)

T3: 1(1,$500); 2(2,$1000); 3(3,$1500); 4(4,$2000); 5(5,$2500)

T4: 1(4,$0); 2(5,$0); 3(6,$0); 4(7,$0); 5(8,$0)

T1 and T2 are taken from the result of GA, while T3 and T4 are chosen manually. Table 5 shows that the social costs from T1 and T2 are less than both T3 and T4. The crime rate for each type of crime, i.e. %C1, %C2, %C3, %C4, and %C5, and the total crime rate %TC are shown. It is shown that there is no specific difference for the total crime rate among T1, T2, T3, and T4. The difference is that the crime rate for type1, type2 and type3 are lower in T1 and T2, while the crime rate for type5 is higher in T1 and T2. Intuitively, criminals in T3 and T4 spend most of their life in prison due to longer imprisonment and therefore have less opportunity to commit crime type5. Moreover, the prisoners in T1 and T2 are lower than T3 and T4, because prisoners in T3 and T4 spend longer time in prison.

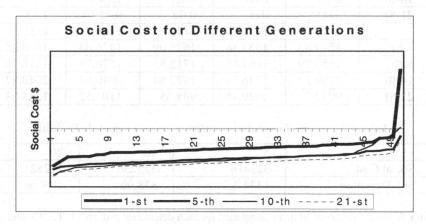

Fig. 5. Shift of social cost within different generations

4   Conclusions

Two main conclusions are drawn from our experiment. First, the repeated evaluation GA outperforms the sub-population GA in term of cost-performance analysis. Second, genetic algorithm is capable of finding the optimal solutions in the agent-based simulation in terms of the convergence of its solutions and better fitness value, and too many repetition may not have impact on the searching of optimal policy.

Table 1. The first 5 individuals in the fifth generation

Social Cost	Y1	F(1)	Y2	F(2)	Y3	F(3)	Y4	F(4)	Y5	F(5)
-20888	1	$500	1	$1,000	1	$1,500	4	$2,500	5	$4,000
-19561	1	$500	1	$500	2	$1,500	5	$2,500	6	$4,000
-19305	1	$500	1	$2,000	2	$2,500	5	$3,500	6	$5,000
-19130	1	$500	1	$2,000	1	$2,500	4	$3,500	5	$5,000
-18703	1	$2,500	2	$3,000	3	$3,500	6	$3,500	9	$5,000

Table 2. The first 5 individuals in the 21-st generation

Social Cost	Y1	F(1)	Y2	F(2)	Y3	F(3)	Y4	F(4)	Y5	F(5)
-24451	1	$2,500	1	$2,500	1	$3,500	1	$4,500	2	$4,500
-22492	1	$3,000	1	$4,000	1	$4,500	1	$6,000	3	$6,000
-22074	1	$2,500	1	$3,000	1	$3,500	2	$4,000	5	$4,500
-21909	1	$1,500	1	$2,000	1	$2,500	1	$3,500	4	$4,000
-20911	1	$2,500	1	$3,000	1	$3,500	1	$4,500	1	$5,000

Table 3. Standard Deviation from the First 20 Individuals in the 1-st, 5-th, 10-th and 21-st Generations

	Y1	Y2	Y3	Y4	Y5
1-St	1.43	1.90	2.04	2.43	2.63
5-th	0.00	0.50	1.40	1.92	2.25
10-th	0.00	0.00	0.75	1.79	2.11
21-St	0.00	0.00	0.00	0.31	1.15
	F(1)	**F(2)**	**F(3)**	**F(4)**	**F(5)**
1-St	1549.83	1353.36	1575.09	1426.03	1455.25
5-th	1550.89	1664.45	1715.83	1576.76	1576.76
10-th	1489.22	1746.24	1972.84	2040.87	2040.87
21-St	993.07	1079.41	998.35	1103.52	1268.03

Table 4. The results from 5 times simulation for each Sample in Evaluation

	5	10	20
Social Cost	321416	323236	322821
Std. Deviation	1334.2	838.96	1030.9

Table 5. The results from 30 times simulation for each deterrence pattern T1, T2, T3, and T4

	Social Cost	Non Prisoner	%C1	%C2	%C3	%C4	%C5	%TC
T1	-17455	994.71	4.87	4.14	2.37	2.43	3.04	16.85
T2	-18961	994.79	4.76	4.10	2.35	2.31	2.90	16.43
T3	-14361	957.26	4.86	4.56	2.47	2.25	2.24	16.38
T4	24612	854.25	6.04	7.35	3.77	2.83	2.03	22.02

References

[1] Conte, R., Hegselmann, R. and Terna, P. (Eds.) Simulating Social Phenomena. Springer, 1997.
[2] Gilbert, N. and Conte, R. (Eds.) Artificial Societies: the computer simulation of social life. UCL Press, London, 1995.

[3] Luna, F. and Stefansson, B. (Eds.) Economic Simulations in Swarm: Agent-based modelling and object oriented programming. Kluwer Academic Publishers, 2000.

[4] McCain, R. A. Agent-Based Computer Simulation of Dichotomous Economic Growth. Kluwer Academic Publishers, 2000.

[5] Sichman, J. S., Conte, R. and Gilbert, N. (Eds.) Multi-Agent Systems and Agent-Based Simulation. Springer, 1998.

[6] Tesfatsion, L. Guest editorial agent-based modeling of evolutionary economic systems. *IEEE Transactions on Evolutionary Computation*, vol. 5(5), Oct. 2001, 437-441.

[7] Winoto, P. and Tang, T. Y. Evaluating the Stochastic Properties of Agent Society from Economics' Perspective. *Proceedings of the 2001 IEEE Systems, Man and Cybernetics Conference*, Tucson, AZ, USA, vol. 5, Oct. 2001, 2905-2910.

[8] Takadama, K., Terano, T. and Shimohara, K., Nongovernance rather than governance in a multiagent economic society. *IEEE Transactions on Evolutionary Computation*, vol. 5(5), Oct. 2001, 535 -545.

[9] Bingül, Z, Sekmen, A•., Palaniappan, S. and Zein-Sabatto, S. Genetic Algorithms Applied to Real Time Multiobjective Optimization Problems. *Proceedings of the IEEE Southeast Con 2000*, Piscataway, NJ. USA, 2000, 95-103.

[10] Stroud, P.D. Kalman-extended genetic algorithm for search in nonstationary environments with noisy fitness evaluations. *IEEE Transactions on Evolutionary Computation*, vol. 5(1), Feb. 2001, 66 -77.

[11] Fitzpatrick, J., and Grefenstette, J. Genetic Algorithms in Noisy Environments. *Machine Learning*, 3, 1988, 101-120.

[12] Miller, B.L. and Goldberg, D.E. Optimal Sampling for Genetic Algorithms. *IlliGAL Report No. 96005,* Univ. of Illinois, Urbana-Champaign, August 1996.

[13] Miller, B.L. Noise, Sampling, and Efficient GA's. Ph.D. dissertation, Univ. of Illinois, Urbana-Champaign, 1997.

[14] Nissen, V. and Propach, J. On the robustness of population-based versus point-based optimization in the presence of noise. *IEEE Transactions on Evolutionary Computation*, vol. 2(3), Sept. 1998, 107 -119.

[15] Smith, R., Dike, B., and Stegmann, S. Fitness Inheritance in Genetic Algorithms. *Proceedings of the ACM Symposium on Applied Computing*, New York, NY, 1995, 345-350

[16] Sastry, K., Goldberg, D.E., Pelikan, M. Don't Evaluate, Inherit. *IlliGAL Report No. 2001013,* Univ. of Illinois, Urbana-Champaign, Jan. 2001.

[17] Albert, L.A. and Goldberg, D.E. Efficient Evaluation Genetic Algorithms under Integrated Fitness Functions. *IlliGAL Report No. 2001024,* Univ. of Illinois, Urbana-Champaign, July 2001.

[18] Becker, G. S. Crime and Punishment: An Economic Approach. The Journal of Political Economy; 76 (2), 1968, pp. 169-217.

[19] Ehrlich, I. The Deterrent Effect of Criminal Law Enforcement. Journal of Legal Studies, Vol. L (2), June 1972, 259-276.

[20] Leung, S. F. Dynamic deterrence theory. Economica, 62, 1995, 65-87.

[21] Polinsky, A. M.. and Shavell, S. On the disutility and discounting of imprisonment and the theory of deterrence. NBER Working Paper, 6259, November 1997. http://www.nber.org/papers/w6259

[22] Sah, Raaj K. Social osmosis and patterns of crime. The Journal of Political Economy, 99(6), 1991, 1272-1295.

Adaptive Directed Acyclic Graphs for Multiclass Classification

Boonserm Kijsirikul[1], Nitiwut Ussivakul[1], and Surapant Meknavin[2]

[1] Department of Computer Engineering, Chulalongkorn University, Thailand.
boonserm.k@chula.ac.th, 42703860@student.chula.ac.th
[2] Siamguru Co.,Ltd. 219/38 Asoke Towers, Bangkok 10110, Thailand.
surapan@siamguru.com

Abstract. This paper presents a method, called Adaptive Directed Acyclic Graph (ADAG), to extend Support Vector Machines (SVMs) for multiclass classification. The ADAG is based on the previous approach, the Decision Directed Acyclic Graph (DDAG), and is designed to remedy some weakness of the DDAG caused by its structure. We prove that the expected accuracy of the ADAG is higher than that of the DDAG, and also empirically evaluate our approach by comparing the ADAG with the DDAG on two data sets.

1 Introduction

Support Vector Machines (SVMs) have been well developed for binary classification [10]. However, many real world problems involve multiclass classification, such as optical character recognition, phoneme classification, text classification, etc. Several approaches of extending SVMs for solving the problem of multiclass classification have been proposed [10,6,3].

The standard approaches for constructing N-class SVMs are to consider the problem as a collection of binary SVMs, such as One-against-the-Rest [10] and One-against-One [6]. The One-Against-the-Rest (1-v-R) approach works by constructing a set of N binary classifiers. The ith classifier is trained with all of the examples in the ith class with positive labels, and all other examples with negative labels. The final output is the class that corresponds to the classifier with the highest output value. On the other hand, the One-Against-One (1-v-1) approach simply constructs all possible binary classifiers from a training set of N classes. Each classifier is trained on only two out of N classes. Thus, there will be $N(N-1)/2$ classifiers. In the Max Wins algorithm [4] which is one of 1-v-1 approaches, a test example is classified by all of classifiers. Each classifier provides one vote for its preferred class and the majority vote is used to make the final output. Although Max Wins offers faster training time compared to the 1-v-R method, it is very inefficient in term of evaluation time. Using a new learning architecture, DDAG, Platt et al. [7] proposed an algorithm that reduces evaluation time, while maintaining accuracy compared to the Max Wins.

In this paper we point out some limitations of the DDAG caused by its structure which needs an unnecessarily high number of node evaluations for the

M. Ishizuka and A. Sattar (Eds.): PRICAI 2002, LNAI 2417, pp. 158–168, 2002.
© Springer-Verlag Berlin Heidelberg 2002

correct class and results in high cumulative error. Our modified version of the DDAG will increase accuracy by minimizing the number of node evaluations for the correct class. This advantage is due to the tournament-based architecture that is structurally flatter than the DDAG. We prove that the expected accuracy of our method is higher than that of the DDAG, and also empirically evaluate our approach by comparing the ADAG with the algorithm of the DDAG on two data sets, i.e. Thai vowel recognition and UCI Letter data sets.

2   Decision Directed Acyclic Graphs

A disadvantage of the 1-v-1 SVMs is their inefficiency of classifying data as the number of SVMs grows superlinearly with the number of classes. Platt et al. introduced a new learning architecture, DDAG, and an algorithm, DAGSVM, to remedy this disadvantage [7].

2.1   The DDAG Architecture & the DAGSVM Algorithm

A Directed Acyclic Graph (DAG) is a graph whose edge has an orientation and no cycles. Platt et al. used a rooted binary DAG, which has a unique node with no arcs pointing into it, and other nodes which have either 0 or 2 arcs leaving them, to be a class of functions used in classification tasks. In a problem with N classes, a rooted binary DAG has N leaves labeled by the classes where each of the $N(N-1)/2$ internal nodes is labeled with an element of Boolean function. The nodes are arranged in a triangular shape with the single root node at the top, two nodes in the second layer and so on until the final layer of N leaves.

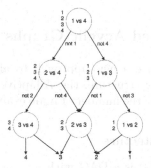

Fig. 1. The DDAG finding the best class out of four classes.

To evaluate a DDAG, starting at the root node, the binary function at a node is evaluated. The node is then exited via the left edge, if the binary function is -1; or the right edge, if the binary function is 1. The next node's binary function is then evaluated. The value of the decision function is the value associated with the final leaf node (see Figure 1). Only $N-1$ decision nodes will be evaluated in order to derive an answer. The DDAG can be implemented using a list, where each node eliminates one class from the list. The implementation list is initialized with a list of all classes. A test point is evaluated against the decision node that corresponds to the first and last elements of the list. If the node prefers one of the two classes, the other class is eliminated from the list, and the DDAG proceeds to test the first and last elements of the new list. The DDAG terminates when only one class remains in the list.

The DAGSVM algorithm creates a DDAG whose nodes are maximum margin classifiers over a kernel-induced feature space. Such a DDAG is obtained by training each 'i vs j' node only on the subset of training points labeled by i or j. The final class decision is derived by using the DDAG architecture. For the DAGSVM, the choice of the class order in the list (or DDAG) is arbitrary.

2.2   Issues on DDAG

Systematically innovated, the DDAG has outperformed the standard algorithm in terms of speed. However, the DDAG has the main weakness that the number of node evaluations for the correct class is unnecessarily high. This results in high cumulative error and, hence, the accuracy. The depth of the DDAG is $N-1$ and this means that the number of times the correct class has to be tested against other classes, on average, scales linearly with N. Let consider a case of 20-class problem. If the correct class is evaluated at the root node, it is tested against other classes for 19 times before it is correctly classified as the output. Despite large margin, there exists probability of misclassification, let say 1%, and this will cause $1 - 0.99^{19} = 17.38\%$ of cumulative error in this situation. This shortcoming becomes more severe if the number of classes increases. The issue raised here motivates us to modify the DDAG.

3   Adaptive Directed Acyclic Graphs

In this section we introduce a new approach to alleviate the problem of the DDAG structure. The new structure, the Adaptive DAG, lowers the depth of the DAG, and consequently the number of node evaluations for the correct class.

3.1   The ADAG Architecture

An Adaptive DAG (ADAG) is a DAG with a reversed triangular structure. In an N-class problem, the system comprises $N(N - 1)/2$ binary classifiers. The ADAG has $N - 1$ internal nodes, each of which is labeled with an element of Boolean function. The nodes are arranged in a reversed triangle with $N/2$ nodes (rounded up) at the top, $N/2^2$ nodes in the second layer and so on until the lowest layer of a final node, as shown in Figure 2(a).

To classify using the ADAG, starting at the top level, the binary function at each node is evaluated. The node is then exited via the outgoing edge with a message of the preferred class. In each round, the number of candidate classes is

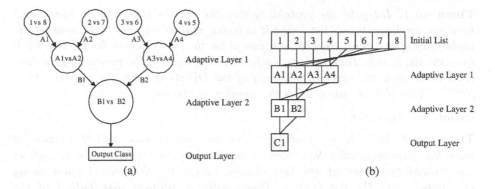

Fig. 2. (a) The structure of an adaptive DAG for an 8-class problem, and (b) the corresponding implementation through the list.

reduced by half. Based on the preferred classes from its parent nodes, the binary function of the next-layer node is chosen. The reduction process continues until reaching the final node at the lowest level. The value of the decision function is the value associated with the message from the final leaf node (see Figure 2(a)). Like the DDAG, the ADAG requires only $N-1$ decision nodes to be evaluated in order to derive an answer. Note that the correct class is evaluated against other classes for log_2N times (rounded up) or less, considerably lower than the number of evaluations required by the DDAG, which scales linearly with N.

3.2 Implementation

An ADAG can be implemented using a list, where each node eliminates one class from the list (see Figure 2(b)). The implementation list is initialized with a list of all classes. A test point is evaluated against the decision node that corresponds to the first and last elements of the list. If the node prefers one of the two classes, the class is kept in the left element's position while the other class will be eliminated from the list. Then, the ADAG proceeds to test the second and the elements before the last of the list. The testing process of each round ends when either one or no class remains untested in the list. In case that there is one class remaining untested, the class will be put at the right-most position of the next round list. After each round, a list with N elements is reduced to a list with $N/2$ elements (rounded up). Then, the ADAG process repeats until only one class remains in the list.

4 Analyses of DDAG & ADAG

The following theorems give the expected accuracy of the DDAG and ADAG. The proofs of the theorems will be given in Appendix.

Theorem 1. *Let p be the probability that the correct class will be eliminated from the implementation list, when it is tested against another class, and let the probability of one of any two classes, except for the correct class, being eliminated from the list be 0.5. Then under a uniform distribution of the position of the true class in the list, the expected accuracy of the DDAG is $(1/N)[(1 - p)/p + (1 - p)^{N-1} - (1 - p)^N/p]$, where N is the number of classes.*

Proof. See Appendix.

Theorem 2. *Let p be the probability that the correct class will be eliminated from the implementation list, when it is tested against another class, and let the probability of one of any two classes, except for the correct class, being eliminated from the list be 0.5. Then under a uniform distribution of the position of the true class in the list, the expected accuracy of the ADAG is $((2N - 2^{\lceil log_2 N \rceil})/N)(1 - p)^{\lceil log_2 N \rceil} + ((2^{\lceil log_2 N \rceil} - N)/N)(1 - p)^{\lceil log_2 N \rceil - 1}$, where N is the number of classes, and $\lceil x \rceil$ is the least integer greater than or equal to x.*

Proof. See Appendix.

The above theorems show that the accuracy of the ADAG decreases much slower than that of the DDAG, with the increase of the number of classes. For example, in case of $p = 0.01$ and $N = 20$, according to the above theorems, the expected accuracy of the ADAG and DDAG are 95.68% and 90.18%, respectively.

5   Experiments

In this section, we evaluate the performance of our method on two different data sets: the Thai vowel data set having 12 classes [9], and the UCI Letter data set having 26 classes [1]. According to the theorems in Section 4, the ADAG should have much advantage over the DDAG when the number of classes increases. Another factor which affects the performance of the ADAG and DDAG is the accuracy of binary classifiers (the value of $(1 - p)$ in the theorems); the more accurate the classifiers are, the smaller differences in performance between the ADAG and DDAG will be. The accuracy of a binary classifier depends heavily on the parameter of the kernel function used to construct the classifier, so in the following experiments, we varied the parameter of the kernel function to observe the differences. Therefore, for each data set with every value of the chosen parameter, several different sequences of nodes were chosen randomly for running a number of experiments evaluating both the DDAG and ADAG. Each time the accuracy using a sequence was recorded, and the average accuracy was taken as the result for each DAG. For every value of the parameter, the numbers of experiments for the Thai vowel data set, and the UCI Letter data set were 20000 and 50000, respectively. All experiments were run using SVM^{Light} [5].

5.1   The Thai Vowel Data Set

The Thai vowel data set consists of 12 classes with 72-dimension features [9]. This data set comprises data from two tests, i.e., inside and outside tests. The

Table 1. Percent accuracy of the ADAG and DDAG for the Thai vowel data set.

	Polynomial						RBF					
	Inside Test			Outside Test				Inside Test			Outside Test	
d	ADAG	DDAG	DIFF	ADAG	DDAG	DIFF	c	ADAG	DDAG	DIFF	ADAG	DDAG	DIFF
6	94.44	94.41	0.03	86.12	86.09	0.03	0.1	85.71	85.71	0.00	74.32	74.31	0.01
7	94.46	94.44	0.02	86.12	86.08	0.04	0.2	94.51	94.52	-0.01	84.50	84.48	0.02
8	94.43	94.41	0.02	85.98	85.91	0.07	0.3	94.66	94.64	0.02	86.55	86.52	0.03
9	94.27	94.26	0.01	85.39	85.33	0.06	0.4	94.35	94.33	0.02	86.77	86.75	0.02
10	94.18	94.16	0.02	85.09	85.05	0.04	0.5	93.51	93.49	0.02	86.64	86.63	0.01
11	93.70	93.68	0.02	84.58	84.55	0.03							
12	93.26	93.23	0.03	84.30	84.27	0.03							

Where, DIFF, d and c denote the differences in accuracy, the parameters in the Polynomial kernel $|\frac{(\mathbf{x} \cdot \mathbf{y}+1)}{72}|^d$ and the RBF kernel $exp(-|\mathbf{x} - \mathbf{y}|^2/72c)$, respectively.

inside test includes 12,384 training examples, while the outside test includes 6,192. Both tests have 3,096 test examples.

As shown in Table 1, the accuracy of the ADAG is higher for all experiments, except for one experiment using $c = 0.2$ as the parameter for the RBF kernel where the accuracy of the ADAG is slightly lower. In this data set, although the ADAG achieves better performance than the DDAG, the accuracy of both methods are not significantly different.

5.2   The UCI Letter Data Set

The UCI Letter data set comprises 26 classes of letter A to Z. Their 15-dimension features are measured statistics of printed font glyphs. The training set consists of first 16,000 examples, and the test set consists of the rest (4,000). The results are shown in Table 2.

Table 2. Percent accuracy of the ADAG and DDAG for the UCI letter data set.

	Polynomial				RBF		
d	ADAG	DDAG	DIFF	c	ADAG	DDAG	DIFF
1	83.83	83.31	0.52****	0.1	90.81	90.64	0.17**
2	95.59	95.17	0.42****	0.2	94.13	93.97	0.16***
3	95.96	95.51	0.45****	0.3	95.46	95.36	0.10**
4	95.88	95.46	0.42****	0.4	96.31	96.21	0.10**
5	95.83	95.34	0.49****	0.5	96.48	96.39	0.09**
6	95.35	94.87	0.48****	0.6	97.38	97.34	0.04*
7	94.78	94.25	0.53****	0.7	97.28	97.22	0.06*
8	93.83	93.14	0.69****	0.8	97.20	97.15	0.05*
9	93.22	92.45	0.77****	1.0	97.38	97.34	0.04
10	92.42	91.62	0.80****	1.5	97.59	97.55	0.04
				2.0	97.63	97.62	0.01
				2.5	97.76	97.76	0.00
				3.0	97.91	97.90	0.01
				3.5	97.84	97.84	0.00
				4.0	97.80	97.79	0.01

Where, DIFF, d and c denote the differences in accuracy between the ADAG and the DDAG, the parameters in the Polynomial kernel $|(\mathbf{x} \cdot \mathbf{y} + 1)|^d$ and the RBF kernel $exp(-|\mathbf{x} - \mathbf{y}|^2/c)$. Superscripts denote confidence levels for the differences in accuracy between the ADAG and DDAG, using a one-tailed paired t-test:* is 90.0%,** is 95.0%, *** is 99.0%, **** is 99.99%; no superscripts denote confidence levels below 90.0%.

As shown in Table 2, when the number of classes increases to 26 in this data set, the differences in accuracy between the ADAG and the DDAG become much larger on average. This shows the effectiveness of the ADAG in case of the data set with a large number of classes. In case of the Polynomial kernel, the ADAG performs significantly better than the DDAG at a 99.99% confidence level, for all value of the parameter d. In case of the RBF kernel, the ADAG yields statistically significantly better than the DDAG for $c = 0.1 - 0.8$. In our experiments, the value of $c = 3.0$ produces highly accurate binary SVMs, as can be seen by the experimental results that the ADAG or DDAG with $c = 3.0$ performs the best among those with different values of c. When the values of c near the best one, i.e. $c = 1.0 - 4.0$, the significance levels of the differences in accuracy between the DDAG and the ADAG are below 90%.

From the above experiments, we may conclude qualitatively that:

- The optimal kernels and parameters for the DDAG and the ADAG are quite similar.
- In general, the RBF kernel outperforms the Polynomial kernel.
- In a problem with a small number of classes, the improvement is insignificant. However, if the number of classes rises, the ADAG is at advantage.
- The improvement comes in the form of higher accuracy with higher confidence of achieving the accuracy. Our approach is empirically proved to increase accuracy and confidence, especially in problems with the higher number of classes.

6 Conclusion

We have proposed a new approach, ADAG, that alleviates the problem of the DDAG caused by its structure which needs an unnecessarily high number of node evaluations for the correct class. We proved that the expected accuracy of our method is higher than that of the DDAG. Our experimental results are also evidence that ADAG yields higher accuracy of classification, especially in such a case that the number of classes is relatively large.

Since the DDAG is one of the SVMs' fastest methods in multiclass classification, this modification of the DDAG will help improve accuracy even further. In our ongoing work, we are performing more experiments on several data sets, and studying the effect of initial sequences of binary classes on the performance of the ADAG.

Appendix

In the following analyses of the DDAG and ADAG, we assume that the probability of the correct class being in any position in the list is a uniform distribution. We also assume that the probability of the correct class being eliminated from the list is p, when it is tested against another class, and that the probability of one of any two classes, except for the correct class, being eliminated from the list is 0.5 when they are tested against each other.

We first illustrate the expected accuracy of the DDAG by the following example.

Example: (Expected accuracy of the DDAG for a 4-class problem).
Consider a four-class problem. Figure 3 shows all *probability calculation paths* where the correct class will be correctly classified by the DDAG. There are 8 calculation paths for this problem. The correct class will be correctly classified if it is not eliminated from the list. This means that when it is at the edge (the first or the last element) of the list in each calculation path, all other classes have to be excluded from the list.

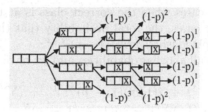

Fig. 3. An example of a four-class problem.

Under a uniform distribution, the probability is $1/4$ that the correct class will be at any position of the *initial* list. In the case that the correct class (indicated by 'X' in the figure) is at the edge of the current list, it will be correctly classified if all other classes are eliminated from the list. The probability of this is $(1 - p)^{N-1}$, where N is the number of elements in the current list. In the case that the correct class is not at the edge, we have two possible choices, i.e. to remove the first element and to remove the last element from the list. This reduces the number of elements one by one. From the above example, the probability that the correct class is correctly classified is:

$$(1/4)(1 - p)^3 + (1/4)(1/2)^1(1 - p)^2 + (1/4)(1/2)^2(1 - p)^1 + (1/4)(1/2)^2(1 - p)^1 +$$
$$(1/4)(1/2)^2(1 - p)^1 + (1/4)(1/2)^2(1 - p)^1 + (1/4)(1/2)^1(1 - p)^2 + (1/4)(1 - p)^3$$
$$= (1/4)[(1 - p)/p + (1 - p)^3 - (1 - p)^4/p] \qquad \square$$

We now give the theorem for expected accuracy of the DDAG as follows.

Proof of Theorem 1 (Expected accuracy of the DDAG). As shown in the above example, the correct class will be correctly classified if when it is at the edge of the list, all other classes have to be excluded from the list. Consider the cases when we *first* obtain a list with i elements where the correct class is at the left-most position, where $2 \le i \le N - 1$. The list can be written as $XO \ldots O$, where X and O represent the correct class and a wrong class, respectively. This list is obtained from a list containing $i + 1$ elements with one wrong class preceding the correct class as shown by $OXO \ldots O$. Before the list $OXO \ldots O$ is obtained, $N - i - 1$ wrong classes must be excluded from an initial list. Thus beginning from all possible different initial lists, the number of possible calculation paths ending with a list of i elements where the correct class is at the left-most position is 2^{N-i-1} (as there are two possible choices for one wrong class; to remove the first element or to remove the last element of the list). Therefore the number of possible calculation paths ending with a list of i elements where the correct class is at the edge (the left-most and right-most positions) is 2^{N-i}. The probability of obtaining the list of i elements where the correct class is at the edge is equal to $(1/N)(0.5)^{N-i}(1-p)^{i-1}$, as $N-i$ wrong classes must be eliminated from the list and after that the correct class is at the edge and $i-1$ wrong classes must be excluded. The total probability that the correct class of this pattern will be correctly classified is thus $2^{(N-i)}(1/N)(0.5)^{N-i}(1-p)^{i-1} = (1/N)(1-p)^{i-1}$.

Next consider the cases when the correct class is at the edge of a list with N elements. For these cases, the total probability that the correct class will be correctly classified is obviously $2(1/N)(1-p)^{N-1}$.

Finally we sum up all above probabilities and we have the expected accuracy as:
$(\sum_{i=2}^{N-1}(1/N)(1-p)^{i-1}) + 2(1/N)(1-p)^{N-1} = (\sum_{j=1}^{N-1}(1/N)(1-p)^{j}) + (1/N)(1-p)^{N-1} = (1/N)[(1-p)(1-(1-p)^{N-1})/p + (1-p)^{N-1}] = (1/N)[(1-p)/p + (1-p)^{N-1} - (1-p)^{N}/p]$ □

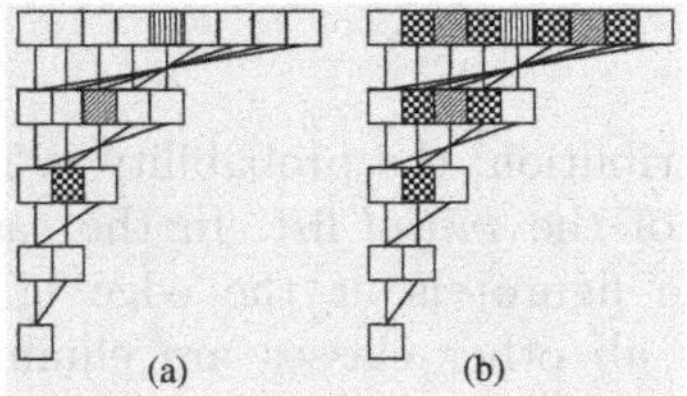

Fig. 4. The positions of classes that can be *bye-getting* elements.

Proof of Theorem 2 (Expected accuracy of the ADAG). Given N classes of examples, the height (the number of adaptive layers and the output layer) of the ADAG is obviously $\lceil log_2 N \rceil$. To be selected as the *winner* (as the output of the ADAG), some elements have to be compared with others for $\lceil log_2 N \rceil$ times, and there are some elements, called *bye-getting* elements that are compared with others for less than $\lceil log_2 N \rceil$ times. As the architecture of the ADAG always puts a bye-getting element (the middle element) of the current list at the edge of the list of the next layer, any element can get at most one bye. Therefore, a bye-getting element will be compared with others for $\lceil log_2 N \rceil - 1$ times. There will be bye-getting elements only when the number of classes cannot be represented by 2^X, where X is a positive integer. These bye-getting elements will be at the middle of the initial list and of the current list representing each adaptive layer; e.g. the 5th, 3rd and 2nd elements in the initial list, the list of the first adaptive layer, and the list of the second adaptive layer in Figure 4(a), respectively. A bye-getting element at the ith adaptive layer can come from *two* elements in the $(i-1)^{st}$ layer, as shown in Figure 4(b). Therefore, 7 elements of the initial list in the figure can possibly be bye-getting ones. Let $F(N)$ be the number of all possible bye-getting elements of the list with N elements. It is obvious that with $F(2) = 0$, and

$$F(N) = (N \bmod 2) + 2 \cdot F(\lceil N/2 \rceil). \tag{1}$$

Next we will prove by induction on X that $F(N) = 2^{\lceil log_2(N) \rceil} - N$, when N is an integer between $2^X + 1$ and 2^{X+1}, and X is a positive integer greater than or equal to 1.

First consider the base case of $X = 1$. In this case, N is equal to 3 or 4. It is obvious that $F(3) = 1$ which satisfies $F(3) = 2^{\lceil log_2(3) \rceil} - 3$, and $F(4) = 0$ satisfying $F(4) = 2^{\lceil log_2(4) \rceil} - 4$.

Next we prove general cases of $X \geq 2$ by induction: suppose $F(N)$ is equal to $2^{\lceil log_2(N) \rceil} - N$ when N is an integer between $2^{X-1} + 1$ and 2^X, and we will show that $F(M)$ is also equal to $2^{\lceil log_2(M) \rceil} - M$ when M is an integer between $2^X + 1$ and 2^{X+1}.

In case of $M = 2N$ (an even number) and $2^X + 2 \leq M \leq 2^{X+1}$, it is clear that $F(M) = 2F(N)$ according to Equation 1 (in case that M is an even number, a bye-getting elements of $F(N)$ can possibly come from two bye-getting elements of $F(M)$). Therefore, we will have the following.

$$F(M) = 2F(N) = 2(2^{\lceil log_2 N \rceil} - N) = 2^{\lceil log_2 N \rceil + 1} - 2N = 2^{\lceil log_2 2N \rceil} - 2N$$
$$= 2^{\lceil log_2 M \rceil} - M$$

This proves the case of M is an even number.

Next in case of $M = 2N - 1$ (an odd number) and $2^X + 1 \leq M \leq 2^{X+1} - 1$, it is also clear that $F(M) = 2F(N) + 1$ according to Equation 1 (in case that M is an odd number, a bye-getting elements of $F(N)$ can possibly come from two bye-getting elements of $F(M)$, and there is one more bye-getting (the middle) elements of $F(M)$ that gets a bye of this round). Therefore, we will have the following.

$$F(M) = 2F(N) + 1 = 2(2^{\lceil log_2 N \rceil} - N) + 1 = 2^{\lceil log_2 N \rceil + 1} - 2N + 1$$
$$= 2^{\lceil log_2 2N \rceil} - (2N - 1)$$

As $2^X + 1 \leq 2N - 1 < 2N \leq 2^{X+1}$, we have $log_2(2^X + 1) \leq log_2(2N - 1) < log_2(2N) \leq log_2(2^{X+1})$, which means $\lceil log_2(2N - 1) \rceil = \lceil log_2(2N) \rceil = X + 1$. The above formula then becomes as follows.

$$F(M) = 2^{\lceil log_2(2N-1) \rceil} - (2N - 1) = 2^{\lceil log_2 M \rceil} - M$$

This proves the case of M is an odd number. The above then proves that $F(N)$ is equal to $2^{\lceil log_2(N) \rceil} - N$ when N is an integer between $2^X + 1$ and 2^{X+1}, where $X \geq 1$.

Having the value of $F(N)$ as above, we then can calculate the expected accuracy of the ADAG. As under a uniform distribution, the probability that the correct class is at any position of the initial list is $1/N$. Therefore, the expected accuracy is calculated by weighting the bye-getting correct elements with $F(N)/N$, and the non-bye-getting correct elements with $(N - F(N))/N$. Finally, we have the expected accuracy of the ADAG as follows.

$$(N - F(N))/N \cdot (1 - p)^{\lceil log_2 N \rceil} + F(N)/N \cdot (1 - p)^{\lceil log_2 N \rceil - 1}$$
$$= ((2N - 2^{\lceil log_2 N \rceil})/N) \cdot (1 - p)^{\lceil log_2 N \rceil} + ((2^{\lceil log_2 N \rceil} - N)/N) \cdot (1 - p)^{\lceil log_2 N \rceil - 1}.$$

This proves the theorem.   □

References

1. Blake, C., Keogh, E., and Merz, C. (1998) *UCI repository of machine learning databases*, Dept. of Information and Computer Science, University of California, Irvine.
2. Burges, C. (1998) *A tutorial on support vector machines for pattern recognition*, Data Mining and Knowledge Discovery, 2(2):121-167.
3. Dietterich, T. G., and Bakiri, G. (1995) *Solving multiclass learning problems via error-correcting output codes*, Journal of Artificial Intelligence Research, 2:263-286.
4. Friedman, J. H. (1996) *Another approach to polychotomous classification*, Technical report, Stanford University, Department of Statistics.
5. Joachims, T. (1999) SVM^{light}, http://ais.gmd.de/ thorsten/svm_light.
6. Knerr, S., Personnaz, L., and Dreyfus, G. (1990) *Single-layer learning revisited: A stepwise procedure for building and training a neural network*, In Fogelman-Soulie and Herault, editors, Neurocomputing: Algorithms, Architectures and Applications, NATO ASI Series. Springer.
7. Platt, J., Cristianini, N., and Shawe-Taylor, J. (2000) *Large margin DAGs for multiclass classification*, Advance in Neural Information Processing System, 12, MIT Press.
8. Schölkopf, B. (1997) *Support vector learning*, Ph.D. Thesis, R.Oldenbourg Verlag Publications, Munich, Germany.
9. Thubthong, N. and Kijsirikul, B. (2001) *Support vector machines for Thai phoneme recognition*, International Journal of Uncertainty, Fuzziness and Knowledge-Based Systems, 9(6):803-813.
10. Vapnik, V. (1998) *Statistical Learning Theory*, New York, Wiley.

Network Optimization through Learning and Pruning in Neuromanifold

Hyunjin Lee[1], Hyeyoung Park[2], and Yillbyung Lee[1]

[1] Dept. of Computer Science, Yonsei University, Seoul, Korea
{dryad,yblee}@csai.yonsei.ac.kr
[2] Institute of Physical and Chemical Research, Saitama, Japan
hypark@brain.riken.go.jp

Abstract. In this paper, we propose an optimization method of neural networks based on the geometrical structure of neuromanifold. The
optimizing process starts from the manifold of sufficiently large network
model. In the manifold of the given network structure, we first find an
optimal point, which achieves good generalization performance. To do
this, we propose an extension of the adaptive natural gradient learning
with regularization term. Using hierarchical structure of neuromanifold,
we then try to optimize the network structure. To do this, we apply
the natural pruning method starting from the current optimal parameter point. The whole optimization process can be explained from the
geometrical point of view. We confirm the generalization performance of
the optimized network by the proposed method through experiments on
benchmark data sets.

1   Introduction

In this paper, we concentrate our interest on the feedforward neural networks
which mean there exist just one-way connections from input units to output
units. Under this assumption, the input-output mapping determined by a structure of neural networks can be described by

$$y = f(x, \theta), \tag{1}$$

where x and y are the input and output vector respectively, and θ is the vector
of weight parameters of the network. From this definition of neural network
structure with parameter $\theta = (\theta_1, ..., \theta_n)$, we can consider a set of all the possible
neural networks realized by specifying the value of parameter θ. This set forms
an n-dimensional manifold S, where θ plays the role of the coordinate system of
S. S is called the manifold of neural networks. From the geometrical viewpoint,
the learning of neural networks is a process of finding the closest point on a
neural manifold to the teacher network which generates the training data. If one
knows the geometrical structure of the neural manifold, one can choose more
efficient path to the optimal point. The geometrical approach thus can give
helpful insight to solve the optimization problems in neural networks.

M. Ishizuka and A. Sattar (Eds.): PRICAI 2002, LNAI 2417, pp. 169–177, 2002.

On the other hand, from statistical point of view, each network is accompanied with a probability density or a conditional probability density function. When an input x is given, the ultimate output y is assumed to be emitted through a stochastic process of the network, which is applied to the deterministic output calculated by $f(x, \theta)$. Therefore, the stochastic process of the network can be represented by the conditional probability density of the form

$$p(x, y; \theta) = p(y|x; \theta)q(x) = r(y|f(x; \theta))q(x), \tag{2}$$

where $r(\cdot)$ defines the stochastic property of the network, and $q(x)$ is the pdf of input x which is given from outside. When we treat a neural network from this stochastic viewpoint, we can describe the behavior of the network with the probability density function $p(x, y; \theta)$. Thus a neuromanifold can be regarded as a manifold of probability density functions.

By taking this geometrical approach, the natural gradient learning and the natural pruning have been developed. These methods are based on the fact that the neuromanifold is a Riemannian space, and the metric is uniquely determined by the Fisher information matrix[2,8]. Amari[1] proposed the concept of natural gradient learning by defining the steepest descent direction of error function using Fisher metric, and proved its asymptotic efficiency. Rattray et al[10] showed that it can solve the plateau problems, by using statistical-mechanical analysis. Amari, Park, and Fukumizu[3] proposed an adaptive version of natural gradient learning, and Park, Amari and Fukumizu[9] introduced explicit learning algorithms for various stochastic neural network models. The natural pruning[8] also use the Fisher metric in order to find unnecessary weight parameters from a trained large network. Heskes[6] mentioned the consistency between the natural gradient learning and the natural pruning in the sense that they uses the same Fisher metric, which is uniquely defined invariant metric in neuromanifolds.

Based on these previous works, in the present paper, we propose a network optimization method through combination of the natural gradient learning and the natural pruning. To this end, we consider one more important geometrical property of neuromanifold, which is the hierarchical structure. Recently, the hierarchical and singular structure of neuromanifold have been actively studied(See [5,12] for details). The hierarchical structure means that manifolds of large networks include submanifolds of smaller networks. Using this hierarchy, we consider the learning and pruning as a single optimization process in the large neuromanifold. From this point of view, we emphasize the necessity of regularization term in learning process, and propose a natural gradient learning method with adaptive regularization. Even though there have been the similar integrating method of learning, regularization, and pruning[7], the present paper gives a geometrical explanation on the previous heuristic approaches.

2   Hierarchical Structure of Neuromanifold

Let us first explain about the hierarchical structure of neuromanifolds. For just simplicity, we consider here about a feedforward neural networks with one hidden layer and one output, which can be written by

$$f(\boldsymbol{x}, \boldsymbol{\theta}) = \sum_{i=1}^{H} v_i \varphi(\boldsymbol{w}_i \cdot \boldsymbol{x}), \tag{3}$$

where the weight parameter $v_i, \boldsymbol{w}_i (i = 1, \ldots, H)$ are summarized to $\boldsymbol{\theta}$. Then we have a neuromanifold S^H, in which $\boldsymbol{\theta}$ plays a role of coordinates.

For this network, when $v_H = 0$ or $\|\boldsymbol{w}_H\| = 0$, the H-th hidden unit has no influence on the behavior of neural network, $f(\boldsymbol{x}, \boldsymbol{\theta})$, and its behavior comes to be same as that of smaller network with $H - 1$ hidden units. Furthermore, when $\boldsymbol{w}_i = \boldsymbol{w}_j (i \neq j)$ satisfies, the ith hidden unit and jth hidden unit can be combined to one hidden units as shown in the Eq. 4 of the form,

$$v_i \varphi(\boldsymbol{w}_i \cdot \boldsymbol{x}) + v_j \varphi(\boldsymbol{w}_j \cdot \boldsymbol{x}) = (v_i + v_j)\varphi(\boldsymbol{w}_i \cdot \boldsymbol{x}). \tag{4}$$

Consequently, the network with H hidden units satisfying one of the above conditions is same as a smaller network with $H-1$ hidden units. This relationship can be easily extended to the case of general number of hidden units, and one can obtain the hierarchy of the manifolds, which can be written as

$$S^1 \subset S^2 \subset \cdots S^{H-1} \subset S^H \subset \cdots. \tag{5}$$

Fukumizu and Amari[5] investigated the hierarchical geometrical structure of neuromanifold, and they proved that a critical point of a network model with $H - 1$ hidden units always gives many critical points of the larger network model with H hidden units, which can cause plateaus in learning of neural networks. In addition, on the critical subspace, the Fisher metric is singular, and the conventional statistical estimation theories cannot be applied. Therefore the classical results on the estimation performance of neural networks does not hold on those singular points. In order to solve these problems and to investigate various phenomena in neural networks, there is no doubt about that the geometrical study on the neuromanifold shoul play more and more important roles. The present paper is one of preliminary and practical studies to exploit the geometrical concept to the network optimization task.

3   Network Optimization in Neuromanifold

3.1   Geometrical Descriptions of Network Optimization

Before going into detail explanation of each part of the method, let us briefly describe the network optimization process based on the geometrical concept. We consider that our network optimization process starts from a sufficiently large network N^{H^+}, which has a corresponding neuromanifold S^{H^+}. As mentioned in previous section, many submanifold corresponding to smaller networks are embedded in the current manifold.

Here, we assume that an optimal network model is smaller than the current one, and we try to find the optimal network N^H and its optimal parameter $\boldsymbol{\theta}_H^*$, through iterating the learning and the pruning process. First, we start learning process in the manifold of large network N^{H^+}, so as to obtain an optimal parameter θ^*_{H+}. Then we conduct pruning, that is, deleting unnecessary element from parameter vector θ^*_{H+}, and obtain a smaller dimensional parameter θ_H. In this point, the dimension of parameter comes to be different and thus the parameter space are different. However, we can still consider the θ_H and θ^*_{H+} together in the space of larger network, due to the hierarchy. By iterating the learning and pruning process, we finally obtain an optimal parameter θ^*_H.

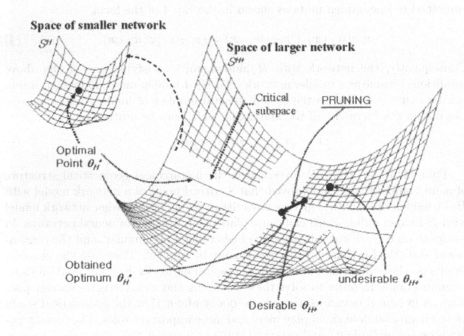

Fig. 1. Network optimization in Neuromanifold

From this geometrical viewpoint, we can intuitively evaluate the goodness of the sub-optimal parameter θ^*_{H+}. Obviously, it is desirable to make θ^*_{H+} close to θ^*_H so that the optimization process converges to the optimum θ^*_H efficiently. However, by using standard learning strategy, it is not rare the case that some elements of parameter vectors fitted to noisy data, and the obtained parameter θ^*_{H+} is far from the desirable θ^*_H.

To overcome this problem, we use a regularization term added to standard error functions, so as to prevent the overfitting. By using the regularization strategy, we hope that the learning converges to a desirable point θ^*_{H+} near to θ^*_H. Figure 1 illustrates these geometrical concepts. Based on this concept, we propose a network optimization method by combining the natural gradient learning, regularization, and the natural pruning. We first propose a natural gradient learning algorithm with adaptive regularization in the next subsection, and then briefly review the natural pruning method.

3.2   Natural Gradient Learning Method

Since the natural gradient learning is a kind of the stochastic gradient descent learning methods, we have to consider a system to be trained as a stochastic system so that it can be represented by a probability density function. Then we can consider a space of the probability density functions $\{p(x, y; \theta)|\theta \in \Re^M\}$, and define an appropriate error function $E(\theta)$ on the space. The typical error function is the loss function defined by the negative logarithm of the likelihood function which is of the form,

$$E(\theta) = -\log p(x, y^*; \theta) \tag{6}$$

$$= -\log p(y^*|x; \theta)q(x) = -\log p(y^*|x; \theta) - \log q(x), \tag{7}$$

where $q(x)$ is the pdf of the input x and $p(y|x; \theta)$ is the conditional pdf of y conditioned on x. The learning is a process of finding an optimal point in the space of the probability density functions, which minimizes the value of the error function.

The natural gradient learning method is based on the fact that the space of $p(x, y; \theta)$ is a Riemannian space in which the metric tensor is given by the Fisher information matrix $G(\theta)$ defined by

$$G(\theta) = \int\int \frac{\partial \log p}{\partial \theta}(\frac{\partial \log p}{\partial \theta})^T p(y|x, \theta)q(x)\, dy\, dx \tag{8}$$

$$= E_x \left[E_{y|x;\theta} \left[\frac{\partial \log p(y|x; \theta)}{\partial \theta}(\frac{\partial \log p(y|x; \theta)}{\partial \theta})^T \right] \right] \tag{9}$$

where $E_x[\cdot]$ and $E_{y|x;\theta}[\cdot]$ denote the expectation with respect to $q(x)$ and $p(y|x; \theta)$, respectively, and T denotes the transposition. Using the Fisher information matrix of Eq. 9, we can obtain the natural gradient $\tilde{\nabla}E$ and its learning algorithm for the stochastic systems;

$$\tilde{\nabla}E(\theta) = G^{-1}(\theta)\nabla E(\theta), \tag{10}$$

$$\theta_{t+1} = \theta_t - \eta_t\tilde{\nabla}E(\theta_t) = \theta_t - \eta_t G^{-1}(\theta_t)\nabla E(\theta_t). \tag{11}$$

We shoul note here about the shape of $p(y|x; \theta)$ and the explicit form of $G(\theta)$. As shown in Eq. 2, the specific form of $p(y|x; \theta)$ is depend on $r(\cdot)$, which can be determined according to the stochastic property of training data. The most common type is the additive Gaussian model, which is defined by the conditional probability distribution of the form,

$$p(y|x; \theta) = \frac{1}{\sqrt{2\pi}\sigma} \exp\left\{ -\frac{1}{2\sigma^2}(y - f(x, \theta))^2 \right\}, \tag{12}$$

where the output y is one dimensional case. We can then optain the corresponding form of $G(\boldsymbol{\theta})$ using Eq. 9. The explicit forms of $G(\boldsymbol{\theta})$ for various type of $p(y|\boldsymbol{x}; \boldsymbol{\theta})$ is given in [9]. Park et al[9] also proposed an adaptive version of natural gradient which eliminates the inverse operation of $G(\boldsymbol{\theta})$, for practical applications.

In this paper, we propose a natural gradient learning method with adaptive regularization, to overcome the overfitting problem. Let us define a new cost function $C(\boldsymbol{\theta})$ with regularization term $R(\boldsymbol{\theta})$ as

$$C(\boldsymbol{\theta}) = E(\boldsymbol{\theta}) + \alpha R(\boldsymbol{\theta}), \tag{13}$$

where α is a regularization parameter. Since the definition of the Fisher information matrix does not depend on the cost function, the natural gradient learning algorithm with regularization term can be written by

$$\boldsymbol{\theta}_{t+1} = \boldsymbol{\theta}_t - \eta_t G^{-1}(\boldsymbol{\theta}_t)\nabla C(\boldsymbol{\theta}_t) \tag{14}$$
$$= \boldsymbol{\theta}_t - \eta_t G^{-1}(\boldsymbol{\theta}_t)(\nabla E(\boldsymbol{\theta}_t) + \alpha\nabla R(\boldsymbol{\theta}_t)). \tag{15}$$

In order to determine the regularization parameter α, we apply the Bayesian evidence, which has the form,

$$p(\boldsymbol{\theta}|D) \propto p(D|\boldsymbol{\theta})p(\boldsymbol{\theta}), \tag{16}$$

where D denotes the whole data set. The optimal parameter α^* maximizing the evidence is given by $n/2NR(\boldsymbol{\theta})$, where the n denotes the number of parameters, and N denotes the number of data (See [4] for details).

3.3   Natural Pruning

The most important thing in the pruning process is to determine the most meaningless element from the current optimal parameter vector $\boldsymbol{\theta}^* = (\theta_1^*, \ldots, \theta_n^*)$. The most popular measure of the importance of each element θ_i^* is the change of the value of error function $E(\boldsymbol{\theta})$ when θ_i^* is set to zero, which is usually called the saliency[4].

On the other hand, the natural pruning applies the Fisher metric to define the measure, which is written by

$$F(\theta_i^*) = (\boldsymbol{\theta}^* - \boldsymbol{\theta}^i)^T G(\boldsymbol{\theta}^*)(\boldsymbol{\theta}^* - \boldsymbol{\theta}^i), \tag{17}$$

where $G(\boldsymbol{\theta}^*)$ is the Fisher information matrix at $\boldsymbol{\theta}^*$, and $\boldsymbol{\theta}^i$ is the parameter vector obtained by setting θ_i^* to zero. In natural pruning, we first find an element that have minimum value of $F(\theta_i^*)$, and delete the element.

Note that the measure $F(\theta_i^*)$ is based on the difference of the probability density function $p(y|\boldsymbol{x}; \boldsymbol{\theta})$ of the neural network, whereas the saliency is depend on the training error. Therefore, by using this measure instead of conventional saliency, we can expect to find the best element to be pruned in the sense of the generalization performance. From this, we again see the necessity of regularization term. Since the pruning is done under the assumption that the current parameter $\boldsymbol{\theta}^*$ is the best one, it is important to optimize the parameter to the generalization error, not the training error.

4 Experimental Results

To check the generalization performance of the proposed learning method, we conducted computational experiments using the Monk problems, which have been widely used as benchmark data. The Monk problems are originally from the UCI repository of machine learning data bases[11]. It is a classification problem, and composed of three sub-problems with different data sets, Monk1, Monk2, and Monk3. Each data set has 432 samples for training and test. In the case of Monk 1 and Monk 2 problems, 124 samples and 169 samples have been selected for training, respectively. In the case of Monk 3, 122 samples with 5% noise have been used for training.

Table 1. Classification results on test data of Monk problems.

Method	Monk1	Monk2	Monk3
Assistant Pro.	100%	81.5%	100%
ID5R	79.7%	69.2%	95.2%
ID3	98.6%	67.9%	94.4%
AQR	95.9%	79.7%	87.0%
PRISM	86.3%	72.7%	90.3%
ECOWEB	82.7%	71.3%	68.0%
BP	100%	100%	93.1%
BP + Weight Decay	100%	100%	97.2%
Cascade Correlation	100%	100%	97.2%
Proposed Method	100%	100%	100%

In Table 1, we compare the classification rates of the proposed method with those of other conventional methods, which are offered by the UCI repository of machine learning databases. The first six methods from Assistant Pro. to ECOWEB are variations of the decision tree method (See [11] for details). The next three method used neural networks with the backpropagation (BP) learning method. The BP + Weight Decay method used BP learning with weight decay as regularization term. The Cascade Correlation is one of the well known growing method for network optimization[4]. The proposed method showed superiority to the other methods in the sense of classification rate, for all Monk problems.

We also compared the proposed method with naive combination method of natural gradient learning and natural pruning. In the experiment, we used 10 fully connected neural networks with random initialization as starting networks, so as to get average performances for each method. Each starting network consists of 17 input units, 5 hidden units and 1 output unit. Including bias parameters, the total number of weight parameter of one network is 96. The average results over 10 independent learning and pruning tasks are shown in Table 2. For all three problems, Monk1, Monk2, Monk3, the proposed method obtained smaller networks comparing to the naive combination method. In addition, for the Monk3 problem, the proposed method showed higher classification rate for test data, implying better generalization performance.

Table 2. Proposed method vs. naive combination method

Method		Monk1	Monk2	Monk3
Naive Combination	Number of Weights	14.2	17	17
	Classification rate(Training)	100%	100%	95.9%
	Classification rate(Test)	100%	100%	97.2%
Proposed Method	Number of Weights	10.2	15.2	10.6
	Classification rate(Training)	100%	100%	96.5%
	Classification rate(Test)	100%	100%	100%

These results agree with our geometrical assumption described in section 3. The difference between two method is the existence of regularization term. By using the regularization term, the proposed method tries to find a (sub)optimal parameter (θ^*_{H+}) near the ultimate optimal parameter (θ^*_H) of smaller neural networks so as to make the pruning process efficient. Thus we can expect to get a compact network with better generalization.

5   Conclusions and Discussions

The generalization problem is closely related to the optimization problem of complexity of the model, such as structure optimization in neural networks. In this paper, we proposed an optimization method of neural networks based on the geometrical structure of neuromanifold. We regard the learning and the structure optimization problem as a single process getting close to the optimal model in the hierarchical neuromanifold. Based on this concept, we construct a combination method of learning, adaptive regularization, and pruning. For the learning and pruning, we used the natural gradient and the natural pruning, which are the most appropriate methods considering the geometrical property of neuromanifold. Through experiments, we confirmed that our learning strategy based on the geometrical concept can achieve better generalization performance.

This work is a preliminary study on construction of optimal network based on the geometrical concept of neuromanifolds. We should note here that the combination of learning with regularization and pruning has been taken as an integrating strategy for network design, with little theoretical study. The present paper discusses some geometrical meaning of the strategy. By taking the geometrical point of view and analysing the structure, it is possible to develop more novel method for network optimization. The present paper is the first step to the ultimate goal.

References

1. S. Amari, Natural Gradient Works Efficiently in Learning, *Neural Computation*, 10, 251-276, 1998.
2. S. Amari and H. Nagaoka, *Information Geometry*, AMS and Oxford University Press, 2001.
3. Amari, S., Park, H., and Fukumizu, F., Adaptive method of realizing natural gradient learning for multilayer perceptrons, *Neural Computation*, 12, 1399-1409, 2000.
4. Bishop, C.,*Neural Networks for Pattern Recognition*, Oxford University Press, 1995.
5. Fukumizu K. and Amari, S., Local Minima and Plateaus in Hierarchical Structures of Multilayer Perceptrons, *Neural Networks*, 13, 317-327, 2000.
6. Heskes, T., On Natural Learning and Pruning in Multilayer Perceptrons, *Neural Compuataion*, 12, 1037-1507, 2000.
7. Hintz-Madsen, M., Hansen, L., Larsen, J., Pedersen, M., and Larsen, M., Neural Classifier Construction using Regularization, Pruning and Test Error Estimation, *Neural Networks*, 11, 1659-1670, 1998.
8. Laar, P.V.D., Heskes, T., Pruning Using Parameter and Neuronal Metrics, *Neural Computation*, 11, 977-993, 1999.
9. Park, H., Amari, S., Fukumizu, F., Adaptive Natural Gradient Learning Algorithms for Various Stochastic Models, *Neural Networks*, 13, 755-764, 2000.
10. M. Rattray, D. Saad, and S. Amari, Natural Gradient Descent for On-line Learning, *Physical Review Letters*, 81, 5461-5464, 1998.
11. Thrun et al., The MONK's Problems A Performance Comparison of Different Learning Algorithm, (CMU-CS-91-197), Carnegie University, 1991.
12. Watanabe, S., Algebraic Analysis for Non-identifiable Learning Machines, Neural Computation, 13, 899-933, 2001.

DIC: A Novel Discrete Incremental Clustering Technique for the Derivation of Fuzzy Membership Functions

W.L. Tung and C. Quek

Intelligent Systems Laboratory, Nanyang Technological University,
School of Computer Engineering, Blk N4 #2A-32, Nanyang Avenue, Singapore 639798
ashcquek@ntu.edu.sg

Abstract. Generally, clustering techniques may be classified into *hierarchical-*based and *partition*-based techniques. Hierarchical-based clustering techniques included *single link* [1], *complete link* [2] and [3][4]. The main drawback of hierarchical clustering is that it is static, and points committed to a given cluster in the early stages cannot be moved to a different cluster. Prototype-based partition clustering techniques, on the other hand, are dynamic and the data points can move from one cluster to another under varying conditions. However, partition-based clustering techniques require *prior* knowledge such as the number of classes, C, in the set of training data. Such information may be unknown and is difficult to estimate in data sets such as traffic flow data [5]. For tasks such as the 2-Spiral problem [6], computing a predefined number of clusters, C, may not be good enough to satisfactorily solve the tasks. Moreover, partition-based clustering techniques suffer from the *stability-plasticity dilemma* [7] where new information cannot be learned without running the risk of eroding old (previously learned) but valid knowledge. Therefore, in the context of *neural fuzzy systems* [8] such as POPFNN [9], hierarchical clustering violates the networks' ability to self-organize and self-adapt with changing environments while current partition-based clustering techniques have some significant shortcomings. These deficiencies serve as the main motivations behind the development of the *Discrete Incremental Clustering* (DIC) technique. The DIC technique is not limited by the need to have *prior* knowledge of the number of clusters C and it preserves the dynamism of partition-based clustering techniques. The proposed DIC technique is implemented in a new neural fuzzy network named Gen-SoFNN [10] to demonstrate its performance.

1 Introduction

Neural fuzzy (or neuro-fuzzy) networks [8] such as POPFNN [9], ANFIS [11] and Falcon-ART [12] are the realisations of the functionality of fuzzy systems using neural techniques. The main advantage of a neural fuzzy network is its ability to model a problem using a linguistic model instead of complex mathematical models. The lin-

M. Ishizuka and A. Sattar (Eds.): PRICAI 2002, LNAI 2417, pp. 178-187, 2002.
© Springer-Verlag Berlin Heidelberg 2002

guistic model is essentially a fuzzy rule base consisting of a set of IF-THEN fuzzy rules. The IF-THEN fuzzy rules are highly intuitive and easily comprehended. In addition, the black-box nature of neural network is resolved as the intuitive IF-THEN fuzzy rules can be used to interpret the weights and connections of the neural structure. Moreover, the embedded fuzzy system in a neural fuzzy network can self-adjust the parameters of the fuzzy rules using neural network learning algorithms.

Generally, the derivation of the fuzzy rules consists of two phases. Firstly, a cluster analysis is performed on the numerical training data to compute the required clusters and subsequently, the appropriate fuzzy rules are formulated through the proper connections of the computed fuzzy sets. During the interpretation of the fuzzy rules, the fuzzy sets are represented as fuzzy labels in the formulated fuzzy rules.

Hence, cluster analysis is a major component in the training of neural fuzzy networks. Clustering is a process to partition a data space or a given data set into different classes/groups so that the data points within the same class are more similar to one another than to data points in other classes. Clustering is an exploratory approach to analyze a given numerical data set by creating a structural knowledge representation of the data set. The clustering techniques proposed in the literature can be categorized into two main groups: *Hierarchical-based* and *Partition-based* clustering techniques.

The main drawback of hierarchical clustering is that it is static, and points committed to a given cluster in the early stages cannot be moved to a different cluster. Prototype-based partition clustering techniques, on the other hand, are dynamic and the data points can move from one cluster to another under varying conditions. However, partition-based clustering techniques require *prior* knowledge such as the number of classes C in the training data. Such information may be unknown and is difficult to estimate in data set such as traffic flow data [5]. For tasks such as the 2-Spiral problem [6], computing a predefined number of clusters C may not be good enough to satisfactorily solve the tasks. Moreover, partition-based clustering techniques suffer from the *stability-plasticity dilemma* [7] where new information cannot be learned without running the risk of eroding old (previously learned) but valid knowledge. Hence, these deficiencies serve as the main motivations behind the development of the proposed *Discrete Incremental Clustering* (DIC) technique. The DIC technique is implemented in a new neural fuzzy network named *Generic Self-organising Fuzzy Neural Network* (GenSoFNN) [10] to demonstrate its performance.

This paper is organised as follows. Section 2 briefly describes the generic structure of the GenSoFNN network. Section 3 introduces the concepts behind the DIC technique and Section 4 presents the experimental results of the DIC technique using the 2-Spiral problem. Section 5 concludes this paper.

2   The GenSoFNN Network

The GenSoFNN network (Fig. 1) consists of five layers of nodes. Each input node IV_i, $i \in \{1,...,n1\}$, has a single input. The vector $X=[x_1,...,x_i,...,x_{n1}]^T$ represents the inputs to the GenSoFNN. Each output node OV_m, where $m \in \{1,...,n5\}$, computes a single output denoted by y_m. The vector $Y=[y_1,...,y_m,...,y_{n5}]^T$ denotes the outputs of the GenSoFNN network with respect to the input stimulus X. In addition, the vector $D=[d_1,...,d_m,...,d_{n5}]^T$ represents the desired network outputs required during the parameter-learning phase of the training cycle. The trainable weights of the GenSoFNN network are found in layers 2 and 5 (enclosed in rectangular boxes in Fig. 1). Layer 2 links contain the parameters of the input fuzzy sets while layer 5 links contain the parameters of the output fuzzy sets. The weights of the remaining connections are unity. The trainable weights (parameters) are interpreted as the corners of the trapezoidal-shaped fuzzy sets computed by the proposed DIC technique. They are denoted as l and r (left and right support points), and u and v (left and right kernel points). The subscripts denote the pre-synaptic and post-synaptic nodes respectively. For clarity in subsequent discussions, the variables i,j,k,l,m are used to refer to arbitrary nodes in layers 1, 2, 3, 4 and 5 respectively. The output of a node is denoted as Z and the subscripts specify its origin.

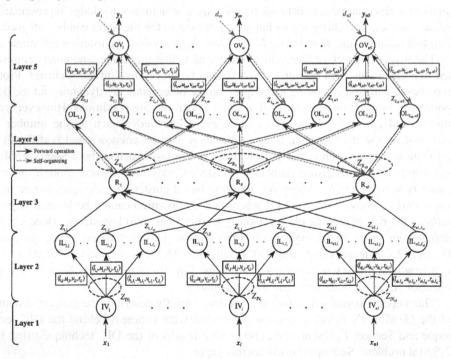

Fig. 1. Structure of the GenSoFNN network

Each input node IV_i may have different number of input terms J_i. Hence, number of layer 2 nodes is "n2", where $n2=\sum_{i=1}^{n1}J_i$. Layer 3 consists of the rule nodes R_k, where $k=\{1,...,n3\}$. At layer 4, an output term node $\mathrm{OL}_{l,m}$ may have more than one fuzzy rule attached to it. Each output node OV_m in layer 5 can have different number of output terms L_m. Hence, number of layer 4 nodes is "n4", where $n4 = \sum_{m=1}^{n5} L_m$. In Fig.1, the solid arrows denote the links that are used during the feed-forward normal operation of the GenSoFNN network. The dashed arrows denote the backward links used during the self-organising phase of the training cycle of the GenSoFNN. The GenSoFNN network adopts the Mamdani's fuzzy rule model [8].

In this paper, the *Compositional Rule of Inference* (CRI) [13] is mapped to the GenSoFNN network to define the node functions. Please refer to [14] for more details on how this mapping is performed. The training cycle of the GenSoFNN network consists of three phases: *Self-organising*, *rule formulation* and *parameter learning*. These are performed sequentially with a single pass of the training data. The proposed DIC technique is responsible for the self-organising phase of the GenSoFNN network and automatically computes the input-output clusters from the numerical training data. The fuzzy rules are subsequently formulated by connecting the appropriate input and output clusters during the rule-mapping phase of the training cycle. Consequently, the parameters of the GenSoFNN network (the links of layer 5 and layer 2) are tuned during the parameter-learning phase.

3 The Discrete Incremental Clustering (DIC) Technique

This novel clustering technique attempts to integrate the merits of the fuzzy ART [15] and the LVQ [16] clustering techniques. Fuzzy ART creates a new category to hold the new inputs when they do not sufficiently resonate with the existing knowledge base. The main strength of fuzzy ART is it does not assume a predefined number of clusters to compute. This allows ART-based systems to handle non-partitionable problems like the XOR and 2-Spiral problems [6][17]. On the other hand, LVQ is a well-established partition-based clustering technique with updating equations that is simple to comprehend and is not computationally intensive.

The proposed DIC technique uses raw numerical values of a training data set with no pre-processing. In the current implementation, DIC computes trapezoidal-shaped fuzzy sets on a local basis. That is, the number of fuzzy sets for each input/output dimension need not be the same. However, unlike fuzzy ART, if the fuzzy label (fuzzy set) for a particular input/output dimension already exists, then it is not "recreated". Hence, DIC ensures that a fuzzy label is uniquely defined by a fuzzy set and this serves as a basis to formulate a *consistent* rule base [8] in the GenSoFNN network. The proposed DIC technique has five parameters: a plasticity parameter β, a tendency parameter TD, an input threshold IT, an output threshold OT and a fuzzy set support parameter *SLOPE*.

3.1 The Fuzzy Set Support Parameter *SLOPE*

Each new cluster in DIC begins as a triangular fuzzy set as shown in Fig. 2(a). The kernel of a new cluster (fuzzy set) takes the value of the data point (Γ) that triggers its creation and its support is defined by the parameter *SLOPE*. As training continues, the cluster "grows" to include more points, but maintains the same amount of buffer regions on both sides of the kernel (Fig. 2(b)). The same applies for the output clusters. With respect to the ith input dimension, $\max(x_i) =$ maximum input and $\min(x_i) =$ minimum input.

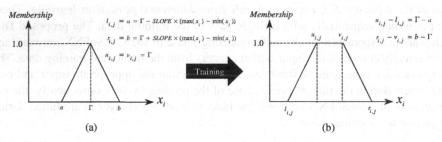

Fig. 2. (a) A newly created cluster $\mu_{i,j}(x_i)$ and (b) Cluster $\mu_{i,j}(x_i)$ undergoes training

3.2 Plasticity Parameter β

A cluster "grows" by expanding its kernel. This expansion is controlled by the plasticity parameter β. A cluster expands its kernel when it is the best-fit cluster (has the highest membership value) to a data point and this data point falls outside its kernel. The plasticity parameter β governs how much a cluster (fuzzy set) expands its kernel to include the new data point. To satisfy the *stability-plasticity dilemma* [7], the initial value of β for all newly formed input/output clusters is pre-set at 0.5. The value of its β parameter decreases as the cluster expands its kernel. The first quadrant of a cosine waveform (Fig. 3a) is used to model the change of β in a cluster. The parameter θ in Fig. 3a is intuitively interpreted as the maximum expansion a cluster (fuzzy set) can have and a parameter *STEP* controls the increment of θ from 0 to 1.57 radians. Hence, the amount of expansion a cluster can adopt decreases with the number of expansions.

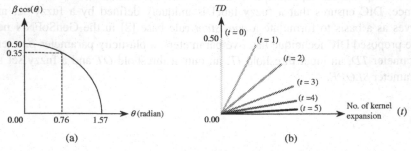

Fig. 3. (a) Modeling of plasticity parameter β and (b) Dynamics of tendency parameter *TD*

3.3 Tendency Parameter *TD*

The tendency parameter *TD* is analogous to a cluster's willingness to "grow" when it is the best-fit cluster to a data point that falls outside its kernel. It complements the use of the plasticity parameter β. Parameter *TD* maintains the relevance of a cluster and prevents it from incorporating too many data points that has low "fitness" or membership values to the cluster. Otherwise, the kernel of a cluster may become overly large and the semantic meaning of the fuzzy label the cluster represents may become obscure and poorly defined. The initial value of *TD* of a newly created cluster is pre-set at 0.5 and the cluster stops expanding its kernel when *TD* reaches zero. The rate of decrease depends on the "fitness" of the data points that the cluster incorporates as shown in equation (1). With respect to node $IL_{i,j}$,

$$TD_{i,j}^{new} = TD_{i,j}^{old} + (A - TD_{i,j}^{old}) \times (1 - \mu_{i,j}(x_i))^2.$$ (1)

Where $\mu_{i,j}$ denotes the membership function of the node $IL_{i,j}$ and A = -0.5.

When *TD* is less than or equal to zero, the cluster stops "growing" and sets its plasticity parameter β to zero. A has to be less than zero, else *TD* can never reach or exceed zero. This is because the value of the term $(1 - \mu_{i,j}(x_i))^2$ is in the range [0, 1) (The case when $\mu_{i,j}(x_i) = 0$ is not valid as the point is then irrelevant to the cluster).

Hence, the less fit the data points (with small membership values) a cluster try to incorporate or absorb; the faster its *TD* decreases and vice-versa. Thus, *TD* and β together maintain the integrity of the input clusters and the fuzzy labels they represent. The same applies for the output clusters. Fig. 3b illustrates the dynamics of *TD*.

3.4 Thresholds (*IT* and *OT*)

The input (output) threshold, *IT* (*OT*), specifies the minimum "fitness" or membership value an input (output) data point must have before it is considered as relevant to any existing input (output) clusters or fuzzy sets. If the fitness of the input (output) data point to the existing best-fit input (output) cluster falls below the predefined *IT* (*OT*), then a new cluster is created. In addition, *IT* (*OT*) determines the degree of overlapping of an input (output) cluster with its immediate neighbors (Fig. 4).

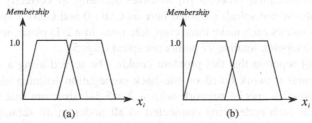

Fig. 4. Effects of *IT* on clusters for the *i*th input (The same applies for *OT* and the output clusters). (a) High *IT* value (*IT* = 0.85) and (b) Low *IT* value (*IT* = 0.5)

Hence, the larger the pre-set value of IT (OT), the closer is the computed input (output) clusters. In order to prevent excessive overlapping of the input (output) clusters (whereby the fuzzy labels become obscure or poorly defined), IT (OT) is predefined at 0.5. The following algorithm performs clustering of the input space (The same applies to clustering of the output space). More details on the DIC technique are reported in [10].

```
Algorithm DIC
    Assume data set  X̄ = {X⁽¹⁾, ... , X⁽ᵖ⁾, ... , X⁽ᴾ⁾}. Initialize STEP,
    SLOPE, IT and TD. Vector X⁽ᵖ⁾ = {x₁⁽ᵖ⁾, ... , xᵢ⁽ᵖ⁾, ... , xₙ₁⁽ᵖ⁾} repre-
    sents the pth input training vector to GenSoFNN.
    ∀p ∈ {1 ... P}
        ∀i ∈ {1 ... n1}
            When Jᵢ is zero, create a new cluster using xᵢ⁽ᵖ⁾.
            Otherwise,
                Determine best-fit cluster Winner such that:
                    Winner = arg max {...ᵢ,ⱼ (xᵢ⁽ᵖ⁾)}
                               j∈{1...Jᵢ}
                Update the kernel of Winner if μᵢ,ᵂⁱⁿⁿᵉʳ(xᵢ⁽ᵖ⁾) > IT
                Otherwise, create a new cluster using xᵢ⁽ᵖ⁾
End.
```

All parameters in DIC are constants except for the $STEP$ and $SLOPE$ parameters. In the current implementation, the selection of these two parameters is heuristic and varies with different tasks. However, there are several guidelines to assist in the selection of suitable values for these two parameters. A small $STEP$ value results in "fat" fuzzy sets with large kernels and vice versa. On the other hand, a small $SLOPE$ value results in steep slopes (nearly crisp fuzzy sets) and the fuzziness of the fuzzy sets (input and output clusters) increases as the value of $SLOPE$ increases.

4 Experimental Results

The 2-Spiral classification problem [6] involves learning to correctly classify the points of two intertwined spirals (denoted here as Class 0 and Class 1 spirals respectively). The two spirals each make three complete turns in a 2-D plane, with 32 points per turn plus an endpoint, totaling 97 points per spiral (Fig. 5).

Lang et al. [6] reported that this problem couldn't be solved using a conventional feed-forward neural network based on the back-propagation learning algorithm. Instead, they proposed a special network with a 2-5-5-5-1 structure that has shortcut connections, with each node being connected to all nodes in all subsequent layers. With one additional bias weight for each node, the system has 138 trainable weights.

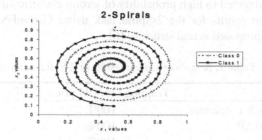

Fig. 5. The 2-Spiral problem

In [17], the fuzzy ARTMAP system is trained using the standard 2-Spiral data set consisting of 194 points [6]. Evaluation of the fuzzy ARTMAP is performed using the training set as well as a test set that consists of two dense spirals, each with 385 points. For the evaluation of the proposed DIC based GenSoFNN network, the training set is the standard 2-Spiral data consisting of 194 points. The test set consists of two dense spirals with 385 points each as in [17].

There are two inputs and a single output. The inputs consist of the co-ordinates of the points (x_1 and x_2) belonging to the two spirals. During a training epoch, the outermost Class 0 point is presented first followed by the outermost Class 1 point and the sequence continues, alternating between the two spirals and moving towards the centre of each spiral. In the experiment, one output is used to define the class of a point. That is, Class 0 is defined as "0" and Class 1 is defined as "1". Fig. 6 shows the effect of the parameter *SLOPE* on the classification rate of GenSoFNN for the 2-Spiral task. Both the training and test sets are used in the evaluation.

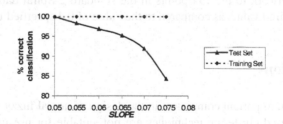

Fig. 6. 2-Spiral classification results of GenSoFNN versus *SLOPE*

It is seen that the classification rate of the training set is not affected by the change in the parameter *SLOPE* that varies from 0.05 to 0.075 and maintains at 100%. That is, all the 194 points are correctly classified. However, the classification rate of the test set decreases rapidly from 100% at *SLOPE* = 0.05 to 84.3% at *SLOPE* = 0.075. It is probably due to the increased fuzziness of the clusters (fuzzy sets) that result from a larger *SLOPE*. As fuzziness of the clusters increases, more uncertainty and ambiguity arises between the fuzzy sets (due to gentler slopes). Hence, the test set, which contains a higher density of points packed into two spirals, gives a poorer classification rate with increasing *SLOPE* as points appearing between the fuzzy (uncertain) regions of clusters are subjected to high probability of wrong classification. Table 1 shows the best classification results for the 2-Spiral task using GenSoFNN, Fuzzy ARTMAP [17] and Lang's proposed neural structure [6].

Table 1. Best classification results in 2-Spiral simulations

Architecture	Training set (194 points)	Test set (770 points)
Lang's 2-5-5-5-1 structure	100%	92.8%
Fuzzy ARTMAP	100%	100%
GenSoFNN	100%	100%

The classification results for Lang's neural structure are obtained from [17]. Lang considered the task as completed when each of the 194 points in the two spirals used for training produces an output within 0.4 of its target output value. That is, zero for Class 0 spiral and one for Class 1 spiral. When the weights of the specialized network are updated using vanilla back-propagation [18], training required an average of 20,000 epochs. Average training time was decreased to 10,000 epochs using the cross-entropy error measure and to 8000 epochs using the quick-prop algorithm [19]. On the other hand, Carpenter *et. al.* uses the most stringent criteria to train the fuzzy ARTMAP system with the standard 2-spiral data set to obtain 100% classification for the dense spirals [17]. As a result, the fuzzy ARTMAP system creates 194 ART categories for the standard 2-spiral data set that contains 194 points. In comparison, DIC trained GenSoFNN achieves 100% classification for both the standard 2-Spiral data set as well as the dense spirals with only 23 fuzzy sets in each of the two input dimensions. This occurs when *SLOPE* is 0.05 and a total of 156 rules are created (as compared to fuzzy ARTMAP's 194 categories). Moreover, the output responses of the GenSoFNN network to the 194 points in the standard 2-Spiral data set are all within 0.01 of the desired value, as compared to the value of 0.4 specified by Lang.

5 Conclusions

Clustering is an important component in the design of neural fuzzy systems. However, hierarchical-based clustering techniques are not suitable for use in neural fuzzy systems such as POPFNN [9] while existing prototype-based clustering techniques encountered several limitations. The proposed DIC technique attempts to overcome such limitations and is fairly successful as demonstrated by the experimental results of the 2-Spiral [6] simulation. DIC does not require the *prior* knowledge of the number of clusters C for a given data set and handles the *stability-plasticity dilemma* [7] by performing the clustering of data on a local basis. Moreover, DIC provides the platform for the GenSoFNN [10] network to formulate a *consistent* fuzzy rule base [8], which is important since the ability to interpret the fuzzy rule base is one of the main reasons why complex hybrid neural fuzzy systems are constructed.

References

1. Gower, J.C., Ross, G.J.S.: Minimum spanning trees and single linkage cluster analysis. Applied Statistic (1969) 18: 54-64
2. Johnson, S.C.: Hierarchical clustering schemes. Psychometrika (1967) 323: 241-254
3. Benkirane, H., Kbir, M.A., Maalmi, K., Benslimane, R.: Hierarchical fuzzy partition for pattern classification with fuzzy if-then rules. Pattern Recog. Letters (2000) 21: 503-509
4. Cunningham, G.A., Lin, Y.H., Coggeshall, S.V.: Using Fuzzy Partitions to Create Fuzzy Systems from Input-Output Data and Set the Initial Weights in a Fuzzy Neural Network. IEEE Trans. Fuzzy Systs (1997) 5(4): 614-621
5. Tan, G.K.: Feasibility of predicting congestion states with neural networks. Final Year Project Thesis, School of Civil and Structural Engineering, Nanyang Technological University, Singapore (1997)
6. Lang, K.J., Witbrock, M.J.: Learning to tell two spirals apart. Proc. 1988 Connectionist Models Summer School (1988) 52-59
7. Lin, C.T., Lee, C.S.G.: Neural Fuzzy Systems – A Neuro-Fuzzy Synergism to Intelligent Systems. Englewood Cliffs, NJ, Prentice Hall (1996)
8. Nauck, D., Klawonn, F., Kruse, R.: Foundations of Neuro-Fuzzy Systems. Chichester, England; New York, John Wiley (1997)
9. Quek, C., Zhou, R.W.: POPFNN: A Pseudo Outer-Product Based Fuzzy Neural Network. Neural Networks 9(9): 1569-1581, Elsevier Science Ltd. (1996)
10. Tung, W.L.: A Generalized Platform for Fuzzy Neural Network. Technical Report, ISL-TR-01/01, School of Computer Engineering, Nanyang Technological University, Singapore (2001)
11. Jang, J.S.: ANFIS: Adaptive-Network-Based Fuzzy Inference Systems. IEEE Trans. Systems, Man & Cybernetics (1993) 23: 665-685
12. Lin, C.J., Lin, C.T.: An ART-Based Fuzzy Adaptive Learning Control Network. IEEE Trans. Fuzzy Systs (1997) 5(4): 477-496
13. Zadeh, L.A.: Calculus of fuzzy restrictions. Fuzzy sets and Their Applications to Cognitive and Decision Processes. Ed. New York: Academic 1-39 (1975)
14. Tung, W.L., Quek, C.: Derivation of GenSoFNN-CRI(S) from CRI-based Fuzzy System. Technical Report, ISL-TR-04/01, School of Computer Engineering, Nanyang Technological University, Singapore (2001)
15. Carpenter, G.A., Grossberg, S., Rosen, D.B.: Fuzzy ART: Fast stable learning and categorization of analog patterns by an adaptive resonance system. Neural Networks (1991) 4: 759-771
16. Kohonen, T.K.: Self-Organized Formation of Topologically Correct Feature Maps. Bio. Cybern. (1982) 43: 59-69
17. Carpenter, G.A., Grossberg, S., Markuzon, N., Reynolds, J.H., Rosen, D.B.: Fuzzy ARTMAP: A Neural Network Architecture for Incremental Supervised Learning of Analog Multidimensional Maps. IEEE Trans. Neural Networks (1992) 3(5): 698-713
18. Rumelhart, D.E., Hinton, G.E., Williams, R.J.: Learning internal representations by error propagation. In Rumelhart, D.E., McClelland, J.L. et al., eds. Parallel Distributed Processing, vol. 1, chap. 8, Cambridge, MA: MIT Press (1986)
19. Fahlman, S.E.: Faster-learning variations on back-propagation: An empirical study. Proc. 1988 Connectionist Models Summer School (1989) 38-51

Application of Episodic Q-Learning to a Multi-agent Cooperative Task

Akira Ito

Gifu University,
1-1, Yanagido, Gifu, 502-0851, Japan
ai@info.gifu-u.ac.jp
http://www.elf.info.gifu-u.ac.jp

Abstract. Episodic Q-learning is successfully applied to a multi-agent cooperative task, which is strongly non-Markovian and for which Q-learning is believed to have poor performance. The 3-hunter game, which is a modified version of the pursuit problem, is employed and the time necessary for hunters to capture the escapee is measured. By restricting the amount of the history used for learning, a significant increase in the speed of learning is realized. The success is not accidental, but based on the *mind-reading* algorithm we have proposed.

1 Introduction

The design and implementation of multi-agent system whose members can act autonomously is a fascinating research theme. If we have to design every detail of the action strategy for each agent, however, it is difficult to program them all. Moreover, the significance of employing autonomous agents would be questioned. To cope with this problem, reinforcement learning, which realizes on-line learning for each agent, seems to be a promising approach. The fact that the constituent agents learn means, however, that the future for each agent cannot be determined by the current state of the system and the action it will take, i.e., the environment is non-Markovian for each agent.

Two types of methods have been developed for the reinforcement learning framework. One is the Q-learning type[1][2], whose formalization is based on the sum of the expected value of the discounted reward in the future (called action/state values). The other is the Profit Sharing (PS) learning type[3], which reinforces successful episodes directly. It has been suggested that the Q-learning method, which was originally developed for learning Markovian environment, is inapplicable to, or have poor performance for a strongly non-Markovian environment[4][5]. Hence PS-learning is often employed for multi-agent reinforcement learning.

However, the meaning of the evaluation function in PS-learning is rather ambiguous. Hence it is difficult to extend or generalize an approximation that proved useful in some situation to another. Conversely, the theoretical framework of Q-learning is clear, and many powerful techniques for its solutions have been developed[6]. If Q-learning is applicable to multi-agent reinforcement learning, various merits will be expected.

M. Ishizuka and A. Sattar (Eds.): PRICAI 2002, LNAI 2417, pp. 188–197, 2002.
© Springer-Verlag Berlin Heidelberg 2002

We have proposed in the previous paper the speeding up of PS-learning by the coarse graining of perceptions[7]. In this paper Q-learning is applied to the same problem, and shown to be effective for some kind of problems that are essentially non-Markovian. The success is not accidental, but rooted in the cooperative nature of the task we employed. The method is based on the idea of the mind-reading algorithm we have proposed[8].

2 N-Hunter Game

We will employ a N-hunter game, a modified version of the pursuit problem proposed by Benda et al[9]. The reason we modified the original problem is as follows. In the original pursuit problem, it is very difficult for hunters to learn to capture a rational escapee. In order to reduce the difficulty of the problem to a tractable level, the number of hunters is often reduced to two or three. However, to capture the rational escapee with less than 4 hunters is unrealistic in the original formulation, for the escapee can always run away in at least one direction. Hence some restrictions on the ability of the escapee (incomplete sight, etc.) are also imposed.

With the adoption of these modifications, we may lose essential elements of the multi-agent reinforcement learning, because these restrictions reduce the freedom of the escapee, and simplify the modeling of the escapee by the chasing hunters. Hence we reformulate the problem as the capture of a rational escapee by a minimum numbers of hunters whose ability (vision, action, etc.) is equal to the escapee. The detailed specification of the N-hunter game is given below:

N-hunter game The N-hunter game is a canonical problem where n hunters chase and capture one escapee on a 2-dimensional $m \times m$ torus as shown in Fig.1. Each hunter and the escapee can move up/down/right/left by one step or stay at the same location. If the escapee and one of the hunters occupy the same location, the escapee is regarded as captured. The hunters and the escapee have complete sights, i.e., they can perceive the exact locations (relative to himself) of the escapee and other hunters. No communication is allowed among the hunters. Obviously a team of two hunters cannot capture a rational escapee. Hence we employ a 3-hunter game in the following.

As the aim of this paper is to make hunters learn to capture a escapee, we do not make the escapee learn, but run away as far as possible from the nearby hunters. Let the location vector of the hunters (viewed by the escapee) be h_i and its norm be $|h_i|$. Then the escapee selects the action that decreases $E = \sum_i (1/|h_i|)$ by the greatest amount. The adoption of the inverse of the norm makes the escapee try to avoid the nearest hunter.

If an escapee takes an action to run away from the hunters, it is not easy for the hunters to capture it. For example, in our preliminary experiments, it takes about 10^5 turns for randomly moving 3 hunters to capture such an escapee on a 7×7 torus. The capture demands rigid cooperative behavior between the hunters. In the worst case scenario, if all the hunters simply chase the escapee in the same direction as that of the escapee, then the capture will never succeed.

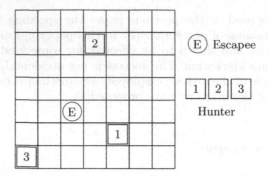

Fig. 1. Three-Hunter Game

3   Q-Learning and PS Learning

We use the term Q-learning for a method to perform action selection based on the expected sum of the discounted reward (state/action value). Sutton[6] is a good textbook for this topic. In the Q-learning framework, a set of system states Σ and a set of possible actions A are given. When an agent takes an action $a_t \in A$ in a state $S_t \in \Sigma$, then the reward r_t is given and the state transits to S_{t+1}. Let the reward at $t + k$ obtained by following the action policy π be r^π_{t+k}, then the sum of the discounted reward (state value) V is given by:
$$V^\pi(S_t) = \sum_{k=0}^\infty \gamma^k r^\pi_{t+k}$$
Here, $\gamma(0 < \gamma < 1)$ is a discount rate, which assures the convergence of the infinite summation, and evaluates the future rewards smaller.

In the standard algorithm for Q-learning, the action-value Q is defined as the sum of the expected reward obtained by taking an action a in a state S.
$$Q^\pi(S_t, a) = r(S_t, a) + \gamma V^\pi(S_{t+1})$$
In a Markovian environment (i.e., one that can be modeled as a Markov Deterministic Process, MDP), r_t and S_{t+1} are determined (in an indeterministic Markovian environment, stochastically determined) by S_t and a_t, and expressed as $r_t = r(S_t, a_t)$ and $S_{t+1} = \delta(S_t, a_t)$.

Conversely, in a multi-agent environment in which a number of learning agents cooperate/compete, each agent can change the future action from the information on how other agents acted in the past, and for each agent the assumption that the future is determined from the current state and the action it takes is violated. This is the main difficulty in applying Q-learning to multi-agent reinforcement learning.

The algorithm for Q-learning is summarized as follows. Suppose that at a state S_t an action a_t is selected, then reward r_t is obtained, and the state transits to S_{t+1}. Then the action-value $Q(S, a)$ is updated according to the following formula:
$$Q(S_k, a_k) \leftarrow r_k + \gamma \max_a Q(S_{k+1}, a)$$
If the reward and the next state is determined only stochastically, a learning rate α is introduced and the update formula is modified to:
$$Q(S_k, a_k) \leftarrow (1 - \alpha)Q(S_k, a_k) + \alpha(r_k + \gamma \max_a Q(S_{k+1}, a)).$$

Under the Markovian assumption, if all the state-action pairs are experienced a sufficient number of times, action-value $Q(S, a)$ is known to converge to that of the optimal policy $Q^\pi(S, a)$. Once obtained, the optimal policy is the action a which maximizes the $Q^\pi(S, a)$ for each S.

However, convergence theorem for Q-learning does not tell us how to learn the Q-value effectively. Ordinarily, the policy that selects every state-action pairs with non-zero probability is required. For example, Boltzmann's probability given below is often adopted.
$$p(a|S) = C \exp(Q(S, a)/T).$$

In PS-learning the evaluation function R is updated not for each action, but for each episode (a sequence of actions ending in a successful capture). That is, let the initial state and the captured state be S_0, S_e, and the sequence of actions leading to the captured state be $\{S_0, a_0, S_1, a_1, \ldots, S_t, a_t, S_e\}$, then for each episode the reward is given following the history backwards from the captured state as $k = t, t - 1, \ldots, 0$.
$$R(S_k, a) \leftarrow R(S_k, a) + r\gamma^{t-k}.$$
Afterward R is normalized to avoid the monotonic increase.
$$\sum_a R(S_k, a) = C_0.$$

As the reward is discounted by the factor γ, the effect of the reward decreases quickly. The policy for action selection in PS-learning is the same as that in Q-learning except for the use of R instead of Q.

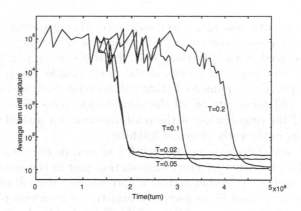

Fig. 2. Learning curve for Standard Q-Learning

The learning curves obtained by the standard Q-learning (SQ-learning) is given in Fig.2, and that of PS-learning in Fig.3 with the same experimental condition. The abscissas represent the time (in turn) and the ordinates represent the average turns (averaged over 5×10^4 turns) necessary for capture. Note that scale of the abscissas in Fig.2 and Fig.3 are different. The parameters used are $\alpha = 0.2$, $\gamma = 0.9$ for SQ-learning, and $\gamma = 0.9$ for PS-learning.

The experiments were conducted with various values of T, which governs the trade off between exploration and exploitation. Generally speaking, if we take a

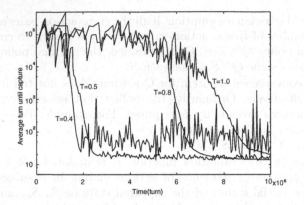

Fig. 3. Learning curve for PS Learning

smaller value of T (exploitation type), the initial learning proceeds quickly, but the asymptotic performance would be poor. In fact, with PS-learning, severe degradation in performance with small T is observed.

4   Episodic Q-Learning

In a hunter game, the reward is given only after the successful capture. While with PS-learning, every state-action pair in the episode leading to the successful capture is reinforced, with Q-learning only the state-action pair just before the capture is first reinforced. Of course, in the next episode, the state-action pair leading to the previously reinforced state will be reinforced, and ultimately, the reinforcement will propagate to all the state-action pairs. But the problem is the slowness of the propagation of the reinforcement, for a single episode takes about 10^5 turns in the early stages of learning.

In order to speed up learning, the reinforcement, or the updating of the Q-value should be performed for every state-action pair in the successful episode. Hence we adopted the following update algorithm. Let the initial state and the captured state be S_0 and S_e respectively, and the state-action pairs leading to the capture be $\{S_0, a_0, S_1, a_1, \ldots, S_t, a_t, S_e\}$. Then the Q-value is updated by:

$$Q(S_k, a_k) \leftarrow (1 - \alpha)Q(S_k, a_k) + \alpha(r_k + \gamma \max Q(S_{k+1}, a)) \qquad (1)$$

where

$$Q(S_e, a) = 0, \text{ and } \quad r_k = \begin{cases} 0 \ (k \neq t) \\ 1 \ (k = t) \end{cases}$$

Q is updated by following the history of the episode in reverse order from S_e as $k = t, t - 1, t - 2, \ldots 0$.

The learning curves obtained by the Episodic Q-learning (EQ-learning) is given in Fig.4, with the same experimental condition as Fig.2 and Fig.3. The parameters used are $\alpha = 0.2$, $\gamma = 0.9$. Interestingly, with EQ-learning, the degradation in performance with small T is small compared to those with SQ-learning and PS-learning.

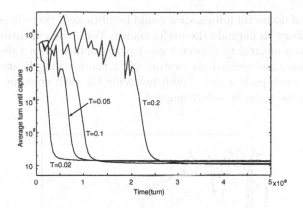

Fig. 4. Learning curve for Episodic Q-Learning

5   Restricting the History Length

From the update formula (1), it is observed that while with PS-learning only the action sequence immediately prior to the capture contributes to the learning, with EQ-learning the entire action sequence contributes to the learning. For the second term in the Q-learning update formula, $\alpha\gamma\max Q(S_{t+1}, a)$, is not necessarily small even at states far from a successful capture. It is therefore natural to question "What is the use of the history far apart from the capture."

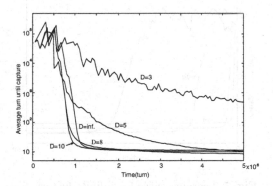

Fig. 5. Effect of maximum history length

Hence the history used for EQ-learning is restricted to the last D turns, and experiments were conducted with various values of D. The obtained learning curves are given in Fig.5. The parameters used are $\alpha = 0.2$, $\gamma = 0.9$, $T = 0.1$. From the graph it is observed that not only the speed of learning, but also the asymptotic performance is improved by restricting the history length to D.

These phenomena cannot be explained under the MDP assumption, for the update formula (1) used for Q-learning holds exactly for the entire sequence of actions. Even if no useful information could be obtained, there is no reason for an additional history to degrade the performance. With the exception of the above reservation, it is natural to expect a good performance for a value of D around 10. The average time needed for capture after the learning is around 10, and if only the last 10 steps is a meaningful behavior for each episode, the remaining part of the episode can be safely ignored.

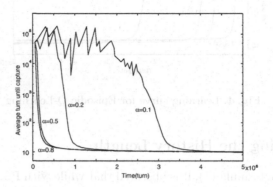

Fig. 6. Learning curve when restricting history size to D=10

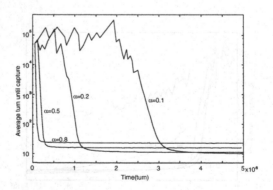

Fig. 7. Learning curve for infinite history size

The learning curve for $D = 10$ with various α is given in Fig.6, and that for $D = \infty$ (using the entire episode for learning) in Fig.7. The parameters used are $T = 0.1$, $\gamma = 0.9$. What is interesting is that the performance degradation for large values of α disappears for $D = 10$. The parameter α is introduced to average the indeterminacy in the reward function $r(S, a)$, and transition function $\delta(S, a)$. If we take large values of α, the learning might speed up but asymptotic performance would degrade. With an appropriate value of D the performance does not degrade even for a large value of α, and as a result a surprisingly high learning speed is achieved. Especially with the value of $\alpha=0.5$ and 0.8 hunters can learn to capture with only several episodes, which counteracts the popular belief that reinforcement learning is too slow to be practical.

The various data so far presented are each a result of a single simulation. Of course, a single trial of the Q-learning process contains many episodes, each of which is started from randomly scattered hunters and the escapee. Even so, the exact shape of the learning curves may change by changing the random number used for the simulation.

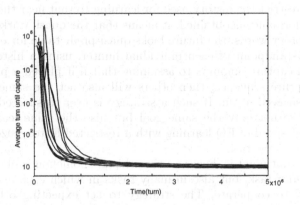

Fig. 8. Dependency on the random numbers used

Figure 8 shows learning curves obtained by changing the initial values of the random numbers. The parameters used are $\alpha = 0.5$, $D = 10$, $T = 0.1$, $\gamma = 0.9$ which we believe is the optimal set of parameters. It is true that there are considerable differences in the speed of learning and asymptotic performance, but the qualitative behavior is the same, and even in the worst case the initial learning stage finishes in less than 10^6 turns, much faster compared to PS-learning and SQ-learning.

6   Discussions — The Algorithm to Read Other's Mind

It is important to question why EQ-learning with an appropriate history size is so powerful for learning cooperative tasks. The task forces hunters to learn from no knowledge. In such a situation, even if one of the hunters acts *correctly*, a good performance can not be expected without cooperation from the other hunters, which seems hopeless in the early stages of learning. Hence Q-value or the expected reward must be very low, when averaged over probable actions of the other hunters.

The cooperation of all the hunters is essential for capture. If randomly moving hunters ever succeeded in capture, it is because they accidentally behaved as if they were cooperating. Of course, if one of the hunters acts in the same way in the next similar situation, there is no reason to expect that the others would act the same way. If the strategy of the other hunters were not known, nothing could be done. Even if one of the hunters knows that the other hunters also *want to capture the escapee*, it will not help, for it does not know itself what action it should take for the capture.

Let us examine what happens when the history size is restricted. The reason for the speeding up of the learning is due to the use of large values of α without the performance degradation. The large values of α are allowed only when the future (the next state and the reward) is determined exactly by the current state and its own action, i.e., the environment is a deterministic Markovian case. If each hunters restrict the history used for learning to that near the capture event and good performance is obtained, it means that the quasi-Markovian property holds, or, in other words, the future looks quasi-predictable for each agent.

From the standpoint of each individual hunter, using a history just before the successful capture amounts to assuming that if it played a part in the past successful capture sequence, then others will also act the same way, and the capture will succeed again. If such a strategy is ever to succeed, it is because the others have not only the same goal but also the same learning strategy. The significant speed of EQ-learning with a restricted history size is due to this special feature of the task.

The important point is, however, that this phenomenon is observed not only in this particular task, but also in many tasks in which each agent must learn independently to cooperate. The strategy to act expecting others to behave in the same way without a sound ground works for many cooperative tasks involving homogeneous learning agents. In fact, this strategy is what we have been proposing as a mind-reading algorithm[8].

> To mindread is, among the agents of comparable computational abilities, to select its own action groundlessly expecting others to take not the most reasonable action but a sort of biased action from the observation of the other's past behavior. Mindreading is possible only when to be mindread by others is mutually profitable.

This proposition is obtained from the investigation on the emergence of cooperative strategies to solve the Prisoner's Dilemma Game in a society of selfish agents[10]. Unexpectedly, this same algorithm makes possible a significant increase in the speed of learning for the 3-hunter game.

However, the above formalization of mindreading suggests that EQ-learning with restricted history size is effective only among cooperative learning agents. This is verified by our preliminary simulation in which the escapee is made to learn.

In Fig.9 are shown learning curves where the escapee also learns (EQ-learning with $D = \infty$). The learning method for hunters are SQ-learning, and EQ-learning ($D = 10, 100, 1000$). The hunters and the escapee start from random actions, but the escapee quickly learns to escape, and later the hunters gradually learns to capture the escapee.

To capture a learning escapee, the history size must be large. EQ-learning with small history size, and SQ-learning has poor performance. Learning with a small history size probably means that its behavior can be easily predicted

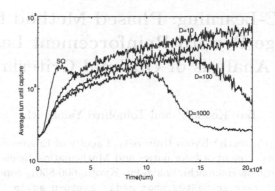

Fig. 9. Learning curve where the escapee also learns

by others agents. Obviously being predictable by others is fine for cooperative situation, but will prove to be miserable for competitive situation. We are going to report on this problem in the next paper.

References

1. Sutton, R. S.: "Learning to Predict by the Methods of Temporal Differences," Machine Learning 3, pp.9-44(1988).
2. Watkins, C.J.C.H. and Dayan, O.: "Technical Note: Q-learning," Machine Learning 8, pp.55-68 (1992).
3. Grefenstette, J.J.: "Credit Assignment in Rule Discovery Systems Based on Genetic Algorithms," Machine Learning, Vol.3, pp.225-245(1988)
4. Arai, S., Miyazaki, K. and Kobayashi, S.: "Methodology in Multi-Agent Reinforcement Learning — Approaches by Q-learning and Profit Sharing —, J. Japanese Society for Artificial Intelligence, Vol.13, No.4, p609-618(1998) (in Japanese).
5. Arai, S., Sycara, K., and Payne, T.R.: "Multi-agent Reinforcement learning for Planning and Scheduling Multiple Goals", Proc. 4th Intern. Conf. on MultiAgent Systems (ICMAS2000), pp.359-360 (2000).
6. Sutton, R.S and Barto, A.G., Reinforcement learning, an introduction, A Bradford Book, The MIT Press(1998).
7. Ito, A. and Kanabuchi, M., Speeding Up Multiagent Reinforcement Learning by Coarse-Graining of Perception: The Hunter Game, Electronics and Communications in Japan, Vol.84, No.12, pp.37-45 (2001).
8. Ito, A., The Emergence of Mindreading Ability — Multi-Player Prisoner's Dilemma Game —, Cognitive Studies, Vol.6, No. 1, pp.77-87 (1999) (in Japanese).
9. Benda, M., Jagannathan, V., and Dodhiawalla, R.: "On Optimal Cooperation of Knowledge Sources", Technical Report BCS-G2010-28, Boeing AI Center (1985).
10. Ito, A. and Yano, H.: "The Emergence of Cooperation in a Society of Autonomous Agents," *First Intl. Conf. on Multi Agent Systems, (ICMAS'95),* pp. 201-208, San Fransisco, 1995.

LC-Learning: Phased Method for Average Reward Reinforcement Learning – Analysis of Optimal Criteria –

Taro Konda[1,2] and Tomohiro Yamaguchi[2]

[1] (Currently) Kyoto University, Faculty of Engineering
Department of Informatics and Mathematical Science
Yoshida-Honmachi, Sakyo-ku, Kyoto, 606-8501, Japan
taro.konda@t02.mbox.media.kyoto-u.ac.jp
[2] Nara National College of Technology, Department of Information Science
22 Yata-cho, Yamato-Koriyama, Nara, 639-1080, Japan
yamaguch@info.nara-k.ac.jp

Abstract. This paper presents an analysis of criteria which measure policy optimality for average reward reinforcement learning. In previous works for undiscounted tasks, two criteria, *gain-optimality* and *bias-optimality* have been presented. The former is one to measure an average reward and the latter is one to evaluate transient actions. However, a limit factor in the definition of the gain-optimality makes real meaning of the criterion unclear, and what si worse, the performance function for the bias-optimality does not always converge. Thus, previous methods calculate an optimal policy with approximation approaches, that is, they don't always acquire the optimal policy because of some finite errors. In addition, the theoretical proof of the convergence to the optimal policy is a difficult task. To eliminate ambiguity over these criteria, we show a necessary and sufficient condition of the gain-optimality: *if and only if a policy is gain-optimal, it includes an optimal cycle*-In other words, we only need to search a stationary cycle that has the highest average reward to find a gain optimal policy. We also make the performance function for the bias-optimality always converge by dividing it into two terms *cycle-bias-value* and *path-bias-value*. Finally, we build foundation of *LC-learning*, an algorithm for computing the bias optimal policy in a cyclic domain.

Keywords: Artificial Intelligence, Machine Learning, Reinforcement Learning, Markov Decision Process, Average Reward Method, LC-learning

1 Introduction

Reinforcement Learning(RL) aims to let an agent compute an optimal policy which maximizes an average reward in an environment. In most RL papers, Q-learning is applied to various problems [3] [12] [14]. It maximizes utility value

M. Ishizuka and A. Sattar (Eds.): PRICAI 2002, LNAI 2417, pp. 198–207, 2002.

Q, that is sum of expected *discounted* rewards. Although the discount factor makes infinite sum of rewards finite, a large number of computational iterations is needed until the value converges, and what is worse, Q-learning does not always acquire the optimal policy.

Average Reward Reinforcement Learning(ARL) gave a solution to these problems. It maximizes utility values without discounting. R-learning is the first undiscounted method [11] and it performs better than the discounted method, Q-learning [5]. The new framework has been well studied and some methods were proposed at two approaches, model-free and model-based. A difference between them is whether an agent builds its internal environment model. The model-based method calculates the optimal policy more rapidly, though it requires an extra cost to update the model. The model-free method is vice versa. For example, a typical model-free method is a Model-free Bias Optimality Algorithm [7], A Model-based Bias-optimality Algorithm [5] and H-learning algorithm [13] are model-based methods.

To measure a performance of the methods, two criteria, *gain-optimality* and *bias-optimality* were suggested. The former is one to measure an average reward and the latter is one to evaluate transient actions. However, a limit factor in the definition of the gain-optimality makes real meaning of the criterion unclear, and what was worse, a performance function for the bias-optimality does not always converge, therefore all of above methods does not always acquire an optimal policy.

In this paper, we eliminate ambiguity over the criteria. Second, following the results, we present some theoretical foundations of *LC-learning*, which guarantees to filter the bias-optimal policy.

2   Markov Decision Process and Policy

A Markov Decision Process (MDP) is a sequential decision model[9]. MDP consists of two sets S, A, a function $P(s, s', a)$ and a matrix R. S is a set of states of an agent in an environment. A is a set of actions for moving between the states. In this paper we assume that both S and A are finite. The function $P(s, s', a)$ (*where* $s, s' \in S, a \in A$) evaluates a probability of the transition from the state s to s' under the action a. The matrix R defines a distribution of rewards in the environment. The factor $r_{ss'}$ of R represents a reward value (nonnegative number) given to the agent moving from the state s to s'. We label a state-action set as a $rule(s, a)$ (*where* $s \in S, a \in A$).

A task of RL is to use rewards to learn a successful agent function[10]. We aim to let an agent learn which action should be selected at each state. A set of decisions is termed policy π and $\pi(s)$ means the action that the agent take at the state s. We assume that MDP is *unichain* whose transition matrix corresponding to every policy contains a single recurrent class and possibly a set of transient states in this paper. We label the recurrent class as *stationary cycle* and the set of transient states as *transient path*. The stationary cycle is a loop chain of states and the transient paths binds any state to the stationary cycle.

3   Analysis of Policy Optimality

The criteria to measure a performance of a policy acquired by ARL agent have been well defined. In this section, we cite some definitions and clarify their natures.

3.1   Necessary and Sufficient Condition of Gain-Optimality

First of all, an agent should compute a policy that yields the highest expected reward per step. The average reward ρ^π associated with a particular policy π at a state s is defined as

$$\rho^\pi(s) \overset{def}{\equiv} \lim_{N \to \infty} E\left(\frac{1}{N} \sum_{t=0}^{N-1} r_t^\pi(s) \right),\tag{1}$$

where the reward $r_t^\pi(s)$ is one which the agent starting from the state x and choosing actions under the policy π receives at time t. E denotes the expected value.

We define a *gain-optimal* policy π^* as one that maximizes the average reward over all states, that is $\rho^{\pi^*}(s) \geq \rho^\pi(s)$ over all policies π and states s. We refer to this criterion as *gain-optimality* [6]. However, the limit factor makes real meaning of the gain-optimality unclear. We clarify a *necessary and sufficient condition* for the gain-optimality by paying attention to a stationary cycle in a policy. If a policy is unichain, the average reward of any policy is state independent. [5][11].

$$\rho^\pi(x) = \rho^\pi(y) = \rho^\pi\tag{2}$$

The agent starting from the state s which belongs to a transient path reaches and stays forever at a stationary cycle. The average reward defined in the equation(1) is transformed as

$$\rho^\pi(s) = \lim_{N \to \infty} E\left(\frac{1}{N} \sum_{t=0}^{N-1} r_t^\pi(s) \right)$$

$$= \lim_{N \to \infty} \left(E\left(\frac{1}{N} \sum_{t=0}^{n-1} r_t^\pi(s) \right) + E\left(\frac{1}{N} \sum_{t=n}^{N-1} r_t^\pi(s) \right) \right)$$

$$= \lim_{N \to \infty} E\left(\frac{1}{N} \sum_{t=n}^{N-1} r_t^\pi(s) \right) = \lim_{(N-n) \to \infty} E\left(\frac{1}{N-n} \sum_{T=0}^{N-n-1} r_T^\pi(s') \right)$$

$$= \lim_{m \to \infty} E\left(\frac{1}{m} \sum_{T=0}^{m-1} r_T^\pi(s') \right) = \lim_{i \to \infty} E\left(\frac{i}{i \times l} \sum_{T=0}^{l-1} r_T^\pi(s') \right)$$

$$= E\left(\frac{1}{l} \sum_{T=0}^{l-1} r_T^\pi(s') \right),\tag{3}$$

where the agent reaches the stationary cycle at the state s' when $t=n$-1. The alternative time parameter T is set 0 then. m means the length of time from when the agent reaches the stationary cycle to the end of the task $(m=N\text{-}n)$. l means the length of the stationary cycle and i corresponds to the number of rounds.

The equation(3) gives the following consequence.

Theorem 1. If and only if a policy is gain-optimal, it includes an optimal cycle that has the highest average.

We only need to search the optimal cycle to find a gain-optimal policy.

3.2   Disambiguation for Bias-Optimality

The equation(3) shows that the gain-optimality is not a sufficient criterion since it only evaluates the stationary cycle. It never gives any guidance for decision which of actions should be chosen at transient paths. A more selective criterion termed *bias-optimality* addresses this problem [6]. The average adjusted sum of rewards earned following a policy π is

$$V^\pi(s) \stackrel{def}{=} \lim_{N\to\infty} E\left(\sum_{t=0}^{N-1}(r_t^\pi(s) - \rho^\pi)\right), \tag{4}$$

where the average reward ρ^π is one associated with the policy π.

A policy π^* is termed *bias-optimal* if it is also gain-optimal. It maximizes the average adjusted values, that is $V^{\pi^*}(s) \geq V^\pi(s)$ over all states s in any policy π. We refer to $V^\pi(s)$ as *bias-value*.

Unfortunately, the definition of the bias-value is not sufficient because the value does not always converge. We divide the bias-value into two terms and analyze each of them as well as the gain-optimality.

$$\lim_{N\to\infty} E\left(\sum_{t=0}^{N-1}(r_t^\pi(s) - \rho^\pi)\right) = \lim_{N\to\infty}\left(E\sum_{t=0}^{n-1}(r_t^\pi(s) - \rho^\pi) + E\sum_{t=n}^{N-1}(r_t^\pi(s) - \rho^\pi)\right),$$
$$\tag{5}$$

where the agent reaches the stationary cycle at $t=n$.

The first term in the equation(5) represents the bias-value which the agent obtains through the transient paths. The second term represents the bias-value that the agent acquires after it reaches the stationary cycle.

The first term is simplified as follows because there is no limit factor N in the equation anymore.

$$\lim_{N\to\infty} E\left(\sum_{t=0}^{n-1}(r_t^\pi(s)-\rho^\pi)\right) = E\left(\sum_{t=0}^{n-1}(r_t^\pi(s)-\rho^\pi)\right) = V_P^\pi(s) , \qquad (6)$$

where $V_P^\pi(s)$ represents bias-value that the agent obtains over the transient path. We call it path-bias-value.

We set an alternative time parameter $T=0$ when the agent reaches the stationary cycle at the state s'. Then the second term in the equation(5) is also simplified as follows.

$$\lim_{N\to\infty} E\left(\sum_{T=0}^{N-n}(r_T^\pi(s')-\rho^\pi)\right)$$

$$= E\left(\frac{1}{l}\left(\sum_{T=0}^{0}(r_T^\pi(s')-\rho^\pi)+\ldots+\sum_{T=0}^{l-1}(r_T^\pi(s')-\rho^\pi)\right)\right)$$

$$= E\left(\frac{1}{l}\sum_{i=0}^{l-1}\sum_{T=0}^{i}(r_T^\pi(s')-\rho^\pi)\right) = E\left(\frac{1}{l}\left(\sum_{i=0}^{l-1}\sum_{T=0}^{i}r_T^\pi(s')-\sum_{i=0}^{l-1}\sum_{T=0}^{i}\rho^\pi\right)\right)$$

$$= E\left(\frac{1}{l}\left((r_T^\pi(s')\times l+\ldots+r_T^\pi(s')\times 1)-\frac{l(l+1)\rho^\pi}{2}\right)\right)$$

$$= E\left(\frac{1}{l}\left(\sum_{T=0}^{l-1}(r_T^\pi(s')(l-T))-\frac{l(l+1)\rho^\pi}{2}\right)\right) = V_C^\pi(s') , \qquad (7)$$

where $V_C^\pi(s')$ is the bias-value at the state s' in the stationary cycle. We call it cycle-bias-value.

The cycle-bias-value is determined by the state s' at which the agent reaches the stationary cycle.

Theorem 2. The bias-value is the sum of the path-bias-value and the cycle-bias-value.

$$V^\pi(s) = V_P^\pi(s) + V_C^\pi(s') \qquad (8)$$

It means that the bias-optimal policy is one which maximizes the sum of two values. The path-bias-value is determined by the transient path which the agent passes until it reaches the stationary cycle. The cycle-bias-value depends on which of the states belonging to the cycle the agent reaches first.

4   Foundation of LC-Learning

We have shown so far that we only need to search the stationary cycle that has the highest average reward to find a gain-optimal policy and that the bias-value could be determined once the stationary cycle is identified. In this section,

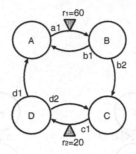

Fig. 1. An example MDP which consists of four states, A, B, C, D and six actions, $a1, b1, b2, c1, d1, d2$. There are two rewards $r_1 = 60$, $r_2 = 20$.

we present foundations of a novel method, LC-learning(Length of the Cycle), which computes the bias-optimal policy with its internal MDP model according to above analyses. The method includes no approximation, therefore it prevents some finite errors from computing the maximized average reward and always finds the bias-optimal policy.

An agent does not know about an environment at the beginning. It builds up an environment model with its experiences. We give the model to the agent so that we could only pay attention to let the agent search the optimal policy with the identified model here. In addition, we focus on a deterministic domain thought the method is capable of applying to a stochastic domain in principle (shown in the equation(3)and(8)).

The basic idea of the method is similar to DG-learning[2][1]. However, it only works for a goal task, but LC-learning is able to address a cyclic task.

4.1   Detect all Cycles

Any unichain policy contains one stationary cycle. We convert a MDP into tree structures to detect all possible cycles in which the agent obtains the reward by setting the reward rules as root of the tree.

The figure1 illustrates an example MDP, which is converted into the tree structures as shown in the figure2. In the MDP, three cycles which contain rewards are detected as shown in the figure 3. Let C correspond to a set of all detected cycles.

4.2   Select Optimal Cycle

After all cycles which contain reward rules are detected, the agent evaluates them to filter an optimal cycle. From the equation(3), the cycle is evaluated as,

$$\rho^\pi(s') = \rho^c(s') = \frac{\sum_{T=0}^{L(c)-1} r_T^c(s')}{L(c)} , \tag{9}$$

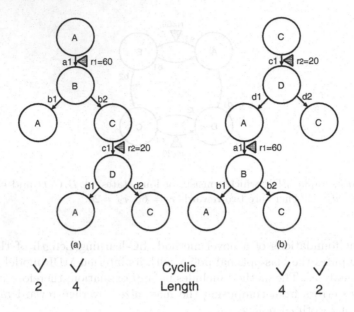

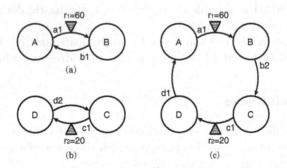

Fig. 2. The tree structures converted from the example MDP. The left tree begins at the rule($A, a1$) with the reward r_1. Two cycles, A-B(Length is 2) and A-B-C-D(Length is 4) are detected. The right tree begins at the rule($C, c1$) with the reward r_2. Two cycles, C-D-A-B(Length is 4) and C-D-C(Length is 2) are detected.

Fig. 3. All detected cycles in the example MDP.

where c corresponds to the stationary cycle in the policy π ($c \in C$). The function $L(c)$ evaluates the length of the cycle c. $r_T^c(s')$ means the reward which the agent entering the cycle c at the state s' obtains at time T.

As shown in the equation(2), the average reward is independent of states. Thus, a policy including the cycle which maximizes the average reward is gain-optimal, that is,

$$\rho^{\pi^*} = \max_{c \in C} \frac{\sum_{T=0}^{L(c)-1} r_T^c}{L(c)}$$

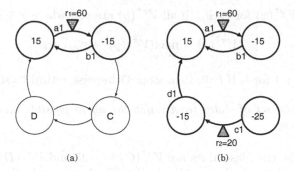

Fig. 4. The left figure(a) shows the cycle-bias-values of optimal cycle. The right figure(b) shows the path-bias-values and the optimal policy.

For example, the cycle A-B in the figure 2 maximizes the average reward $\rho^{\pi^*}=30$.

We refer to the cycle as *optimal cycle*, which is represented as $c^*(\in C)$.

4.3   Evaluate Cycle-Bias-Value

As shown in the equation(7), the cycle-bias-value is affected by the state at which the agent enters the stationary cycle. It is calculated as,

$$
V_C^{\pi^*}(s') - \frac{1}{L(c^*)}\left(\sum_{T=0}^{L(c^*)-1}(r_T^{c^*}(s')(L(c^*)-T)) - \frac{L(c^*)(L(c^*)+1)\rho^{\pi^*}}{2}\right)
$$

where c^* corresponds to the optimal cycle and ρ^{π^*} is the average reward generated by the gain-optimal policy.

For example, as shown in the figure 4(a), the cycle-bias-values are $V_C^{\pi^*}(A) = 15$, $V_C^{\pi^*}(B) = -15$.

If more than two cycles which maximize the average reward are detected, the cycle-bias-values for each cycle have to be calculated to decide the bias-optimal policy. The action which maximizes the cycle-bias-value should be chosen at the state that holds more than two cycle-bias-values.

4.4   Evaluate Bias-Value

The agent has to evaluate the bias-value to compute the bias-optimal policy. The Backward Induction [9] is useful in propagating the cycle-bias-values over the transient paths.

1. Set $t=n$, $V^{\pi^*}(s') = V_C^{\pi^*}(s')$ for all $s'(\in c^*)$.
2. Substitute s' for s_t.

3. Compute $V^{\pi^*}(x)$ for each x if all $V^{\pi^*}(y)$ are set, where $x \in s_{t-1}$, $y \in s_t$,

$$V^{\pi^*}(x) = \max_{y \in s_t}(V^{\pi^*}(y) + r_{xy}) - \rho^{\pi^*}$$

4. Substitute t-1 for t. If t=0, then stop. Otherwise return to step 3.

where s_{t-1} is the set of states from which the agent possibly move to the set s_t under one action.

For example, the bias-values are $V^{\pi^*}(C) = -25$ and $V^{\pi^*}(D) = -15$ at the transient path under the bias-optimal policy as shown in the figure 4(b).

5 Conclusion

In this paper, we eliminated ambiguity over the previous criteria. We showed that we only need to search the stationary cycle that has the highest average reward to find a gain-optimal policy by relying upon the notion that all unichain policies consist of two factors, a set of transient paths and a stationary cycle. We also made the performance function for the bias-optimality always converge by dividing it into *cycle-bias-value* and *path-bias-value*. Finally, following these analyses, we presented a foundation of model-based ARL named *LC-learning*, which strictly computes the bias-optimal policy without some finite errors. The agent detects the optimal cycle to figure the maximum average reward. Then it calculates the bias-values of the states belonging to the cycle propagates the values over the transient paths.

6 Related Work

Evaluation of Performance. Will LC-learning have great potentialities? It may seem to have a large complexity, since it searches most combinations of the actions to detect all cycles. However we can dramatically reduce the complexity of LC-learning with two staged processes, *pruning* [4]. In the paper, we implement the methods and evaluate the performance of LC-learning by comparing it with one of the most rapid method, *Prioritized Sweeping* [8].

Application to Stochastic Domain. Some realistic problems are represented as stochastic MDPs. Most complex phase will be one to detect the optimal cycle. As shown in the equation(3) and (8), it is possible in principle. Now we are checking up some approaches.

Acknowledgement. We would like to thank to Kenji Ishimura for his work building up basis of this work. We must express my gratitude to Shinjiro Tensyo for his helpful comments. The technical aspect of this work was supported by Yuta Ochi.

References

1. Leslie P. Kaelbling. Hierarchical learning in stochastic domains: Preliminary results. In *Proceedings of the Tenth International Conference on Machine Learning (ICML-1993)*, pages 167–173, 1993.
2. Leslie P. Kaelbling. Learning to achieve goals. In *Proceedings of the Thirteenth International Joint Conference on Artificial Intelligence (IJCAI-1993)*, pages 1094–1099, 1993.
3. Leslie P. Kaelbling, Michael L. Littman, and Andrew P. Moore. Reinforcement learning: A survey. *Journal of Artificial Intelligence Research*, 4:237–285, 1996.
4. Taro Konda, Tensyo Shinjiro, and Tomohiro Yamaguchi. Lc-learning: In-stages model-based average reward reinforcement learning : Complexity and empirical results. In *Proceedings of the Seventh Pacific Rim International Conference on Artificial Intelligence (PRICAI-2002)*, 2002.
5. Sridhar Mahadevan. An average-reward reinforcement learning algorithm for computing bias-optimal policies. In *Proceedings of the Thirteenth AAAI (AAAI-1996)*, pages 875–880, 1996.
6. Sridhar Mahadevan. Average reward reinforcement learning: Foundations, algorithms, and empirical results. *Machine Learning*, 22(1-3):159–195, 1996.
7. Sridhar Mahadevan. Sensitive-discount optimality: Unifying average-reward and discounted reinforcement learning. In *Proceedings of the Thirteenth International Conference on Machine Learning (ICML-1996)*, pages 328–336, 1996.
8. Andrew W. Moore and Christopher G. Atkeson. Prioritized sweeping: Reinforcement learning with less data and less time. *Machine Learning*, 13:103–130, 1993.
9. Martin L. Puterman. *Markov Decision Processes: Discrete Dynamic Stochastic Programming, 92–93*. John Wiley, 1994.
10. Stuart J. Russell and Peter Norvig. *Artificial Intelligence: A Modern Approach*. Prentice Hall, 1995.
11. Anton Schwartz. A reinforcement learning method for maximizing undiscounted rewards. In *Proceedings of the Tenth International Conference on Machine Learning (ICML-1993)*, pages 298–305, 1993.
12. Richard S. Sutton and Andrew G. Barto. *Reinforcement Learning: An Introduction*. MIT Press, 1998.
13. Prasad Tadepalli and DoKyeong Ok. Model-based average reward reinforcement learning. *Artificial Intelligence*, 100(1-2):177–223, 1998.
14. Christopher J. Watkins and Peter Dayan. Q-learning. machine learning. *Machine Learning*, 3(8):279–292, 1992.

LC-Learning: Phased Method for Average Reward Reinforcement Learning – Preliminary Results –

Taro Konda[1,3], Shinjiro Tensyo[2], and Tomohiro Yamaguchi[3]

[1] (Currently) Kyoto University, Faculty of Engineering
Department of Informatics and Mathematical Science
Yoshida-Honmachi, Sakyo-ku, Kyoto, 606-8501, Japan
`taro.konda@t02.mbox.media.kyoto-u.ac.jp`

[2] Nara National College of Technology
Department of Advanced Electronic and Information Engineering
22 Yata-cho, Yamato-Koriyama, Nara, 639-1080, Japan
`tensyo@info.nara-k.ac.jp`

[3] Nara National College of Technology, Department of Information Science
22 Yata-cho, Yamato-Koriyama, Nara, 639-1080, Japan
`yamaguch@info.nara-k.ac.jp`

Abstract. This paper presents two methods to accelerate LC-learning, which is a novel model-based average reward reinforcement learning method to compute a bias-optimal policy in a cyclic domain. The LC-learning has successfully calculated the bias-optimal policy without any approximation approaches relying upon the notion that we only need to search the optimal cycle to find a gain-optimal policy. However it has a large complexity, since it searches most combinations of actions to detect all cycles. In this paper, we first implement two pruning methods to prevent the state explosion problem of the LC-learning. Second, we compare the improved LC-learning with one of the most rapid methods, the Prioritized Sweeping in a bus scheduling task. We show that the LC-learning calculates the bias-optimal policy more quickly than the normal Prioritized Sweeping and it also performs as well as the full-tuned version in the middle case.

Keywords: Artificial Intelligence, Machine Learning, Reinforcement Learning, Markov Decision Process, Average Reward Method, LC-learning

1   Introduction

Reinforcement Learning(RL) originally aims to let the agent compute the policy which maximizes an average reward in an environment [1] [9].

Recently, a novel framework has been arresting the attention. It is called average reward reinforcement learning(ARL), which maximizes the utility value

M. Ishizuka and A. Sattar (Eds.): PRICAI 2002, LNAI 2417, pp. 208–217, 2002.

without discounting. The previous methods calculate an optimal policy with approximation approaches. Thus, they don't always acquire the optimal policy because of some finite errors. What is worse, the theoretical proof of the policy convergence is a difficult task.

Our new straightforward method called *LC-learning* gave a clue to these problems[2]. It strictly computes *bias-optimal policy*[4] with its internal MDP model in stages.

In this paper, we first present two methods to accelerate the LC-learning. Second, we evaluate the performance of the LC-learning in the worst cases for it. Finally, we compare it with one of the most rapid method in a *Bus Scheduling Task* shown below.

2   Bus Scheduling Task

ARL have applied to many cyclic control tasks [4] such as a robot avoiding obstacles[3], an automatic guided vehicle [5] [10]. We suggest a bus scheduling task here (The figure1).

There are some BUS STOPS, INTERSECTIONS, CROSSINGS and STREETS in a domain. Some streets are ONE-WAY. The intersections and the crossings obstruct a bus. A figure in the bus stop corresponds to the number of passengers waiting the bus at the stop. The task is to calculate the most effective schedule, which maximizes the number of passengers per step. We can make many versions of this task: people crossing the street and signs changing at random (A stochastic domain) or more than two buses on the town (A multi-agent domain). But we treat deterministic single-agent version so that we can measure a basic ability of methods in this paper.

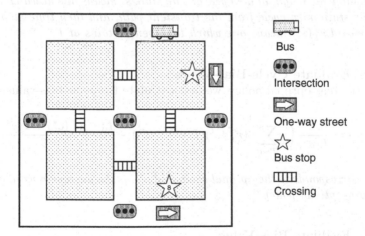

Fig. 1. This is an illustration of the bus scheduling task.

3 LC-Learning

The LC-learning computes the bias-optimal policy with its internal MDP model in stages [2]. It includes no approximation, therefore it prevents some finite errors from computing the policy which maximizes average reward and always finds the bias-optimal policy.

3.1 Framework

The LC-learning acquires the bias-optimal policy with the following procedures.

Phase 1. Detect all Cycles

The MDP is converted into tree structures by setting reward rules as root to detect all possible cycles in which the agent obtains the reward. The set of the cycles is represented as C.

Phase 2. Select an Optimal Cycle

The average reward of all cycles detected at phase1 are calculated to filter *gain-optimal policy*[2][4]. All policies including the *optimal cycle* which maximizes the average reward are gain-optimal. The optimal cycle is represented as $c^*(\in C)$.

$$\rho^{\pi^*} = \max_{c \in C} \frac{\sum_{T=0}^{L(c)-1} r_T^c}{L(c)},$$

where the cycle c corresponds to the stationary cycle in the policy π. The function $L(c)$ evaluates the length of the cycle c. The state s' means one at which the agent enters the stationary cycle from the transient path, and then time step T is set 0. The reward $r_T^c(s')$ means one which the agent obtains at T.

Phase 3. Evaluate Cycle-Bias-Value

To filter the bias-optimal policy, we first calculate the cycle-bias-value.

$$V_C^{\pi^*}(s') = \frac{1}{L(c^*)} \left(\sum_{T=0}^{L(c^*)-1} (r_T^{c^*}(s')(L(c^*) - T)) - \frac{L(c^*)(L(c^*) + 1)\rho^{\pi^*}}{2} \right),$$

where c^* corresponds to the optimal cycle and ρ^{π^*} is the average reward generated by the gain-optimal policy.

Phase 4. Evaluate Bias-Value

To determine the actions in the transient path, we finally propagate the cycle-bias-value and calculate the bias-value over the transient path. Backward Induction[8] is applied to the LC-learning.

1. Set $t=n$, $V^{\pi^*}(s') = V_C^{\pi^*}(s')$ for all $s'(\in c^*)$.
2. Substitute s' for s_t.
3. Compute $V^{\pi^*}(x)$ for each x if all $V^{\pi^*}(y)$ are set, where $x \in s_{t-1}$, $y \in s_t$,

$$V^{\pi^*}(x) = \max_{y \in s_t}(V^{\pi^*}(y) + r_{xy}) - \rho^{\pi^*}$$

4. Substitute t-1 for t. If $t=0$, then stop. Otherwise return to step 3.

where s_{t-1} is the set of states from which the agent possibly move to the set s_t under one action. s_t consists of the states in the stationary cycle when the procedure begins. The state whose bias-value is determined is add to s_t sequentially.

3.2 Pruning

The *plane* LC-learning seems to have a large complexity, since it searches all combinations of actions to detect all cycles. We can dramatically reduce the complexity of the LC-learning with two pruning methods. One is to prevent same cycles from being detected tautologically. The other is closing the process in the middle.

Obviously, the phase1 to detect all cycles has the largest complexity over the processes. Thus, we focus our discussions on it.

The MDP whose all states completely communicate each other(the figure 2) is one of the worst classes for the LC-learning. In this domain, if all combinations are searched, time $O(|S||S|!)$ and space $O(|S|!)$ are needed ($|S|$ is the number of states). The table1 shows a preliminary result of calculation by the plane LC-learning. The state explosion problem occurs.

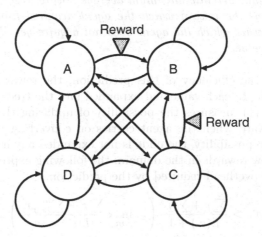

Fig. 2. The example MDP whose four states completely communicate each other.

Table 1. The preliminary result of the plain LC-learning in the MDP communicating completely. $|r|$ is the number of rewards, $|A|$ is the number of actions and $|S \times A|$ is the number of rules. *Step* means the time step when the process ends. *Max queue* corresponds to the maximum length of the queue during the process.

$|S|$	$|r|$	$|S \times A|$	Steps	Max queue
4	2	16	40	2
6	2	36	780	24
8	2	64	31312	720

Method 1. Avoidance of Tautological Detection

The same cycles are detected over the process when there are more than two rewards in the domain, since the MDP is converted into the tree by setting each reward rule as root and all combinations are searched at each tree. When the second or later tree is converted, we should stop expanding the node at the rule which was set as root once. It prevents all tautological detections of cycles.

Method 2. Prediction based on the Reward

We pay attention to capability of updating the currently maximum average reward. At any node over the process, the possible maximum average reward by continuing the conversion can be predicted because the agent knows how rewards are distributed in the MDP. The node should be expanded if

$$\rho^{*'} > \max_m \frac{\sum r^* + \sum_{i=0}^m r'_i}{L(c') + m} \quad (0 \le m \le |r'|) , \tag{1}$$

where $\rho^{*'}$ means the currently maximum average reward which the agent already acquired. r^* means the reward which the agent acquired from the root to the node. r'_i is the reward which the agent does not acquire yet. They are arranged according to the value.

To maximize the efficiency of this prediction, the reward rules should be arranged according to each value and expanded into the tree in order.

The condition(1) measures the possibility of updating the currently maximum average reward when the agent carries on converting the node into the tree. If there is no possibility, the node is not expanded anymore.

If there is a few rewards in the domain, the following expression lightens the process to reduce overhead required by the prediction.

$$\rho^{*'} > \frac{\sum r + \sum r'}{L(c') + 1} \left(\ge \max_m \frac{\sum r + \sum_{i=0}^m r'_i}{L(c') + m} \right)$$

The value calculated in the prediction process can be also utilized to make the present horizontal search into *best-first* one. The detail is discussed in the *Future Work*.

3.3   Preliminary Results

The efficiency of two above methods are shown in the table2 and 3. The former shows the cost according to the number of rules. Compare it with the table1. We can see much cost is cut down. The latter shows the cost according to the number of rewards. These results show that the pruning methods successfully prevent state explosion of the LC-learning despite of the fact that the MDP communicating completely is one of the worst case.

Table 2. The number of rules and the learning cost of LC-learning with two pruning methods. Almost 99% of steps is cut down and much less space is required.

$|S|$	$|A|$	$|r|$	$|r||S \times A|$	Steps	Max queue
4	4	2	32	29	2
6	6	2	72	151	13
8	8	2	128	409	33

Table 3. The number of rewards and the learning cost of LC-learning with two pruning methods.

$|S|$	$|A|$	$|r|$	$|r||S \times A|$	Steps	Max queue
8	8	2	128	409	33
8	8	4	256	1467	122
8	8	6	384	4533	361

3.4   Dynamic Value Domain

The LC-learning is robust in a dynamic value domain, which changes the reward value, since it holds the length of the cycle and the sum of rewards separately. In such a domain, once let the agent find all cycles, there is no need to make the tree anymore. New optimal cycle is easily recalculated with few processes.

3.5   Comparative Experiments with Prioritized Sweeping

Prioritized Sweeping(PriSwp) is an asynchronous model-based method which processes a *policy iteration* and a *value iteration* alternately [6]. We compare the LC-learning with the PriSwp to evaluate its performance in the bus scheduling task: the number of rules are 112 and the number of rewards are 4.

We compare the number of steps of the LC-learning with the number of up-dates of the utility values of the PriSwp. The complexity and the policy quality of the PriSwp mostly depend on the discounting rate γ and the queue threshold ϵ. The γ set smaller, the policy quality becomes worse, although fewer costs are required. The table4 shows the results. With the low γ, the *full tuned* PriSwp takes advantage of the LC-learning little bit. However, we can say the LC-learning calculates the optimal cycle much quickly, since the γ generally ranges from 0.900 to 0.990 . The full tuned PriSwp with low γ can't be in use because the optimal policy are not always guaranteed to be acquired. The figure3 shows all cycles detected by the LC-learning **with** two pruning methods. For reference, we present the figure4 and 5. The former shows that the LC-learning with one pruning method (avoidance of tautological detection) needed about 12000 steps to detect all cycles. And the latter shows the LC-learning **without** pruning method required 18000 steps. They indicate the efficiency of the pruning methods.

Table 4. The result of comparison the LC-learning with the Prioritized Sweeping. The threshold is $\epsilon=0.001$.

	γ	Steps	Updates	Optimal cycle
LC	-	**817**	-	Detected
PriSwp	0.999		219196	Detected
	0.990		22352	Detected
	0.900	-	**2192**	Detected
	0.700		740	Detected
	0.620		588	Undetected

4   Conclusion

In this paper, we reduced the cost of the LC-learning dramatically and evaluated the performance of the LC-learning.

The two pruning methods, the *avoidance of tautological detection* and the *prediction based on the reward* to accelerate the LC-learning successfully prevented the state explosion in the worst cases for it.

Then, we compared the improved LC-learning with one of the most rapid methods, the Prioritized Sweeping in the bus scheduling task. In the middle domain (the number of rules is 112 and the number of rewards is 4), The LC-learning calculated the bias-optimal policy more quickly than the normal PriSwp and it also performed as well as the full-tuned version.

5   Future Work

Application to Stochastic Domain. The algorithm to solve a stochastic domain is required for some realistic problems. It is possible in principle and we are checking up some approaches.

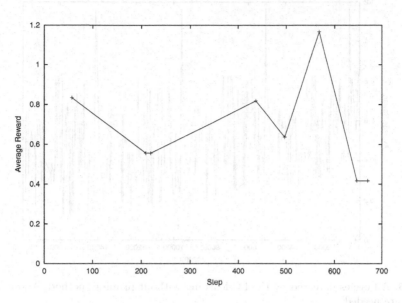

Fig. 3. All cycles detected by the LC-learning with two pruning methods. Only 700 steps are needed.

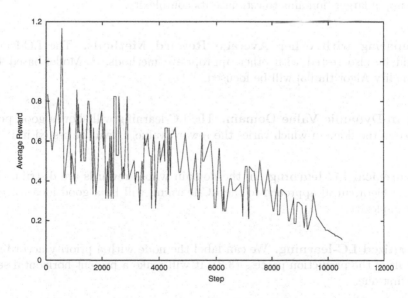

Fig. 4. All cycles detected by the LC-learning with a pruning method (avoidance of tautological detection). About 12000 steps are needed.

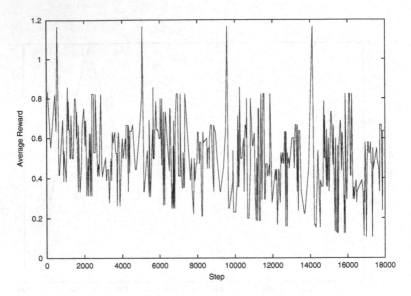

Fig. 5. All cycles detected by the LC-learning without pruning method. About 18000 steps are needed.

Scale-up Test. In the past works, deterministic average cost (possible applied to average reward) MDPs were shown to be in NC[7]. We will test the LC-learning in larger domains to estimate its complexity.

Comparing with other Average Reward Methods. The LC-learning should be also tested with other appropriate methods. A Model-based Bias-optimality Algorithm[3] will be focused.

Test in Dynamic Value Domain. The LC-learning will show a good performance in the domain which varies the reward value. It will be tested in it.

Hierarchical LC-learning. In the domain whose rewards are distributed locally, a hierarchical approach to the LC-learning will be a good idea to reduce the complexity.

Prioritized LC-learning. We can label the node with a priority according to a result of the prediction process (3.2). It will make a present horizontal search best-first one.

Acknowledgement. We must express my gratitude to Kenji Ishimura for his work building up basis of this work. The technical aspect of this work was supported by Yuta Ochi.

References

1. Leslie P. Kaelbling, Michael L. Littman, and Andrew P. Moore. Reinforcement learning: A survey. *Journal of Artificial Intelligence Research*, 4:237–285, 1996.
2. Taro Konda and Tomohiro Yamaguchi. Lc-learning: In-stages model-based average reward reinforcement learning :foundations. In *Proceedings of the Seventh Pacific Rim International Conference on Artificial Intelligence (PRICAI-2002)*, 2002.
3. Sridhar Mahadevan. An average-reward reinforcement learning algorithm for computing bias-optimal policies. In *Proceedings of the Thirteenth AAAI (AAAI-1996)*, pages 875–880, 1996.
4. Sridhar Mahadevan. Average reward reinforcement learning: Foundations, algorithms, and empirical results. *Machine Learning*, 22(1-3):159–195, 1996.
5. Toshimi Minoura, S. Choi, and R. Robinson. Structural active-object systems for manufacturing control. *Integrated Computer-Aided Engineering*, 1(2):121–136, 1993.
6. Andrew W. Moore and Christopher G. Atkeson. Prioritized sweeping: Reinforcement learning with less data and less time. *Machine Learning*, 13:103–130, 1993.
7. C. H. Papadimitriou and J. N. Tsitsiklis. The complexity of markov decision processes. *Mathematics of Operations Research*, 12(3):441–450, 1987.
8. Martin L. Puterman. *Markov Decision Processes: Discrete Dynamic Stochastic Programming, 92–93*. John Wiley, 1994.
9. Richard S. Sutton and Andrew G. Barto. *Reinforcement Learning: An Introduction*. MIT Press, 1998.
10. Prasad Tadepalli and DoKyeong Ok. Model-based average reward reinforcement learning. *Artificial Intelligence*, 100(1-2):177–223, 1998.

Extension of the RDR Method That Can Adapt to Environmental Changes and Acquire Knowledge from Both Experts and Data

Takuya Wada, Tetsuya Yoshida, Hiroshi Motoda, and Takashi Washio

Institute of Scientific and Industrial Research,
Osaka University
8-1, Mihogaoka, Ibaraki, Osaka 567-0047, JAPAN

Abstract. A Knowledge Acquisition method "Ripple Down Rules" can directly acquire and encode knowledge from human experts. It is an incremental acquisition method and each new piece of knowledge is added as an exception to the existing knowledge base. There is another type of knowledge acquisition method that learns directly from data. Induction of decision tree is one such representative example. Noting that more data are stored in the database in this digital era, use of both expertise of humans and these stored data becomes even more important. Further, it is not appropriate to assume that the knowledge is stable and maintains its usefulness. Things change over time. It is not good to keep old useless knowledge in the knowledge base when such change happens. This paper attempts to integrate inductive learning and knowledge acquisition under a situation in which we can't assume a stable environment. We show that using the minimum description length principle (MDLP), the knowledge base of Ripple Down Rules is automatically and incrementally constructed from data. We, thus, can use both human expertise and data simultaneously. When it is found that some change takes place, useless knowledge is automatically deleted based on MDLP, still keeping the consistency of knowledge base. Experiments are carefully designed and tested to verify that the proposed method indeed works for many data sets having different natures.

1 Introduction

With the recent development of computer network, huge amount of information with various forms is communicated over the network. It is required to provide a methodology to construct a reliable and adaptive knowledge-based system (KBS), which is accessible to both human experts and users over the network. Two functions are required to realize such a reliable and adaptive KBS. One is the capability to reconstruct the internal structure of the KBS so that it can adapt to the environmental changes in the domain while sustaining its performance. The other is to acquire knowledge from both data and human experts concurrently or alternately by incorporating the recent development in the research on machine learning. "Ripple Down Rules [2] (RDR)" method has the capability to realize

M. Ishizuka and A. Sattar (Eds.): PRICAI 2002, LNAI 2417, pp. 218–227, 2002.

the above two functions. In the RDR method knowledge is directly acquired and encoded from human experts without requiring high-level models of knowledge. In addition, since it is an incremental KA method, there is no clear distinguish between knowledge acquisition and knowledge maintenance.

This paper proposes to incorporate the concept of the Minimum Description Length Principle [7] (MDLP) into the RDR method. The proposal consists of two parts: (1) an extension of the RDR method to cope with changes in class distribution on a problem domain (2) a method for integrating both Inductive Learning method (a machine learning method that builds an RDR knowledge base incrementally from data) and the standard RDR method (a KA method that captures expertise incrementally from a human expert). Data sets from UCI repository [1] are utilized to evaluate the proposed method with respect to acquiring knowledge from both data and experts and to coping with the changes in the class distribution on a problem domain.

This paper is organized as follows. Section 2 briefly explains RDR. Section 3 describes the use of MDLP for the construction of RDR KB. Section 4 explains the proposed KA method based on MDLP. Section 5 describes how to delete useless knowledge based on MDLP to cope with the environmental changes. Section 6 reports the result of experiments to verify the proposed method.

2   Ripple Down Rules Revisited

The basis of this method is the maintenance and retrieval of cases. When a case is incorrectly retrieved by an RDR system, the KA (maintenance) process requires the expert to identify how a case stored in a KBS differs from the present case. The structure of an RDR knowledge base is a binary tree [8]. Each node in the tree is a rule with a desired conclusion. Each node has a "cornerstone case (CS-case)" associated with it, that is, the case that prompted the inclusion of the rule. The algorithm of an inference process for incoming cases is mentioned in [8]. Note that a node which has induced a conclusion for the case is called "last satisfied node (LSN)".

If the conclusion is different from the one which an expert judges the case to be, knowledge (new rule) must be acquired from the human expert, and this rule must be added to the existing binary tree. When the expert wants to add a new rule, there must be a case that is misclassified by a rule in RDR. The system asks him to select conditions for the rule from the "difference list (D-list)" between these two cases: the misclassified case and the CS-case. Then the misclassified one is stored as the refinement case (new CS-case) with the new rule whose condition part distinguishes these cases. Depending on whether the LSN is the same as the end node (the last node in the inference path), the new rule and its CS-case are added at the end of YES or NO branch of the end node. Knowledge is never removed or changed, simply modified by the addition of exception rules.

3   The Minimum Description Length Principle

This principle is the normal practice for selecting the most plausible probabilistic model from many alternatives, based on individual observational data for those alternatives. "Description length (DL)" can measure the complexity of the hypothesis. When the hypothesis is a classifier of some representation (decision tree [6] or neural network [4]), given some appropriate encoding method, the value can be the sum of (1) a DL for encoding the hypothesis itself and (2) a DL for encoding the misclassified cases by the hypothesis. According to the MDLP, the model with the smallest total DL should be selected. The following weighted sum is used to estimate the total DL:

$$Total\ DL = (DL\ of\ Subsection\ 3.2) + W \times (DL\ of\ Subsection\ 3.1) \quad (1)$$

W is a weight and set to 0.3 based on our experience [8].

One of the differences between the proposed system and the standard one is that each node in the former keeps not only the CS-case but also the cases whose last satisfied node is assigned to that node. Let P be a set consisting of m cases that has passed a node α in the inference process, and let O be a subset of P ($O \subseteq P$), consisting of r cases for which the node α is the last satisfied node. In our encoding the DL of the tree is calculated first and then the one for the misclassified cases is calculated. The DL of the tree is calculated based on the pairs of an attribute and its value in P for the knowledge base. On the other hand, the one for the misclassified cases is based on the class information in O.

3.1   The DL of a Binary Tree

Two kinds of information to be encoded at the node α are the branch information and the If-Then rule information. The DL for the former is mentioned in [8]. The information for the rule [1] consists of 4 components: (1) {the number of attributes used in the condition part}, (2) {attributes used in the part}, (3) {the attribute value for each attribute in (2)} and (4) {the class in the conclusion part}. Before calculating the DL of (1),we need the "attribute-space" of each node in the binary tree. From m cases in P, we obtain the frequency distribution of each attribute-value. The corresponding attribute-space consists of a set of attributes each having at least 2 attribute-values with its frequency of at least 1 case.

Suppose the space for node α has n attributes $\{A_i | i = 1, 2, ..., n\}$, resulting from P. The way to calculate the DLs for information (1), (2) and (4) are same as in [8], and the paper explains how to calculate the DL of (3) in case of nominal attribute only. Thus, we explain here how to calculate the DL for numerical attribute. For numerical attribute A_i, the condition can be $\{? < A_i\}$, $\{A_i \leq?\}$ or $\{? < A_i \leq?\}$. Thus, $\log_2 3C_1$ bits are necessary to identify which one to use. Suppose that m_i is the number of candidates for a cut-off value for the attribute A_i. When the condition is $\{? < A_i\}$ or $\{A_i \leq?\}$, another $\log_2 m_i C_1$

---

[1] In RDR, the rule consists of multiple attribute-value pairs and one class-value pair.

bits are necessary. On the other hand, when it is $\{? < A_i \leq?\}$, $\log_2 2C_1$ bits are needed to indicate which is encoded first lower bound or upper bound. In the former case, the upper one is encoded with $\log_2 {}_{m_i - k_i}C_1$ bits after the lower one is done with $\log_2 {}_{m_i}C_1$ bits. In the latter, the lower one is encoded with $\log_2 {}_{m_i - l_i}C_1$ bits after the upper one is encoded with $\log_2 {}_{m_i}C_1$ bits. Here, k_i (l_i) means that the lower (upper) cut-off value is the k_i-th (l_i-th) one from the left edge (right edge).

3.2   The DL for Class Labels of Misclassified Cases

Suppose that k cases in O has the same class label with the consequence part of the rule in node α. First, $\log_2 {}_rC_1$ bits are necessary to express that $r - k$ cases have different classes from the consequence part. If $k = r$, there is no misclassified case and no further encoding is required. If $k < r$, it is necessary to represent which class the remaining $r - k$ cases have. Suppose that the number of classes which are different from that for the CS-case is s and the number of cases for each class is $p_i(i = 1, 2, ..., s)$. The class labels are sorted in descending order with p_i i.e. $p_s \geq p_{s-1} \geq ... \geq p_2 \geq p_1$. The DL for misclassified cases is calculated using the algorithm shown in Table 1. The function **ceil()** in the table returns the least greatest integer for the argument.

Table 1. Algorithm for DL to specify true classes of misclassified cases

> **initialize** DL **to** 0,   : reset
> all_num **to** r,   : the # of O
> $right\_num$ **to** k,   : the # of right cases
> j **to** $class\_num - 1$,   : the # of class candidates
> i **to** s, and   : the # of different classes
> max_i **to** ∞.
> **repeat while** ($all\_num \neq right\_num$)
>   **if** $all\_num - right\_num < max_i$,
>   **then** $candi = all\_num - right\_num$,
>   **else** $candi = max_i$,
>   **if** $all\_num - right\_num > j$
>   **then** $candi = candi - \textbf{ceil}((all\_num - right\_num) \div j)$.
> $DL = DL + log_2(j) + log_2(candi) + log_2({}_{all\_num}C_{p_i})$.
> $all\_num = all\_num - p_i$.
> $max_i = p_i$.
>   **decrement** j **and** i.

The DL for the i-th different class is calculated at the line "$DL = DL + \log_2(j) + ...$". The first term is for specifying which class label the case has, the second one is for the number of cases p_i with the class, and the last one is to encode the locations for p_i cases. With this encoding it is possible to identify the true class labels for $r - k$ cases if the encoded bits are decoded. Encoding the entire binary tree in top-down produces the bit string for the class labels which are attached to each misclassified case in the tree.

4   Knowledge Acquisition Based on MDLP

4.1   Knowledge Acquisition from Data Alone

In this method, based on the MDLP, we want to search all possible sets of elements from the D-list for a set with the minimum total DL.

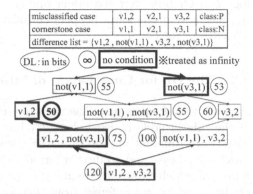

The objective in our approach is to search for the set of conditions from the D-list so that the total DL is minimized when it is utilized as the condition part in the newly created node. In our proposed search strategy, the greedy search is carried out both from the most specialized condition to the misclassified case

Fig. 1. Search by data alone

and from the most general condition to it. The search process is terminated when the total DL is captured in a local minimum. The proposed method enables to construct a knowledge base from data inductively without human experts. Admittedly exhaustive search will enable the construction of more accurate knowledge bases at the cost of much more computational cost. However, greedy search is employed to narrow the search space and to open the possibility for human experts to intervene with their high-level information management capability.

Figure 1 is an example in which an input case misclassified by the so far grown RDR tree is $\{v_{1,2}, v_{2,1}, v_{3,2}\}$ and a CS-case whose node has derived the false conclusion is $\{v_{1,1}, v_{2,1}, v_{3,1}\}$. A detail of the search algorithm in the lattice of elements in the D-list is omitted due to the space limitation, but it is a greedy search. The condition $\{v_{1,2}\}$ found by the search from the most specialized one $\{v_{1,2}, v_{3,2}\}$ has smaller total DL than the one $\{not(v_{3,1})\}$ by the search from the most general condition.

4.2   Knowledge Acquisition from Both Data and Human Experts

We can imagine situations that integrate IL and KA under the RDR knowledge base. For example, during the KBS development, there can be periods that as not to use human experts but use data. On the other hand, there can be periods that as not use data but use experts. In this case, what is necessary is just to switch between IL and KA.

When both human experts and data are available, it is possible to integrate both knowledge sources to construct a knowledge base. One way is to start the search for condition part which is selected from the D-list by the experts so that both knowledge sources can be utilized effectively. This can lead to find out better conditions from the viewpoint of MLDP, compared with the ones selected by experts. Notice that we estimate only this integrating method in Section 6.

5   The Knowledge Deletion for the Environmental Changes

Part of knowledge acquired previously might become useless when the class distribution for the domain or the noise rate for the cases changes dynamically. Moreover, such invalid knowledge might hinder efficient acquisition of new knowledge and thus can be harmful. A naive way to cope with this issue is to discard the constructed knowledge base completely when such a change is detected and to re-construct a new knowledge base under new environment. However, when the change is slow, it is difficult to detect. Moreover, since some knowledge might be still valid for new environment, it would be reasonable to reuse such knowledge as much as possible.

5.1   The Criterion to Estimate the Value of Knowledge

When the class distribution changes, the D-list might have no element even if the input case is misclassified by the current KBS. In such a case, the standard RDR method can't add a new node. Even if the list is not empty, it does not make sense to add a node when no element in the list is judged as important by the expert. It might be reasonable to treat the node that induced the misclassification as useless. However, if the misclassification is brought about due to some noise in the input case, the knowledge stored at that node can be still valid and the deletion might lead to inconsistency of the knowledge base. Since the policy of the RDR method is to acquire new exceptional knowledge based on the inconsistency of the input case with the current knowledge base, the deletion of node should be carried out with caution: otherwise, acquisition of exceptional knowledge cannot be carried out if such inconsistency always trigger the deletion.

The proposed criterion in our approach is based on the assumption that a new node is not to be added even if the input case is misclassified from the viewpoint of MDLP in Section 3, when adding the node does not decrease the DL. First, tentatively delete the node which induces the wrong conclusion. The cases of the same class as the conclusion part of the deleted node are also deleted (These cases are in O for the node α in Section 3). Other cases of different classes, which were in the deleted node, are restored and redistributed in the tree to their new last satisfied nodes. If the normalized [2] total DL for the knowledge base after deletion is smaller than that of the current one, accept the deletion. Otherwise, recover the current knowledge base by retracting the deletion process.

---

[2] Because the DL monotonically increases in proportion to the number of cases, comparing the total DLs for knowledge bases with different number of cases makes no sense. Since the number of cases stored in the knowledge base is different before and after the deletion, the total DL in comparison is normalized as DL_α/DL'_α and DL_β/DL'_β. Here, DL' denotes the DL for encoding the true class information for the whole cases in the current binary tree without using the tree information, i.e. using the root node information alone.

5.2 Deletion of Node from a Binary Tree

A method for deleting a node is illustrated in Fig. 2. Suppose that node No.2 is judged as contradictory. First, the node is deleted from the tree. Then, node No.4, which is the child node of the Yes branch, is connected to the Yes branch of node No.1. At the same time, the condition "a", which is the premise of the If-Then rule in node No.2, is added to node No.4. Next, the subtree below node No.3 is connected to the No branch of node No.7. Finally, the con-

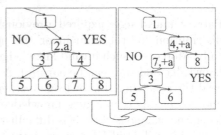

Delete No.2 node. "a" expresses a condition of If-Then rule in No.2 node.

Fig. 2. Deletion Algorithm

dition "a" is added to node No.7. It is easy to confirm that no consistency arises for the stored CS-cases by this reconstruction of the tree. The illustrated process achieves the deletion of the CS-cases in a KBS and the cases which support the If-Then rule attached to the case simultaneously.

6 Experiment

Experiments were carried out to investigate the effectiveness of the proposed method, using 15 databases from University of California Irvine Data Repository [1]. The class distribution of the problem domain were changed abruptly twice during a simulation for the RDR system to acquire knowledge from the data and a human expert incrementally. The accuracy of the knowledge base and the ratio of total DL for the knowledge base are reported for comparison.

[**Generation of change of class distribution**].   A set of cases X_{chg} with different class distribution from the original dataset X_{org} were generated [3]. Then, they are individually divided into the 75% training data $(X_{org}^{train}, X_{chg}^{train})$ and the 25% test data $(X_{org}^{test}, X_{chg}^{test})$. First, by treating X_{org} as the original population, input cases which are selected randomly from X_{org}^{train} are passed to the RDR system. When the total number of cases passed to the system becomes equal to three times large as that of the original population, the population is changed to X_{chg}. After that the system receives the cases drawn from the X_{chg}^{train}. When the total number of cases drawn from X_{chg}^{train} becomes three times large as that of the population, it is changed to X_{org} again.

---

[3] To make X_{chg}, first, all cases in X_{org} are sorted with respect to values in lexical order for nominal attributes and in ascending order for numerical attributes. Then, they are sorted in lexical order for class label. Finally, the labels for (#of all cases ÷ #of classes ÷ 10) cases are changed by shifting them so that the class label for about 10% in X_{org} is changed to neighboring class.

[**Simulated Expert**].   Simulated Expert [3] (SE) is usually used instead of a human expert for the reproduction of experiments and consistent performance estimation in the RDR research community. Therefore, this paper follows this tradition. Note that when $X_{org}^{train}(X_{chg}^{train})$ is the population, we make a If-Then rule set derived from a decision tree constructed by standard C4.5 [5] using $X_{org}(X_{chg})$ to be the SE. A set of elements selected from the D-list by the SE is defined as the intersection between the list and the condition part of the If-Then rule in the SE which predicts correctly the case misclassified by the RDR system at the KA stage.

[**Accuracy of the knowledge base**].   We examine the error rate of misclassified case for the test data using the knowledge base at prespecified time points. Note that we use the $X_{org}^{test}(X_{chg}^{test})$ as the test data when the population is the $X_{org}^{train}(X_{chg}^{train})$. We repeated the simulation 10 times, changing the parameter of random sampling for the input case from the population at each simulation.

6.1   Results and Discussions

Figures 3 and 4 show one result out of 10 simulations for the dataset "PenDigits". For each simulation the RDR system received 75000 cases. Two lines with marks in Fig. 3 indicate the change of accuracy of the proposed methods described in Subsections 4.2 and 4.1. The other two lines with no marks are for the proposed methods without the deletion of nodes. By comparing two lines for "SE&Data" and "Data" ("SE&Data&No_Deletion" and "Data&No_Deletion") the error rate for the former method is fewer than that for the latter up to the 25000th input case. The result shows that the condition which is selected by SE is a good starting condition for the lattice search.

The class distribution was changed abruptly at the 25000th case and 50000th case in the simulation. Such changes are reflected as the sharp increase in the error rate in the figures, since the rate increases with the change of class distribution. The figures also show that deleting the inconsistent knowledge from the knowledge base contributes to reducing the rate.

The change in the ratio of DL for each RDR knowledge base is shown as the four lines in Fig. 4. The two lines without marks show that the ratio decreases monotonously through KA process while the class distribution does not change. Although the ratio increases when the distribution is changed, however, it decreases after the 25000th case in two lines: "DL for se&data" and "DL for data". This also suggests that our delete algorithm works well to keep the size of knowledge base concise. Note that the method with the lowest ratio of DL has the lowest error rate, which confirms the validity of the MDLP in RDR.

Table 2 summarizes the results for 15 data sets at the end of each simulation when the RDR system received all the cases. Out of the four methods, only the results for two with deletion are shown here. The columns for **% of cases** represent the ratio of cases which were kept inside the knowledge base with respect to the whole cases. The ones for **RDR** represent the error rate of the knowledge base for the test data. The decision trees were constructed by C4.5

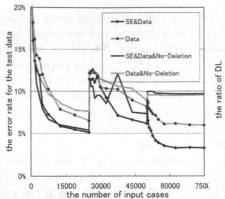

Fig. 3. One of 10times Simulation for "PenDigits" (error)

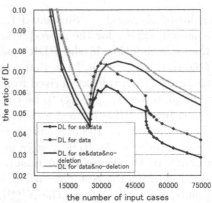

Fig. 4. One of 10times Simulation for "PenDigits" (DL)

Table 2. Summary of experimental results

Data Set	RDR from SE and data			RDR from only data			C4.5 with
	% of cases	RDR	C4.5	% of cases	RDR	C4.5	whole cases
Car	95.3%	4.2%	6.3%	95.2%	4.3%	6.4%	6.8%
Nursery	94.1%	3.0%	2.7%	93.9%	2.9%	2.7%	3.2%
Mushrooms	93.0%	3.7%	2.3%	93.9%	5.0%	2.4%	4.5%
Krvkp	93.5%	2.3%	3.1%	92.7%	2.0%	2.2%	3.9%
VotingRecord	95.6%	6.3%	3.7%	95.3%	6.1%	3.5%	3.2%
BreastCancer	95.1%	4.6%	5.3%	93.5%	4.9%	4.7%	5.6%
Splice	90.4%	7.9%	6.2%	74.9%	8.8%	10.4%	9.1%
Image	93.9%	2.6%	3.3%	94.7%	5.4%	3.8%	8.0%
PageBlocks	93.0%	4.4%	5.1%	90.9%	4.9%	5.2%	5.8%
PenDigits	93.9%	3.5%	3.8%	94.2%	5.0%	4.5%	8.4%
Yeast	56.6%	42.9%	40.0%	62.2%	41.5%	37.3%	24.2%
PimaIndians	62.4%	26.0%	23.0%	41.7%	33.3%	24.5%	15.2%
GermanCredit	72.2%	22.5%	19.4%	73.5%	20.6%	17.1%	14.4%
Cmc	44.6%	47.9%	43.5%	46.3%	47.4%	42.5%	29.1%
AnnThyroid	95.9%	1.2%	2.2%	95.2%	1.8%	2.7%	5.0%

using the cases held in the knowledge bases at the end of simulation. The columns for **C4.5** represent the error rate of such decision trees. Moreover, the column for **C4.5 with whole cases** shows the error rate of a decision trees using all input cases. For instance, the result for the dataset "Mushrooms" suggests that knowledge from SE is effective since the method **RDR from SE and data** shows the lower error rate than the other method.

It is interesting to see whether cases matching to the current class distribution are held in the knowledge base when all cases are input to the RDR system. For the dataset "AnnThyroid", more accurate knowledge bases were constructed for **RDR from SE and data** compared with **C4.5 with whole cases**. This probably is the result that the deletion algorithm works well, and can delete the worthless knowledge with node holding it. Other data sets where such a tendency is shown are "Nursery", "Krvkp" and "Image".

Unfortunately, the error rate for **RDR** was high for some data sets with relatively small number of cases (e.g., "Cmc" and "Yeast") compared with **C4.5 with whole cases**. Since the KA and deletion in our approach are based on the MDLP, if only small amount of cases are available, it is difficult to construct a knowledge base with high prediction accuracy. Thus, our current conjecture is that the deletion algorithm tends to delete too many cases, especially when the size of the original datasets is relatively small. For instance, only 44.6% of the original cases were held in the knowledge base for "Cmc" after deletion. In addition, C4.5 constructs a classifier in batch, contrary to the incremental construction of RDR KB. If C4.5 were modified to construct a decision tree incrementaly, the error rate of the constructed decision tree would increase. Thus, the result indicates that the proposed method can construct a reasonable KB with slightly larger error rate.

7 Conclusion

This paper has proposed a KA method which can adapt to the change in class distribution. The proposed method can be used to acquire knowledge either from both human experts and data or from data alone. Experiments with artificial data showed the effectiveness of the method. However, for some dataset with small number of cases the results were actually bad. In addition, the experimental results suggest that deletion of knowledge (nodes in the binary tree) contributes to holding the necessary cases in the RDR system.

Acknowledgements. This work was partially supported by the grant-in-aid for scientific research on priority area "Active Mining" funded by the Japanese Ministry of Education, Culture, Sport, Science and Technology.

References

1. C.L. Blake and C.J. Merz. UCI repository of machine learning databases, 1998. http://www.ics.uci.edu/~mlearn/MLRepository.html.
2. P. Compton, G. Edwards, G. Srinivasan, et al. Ripple down rules: Turning knowledge acquisition into knowledge maintenance. *Artificial Intelligence in Medicine*, pages 47–59, 1992.
3. P. Compton, P. Preston, and B.H. Kang. The use of simulated experts in evaluating knowledge acquisition. In *Proc. of the 9th Knowledge Acquisition for Knowledge Based Systems Workshop*, 1995.
4. D.K. Gary and J.H. Trevor. Optimal network construction by minimum description length. *Neural Computation*, pages 210–212, 1993.
5. J.R. Quinlan, editor. *C4.5: Programs for Machine Learning*. Morgan Kaufmann, 1993.
6. J.R. Quinlan and R.L. Rivest. Inferring decision trees using the minimum description tion length principle. *Information and Computation*, pages 227–248, 1989.
7. J. Rissanen. Modeling by shortest data description. *Automatica*, pages 465–471, 1978.
8. T. Wada, H. Motoda, and T. Washio. Knowledge acquisition from both human expert and data. In *Proc. of the Fifth Pacific-Asia Conference on Knowledge Discovery and Data Mining*, pages 550–561, HongKong China, April 2001. Springer-Verlag.

Case Generation Method for Constructing an RDR Knowledge Base

Keisei Fujiwara, Tetsuya Yoshida, Hiroshi Motoda, and Takashi Washio

Institute of Scientific and Industrial Research,
Osaka University
Mihogaoka, Ibaraki, Osaka 567-0047, JAPAN

Abstract. Ripple Down Rules (RDR) Method is an incremental Knowledge Acquisition (KA) approach that is able to capture human expertise efficiently. The expert's KA tasks in RDR are 1) to identify the correct class label of each misclassified case and 2) to select important attributes that distinguish the misclassified case from the previous correctly classified case. The latter task is more difficult than the former one since it requires much thought on human expert. This paper proposes a method for reducing the task on human expert by generating context-bounded cases and utilizing them to replace the latter task with the former one. Experiments on the datasets from UCI were carried out to evaluate the proposed method and the result confirmed that it is effective and as good as the standard RDR method on most datasets.

1 Introduction

Ripple Down Rule (RDR) method[2] is one of the methodologies for realizing efficient knowledge acquision and maintenance. It is effective since it allows the incremental acquisition of knowledge. In addition, no knowledge engineers are required since the consistency of knowledge base is also maintained during the knowledge acquision phase.

The following two tasks are required for human experts during the knowledge acquision process in the standard RDR system:

task 1: identify the correct class label of a case

task 2:induce the condition which distinguishes between two cases with different class labels based on the difference in the attribute values.

Compared with **task1**, **task2** is much harder for experts since there can be many candidates for the condition with different generalization capability. Thus, selecting an approporiate one can be very difficult for experts.

This paper proposes an efficient knowledge acquision method in which **task2** is replaced with **task1**. In the proposed method the expert is required only to carry out task1 on cases which are generated by the method to induce the condition in task2. Since the expert does not need to carry out task2, it is expected that his/her cognitive load can be reduced.

M. Ishizuka and A. Sattar (Eds.): PRICAI 2002, LNAI 2417, pp. 228–237, 2002.

Experiments were carried out to compare the proposed method with the standard RDR method which requires the expert to carry out **task2** in addition to **task1**.

2   Ripple Down Rules

The characteristics of RDR are summarized as follows:

- incremental and consistent: allowing incremental addition of exceptional rules contributes to maintaing the consistency of knowledge base.
- direct interface: knowledge is acquired through the interaction between experts and computers and no knowledge engineers are required.

Structure of knowledge base: a binary tree with Yes and No branches is utilized to represent the knowledge base in RDR as shown in Fig.1. Each node stores an If-Then rule and a "cornerstone case (CS-case)" which triggered the addition of the node into the knowledge base.

Inference: suppose the class label of a case (which is called "current case" in RDR) is asked for the knowledge base. The inference starts from the root node and repeats the following process. At each node when the condition in the If-Then rule of the node is satisfied, Yes branch is followed; if not, No branch is followed. When there is no branch to follow, the RDR system returns the conclusion in the If-Then rule of the last satisfied node. The conclusion for the current case is given by the conclusion part of the node in the inference path for the case whose condition part is lastly satisfied.

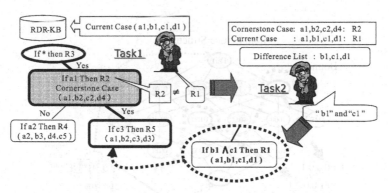

Fig. 1. Knowledge acquisition in RDR.

Knowledge acquision from experts: knowledge acquision is carried out when the expert does not agree with the result of the RDR system. First, the system returns the CS-case for the invoked If-Then rule. Second, the system creates a "difference list (D-List)", which enumerates all the attributes with different values between the current case and the CS-case. Third, the expert is required to select a set of attributes which best distinguishes the current case from the

CS-case. Note that any element in the list satisfies the current case but does not satisfy the CS-case. Fourth, the selected attributes and their values in the current case are utilized to create the condition part for the If-Then rule. Fifth, by treating the class label from the expert as the conclusion, a new node is created with the If-Then rule and the current case as its CS-case. Finally, the new node is attached as a child node to the end node in the inference process.

The difference between 2 cases is represented as the Difference List in Fig. 1. In the RDR system, knowledge constrained within the context of D-List is acquired efficiently in the form of If-Then rule with task2 [6]. However, deciding the appropriate pairs of attribute and its value can be difficult and thus task2 can be hard for human experts.

3   Concept for Case Generation

In our approach cases to be asked for experts in **task1** are generated along with the work for the approximate construction of case base [5]. In this approach a case base for unknown logic function can be constructed approximately with the minimum number of cases. From a negative case and its nearest neighbor positive case, an item lattice shown in Fig.2 is constructed based on their difference. The cases in the lattice are generated and experts are asked to identify their class labels. The case base is refined gradually based on the class labels while its consistency being maintained. Furthermore, the uppor bound for the number of necessary questions (i.e., cases) is estimated analytically to determine the boundary for distinguishing between the positive and negative cases.

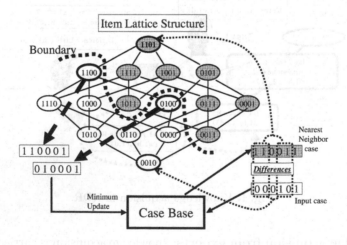

Fig. 2. Estimation of the boundary in item lattice.

In the context of RDR the current case for which the RDR system induced the wrong class label corresponds to the negative case. The CS-case for the induced class label corresponds to the nearest neighbor positive case. Thus, based on the D-List between these cases, the cases which lie in the item lattice for the D-List are generated and the boundary to distinguish between the CS-case and the current case in the lattice is estimated based on the class label from experts through **task1**.

4   Six Algorithms for Generating Cases

This section describes 6 algorithms for generating cases based on the concept in Section 3 in order to replace **task2** with **task1**. The algorithms for generating cases in the item lattice are designed with respect to how many and what kind of cases should be generated to estimate the boundary in the lattice. Cases are represented as the pairs of attribute-values and the proposed algorithms can deal with datasets with both numerical and nominal attributes.

4.1   Knowledge Aquisition in RDR

This section describes the algorithm for knowledge acquision from experts in the conventional RDR system. Notations in the algorithm are as follows:

C_{cu} : current case
C_{co} : cornerstone case
CB : the set of cases which are already encountered
$class(C)$: class label of case C
$DiffList(C_1, C_2)$: different list between cases C_1 and C_2
$RdrClassify(C)$: class label of case C from RDR
$ExpertClassify(C)$: class label of case C from an expert (**task1**)
$ExpertCondition(DiffList)$: condition specified by the expert (**task2**) to distinguish between C_1 and C_2. [1] The condition must satisify C_1.
$QueryNum$: the number of interactions between the expert and RDR

Algorithm for knowledge acquision

Step 1 : If no case is available to acquire knowlege, terminate the knowledge acquision process. If not, classify a case with the RDR system. If $C_{cu} \in CB$, return $class(C_{cu})$. If $C_{cu} \notin CB$, get the class label through $ExpertClassify(C)$ (**task1**) and add C_{cu} into CB.

Step 2 : If $class(C_{cu}) = RdrClassify(C_{cu})$, go to Step 1, since knowledge acquision is not necessary.

Step 3 : (a) calculate $DiffList(C_{cu}, C_{co})$ and show it to the expert, (b) get the condition $Condition$ from the expert through $ExpertCondition(DiffList)$ (**task2**), (c) if $Condition$ is empty, go to Step 1.

---

[1] In this paper the difference list is calculated as the list of values in C_1 which are different from those in C_2. For instance, for the current case $C_{cu} = (0,0,0,1,0,1)$ and cornerstone case $C_{co} = (1,1,0,0,1,1)$ in Fig.1, the difference list $DiffList(C_{cu}, C_{co})$ = (0,0,1,0).

Step 4 : Create If-Then rule with $Condition$ as the condition and $class(C_{cu})$ as its conclusion (i.e., a rule $Condition \Rightarrow class(C_{cu})$). Add a new node with that rule and C_{cu} as its cornerstone case into the RDR binary tree. Go to Step 1.

4.2   Six Algorithms for Generating Cases

Knowledge acquision in RDR with the proposed algorithms is carried out by replacing **Task2** (Step 3(b)) in Subsection 4.1 with **case generation + Task1** as:

- Input: C_{cu}, C_{co}
- In the item lattice based on $DiffList(C_{cu}, C_{co})$ (see Fig.3)
  1. Generate a case C_x based on the search strategy. Ask an expert to perform $ExpertClassify(C_x)$ and get $class(C_x)$ (**task1**).
  2. When the class boundary is found, create the $Condition$ which represent the boundary.
  3. Exit when the search is finished. If not, go to 1.
- Output: $Condition$

The generated case has the value in C_{cu} or C_{co} for each attribute depending on the position in the lattice structure. The $Condition$ for the If-Then rule is represented in Disjunctive Normal Form (DNF). Each conjunct is created such that the current case satisfies it and the CS-case does not. For numerical attribute A_i, the condition is represented as either $\{ ? < A_i \}$ or $\{ A_i \leq ? \}$, as in C4.5. The cut-off value ? is determined as follows. Let R be the range between the value in CS-case and that in the current case for attribute A_i. When no case with the value $\in R$ for A_i has yet been encountered, the cut-off value is set to the middle value in R. When there are some cases with the value $\in R$ for A_i the cut-off value is set to the one which is nearest to the middle value in R.

Different search strategies can be used for generating cases in the item lattice. Different boundaries can be estimated in the item lattice depending on how cases are generated in the search for the boundary. Six algorithms are proposed. They differ in from which case the search is started and how the lattice is searched. Search is started either from the current case C_{cu} or the cornerstone case C_{co}. The lattice is searched as breadth-first like, depth-first like, or just for 1 step. For instance, in Fig. 2 algorithm 1FCU searches the lattice just 1 step From the CUrrent case, BFCO in Breadth-first From the COrnerstone case, and DFCU in Depth-first From the CUrrent case. Search is terminated when the exact boundary is found, or when an approximate one is estimated. Here, the latter is appoximate since it does not guarantee that the cases which satisfy $Condition$ necessarily have the same class label with the current case. The characteristics for the proposed 6 algorithms are summarized in Table 1.

The characteristics of the proposed 6 algorithms are illustrated in Figs. 3, 4 and 5. Each node in the figures represents the possible case to be generated and the search is carried out in the order of the number on the node. The bold dotted curve in each figure represents the condition which is determined through the case generation and task1 on the generated cases.

Table 1. Characters of 6 Algotithms

Algorithm	Start Case	Search Method	Worst Q num
1FCU	C_{cu}	1step	N
1FCO	C_{co}	1step	N
BFCU	C_{cu}	BFS	2^N
BFCO	C_{co}	BFS	2^N
DFCU	C_{cu}	DFS	N^2
DFCO	C_{co}	DFS	N^2

N: number of different attributes, Worst Q num: the maximum number of questions asked for an expert in the worst case

Table 2. Datasets Used in the Experiment

dataset	# cases	# classes	# attributes	dataset	# cases	# classes	# attributes
Samp[+]	4096	2	Nom.[*]12	Pen-Digits	10992	10	Num. 16
Car Evaluation	1728	4	Nom. 6	Pima Indians	768	2	Num. 6
Nursery	12960	5	Nom. 8	Shut	14500	7	Num. 9
Tic Tac Toe	956	2	Nom. 9	Yeast	1484	10	Num. 8
Voting Records	435	2	Nom. 16	Ann-thyroid	7200	3	Mixed.[***] 15/6
Page Blocks	5473	5	Num.[**] 9	Cmc	1473	3	Mixed. 7/2
Iris	150	3	Nom.[**]4	German	1000	2	Mixed. 13/7

[+]Artificial dataset, [*]nominal attributes, [**]numerical attributes, [***]nominal and numerical attributes : #nominal/#numerical

5 Experiment and Discussion

5.1 Experiment

Datasets
Experiments were carried out on one artificial dataset and 13 datasets from UCI repository[1]. On each dataset randomly selected 75% cases were used as the training cases and the remaining 25% cases were used as the test cases. Note that the cases which were encountered in training were removed from the test cases. The above process is repeated 10 times for each dataset and the average is taken for the evaluation.

Simulated Expert
A simulated expert which is constructed by C4.5 was utilized in the experiment for each dataset. C4.5 is used to construct the decision tree for each dataset. Then the decision tree is transformed into a set of If-Then rules (C4.5rules), which is treated as a simulated expert. For each case **Task2** is simulated by

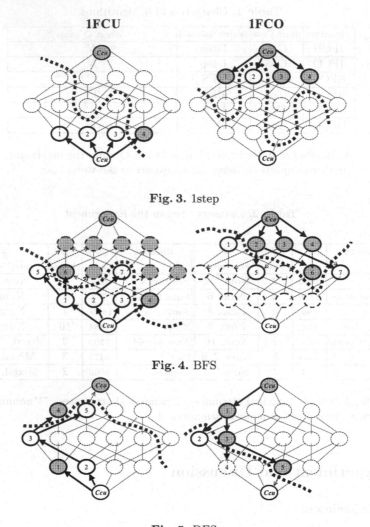

Fig. 3. 1step

Fig. 4. BFS

Fig. 5. DFS

taking the intersecion of the diffrecence list for the case and the If-Then rule which is used to judge its class label [3].

Experiments were carried out for the RDR method with the proposed case generation algorithms and the conventional RDR method in which **task2** is carried out by the simulated expert. The results were analyzed with regard to:

Error Rate: the rate of misclassified cases in the test cases

Size: the number of nodes in the constructed RDR binary tree

Knowledge acquisition from the simulated expert for the training cases was terminated when the number of interaction reached the predefined number[2]. Here, the number of interaction is defined as the sum of the number of *ExpertClassify* and that of *ExpertRule*. Note that in the proposed method the number is equal to that of *ExpertClassify* since *ExpertCondition* is not utilized.

5.2   Results and Discussions

Results are summarized in Table. 3.

Table 3. Results of experiment.

Data set	Error rate(%)							KB size						
	RDR	1FCU	1FCO	BFCU	BFCO	DFCU	DFCO	RDR	1FCU	1FCO	BFCU	BFCO	DFCU	DFCO
Samp	0.17	0.10	0.23	0.14	0.04	0.10	1.19	79	60	80	69	75	84	182
CarEvaluation	4.00	0.78	1.18	0.62	0.94	0.71	5.20	96	67	72	66	73	74	161
Nursery	2.45	1.29	1.29	1.30	1.44	1.53	4.76	478	372	406	370	434	406	1063
TitTacToe	5.46	7.42	12.00	12.84	13.72	11.49	25.70	63	64	74	54	61	77	121
Voting Records	0.26	1.03	0.00	4.29	3.43	0.39	4.36	6	5	5	4	4	6	11
Page Blocks	0.87	1.94	1.98	5.59	5.83	1.83	3.03	35	79	60	13	11	87	143
Iris	0.00	0.00	0.81	1.08	1.60	0.00	5.38	4	7	6	6	6	7	15
Pen Digit	2.66	7.07	13.50	-	-	6.97	44.96	282	293	144	-	-	251	539
Pima Indians	7.29	10.31	7.86	12.50	13.33	7.71	15.94	17	29	28	8	9	30	47
Shut	0.11	0.09	2.18	0.09	0.96	0.15	0.28	21	35	25	31	31	34	95
Yeast	11.55	22.36	23.05	26.88	25.67	23.24	39.87	92	118	89	53	49	109	166
Ann-thyroid	0.46	0.46	0.51	0.50	0.62	0.44	2.28	14	40	38	27	36	42	147
Cmc	16.92	14.79	18.19	16.96	19.57	17.53	22.80	84	116	123	89	91	134	175
German	9.76	10.84	9.24	-	-	10.00	13.00	36	40	38	-	-	34	51

Comparison with the standard RDR method

Error Rate: In 12 datasets the error rate for the proposed RDR method is equivalent to or smaller than that for the standard one.

Size: In 9 datasets the size for the proposed RDR method is equivalent to that for the standard one.

Number of interactions with the expert: Note that the number of **task1** and that of **task2** are equally counted as 1 interaction, albeit the latter is much harder for the expert. This means that the proposed method enables the construction of an equivalent RDR Knowledge Base with the standard one with respect to the error rate and size by reducing the load on the expert.

Effect of the number of classes: Unfortuntaly the proposed method did not work well for PenDigit and Yeast, both of which has 10 classes. Since the proposed method tries to find the boundary under which the the class label is the same with the current case, the estimated condition might be too specific when the number of class gets large.

---

[2] In the experiment the number is set to the number of 75% cases in each dataset.

Table 4. Comparation of the proposal method with the standard RDR.

Data set	Property				Comparison					Rating
					RDR		Best of Algorithms			
	CaseNum	Nominal	Numerical	Class	error	size	error	size	Algorithm	
Samp	4096	12		2	0.17	79	0.04	75	BFCO	◎
Car Evaluation	1728	6		4	4.00	96	0.62	66	BFCU	◎
Nursery	12960	8		5	2.45	478	1.29	372	1FCU	◎
TicTacToe	956	9		3	5.46	63	7.42	64	1FCU	○
Voting Records	435	16		2	0.26	6	0.00	5	1FCO	◎
Page Blocks	5473		10	5	0.87	35	1.83	87	DFCU	○
Iris	150		4	3	0.00	4	0.00	7	1FCU,DFCU	◎
Pen Digit	10992		16	10	2.66	282	6.97	251	DFCU	×
Pima Indians	768		8	2	7.29	17	7.71	30	DFCU	○
Shut	14500		9	7	0.11	21	0.09	31	BFCU	◎
Yeast	1484		8	10	11.55	92	22.36	118	1FCU	×
Ann-thyroid	7200	15	6	3	0.46	14	0.44	42	DFCU	◎
Cmc	1473	7	2	3	16.92	84	14.79	116	1FCU	◎
German	1000	13	7	2	9.76	36	9.24	38	1FCO	◎

◎ means the proposed method is better than, ○ as equivalent to, and × as worse than the standard RDR method.

Comparison of Six Algorithms

From which case the search should be started?: From Table 3 the current case should be used as the starting point in the search since the error rate tends to be low (in 34 combinations out of 40). For instance, DFCU is the best and DFCO is the worst as a whole. Since the current case is misclassified by the RDR KB, it would be better to carry out knowledge acquision so that the KB can be refined around that case. Ggenerating cases which are similar to the current case playes the role of the above process. In the following discussion the current case is used as the starting point in search.

Search strategy: As for 1FCU (maximum N cases are generated) or DFCU (maximum N^2 cases are generated), the error rate and size are equivalent to the standard RDR method. On the other hand, RFCU(BFS-Recursive, maximum 2^N cases are generated) was not effective and did not even work for Pen Digit(16 attributes) and German (21 attributes). The number of interactions required for adding just one node to the RDR binary tree exceeded predefined threshold in these datasets. When the number of attributes are large as in these datasets, the search space in the item lattice becomes huge and thus is difficult to find out the boundary. As a future direction we plan to utilize the feature selection method [4] to reduce the size of item lattice.

Difference in the nominal and numerical attributes: Although the proposed algorithms worked well for the datasets with nominal attributes, they did not work well for some datasets with numerical attributes. With numerical attributes the number of questions per node tend to increase since it is possible to consider a lot of cases with subtle difference in the values. For instance, for a nominal attribute "traffic light" the number of candidates for the value is usually quite limited as "red, yellow, yello". On the other hand, for a numerical attribute as "weight of car" the number of candidates for possible value tends to increase, such as "650, 660,870,...". Thus, many cases can be generated in the item lattice, which results in the increase in the number of interactions to reduce the error rate. DFCU seems better for numerical attributes from Table 4. The difference between DFCU and 1FCU, is due to the different characteristics of the boundary found in these algorithms. In DFCU the boundary is determined based on two cases with different class labels. On the other hand, in 1FCU the boundary is determined based on the neighboring cases for the current case. It is conjectured that such a difference in the boundaries might bring about the different result for the datasets with numerical attributes.

Which is best?: 1FCU and DFCU are the two best algorithms from the experiment, both of which utilize the current case as the start point in search. These are equivalent with respect to the error rate and size. Since Table 4 indicates that DFCU is better than 1FCU for datasets with numerical attributes, DFCU is the best. However, since the difference is quite small, it is necessary to carry out more experiments to draw more definite conclusion.

6 Conclusion

This paper has proposed a case generation method for constructing an RDR Knowledge Base only through the classification of the generated cases by the expert. The experiment showed that the proposed method can construct an RDR knowledge base which is as good as the one with the standard RDR method that requires an expert to induce the condition for distinguishing cases. Our immediate future plan is to utilize the feature selection [4] to scale up the number of attributes.

Acknowledgements. This work was partially supported by the grant-in-aid for scientific research 1) on priority area "Active Mining" and 2) No. 13558034 funded by the Japanese Ministry of Education, Culture, Sport, Science and Technology.

References

1. C.L. Blake and C.J. Merz. UCI repository of machine learning databases, 1998. http :// www.ics.uci.edu / ~mlearn / MLRepository.html.
2. P. Compton, G. Edwards, B. H. Kang, and et al. Ripple down rules: Possibilities and limitations. In *Proc. of the 5th Knowledge Acquisition for Knowledge Based Systems Workshop*, 1991.
3. P. Compton, P. Preston, and B.H. Kang. The use of simulated experts in evaluating knowledge acquisition. In *Proc. of the 9th Knowledge Acquisition for Knowledge Based Systems Workshop*, 1995.
4. Huan Liu and Hiroshi Motoda, editors. *FEATURE SELECTION FOR KNOWLEDGE DISCOVERY AND DATA MINING*. Kluwer academic publishers, 1998.
5. Ken Satoh and Ryuichi Nakagawa. Discovering critical cases in case-based reasoning. In *Online Proceedings of the Sixth International Symposium on Artificial Intelligence and Mathematics*, Florida, 2000.
6. Takuya Wada, Tadashi Horiuchi, Hiroshi Motoda, and Takashi Washio. A description length based decision criterion for default knowledge in the ripple down rules method. *Knowledge and Information Systems*, 3(2):146–167, 2001.

Association Rules Using Rough Set and Association Rule Methods

Defit Sarjon [1,2] and Noor Md Sap Mohd [1]

[1]Faculty of Computer Science and Information System
University of Technology Malaysia, KB. 791
80990 Johor Bahru, Malaysia
Telp: (07)-5576160, Fax: (07)-5566155

[2] Faculty of Computer Science
University of Putera Indonesia "YPTK" Padang
West Sumatera, Indonesia
Telp : (62-751-776666), Fax : (62-751-71913)
{sarjon_d@hotmail.com}, {mohdnoor@fsksm.utm.my}

Abstract. With the wide applications of computers, database technologies and automated data collection techniques, large amount of data have been continuously collected into databases. It creates great demands for analyzing such data and turning them into useful knowledge. Therefore, it is necessary and interesting to examine how to extract hidden information or knowledge from large amounts of data automatically and intelligently. In this paper, we propose an MML-AR (Mining Multiple Level Association Rules), which integrates rough set and association rule methods. MML-AR model has been implemented and tested using Jakarta Stock Exchange (JSX) databases. Our study concludes that MML-AR model can improve the performance ability of generated interesting rules.

1   Introduction

With the wide applications of computers, database technologies and automated data collection techniques, large amount of data have been continuously collected into databases. It creates great demands for analyzing such data and turning them into useful knowledge. Understanding or learning about the implicit or hidden information in the data is important for strategic decision support or technical operations [1], [2], [3]. Therefore, it is necessary and interesting to examine how to extract hidden information or knowledge from large amounts of data automatically and intelligently.

Association rule, introduced by Agrawal, Imielinski and Swami [4], is one of data mining technique to discover interesting rules or relationships among attributes in databases. It has attracted great attention in database research communities in recent years.

M. Ishizuka and A. Sattar (Eds.): PRICAI 2002, LNAI 2417, pp. 238–243, 2002.

In the past research, a multitude of promising association rule methods have been developed. For example, [5] proposed and developed an interesting association rule mining approach, called on-line analytical mining of association rules, which integrates the recently developed OLAP (on-line analytical processing) technology with some efficient association mining methods. This approach gives great advantages over many existing algorithm in term of flexibility and efficiency.

However, these approaches still have several weaknesses and need further improvement. Some of weaknesses are as follows:

1. Did not apply a special data preprocessing techniques [2], [7], [8].
2. The number of rules grows exponentially with the number of items [4].
3. Quite costly to pick interesting rules from the set of generated rules [6].

Based on the above mention problems, at the present stage we propose a MML-AR (Mining Multiple Level Association Rules) model to overcome these problems. This model integrates rough set and association rule methods.

The rest of the paper is organized as follows. The proposed Mining Multiple Level Association Rule (MML-AR) model is given in section 2. Experimental results and conclusion are given in section 3 and 4 respectively.

2   Mining Multiple Level Association Rule (MML-AR) Model

MML-AR model consists of two main modules called pre-processing and processing module. The first module is used to transform continuous values into discrete values and data cleaning. Next, the second module is executed to generate and evaluate interesting rules. Description of each module is given in following sub section.

2.1   Pre-processing Module

Preprocessing module consists of two main steps, called data transformation and data cleaning. The explanations of these steps are given in section 2.1.1 and 2.1.2 respectively.

2.1.1   Data Transformation
The raw data in a database is called at its primitive level and the knowledge is said to be at a primitive level if it is discovered using raw data only. Abstracting raw data to a higher conceptual level and discovering and expressing knowledge at higher abstraction level have superior advantages over data mining at a primitive level.

In this paper, we apply Discretization using boolean reasoning method, one of the discretization method based on rough set, to transform the raw data into higher levels concept. The detail of this algorithm is given in algorithm 2.1.

Algorithm 2.1: Discretization Algorithm

Input   : Initial Databases

Output: Discrete Values

Method :

  1. Sort raw data into ascending order based on conditional attribute

  2. Define interval of each conditional attribute

  3. Generate discernibility matrix, A

  4. Copy A to A* to construct a new decision A*

  5. For each column, find the total number of occurrence of 1, and sort them into descending order

  6. Choose column for A* with the maximal number of occurrence of 1's

  7. Delete from A* the column choose in step (6)

  8. If row is not empty, go to (5), else define set of cuts to define interval of discrete value.

  9. Creation of segments. A set of segments are created based on the value of set of cuts.

2.1.2   Data Cleaning

Imperfection is one of the common characteristics of the information available to human experts. Information can be incomplete, inconsistent, uncertain, or all three. It is important task in many contexts such as data warehousing and data integration [9], [10]. The detail of Data cleaning algorithm is given in algorithm 2.2.

Algorithm 2.2: Data Cleaning Algorithm to Remove Inconsistencies Data

Input : inconsistent raw data

Output: consistent raw data

Method:

1. Sort raw data into ascending order based on conditional attribute

2. Generate indiscernibility of pairs conditional attributes

3. Compare indiscernibility of pair attributes with decision attribute. If pairs of conditional attributes have different decision attribute, it is called inconsistent else inconsistent.

4. Generate approximation, i.e., lower and upper approximation, to remove inconsistencies in data.

2.2 Processing Module

Processing module is also called association rule module. This module consists of two main steps, called rule generation and evaluation. Description of these steps is given in following 2.2.1 and 2.2.2 respectively.

2.2.1 Rule Generation

Multiple level association rules are rules in which the concepts at multiple levels in conceptual hierarchies. In general, mining knowledge at multiple levels is divided into two categories, namely multiple level single dimension and multiple level multi dimensions. In this paper, we focus on multiple level multi dimensional association rules.

Multiple level multi dimensional algorithm for MML-AR is given in algorithm 2.3.

Algorithm 2.3: Multiple Level Multi Dimensional Algorithm

Input : A hierarchy information encoded and task relevant set of a transaction database in the format (tid, itemset)

Output : Multiple level large itemset

Method : A top down

1. Derive Minimum support, σ', of each items of attributes at each conceptual level, i.e., σ'(A₁) is 5, σ' (A₂) is 4, …., σ'(Aₙ) is 2.

2. Sort the Minimum support into ascending or descending order, i.e., σ'(A₁) > σ'(A₂ > ….> σ'(Aₙ).

3. Derive for each level l, start at level 1, the large k itemset, L[l,(i,p)], for each I and p, and the set of large itemset for all i's and p's. For every large itemset, the actual support must greater than or equal to minimum support.

4. Derive the set of association rules from the every large itemsets for each level based on the minimum confidence at this level, Minconf (l).

2.2.2 Rule Evaluation

After frequent itemsets and discover rules are generated, the next process in MML-AR is to measure the interestingness of the rules. A rule is interesting or not can be identified either subjectively or objectively.

To help filter out such incomplete and misleading strong association rules $X \rightarrow Y$, we need to study how the two items X and Y are correlated. The detail of rule evaluation algorithm is given in [10].

3   Experimental Results

We have tested and studied MML-AR model using Jakarta Stock Exchange (JSX). The values are organized into a conceptual hierarchy with three levels. The data samples of inconsistent and consistent data are given in [10].

Table 4.1 and 4.2 show the experimental results of MML-AR model using inconsistent and consistent data at level 1 and 2 respectively.

Table 4.2 shows some improvement from several aspects. First, the valid rule is improved from 37.5% to 50% at level 2, an increment of 16.45%. Second, invalid rules percentage drops from 62.% to 50%, a decrement of 12.5%. These great improvements prove that consistent data will give us better valid rules.

Table 4.1: The Performance Comparison at Level-1

Data	Generated Ruled	Valid Rules	Invalid Rules
Inconsistent	83	49.8	33.2
Consistent	67	50.25	16.75

Table 4.2: The Performance Comparison at Level-2

Data	Generated Ruled	Valid Rules	Invalid Rules
Inconsistent	100	37.5	62.5
Consistent	100	50	50

4   Conclusion

A number of mining association rules methods have been developed and studied. However, a single association rules method has not proven appropriate for every domain and data sets. Instead, several techniques need to be integrated into hybrid system – two or more techniques are combined in a manner that overcomes the limitation of the individual technique. In this paper, we propose a MML-AR (Mining Association Rules) model, which integrates rough set and association rule methods. This model has been successfully implemented and studied using JSX (Jakarta Stock Exchange). Our results show that MML-AR model could give us a better rules or knowledge.

References

Mika, K., and Heikki, M., et.al (1994). „Finding Interesting Rules From Large Sets of Discovered Association Rules". The 3rd Conference on Information and Knowledge Management, November 29 – December 2, 1994, Gainthersburg, Maryland.

Wei, W., (1999). „Predictive Modeling Based on Classification and Pattern Matching Method". MSc Thesis, Computing Science, Simon Fraser University, Augustus 1999.

Sarjon, D., Mohd, N., (2001a). „A Stock Price Prediction Based on Association Rules and Neural Network", KMICE 2001, Langkawi, 14-15 May 2001

Juchen, H., Ulrich, G., et.al (2000). „ Algorithm For Association Rule Mining : A General Survey and Comparison", ACM SIGMODKDD, July 2000.

Hua, Z., (1998). „On-Line Analytical Mining of Association Rules", MSc Thesis,Simon Fraser University, 1998.

Bing, L., Wynne, H., et.al., (1999). „Mining Association Rules With Multiple Minimum Support", ACM SIGMODKDD, Augustus 1999.

Shan, C., (1998). „ Statistical Approaches to Predictive Modeling in Large Databases", MSc Thesis, Computing Science, Simon Fraser University, March 1998.

Sarjon, D., Mohd, N., (2000). „Data Mining : A Preview", Journal of Information Technology, Volume 12, Number 1, June 2000.

Vijayshankar, R., and Josep, M.H., (2001). „Potter's Wheel : An Interactive Data Cleaning System", Proceedings of the 27th VLDB Conference, Roma, Italy 2001

Sarjon, D., Mohd, N., (2002). „Mining Association Rule From Large Databases", Journal of Information Technology, Volume 13 Number 2, December 2001

Change-Point Estimation Using New Minimum Message Length Approximations

Leigh J. Fitzgibbon, David L. Dowe, and Lloyd Allison

School of Computer Science and Software Engineering
Monash University, Clayton, VIC 3168 Australia
{leighf,dld,lloyd}@bruce.csse.monash.edu.au

Abstract. This paper investigates the coding of change-points in the information-theoretic Minimum Message Length (MML) framework. Change-point coding regions affect model selection and parameter estimation in problems such as time series segmentation and decision trees. The Minimum Message Length (MML) and Minimum Description Length (MDL78) approaches to change-point problems have been shown to perform well by several authors. In this paper we compare some published MML and MDL78 methods and introduce some new MML approximations called 'MMLDc' and 'MMLDF'. These new approximations are empirically compared with Strict MML (SMML), Fairly Strict MML (FSMML), MML68, the Minimum Expected Kullback-Leibler Distance (MEKLD) loss function and MDL78 on a tractable binomial change-point problem.

1 Introduction

Change-points can be found in many machine learning problems. They arise where there is a need to partition data into *contiguous* groups which are to be modelled distinctly. The inference of change-points (the boundaries of the contiguous groups) is important since change-points describe a point of transition between different states of stochastic behaviour of the data. They can be used to explain the generating process and also for prediction of future data.

The Minimum Message Length (MML) principle [1,2,3] is an invariant Bayesian point estimation technique based on information theory. MML selects regions from the parameter space which contain models that can justify themselves with high posterior probability mass [3, page 276]. Using MML we are able to capture the important information in the posterior. For example, the best explanation of the data might be that "a change-point occurred between times t_1 and t_2 and the point estimate that best summarizes this region is $\hat{t}$". The MML method is especially useful when many change-points are being estimated and on large data-sets - for example, segmentation of a DNA string. DNA strings can be very large, containing millions of characters. It would be impractical to deal with a posterior distribution over such strings using contemporary computational techniques.

M. Ishizuka and A. Sattar (Eds.): PRICAI 2002, LNAI 2417, pp. 244–254, 2002.

Previous work on coding change-point parameters in the MML framework has resulted in analytical approximations which treat the change-point as a continuous parameter [4,5,6,7] or avoid stating them altogether [8]. These methods work well in practice. However, change-points are realized as discrete parameters since they partition a data sample, and in this paper we investigate new MML approximations which treat them discretely.

The paper proceeds by describing a binomial change-point problem. We then consider the two computationally infeasible MML criteria: Strict MML (SMML) and Fairly Strict MML (FSMML) in Section 3.1 and 3.2. The algorithms to compute the SMML and FSMML codes have exponential time complexity for the binomial problem, which limits the experiments to small samples, but the results still give insight into the behaviour of the methods. We then describe two new approximations called MMLDc and MMLDF. These are practical methods that are motivated by SMML (in part), FSMML and MML87 [2]. In Section 5 we empirically compare these new approximations with SMML, FSMML and other existing methods.

2 Binomial Problem

A Bernoulli trial is conducted with K independent coin tosses. The results are recorded in a binary string x, where $T = 0$ and $H = 1$. It is suspected that the bias of the coin may have changed at some point in time, ϕ, during the trial. Given the data from the trial, we wish to infer the best explanation: was there a change-point and, if so, where was it? We denote the change-point parameter by ϕ and its parameter-space by Φ. We often speak in terms of the number of groups of data rather than the number of change-points. And, in our notation, we use G for the number of groups ($G = \{1,2\}$).

The likelihood for the change-point model is:

$$f(x|G) = \begin{cases} f(x) = f_{null}(x) & G = 1 \\ f(x|\phi) = f_L(x_1^\phi)f_R(x_{\phi+1}^K) & G = 2 \end{cases} \tag{1}$$

where f_{null} is the model for the $G = 1$, no change-point hypothesis; and f_L and f_R are the models for groups to the left and right of the change-point.

The likelihood function for an ordered Bernoulli trial, which we will be using for f_{null}, f_L and f_R is:

$$f_{bin}(x|p) = p^{\sum x_i}(1 - p)^{K - \sum x_i} \quad x_i = 0, 1 \tag{2}$$

To make the SMML and FSMML solutions computationally feasible, the experiments are simplified as follows. For $G = 2$, we use a uniform prior over the change-point location (i.e. $h(\phi) = \frac{1}{K-1}$), and we have a uniform prior for the number of change-points (i.e. h(G=1) = h(G=2) = 0.5). The f_{null}, f_L and f_R likelihood functions that we have chosen to use have fixed biases, and therefore have no free parameters. The biases we use are 0.25, 0.15 and 0.75 for f_{null}, f_L and f_R respectively. We use fixed coins to reduce the estimation problem to the two discrete parameters of interest: G and ϕ. This is necessary to make the construction of the SMML and FSMML (code-books and) estimators feasible. However, even though we are using such a simple model there is still an exponential step (see Section 3.1), so experimenting with large amounts of data is not possible.

3   The Minimum Message Length Principle

In the Minimum Message Length (MML) framework [1,2,3], inference is framed as a coding process. The aim is to construct a code-book that would (hypothetically) allow for the transmission of the data in a two-part message over a noiseless channel as briefly as possible. From coding theory we know that an event with probability p can be encoded in a message with length $-\log_2(p)$ bits using an ideal Shannon code. Using a Bayesian setting, the sender and receiver agree on a prior distribution $h(\theta)$ and likelihood function $f(x|\theta)$ over the parameter space Θ and data-space X. An estimator is a function from the data-space to the parameter-space, denoted $m : X \rightarrow \Theta$. After observing some data x, we can use an estimator to construct a two-part message encoding the estimate $\hat{\theta} = m(x)$ in the first part and then the data using the estimate, $x|m(x)$, in the second.

3.1   Strict Minimum Message Length (SMML)

The probability that $m(.)$ returns an estimate $\hat{\theta}$ is $q(\hat{\theta}) = \sum_{x:m(x)=\hat{\theta}} r(x)$, where $r(x)$ is the marginal probability of the data, x. The length of the first part of the message is therefore $-\log q(m(x))$, and the length of the second part of the message is $-\log f(x|m(x))$. The sender and receiver will use the code-book with estimator, $m(.)$, which minimises the expected message length:

$$I_1 = -\sum_{x \in X} r(x) \left(\log q(m(x)) + \log f(x|m(x)) \right) \qquad (3)$$

The estimator which minimises I_1 is called the Strict Minimum Message Length (SMML) estimator [2, page 242] [9,10,3]. The construction of I_1 is NP-hard for most distributions. The only distributions that it has reportedly been constructed for are the binomial and trinomial (trinomial using a heuristic) [9] and $N(\mu, 1)$ [11, page 22].

The construction of SMML estimators is simplified when there exists a sufficient statistic of lesser dimension than the data-space. Unfortunately, for univariate change-point parameters, the minimal sufficient statistics are of the same dimension as the data. Since we therefore cannot reduce the dimensionality of the data-space, we are left with the SMML code-book construction problem of trying to optimally assign the 2^K elements of the data-space to estimates. For the experiments in this paper we use an EM algorithm which randomly selects an element of the data-space and then finds the optimal code-book assignment $\hat{\theta} = m(x)$ using: $\hat{\theta} = argmax_{\theta \in \Theta} [q(\theta)f(x|\theta)]$.

This is not guaranteed to minimise I_1 since the algorithm can easily get stuck in local optima. To try and avoid this, we iterate the SMML algorithm a number of times with and without seeding the algorithm with the FSMML partition discussed in the next section. The resulting algorithm still has exponential time complexity. The SMML estimates for up to $K = 15$ can be seen in Figure 1. The bold dots in the diagram illustrate the point estimates that are used in the code-book. We can see that for up to, and including, $K = 7$ the estimator always infers that there was no change-point. As the data-space gets larger, point estimates start appearing to the left of the change-point parameter space. This asymmetry is explained by the choice of biases used.

3.2 Fairly Strict Minimum Message Length (FSMML)

The FSMML [12] estimator is an approximation to SMML based on a partition of the parameter space. The FSMML expected message length is:

$$I_{1a} = - \sum_{\hat{\theta} \in \Theta^*} q(\hat{\theta}) \log q(\hat{\theta}) - \sum_{\hat{\theta} \in \Theta^*} \int_{\theta \in s(\hat{\theta})} h(\theta) \sum_{x \in X} f(x|\theta) \log f(x|\hat{\theta}) \, d\theta \quad (4)$$

where $q(\hat{\theta})$ is approximated as $q(\hat{\theta}) = \int_{\theta \in s(\hat{\theta})} h(\theta) \, d\theta$, Θ^* is the set of point estimates, and $s(\hat{\theta})$ is the region of the parameter-space which is grouped with point estimate $\hat{\theta}$.

We minimise I_{1a} by searching for the optimal partition of the parameter-space and the $\hat{\theta}$ for each segment of the partition. Since I_{1a} consists of a sum over independent partitions, we can use W. D. Fisher's [13] polynomial time dynamic programming algorithm[1]. We therefore seek the partition of change-points and the estimates which minimise I_{1a}. We allow the partition to contain models from different subspaces since all we are attempting to do is group similar models in such a way that minimises the expected two-part message length.

The algorithm we use is guaranteed to find the optimal solution. It consists of a high-order polynomial step to find the partition (using Fisher's algorithm), and an exponential step to compute a revised version of the message length (I_{1b} in the Figures). The FSMML partitions for up to $K = 15$ can be seen in Figure 2. The partition is represented by the solid shapes, and the bold dots represent the point estimates used in each region. We can see that once K is greater than eight, the partitions consist of models from different subspaces. This allows data generated by change-points on the right to be modelled by the no change-point model. What the FSMML partition is saying is that we cannot

---

[1] This is the same algorithm that has been used for partitioning the data-space in the SMML binomial case [9].

reliably distinguish between models in this region, and they are best modelled with the no change-point model. In the figures, the FSMML code-book looks very similar to the SMML code-book. However, as expected, for many values of K, the SMML estimator has a slightly better message length. This is because it is able to individually assign elements of the data-space to estimates.

3.3   MML68 Change-Point Approximation

Oliver, Baxter and co-workers have applied the MML68 [1] estimator methodology to the segmentation problem with Gaussian segments [4] [11, chapter 9] [5,6]. They have derived MML formulas for stating the change-point locations to an optimal precision independently of the segment parameters. The same method has been used [7] for the problem of finding change-points in noisy binary sequences [14] - where it compared favourably with Akaike's Information Criterion (AIC), Schwarz's Bayesian Information Criterion (BIC), an MDL-motivated metric of Kearns et al. [14] and a more correct version of Minimum Description Length[7].

We apply the MML68 approximation to the binomial problem in this paper. Assuming that the true change-point is uniformly distributed in some range of width, R, we encode the data using the point estimate $\hat{\phi}$ at the centre of this region. The true change-point is equally likely to be to the right or to the left of the point estimate. If it is located to the right then its expected value is $\hat{\phi} + \frac{R}{4}$, and if it is located to the left its expected value is $\hat{\phi} - \frac{R}{4}$. The expected message length is computed by averaging the expected coding inefficiency of these two scenarios which for our Bernoulli problem simplifies to an expression involving the Kullback-Leibler distance, $KL(.\|.)$:

$$MessLen \approx -\log(\frac{R}{K-1}) + \frac{R}{8}\left(KL(p_R\|p_L) + KL(p_L\|p_R)\right) - \log f(x|\hat{\phi}) \quad (5)$$

where p_L and p_R correspond to the distributions of the coins to the left and right of the change-point respectively. Using Equation 5, the size of the region which minimises the message length is easily derived.

4   A New Approximation to FSMML: MMLD

Minimum Message Length approximation D (MMLD) can be thought of as a numerical approximation to FSMML. It was proposed by D. L. Dowe and has been investigated by his student [15]. MMLD is based on choosing a region R of the parameter space after observing some data. It was partly motivated by improving the Taylor expansion approximation of MML87 [2] while retaining invariance and, like MML87, avoids the problem of creating the whole code-book, which would typically require enumeration of the data and parameter spaces in SMML and FSMML. Given an uncertainty region, R, MMLD approximates the length of the first part of the message as the negative log integral of the prior over R (like FSMML). The length of the second part is approximated by the

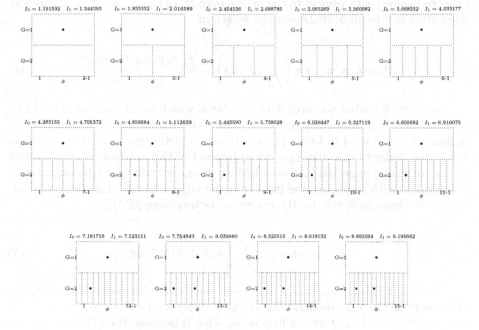

Fig. 1. SMML Estimates K = 2..15

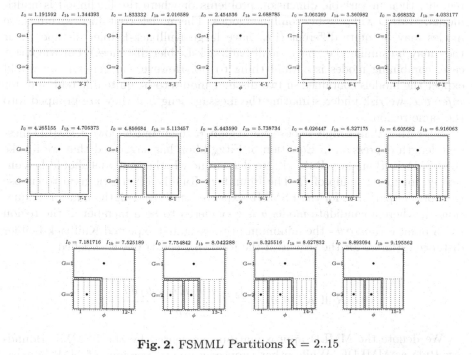

Fig. 2. FSMML Partitions K = 2..15

expected value (with respect to the prior), over R, of the negative log-likelihood. This gives rise to an MMLD message length of

$$MessLen \approx -\log \left(\int_R h(\theta)\, d\theta \right) - \frac{\int_R h(\theta) \log f(x|\theta)\, d\theta}{\int_R h(\theta)\, d\theta} \tag{6}$$

Equation 6 makes no explicit claim about which point estimate should be used to encode data for the region, R. Once the region has been found which minimises it, we need to find a point estimate which summarizes the models in the region. Since the estimates produced by the FSMML estimator are equivalent to the minimum expected Kullback-Leibler distance estimator (the expectation being taken with respect to the prior over the region, rather than the posterior) [12,10], we have used this for the experiments involving MMLD:

$$\hat{\theta} = argmin_{\hat{\theta} \in R} \int_{\theta \in R} h(\theta) KL(\theta, \hat{\theta})\, d\theta \tag{7}$$

Whereas FSMML can build code-books consisting of non-contiguous regions (i.e., combine modes or models from different subspaces) with minimum expected message length, MMLD cannot in general. This is because MMLD does not take into account the similarity of the models it combines in R - it only cares about their prior probability and likelihood. If we attempt to build non-contiguous regions, then in variable dimension problems or where the likelihood is multi-modal, MMLD will possibly combine modes. The models contained within these modes may be quite different (i.e., have large Kullback-Leibler distances), or they may be similar (i.e., have small Kullback-Leibler distances). For the latter case, combining modes is a valid thing to do. However, in general, we would expect the models contained in two distinct modes to be quite different and, for *inference*, we risk underestimating the message length if they are grouped into the same region.

So, rather than simply choose the region R to optimise Dowe's MMLD message length expression in Equation 6, Fitzgibbon has suggested that we invoke the FSMML 'Boundary Rule' [12] to determine whether a model should be considered for membership of R. The Boundary Rule is a heuristic used to choose the optimal partition for the FSMML expected message length equation (Equation 4), where a candidate model θ is considered to be a member of the region (with point estimate $\hat{\theta}$ - the minimum prior-weighted expected Kullback-Leibler distance estimate for the region) if the following constraint is satisfied:

$$\theta \in R \text{ iff } KL(\theta, \hat{\theta}) \leq \frac{\int_{\theta \in R} h(\theta) KL(\theta, \hat{\theta})\, d\theta}{\int_{\theta \in R} h(\theta)} + 1$$

We denote the MMLD approximation augmented by the FSMML Boundary Rule as MMLDF. While other (non-contiguous) versions of MMLD exist, throughout the remainder of this paper, MMLDc will refer to using a contiguous region (i.e. R contains only models of the same dimension and from a single mode). We include both MMLDc and MMLDF in the experiments to compare the advantage of allowing the region to consist of models from different subspaces. For the binomial problem with known biases, the parameter space is discrete - so an exhaustive search for the optimal region was performed.

5   Empirical Comparison and Discussion

Compact coding methods attempt to minimise the expected length of a two-part message. However, they cannot be judged on this criterion since - other than SMML and FSMML - the methods only approximate the message length. Furthermore, we are not really interested in creating short messages per se but rather in how good the inferred statistical model is. The definition of a good model will depend on what use the model will be put to. We therefore use the following general criteria: the Kullback-Leibler (KL) distance between the true and inferred models; and the mean squared error in estimation of the change-point location (if it exists). We have compared the MMLD approximation both with and without the FSMML Boundary Rule (MMLDF and MMLDc respectively) with SMML, FSMML, MML68 (as described in Section 3.3), Minimum Description Length (MDL78) [16] and the Minimum Expected KL Distance loss function (MEKLD) [10]. We ran 10^4 trials for each $K = 2..15$ where we sampled from the prior and then generated data. Each method was given the data and the biases of the coins used to generate the data and then asked to infer whether or not a change-point occurred and, if so, where it was located.

We have plotted the average KL distance for each method in Figure 3. The SMML and FSMML estimators had significantly higher KL distances than the other methods for $K > 4$. MEKLD had the lowest on average, as expected. MML68 performed well and was not far behind MEKLD. Our MMLDF estimator was close behind MML68 and slightly better than our MMLDc estimator.

Figure 4 shows the average squared error in estimating the change-point location for each method. The average is taken over the instances where the method correctly inferred that there was a change-point. The SMML and FSMML estimators performed exceptionally well. Their good performance here and poor KL distance performance indicates that they prefer not to infer a change-point unless they are reasonably certain of its location. The MMLDF estimator comes second to SMML and FSMML for $K < 13$. The MML68 method, which had very good KL distance performance, performed poorly for this criterion.

We note that MMLDF outperforms MMLDc for both criteria, therefore providing evidence that building non-contiguous coding regions - which SMML theory and FSMML theory both advocate - is advantageous. The MMLDF estimator appears to be robust and has good explanatory (i.e., has small squared error in change-point location when correctly inferring change-points) and predictive powers (i.e., has small KL distances).

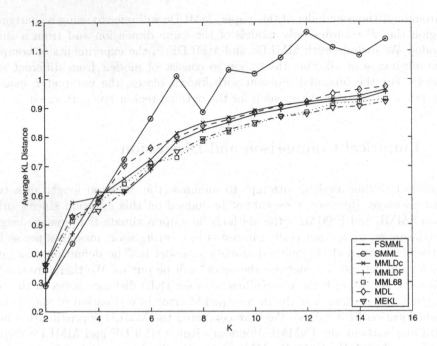

Fig. 3. Average Kullback-Leibler Distance (10^4 trials)

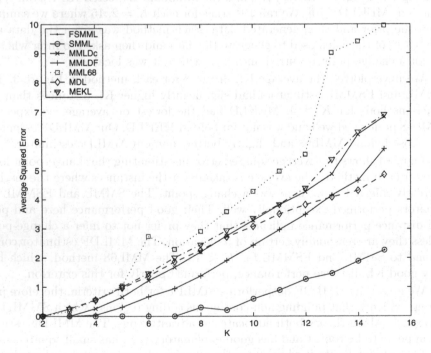

Fig. 4. Average Squared Error of Change-Point Location (10^4 trials)

6   Conclusion

We have empirically compared a number of information-theoretic methods for estimating change-points including two new Minimum Message Length approximations. The comparison was based on a binomial problem using small sample sizes which allowed us to include the computationally impractical Strict MML (SMML) and Fairly SMML (FSMML) estimators. In the comparison we found that the performance of the MMLDc approximation was improved by incorporating the Kullback-Leibler Boundary Rule, therefore allowing coding regions to contain models from different subspaces (MMLDF) whilst still approximating an efficient FSMML code-book. MMLDF was robust and performed well in terms of Kullback-Leibler distance and (squared) error in estimation of the change-point location (where inferred). Use of MMLD and variations for more difficult problems will be investigated in forthcoming work.

References

1. Wallace, C.S., Boulton, D.M.: An information measure for classification. Computer Journal **11** (1968) 185–194
2. Wallace, C.S., Freeman, P.R.: Estimation and inference by compact encoding (with discussion). Journal of the Royal Statistical Society. Series B (Methodological) **49** (1987) 240–265
3. Wallace, C.S., Dowe, D.L.: Minimum message length and Kolmogorov complexity. Computer Journal **42** (1999) 270–283
4. Baxter, R.A., Oliver, J.J.: The kindest cut: minimum message length segmentation. In Arikawa, S., Sharma, A.K., eds.: Proceedings of the Seventh International Workshop on Algorithmic Learning Theory. Volume 1160 of LNCS., Springer-Verlag Berlin (1996) 83–90
5. Oliver, J.J., Forbes, C.S.: Bayesian approaches to segmenting a simple time series. Technical Report 97/336, Department Computer Science, Monash University, Australia 3168 (1997)
6. Oliver, J.J., Baxter, R.A., Wallace, C.S.: Minimum message length segmentation. In Wu, X., Kotagiri, R., Korb, K., eds.: Research and Development in Knowledge Discovery and Data Mining (PAKDD-98), Springer (1998) 83–90
7. Viswanathan, M., Wallace, C.S., Dowe, D.L., Korb, K.: Finding cutpoints in noisy binary sequences - a revised empirical evaluation. In: Australian Joint Conference on Artificial Intelligence. (1999)
8. Fitzgibbon, L.J., Allison, L., Dowe, D.L.: Minimum message length grouping of ordered data. In Arimura, H., Jain, S., eds.: Proceedings of the Eleventh International Conference on Algorithmic Learning Theory (ALT2000). LNAI, Springer-Verlag Berlin (2000) 56–70
9. Farr, G.E., Wallace, C.S.: Algorithmic and combinatorial problems in strict minimum message length inference. In: Research on Combinatorial Algorithms. (1997) 50–58
10. Dowe, D.L., Baxter, R.A., Oliver, J.J., Wallace, C.S.: Point estimation using the Kullback-Leibler loss function and MML. In: Pacific-Asia Conference on Knowledge Discovery and Data Mining (PAKDD98). Volume LNAI of 1394., Springer-Verlag (1998) 87–95

11. Baxter, R.A.: Minimum Message Length Inductive Inference: Theory and Applications. PhD thesis, Department of Computer Science, Monash University (1996)
12. Wallace, C.S.: PAKDD-98 Tutorial: Data Mining. Monash University, Australia (Book in preparation) (1998)
13. Fisher, W.D.: On grouping for maximum homogeneity. Journal of the American Statistical Society **53** (1958) 789–798
14. Kearns, M., Mansour, Y., Ng, A.Y., Ron, D.: An experimental and theoretical comparison of model selection methods. Machine Learning **27** (1997) 7–50
15. Lam, E.: Improved approximations in MML. Honours thesis, Monash University, School of Computer Science and Software Engineering, Monash University, Clayton, Australia (2000)
16. Rissanen, J.J.: Modeling by shortest data description. Automatica **14** (1978) 465–471

Knowledge Discovery from Structured Data by Beam-Wise Graph-Based Induction

Takashi Matsuda, Hiroshi Motoda, Tetsuya Yoshida, and Takashi Washio

Institute of Scientific and Industrial Research,
Osaka University
8-1, Mihogaoka, Ibaraki, Osaka 567-0047, JAPAN

Abstract. A machine learning technique called Graph-Based Induction (GBI) extracts typical patterns from graph data by stepwise pair expansion (pairwise chunking). Because of its greedy search strategy, it is very efficient but suffers from incompleteness of search. We improved its search capability without imposing much computational complexity by incorporating the idea of beam search. Additional improvement is made to extract patterns that are more discriminative than those simply occurring frequently, and to enumerate identical patterns accurately based on the notion of canonical labeling. This new algorithm was implemented (now called Beam-wise GBI, B-GBI for short) and tested against a DNA data set from UCI repository. Since DNA data is a sequence of symbols, representing each sequence by attribute-value pairs by simply assigning these symbols to the values of ordered attributes does not make sense. By transforming the sequence into a graph structure and running B-GBI it is possible to extract discriminative substructures. These can be new attributes for a classification problem. Effect of beam width on the number of discovered attributes and predictive accuracy was evaluated, together with extracted characteristic subsequences, and the results indicate the effectiveness of B-GBI.

1 Introduction

There have been quite a number of research work on data mining in seeking for better performance over the last few years. Better performance includes mining from structured data, which is a new challenge, and there have only been a few work on this subject. Since structure is represented by proper relations and a graph can easily represent relations, knowledge discovery from graph structured data poses a general problem for mining from structured data. Some examples amenable to a graph mining are finding typical web browsing pattern, identifying typical substructure of chemical compounds, finding typical subsequences of DNA and discovering diagnostic rules from patient history records.

Majority of the methods widely used are for data that do not have structure and are represented by attribute-value pairs. Decision tree[10,11], and induction rules[8,3] relate attribute values to target classes. Association rules often used in data mining also uses this attribute-value pair representation. However, the

M. Ishizuka and A. Sattar (Eds.): PRICAI 2002, LNAI 2417, pp. 255–264, 2002.

attribute-value pair representation is not suitable to represent a more general data structure, and there are problems that need a more powerful representation. Most powerful representation that can handle relation and thus, structure, would be inductive logic programming (ILP) [9] which uses the first-order predicate logic. It can represent general relationship embedded in data, and has a merit that domain knowledge and acquired knowledge can be utilized as background knowledge. However, its state of the art is not so matured that anyone can use the technique easily.

AGM (Apriori-based Graph Mining)[6] is one of the representative recent work that can mine the association rules among the frequently appearing substructures in a given graph data set. A graph transaction is represented by an adjacency matrix, and the frequent patterns appearing in the matrices are mined by an extended algorithm of the basket analysis. This algorithm can extract all connected/disconnected induced subgraphs by complete search. However, its computation time increases exponentially with input graph size and support threshold. AGM can use only frequency for the evaluation function. SUBDUE[4] is also well known. It extracts a subgraph which can best compress an input graph based on MDL principle. The found substructure can be considered a concept. This algorithm is based on a computationally-constrained beam search. It begins with a substructure comprising only a single vertex in the input graph, and grows it incrementally expanding a node in it. At each expansion it evaluates the total description length (DL) of the input graph, and stops when the substructure that minimizes the total description length is found. After the optimal substructure is found and the input graph is rewritten, next iteration starts using the rewritten graph as a new input. This way, SUBDUE finds a more abstract concept at each round of iteration. As is clear, the algorithm can find only one substructure at each iteration.

Graph-Based Induction (GBI) [13,7] is a technique which was devised for the purpose of discovering typical patterns in a general graph data by recursively chunking two adjoining nodes. I can handle a graph data having loops (including self-loops) with colored/uncolored nodes and links. There can be more than one link between any two nodes. GBI's expressiveness lies in between the attribute-value pair representation and the first-order logic. The computation time for GBI is very short because of its greedy search, and it does not lose any information of graph structure after chunking. GBI can use various evaluation functions based on frequency. It is not, however, suitable for pattern extraction from a graph structured data where many nodes share the same label because of its greedy recursive chunking without backtracking. However, it is still effective in extracting patterns from such graph structured data where each node has a distinct label (*e.g.*, World Wide Web browsing data) or where some typical structures exist even if some nodes share the same labels (*e.g.*, chemical structure data containing benzene rings etc).

Efficiency of GBI comes from its greedy search in exchange of search incompleteness. There is no guarantee that it can find all the important typical patterns although our past application to various domains produced acceptable results [7]. In this paper we report how we attacked this problem. We improved its search capability without imposing much computational complexity by incorporating the idea of beam search. Furthermore, two other improvements are made: one for criterion to define typical patterns in a more natural way and the other for accurate enumeration of typical patterns based on the notion of canonical labeling. This new algorithm was implemented (now called Beam-wise GBI, B-GBI for short) and tested against a DNA data set from UCI repository and its results were evaluated in terms of predictive accuracy and discovered typical subsequences, showing the effectiveness of the improvement.

The paper is organized as follows. In section 2, we briefly describe the framework of GBI and its improvement made to extracting discriminative patterns. In section 3, we describe B-GBI, which is the main contribution over the existing GBI, followed by canonical labeling treatment. In section 4, we show the experimental results of B-GBI. In section 6 we conclude the paper by summarizing the results and the future work.

2 Graph-Based Induction

2.1 GBI Revisited

GBI employs the idea of extracting typical patterns by stepwise pair expansion as shown in Fig. 1. In the original GBI an assumption is made that typical patterns represent some concepts/substructure and "typicality" is characterized by the pattern's frequency or the value of some evaluation function of its frequency. We can use statistical indices as an evaluation function, such as frequency itself, Information Gain [10], Gain Ratio [11] and Gini Index [2], all of which are based on frequency.

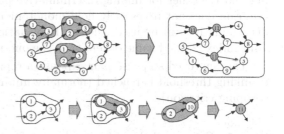

Fig. 1. The basic idea of the GBI method

The stepwise pair expansion (pairwise chunking) repeats the following three steps until no more typical patterns are found.

Step 1. Extract all the pairs consisting of connected two nodes in the graph.

Step 2. Select the most typical pair based on the criterion from among the pairs extracted in Step 1 and register it as the pattern to chunk. If either or both nodes of the selected pair have already been rewritten (chunked), they are restored to the original patterns before registration. Stop when there is no more pattern to chunk.

Step 3. Replace the selected pair in Step 2 with one node and assign a new label to it. Rewrite the graph by replacing all the occurrence of the selected pair with a node with the newly assigned label. Go back to Step 1.

It is possible to extract typical patterns of various sizes by repeating the above three steps. Note that the search is greedy. No backtracking is made. This means that in enumerating pairs no pattern which has been chunked into one node is restored to the original pattern. Because of this, all the "typical patterns" that exist in the input graph are not necessarily extracted. The problem of extracting all the isomorphic subgraphs is known to be NP-complete. Thus, GBI aims at extracting only meaningful typical patterns of a certain size. Its objective is not finding all the typical patterns nor finding all the frequent patterns.

2.2   Extracting Discriminative Patterns

GBI can use any criterion that is based on the frequency of paired nodes. However, for finding a pattern that is of interest any of its subpatterns must be of interest because of the nature of repeated chunking. Frequency measure satisfies this monotonicity. However, if the criterion chosen does not satisfy this monotonicity, repeated chunking may not find good patterns even though the best pair based on the criterion is selected at each iteration. This motivated us to improve GBI allowing to use two criteria, one for frequency measure for chunking and the other for finding discriminative patterns after chunking. The latter criterion does not necessarily hold monotonicity property. Any function that is discriminative can be used, such as Information Gain [10], Gain Ratio [11] and Gini Index [2], and some others (e.g. the one used in Section 4).

The improved stepwise pair expansion repeats the following four steps until chunking threshold is reached (normally minimum support value is used as the stopping criterion).

Step 1. Extract all the pairs consisting of connected two nodes in the graph.

Step 2a. Select all the typical pairs based on the criterion from among the pairs extracted in Step 1, rank them according to the criterion and register them as typical patterns. If either or both nodes of the selected pairs have already been rewritten (chunked), they are restored to the original patterns before registration.

Step 2b. Select the most frequent pair from among the pairs extracted in Step 1 and register it as the pattern to chunk. If either or both nodes of the selected pair have already been rewritten (chunked), they are restored to the original patterns before registration. Stop when there is no more pattern to chunk.

Step 3. Replace the selected pair in Step 2b with one node and assign a new label to it. Rewrite the graph by replacing all the occurrence of the selected pair with a node with the newly assigned label. Go back to Step 1.

The output of the improved GBI is a set of ranked typical patterns extracted at Step 2a. These patterns are typical in the sense that they are more discriminative than non-selected patterns in terms of the criterion used.

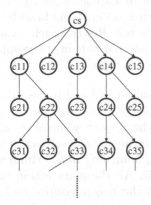

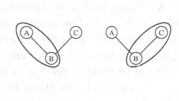

Fig. 2. An Example of State Transition of B-GBI when the beam width = 5

Fig. 3. Two Different Pairs Representing Identical Pattern

3   Beam-Wise Graph-Based Induction

3.1   Algorithm of B-GBI

The improved GBI still has disadvantages. When each node has a distinct label in the input graph, no ambiguity arises in selecting a pair to be chunked and GBI performs well. However, since the search in GBI is greedy, when the same label is shared by plural nodes in the input graph, there arises ambiguity when there are ties in the frequency or there is a chain of nodes of the same label. For example, in the case of the structure like $a \rightarrow a \rightarrow a$, we don't know which $a \rightarrow a$ is best to chunk.

To relax this ambiguity problem, a beam search is incorporated to GBI within the framework of greedy search. A certain fixed number of pairs ranked from the top are allowed to be chunked in parallel. To prevent each branch from growing exponentially, the total number of pairs to chunk is fixed at each level of branch. Thus, at any iteration step, there is always a fixed number of chunking that is performed in parallel.

The new stepwise pair expansion repeats the following four steps.

Step 1. Extract all the pairs consisting of connected two nodes in all the graphs.

Step 2a. Select all the typical pairs based on the criterion from among the pairs extracted in Step 1, rank them according to the criterion and register them as typical patterns. If either or both nodes of the selected pairs have already been rewritten (chunked), they are restored to the original patterns before registration.

Step 2b. Select, from among the pairs extracted in Step 1, a fixed number of frequent pairs from the top and register them as the patterns to chunk. If either or both nodes of the selected pairs have already been rewritten (chunked), they are restored to the original patterns before registration. Stop when there is no more pattern to chunk.

Step 3. Replace each of the selected pairs in Step 2b with one node and assign a new label to it. Delete a graph for which no pair is selected and branch (copy) a graph for which more than one pair are selected. Rewrite each remaining graph by replacing all the occurrence of the selected pair in the graph with a node with the newly assigned label. Go back to Step 1.

An example of state transition of B-GBI is shown in Fig.2 in case that the beam width is 5. The initial condition is the single state cs. All the pairs in cs are enumerated and ranked according to both the frequency measure and the typicality measure. Top 5 pairs according to the frequency measure are selected, and each of them is used as a pattern to chunk, branching into 5 children c_{11}, c_{12}, ..., c_{15}, each rewritten by the chunked pair. All the pairs within these 5 states are enumerated and ranked according to the two measures, and again the top 5 ranked pairs according to the frequency measure are selected. The state c_{11} is split into two states c_{21} and c_{22} because two pairs are selected, but the state c_{12} is deleted because no pair is selected. This is repeated until the stopping condition is satisfied. This increase in the search space improves the pattern extraction capability of GBI.

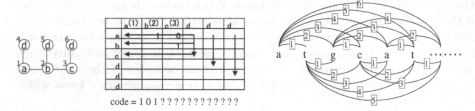

code = 1 0 1 ? ? ? ? ? ? ? ? ? ? ? ?

Fig. 4. Determination of Node Ordering within a Group

Fig. 5. Conversion of DNA Sequence Data to a graph

3.2 Canonical Labeling

Another improvement made in conjunction with B-GBI is canonical labeling. GBI assigns a new label for each newly chunked pair. Because it recursively chunks pairs, it happens that the new pairs that have different labels happen to be the same pattern (subgraph). A simple example is shown in Fig. 3.

To identify whether the two pairs represent the same pattern or not, each pair is represented by canonical label[12,5] and only when the label is the same, they are regarded as identical. The basic procedure of canonical labelling is as follows. Nodes in the graph are grouped according to their labels (node colors) and the degrees of node (number of links attached to the node) and ordered lexicographically. Then an adjacency matrix is created using this node ordering. When the graph is symmetric, the upper triangular elements are concatenated scanning either horizontally or vertically to codify the graph. When the graph is asymmetric, all the elements in both triangles are used to codify the graph in a similar way. If there are more than one node that have identical node label and the degrees of node, the ordering which results in the maximum (or minimum) value of the code is searched. The corresponding code is the canonical label. Let M be the number of nodes in a graph, N be the number of groups of the nodes, and $p_i(i = 1, 2, \ldots, N)$ be the number of the nodes within group i. The search space can be reduced to $\prod_{i=1}^{N}(p_i!)$ from $M!$ by using canonical labeling. The code of an adjacency matrix for the case in which elements in the upper triangle are vertically concatenated is defined as

$$A = \begin{pmatrix} a_{11} & a_{12} & \cdots & a_{1n} \\ & a_{22} & \cdots & a_{2n} \\ & & \ddots & \vdots \\ & & & a_{nn} \end{pmatrix}$$

$$code(A) = a_{11}a_{12}a_{22}a_{13}a_{23}\ldots a_{nn} \tag{1}$$

$$= \sum_{j=1}^{n}\sum_{i=1}^{j}((L+1)^{\sum_{k=j+1}^{m} k+j-i}a_{ij}). \tag{2}$$

Here L is the number of link label kinds. It is possible to further prune the search space. We choose the option of vertical concatenation. Elements of the adjacency matrix of higher ranked nodes form higher elements of the code. Thus, once the locations of higher ranked nodes in the adjacency matrix are fixed, corresponding higher elements of the code are also fixed and are not affected by the order of elements of lower ranks. For example, in Eq. 1 elements that the first two ranked nodes can decide are the first 3 elements in the $code(A)$ and no elements corresponding to the nodes of the lower ranks are included. This reduces the search space of $\prod_{i=1}^{N}(p_i!)$ to $\sum_{i=1}^{N}(p_i!)$.

However, there is still a problem of combinatorial explosion for a case where there are many nodes of the same labels and the same degrees of node such as the case of chemical compounds because the value of p_i becomes large. What we can do is to make the best of already determined nodes of higher ranks. Assume that the nodes $v_i \in V(G)(i = 1, 2, \ldots, N)$ are already determined in a graph G. Consider finding the order of the nodes $u_i \in V(G)(i = 1, 2, \ldots, k)$ of the same group that gives the maximum code value. The node that comes to v_{N+1} is the one in $u_i(i = 1, \ldots, k)$ that has a link to the node v_1 because the highest element that v_{N+1} can make is a_{1N+1} and the node that makes this element not 0, that is, the node that is linked to v_1 gives the maximum code. If there are more than one node or no node at all that has a link to v_1, the one that has a link to v_2 comes to v_{N+1}. Repeating this process determines which node comes to v_{N+1}. If no node can't be determined after the last comparison at v_N, permutation within the group is needed.

This is explained using an example in Fig. 4. Assume that nodes 1, 2 and 3 have already been determined. Nodes 4, 5 and 6 are in the same group. The fourth node is the node that has a link to the highest ranked node 1, which is the node 4. Likewise, the fifth and the sixth nodes are the nodes 5 and 6 respectively. In this case, node ordering is uniquely determined. If l nodes can be determined by this procedure, the search space can be reduced from $k!$ to $(k - l)!$.

4   Experimental Evaluation of B-GBI

The proposed method is implemented as B-GBI and tested against the promoter dataset in UCI Machine Learning Repository [1]. A promoter is a genetic region which initiates the first step in the expression of an adjacent gene (*transcription*). The promoter dataset consists of strings that represent nucleotides (one of A, G, T or C). The input features are 57 sequential DNA nucleotides and the total number of instances is 106 including 53 positive instances (sample promoter sequences) and 53 negative instances (non-promoter sequence). Direct encoding of this data to the standard attribute-value format assigning the n-th attribute to the n-th nucleotide in the sequence does not make sense. Encoding the data this way and running C4.5[11] gives a predictive error of 16.0% by leaving one out cross validation. Randomly shifting the sequence by 3 elements gives 21.7% and by 5 elements 44.3%. Graph representation resolves this problem. Since it is not known in advance how strong the interaction among the elements are for determining the class label, it is assumed that an element interacts up to 10 elements on both sides (See Fig. 5.). Each sequence results in a graph with 57 nodes and 515 links.

The minimum support for chunking is set at 20%. The normalized class probability of Eq. 3 is used as a criterion to select typical patterns. Here, p and n indicate respectively the number of positive and negative instances that have a typical pattern and P and N the total number of positive and negative instances (*i.e.*, $P = N = 53$).

$$Max. \left\{ \frac{\frac{p}{P}}{\frac{p}{P} + \frac{n}{N}}, \frac{\frac{n}{N}}{\frac{p}{P} + \frac{n}{N}} \right\} \tag{3}$$

Three threshold values are used: 0.6, 0.7 and 0.8. The beam width is set at 1, 5, 10, ..., 50. The number of typical patterns and their sizes (nodes) are listed in Table 1.

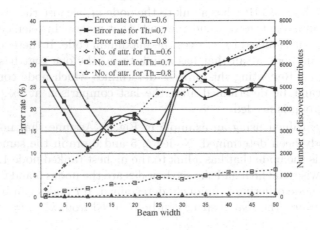

Fig. 6. Effect of Beam Width for the Final Decision Tree

Table 1. Number of Typical Patterns and Average Sizes

Beam width		1	5	10	15	20	25	30	35	40	45	50
Thres.	Pattern	355	1442	2125	3174	3688	4733	4697	5604	6293	6780	7342
0.6	Size	3.8	3.9	3.8	3.8	3.9	3.9	3.8	3.9	3.9	3.9	3.9
Thres.	Pattern	81	282	399	590	645	896	815	992	1136	1162	1249
0.7	Size	3.9	4.1	4.0	4.0	4.1	4.0	4.0	4.1	4.0	4.1	4.1
Thres.	Pattern	16	41	38	72	73	117	115	145	163	161	178
0.8	Size	4.1	4.3	4.0	4.1	4.1	4.2	4.2	4.3	4.2	4.2	4.3

To evaluate these patterns, they are used as binary attributes of each sequence to build a classifier by C4.5[11]. Predictive error rate is evaluated by leaving one out. Results are shown in Fig. 6.

It is noted that the error reduces as the beam width is increased from 1 to 10, levels off to 25 and then increases. Number of extracted patterns increases monotonically with the beam width. Too many beams affect adversely due to overfitting/oversearching. Sharp reduction of the error up to beam width of 10 indicates that important typical patterns that contribute to discriminative power are indeed extracted.

The induced decision tree for which the error is minimum (11.3%) is shown in Fig. 7. The threshold of Eq. 3 is 0.8 and the beam width is = 10. There are 38 typical patterns in this case and C4.5 chooses 6 patterns from among them. These are shown in the nodes of the tree. The tree shown in Fig. 8 is for the case where the threshold of Eq. 3 is 0.6 and the beam width is = 10. The error of this tree is 20.8%. There are 2125 typical patterns but C4.5 chooses only 7 patterns, out of which 4 patterns also appear in the first tree. These 4 are the most discriminative patterns. Graph representation is not affected by random shifting of sequences.

5   Conclusion

Graph based induction GBI is improved in three aspects by incorporating: 1) two criteria, one for chunking and the other for task specific criterion to extract more discriminative patterns, 2) beam search to enhance search capability and 3) canonical labeling to accurately count identical patterns. The improved B-GBI is applied to a classification problem of DNA promoter sequence and the results indicate that it is possible to extract discriminative patterns which otherwise are hard to extract.

Immediate future work includes to use feature selection method to filter out less useful patterns.

Acknowledgements. This work was partially supported by the grant-in-aid for scientific research on priority area "Active Mining" funded by the Japanese Ministry of Education, Culture, Sport, Science and Technology.

264   T. Matsuda et al.

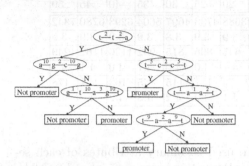

Fig. 7. Decision Tree (Threshold value of Eq. 3 = 0.8 and Beam width = 10)

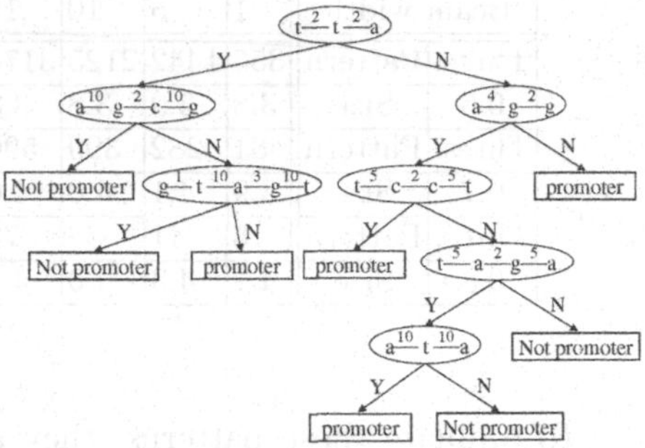

Fig. 8. Decision Tree (Threshold value of Eq. 3 = 0.6 and Beam width = 10)

References

1. C. L. Blake, E. Keogh, and C.J. Merz. Uci repository of machine leaning database, 1998. http://www.ics.uci.edu/~mlearn/MLRepository.html.
2. L. Breiman, J. H. Friedman, R. A. Olshen, and C. J. Stone. *Classification and Regression Trees*. Wadsworth & Brooks/Cole Advanced Books & Software, 1984.
3. L. Breiman, J. H. Friedman, R. A. Olshen, and C. J. Stone. The cn2 induction algorithm. *Machine Learning*, 3:261–283, 1989.
4. D. J. Cook and L. B. Holder. Graph-based data mining. *IEEE Intelligent Systems*, 15(2):32–41, 2000.
5. S. Fortin. The graph isomorphism problem, 1996.
6. A. Inokuchi, T. Washio, and H. Motoda. An apriori-based algorithm for mining frequent substructures from graph data. In *Proc. of the 4th European Conference on Principles of Data Mining and Knowledge Discovery*, pages 13–23, 2000.
7. T. Matsuda, T. Horiuchi, H. Motoda, and T. Washio. Extension of graph-based induction for general graph structured data. In *Knowledge Discovery and Data Mining: Current Issues and New Applications, Springer Verlag, LNAI 1805*, pages 420–431, 2000.
8. R. S. Michalski. Learning flexible concepts: Fundamental ideas and a method based on two-tiered representaion. *In Machine Learning, An Artificial Intelligence Approiach*, 3:63–102, 1990.
9. S. Muggleton and L. de Raedt. Inductive logic programming: Theory and methods. *Journal of Logic Programming*, 19(20):629–679, 1994.
10. J. R. Quinlan. Induction of decision trees. *Machine Learning*, 1:81–106, 1986.
11. J. R. Quinlan. *C4.5:Programs For Machine Learning*. Morgan Kaufmann Publishers, 1993.
12. R. C. Read and D. G. Corneil. The graph isomorphism disease. *Journal of Graph Theory*, 1:339–363, 1977.
13. K. Yoshida and H. Motoda. Clip : Concept learning from inference pattern. *Journal of Artificial Intelligence*, 75(1):63–92, 1995.

BackPOLE: Back Propagation Based on Objective Learning Errors

W.L. Tung and C. Quek

Intelligent Systems Laboratory, Nanyang Technological University
School of Computer Engineering, Blk N4 #2A-32, Nanyang Avenue, Singapore
639798
ashcquek@ntu.edu.sg

Abstract. A new variant of the *back propagation* (BP) [1,2] algorithm is proposed in this paper. The BP algorithm is widely used to tune the parameters of multi-layered neural networks and hybrid *neural fuzzy systems* [3]. Most applications of the BP algorithm are based on the *negative gradient descent* approach (NGD-BP) [2]. However, NGD-BP may not be suitable for use in neural fuzzy systems due to the poor interpretations of its error signals and over-reliance on *prior* knowledge of the node functions (i.e. the aggregation and activation functions of individual nodes). In neural fuzzy systems such as the POPFNN [4], the node functions are defined by the inference scheme adopted. This results in the NGD-BP algorithm being overly dependent on the gradient definition defined by the inference engine. That is, a set of customized learning equations is required for a given inference scheme. Hence, a change of the inference scheme requires a re-computation of the back propagation learning equations. This makes the neural fuzzy structure and learning highly dependent on the type of fuzzy inference engine employed. In contrast, the proposed BackPOLE algorithm generates intuitive error signals using a set of pre-defined objectives and is resilient to the change of inference schemes. This is highly desirable since the *parameter-learning* phase [2] of neural fuzzy systems can then be generalized and be independent of the fuzzy inference scheme. The BackPOLE algorithm has been implemented in a new neural fuzzy architecture named GenSoFNN [5] to demonstrate its effectiveness.

1 Introduction

The back propagation (BP) algorithm [1] has been widely used to tune the parameters of multi-layered neural networks such as the multi-layered perceptron (MLP) [2] and *neural fuzzy systems* such as POPFNN [4], Falcon-ART [6] and Falcon-MART [7]. The BP algorithm is a supervised training algorithm and generates error signals based on a cost error function $CError$ defined in equation (1).

$$CError = \frac{1}{2} \sum_{m=1}^{\#output} (d_m - y_m)^2. \tag{1}$$

Where d_m and y_m are the mth desired and actual outputs.

M. Ishizuka and A. Sattar (Eds.): PRICAI 2002, LNAI 2417, pp. 265–274, 2002.

Neural fuzzy networks, on the other hand, are the realizations of the functionality of fuzzy systems using neural techniques. The main advantage of a neural fuzzy network is its ability to model a problem using a linguistic model instead of complex mathematical models. The linguistic model is essentially a fuzzy rule base consisting of a set of IF-THEN fuzzy rules. The IF-THEN fuzzy rules are highly intuitive and comprehensible by the human users. In addition, the black-box nature of neural network is resolved as the intuitive IF-THEN fuzzy rules are used to interpret the weights and connections of the neural structure. Moreover, the embedded fuzzy system can self-adjust the parameters of the fuzzy rules using neural-learning algorithms.

The *Generic Self-organising Fuzzy Neural Network* (GenSoFNN) [5] is one such neural fuzzy system. The GenSoFNN network automatically formulates the fuzzy rules from the numerical training data and crafts a *consistent* rule base [3]. Each fuzzy label in the input/output dimensions is uniquely represented by only one cluster. The GenSoFNN network employs a new clustering technique known as *Discrete Incremental Clustering* (DIC) to resolve the *stability-plasticity dilemma* [2]. In addition, the GenSoFNN network does not require *prior* knowledge of the number of fuzzy rules as the rule formulation process is entirely data-driven. The training cycle of the GenSoFNN network consists of three phases: *Self-organising, rule formulation* and *parameter learning*. The back-propagation [1] learning algorithm based on negative gradient descent is initially used to tune the parameters of the GenSoFNN network.

This paper is organised as follows. Section 2 describes the general structure of the GenSoFNN and the drawbacks of NGD-BP based parameter-learning phase. Section 3 presents the proposed BackPOLE algorithm. In Section 4, the BackPOLE trained GenSoFNN network is evaluated using the iris experiment and its performance is benchmarked against its NGD-BP trained counterpart. Section 5 concludes this paper.

2   The GenSoFNN Network

The GenSoFNN network (Fig. 1) consists of five layers of nodes. Each input node IV_i, $i \in \{1, \ldots, n1\}$, has a single input. The vector $X = [x_1, \ldots, x_i, \ldots, x_{n1}]^T$ represents the inputs to the GenSoFNN. Each output node OV_m, where $m \in \{1, \ldots, n5\}$, computes a single output denoted by y_m. The vector $Y = [y_1, \ldots, y_m, \ldots, y_{n5}]^T$ denotes the outputs of the GenSoFNN network with respect to the input stimulus X. In addition the vector $D = [d_1, \ldots, d_m, \ldots, d_{n5}]^T$ represents the desired network outputs required during the parameter-learning phase of the training cycle. Layer 2 links contain the parameters of the input trapezoidal fuzzy sets while layer 5 links contain the parameters of the output trapezoidal fuzzy sets. They are denoted as l and r (left and right support points), and u and v (left and right kernel points). The subscripts denote the pre-synaptic and post-synaptic nodes respectively. The weights of the remaining connections are unity. In subsequent discussions, the variables i, j, k, l, m are used to refer to arbitrary nodes in layers 1, 2, 3, 4 and 5 respectively. The output of a node is denoted as Z and the subscripts specify its origin.

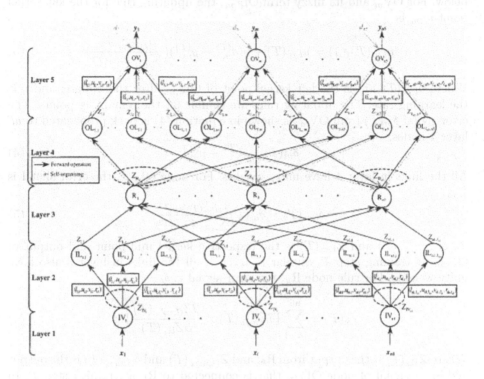

Fig. 1. Structure of the GenSoFNN network

Each input node IV_i may have different number of input terms J_i. Hence, the number of layer 2 nodes is $n2 = \sum_{i=1}^{n1} J_i$. Layer 3 consists of the rule nodes R_k, where $k = \{1, \ldots, n3\}$. At layer 4, an output term node $OL_{l,m}$ may have more than one fuzzy rule attached to it. Each output node OV_m in layer 5 can have different number of output terms L_m. Hence, the number of layer 4 nodes is $n4 = \sum_{m=1}^{n5} L_m$. In this paper, the GenSoFNN network adopts the Mamdani's fuzzy model [3] and the *Compositional Rule of Inference* (CRI) [8] is mapped to the GenSoFNN network to define the node functions. Please refer to [9] for more details of how this mapping is performed.

2.1 NGD-BP Based Parameter Learning of GenSoFNN

Initially, the NGD-BP algorithm is used to tune the parameters of layers 2 and 5 of the GenSoFNN network to minimize the cost function *MSE* defined in equation (2).

$$MSE^{(p)} = 1/2 \sum_{m=1}^{n5} (d_m^{(p)} - y_m^{(p)})^2. \tag{2}$$

Where $d_m^{(p)}$ and $y_m^{(p)}$ are the mth desired and network outputs based on the pth input training vector. The derived error signals for layer 5 to layer 2 are shown below. For OV_m and its fuzzy term $OL_{l,m}$, the updating rule for the left kernel point $u_{l,m}$ is

$$u_{l,m}(T+1) = u_{l,m}(T) + \eta(d_m^{(T)} - y_m^{(T)})(\frac{\frac{1}{2}Z_{l,m}(T)}{\sum_{l=1}^{L_m} Z_{l,m}(T)}). \tag{3}$$

Where $u_{l,m}(T+1)$ is the left kernel point of $OL_{l,m}$ after the update; and η is the learning rate. The updating rules are similar for the remaining points. The error signal $\delta_m(T)$ from OV_m as shown in equation (4) is back propagated to all layer 4 nodes.

$$\delta_m(T) = d_m^{(T)} - y_m^{(T)}. \tag{4}$$

All the links in layer 4 have unity weights. For node $OL_{l,m}$, the error signal is $\delta_{l,m}$.

$$\delta_{l,m}(T) = \delta_m(T)\frac{\widetilde{m_{l,m}}(T) - y_m^{(T)}}{\sum_{l=1}^{L_m} Z_{l,m}(T)}. \tag{5}$$

Where $\widetilde{m_{l,m}}(T)$ and $Z_{l,m}(T)$ is the respective kernel mid-point and output of $OL_{l,m}$ at training step T. Similar to layer 4, all the links in layer 3 also have unity weights. For rule node R_k, the error signal is δ_k.

$$\delta_k(T) = \sum_{m=1}^{n5} \{\delta_{(l,m)_k}(T) \times \frac{\partial Z_{(l,m)_k}(T)}{\partial Z_{R_k}(T)}\}. \tag{6}$$

Where $Z_{R_k}(T)$ is the output from R_k; and $Z_{(l,m)_k}(T)$ and $\delta_{(l,m)_k}(T)$ is the output and error signal of node $OL_{l,m}$ that is connected to R_k at training step T. In addition,

$$\frac{\partial Z_{(l,m)_k}(T)}{\partial Z_{R_k}(T)} = \begin{cases} 1, & \text{if } Z_{(l,m)_k}(T) = Z_{R_k}(T) \\ 0, & \text{otherwise} \end{cases}. \tag{7}$$

Thus $\delta_k(T)$ sums the error signals from the layer 4 nodes to which R_k contributes the maximum input at training step T. The error signal $\delta_{i,j}(T)$ of layer 2 node $IL_{i,j}$ is

$$\delta_{i,j}(T) = \sum_{m=1}^{n5} (\frac{1}{\tau_m} \sum_{\theta=1}^{\tau_m} \delta_{l_\theta,m}(T)). \tag{8}$$

Where $\delta_{l_\theta,m}(T)$ and τ_m is the error signal from the θth term node $OL_{l_\theta,m}$ and the total number of term nodes of OV_m that $IL_{i,j}$ contributes to through some rule node R_k respectively. The updating rule for the left kernel point $u_{i,j}$ of $IL_{i,j}$ is defined as:

$$u_{i,j}(T+1) = \begin{cases} u_{i,j}(T) - \eta\delta_{i,j}(T)\frac{x_i^{(T)} - l_{i,j}(T)}{(u_{i,j}(T) - l_{i,j}(T))^2} & \text{If } \delta_{i,j}(T) > 0 \text{ and } l_{i,j}(T) < x_i^{(T)} < u_{i,j}(T) \\ u_{i,j}(T) & \text{Otherwise} \end{cases}. \tag{9}$$

Where $u_{i,j}(T+1)$ is the left kernel point of $IL_{i,j}$ after the update; $x_i^{(T)}$ is the ith input at training step T; and η is learning rate.

2.2   Shortcomings of NGD-BP in GenSoFNN

From the computed error signals, three major deficiencies of the NGD-BP algorithm are identified. Firstly, output labels $OL_{l,m}$ with $Z_{l,m}(T) > 0$ moved in a *uniform* direction to reduce the output error at y_m. From equation (3), the amount of update is

$$\eta(d_m^{(T)} - y_m^{(T)})(\frac{1/2 Z_{l,m}(T)}{\sum_{l=1}^{L_m} Z_{l,m}(T)}). \tag{10}$$

The term $(d_m^{(T)} - y_m^{(T)})$ determines the direction of the update. However, $Z_{l,m}(T) > 0$ does not sufficiently justify that $OL_{l,m}$ should contribute to the output y_m. This is because the desired output d_m may be outside the support set of $OL_{l,m}$.

Secondly, *all* layer 4 nodes $OL_{l,m}$ receive the error signal $\delta_m(T)$ from OV_m of layer 5 regardless of their contribution to output y_m. Label $OL_{l,m}$ subsequently computes $\delta_{l,m}(T)$. Equation (5) indicated that $\delta_{l,m}(T)$ consists of three terms: $\delta_m(T)$, $\widetilde{m_{l,m}}(T) - y_m^{(T)}$ and $\sum_{l=1}^{L_m} Z_{l,m}(T)$. It is certain that $\delta_m(T) \neq 0$ when $d_m^{(T)} \neq y_m^{(T)}$. In addition $\sum_{l=1}^{L_m} Z_{l,m}(T) \neq 0$; else it violates the objective of the rule formulation phase of the GenSoFNN network. Moreover, it is highly possible that $\widetilde{m_{l,m}}(T) - y_m^{(T)} \neq 0$ since the condition $Z_{(l,m)}(T) \gg Z_{(l_a,m)}(T), \forall l_a \in \{1 \ldots L_m\} \wedge l_a \neq l$ must be satisfied in order for $\widetilde{m_{l,m}}(T) - y_m^{(T)} \to 0$. Hence, one may assume that $\delta_{l,m}(T) \neq 0$ when $d_m^{(T)} \neq y_m^{(T)}$. Moreover, $\left|\widetilde{m_{l,m}}(T) - y_m^{(T)}\right| \gg 0$ when $\widetilde{m_{l,m}}(T)$ and $y_m^{(T)}$ differs a lot. Hence, $\delta_{l,m}(T)$ could be very large. From equation (6) and (7), $\delta_{l,m}(T)$ is back propagated to rule node R_k and subsequently to layer 2 nodes even though the antecedents of R_k (*input space partition ISP_k of R_k*) may have minimal correlation to the desired output d_m. That is, $Z_{R_k}(T) = Z_{(l,m)_k}(T) \to 0^+$. As a result, ISP_k of R_k is indiscriminately tuned.

Thirdly, $\delta_{l,m}(T)$ is very sensitive to the location of the output label $OL_{l,m}$ with respect to the computed $y_m^{(T)}$. Fig. 2 illustrates this.

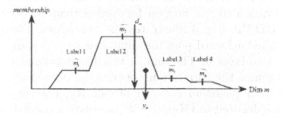

Fig. 2. Computing the error signal $\delta_{l,m}(T)$

Fig. 2 shows that $\delta_m(T) = d_m^{(T)} - y_m^{(T)} < 0$. For Labels 1 and 2, $\delta_{l,m}(T) > 0$ since $\widetilde{m_{l,m}}(T) < y_m^{(T)}$. For Labels 3 and 4, $\delta_{l,m}(T) < 0$ since $\widetilde{m_{l,m}}(T) > y_m^{(T)}$ and is valid when one regards a negative error signal as an indication to reduce a label's contribution to the output. However, the problem lies with the error signals of Labels 1 and 2. This is because while increasing Label 2's contribution to output y_m since error signal $\delta_{l,m}(T)$ is positive, Label 1's contribution to y_m also increases. However, Label 1 is an irrelevant output label (cluster) with respect to the desired value d_m.

3   The Proposed BackPOLE Algorithm

In lieu of the deficiencies of the NGD-BP algorithm, a new back propagation algorithm based on *objective learning errors* (OLEs) is proposed. A set of objectives unique to each layer of the GenSoFNN network is defined and the required error signals are computed on the basis of these objectives. The term OLE refers to the error signal that is back propagated from a forward to a preceding layer. The new learning algorithm is thus named *Back Propagation with Objective Learning Errors* (BackPOLE). The formulation of BackPOLE begins from layer 5 and terminates at layer 2.

Layer 5
The objectives for node OV_m are:

1. Detect output error using function *Err* defined in equation (11);
2. Identify the output label(s) $OL_{l,m}$ that contributes to the output error;
3. Compute the amount of update for each output label;
4. Update the output label(s) $OL_{l,m}$ so that $y_m^{(T)} \to d_m^{(T)}$ as $T \to \infty$ when the training pair (X, D) is clamped at layer 1 and layer 5 of the GenSoFNN network; and
5. Compute the error signal $\delta_m(T)$ and back propagates it to layer 4 nodes.

$$Err(d_m^{(T)}, y_m^{(T)}) = \begin{cases} 1, & \left| d_m^{(T)} - y_m^{(T)} \right| > 0 \\ 0, & \text{otherwise} \end{cases}. \qquad (11)$$

To fulfill objectives 2 to 4, the BackPOLE algorithm performs a backward *partial firing* pass in addition to the normal forward activation (forward firing) pass performed by NGD-BP. Fig. 3 illustrates the two passes. Please refer to [5] for greater details. The backward pass terminates at layer 3 while the forward pass goes from layer 1 to layer 5. The aim of this bi-directional network activation process is to determine the correlation between the *input space partition* (ISP_k) and the *output space partition* (OSP_k) of rule R_k. For the output label that R_k contributes to, denoted as $OL_{(l,m)_k}$, its correlation coefficient $CCoef_{(l,m)_k}$ is defined in equation (12).

$$CCoef_{(l,m)_k} = Z_{(l,m)_k}^{(backward)} \times F_{ISP_k}. \qquad (12)$$

Where $Z_{(l,m)_k}^{(backward)}$ is the backward output of $OL_{(l,m)_k}$; and F_{ISP_k} is the aggregated input to R_k due to the forward pass.

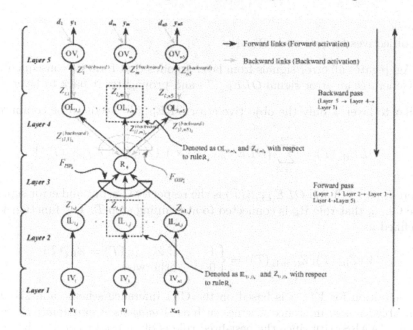

Fig. 3. Forward and partial backward activation passes performed by BackPOLE

The amount of update to the four parameters of $OL_{l,m}$ (denoted as Δ) is defined in terms of $CCoef_{(l,m)_k}$ as in equation (13).

$$\Delta = \eta \{ d_m^{(T)} - \widetilde{m_{l,m}}(T) \} \{ \max_{k \in \{1...n3\}} (CCoef_{(l,m)_k}) \times Z_{l,m}^{(backward)}(T) \} Err(d_m^{(T)}, y_m^{(T)}). \tag{13}$$

Finally, the OLE to be back propagated to layer 4 is defined in equation (14).

$$OLE_m(T) = Err(d_m^{(T)}, y_m^{(T)}) = \begin{cases} 1, & \left| d_m^{(T)} - y_m^{(T)} \right| > 0 \\ 0, & \text{otherwise} \end{cases}. \tag{14}$$

Layer 4
The objectives are defined as follows:

1. Determine whether node $OL_{l,m}$ contributes to the output y_m;
2. If $OL_{l,m}$ contributes to the output y_m, then determine whether to increase, reduce or maintain its contribution to y_m; and
3. Generates an error signal $OLE_{l,m}(T)$ for $OL_{l,m}$ to be back propagated to layer 3.

Since all the links in layer 4 have unity weights (Fig. 1), only the error signal $OLE_{l,m}(T)$ of $OL_{l,m}$ as defined by equation (15) needs to be computed.

$$OLE_{l,m}(T) = OLE_m(T) \times \{ \tfrac{Z_{l,m}^{(backward)}(T)+1}{Z_{l,m}(T)+1} - 1 \} \times \{ Z_{l,m}^{(backward)}(T) - Z_{l,m}(T) \}^2. \tag{15}$$

Layer 3
The objectives for rule node R_k are:

1. Aggregates all error signals from layer 4 nodes that form its consequent; and
2. Generates an error signal $OLE_{R_k}(T)$ and propagates it back to layer 2.

Similar to layer 4, only the objective error $OLE_{R_k}(T)$ needs to be computed.

$$OLE_{R_k}(T) = \sum_{m=1}^{n5} \{OLE_{(l,m)_k}(T) \times V(Z_{R_k}(T), Z_{(l,m)_k}(T))\}. \tag{16}$$

Where $Z_{(l,m)_k}(T)$ and $OLE_{(l,m)_k}(T)$ is the respective output and error signals of node $OL_{l,m}$ that rule R_k is connected to at training step T. The function $V(\cdot, \cdot)$ is defined as

$$V(Z_{R_k}(T), Z_{(l,m)_k}(T)) = \begin{cases} 1, & \text{if } Z_{(l,m)_k}(T) = Z_{R_k}(T) \\ 0, & \text{otherwise} \end{cases}. \tag{17}$$

The definition for $V(\cdot, \cdot)$ is based on the CRI inference scheme and should be applicable to most inference schemes such as *Analogous Approximate Reasoning Schema* (AARS) [10] since the best-fired rule is often used to derive the best-fit consequent at layer 4. Else, $V(\cdot, \cdot)$ can be conveniently redefined.

Layer 2
The objectives are:

1. Determine whether the node $IL_{i,j}$ contributes to the firing of the fuzzy rules;
2. Compute the error signal $OLE_{i,j}(T)$ for $IL_{i,j}$; and
3. Perform parameter tuning using the computed $OLE_{i,j}(T)$.

The objective error $OLE_{i,j}(T)$ for node $IL_{i,j}$ is defined as:

$$OLE_{i,j}(T) = \frac{1}{A_{i,j}} \sum_{\Omega=1}^{A_{i,j}} \{OLE_{R_{k_\Omega}}(T) \times Q(Z_{R_{k_\Omega}}(T), Z_{i,j}(T))\}. \tag{18}$$

Where $A_{i,j}$ denotes the number of rules $IL_{i,j}$ contributes to and $Q(\cdot, \cdot)$ is defined as

$$Q(Z_{R_{k_\Omega}}(T), Z_{i,j}(T)) = \begin{cases} 1, & \text{if } Z_{R_{k_\Omega}}(T) = Z_{i,j}(T) \\ 0, & \text{otherwise} \end{cases}. \tag{19}$$

Function $Q(\cdot, \cdot)$ has been defined based on CRI but can be conveniently redefined.

4 Experimental Results

The *Iris* data set [11] consists of 150 instances of iris flowers belonging to three classes, namely Setosa, Virginica and Versicolor. For the experiment, the data set is partitioned into a training and a test set. The training set consists of 17 instances from each of the three classes. The test set contains the remaining 33 instances from each of the three classes, totaling 99 data instances. The training and test sets are randomly generated. The simulation results of the GenSoFNN network are cross-validated using three different groups of training and test sets. These are denoted as CV1, CV2 and CV3. Two indicators tracked the performance of the GenSoFNN network for the experiment. They are the *mean classification rate* (Mean c rate) and the *standard deviation* (Std Dev) of the classification rates across the three cross-validation groups. A higher "mean c rate" reflects better classification result and the "Std Dev" tracks the consistency of the results across the three cross-validation groups. Hence, a small "Std Dev" indicates strong tolerance by GenSoFNN to variations across the three cross-validation groups. The classification results of GenSoFNN trained using both NGD-BP and BackPOLE are summarised in Table 1.

Table 1. Experimental results of GenSoFNN for Iris classification (c rate = classification rate; m rate = misclassification rate; u rate = unclassification rate; and TC = # training cycle)

Network: GenSoFNN								
NGD-BP trained					BackPOLE trained			
	c rate (%)	m rate (%)	u rate (%)	TC		c rate (%)	m rate (%)	u rate (%)	TC
CV1	98.99	1.01	0.00	26	CV1	98.99	1.01	0.00	14
CV2	93.14	6.86	0.00	23	CV2	93.14	6.86	0.00	15
CV3	95.96	4.04	0.00	23	CV3	95.96	4.04	0.00	15
Mean c rate = 96.03%	Std Dev = 2.93%				Mean c rate = 96.03%	Std Dev = 2.93%			

Table 1 indicates that the GenSoFNN network (regardless of whether it has been trained using NGD-BP or BackPOLE) has good performance across the three cross-validation groups. For group CV1, GenSoFNN almost has 100% classification (98 out of the 99 test points are correctly classified). The "Mean c rate" for the GenSoFNN network is 96.03%. However, from the number of training cycle (TC) required, it is obvious that when GenSoFNN is trained using BackPOLE, it requires far fewer cycle than when it is trained using the NGD-BP algorithm. On average, the proposed BackPOLE required only 58% of the total time the NGD-BP algorithm used to train the GenSoFNN on a PIII-450 machine.

5   Conclusions

A new variant of the popular back propagation (BP) algorithm is proposed in this paper. Although negative gradient descent based back propagation (NGD-BP) algorithm has been widely used to tune the parameters of multi-layered neural networks, it is not so suitable when applied to the tuning of neural fuzzy systems such as POPFNN and has some major shortcomings. The error signals computed using the NGD-BP algorithm are not intuitive and may even upset the equilibrium of a neural fuzzy system as highlighted in Section 2.2. In addition, since the nodal operations of a neural fuzzy system such as POPFNN are defined by the fuzzy inference scheme adopted, a set of customized back propagation learning equations is required when NGD-BP is employed to tune the parameters. As a result, the parameter-learning phase of the neural fuzzy system is overly dependent on the choice of inference scheme; and a change of inference scheme usually requires a re-computation of the learning NGD-BP equations. Thus, the BackPOLE algorithm is proposed and the GenSoFNN network is used to demonstrate the effectiveness of the new algorithm. Preliminary results have demonstrated that BackPOLE is more intuitive and achieves the same level of classification performance as the NGD-BP algorithm (which is specially crafted based on the inference engine) in a shorter training time.

References

1. Rumelhart, D.E., Hinton, G.E., Williams, R.J.: Learning internal representations by error propagation. In Rumelhart, D.E., McClelland, J.L. et al. eds. Parallel Distributed Processing, vol. 1, chap. 8, Cambridge, MA: MIT Press (1986)
2. Lin, C.T., Lee, C.S.G.: Neural Fuzzy Systems – A Neuro-Fuzzy Synergism to Intelligent Systems. Englewood Cliffs, NJ: Prentice Hall (1996)
3. Nauck, D., Klawonn, F., Kruse, R.: Foundations of Neuro-Fuzzy Systems. Chichester, England; New York: John Wiley (1997)
4. Quek, C., Zhou, R.W.: POPFNN: A Pseudo Outer-Product Based Fuzzy Neural Network. Neural Networks (1996) 9(9): 1569-1581
5. Tung, W.L.: A Generalized Platform for Fuzzy Neural Network. Technical Report, ISL-TR-01/01, School of Computer Engineering, Nanyang Technological University, Singapore (2001)
6. Lin, C.J., Lin, C.T.: An ART-Based Fuzzy Adaptive Learning Control Network. IEEE Trans. Fuzzy Systs. (1997) 5(4): 477-496
7. Quek, C., Tung, W.L.: A Novel Approach to the Derivation of Fuzzy Membership Functions Using the Falcon-MART Architecture. Pattern Recog. Letters (2001) 22(9): 941-958
8. Zadeh, L.A.: Calculus of fuzzy restrictions. Fuzzy sets and Their Applications to Cognitive and Decision Processes; New York: Academic 1-39 (1975)
9. Tung, W.L., Quek, C.: Derivation of GenSoFNN-CRI(S) from CRI-based Fuzzy System. Technical Report, ISL-TR-04/01, School of Computer Engineering, Nanyang Technological University, Singapore (2001)
10. Turksen, I.B., Zhong, Z.: An approximate analogical reasoning scheme based on similarity measures and interval valued fuzzy sets. Fuzzy Sets and Syst. (1990) 34: 323-346
11. Fisher, R. A.: The Use of Multiple Measurements in Taxonomic Problems. Annals of Eugenics 7 (1936) Part II: 179-188

A Method on Improvement of the Online Mode Error Backpropagation Algorithm for Pattern Recognition

Tae-Seung Lee[1], Ho-Jin Choi[2], Young-Kil Kwag[1], and Byong-Won Hwang[1]

[1] School of Electronics, Telecommunication and Computer Engineering, Hankuk Aviation University, Seoul, Korea
[2] School of Engineering, Information and Communications University, Taejon, Korea
thestaff@hitel.net, hjchoi@icu.ac.kr,
{ykwang, bwhwang}@mail.hangkong.ac.kr

Abstract. Having a variety of good characteristics against other pattern recognition techniques, the multilayer perceptron (MLP) has been used in many applications. But, it is known that the error backpropagation (EBP) algorithm that the MLP uses in learning has the defect that requires relatively long learning time. In order to increase learning speed it is very effective to use the online-based learning methods, which update the weight vector of the MLP pattern by pattern, because the learning data for pattern recognition contain high redundancy. A typical online EBP algorithm applies the fixed learning rate for each update of the weight vector. Though a large amount of speedup with the online EBP can be obtained just by choosing the appropriate fixed rate, fixing the rate has the inefficiency that doesn't fully utilize the instant updates of the online mode. And, although the patterns come to be divided into the learned and the unlearned during learning process and the learned have no need to go through the computation for learning, the existing online EBP uniformly computes the whole patterns during an epoch. To remedy these inefficiencies, this paper proposes a Changing rate and Omitting patterns in Instant Learning (COIL) method to apply the appropriate rate for each pattern and put only the unlearned into learning. To verify the efficiency of the COIL, experimentations are conducted for speaker verification and speech recognition as the applications of pattern recognition and the results are presented.

1 Introduction

Among recognition methods for pattern recognition, the multilayer perceptron (MLP) is applied to various problems due to the advantages as follows [1][2]:

- Being nonparametric, it doesn't require the underlying statistical distributions to be assumed;
- Having the inhibitory-excitatory learning ability that maximizes the discrimination between the learning models, it minimizes error probability;
- When the targets +1 and 0 (or −1) are used, it has a feature space transferring ability similar to linear discriminant analysis (LDA).

M. Ishizuka and A. Sattar (Eds.): PRICAI 2002, LNAI 2417, pp. 275-284, 2002.
© Springer-Verlag Berlin Heidelberg 2002

The MLP consists of more than zero hidden layer(s) and one output layer, where the hidden layers control learning complexity of the MLP and the output layer determines the number of learning models. The error backpropagation (EBP) algorithm used for MLP learning is based on the steepest gradient descent method, and achieves an ultimate target by propagating the error between the current output and the target of the MLP back from output layer into hidden layers and adjusting the weight vector of MLP [2]. The delta for each the current weight to approach a target in the fastest manner is determined by

$$\frac{\partial e_p}{\partial w_{ij}} = \frac{\partial e_p}{\partial s_i} \frac{\partial s_i}{\partial n_i} \frac{\partial n_i}{\partial w_{ij}} \ . \tag{1}$$

where e_p is the error function of output layer neurons for the current pattern p, w_{ij} the weight of the link between the j-th and the i-th neurons, s_i the activation of the i-th neuron, and n_i the sum of the weighted inputs into the i-th neuron. A value nearer to target can be acquired by applying the deltas to the weight vector, and the method of applying this delta to the weight vector is

$$w_{ij}(t+1) = w_{ij}(t) - \eta \frac{\partial e_p(t)}{\partial w_{ij}(t)} \ . \tag{2}$$

where t is the time for specific status of the weight vector and η the learning rate determining how much this delta is reflected.

As seen in Eqn. 2, the delta in order to reach a target is affected seriously by the learning rate η. If η is large, learning is fast, though the possibility not converging to a target increases as the outputs of MLP oscillate nearby to the target. On the other hand, if η is small, the possibility converging to a target increases, though much updates are required until converging to the target, especially for a certain case learning falls into a local minima and might not achieve the target. So in general, in order to determine the most appropriate learning rate, the maximum value is selected to ensure convergence after changing η variously and examining it.

It is general that MLP learning needs long time even if the maximum learning rate is selected. This results from the fact that the steepest descent gradient uses only the local information for the current weight. To improve the learning speed of the MLP, two directions have been tried. The first is based on the experiences and experimentations in which η is increased when the current output is distant from a target and decreased when close to the target. This direction is divided into the method changing the global η that affects the whole weight vector [3], and the method changing the local η as to the result of Eqn. 1 for each weight [4]. The second borrows the idea from the optimal theory in which the second derivative information to each weight is used. It includes the method that applies the learning tendency of the previous epochs to the current update through momentum [3], and the method that computes the deltas to the weight vector converging to a target in the fastest manner using the Newton's method [5] or its derivatives [6][7].

The updates of Eqn. 2 are conducted in two modes. One is that applying the averaging the deltas to weight vector follows presenting all learning data with the MLP. The other is that the delta is once applied whenever one data is presented. The former is called offline (or batch) mode and the latter online (or stochastic) mode. In both one period that all learning data are presented is defined as an epoch. The decision whether or not continuing learning is implemented based on the difference between the targets and outputs of the MLP on each of the whole epoch.

In pattern recognition, all models given by the problem have a number of patterns belonging to themselves, and learning is conducted so as to classify the patterns newly-input into their own models. In general, the difference between patterns within a model is smaller than in different models. When the MLP is used in pattern recognition, the online mode learning is implemented faster than the offline mode, and the reasons of this can be found as follows [8]:

- Since all the patterns in a model have high redundancy with each other, all of them contribute to the maximum gradient computation in Eqn. 1. From this, the more such patterns are included in a model, the faster learning by the epoch is;
- While the maximum gradients of the patterns within a model computed with Eqn. 1 are within $90°$ to each other, learning is done toward minimizing error;
- The possibility falling in a local minima is dramatically decreased. This is because when the weight vector is updated for each model pattern, a random learning oscillation deviated from the whole learning direction occurs. The oscillation results from the patterns relatively far from the center location of a model.

The online mode learning has the advantages mentioned above against the offline mode, but there are yet possibilities that can improve learning speed. In the existing online mode learning, a fixed learning rate has been used. But it is not efficient for fast learning because it cannot utilize the contribution of the model patterns to learning that varies as learning progresses. The MLP learned with the EBP algorithm goes through three phases: (1) the center location; (2) the area variance; and (3) the area contour of a model. As learning proceeds from (1) to (3), the number of patterns contributing to learning decreases and the appropriate learning rate for the current learning phase changes in the decreasing manner. In addition, the inefficiency occurs that the patterns not contributing to the learning are sustained in the computation of learning. Since the online mode learning using a fixed learning rate does not deal with such variability, it does not achieve a goal in the optimal speed.

Taking these facts into consideration, this paper adopts the varying learning rate applied to each pattern to remedy the defect of the fixed learning rate of the online mode, and proposes omitting the computation of the patterns not contributing to learning as learning progresses.

2 Analysis of the Offline and Online EBP Learning Using the Repulsive Force Concept

All the models in the EBP learning for pattern recognition are learned by an iterative manner with Eqn. 2, and go through the following phases:

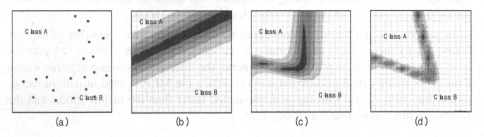

(a)   (b)   (c)   (d)

Fig. 1. (a) data distribution in two models, (b) learning model center locations, (c) learning model area variations, and (d) learning model contours.

The three phases in EBP learning

(1) The model center location learning
(2) The model area variance learning
(3) The model area contour learning

Fig. 1 shows the procedure in the problem of classifying two models. In (b) ~ (d) of this figure, the black line represents the decision boundary of the two models, and darker shade means more concrete boundary. In this figure the boundary is crossing the midway of the models in (b) and showing the area variances of the models in (c), and determining the precise contours of the models in (d).

The e_p of Eqn. 1 is defined as

$$e_p(t) = \frac{1}{2} \sum_{o=1}^{N} e_{o,p}^2(t) \cdot \tag{3}$$

where $e_{o,p}$ is the error of the individual output neuron for the current pattern, and N the number of output neurons. The $e_{o,p}$ is in turn defined as

$$e_{o,p}(t) = d_{o,p}(t) - y_{o,p}(t) \cdot \tag{4}$$

where $d_{o,p}$ is the learning target, and $y_{o,p}$ the current output. In the each phase of Fig. 1, the error presented by each pattern with Eqn. 4 might be considered as the repulsive force to move the decision boundary, and also as a contribution to learning in each phase. Fig. 2 demonstrates the repulsive force concept corresponding to Fig. 1.

In this figure, the dash line represents the decision boundary, and the arrows the repulsive forces for each pattern. In the pre-learning phase corresponding to (a), the strong repulsive forces excited by all the patterns enable learning the center locations of the models. In phases from (b), the strong repulsive forces excited by the patterns adjacent to and over the decision boundary change the shape and location of the boundary.

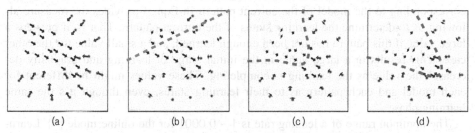

(a)   (b)   (c)   (d)

Fig. 2. The repulsive force of each pattern in the EBP learning

In pattern recognition, the reason why the online mode achieves the faster learning than the offline mode can be analyzed by the difference of the applying manners of the repulsive forces of patterns. While the offline mode applies the vector sum of all the repulsive force vectors, the online mode applies the vectors respectively. So the online mode has more opportunities to change decision boundaries, and makes even more effective if models show complicate shapes.

3 Possibility of Improving the Online EBP Learning Speed

The online mode has an advantage with respect to learning speed against the offline mode, but the optimum speed has not been reached yet.

In EBP learning methods for pattern recognition, the inter-model learning with each pattern changes as the learning progresses. That is, at the initial stage of learning, all the patterns of models participate in inter-model discriminating. And as the learning progresses, the patterns nearby to the center of each model come to fail to participate in the learning. For the fast learning, the followings are helpful: (a) the patterns have large η at the initial stage of learning when the whole patterns of models participate in the learning; (b) the ηs have to be smaller gradually to avoid the oscillation of the learning when the precise contours of the models come to be learned; (c) because the patterns already learned do not contribute to the learning and their learning raise inefficiency with respect to time, they have to be excluded from the learning computation.

The existing online EBP learning doesn't deal with such variability of η since it sets η the fixed value before learning. And as learning progresses, the patterns not contributing to the learning spend time on unnecessary learning computation. As a result, these prevent the online mode EBP algorithm from achieving the faster learning.

4 Proposals

So as to implement the ideas expressed in section 3 to improve the learning speed of the online mode EBP algorithm, this paper proposes two methods.

The first method is to change learning rate for each pattern. A learning rate needs to vary from a large value to a small value as model learning progresses. The $e^{\prec}_{o,p}(t)$ corresponding to the model of the current pattern in Eqn. 3 provides the measure allowing us to determine the learning status of the current pattern. That is, it presents a large value if this pattern has not been enough learned, and a small value for the other case. This results in a large value in the initial stage of learning and gradually decreases the value as the learning is completing. These values might be different for each model and each pattern as to their learning status, even though it's the same learning phase.

The common range of a leaning rate is $1 \sim 0.0001$ for the online mode [9]. Learning is diverged when the learning rate is over the upper limit, and is prolonged unnecessarily when under the lower limit. But because the appropriate ranges are various as to cases, it needs to be determined through repetitive experiments. Since using the $e^{\prec}_{o,p}(t)$ in Eqn. 3 enables us not to concern the lower limit, it is required only to know the proper upper limit. After this, the rate range has to be transformed using the below equation, making it smooth curve:

$$y'(x) = \frac{2 \cdot V_{UL}}{1 + e^{-2x}} - V_{UL} \cdot \qquad (5)$$

where V_{UL} is the upper limit of the range determined through experiments and x the output value from the $e^{\prec}_{o,p}(t)$. The reason of letting Eqn. 5 be of sigmoid type is to avoid the rapid changes of values nearby to the upper limit and 0 while suppress the range to the upper limit.

But, Eqn. 5 uses the error information restricted to the current pattern. If the learning models have inherently large error, i.e. if the distributions of the models overlap considerably each other, the $e^{\prec}_{o,p}(t)$s of those distributions represent large values nearly independent of the current learning phase, resulting in the disturbance of the learning that uses the rate from Eqn 5. So as to deal with such situations, the value from Eqn. 5 is constrained with the averaging error of one epoch before:

$$y(x) = \begin{cases} V_{ASEE} \cdot V_{UL} & \text{if } y'(x) \geq V_{ASEE} \cdot V_{UL} \\ y'(x) & \text{otherwise} \end{cases} \cdot \qquad (6)$$

where V_{ASEE} is the averaging squared error energy [2] represented as below:

$$V_{ASEE} = \frac{1}{NM} \sum_{p=1}^{M} e_p(t-1) \cdot \qquad (7)$$

where M is the number of patterns involved with one learning epoch.

The second method is to omit learning of patterns. The major computations involved in the online mode EBP are error calculations, error backpropagations, and weight updates of patterns. Now that the contribution of the current pattern to learning can be detected by the $e^4_{o,p}(t)$, when the value of the $e^4_{o,p}(t)$ moves down from less than the target value of Eqn. 7 set before the learning, it is decided that the contribution of the current pattern is slight, and we could make omission of the two computations after that point, which are the error backpropagation and the weights update. After this, if the contribution of the pattern comes to increase by the influence of the other patterns' learning, this status will be found by the $e^4_{o,p}(t)$ of the pattern, thus enabling the pattern to involve the learning again. This idea can be presented as follows:

$$P(e^2_{o,p}(t)) = \begin{cases} \textit{The learning of the current pattern is canceled,} \\ \qquad\qquad\qquad \textit{if } e^2_{o,p}(t) < V_{ASEE}(t-1) \\ \textit{The learning of the current pattern is continued,} \\ \qquad\qquad\qquad \textit{if } e^2_{o,p}(t) \geq V_{ASEE}(t-1) \end{cases} \qquad (8)$$

where, P is the learning process of the current pattern.

In this paper, these two methods are called as a Changing rate and Omitting patterns in Instant Learning (COIL) method.

5 Experimentations

To verify the performance of the COIL, MLP learning speeds in speaker verification [10] and speech recognition [11] are examined.

First, pattern matching with medium-small data is performed, comparing different learning methods with each other, where the MLP is used as the verifier that enrolls speakers with the verification system and processes the verifying tests by using speech. The data used in this experiment are the four digits recordings continuously spoken by 40 Korean male and female speakers, in which each speaker utters total 35 words of different digit arrays four times. Three times of them are used as the enrolling utterances, and the other is used as the verifying utterance. The nine Korean constituants (/a/, /e/, /□/, /o/, /u/, /ʌ/, /i/, /l/, nasals) extracted from the enrolling utterances are used for training MLPs, in which nine MLPs correspond to the nine constituents respectively, and the number of the learning data presented with each MLP is 580 per epoch. The count of MLPs' learning times during the experiment is about 9,600, and the averaging for all the speakers and digit arrays is recorded. The each MLP consists of 50 input neurons, 2 hidden neurons, and 1 output neuron, namely 2-layer structure.

Next, pattern matching with large data is performed, where MLP is used as the recognizer that recognizes seven Korean mono-vowels (/a/, /e/, /□/, /o/, /u/, /ʌ/, /i/) in speaker-independent mode. The data used in this experiment are the mono-vowels extracted from the phone-balanced words of 70 Korean male and female speakers. In this experiment, single MLP is learned ten times, and the averaging is recorded. The number of the learning data presented with MLP is 20,748 per epoch, and the MLP consists of 16 input neurons, 20 hidden neurons, and 7 output neurons, namely 2-layer structure.

The records of the experiments are written for the offline EBP, RPROP [3], online EBP, CIL, and COIL. Here the offline EBP is marked as OffEBP, the online EBP as OnEBP, the method using only the first proposed method as CIL, and the method using both as COIL. The measures recorded are the number of epochs, learning time, and recognition rate.

The Fig. 3 presents the result of the speaker verification experiment. It can be found from the figure that the number of epochs and the learning time improve in order of OffEBP, RPROP, OnEBP, CIL and COIL. The RPROP is the offline mode learning method to improve the OffEBP which is determined the slowest method of all. It marks near two times faster speed than the OffEBP. The OnEBP shows more than two times faster speed than such RPROP. This result tells the significance of how important the using of the redundancy in the data for pattern recognition is. The CIL, in turn, confirms the effectiveness of applying the variable learning rate as well as using the data redundancy, by making improvement little short of two times faster than the OnEBP. The COIL improves little on the CIL with respect to the number of epochs, but shows the speedup near two times faster in learning time. From this result, it is evident that while the omitting method does not change the phase transition of learning process, it skips efficiently the patterns' learning seldom contributing to the learning.

In the Fig. 4, which presents the result of the speech recognition experiment, the improvement transitions are similar to the Fig. 3 but the improving rates of the CIL and COIL are relatively low against other learning methods. Such phenomenon seems to result from a fact that the data size in an epoch used in the speech recognition experiment is 35 times larger than in the speaker verification experiment. The speedup in the online mode learning using data redundancy takes more effect as the data size increases. The reason that the improvements of the CIL and COIL are relatively low can be guessed as they stem from the OnEBP algorithm and the large amount of speedup is already obtained in the OnEBP basis.

The final phenomenon detected in the Fig. 3 and 4 is that each learning method shows different recognition rates. The online learning methods record higher rates than the offlines in large. This result appears to originate from the difference that while the offline mode averages the errors from all patterns and reflects the average to learning, the online mode reflects the each error of all patterns. If the data distribution of the learning model shows a complicate shape, the recognition error can increase since the averaging makes the shape stumpy.

6 Conclusion

Based on the experiments conducted above, it is evident that the online mode EBP learning algorithm for the MLP in pattern recognition does achieve a goal faster than the offline mode, resulting from much redundancy in the data of pattern recognition. However, as learning progresses, the faster speed can be obtained if the property is utilized that the contribution of the model patterns to learning varies. This paper proposed the COIL method that applied the variable learning rate for each pattern instead

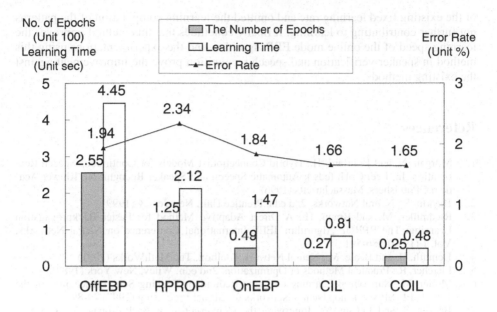

Fig. 3. The comparison of the numbers of epochs, learning duration times, and error rates with each learning method

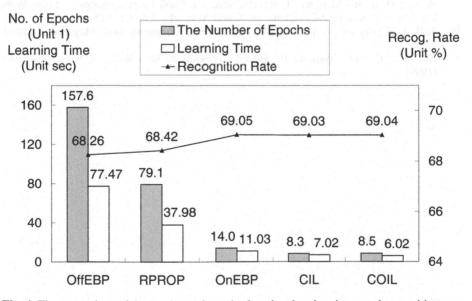

Fig. 4. The comparison of the numbers of epochs, learning duration times, and recognition rates with each learning method

of the existing fixed learning rate and omitted the learning computation of the patterns not further contributing to learning. It finally concludes that this method improves the learning speed of the online mode EBP algorithm and the experimentations using this method in speaker verification and speech recognition prove the improvement against the existing methods.

References

1. Morgan, N. and Bourlard, H.: Hybrid Connectionist Models for Continuous Speech Recognition. In: Lee, C. H. (eds.): Automatic Speech and Speaker Recognition. Kluwer Academic Publishers, Massachusetts (1996)
2. Haykin, S.: Neural Networks. 2nd edn. Prentice Hall, New Jersey (1999)
3. Riedmiller, M. and Braun, H.: A Direct Adaptive Method for Faster Backpropagation Learning: The RPROP Algorithm, IEEE International Conference on Neural Networks. Vol. 1 (1993) 586-591
4. Demuth, H. and Beale, M.: Neural Network Toolbox. The MathWorks (2001)
5. Fletcher, R.: Practical Methods of Optimization. 2nd edn. Wiley, New York (1987).
6. Moller, M.: Supervised Learning on Large Redundant Training Sets. Proceedings of the 1992 IEEE-SP Workshop Neural Networks for Signal Processing (1992) 79-89
7. Becker, S. and LeCun, Y.: Improving the Convergence of Back-Propagation Learning with Second-Order Methods. Proceedings of the 1988 Connectionist Models Summer School (1988) 29-37
8. Bengio, Y.: Neural Networks for Speech and Sequence Recognition. International Thomson Computer Press, London (1995)
9. Wilson, D. R. and Martinez, T. R.: The Need for Small Learning Rates on Large Problems. International Joint Conference on Neural Networks. 1 (2001) 115-119
10. Naik, J. M.: Speaker Verification: A Tutorial. IEEE Communications Magazine. 1 (1990) 42-48
11. Becchetti, C. and Ricotti, L. P.: Speech Recognition. John Wiley & Sons, Chichester (1999)

Optimizing a Multiple Classifier System

Hirotaka Inoue[1] and Hiroyuki Narihisa[2]

[1] Department of Electrical Engineering and Information Science,
Kure National College of Technology,
2-2-11 Agaminami, Kure-shi, Hiroshima, 737-8506 Japan
hiro@kure-nct.ac.jp
[2] Department of Information and Computer Engineering,
Okayama University of Science,
1-1 Ridai-cho, Okayama-shi, Okayama, 700-0005 Japan
narihisa@ice.ous.ac.jp

Abstract. Recently, multiple classifier systems (MCS) have been used for practical applications to improve classification accuracy. Self-generating neural networks (SGNN) are one of the suitable base-classifiers for MCS because of their simple setting and fast learning. However, the computation cost of the MCS increases in proportion to the number of SGNN. In this paper, we propose a novel optimization method for the structure of the SGNN in the MCS. We compare the optimized MCS with two sampling methods. Experiments have been conducted to compare the optimized MCS with an unoptimized MCS, the MCS based on C4.5, and k-nearest neighbor. The results show that the optimized MCS can improve its classification accuracy as well as reducing the computation cost.

1 Introduction

Classifiers need to find hidden information in the given large data effectively and classify unknown data as accurately as possible [1]. Recently, to improve the classification accuracy, multiple classifier systems (MCS) such as neural network ensembles, bagging, boosting, and a mixture of experts have been used for practical data mining applications [2,3,4]. In general, the base classifiers of the MCS use traditional models such as neural networks (backpropagation network and radial basis function network) [5] and decision trees (CART and C4.5) [6].

Neural networks have great advantages of adaptability, flexibility, and universal nonlinear input-output mapping capability. However, to apply these neural networks, it is necessary to determine the network structure and some parameters by human experts, and it is quite difficult to choose the right network structure suitable for a particular application at hand. Moreover, they require a long training time to learn the input-output relation of the given data. These drawbacks prevent neural networks being the base classifier of the MCS for practical applications.

Self-generating neural networks (SGNN) [7] have simple network design and high speed learning. SGNN are an extension of the self-organizing maps (SOM)

M. Ishizuka and A. Sattar (Eds.): PRICAI 2002, LNAI 2417, pp. 285–294, 2002.
© Springer-Verlag Berlin Heidelberg 2002

of Kohonen [8] and utilize the competitive learning which is one of many un-supervised learning methods. SGNN is implemented as a tree structure that is called a self-generating neural tree (SGNT). The abilities of SGNN make it suitable for the base classifier of the MCS. In order to improve in the accuracy of SGNN, we proposed ensemble self-generating neural networks (ESGNN) for classification [9] as one of the MCS. Although the accuracy of ESGNN improves by using various SGNN, the computation cost, that is, the computation time and the memory capacity increases in proportion to the increase in number of SGNN in the MCS.

In this paper, we propose a novel MCS optimizing method to reduce the computational cost for classification. We optimize the structure of SGNT in MCS by pruning the tedious leaves. We introduce a threshold value as a pruning parameter to decide which subtree's leaves to prune and estimate with 10-fold cross-validation [10]. After the optimization, the MCS can improve its classifi-cation accuracy as well as reducing the computation cost. We use two sampling methods for the optimizing MCS; shuffling and bagging. Shuffling uses all the training data by changing randomly the order of the training data on each clas-sifier. Bagging [11] is a resampling technique which permits the overlap of the data. We investigate the improvement performance of the optimized MCS by comparing it with the MCS based on C4.5 [12] using ten problems in the UCI repository [13]. Moreover, we compare the optimized MCS with k-nearest neigh-bor (k-NN) [14] to investigate the computational cost and the classification accuracy. The optimized MCS demonstrates higher classification accuracy and faster processing speed than k-NN on average.

2   Self-Generating Neural Networks

SGNN are based on SOM and implemented as a SGNT architecture. The SGNT can be constructed directly from the given training data without any intervening human effort. The SGNT algorithm is defined as a tree construction problem of how to construct a tree structure from the given data which consist of multiple attributes under the condition that the final leaves correspond to the given data.

Before we describe the SGNT algorithm, we denote some notations.

- input data vector: $e_i \in \mathbb{R}^m$.
- root, leaf, and node in the SGNT: n_j.
- weight vector of n_j: $w_j \in \mathbb{R}^m$.
- the number of the leaves in n_j: c_j.
- distance measure: $d(e_i, w_j)$.
- winner leaf for e_i in the SGNT: n_{win}.

The SGNT algorithm is a hierarchical clustering algorithm. The pseudo C code of the SGNT algorithm is given as follows:

Algorithm (SGNT Generation)

```
Input:
  A set of training examples E = {e_i}, i = 1, ... , N.
  A distance measure d(e_i,w_j).
Program Code:
  copy(n_1,e_1);
  for (i = 2, j = 2; i <= N; i++) {
    n_win = choose(e_i, n_1);
    if (leaf(n_win)) {
      copy(n_j, w_win);
      connect(n_j, n_win);
      j++;
    }
    copy(n_j, e_i);
    connect(n_j, n_win);
    j++;
    update(e_i, w_win);
  }
Output:
  Constructed SGNT by E.
```

In the above algorithm, several sub procedures are used. Table 1 shows the sub procedures of the SGNT algorithm and their specifications.

In order to decide the winner leaf n_{win}, competitive learning is used. If an n_j includes the n_{win} as its descendant in the SGNT, the weight w_{jk} ($k = 1, 2, \ldots, m$) of the n_j is updated as follows:

$$w_{jk} \leftarrow w_{jk} + \frac{1}{c_j} \cdot (e_{ik} - w_{jk}), \quad 1 \leq k \leq m. \tag{1}$$

After all training data are inserted into the SGNT as the leaves, the weights of each node are the averages of the corresponding weights of all its leaves. The whole network of the SGNT reflects the given feature space by its topology. For more details concerning how to construct and perform the SGNT, see [7]. Note, to optimize the structure of the SGNT effectively, we remove the threshold value of the original SGNT algorithm to control the number of leaves based on

Table 1. Sub procedures of the SGNT algorithm

Sub procedure	Specification
$copy(n_j, e_i/\boldsymbol{w}_{win})$	Create n_j, copy attributes of $e_i/\boldsymbol{w}_{win}$ as weights $\boldsymbol{w}_j$ in n_j.
$choose(e_i, n_1)$	Decide n_{win} for e_i.
$leaf(n_{win})$	Check n_{win} whether n_{win} is a leaf or not.
$connect(n_j, n_{win})$	Connect n_j as a child leaf of n_{win}.
$update(e_i, \boldsymbol{w}_j)$	Update $\boldsymbol{w}_j$ of n_j.

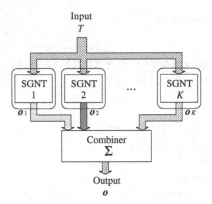

Fig. 1. An MCS which is constructed from K SGNTs. The test dataset T is entered each SGNT, the output o_i is computed as the output of the winner leaf for the input data, and the MCS's output is decided by voting outputs of K SGNTs

the distance because of the trade-off between the memory capacity and the classification accuracy. In the next section, we describe how to optimize the structure of the SGNT in the MCS to avoid the above problem.

3   Optimization of a Multiple Classifier System

We showed the SGNT generation algorithm in the previous section. The SGNT has the capability of high speed processing. However, the accuracy of the SGNT is inferior to the conventional approaches, such as nearest neighbor, because the SGNT has no guarantee to reach the nearest leaf for unknown data. Hence, we construct an MCS by taking the majority of plural SGNT's outputs to improve the accuracy (Figure 1).

Although the accuracy of the MCS is superior or comparable to the accuracy of conventional approaches, the computational cost increases in proportion

```
1 begin     initialize j = the height of the SGNT
2    do for each subtree's leaves in the height j
3      if the ratio of the most class ≥ the threshold value α,
4      then merge all leaves to parent node
5      if all subtrees are traversed in the height j,
6      then j ← j - 1
7    until j = 0
8 end.
```

Fig. 2. The pruning algorithm

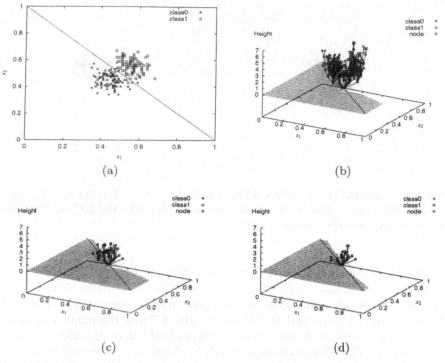

(a)   (b)

(c)   (d)

Fig. 3. An example of the SGNT's pruning algorithm, (a) a two dimensional classification problem with two equal circular Gaussian distribution, (b) the structure of the unpruned SGNT, (c) the structure of the pruned SGNT ($\alpha - 1$), and (d) the structure of the pruned SGNT ($\alpha = 0.6$). The shaded plane is the decision region of class 0 by the SGNT and the dotted line shows the ideal decision boundary

to the increase in the number of SGNTs in the MCS. In particular, the huge memory requirement prevents the use of MCS for large datasets even with latest computers.

In order to reduce the memory requirement, we propose an optimization method of the MCS for classification. We introduce a pruning method of the SGNT to optimize the MCS. This method has two parts, the merge phase and the evaluation phase. The merge phase is performed as the pruning algorithm to reduce dense leaves (Figure 2). This phase uses the class information and a threshold value α to decide which subtree's leaves to prune or not. For leaves that have the same parent node, if the proportion of the most common class is greater than or equal to the threshold value α, then these leaves are pruned and the parent node is given the most common class.

We show an example of the pruning algorithm in Figure 3. This is a two-dimensional classification problem with two equal circular Gaussian distributions that have an overlap. The shaded plane is the decision region of class 0 and the other plane is the decision region of class 1 by the SGNT. The dotted line is

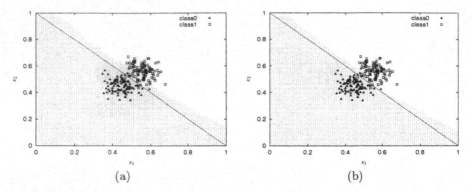

Fig. 4. An example of the MCS's decision boundary ($K = 25$), (a) $\alpha = 1$, and (b) $\alpha = 0.6$. The shaded plane is the decision region of class 0 by the MCS and the doted line shows the ideal decision boundary

the ideal decision boundary. The number of training samples is 200 (class0: 100,class1: 100) (Figure 3(a)). The unpruned SGNT is given in Figure 3(b). In this case, 200 leaves and 120 nodes are automatically generated by the SGNT algorithm. In this unpruned SGNT, the height is 7 and the number of units is 320. In this, we define the unit to count the sum of the root, nodes, and leaves of the SGNT. The root is the node which is of height 0. The unit is used as a measure of the memory requirement in the next section. Figure 3(c) shows the pruned SGNT after the merge phase in $\alpha = 1$. In this case, 159 leaves and 107 nodes are pruned away and 54 units remain. The decision boundary is the same as the unpruned SGNT. Figure 3(d) shows the pruned SGNT after the merge phase in $\alpha = 0.6$. In this case, 182 leaves and 115 nodes are pruned away and only 23 units remain. Moreover, the decision boundary is improved more than the unpruned SGNT because this case can reduce the effect of the overlapping class by pruning the SGNT.

In the above example, we use all training data to construct the SGNT. The structure of the SGNT is changed by the order of the training data. Hence, we can construct the MCS from the same training data by changing the input order. We call this approach "shuffling".

To show how well the MCS is optimized by the pruning algorithm, we show an example of the MCS in the same problem used above. Figure 4(a) and Figure 4(b) show the decision region of the MCS in $\alpha = 1$ and $\alpha = 0.6$, respectively. We set the number of SGNTs K as 25. The result of Figure 4(b) is a better estimation of the ideal decision region than the result of Figure 4(a).

The optimum threshold values α of the given problems are different from each other. The evaluation phase is performed to choose the best threshold value by introducing 10-fold cross validation. We investigate the optimization method for more complex problems in the next section.

4   Experimental Results

We investigate the computational cost (the memory capacity and the computation time) and the accuracy of MCS based on SGNN with two sampling methods, shuffling and bagging for ten benchmark problems in the UCI repository [13]. We evaluate how the MCS is optimized using 10-fold cross-validation for the ten benchmark problems. In this experiment, we use a modified Euclidean distance measure for the MCS. To select the optimum threshold value α, we set the different threshold values α which are moved from 0.5 to 1; $\alpha = [0.5, 0.55, 0.6, \ldots, 1]$. We set the number of SGNT K in the MCS as 25 and execute 100 trials by changing the sampling order of each training set. All computations of the MCS are performed on an IBM PC-AT machine (CPU: Intel Pentium II 450MHz, Memory: 323MB).

Table 2 shows the average memory requirement of 100 trials for the shuffled SGNT and the bagged SGNT in the MCS. As the memory requirement, we count the number of units which is the sum of the root, nodes, and leaves of the SGNT. The memory requirement is reduced from 50% to 96.2% in shuffling, and from 57.6% to 96.7% in bagging, by optimizing the MCS. It is found that the bagged SGNT can be a higher memory compression than the shuffled SGNN. This supports that bagged SGNN can be effectively used for large scale datasets.

Table 3 shows the average classification accuracy of 100 trials for the MCS with shuffling and bagging. It is clear that over 10 datasets, both optimized MCS with shuffled and bagged SGNT lead to more accurate or comparable classifiers than the unoptimized MCS. In comparison with shuffling, bagging is superior or comparable to shuffling on 7 of the 10 datasets. In short, bagging is better than shuffling in terms of the computational cost and the classification accuracy in the MCS.

To evaluate the optimized MCS's performance, we compare the optimized MCS with the MCS based on C4.5. We set the number of classifiers K in the MCS as 25 and we construct both MCS by bagging. Table 4 shows the improved performance of the optimized MCS and the MCS based on C4.5. The results of the SGNT and the optimized MCS are the average of 100 trials. The optimized MCS has a better performance than the MCS based on C4.5 for 6 of the 10 datasets. Although the MCS based on C4.5 degrades the classification accuracy for iris, the optimized MCS can improve the classification accuracy for all problems. Therefore, the pruned SGNT is a good base classifier for the MCS on the basis of both the scalability for large scale datasets and the robust improving generalization capability for the noisy datasets comparable to the MCS with C4.5.

To show the advantages of the optimized MCS, we compare it with k-NN on the same problems. In the optimized MCS, we choose the best classification accuracy of 100 trials with bagging. In k-NN, we choose the best accuracy where k is 1,3,5,7,9,11,13,15,25 with 10-fold cross-validation. All methods are compiled by using gcc with the optimization level -O2 on the same computer.

Table 5 shows the classification accuracy, the memory requirement, and the computation time achieved by the optimized MCS and k-NN. Since k-NN does

Table 2. The average memory requirement of 100 trials for the shuffled SGNT and the bagged SGNT in the MCS. The average optimum threshold value α is given inside the bracket

	shuffled SGNT			bagged SGNT		
Dataset	optimized	unoptimized	ratio	optimized	unoptimized	ratio
balance-scale	133.98(0.577)	846.63	15.8	113.68(0.609)	860.85	13.2
breast-cancer-w	34.4(0.641)	889.24	3.8	30.32(0.665)	897.55	3.3
glass	147.85(0.671)	295.59	50	126.43(0.723)	297.59	42.4
ionosphere	100.46(0.692)	454.19	22.1	78.93(0.689)	472.15	16.7
iris	24.74(0.695)	207.76	11.9	21.11(0.699)	208.67	10.1
letter	8956.12(0.926)	26537.59	33.7	7576.84(0.919)	27050.51	28
liver-disorders	257.26(0.624)	464.25	46.4	162.79(0.649)	471.73	34.5
new-thyroid	90.38(0.889)	296.54	30.4	77.3(0.899)	298.23	25.9
pima-diabetes	266.49(0.612)	1023.47	26	217.31(0.64)	1045.18	20.7
wine	18.4(0.643)	229.14	8	14.71(0.63)	239.04	6.1
Average	1003.01	3124.44	24.8	841.94	3184.15	20.1

Table 3. The average classification accuracy of 100 trials for the MCS with shuffling and bagging. The standard deviation is given inside the bracket ($\times 10^{-3}$)

	MCS with shuffled SGNT			MCS with bagged SGNT		
Dataset	optimized	unoptimized	ratio	optimized	unoptimized	ratio
balance-scale	0.868(5.23)	0.837(7.45)	+3.1	0.870(5.86)	0.848(7.93)	+2.2
breast-cancer-w	0.971(1.61)	0.968(2.05)	+0.3	0.972(2.02)	0.968(2.66)	+0.4
glass	0.727(11.6)	0.717(11.95)	+1	0.722(11.38)	0.716(13.73)	+0.6
ionosphere	0.897(5.22)	0.882(5.53)	+1.5	0.877(5.54)	0.868(7.79)	+0.9
iris	0.966(3.24)	0.964(3.94)	+0.2	0.965(4.16)	0.961(4.74)	+0.4
letter	0.958(0.7)	0.958(0.68)	0	0.956(0.75)	0.956(0.75)	0
liver-disorders	0.623(11.59)	0.605(13.03)	+1.8	0.625(13.6)	0.608(17.01)	+1.7
new-thyroid	0.957(5.82)	0.957(5.92)	0	0.949(6.74)	0.949(6.76)	0
pima-diabetes	0.746(6.17)	0.72(8.18)	+2.6	0.748(7.66)	0.730(8.71)	+1.8
wine	0.964(3.98)	0.958(5.29)	+0.6	0.964(4.49)	0.96(4.2)	+0.4
Average	0.867	0.856	+1.1	0.864	0.856	+0.8

not discard any training sample, the size of this classifier corresponds to the training set size. The results of k-NN correspond to the average measures obtained by 10-fold cross-validation that is the same experimental procedure of the MCS. Next, we show the results for each category.

First, with regard to the classification accuracy, the optimized MCS is superior to k-NN for 7 of the 10 datasets and gives 0.7% improvement on average. Second, in terms of the memory requirement, even though the optimized MCS includes the root and the nodes which are generated by the SGNT generation algorithm, this is less than k-NN for all problems. Although the memory requirement of the optimized MCS is totally used K times in Table 5, we release the memory of SGNT for each trial and reuse the memory for effective computation. Therefore, the memory requirement is suppressed by the size of the single

Table 4. The improved performance of the optimized MCS and the MCS based on C4.5 with bagging

Dataset	MCS based on SGNT			MCS based on C4.5		
	SGNT	MCS	ratio	C4.5	MCS	ratio
balance-scale	0.789	**0.87**	+8.1	0.795	0.827	+3.2
breast-cancer-w	0.961	**0.972**	+0.9	0.946	0.963	+1.7
glass	0.665	0.722	+5.7	0.664	**0.757**	+9.3
ionosphere	0.866	0.877	+1.1	0.897	**0.92**	+2.3
iris	0.951	**0.965**	+1.4	0.953	0.947	−0.6
letter	0.894	**0.956**	+6.2	0.880	0.938	+5.8
liver-disorders	0.59	0.625	+3.5	0.635	**0.736**	+10.1
new-thyroid	0.942	**0.949**	+0.7	0.93	0.94	+1
pima-diabetes	0.708	0.748	+4	0.749	**0.767**	+1.8
wine	0.952	**0.964**	+1.2	0.927	0.949	+2.2
Average	0.831	0.864	+3.3	0.837	**0.874**	+3

Table 5. The classification accuracy, the memory requirement, and the computation time of ten trials for the best optimized MCS and k-NN

Dataset	classification acc.		memory requirement		computation time (s)	
	MCS	k-NN	MCS	k-NN	MCS	k-NN
balance-scale	0.885	**0.899**	**118.7**	562.5	**1.43**	2.52
breast-cancer-w	**0.976**	0.973	**20.9**	629.1	2.19	**1.31**
glass	**0.747**	0.706	**123.47**	192.6	0.5	**0.04**
ionosphere	**0.889**	0.875	**37.4**	315.9	1.86	**0.25**
iris	**0.973**	0.960	**22.6**	135	0.26	**0.05**
letter	0.957	**0.961**	**7627.5**	18000	**215.23**	845.44
liver-disorders	**0.658**	0.647	**221.6**	310.5	0.82	**0.6**
new-thyroid	0.963	**0.968**	**76.8**	193.5	0.39	**0.05**
pima-diabetes	**0.763**	0.753	**181**	691.2	**2.59**	3.41
wine	**0.978**	0.977	**12.3**	160.2	0.44	**0.13**
Average	**0.879**	0.872	**844.23**	2119.1	**22.6**	85.38

SGNT. Finally, in view of the computation time, although the optimized MCS consumes the cost of K times of the SGNT, the average computation time is faster than k-NN. In the case of letter, in particular, the computation time of the optimized MCS is faster than k-NN by about 3.9 times. We need to repeat 10-fold cross validation many times to select the optimum parameters for α and k. This evaluation consumes much computation time for large datasets such as letter. Therefore, the optimized MCS based on the fast and compact SGNT is useful and practical for large datasets. Moreover, the optimized MCS has the ability of parallel computation because each classifier behaves independently. In conclusion, the optimized MCS is practical for large-scale data mining compared with k-NN.

5 Conclusions

In this paper, we proposed a new optimizing method for the MCS based on SGNN and evaluated the computation cost and the accuracy. We introduced a threshold value for pruning the SGNT and evaluated the optimized MCS by 10-fold cross-validation. We investigated the difference of two sampling methods; shuffling and bagging. Experimental results showed that the memory requirement reduces remarkably, and the accuracy increases by using the pruned SGNT as the base classifier of the MCS. Bagging is better than shuffling in view of the memory reduction and the improvement to the classification accuracy. The optimized MCS is a useful and practical tool to classify large datasets. In future work, we will study an on-line pruning method of the SGNT in the MCS for effective processing.

References

1. J. Han and M. Kamber. *Data Mining: Concepts and Techniques*. Morgan Kaufmann Publishers, San Francisco, CA, 2000.
2. J. R. Quinlan. Bagging, Boosting, and C4.5. In *Proceedings of the Thirteenth National Conference on Artificial Intelligence*, pages 725–730, Portland, OR, Aug. 4–8 1996.
3. G. Rätsch, T. Onoda, and K.-R. Müller. Soft margins for AdaBoost. *Machine Learning*, 42(3):287–320, March 2001.
4. H. Mamitsuka and N. Abe. Efficient mining from large databases with query learning. In *Proceedings of the 16th International Conference on Machine Learning*, pages 575–582, 2000.
5. C. M. Bishop. *Neural Networks for Pattern Recognition*. Oxford University Press, New York, 1995.
6. R. O. Duda, P. E. Hart, and D. G. Stork. *Pattern Classification*. John Wiley & Sons Inc., New York, 2nd ed., 2000.
7. W. X. Wen, A. Jennings, and H. Liu. Learning a neural tree. In *International Joint Conference on Neural Networks*, Beijing, China, 1992. This paper available at ftp://ftp.cis.ohio-state.edu/pub/neuroprose/wen.sgnt-learn.ps.Z.
8. T. Kohonen. *Self-Organizing Maps*. Springer-Verlag, Berlin, 1995.
9. H. Inoue and H. Narihisa. Improving generalization ability of self-generating neural networks through ensemble averaging. In Takao Terano, Huan Liu, and Arbee L P Chen, editors, *Knowledge Discovery and Data Mining: Current issues and new applications*, volume 1805 of *LNAI*, pages 177–180, Springer-Verlag, Berlin, 2000.
10. M. Stone. Cross-validation: A review. *Math. Operationsforsch. Statist., Ser. Statistics*, 9(1):127–139, 1978.
11. L. Breiman. Bagging predictors. *Machine Learning*, 24:123–140, 1996.
12. J. R. Quinlan. *C4.5: Programs for Machine Learning*. Morgan Kaufmann, San Mateo, CA, USA, 1993.
13. C.L. Blake and C.J. Merz. UCI repository of machine learning databases, University of California, Irvine, Dept. of Information and Computer Sciences, 1998. Datasets available at http://www.ics.uci.edu/~mlearn/MLRepository.html.
14. E. A. Patrick and F. P. Fischer. A generalized k-nearest neighbor rule. *Information and Control*, 16(2):128–152, 1970.

Generalization of Iterative Learning Control for Multiple Desired Trajectories in Robotic Systems

M. Arif, T. Ishihara, and H. Inooka

Graduate School of Information Sciences, Tohoku University,
Aramaki aza Aoba 01, Aoba-ku, Sendai 980-8579, JAPAN
Tel: +81-22-217-7021
{arif,ishihara,inooka}@control.is.tohoku.ac.jp

Abstract. Iterative learning controllers are found to be effective for trajectory tracking tasks in the robotic systems especially when the system model is not known. One of the drawback of iterative learning control is its slow convergence and high tracking errors in the initial iterations because of zero knowledge about the system for each new desired trajectory. In this paper, importance of the initial control input in the convergence of error is highlighted. Experience of iterative learning controller for different desired trajectories is modelled using neural network. For a new desired trajectory, this neural network generates the initial control input which is used by the learning controller. This approach is proved to be very effective in improving the convergence of the tracking error. The proposed method is very general and applicable to most of the iterative learning controller without modifying their simple learning structures.

1 Introduction

In the control theory, especially for the applications related to robots, tracking of a desired trajectory with high precision is one of the main research issues. In many robotic applications, the task is to track a pre-specified desired trajectory many times. In this situation, iterative learning control is a good choice. The implementation of the controller is easy because of its structural simplicity and it does not require the identification of the system. An iterative learning controller modifies the control input using the experience of the previous iterations in a way that the control input converges to the desired control input. Iterative learning control algorithm was first proposed by Arimoto et al. [2] when he presented the idea of the first order D type Iterative learning controller using differential of the tracking error to update the control input. Since then many researchers has proposed different ideas for the application of iterative learning controller for robotic applications to improve its convergence properties [3,9].

Because learning controller does not incorporate any knowledge about the system parameters for generating the control input, the tracking error in the initial iterations is always large for each new desired trajectory. It requires certain

M. Ishizuka and A. Sattar (Eds.): PRICAI 2002, LNAI 2417, pp. 295–304, 2002.

number of iterations for each trajectory to reduce the tracking error below certain acceptable bound. In this respect, Arif et al. [1] illustrated that proper selection of the initial control input can effectively reduce the number of iterations required to decrease the tracking error below certain acceptable bound. They have used local modelling technique to model the inverse dynamics of the nonlinear system. A database of the system states and the control inputs gathered from different trajectory tracking tasks by the iterative learning controller is used to generate the local models. This idea works well but requires large amount of memory to store the data points and is time consuming to search the required data points for fitting a local model near a query point. In this paper, we have used neural network to store the experience of the learning controller by learning the inverse dynamics of the system. Hence, experience can be stored in less amount of memory in terms of the weights of the neural network. Once the neural network is trained, generation of the desired control input is not time consuming. Many researchers have used the idea of neural network in iterative learning controller but their main emphasis was on implementing neural network online to calculate the next control input for which neural network takes long time for training and are difficult to be implemented [4,5]. In our proposed method, neural network are only used to model the experience of the iterative learning controller and therefore can be trained offline. This method can be applied to any iterative learning control without effecting its structural complexity.

2   Problem Formulation

The dynamic equation of a robotic manipulator having n degree of freedom can be described as follows,

$$M(\mathbf{q})\ddot{\mathbf{q}} + C(\mathbf{q}, \dot{\mathbf{q}})\dot{\mathbf{q}} + G(\mathbf{q}) = \mathbf{u} \qquad (1)$$

where $\mathbf{q}(t) \in R^n$ is the angular joint positions, $M(\dot{\mathbf{q}})$ is the inertia matrix, $C(\mathbf{q}, \dot{\mathbf{q}})\dot{\mathbf{q}}$ is the Coriolis and centripetal forces, $G(\mathbf{q})$ are the gravitational torques and $\mathbf{u} \in R^n$ are the input torques applied to the joints of manipulator. Let $\mathbf{q}_d(t)$ be the desired trajectory which is achievable and continuously differentiable on a finite time interval $t \in [0, t_f]$, such that for a bounded desired trajectory, there exist bounded input torques $\mathbf{u}_d(t)$.

The problem can be stated as follows: For a desired trajectory $\mathbf{q}_d(t)$, find a sequence of piecewise continuous control input $\mathbf{u}(t)$ such that the system's output $\mathbf{q}(t)$ converges to $\mathbf{q}_d(t)$.

In the context of iterative learning control, the problem is solved by modifying the control input $\mathbf{u}_i(t)$ in each iteration i such that the control input $\mathbf{u}_i(t)$ converges to the desired control input $\mathbf{u}_d(t)$.

3   Generalization of Experience for Multiple Desired Trajectories

An iterative learning controller learns from the error information of the previous iteration. But it learns and then forgets when the tracking is shifted from one desired trajectory to another desired trajectory. A simple iterative learning control algorithm can be represented in series form as

$$\mathbf{u}_{i+1}(t) = \mathbf{u}_0(t) + \sum_{j=0}^{i} \mathbf{g}(\dot{\mathbf{e}}_j(t), \mathbf{e}_j(t)), \forall t \in [0, t_f] \tag{2}$$

Most of the research related to iterative learning control is concentrated on how to design a better function $\mathbf{g}(.)$ to get a faster and smooth convergence of the error to zero.

Our emphasis in this paper is to use the experience of the previous tracking tasks by iterative learning controller to reduce the tracking error to an acceptable level in less number of iterations. In the iterative learning control algorithm, the data of the last iteration or in some cases data of more than one past iterations is used in the construction of the control input for the current iteration. Data about the past iterations is stored in the computer memory. But as the iterations proceed, only the data of one or two past iterations, which are required in constructing the control input, is remembered. The past data of the old iterations, which will not be used in the future iterations, is discarded. This mechanism works well if the task is bounded to a single desired trajectory tracking task. But if the task is to track multiple desired trajectories or the desired trajectory may change over the time, the learning that was acquired in the tracking task of the previous desired trajectory will be lost and for a new desired trajectory, iterative learning control algorithm will start from zero learning.

In our approach, the experience gained by the learning controller in an specific trajectory tracking task is stored in a neural network in the form of its weights and later is used to predict the initial control input for a new trajectory tracking task. The approximation error of the initial control input will be corrected by the iterative learning controller when applied to the system.

The convergence condition quoted by many researchers in the field of iterative learning control is,

$$\|\mathbf{e}_{i+1}\|_\lambda \leq \rho \|\mathbf{e}_i\|_\lambda \quad for\ \rho < 1 \tag{3}$$

To illustrate the effectiveness of our proposed method, the above inequality can be rewritten as,

$$\|\mathbf{e}_{i+1}\|_\lambda \leq \rho^i \|\mathbf{e}_0\|_\lambda \quad for\ \rho < 1 \tag{4}$$

Hence the error at the ith iteration depends on two parameters. One is the selection of the parameter ρ which controls the convergence rate and the other parameter is the initial error $\mathbf{e}_0(t)$. By selecting the initial control input $\mathbf{u}_0(t)$

using the previous experience of the controller, the initial error $\mathbf{e}_0(t)$ will be less and subsequently reduce the error more effectively at the ith iteration. Hence the error at the ith iteration can be improved without modifying the structure of the algorithm. In this way, our method can be extended to all types of iterative learning control algorithms which were proposed for different systems and applications by just selecting an initial control input without modifying the original structure of the learning controller.

3.1   Selection of Initial Control Input

Let the dynamic equation mentioned in equation (1) can be rewritten as,

$$\mathbf{u}(t) = \mu(\mathbf{q}, \dot{\mathbf{q}}, \ddot{\mathbf{q}}) \tag{5}$$

The function $\mu(.)$ given in the above equation can be learnt by the neural network. This function can be very complicated and we do not expect that we can approximate it correctly for all input space. But from some input-output data we assume that we can approximate the function in a compact subset of input space. Neural network model is considered as classes of functions $\mathbf{F}(\mathbf{W}, \mathbf{s})$ in our paper that can approximate the function $\mu(.)$ with certain arbitrary accuracy. Each time when a new desired trajectory has to be tracked, an approximate desired control input $\tilde{\mathbf{u}}_d(t)$ can be generated by the neural network which will then be used as an initial control input $\mathbf{u}_0(t)$ for iterative learning control in a way that the control input $\mathbf{u}_i(t)$ converges to the desired control input $\mathbf{u}_d(t)$ as number of iteration increases.

3.2   NN as a Universal Function Approximator

Neural network are considered as a good candidate for learning the inverse mapping due to their universal function approximation capability with sufficient number of hidden layer neurons. A two-layer neural network is used to approximate the non-linear input-output mapping with some supervised learning (adjustment of weights) from the given training patterns. From real algebra, we know that a function $\tilde{\mathbf{f}}(\mathbf{s})$ approximate the function $\mathbf{f}(\mathbf{s})$ uniformly on $S \subset R^n$ if

$$\left\| \mathbf{f}(\mathbf{s}) - \tilde{\mathbf{f}}(\mathbf{s}) \right\| \leq \varepsilon \qquad \forall \mathbf{s} \in S \tag{6}$$

where ε is an approximation error bound and $\varepsilon > 0$. Where the unknown function

$$\mathbf{f} : S \to T \quad ; \mathbf{s} \in S \subset R^n, \quad T \subset R^m \tag{7}$$

is described by the set of input output data. When approximating with neural network, we assume that

$$\tilde{\mathbf{f}}(\mathbf{s}) = \tilde{\mathbf{F}}(W, \mathbf{s}) \tag{8}$$

will approximate the actual function $\mathbf{f}(\mathbf{s})$ by selecting proper weights W such that the approximation error $\left\|\mathbf{f}(\mathbf{s}) - \widetilde{\mathbf{f}}(\mathbf{s})\right\|$ will be minimized. For a two layer neural network with linear activation function on the output, $\widetilde{f}_k(\mathbf{s})$ will be

$$\widetilde{f}_k(\mathbf{s}) = \sum_{i=1}^{N} c_{ik}\sigma \left(\sum_{j=1}^{n} w_{ij}s_j + \theta_i \right) \tag{9}$$

where c_{ik} and w_{ij} are the weights of the output and hidden layers respectively and $k = 1, 2...., m$. The universal approximation property of neural networks is presented in a theorem by Funahashi [6],

Theorem 1. *Let $\sigma(.)$ be a non-constant, bounded and monotonically increasing function. Let K be a compact subset of R^n and $\mathbf{f}(s_1, s_2, ...s_n)$ be a real valued continuous function on K. Then for arbitrary $\varepsilon > 0$ there exists an integer N and real constants $c_i, \theta_i, i = 1, ..., n, w_{ij}, i = 1, ..., N, j = 1, ..., n$, such that*

$$\widetilde{f}_k(s_1, s_2, ...s_n) = \sum_{i=1}^{N} c_{ik}\sigma \left(\sum_{j=1}^{n} w_{ij}s_j + \theta_i \right) \tag{10}$$

for $k = 1, 2, ...m$ satisfies

$$\max_{\mathbf{s} \in K} \left| \mathbf{f}(s_1, s_2, ...s_n) - \widetilde{\mathbf{f}}(s_1, s_2, ...s_n) \right| < \varepsilon \tag{11}$$

The above approximation property for two layer perceptron neural network can be guaranteed by the selection of the activation function $\sigma(.)$ for the hidden layer. For a set of p training patterns $(\mathbf{s}^l : \mathbf{t}^l)$ for $l = 1, 2, ..., p$, where $\mathbf{s}^l \in S \subset R^n$ and $\mathbf{t}^l \in T \subset R^m$, Itoo and Saito [8] proved that if $\sigma(.)$ is sigmoidal, continuous and non-decreasing function, the neural network can interpolate some unknown data point $\mathbf{s}^d \in S \subset R^n$. Due to the universal function approximation property of the neural networks, it can be used to approximate the nonlinear mapping given in equation (5).

3.3   Modelling of Experience

The training data determines the region of the approximation $S \subset R^n$. For a new desired trajectory, let the set of desired states $(\mathbf{q}_d(t), \dot{\mathbf{q}}_d(t), \ddot{\mathbf{q}}_d(t))$ lies in the state space region S_d. The desired states region S_d should be a subset of S to ensure that the approximation property given in equation (11) holds. If the desired trajectory lies outside the region S, then the neural network may not approximate the inverse mapping very well and the initial control input $\mathbf{u}_0(t)$ generated by the neural network can produce large initial errors by the iterative learning controller in the initial iterations. Experience supervisor keep the record of the state region S of the training patterns of the neural network. Whenever a new desired trajectory is presented for the tracking, the experience supervisor

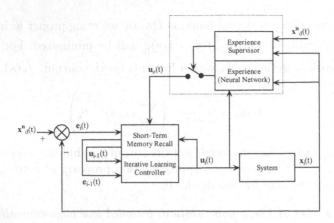

Fig. 1. Intelligent iterative learning controller

checks whether the state region S_d, in which the new desired trajectory lies, is a subset of the region S. If the new desired trajectory lies within the region S of the training pattern, then the experience supervisor let the neural network to approximate the initial control input $\mathbf{u}_0(t)$ for the new desired trajectory and provide this initial control input $\mathbf{u}_0(t)$ to the iterative learning controller. If the state region S_d is not the subset of S, the experience supervisor forces the iterative learning controller to start from the zero knowledge. The purpose of the experience supervisor is to make sure that neural network is always interpolating.

3.4   Convergence Property

The approximation error of the initial control input generated by neural network will be

$$\delta \mathbf{u}_0(t) = \mathbf{u}_d(t) - \mathbf{u}_0(t)$$
$$= \mu(\mathbf{q}_d, \dot{\mathbf{q}}_d, \ddot{\mathbf{q}}_d) - \widetilde{\mu}(\mathbf{q}_d, \dot{\mathbf{q}}_d, \ddot{\mathbf{q}}_d) \tag{12}$$

where $\widetilde{\mu}(\mathbf{q}_d, \dot{\mathbf{q}}_d, \ddot{\mathbf{q}}_d)$ is the approximation of the inverse mapping by neural network and $\mathbf{u}_d(t)$ is the desired control input that can force the system to track the desired trajectory.

Taking norm of both side of equation (12),

$$\|\delta \mathbf{u}_0(t)\| = \|\mathbf{u}_d(t) - \mathbf{u}_0(t)\|$$
$$= \|\mu(\mathbf{q}_d, \dot{\mathbf{q}}_d, \ddot{\mathbf{q}}_d) - \widetilde{\mu}(\mathbf{q}_d, \dot{\mathbf{q}}_d, \ddot{\mathbf{q}}_d)\| \leq \epsilon \tag{13}$$

Hence the approximation error of the initial control input $\mathbf{u}_0(t)$ is bounded. Using this intial control input $\mathbf{u}_0(t)$ and assuming that the system mentioned in equation (1) is stable, the output of the system will also be bounded such that,

$$\|\mathbf{e}_0(t)\| = \|\mathbf{q}_d(t) - \mathbf{q}(t)\| \leq \zeta \tag{14}$$

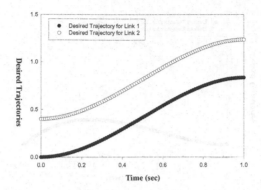

Fig. 2. A set of desired trajectories $TR1$ for the training of the neural network

where ζ is bounded to a small constant. Putting $\|\mathbf{e}_0(t)\|$ in equation (4), we get

$$\|\mathbf{e}_i\|_\lambda \leq \rho^{i-1}\zeta \tag{15}$$

For $\rho < 1$, the error in i^{th} iteration $\|\mathbf{e}_i\|_\lambda$ will decrease to zero as number of iterations i tends to ∞.

4 Numerical Illustration – An Example of Two Link Robot

In this section, we will demonstrate the effectiveness of the proposed method. For this purpose, simulations of a nonlinear model of a two link robot has been done.

The dynamic equation of the system is

$$M(\mathbf{q})\ddot{\mathbf{q}} + N(\mathbf{q}, \dot{\mathbf{q}}) = \tau \tag{16}$$

where

$$N(\mathbf{q}, \dot{\mathbf{q}}) = V(\mathbf{q}, \dot{\mathbf{q}}) + F(\dot{\mathbf{q}}) + G(\mathbf{q}) \tag{17}$$

In the above equation, $M(\mathbf{q})$ is the inertia matrix, $V(\mathbf{q}, \dot{\mathbf{q}})$ is the coriolis/centripetal term, $F(\dot{\mathbf{q}})$ are the friction terms and $G(\mathbf{q})$ is the gravity vector. The control input to the systems is the torque vector τ. For two link robot, the inertia matrix $M(\mathbf{q})$ is

$$M(\mathbf{q}) = \begin{bmatrix} M_{11} & M_{12} \\ M_{21} & M_{22} \end{bmatrix} \tag{18}$$

where

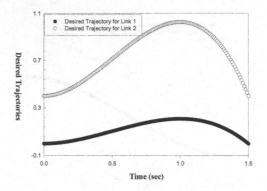

Fig. 3. Another set of desired trajectories $TR2$

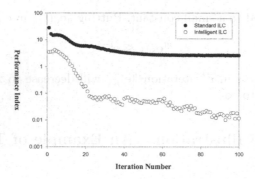

Fig. 4. Performance index J for the desired trajectories $TR2$

$$M_{11} = m_2(l_1^2 + 2l_1l_{c2}\cos q_2 + l_{c2}^2) + m_1l_{c1}^2 + I_1 + I_2$$
$$M_{12} = M_{21} = I_2 + m_2l_{c2}^2 + m_2l_1l_{c2}\cos q_2$$
$$M_{22} = I_2 + m_2l_{c2}^2 \tag{19}$$

m_i, I_i, l_{ci} and l_i are the mass, moment of inertia, length from center of the mass and total length of the link i respectively. The term $V(\mathbf{q}, \dot{\mathbf{q}})$ is

$$V(\mathbf{q}, \dot{\mathbf{q}}) = \begin{bmatrix} -m_2l_1l_{c2}(2\sin q_2 \dot{q}_1 \dot{q}_2 + \sin q_2 \dot{q}_2^2) \\ m_2l_1l_{c2}\sin q_2 \dot{q}_2^2 \end{bmatrix} \tag{20}$$

For simplicity, we ignore the friction term and consider the system as gravity compensated. The parameters of the two link robot are given in Table 1. The sampling period is set to be 0.01 seconds.

Table 1. Parameters of the two link robotic manipulator

Variable Name	Link 1	Link 2
Mass m_i (Kgs)	0.5	0.5
Length l_i (m)	0.5	0.5
Length from Centre of Mass l_{ci} (m)	0.25	0.25
Inertia I_i (Kg-m^2)	0.011	0.011

Performance index J for one iteration is defined as follows to evaluate the performance.

$$J = \int_0^{t_f} \mathbf{e}^2(t)dt = \sum_{j=0}^{N} \left(e_1^2(j) + e_2^2(j) \right) \tag{21}$$

where $\mathbf{e}(t) = \mathbf{q}_d(t) - \mathbf{q}(t)$. A D-type Iterative learning controller is chosen for this numerical illustration and given as,

$$\tau_{i+1}(t) = \tau_i(t) + \mathbf{\Gamma}\dot{\mathbf{e}}_i(t) \tag{22}$$

where $\mathbf{\Gamma}$ is the learning gain vector and is equal to $\begin{bmatrix} 0.01\ 0.01 \end{bmatrix}$ for the smooth error convergence. In this example we have used two layer back propagation neural network for the approximation of the inverse dynamics of the two link robot. Number of hidden layers used are 12 with tangent sigmoid activation function. The activation function for the output layer is a pure linear function. We have used Levenberg-Marquardt algorithm [7] for the batch training of the neural network. This algorithm is ideal for training moderate sized neural networks faster.

Standard D type iterative learning controller is applied to the system and trained the neural network simultaneously on the data received from the system for 100 iterations for the desired trajectories $TR1$ for the joint angles of the two link robot manipulator shown in Figure 2. After training the neural network with this desired trajectory, we have applied the proposed intelligent controller with experience stored in its neural network to a different set of desired trajectories $TR2$ for the joint angles of the two links as shown in Figure 3. This set of trajectories are very different from the original trajectories on which neural network is trained in not only shape but also amplitude and time scale. The performance index J is plotted in Figure 4 for the standard D type iterative learning controller without experience mentioned in equation (22) and our proposed method (D type iterative learning control with experience) on logarithmic scale. It can be observed from the profile of both performance indices that incorporation of experience in learning controller has improved the performance of the controller considerably than standard D type iterative learning controller.

5 Conclusions

In this paper, we have proposed a new method of incorporating the experience of the iterative learning controller about the tracking of previous trajectories in the tracking task of some new desired trajectory. Experience of the iterative learning controller is stored in a two layer back propagation neural network. Neural network learns the inverse dynamics of the system in the neighborhood of the trajectories that the iterative learning controller has tracked successfully in the past. For a new desired trajectory, the experience of iterative learning controller is used to predict a better initial control input for the iterative learning controller and hence the tracking error converges to an acceptable level in less number of iterations.

Our proposed method does not effect the convergence rate but it reduces the initial error bound. Hence, starting with less initial error bound, the error bound in each succeeding iteration will reduce for a certain convergence rate determined by the learning gains. In this way, it is possible to get better performance without sacrificing the simplicity of the iterative learning control schemes. The selection of the initial input is independent of the structure of the controller, therefore this method is very general for all class of the iterative learning control schemes. Numerical illustrations have shown the effectiveness of the proposed method.

References

1. Arif M., T. Ishihara and H. Inooka (2001). Incorporation of Experience in Iterative Learning Controllers using Locally Weighted Learning, Automatica, Vol **37(6)**, pp. 881-888.
2. Arimoto S., S. Kawamura and F. Miyazaki (1984). Bettering operation of robots by learning, J. Robotic Systems, Vol. **1(2)**, pp.123-140.
3. Bien Z., D.H. Hwang and S.R. Oh (1991). A nonlinear iterative learning method for robot path control. Robotica, Vol. **9**, pp. 387-392.
4. Chow W. S. T. and Y. Fang (1998), A recurrent neural network based real time learning control strategy applying to nonlinear systems with unknown dynamics, IEEE Trans. on IE, Vol. **45(1)**, pp. 151 - 161.
5. Fu J. and N.K. Sinha (1993). An iterative learning scheme for motion control of robots using neural networks: A case study, Journal of Intelligent and Robotic Systems, Vol. **8**, pp. 375 - 398.
6. Funahashi, K.I. (1989), On the approximation realization of continuous mappings by neural networks, Neural Networks, Vol. **2**, pp. 183-192.
7. Hagan M. T. and M. Menhaj (1994). Training feedforward networks with the Marquardt algorithm. IEEE trans. on Neural Networks, Vol. **5(6)**, pp. 989 - 993.
8. Itoo Y. and K. Saito (1996). Superposition of linearly independent functions and finite mappings by neural networks, Math. Scient. Vol. **21**, pp. 27 - 33.
9. Oh S. R., Z. Bien and I.H. Suh (1988). An iterative learning control method with application for the robot manipulator, IEEE J. of Robotics and Automation, pp. 508-514.

Learning Topological Maps from Sequential Observation and Action Data under Partially Observable Environment

Takehisa Yairi, Masahito Togami, and Koichi Hori

Research Center for Advanced Science and Technology, University of Tokyo
4-6-1 Komaba, Meguro-ku, Tokyo 153-8904, Japan
{yairi, togami, hori}@ai.rcast.u-tokyo.ac.jp

Abstract. A *map* is an abstract internal representation of an environment for a mobile robot, and how to learn it autonomously is one of the most fundamental issues in the research fields of intelligent robotics and artificial intelligence. In this paper, we propose a *topological* map learning method for mobile robots which constructs a *POMDP*-based discrete state transition model from time-series data of observations and actions. The main point of this method is to find a set of states or nodes of the map gradually so that it minimizes the three types of entropies or uncertainties of the map about "what observations are obtained","what actions are available" and "what state transitions are expected". It is shown that the topological structure of the state transition model is effectively obtained by this method.

1 Introduction

Map learning problem of autonomous mobile robots has attracted a number of researchers in the two fields of robotics and artificial intelligence for many years.

From the former viewpoint, *metric* map construction methods such as occupancy grid map[6] and object location map[9] have been mainly studied. The main purpose of the metric maps is to capture the quantitatively accurate features of the environment geometry. Therefore, it requires a lot of *a priori* knowledge such as a quantitative computation model to estimate the geometric features from the robots' sensor inputs.

On the other hand, from the viewpoint of artificial intelligence, *topological* map construction methods have been actively studied [5,4,3,8,11]. A topological map is represented as a graph structure, where the *nodes* correspond to some *characteristic* or *distinctive* places the robot visited, and the *arcs* correspond to the travel paths or motor behaviors connecting the places. Topological map learning is important for artificial intelligence research because it is closely related to the issue of *abstraction* or internal representation acquisition based on the interaction between the robots' sensorimotor system and the environment.

A remarkable trend in the recent topological map research is the use of the representation based on the probabilistic state transition models such as Hidden Markov Model (HMM)[10] and Partially Observed Markov Decision Process

M. Ishizuka and A. Sattar (Eds.): PRICAI 2002, LNAI 2417, pp. 305–314, 2002.

(POMDP)[11]. In this approach, the sequence data of the robot's observation and action is used to estimate the parameters of those probabilistic models by EM algorithm. Though these methods are general and theoretically grounded, the computational cost of them is considered to be very high. Furthermore, the effectiveness of estimating the *structure* of the model is unclear, especially in the practical situation where the robot has a number of sensors and actions.

In this paper, we propose an alternative approach to the topological map learning problem. This method also employs a POMDP-based state transition model for the map representation. However, the emphasis of this method is not on estimating the parameters which maximize the likelihood unlike EM algorithm, but on learning the structure of the map model effectively by locally maximizing three kinds of information (or minus entropies) about "what observations are obtained","what actions are available" and "what state transitions are expected". Specifically, it obtains an initial set of states (or nodes in the map) by applying a distance-based clustering to the whole set of instantaneous observation vectors at first. Then it repeatedly and selectively divides compound states into two so that it locally minimizes the uncertainty or entropy of the state transition probability distribution.

In the next section, we formalize the topological map learning problem more strictly. Then we describe the detail of the proposed method in section 2, and show some simulation results in section 4.

2   Problem Definition

2.1   Observation Data and Map Model

First, we assume a robot is given a series of observation and action data D:

$$D = \{o_1, u_1, o_2, u_2, \cdots, o_t, u_t, \cdots, o_T, u_T\}$$

where,

- o_t is an observation vector obtained from the robot's sensors at time t. o_t is a point in a continuous and multi-dimensional observation space $\mathcal{O}$.
- u_t is an action executed by the robot at time t. u_t takes a value in a predefined action set $\mathcal{A} = \{a_1, a_2, \cdots, a_{n_a}\}$.

We make a POMDP assumption on this data, where the robot's *hidden* state at time t is denoted by x_t. Under this assumption, o_t and u_t depend only on x_t, and x_{t+1} depends only on x_t and u_t.

Next, we consider a topological map model M is composed of 3 elements - $\mathcal{Q}$, $\boldsymbol{P}_M(o_t|x_t)$, $\boldsymbol{P}_M(x_{t+1}|x_t, u_t)$, where,

- $\mathcal{Q} = \{q_1, q_2, \cdots, q_{n_q}\}$ is a set of discrete states the robot can occupy. Each state q_i corresponds to a node in the graph.
- $\boldsymbol{P}_M(o_t|x_t)$ is a conditional probability distribution model of observation at time t o_t given $x_t = q_i$ $(i = 1, 2, \cdots, n_q)$.

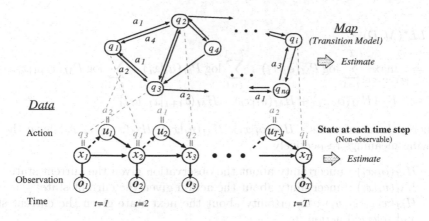

Fig. 1. Relationship among data, states and map model

- $\boldsymbol{P}_M(x_{t+1}|x_t, u_t)$ is a conditional probability distribution model of state at time $t+1$ x_{t+1} given $x_t = q_i$ $(i = 1, 2, \cdots, n_q)$ and $u_t = a_j$ $(j = 1, 2, \cdots, n_a)$.

Fig.1 illustrates the relationship among the map model M, data D and a time sequence of states $\{x_t\}$.

Now, the topological map learning problem can be defined as estimating the model M when the data D is given. If Q were completely defined and $\{x_t\}$ were given beforehand, this estimation problem would be relatively easy. The difficulty is in that neither of them is given in advance. That is to say, it is required not only to estimate the parameters of $\boldsymbol{P}_M(o_t|x_t)$ and $\boldsymbol{P}_M(x_{t+1}|x_t, u_t)$, but also to define the state set Q and estimate the value at each time $\{x_t\}$. In a sense, the map learning problem considered here is a kind of *unsupervised classification* or clustering problem.

2.2 Model Likelihood and Entropies as Criteria

A most reasonable evaluation criterion for estimated M and $\{x_t\}$ is the *likelihood* of the model M given the data D, which can be written as:

$$L(M|D) = P(D|M) = P_M(\boldsymbol{o}_1, \cdots, \boldsymbol{o}_T, u_1, \cdots, u_{T-1})$$

$$= \sum_{[x_1, \cdots, x_T]} \{\prod_{t=1}^{T} P_M(\boldsymbol{o}_t|x_t) \cdot \prod_{t=1}^{T-1} P_M(u_t|x_t) \cdot \prod_{t=1}^{T-1} P_M(x_{t+1}|x_t, u_t)\} \tag{1}$$

While [10] and [11] have proposed methods of estimating the model M which locally maximizes this criterion by EM algorithm, we consider that replacing the operator $\sum_{[x_1, \cdots, x_T]}$ in Eq.1 with $\max_{[x_1, \cdots, x_T]}$ is more suitable because it prefers to a model which crisply assigns the robot's state at each time to a place in the map. Transforming the equation based on this idea and taking the logarithm of it leads to:

$LL^*(M|D)$

$$= \max_{[x_1,\cdots,x_T]} \sum_{t=1}^{T} \log P_M(o_t|x_t) + \sum_{t=1}^{T-1} \log P_M(u_t|x_t) + \sum_{t=1}^{T-1} \log P_M(x_{t+1}|x_t, u_t)$$

$$\approx -T \cdot \{H_M(o_t|x_t) + H_M(u_t|x_t) + H_M(x_{t+1}|x_t, u_t)\} \qquad (2)$$

where, three entropies - $H_M(o_t|x_t)$, $H_M(u_t|x_t)$, $H_M(x_{t+1}|x_t, u_t)$ have the following meanings respectively.

- $H_M(o_t|x_t)$: uncertainty about the observation given the current state.
- $H_M(u_t|x_t)$: uncertainty about the action given the current state.
- $H_M(x_{t+1}|x_t, u_t)$: uncertainty about the next state given the current state and selected action.

It implies that finding a map model maximizing the value of equation 2 can be regarded as learning the map most *informative* about (a) "what observation is to be obtained", (b) "which action is to be selected" and (c) "what state transition is to be expected" at each time step. This information theoretic interpretation of the map criterion is reasonable from the viewpoint of our general notion of *maps*.

2.3 Globally Distinctive States

If none of the elements of the state set $\mathcal{Q}$ is given beforehand, the robot must define them all by itself. Though this problem setting is interesting, it is more natural to assume that there are several *distinguishable predefined* states in the environment depending on the tasks and goals of the robot.

In this paper, we call such special places or states *globally distinctive states* (GDS). While the notion of GDS is similar to those of *distinctive places*[4] and *significant points*[11], GDS is meant to emphasize that those states are uniquely distinguishable in the environment. Introducing GDS, our problem assumption previously described is slightly modified. Some elements of the state set $\mathcal{Q}$ are defined in advance, and the state sequence $\{x_t\}$ is *partially* labeled by them.

An important feature of GDS is that they are *fixed* nodes in the topological map and have the effects of "boundary conditions" in deciding other states. In other words, GDS is similar to *reward* in the framework of reinforcement learning.

3 Proposed Method

3.1 Overview

Our method divides the topological map construction problem defined in the previous section into two phases as below:

1. Discretization of observation space and construction of initial state set by distance-based clustering of observation vectors.

2. Repeated state splitting and structure updates based on the similarity of the state transition probability distribution.

Fig.2 illustrates the whole process. It is important that these two phases locally and greedily minimize $H_M(o_t|x_t)$ and $H_M(u_t|x_t) + H_M(x_{t+1}|x_t, u_t)$ in Eq.2 respectively. In the rest of this section, we describe these procedures in detail.

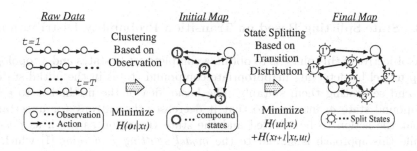

Fig. 2. Outline of proposed method

3.2 Discretization of Observation Space by Distance-Based Clustering

The objective of this phase is to construct an initial map model by disretizing the multi-dimensional continuous observation space $\mathcal{O}$ into a finite set of symbols. The detail of the procedure is described as follows:

1. Pick up all observation vectors $\{o_t\}$ from D except ones labeled with GDS.
2. Apply *K-means* algorithm to the set above, and divide it into a specified number n_s of subsets or clusters.
3. Assign a *symbol* to each of the clusters, and discretize the observation space $\mathcal{O}$ into a finite set of symbols $\mathcal{S} = \{s_1, s_2, \cdots, s_{n_s}\}$.
4. Generate a set of states whose element corresponds to each symbol, and define an initial state set $\mathcal{Q}_0$ by merging it with the set of GDS.
5. Classify all unlabeled elements of $\{x_t\}$ to a state in $\mathcal{Q}_0$ based on o_t.
6. Estimate the values of parameters $\boldsymbol{P}_M(o_t|x_t)$ and $\boldsymbol{P}_M(x_{t+1}|x_t, u_t)$.

As is well known, *K-means* algorithm is a clustering method which locally minimizes *distortion* or *quantization error* on the data. In the special case where the probability densities of all the clusters are multivariate Gaussians with identity covariance matrices, it is equivalent to locally minimizing the *partition loss*[2]. Roughly speaking, it means that this clustering process generates a set of states which locally minimizes $H_M(o_t|x_t)$ in Eq.2.

Currently we are using the ordinary Euclid norm as a distance measure in $\mathcal{O}$. In case it is not appropriate, other distance measures should be used instead. In addition, we must specify the number of clusters n_s beforehand in this algorithm. However, this limitation will be relieved by incorporating some information criteria such as *Bayesian Information Criterion* (BIC)[7].

The initial map obtained in this phase is expected to be *incomplete*, because it defines the set of states $\mathcal{Q}_0$ considering only the instantaneous observation inputs $\{o_t\}$. As a result, it is possible that several different real states are mapped into one compound state in $\mathcal{Q}_0$. This issue is known as *perceptual aliasing*.

3.3   State Splitting Based on Transition Probability Distribution

The objective of this phase is to obtain a complete set of states and a topological map model by detecting inappropriate compound states in the initial state set $\mathcal{Q}_0$ and separating them suitably. The basic idea of the method is to split a compound state q_i into two so that it decreases the entropy (or uncertainty) about the action to be selected and the state transition as much as possible. While this approach is similar to the *model splitting / merging* [1] which is a learning method of *hidden Markov model* (HMM) structures, our method requires more complicated processes because it deals with POMDP model structures and takes actions u_{t-1}, u_t into account necessarily. Specifically, it consists of two major steps. One is the *grouping* by the values of x_{t-1} and u_{t-1}. The other is *merging* based on the similarity of the distribution of u_t and x_{t+1}. Fig.3 illustrates these two steps.

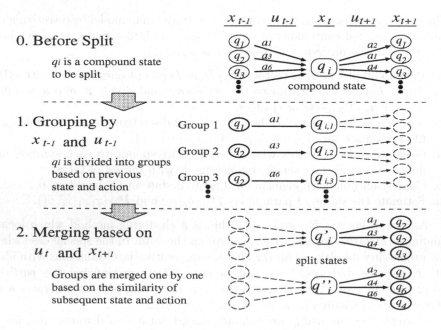

Fig. 3. Procedure of state splitting

To describe the algorithm, we define several notions:

- ι_t is a *transition instance* at time t, which denotes a two-step state transition subsequence $(x_{t-1}, u_{t-1}, x_t, u_t, x_{t+1})$ in D.
- $\mathcal{I}$ is a set of transition instances, and $|\mathcal{I}|$ denotes the number of elements.
- $H_{\mathcal{I}}(u_t) = -\sum_{k=1}^{n_a} p_{\mathcal{I}}(u_t = a_k) \log p_{\mathcal{I}}(u_t = a_k)$ is the entropy of u_t in $\mathcal{I}$.
- $H_{\mathcal{I}}(x_{t+1}|u_t) = -\sum_{k,j} p_{\mathcal{I}}(x_{t+1} = q_j, u_t = a_k) \log p_{\mathcal{I}}(x_{t+1} = q_j | u_t = a_k)$ is the average entropy of x_{t+1} given u_t in $\mathcal{I}$.
- $\mathcal{H}(\mathcal{I})$ denotes the sum of $H_{\mathcal{I}}(u_t)$ and $H_{\mathcal{I}}(x_{t+1}|u_t)$ for a set of instances.

Now the state splitting algorithm for a state q_i can be described as below:

1. Pick up all transition instances whose state at time t (x_t) is q_i, and form a instance set $\mathcal{I}_i$ ($= \{\iota_t | x_t = q_i\}$). Compute and store the value of $\mathcal{H}(\mathcal{I}_i)$.
2. Divide the set $\mathcal{I}_i$ into groups or subsets according to the values of x_{t-1} and u_{t-1}. For example, $\mathcal{I}_{i,j,k}$ is a subset of instances whose x_{t-1} is q_j and u_{t-1} is a_k respectively, i.e., $\mathcal{I}_{i,j,k} = \{\iota_t | \iota_t \in \mathcal{I}_i . x_{t-1} = q_j, u_{t-1} = a_k\}$. For each subset $\mathcal{I}_{i,j,k} (j = 1, \cdots, k = 1, \cdots)$, compute the values of $\mathcal{H}(\mathcal{I}_{i,j,k})$.
3. Repeat merging the subsets one by one in a bottom-up way so that it increases the value of $\mathcal{H}(\mathcal{I}_{i,j,k})$ as little as possible, until the number of subsets reaches two. Define the x_t values of the two subsets as split states q_i', q_i''.
4. Compute the *entropy gain* of this splitting $Gain(q_i)$, which is, $Gain(q_i) = \mathcal{H}(\mathcal{I}_i) - (\frac{|\mathcal{I}'|}{|\mathcal{I}|} \mathcal{H}(\mathcal{I}_i') + \frac{|\mathcal{I}''|}{|\mathcal{I}|} \mathcal{H}(\mathcal{I}_i''))$

In practice, this state splitting is tested on each state $q_i (i = 1, \cdots, n_q)$ and the one with largest *entropy gain* is employed at one time. Along with updating the contents of $\mathcal{Q}$, this splitting process is repeated until the number of states reaches a specified number.

It is almost obvious that this series of state splittings locally minimizes the sum of $H_M(u_t|x_t)$ and $H_M(x_{t+1}|x_t, u_t)$ in equation 2. In addition, it should be noted that this state splitting *never* increase (or worsen) the value of $H_M(o_t|x_t)$, which was locally minimized in the previous phase.

4   Simulation

4.1   Assumed Environment and Robot

In this simulation, we assume an *indoor* environment containing a lot of objects (Fig.4 left). There are 25 objects of 15 types, such as "blue desk", "red wall".

We assume the robot has a panoramic camera for observation and wheels for transportation. The robot processes the image by template matching based on shape and color, and obtains the sizes of the 15 types of objects. Therefore the dimension of the observation vector is **15**. The influences of noise and occlusion are also taken into account. As to the action set, two categories of actions are available. An action in the fist category is "approaching a *xxx* object", where *xxx* is any of the 15 types of objects mentioned above. The other category of contains two actions of "following left / right wall". Therefore, the total number

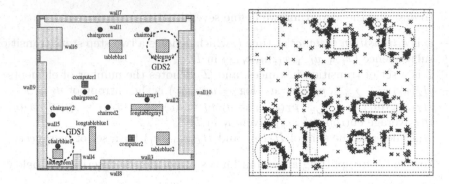

Fig. 4. Simulation environment(left) and all observation points(right)

of actions becomes **17**. Each action is stopped when the robot approaches an object within a certain distance or changes its direction by more than 90 degrees.

In this environment, two globally distinctive states(GDS) are set (dashed circles in Fig.4 left). It is assumed that the robot can distinguish either of the two GDS when it reaches there.

The robot explores this environment by selecting an action randomly among the executable ones at each place, and obtaining observation vector there (Fig.4 right). The number of observation points is **2000** ($T = 2000$).

4.2 Clustering of Observation Vectors

First, we obtained an initial state set Q_0 by clustering the set of observations $\{o_t\}$ based on the method in 3.2. The number of states in Q_0 was set to **20**.

In this environment, different places present a similar observation to the robot, because there are more than one objects with the same object type (i.e., 25 objects for 15 types). That is to say, the robot is subject to *perceptual aliasing*. As a result, there are a lot of compound states in Q_0 which contain observation vectors obtained in different places.

Fig.5 shows *State 11* which is an example of the compound states. The left figure shows the real locations of the observation points classified into this state. The right figure shows the transition probability distribution $P(x_{t+1}|x_t = state11, u_t)$ for each action in this state. We can see that diversity or entropy of this state about the selected action (u_t) and the next state (x_{t+1}) is high.

4.3 State Splitting

Next we applied the state splitting method in 3.3 to the initial state set Q_0 repeatedly until the number of states becomes *30*.

As a result, most of the compound states are detected and split into right pieces. For example, Fig.6 illustrates two split states (*State 11' and 20*). It is shown that they have different transition probability distributions (Fig.6 right).

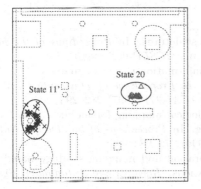

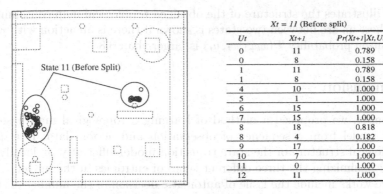

$X_t = 11$ (Before split)		
U_t	X_{t+1}	$Pr(X_{t+1}|X_t, U_t)$
0	11	0.789
0	8	0.158
1	11	0.789
1	8	0.158
4	10	1.000
5	1	1.000
6	15	1.000
7	15	1.000
8	18	0.818
8	4	0.182
9	17	1.000
10	7	1.000
11	0	1.000
12	11	1.000

Fig. 5. Initial *State 11* after observation-based clustering (left) and state transition probability distribution (right)

$X_t = 11'$ (After split)		
U_t	X_{t+1}	$Pr(X_{t+1}|X_t, U_t)$
0	11	0.882
1	11	0.937
6	15	1.000
7	15	1.000
8	18	0.818
9	17	1.000
11	0	1.000
12	11	1.000

$X_t = 20$ (New state)		
U_t	X_{t+1}	$Pr(X_{t+1}|X_t, U_t)$
0	8	1.000
1	8	1.000
4	10	1.000
5	1	1.000
10	7	1.000

Fig. 6. Split states (11' and 20) (left) and state transition probability distributions (right)

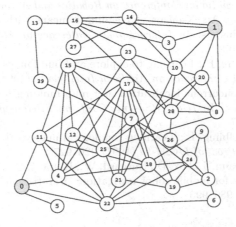

Fig. 7. Obtained topological map after state splitting (actions are omitted)

Fig.7 illustrates the structure of the obtained topological map containing 30 states, where an arc between two states is shown if there is an action with which the transition probability $P(x_{t+1}|x_t, u_t)$ is larger than 0.8.

5   Conclusion

In this paper, we proposed a method of learning a topological map based on POMDP model from a sequence of observation and action data. It acquires the topological structure of the state transition model efficiently by locally and gradually minimizing the three different types of entropies in the model.

Future works include the issue of automatic decision of the number of states in the two phases, quantitative comparison with the conventional methods especially with the *EM algorithm* approaches[10,11].

References

1. Brants, T.: Estimating markov model structures. In *Proceedings of the Fourth Conference on Spoken Language Processing (ICSLP-96)* (1996)
2. Kearns, M., Mansour, Y., Ng, A.: An information-theoretic analysis of hard and soft assignment methods for clustering. In *Proceedings of Thirteenth Conference on Uncertainty in Artificial Intelligence (UAI-97)* (1997) 282–293
3. Kortenkamp, D., Weymouth, T.: Topological mapping for mobile robots using a combination of sonar and vision sensing. In *Proceedings of the Twelfth National Conference on Artificial Intelligence* (1994) 979–984
4. Kuipers, B., Byun, Y.: A robot exploration and mapping strategy based on a semantic hierarchy of spatial representations. *Robotics and Autonomous Systems* Vol.8 (1991) 47–63.
5. Mataric, M.: Integration of representation into goal-driven behavior-based robots. *IEEE Transactions on Robotics and Automation*, Vol.8 No.3 (1992) 304–312,
6. Moravec, P., Elfes, A.: High resolution maps from wide angle sonar. In *Proceedings of the IEEE International Conference on Robotics and Automation* (1985) 116–121
7. Pelleg, D., Moore, A.: X-means: Extending k-means with efficient estimation of the number of clusters. In *International Conference on Machine Learning, 2000 (ICML2000)* (2000)
8. Pierce, D., Kuipers, B.: Learning to explore and build maps. In *Proceedings of the Twelfth National Conference on Artificial Intelligence* (1994) 1264–1271
9. Rencken, W: Concurrent localization and map building for mobile robots using ultrasonic sensors. In *IEEE/RSJ Int. Conf. on Intelligent Robots and Systems* (1993) 2192–2197
10. Shatkay, H., Kaelbling, L.: Learning topological maps with weak local odometric information. In *Proc. of IJCAI-97* (1997) 920–927
11. Thrun, S., Gutmann, J., Fox, D., Burgard, W., Kuipers, B.: Integrating topological and metric maps for mobile robot navigation: A statistical approach. In *Proc. of AAAI-98* (1998) 989–995

A Saliency Map Model for Active Perception Using Color Information and Local Competitive Mechanism

Kyungjoo Cheoi and Yillbyung Lee

Dept. of Computer Science, Yonsei University,
134 Sinchon-Dong, Seodaemun-Gu, Seoul, 120-749, Korea
{kjcheoi,yblee}@csai.yonsei.ac.kr

Abstract. We present a biologically motivated saliency map model for active perception, and its applications to locate candidate regions of interest on various real images for further high-level analysis. The model is based on the idea that an image is memorized and recognized by the way of consecutive fixations of moving eyes on the most informative image fragments. The model suggested herein guides selecting the most informative regions of an image purely based on the properties of the input image. In order to evaluate the performance of our model, we first simulated it on various color images of natural environment, then, performed psychological human test with the same test image which were inputted to the model, and finally compared the two results to verify whether the output of the model is right. Experimental results were shown and they indicate the practicality and the promise of the model in complicated vision applications.

1 Introduction

Current methods in image analysis are rather inefficient. Even if very effective technologies were developed for early visual processing in computer vision, some more high-level process such as feature binding and object recognition based on these extracted early visual features needs some a-priori knowledge about the objects. Because of this reason, it is very hard to extend the system to other applications. In addition, there are still more problems such as limited capability to scale up with the images, and the computational complexity problem, which give much trouble to apply the system to actual computer vision problem.

Active perception seeks regions of interest in an image in order to reduce the computational complexity associated with time-consuming process. It is desirable from an engineering point of view to achieve good performances with limited resources. An early reference to active perception is the work done by Bajcsy [1] who addressed active perception as a selective and task-oriented gathering of information.

From these backgrounds, we describe here a saliency map model for active perception based on the primate's bottom-up selective visual attention mechanism, and which requires no a-priori knowledge. The idea in selective attention is that just analyzing only the part of the image in detail not all parts is sufficient enough for us to

M. Ishizuka and A. Sattar (Eds.): PRICAI 2002, LNAI 2417, pp. 315–324, 2002.
© Springer-Verlag Berlin Heidelberg 2002

recognize and analyze the image more quickly with using less computational resources.

In engineering, visual attention mechanism can be very efficiently applied to the problems of background/foreground separation, object recognition, and etc., but is not utilized enough yet. Most computer vision systems employ filtering techniques in order to reduce computational complexity. And they provide basic standard form-invariant object representations such as multi-resolution representation formed within pyramid, or space-variant representation which were modeled after non-uniform sampling technique of retina. Applied filter based on such above two representations could be the low-pass or band-pass filter, however cannot be used as a generalized visual attention mechanism in a computer vision system because of its insufficient ability of finding interest regions in a given image.

Visual attention has become the topic of much interest and has long been studied by researchers in psychology [2,10,11,12] as well as in computer vision [3,5,6,8,9].

A widely accepted computational model of human attention is based on the "spotlight" metaphor. The main idea of this model is that visual processing would rather occur in two ways, a pre-attentive unlimited-capacity stage where basic features of each location in the scene are subjected to local mismatch detection, followed by an attentive limited-capacity stage that combines and integrates the different basic features to produce 'whole' percepts of the attended items [10]. The "Guided Search" [12] is one of these spotlight models, which tried to explain the principle of the determination of the scanning sequence of the image. A variation of the spotlight metaphor, called the attentional beam, has been developed by Tsotsos [11]. It is based on a hierarchical information representation where a serial light on the top is passed downwards in the hierarchy to all processing units that contribute to the attended unit. Neighboring units are inhibited, and the information in the 'beam' part of the hierarchy is reprocessed without the interference from the neighbors. The beam is then used to inhibit the processing elements and a new beam is chosen. Eriksen and St. James [4] extended the concept of a spotlight by proposing an analogy of a zoom-lens or variable magnification system. A low power setting of the lens would correspond to a wide field, where attentional resources would be evenly distributed. A higher setting would result in a more restricted field of view but would also increase the concentration of resources in that field. This kind of model which is based on the 'zoom-lens' metaphor, were founded on the assumption that visual processing would always be performed in parallel, either over the entire field of view, or in a more restricted area. However, this model also implies a trade-off. If the visual scene is attended to at large, it is done with relatively low resolution of detail, and similarly, if it is attended to in detail, it is done with relatively high resolution of detail. Thus the problem is to allocate the resources properly.

Some biologically plausible systems for computer vision have also been proposed, which can be applied to synthetic images, or other simple images containing alphabetical characters [3,9]. In most of these systems, the selection of "locations" of interest is based on simple features, such as intensity and edges and hard to be extended to apply the system to complex natural color images. Another model which Milanese and his colleague proposed, extracts regions of interest by integrating bottom-up and top-down cues [8], and has been tested with some real images. In their model, bottom-up cues are obtained by decomposing the image into a number of feature and conspicuity maps, while top-down cues are obtained from a-priori knowledge about the targets. Bottom-up and top-down cues are then combined through a non-linear relaxation technique using energy minimization-like procedures. Although they tried to test their system with some real images, the model yielded rare examples that can be applied to natural color images, and very slow convergence of the relaxation algorithm caused the speed of the overall working of the system slowed down.

As seen, most of the attention systems in computer vision reviewed here are not general purpose enough, and has not been widely applied to real actual problem of visual world yet. And the models in psychology do put too much emphasis on the theoretical aspects of human visual attention. Therefore it is inadequate to apply the model to complicated vision applications.

The focus of the model presented in this paper is in expanding the capabilities of previous models by extracting and integrating more complex information, and in simulating our model with lots of complex real images. The location of the attention region resulted from our model can be used to change the gaze of a non-uniform sensor, and it implies that our model would be widely used to complicated vision applications including active perception tasks.

In Section 2 we will describe overall architecture of our model, and detailed components of the model will be described in Section 3 and 4. In Section 5 we will present our experiments and some examples of the results on various color images of natural environment, and its comparison with those of human attention. Some discussion and conclusion will be made in Section 6.

2   The Saliency Map Model

The block diagram of the model is given in Fig. 1. It is composed of two main levels, feature extraction level and combination level.

In feature extraction level, the raw image is initially decomposed into multiple independent retinotopic feature maps. Each map represents the value of a certain attribute computed on a set of low-level features. Here, two chromatic feature maps and one achromatic feature map are generated based on the fundamental color perception mechanism of human visual system.

In Feature combination level, all feature maps are combined into one single saliency map. In this level, computed feature maps are first converted into corresponding number of importance map by the bank of difference of oriented Gaussian filter which simulates lateral inhibition schemes, in order to extract the measure of "perceptual importance" of pixels in each of the feature map and also to detect orientation. Thereafter, iterative non-linear mechanism using local competition and statistical information of pixels in importance map is ran on all of the importance maps. And at last, the computed result maps are just simply summed to generate single saliency map.

In Section 3 and 4, more detailed processing of these two levels will be described.

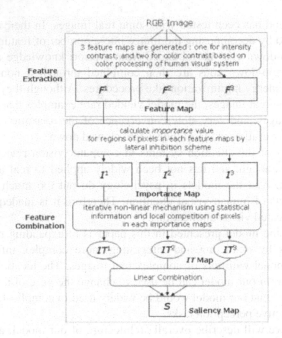

Fig. 1. The Block Diagram of the Model

3 Feature Extraction

In the first step of the model, several visual features known to influence human visual attention are first extracted from the input image, and a set of features are then evaluated for each feature and represented into a set of topographic feature maps. Here, two kinds of feature maps are generated : one for achromatic feature map representing intensity contrast and two for chromatic feature maps representing color contrast. In addition, generated multiple three independent feature maps are normalized in the range [0,1] in order to eliminate across-modality differences due to dissimilar feature extraction mechanisms, and to simplify the map for the further processing.

3.1 Color Processing in Human Visual System

In human retina, there are two types of photoreceptors, rods and cones. They respond differently to light, having different sensitivities to wavelengths. Especially cones are associated to color vision, whereas rods are associated to vision in darkness.

Human display his capability of color perception basically by the collective responses of three types of cones(R,G,B) in the normal trichromat's retina, each of which contains a different light-absorbing pigment. These three cone types often called "red", "green", and "blue" cones, however is not right. Because, each of cone's maximal responses at wavelengths of light is not matched to the corresponding pure hue. Any way, human visual system can discriminate different wavelengths of lights, because of their overlapped and collected responses. The color information gathered by these cones is then processed by the retinal ganglion cell, and is then routed through the lateral geniculate nucleus(LGN) to the visual cortex. The neural circuits that convey color information to the visual cortex, convert the information of three types of cones into 'red/green', and 'yellow/blue'.

In primary visual cortex(V1), it appears that there are three types of cells with center-surround receptive fields, homogeneous receptive fields, and more complex receptive fields which were the combination of above mentioned two types. The cells with center-surround receptive fields respond very strongly when the center and the surround of their receptive fields receives stimuli of different wavelength, whereas the cells with homogeneous receptive fields respond the highest when both the center and the surround receive the same stimuli of a specific wavelength. This means that the cells with homogeneous receptive fields are not spatially selective but respond very strongly to color contrast.

From these backgrounds, we selected three features (1) intensity, (2) red minus green, and (3) blue minus yellow. Intensity information was used to generate achromatic feature map, and the two types of color-opponency filter exhibited by the cells with homogeneous receptive fields in visual cortex were used to generate two chromatic feature maps.

3.2 The Feature Maps

Intensity image plays an important role in detecting interesting objects, and actually represents the unique feature map for the extraction of regions of interest. To generate one achromatic feature map F^1, red, green and blue components of the original input color image are first extracted as R, G, B. Then an intensity image I is obtained as $(R+G+B)/3$, and this becomes an achromatic feature map F^1.

To generate two chromatic feature maps F^2 and F^3, broadly tuned color channels are first extracted as r, g, b, and y by $r=R-(G+B)/2$, $g=G-(R+B)/2$, $b=B-(R+G)/2$, $y=R+G-2(|R-G|+2)$. Each of which indicates red, green, blue, and yellow channel respectively, and each yields maximal response for corresponding pure hue. And then, F^2 is computed to account for red/green color-opponency by $F^2= r - g$ and F^3 for blue/yellow color-opponency by $F^3= b - y$.

4 Feature Combination

4.1 The Need for the Saliency Map

In order to obtain a single representation which could be the basis of detecting attention regions, multiple feature maps must be merged into a unique saliency map. The idea of "saliency map" which is an explicit two-dimensional map that encodes the saliency of objects in the visual environment was introduced by Koch and Ullman [7]. Since feature maps were derived from different visual modalities, combining these maps into one single map is not a trivial work. Previously, this could be done by weighted summation of all information in the maps [5,12]. However, in this case the performance of the model would highly rely on the appropriate choice of the weight. In what follows, we will describe our simple combining method that promoting those maps where a small number of meaningful high activity areas are present while suppressing others, using local competition relations and statistical information of pixels in pre-computed maps(Fig. 2).

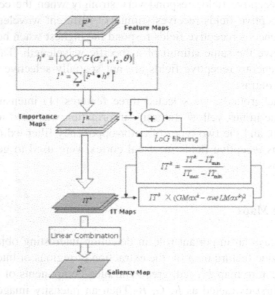

Fig. 2. Combination process of multiple feature maps into a saliency map(see text below)

4.2   Combination Process

The saliency map has been generated through following four steps.

First Step. Three feature maps F^k(where k=1,2,3), which were computed in Section 3 are inputted. Since each feature map has the special meaning at every locations of original input image, we first assigned measure of interest to each of the feature maps, i.e. generated three importance maps I^k. We used a kind of ON-center, OFF-surround operator which is based on the $DOOrG$(Difference-Of-Oriented-Gaussians) model [8]. The $DOOrG$ model is the difference of two oriented Gaussians of different sizes with the width of positive Gaussian being smaller than the width of the negative one. The two Gaussians may have an elliptic shape characterized by different width of the two Gaussians while the DoG(Difference-of-Gaussian) model has isotropic shape of Gaussians. The *DOOrG* model is defined as Eq. 1, where $G(\cdot,\cdot,\cdot)$ denotes 2-D oriented Gaussian function, and K_1 and K_2 denote positive constants.

$$DOOrG(\sigma,r_1,r_2,\theta) =$$
$$K_1 \cdot G(\sigma,r_1 \cdot \sigma,\theta) - K_2 \cdot G(r_2 \cdot \sigma, r_1 \cdot r_2 \cdot \sigma,\theta) \tag{1}$$

In general, the eccentricity of the two Gaussians(r_1), is the same as $r_1 = \sigma_y/\sigma_x$, and the ratio between the width of the ON and OFF Gaussians(r_2) is also fixed as $r_2 = \sigma_{off}/\sigma_{on}$. In addition, σ_x, σ_y denotes the width of the two Gaussians.

The three importance maps are computed as following. First, the bank of filter h^θ at 8 orientations($\theta \in \{0, \pi/8, 2\pi/8, \cdots, 7\pi/8\}$) is generated by taking the absolute value of the result of Eq. 1. And then, each feature map is convolved with the bank of h^θ filter. Then the results are squared to enhance the contrast. Finally we take the summation of the results to factor out θ. Total process of computing importance map is expressed as

$$I^k = \sum_\theta \left[F^k \bullet h^\theta \right]^2 \tag{2}$$

where $\bullet$ denotes convolution. Since the importance maps computed in this step are generated by the filter bank based on the *DOOrG* model at 8 orientations, each importance map can detects orientations in addition, and also reduces noise.

Second Step. Each computed importance map is convolved with the large size of the *LoG* filter and the result is added with the original one. This work is iterated 4 times and three IT^k maps are generated as a result. This procedure causes the effect of short range cooperation and long-range competition among neighboring values of the map.

Third Step. Each IT^k map is evaluated iteratively by statistical information of the map to enhance the values associated with strong peak activities in the map while suppress uniform peak activities. For each IT^k map, the map is multiplied by the squared subtraction of the $aveLMax^k$, which is the average of all the values except the global maximum value of the map, from the global maximum value $GMax^k$, and is normalized by

$$IT^k = \frac{IT^k - IT_{min}}{IT_{max} - IT_{min}} \tag{3}$$

where IT_{min} and IT_{max} denote the global minimum and the maximum value out of all IT^k maps, respectively. Through this, relative importance of an IT^k map with respect to other ones would be remained, and irrelevant information extracted from ineffective IT^k maps would be suppressed. This procedure of this step is iterated 4 times.

Fourth Step. Three IT^k maps are just simply summed into one saliency map S.

5 Experimental Results

We applied the model to target detection problem in order to study overall behaviors of the model with various color images of natural environment.

As test images, we used 124 complex natural outdoor scenes taken from different domains. Most of the scenes were photographed in high-resolution, in which the target appears very small(113 out of 124). And each of the scenes contains the 'target'(salient object) such as signboard, signal lamp, traffic sign, mailbox, placard, and etc, and also contains the 'distractors' such as strong local variations in illumination, textures, and large number of other 'non-targets'. In addition, we intentionally added high amount of noise(about 35% to 90%) on 30 images(see Fig. 4(b)). The noise has some properties : its distribution would be gaussian or uniform distribution, and would have color information not only intensity information.

Fig. 3 and Fig 4 show some examples of the results obtained through our model. Fig. 3 shows the overall working of our model. Three feature maps are extracted from the input image and combined into the single saliency map. Fig. 3(a) shows the application of our model to detecting red mailbox and Fig 3(b), blue signboard. The targets in each of the test images are salient by their unique color contrast. In Fig. 3(a), the features in F^2 win among other feature maps through generating the saliency map, and in Fig 3(b), the features in F^3 win among other feature maps. Fig. 4 shows the more examples of results with real and noisy images. As we can see, the results were very promising.

By the way, evaluating the performance our model with such real images is not easy, because there are no objective criteria to evaluate the model. Thus it is very difficult to determine the basic ideal output of the model. For these reasons, we used a subjective evaluation, i.e. we compared the output of the model with the maximum measured behaviors of human subjects. Forty human subjects(19 were girl and 21 were boy) aged 12 years were participated in the test. Subjects were first presented with the same test images which were inputted to the model, and we asked them to mark the most attended region or object as soon as they found it during each trial. According to the results of human test, when subjects were presented with Fig. 3(a) and Fig. 3(b), 28 human subjects marked the red mailbox(4:gray car, 2:child, 6:small placards) of Fig. 3(a), and 39 human subjects marked the blue signboard of Fig. 3(b) as the most attended region. The results of the model with the images of the type shown in Fig. 3 and Fig. 4(except the third image of Fig. 4(a)) were always good compared to human attention, however it fails when salient objects were overlapped like the third image of Fig. 4(a). With this image, 20 human subjects marked red car(13:white wall, 7 :the front of the house), although the model detected white wall because of its salient color contrast. It seems that the fact that our model proposed here only concerned with bottom-up component while human attention depends on both bottom-up and top-down component causes the main differences between the model and human(see Table 1.). However, the false detection rate will be easily decreased if we implement dedicated feature maps and insert them into the model. Besides, we are now conducting further systematic evaluation of the model using more complex real images and especially noisy images taken from different domains, including synthetic images. And we are expecting better performance.

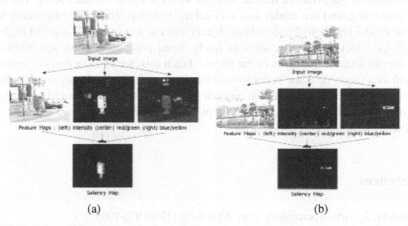

(a)   (b)

Fig. 3. Examples of the overall working of our model : application to target detection on real-world images. The target is (a) red mailbox (b) blue signboard

(a)   (b)

Fig. 4. More examples of the model with (a) noiseless images(salient object is a traffic sign for first two images(left:yellow,center:blue), and right image is an example of false detection of the model compare to human attention), (b) noisy images(left:color noise with uniform distribution(noisy density:60%), right:intensity noise with gaussian distribution(noisy density:35%))

Table 1. The results of the model compared to human attention(total 124 images)

Test Image(no.)	No. of Right Detection	No. of False Detection
Non-Noisy(94)	78	16
Noisy(30)	27	3

6   Discussion and Conclusions

The use of saliency map model for active perception has been proposed. The model proposed here detects the regions of interest by properties of the input image. We have tested the model on a variety of color images, each containing salient objects as well as obstacles such as noises, shadows, and other non-interesting objects. In present study we presented some examples of the results of the model's application to target detection. To verify the results, we performed human test, and compared the maximum measured behaviors of human subjects with the results of the model. The results were promising, and the model was very robust to noise. The more interesting fact is that our model is able to detect salient objects without any tuning or a-priori high-level knowledge about the targets, whereas finely tuned computer vision algorithms typically cannot detect other types of the targets. From this, we can say that our model can be used as a target detector in complex natural scene for general purpose. In addition, the location of the attention region resulted from our model can be used to change the gaze of a non-uniform sensor, and this implies that our model can be used in active vision including active perception tasks.

References

1. Bajcsy, R.: Active perception. Proc. IEEE 76(8) (1998) 996-1005
2. Duncan, J., Humphreys, J.: Visual search and stimulus similarity. Psychological Reviews 96 (1989) 433-458
3. Fukushima, K., Imagawa, T.: Recognition and Segmentation of Connected Characters with Selective Attention. Neural Networks 6 (1993) 33-41
4. Eriksen, C., At.James, J.: Visual attention within and around the field of focal attention:a zoom lens model. Perception Psychology 40(4) (1986) 225-240
5. Giefing, G., Mallot, H.: Saccadic Object Recognition with an Active Vision System., 10th European Conf. on Artificial Intelligence (1992) 803-805
6. Itti, L., Koch, C.,: A saliency-based search mechanism for overt and covert shifts of visual attention. Vision Research 40(10-12) (2000) 1489-1506
7. Koch, C., Ullman, S.: Shifts in Selective Visual Attention : Towards the Underlying Neural Circuitry. Human Neurobiology 4 (1985) 219-227
8. Milanese, R., Wechsler, H., Gil, S., Bost, J.,Pun, T.: Integration of Bottom-up and Top-down Cues for Visual Attention Using Non-Linear Relaxation. Proc. of IEEE Conf. on Computer Vision and Pattern Recognition (1994) 781-785
9. Mozer, M.: The Perception of Multiple Objects : a Connectionist Approach. MIT Press, Cambridge, MA (1991)
10. Treisman, A., Gelade, G.: A Feature-integration theory of Attention. Cognitive Psychology 12(1) (1980) 97-136
11. Tsotsos, J., Culhane, S., Winky, Y., Yuzhong, L., Davis, N., Nuflo, F.: Modeling Visual Attention via Selective Tuning. Artificial Intelligence 78 (1995) 507-545
12. Wolfe, J., Cave, K.: Guided Search : An Alternative to Feature Integration Model of Visual Search. Journal of Experimental Psychology : Human Perception and Performance 15 (1989) 419-433

Generation of Optimal Biped Walking for Humanoid Robot by Co-evolving Morphology and Controller

Ken Endo[1,2], Funinori Yamasaki[1,3], Takashi Maeno[2], and Hiroaki Kitano[1,4]

[1] Kitano Symbiotic Systems Project, ERATO, JST, Corp.
6-31-15 Jingumae, M31 Suite 6A, Shibuya-ku, Tokyo, Japan
{endo, yamasaki, kitano}@symbio.jst.go.jp
http://www.symbio.jst.go.jp
[2] Keio University
maeno@mech.keio.ac.jp
[3] Osaka Uvinersity
[4] Sony Computer Science Laboratories

Abstract. In this paper, a method for co-evolving morphology and controller of bi-ped humanoid robots is proposed. Currently, structure and walking pattern of humanoid robots are designed manually on trial-and-error basis. Although certain control theory exists, for example zero moment point (ZMP) compensation, these theories do not constrain structure of humanoid robot or detailed control. Thus, engineers has to design control program for apriori designed morphology, neither of them shown to be optimal within a large design space. Therefore, evolutionary approaches that enables co-evolution of morphology and control can be useful for designing the humanoid robot. Co-evolution was achieved in a precision dynamics simulator, and discovered unexpected optimal solutions. This indicate that a complex design task of bi-ped humanoid can be performed automatically using evolution-based approach, thus varieties of humanoid robots can be design in speedy manner. This is a major importance to the emerging robotics industries.

1 Introduction

Traditionally, robotics systems has been used dominantly in factories for high-precision routine operations. In recent years, there are increasing interest in robotics systems for non-traditional use, as represented by Sony's AIBO, several prototype attempts for home robotics, rescue robots, etc. Among various possible robot shapes, human-like robots, humanoids, are of particular interests because of its visual appeal and less need to modify environment since robots has same degree of freedom to fit into the operational space. Numbers of humanoid robots have been developed aiming at possible deployment of humanoid for office and home [6],[5]. However, all of them requires expensive components and extensive time to design and construct elaborate humanoids.

M. Ishizuka and A. Sattar (Eds.): PRICAI 2002, LNAI 2417, pp. 325–334, 2002.

For humanoid to share a serious proportion of robotics industry, however, low-cost and faster design cycle is required. Research for low-cost and easy-to-design humanoid is essential for industrial exploration. To promote this avenue of research a humanoid robot PINO [17] was developed with well designed exterior. and only using off-the-shelf components. In addition, all technical information for PINO was disclosed under GNU General Public License, as OpenPINO (http://www.openpino.org/), to facilitates open evolution.

There are several interesting issues have emerged. First, one of the challenges is to identify methods to control such robots to walk and behave in a stable manner by overcoming lack of torque and non-trivial backrush, because only cheap servomotor for radio-controlled toys are used to lower the cost. Assuming the current structural design of PINO, the use of traditional ZMP-compensation method did not fits well as it requires sufficient torque and precision to stably control the robot[15]. A new control methods need to discovered to control it to walk in a stable manner.

Second, a current structural design is not proven to be optimal, and it will never be proven to be optimal because control methods are generally designed assuming specific hardware is given. What we wish to attain is to optimize both morphology and control at the same time, so that it is optimized for the walking behavior, instead of optimizing walking behavior for the given hardware. This is important for open evolution of robotics system, such as OpenPINO.

Our position is that we can learn from evolution of living systems on how they have developed morphology and control systems at the same time. What we should learn from the living creatures is not the structures and components themselves but how they have been emerged during evolution. Optimum structures of robots can be designed only when the suitable components and locomotions for the robots are selected appropriately through evolution. Design of the robots, by the robots, for the robots, should be achieved using evolutionary method, whereas designers of the robots should only set up an environmental constraint condition for the robots.

An artificial life is one of the answers. Sims [10] generated robots that can walk, jump and swim in computer simulation. He also generated virtual creatures which compete each other to obtain one resource [9]. Ventrella [8] presented evolutionary emergence of morphology and locomotion behavior of animated characters. Kikuchi and Hara [14] studied a method of evolutionary design of robots having tree structure that change their morphology in order to adapt themselves to the environmental conditions. However, all of them do not consider how to make practical robots.

On the other hand, evolutionary method has been tried to apply to the practical robots. Kitamura [16] used Genetic Programming, GP [7], to emerge the simple linked-locomotive robot in virtual space. Lipson [1] adopted the rapid prototyping to produce the creatures that were generated in three-dimensional virtual space. However, all of the are far from practical robots.

Until now, we have developed the method for designing the morphology and neural systems of multi-linked locomotive robots [12][11]. Both the morphology and neural systems are represented as a simple large tree structure and both of them are optimized simultaneously using evolutionary computation. This method can be applied to development of the humanoid robot. In this paper, co-evolution were achieved in a precision dynamics simulator. Moreover the validness of the solution is confirmed considering the efficiency and stability.

2   Materials and Methods

2.1   Morphology

Humanoid robots are composed of large numbers of components such as sensors, actuators and so on. It is difficult to consider optimal choice for all of them simultaneously. At first, the simple models are needed in order to develop the basic method for generating the both of morphology and controller. Therefore The multi-link model of robot as shown in Fig. 1 is used here. This three-dimensional robot is composed of 10 links for body and legs and two plates for each foot. The length of five links for upper body, upper limbs and lower limbs change through the evolution though the total length of all links is constant. Joints are numbered as joint 1 to 10 as shown in Fig. 1. Driving torque of each joint can be change from -30kgfcm to 30kgfcm reflecting the real robots. The joint 3 and 8 have the range of motions between 0 and $\pi/2$ and other joints have between $-\pi/2$ and $\pi/2$ respectively. Densities of the links of leg and upper body are 0.314kg/m and 4.557kg/m, respectively, and the length of one leg is 0.28 m. These parameters are based on PINO, so as to improve the structure of PINO in the future.

2.2   Controller

A lot of researches about generating the locomotion of artificial lives or robots with neural network and evolutionary computation have been conducted[4][2].

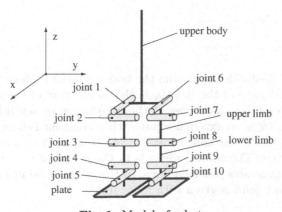

Fig. 1. Model of robot

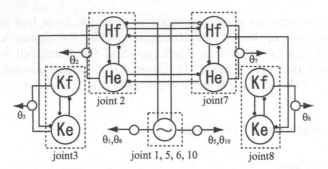

Fig. 2. Structure of control system

However the size of chromosomes becomes too large to generate the valid solution considering the both morphology and locomotion simultaneously. Moreover we have to take the velocity of all joints and external force from the ground in account to control the robots. In the biomechanics field, pattern generators are often used for generating the walking pattern of human because the bi-ped walking is the periodical and symmetrical motion, and the structure of the control system can be decided in advance. Until now, many studies of neural oscillators have been conducted. The control system composed of neural oscillators can generate the rhythm for the bi-ped walking. Unlike the recurrent neural network, not so large length of chromosome is needed. However any application for the real robots has not been accomplished. Our goal is to propose the designing method that can generate detail structure and controller of bi-ped humanoid robot. Therefore we can make the difference between the real world and computer simulation minimal with our method.

The structure of control system is decided according to the basic locomotion of bi-ped walking as shown in Fig. 2. Hf and He are neurons for the hip joints. Kf and Ke are neuron for knees. The action of each neuron is expressed as follow,

$$T_i \dot{u}_i = -u_i - \sum_{ij} w_{ij} y(u_j) - \beta y(v_i) + U_0 + \sum_k FB_k \tag{1}$$

$$T_i' \dot{v} = -v_i - y_i \tag{2}$$

$$y(x_i) = \frac{1}{1 + e^{-\tau(x_i)}} \tag{3}$$

where FB_k is a feedback signal from the body of robot such as the angle of each joint or external force of the feet, u_i is the inner state of the ith neuron, v_i is a variable representing the degree of the adaptation or self-inhibition effect of the ith neuron, U_0 is an external input with a constant rate, w is a connecting weight, and T_i and T_i' are time constants of the inner state and the adaptation effect, respectively. The neuron which is in the center of Fig. 2 is for joint 1, 5, 6, and 10 that generates just sine wave. In the white circle in Fig. 2, the desired trajectory of each joint is given with following,

$$\theta_k = p_k(y(u_{k1}) - y(u_{k2})) \tag{4}$$

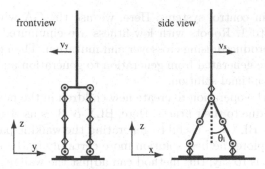

Fig. 3. Initial state

where, θ_k is the desired trajectory and p_k is the gain for the joint k. The desired trajectory of joint is given from the output of neurons. Thus the driving torque of each joint is given with controlling the angle of joints to desired trajectory with PD control. However the maximum driving torque is ± 30 kgfcm and each gain for PD control are decided in advance. This value is decided based on the PINO. The plates of feet are kept parallel to the ground. This method is often used for bi-ped humanoid robot in order to make the problem simple.

3 Method

3.1 Simulation

The environment which robots walk on is the flat ground. When the dynamic simulation starts, the posture of the robot is in the state of the initial position as show in Fig. 3. Initial angle of θ_i and velocity v_x, v_y are decoded from chromosomes. When the dynamic simulation begins, the controller starts to work and generate driving torque at the each joint. The only robots with controller that generates the rhythm for walking can keep walking. If the knee, hip and other parts of body of robots gets contact with the ground or the motion of robot continue staying at the same place for 0.5 s, simulation is over and next one begins in order to avoid wasting the time.

Dynamic simulation is conducted for 5 s per a robot. the movement of robots resulting from their interaction with the environment. Motions of the robot are calculated by the forth order Runge-Kutta method. One time step is 0.2 ms. Contact response with ground of the links is accomplished by a hybrid model using spring and damper under the influence of friction and gravity. The friction is large enough for robots not to slip while they are walking.

3.2 Evolutionary Computation

GA is the method for optimization based on the evolution of creature. GA has been used for many complex problems[13]. In this paper, a fixed length genetic algorithm is used to evolve the controllers and morphologies. Each chromosome includes the information of initial angle, velocity, length of each link and weights of each neuron in control systems. Here, we use the GA which deal with real number from 0 to 1. Robots with low-fitness are eliminated by selection, and new robots are produced using crossover and mutation. Then their morphologies and controller are generated from generation to generation and ,finally, converge to a reasonably optimal solution.

Crossover is the operation to create new children in the next generation from parents selected due to their fitness. Here, BLX-α [3] is used as the crossover for real number GA. BLX-α is useful to generating the walking pattern because this crossover can explore the best solution more certainly in the middle or latter of calculation, that is to say, this method can adjust the walking pattern in detail. Each factor in the chromosomes is decided as follow:

$$c_{1i,2i} = u(min(p_{1i}, p_{2i}) - \alpha I_i, max(p_{1i}, p_{2i}) + \alpha I_i) \tag{5}$$
$$I_i = |p_{1i} - p_{2i}| \tag{6}$$

where $p_1 = (p_{11} \cdots p_{1n})$, $p_2 = (p_{21} \cdots p_{2n})$ are parents, $c_1 = (c_{11} \cdots c_{1n})$, $c_2 = (c_{21} \cdots c_{2n})$ are children, and $u(x, y)$ is the uniform deviates from x to y. Here α is set to 0.05. In this way, the length of total chromosomes does not change. Selection is operated due to finesses of the robots. The larger the fitness is, the easier the robot is selected. Mutation is the operation to change the part of some chromosomes of robots selected randomly. When mutation occurred to c_i, the new factor c_n is given as follow:

$$c_n = c_i + \frac{rand_g}{10} \tag{7}$$

where $rand_g$ donates the gaussian deviates. This operation also works without changing the total length of chromosomes. With these operations, the only robots with large fitness can survive.

Through the evolution, walking distance of all robots are evaluated. As the evaluate function,

$$fitness = l_g \tag{8}$$

is used, where l_g is distance of the center of mass of robots from the initial point. With this function, robots are evaluated just the walking distance.

The parameters of GA is as shown in Table 1. Moreover we use the elite preservation strategy at the same time.

Table 1. GA parameters

population size	100
generation	300
crossover ratio	0.8
mutation ratio	0.05

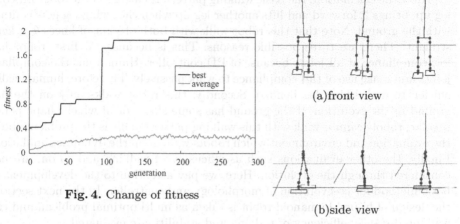

Fig. 4. Change of fitness

(a)front view

(b)side view

Fig. 5. Walking pattern of the best robot

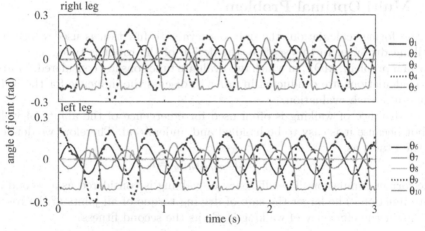

Fig. 6. Angle of joint during walking

4   Results and Discussions

Calculation using GA is conducted for the models mentioned above. The best fitness and average of all is shown in Fig. 4. At first, all robots can walk only a little distance and fitnesses are low. Gradually, the robots that can walk are emerged and their walking distance increases. Finally, some robots keep walking till the end of dynamic simulation.

The walking pattern of the best robot at the final generation is shown in Fig. 5, and angle of each joint during walking is shown in Fig. 6. This robot has 0.667 m of upper body, 0.1309 m of upper limbs and 0.0726 m of lower limbs. When the real robot is constructed, these parameters can be more useful than intuitions.

After the calculation, the basic walking pattern is emerged that robot lifts one leg up, brings it forward and lifts another leg up when the swing leg gets contact with the ground. Note that this robot walk with both of joint of knees $\theta_{3,8}$ kept straight. There are three possible reasons. This is because, At first, robot has low compliance at all joints because of PD controller. Human has the compliant joints and make use of this compliance to walk passively. Therefore, human walks efficiently with swing leg bended. Secondly, this robot walks only on the flat ground in the evolution. If the ground has some slope, or of which shape is not regular, robots cannot walk with this walking pattern. This is the problem about the evaluation and environment which robots walk on in the dynamic simulation. Finally, the other evaluations such as efficiency of walking and so on, are not considered through the evolution. Here, we pay attention to the development of basic method for co-evolution of morphology and controller. In the next section, the design of bi-ped humanoid robot is taken as multi optimal problem, and the walking distance, efficiency of walking and stability are evaluated.

5   Multi Optimal Problem

In the former calculation, the only one evaluate function is used which is the walking distance. In this section, the design of the robot is taken as the multi optimal problem, MOP, in which two evaluate functions are considered. Moreover two calculations are conducted in order to discuss the influence for the walking pattern of each evaluation.

A distance of walking is often used for emergence of the ability of walking robot because it is easy to be handled and understood. Therefore we define one of the fitness as,

$$fitness_{movability} = l_g \tag{9}$$

like former simulation. The efficiency of walking is considered as a second evaluate function. The larger the sum of driving torque of all joints of the robot is, the lower the efficiency of walking is. So as the second fitness,

$$fitness_{efficiency} = \frac{1}{1 + \int_t \Sigma_i |\tau_i| dt} \tag{10}$$

is defined, where, τ_i is driving torque of joint i per a unit time step. The third evaluation function is

$$fitness_{stability} = \frac{1}{\int |\dot{\theta}_{upper}|} \tag{11}$$

, where $\dot{\theta}_{upper}$ donates the angle velocity of upper body. This fitness means the stability of upper body. With these functions, two calculations are conducted, which one is with $fitness_{movability}$ and $fitness_{efficiency}$ (calculation 1), and the other is with $fitness_{movability}$ and $fitness_{stability}$ (calculation 2). Moreover, we use the method combined with pareto preserving strategy and vector evaluated GA. The parameters of GA is the same as the former calculation as shown in Table 1.

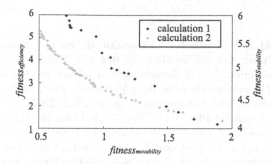

Fig. 7. Pareto optimal solutions of final generation

6   Results and Discussions

After the calculation, pareto optimal solution which are 73 for calculation 1 and 19 for calculation 2, are emerged at the final generation as shown in Fig. 7. However all of them walk with the leg kept straight like the robot in Fig. 5. The value of $fitness_{movability}$ means just the point which the robot falls down in the calculation 1. In fact, the robot which falls down as soon as the dynamic simulation begins can get high $fitness_{efficiency}$. if other efficient walking pattern dose not would exist, the robot with it could survive. This means that the efficiency of walking has no relationship with the way to walk like this. In the calculation 2, the robot which just stand without walking can get high $fitness_{stability}$ if other stable walking pattern dose not exist because upper body does not move. Like efficiency, the stability has no relationship with this walking pattern. Therefore we can say that this walking pattern is the best solution under the condition which robot with this controller walk on the flat ground.

7   Conclusions

In this paper, we present a method for co-evolving morphology and controller of bi-ped humanoid robots. We propose evolutionary approaches that enables that co-evolution of morphology and control. Co-evolution are achieved and discovered unexpected optimal solutions. It is that robot walk with both swing and supporting legs kept straight. Moreover, the validness of the solution was confirmed considering the efficiency and stablitity.

In this paper, the walking distance, efficiency of walking and stability of upper body are evaluated for just walking. However we can use many other evaluation functions for other tasks. Secondly, we use the simple multi-link model. More detail structure have to be used in order to improve PINO or make the other type of robots. Finally, the movement of the other parts such as arms can be considered for walking or the other tasks. The size of chromosomes of our method is so short that all of them are possible to be conducted.

References

1. H. Lipson and J. B. Plollack. "Automatic design and manufacture of robotic lifeforms". *Nature*, Vol.406(No.6799):pp. 974–978, 2000.
2. Cao, M., Kawamura, A. "A Design Method of Neural Oscillatory Networks for Generation of Humanoid Biped walking Patterns". *Proc. of the International Conference on Robotics and Automation*, pages pp.2357–2362, 1998.
3. Eshleman, L. J. and Schaffer, J. D. "Real-Coded Genetic Algorithms and Interval-Schemata". *Foundations of Genetic Algorithms 2*, pages pp.187–202, 1993.
4. Fukuda, T., Komata, Y., Arakawa, T. "Stabilization Control of Biped Locomotion Robot based learning with GAs having Self-adaptive Mutation and Recurrent Neural Networks". *Proc. of the International Conference on Robotics and Automation*, pages pp.217–222, 1997.
5. Hashimoto, S. Narita, S., Kasahara, K., Shirai, K., Kobayashi, T., Takanishi, A., Sugano, S., et. al. "Humanoid Robots in Waseda University – Hadaly-2 and WABIAN". *Proc. of The First IEEE-RAS International Conference on Humanoid Robots*, CDROM, 2000.
6. Inaba, M., Kanehiro, F., Kagami, S. and Inoue, H. "Two-armed Bipedal Robot that can Walk, Roll Over and Stand up". *Proc. of International Conference on Intelligent Robots and Systems*, 1995.
7. J. Koza. *"Genetic Programming II"*. MIT Press, 1994.
8. J. Ventrella. "Exploration in the Emergence of Morphology and Locomotion Behavior in Animated Characters". *Artificial Life IV*, pages pp. 436–441, 1994.
9. Karl Sims. "Evolving 3D Morphology and Behavior by Competition". *Artificial Life IV*, pages pp.28–39, 1994.
10. Karl Sims. "Evolving Virtual Creatures", Computer Graphics Proceedings". *Computer Graphics Proceedings*, pages pp.12–22, 1994.
11. Ken Endo, Takashi Maeno. "Simultaneous Design of Morphology of Body, Neural Systems and Adaptability to Environment of Multi-Link-Type Locomotive Robots using Genetic Programming". *Proc. IEEE/RSJ International Conference on Intelligent Robots and Systems*, pages pp.2282–2287, 2001.
12. Ken Endo, Takashi Maeno. "Simultaneous Generation of Morphology of Body and Neural System of Multi-Linked Locomotive Robot using Evolutionary Computation". *Proceedings of the 32nd International Symposium on Robotics*, CDROM, 2001.
13. Kitano, H. "Designing neural networks using genetic algorithms with graph generation system". *Complex System*, pages pp.454–461, 1990.
14. Kohki Kikuchi and Fumio Hara. "Evolutionary Design of Morphology and Intelligence in Robotic System". *Proceedings of the fifth international conference on SAB*, pages pp. 540–545, 1998.
15. M. Vukobratović, B. Borovac and D. Šurdilović. "Zero-Moment Point – Propoer Interpretation and New Apprications". *Proc. of The Second IEEE-RAS International Conference on Humanoid Robots*, CD-ROM, 2001.
16. Shinzo Kitamura, Yuzuru Kakuda, Hajime Murao, Jun Gotoh and Masaya Koyabu. "A Design Method as Inverse Problems and Application of Emergent Computations". *SICE*, Vol.36(No.1):pp. 90–97, 2000.
17. Yamasaki, F., Matsui, T., Miyashita, T. and Kitano, H. "PINO The Humanoid that Walk". *Proc. of The First IEEE-RAS International Conference on Humanoid Robots*, CDROM, 2000.

Multi-agent Coordination in Planning

Jeroen Valk* and Cees Witteveen

Delft University of Technology,
Dept of Information Technology and Systems,
P.O.Box 356, 2600 AJ Delft, The Netherlands

Abstract. We consider coordination problems where several agents, each assigned to some subtask of a complex task, solve their own subtask by making minimal plans and want to find a common plan based on their individual plans. A task is conceived as a set of primitive tasks (operations), partially ordered by a set of precedence constraints. Operations are distributed among agents dependent on their capabilities and constitute the subtasks the agents have to solve. The precedence constraints between operations in subtasks are inherited from the overall precedence constraints occurring in the task. Since it is assumed that every agent is capable to find a suitable (minimal) plan for its own subtask, the main problem for the agents to coordinate their plans in order to solve the complete task. First, we characterize situations in which an optimal coordinated plan can be constructed by simple plan coordination. Since, in general, obtaining optimal global plans is intractable, we therefore introduce two simple and efficient distributed approximation algorithms to achieve plan coordination. The first algorithm can be used as a d-approximation of a globally optimal plan for the agents, where d is the depth of the original task, i.e. the length of the longest chain in the set of precedence constraints constituting the task. This algorithm assumes almost no knowledge about the distribution of tasks over the agents. If such knowledge, however, is available, a second, more refined algorithm can be used, that is based on elaborate inter-agent negotiation and is able to achieve a better approximation ratio.

1 Introduction

Multi-agent systems that are able to cooperate in order to accomplish a joint set of tasks, are becoming increasingly important. Unfortunately, however, achieving an optimal coordination usually is not feasible. One reason is that actions improving the performance of the system as a whole need not be beneficial from the viewpoint of the individual agent or organization and therefore, negotiation processes intended to overcome this problem might fail. A second reason is that coordination of the activities of all agents at the operational level might involve an excessive computational and communication overhead.

---

* Jeroen Valk is supported by the TNO-TRAIL project *IT-architecture and coordination in transport chains* carried out within the research school for Transport, Infrastructure and Logistics (TRAIL).

M. Ishizuka and A. Sattar (Eds.): PRICAI 2002, LNAI 2417, pp. 335–344, 2002.

This *agent coordination problem*, therefore, has received much attention. A particular kind of coordination, extensively studied, is *coalition formation*, i.e., the process of partitioning agents into groups called coalitions. Agents that are within the same coalition coordinate their actions, while agents in different coalitions do not. The aim is to find processes for coalition formation that maximize to sum of the values each coalition can at least obtain regardless of the activities of the agents outside the coalition. Coalition formation has been studied in game theory [7,2], and recently, models of bounded rationality have received much attention [1,4,3]. In task-oriented domains, coalition formation can be combined with *task allocation* [8,5]. In such an approach, the tasks that have to be performed are distributed among the agents. Task allocation is a form of coordination where the attention of each agent is restricted to its own tasks. Whenever the tasks to be executed are subject to *precedence constraints*, however, additional plan coordination is necessary in order to respect these constraints.

In previous work on coalition formation and task allocation this kind of coordination has been addressed only implicitly [5]. In this paper we will study some simple but efficient approximation algorithms for plan coordination and compare them to the outcome of optimal strategies. To the best of our knowledge, explicit models of the coordination of precedence constraints as will be studied in this paper have received little or no attention, yet. In previous papers [6] we have designed some protocols restricted to particular agent configurations to solve this problem. These protocols ensured that the plans of each of the parties involved were split up in subplans. The protocol ensured that while each of the agents was completely free in coming up with its own private plan and had to reveal not any detail about it to the other agents, the complete task could be executed by a careful scheduling of the agents. In this paper this approach is generalized significantly, allowing the parties to interact in order to come up with more refined protocols for coordinating their individual plans.

2   A Framework for Multi-agent Planning

We consider a multi-agent approach to planning problems where completing a task requires the cooperation between several parties. Here, a task T will be specified as a partial order of some set of operations, or *primitive tasks*, t. These primitive tasks have to be executed in a sequence specified by the partial order. *Agents* are systems capable to perform those primitive tasks t and to make plans for executing them. Every single agent, however, is only capable to perform some subset of primitive tasks. Therefore, usually, execution of the complete task will require several agents to cooperate on performing all operations. In real life, agents will accept several tasks T simultaneously. We therefore consider problems where agents have to execute several tasks T, each requiring the joint cooperation of agents. We therefore consider multi-agent planning and scheduling problems characterized by

- a set Tp of types of *primitive tasks* agents are capable to perform.
- a set $\mathcal{A}$ of agents, each agent $A \in \mathcal{A}$ capable of performing a subset $Tp_A \subseteq Tp$ of (types of) primitive tasks. The subset Tp_A specifies the *skills* of agent A.

– a family of *tasks* $\{T_k\}_{k=1}^n$ to be executed, where each task T_k is specified by a set of instances of primitive tasks in Tp, together with a specification of a set of *precedence constraints* $\prec_k$ on this set of instances. These precedence constraints specify the partial order to be respected when executing the task T_k.

For every task instance t, $type(t) \in Tp$ refers to the type of primitive task t is an instance of.

To avoid cumbersome notation, without loss of generality, we may assume that the set of tasks $\{T_k\}_{k=1}^n$ just contains one single *complex task* T, since the union $T = \bigcup_{k=1}^n T_k$, together with the union of their precedence constraints $\prec_k$, is just a partially ordered set of tasks. Therefore, in the sequel we will specify a (complex) *task* by a single tuple $(T, \prec)$. Such a task $(T, \prec)$ can be completed by a set of agents $A_i \in \mathcal{A}$ if *(i)* all primitive tasks contained in T have been assigned to agents A_i capable of performing them and *(ii)* the agents have agreed upon a joint plan $P_{\mathcal{A}}$ to execute the tasks in T, respecting the precedence constraints $\prec$. Given a set of agents $\mathcal{A}$ and a task $(T, \prec)$, we will assume that agents have already agreed upon a particular assignment of subsets $T_i \subseteq T$ to agents $A_i \in \mathcal{A}$ such that $type(T_i) \subseteq Tp_{A_i}$, $\bigcup_{A_i \in \mathcal{A}} T_i = T$ and $T_i \cap T_j = \emptyset$, whenever $i \neq j$.

By distributing the set T of tasks, the total set of precedence constraints $\prec$ is split up into sets $\prec_i$ of *intra*-agent constraints and a set $\prec_{inter}$ of *inter*-agent constraints, that is,

– $\prec_i = \prec \cap (T_i \times T_i)$ is the set of constraints agent A_i has to take into account, while
– $\prec_{inter} = \prec - (\bigcup_{i=1}^n \prec_i)$ is the set of constraints *between* the agents.

So $(T_i, \prec_i)$ denotes the *subtask* assigned to agent $A_i \in \mathcal{A}$. Note that $\prec_i$ and $\prec_{inter}$ again are partial orders. We call d_i the *depth* of $(T_i, \prec_i)$, that is the length of the longest chain in $(T_i, \prec_i)$.

Our agents are planning agents and therefore want to come up with a *plan* P_i to perform their local subtask. A plan P_i must specify a partial order the agent has in mind to execute the primitive tasks t_j occurring in its subtask T_i. A minimal requirement for such a plan, of course, is that it satisfies all the local constraints $\prec_i$. Hence, we simply define a single agent plan for task $(T_i, \prec_i)$ as a partial order $P_i = (T_i, \prec_i^p)$ where $\prec_i^p$ *extends* $\prec_i$. Note that we do not require P_i to be totally ordered, since some agents might be capable to perform elementary tasks t_j concurrently.

Example 1. Suppose we have eight tasks t_i with the following precedence constraints and distribution over three agents A_1, A_2 and A_3 (see Figure 1): $t_0 \prec t_1, t_2$; $t_1, t_2 \prec t_3$; $t_1 \prec t_5$; $t_5 \prec t_7$; $t_3 \prec t_4$; $t_4 \prec t_6$. Agent A_1 receives the tasks t_0, t_4 and t_5 and constructs a plan $t_0 < t_4 < t_5$. Agent A_2 has to execute t_1, t_2 and t_3 and orders them as $t_1 < t_2 < t_6$ in his plan. Finally, agent A_3 receives t_7 and t_3 and plans to execute them concurrently. Note that the plans P_i of all agents are feasible.

For every agent A_i it is important to execute its task efficiently. We assume each primitive task t_i to have a fixed (time) cost $c(t_i)$. Given a plan $P_i = (T_i, \prec_i^p)$,

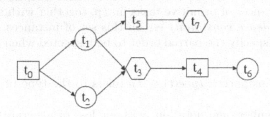

a. Ordered set of tasks to execute

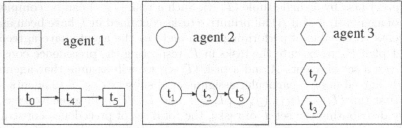

b. Distribution of tasks over agents and their plans

Fig. 1. Task distribution among three agents and their plans.

the cost $c(p)$ of a *chain* c of tasks in P_i is simply the sum $\Sigma c(t_j)$ of the costs of all primitive tasks contained in c. The cost of a plan P_i, denoted by $c(P_i)$, is the maximum of the costs of all (maximal) chains in P_i. A plan P_i is *minimal* if its cost $c(P_i)$ is minimal among all plans P_i' for $(T_i, \prec_i)$. Note that by definition of the depth d_i we always have $c(P_i) \geq d_i \times min_{t \in T_i}\{c(t)\}$. From now on we assume that every agent is able to construct locally optimal and feasible plans, i.e. the plan P_i chosen by agent A_i is locally optimal.

3 Plan Coordination

Given this simple set-up we would like to investigate how agents A_i might effectively coordinate their local plans P_i, i.e. how their local plans can be tuned such that a global plan P_A can be constructed satisfying all precedence constraints and how these coordination methods affect the quality of the resulting plan, i.e., what the costs are of the resulting coordinated plan compared with a globally optimal plan for the task at hand.

Ideally, every agent A_i should come up with its minimal plan P_i. Hereafter, by a simple cooperation protocol, the agents would coordinate their plans to satisfy also the inter-agent precedence constraints without affecting their own local plan, i.e. the coordination should be accomplished in such a way that it only affects the ordering in which *agents* are allowed to execute their plan. That is, ideally, such a global plan P should consist of a simple ordering of the *plans* P_i of the agents instead of ordering the primitive tasks of the agents.

Example 2. Take the set of tasks given in Figure 1 (a). Assume that we have two agents A_1 and A_2. Let A_1 receive the tasks t_0, t_1, t_2, t_3 and let A_2 receive the tasks t_4, t_5, t_6 and t_7. Suppose that A_1 comes up with a feasible plan P_1 and A_2 with a feasible plan P_2. Without knowing the details of these plans, there is a simple coordinated feasible plan: $P_1 < P_2$, i.e., let first A_1 execute his plan and then A_2. So, in this example a coordinated plan is a simple ordering of the (plans of the) agents.

Note that such cooperation protocols would not assume any knowledge about the details of the local plans made by the agents; it should be sufficient to have knowledge about the (task) *dependencies* between the *agents*. To represent such agent dependencies explicitly, we therefore define the *agent dependency graph* G_A w.r.t. the task $(T, \prec)$:

Definition 1. *Let $(T, \prec)$ be a task and $(T_i, \prec_i)$ be the subtasks assigned to the agents $A_i \in \mathcal{A}$. The agent dependency graph G_A is the graph $G_A = (\mathcal{A}, \prec_A)$, where $(A_i, \prec_A A_j)$ iff[1] there exists primitive tasks $t \in T_i$ and $t' \in T_j$ such that $t \prec t'$.*

We say that a global plan $P_A = (T, \prec_P)$ for $(T, \prec)$ can be constructed by *simple plan coordination* from the plans $P_i = (T_i, \prec_i^p)$ of the agents A_i if

1. $\prec_P = \bigcup_i \prec_i^p \cup \{(t, t') \mid t \in T_i, t' \in T_j \text{ and } A_i \prec_A A_j\}$
2. $\prec_P$ is a partial order.

That is, P_A is the result of simply ordering the plans of the agents. It is easy to see that P_A exists iff G_A is a directed acyclic graph (DAG):

Observation 1 *The relation* $\prec_P = \bigcup_i \prec_i^p \cup \{(t, t') \mid t \in T_i, t' \in T_j \text{ and } A_i \prec_A A_j\}$ *is a partial order iff G_A is acyclic.*

Note that whenever simple plan coordination is possible, the result is an optimal plan (given the task assignment) since every agent is assumed to be able to produce a minimal plan. Hence the following result is immediate:

Proposition 1. *An optimal plan $P_A = (T, \prec_P)$ for $(T, \prec)$ can be obtained from optimal local plans $P_i = (T_i, \prec_i^p)$ by simple plan coordination iff G_A is acyclic.*

In most cases, however, global plans cannot be obtained by simple plan coordination the reason being that, in general, an agent A_i will come up with a local plan *extending* $\prec_i$. It may then be the case that, no matter how these local plans are ordered, the global precedence constraints are violated.

Example 3. Consider the previous example and the task assignment to the three agents A_1, A_2 and A_3. This task assignment induces the following agent dependency graph (see Figure 2). This agent dependency graph clearly is not acyclic and therefore, no simple plan coordination is possible.

---

[1] That is, $\prec_A$ is the *lifting* of $\prec_{inter}$ from $T \times T$ to $\{T_i\}_{i=1}^n \times \{T_i\}_{i=1}^n$.

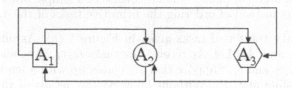

Fig. 2. The agent dependency graph corresponding to Figure 1.

In the following section we will discuss two algorithms to enable agents to come up with a global plan respecting all constraints while affecting their original local plans as little as possible. The price to be paid however is a loss of plan quality. We present some upper bounds on this loss of plan quality.

4   Plan Coordination by Partitioning Local Plans

By the previous example, it will not always suffice to add constraints to the local plans of the agents in order to guarantee a successful simple coordination process. Hence, in some cases it seems to be inevitable to apply a *partitioning strategy*: in order to get rid of circular dependencies between the (plans of) the agents, local plans have to be partitioned in separate subplans such that circular dependencies are removed. The coordination process then should only pertain the ordering of subplans between and within agents. In principle, since the original task is a partially ordered set, such a strategy should succeed: take a partitioning in which every agent has to execute a set of subplans each containing exactly one elementary task. In that case every global plan extending $\prec$ is a simple coordinated plan. But, clearly, such a solution could increase the costs of such a plan to its maximal value: since every agent has to execute every elementary task sequentially, the total cost of such plan P would be equal to $\Sigma_{t_i \in T} c(t_i)$ and could be $|T|$-times the optimal cost of a coordinated plan. Therefore, in this section we will present two algorithms that guarantee a better performance: the first algorithm obtains a plan whose costs are never more than d times the cost of an optimal plan where d is the depth of the task order and the second algorithm realizes an even better ratio, but assumes more knowledge from the participating agents.

4.1   Partitioning Using Only Local Dependency Information

We construct a polynomial-time distributed algorithm capable of adding sufficient constraints between the tasks an agent has to perform such that simple plan coordination becomes possible. The intuitive idea behind the algorithm is that each agent (only knowing from which other tasks its own tasks are dependent) tries to schedule a task t_i whenever all tasks preceding it are already scheduled by the other agents. It then separates those tasks from the remaining tasks, adds them to a common store **done** and splits its local task into two subtasks: one containing all tasks that can be scheduled now and the set of remaining tasks to be scheduled. As a result, the agent dependency graph will be refined to a new graph where instead of one node per agent several nodes per agent are created that are linearly ordered. It can be easily shown that the resulting refined agent dependency graph is acyclic, offering an easy way to construct a plan by simple plan coordination.

The algorithm uses a global store **done** that is distributed among all the agents. Initially this store is empty. Each agent is capable of inspecting and updating ($update(\textbf{done}, \phi)$ means that ϕ is added to the store) the store. Each agent only knows that in performing some tasks it is dependent upon other agents whose identity may be unknown. We specify for each agent A_i a procedure to find out how to split its current task assignment T_i into a number k_i of linearly ordered task assignments $(T_{i_1}, \ldots T_{i_{k_i}})$ such that simple plan coordination on the resulting set of subtasks becomes possible:

Algorithm 4.1
(partitioning for agent A_i)

Input: a subtask $(T_i, \prec_i)$ and a plan $P_i = (T_i, \prec_i^p)$ for agent A_i;
Output: a set of task assignments $P_{i,j}$ ordered by $\tilde{\prec}_i^p$;
begin

   1. $k_i := 1$ $\tilde{\prec}_i^p := \emptyset$;
   2. **while** $T_i \neq \emptyset$ **do**
      2.1. $T_{i,k_i} := \{t \in T_i \mid \forall t' \notin T_i[t' \prec t \implies t' \in \textbf{done}]\}$
      2.2. **while** $T_{i,k_i} = \emptyset$ **do**
           2.2.1. skip; % wait for tasks to occur in T_{i,k_i}
           2.2.2. $T_{i,k_i} := \{t \in T_i \mid \forall t' \notin T_i[t' \prec t \implies t' \in \textbf{done}]\}$
      2.3. $P_{i,k_i} := (T_{i,k_i}, \prec_i^p \cap T_{i,k_i}^2)$;
      2.4. $T_i := T_i \setminus T_{i,k_i}$;
      2.5. $update(\textbf{done}, T_{i,k_i})$;
      2.6. $\tilde{\prec}_i^p := \tilde{\prec}_i^p \cup (T_{i,k_i-1}, T_{i,k_i})$ if $k_i > 1$;
      2.7. $k_i := k_i + 1$;
end

As a result of this algorithm, a single agent plan P_i of agent A_i is refined to a linear sequence of subplans $P_{i,1}, \ldots, P_{i,k_i}$. Let us associate each such a plan $P_{i,j}$ with a subagent $A_{i,j}$ of A_i. Now construct the refined dependency graph $G_{\mathcal{A}}^* = (\bigcup A_{i,j}, \prec_{\mathcal{A}}^*)$, where $\prec_{\mathcal{A}}^* = \bigcup_i \tilde{\prec}_i \cup \{(A_{i,j}, A_{i',j'}) \mid i \neq i', \exists t \in T_{i,j}, t' \in T_{i',j'}[t \prec t']\}$. The following result is obvious, observing that as soon as subplan $P_{i,j}$ is created, all tasks in plans it depends upon occur in **done**:

Lemma 1. *The refined agent dependency graph $G_{\mathcal{A}}^*$ is an acyclic graph.*

Hence, by a simple version of e.g. distributed topological sort, a global plan P found by simple coordination of all subplans can be easily obtained. The price of course to be paid is loss of plan efficiency. This loss of efficiency can be derived from the following general proposition:

Proposition 2. *Let* $(T_i, \prec)$ *is partitioned into a totally ordered set of tasks* $T_i^* = ((T_{i,1}, \prec_{i,1}), \ldots , (T_{i,k}, \prec_{i,k}))$, *let* P_i *be an optimal plan for* $(T_i, \prec_i)$ *and let* P_i^* *an optimal plan for the totally ordered set of tasks* T_i^*. *Then* $c(P_i^*) \leq k \times c(P_i)$.

Proof. Note that $\prec_{i,j} = \prec_i \cap (T_{i,j} \times T_{i,j})$. Hence, from the definition of $c(P_i)$, it follows that $c(P_{i,j}) \leq c(P_i)$. Hence, $c(P_i) \geq max_{j=1}^k \{c(P_{i,j})\}$ and, therefore, since $c(P_i^*) = \Sigma_{j=1}^k c(P_{i,j})$, it follows that $c(P_i^*) \leq k \times c(P_i)$.

Hence, we immediately obtain the following result:

Theorem 1. *Algorithm 4.1 is a d-approximation algorithm for obtaining an optimal plan P for completing a task* $(T, \prec)$, *where d is the depth of the task.*

Proof. Every time a single agent splits his original plan, it does so because a set of nodes is added to **done**. It is easy to see that that **done** is updated at most $d = depth(T, \prec)$ times by each agent. Hence, an agent plan cannot be split more than d-times. Now apply the previous proposition.

4.2   A Refined Partitioning Strategy

A problem with the previous algorithm is that sometimes an agent puts its tasks on the global store too soon. If an agent waits until other agents have put a sufficient amount of tasks on the global store, more prerequisites will be satisfied allowing the agent to put more tasks on the global store, simultaneously, and thereby, reducing the number of plan splits. On the other hand, waiting too long may result in a deadlock situation in which none of the agents puts tasks on the global store. A better approximation of an optimal global plan therefore might be obtained if the agents also have knowledge about *direct inter-agent dependencies*, i.e., each agent A_i exactly knows upon which tasks t' assigned to other agents A_j his own tasks t are dependent. For each task t, the direct inter-agent dependencies for an agent consists of the following components : (i) the direct prerequisites t' for each task t, and (ii) the agents assigned to these prerequisites. Using these information components, like in the previous algorithm, each agent A_i, iteratively selects a subset of its tasks T_i and puts it on the global store **done** while respecting the constraint that T_i may only be put there if all its prerequisites are already there. The following algorithm uses this dependency information and offers a suitable trade-off between efficiency and deadlock prevention.

Algorithm 4.2
(refined partitioning for agent A_i **)**

Input: a task assignment $(T_i, \prec_i)$ for agent A_i,
Output: an ordered set of task assignments $(T_{i,j}, \hat{\prec}_i)$;

begin
    1. $k_i := 1$; $\hat{\prec}_i := \emptyset$;
    2. **while** $T_i \neq \emptyset$ **do**
        2.1. $\mathcal{R}_i := \emptyset$; **todo**$_i := \emptyset$; $\lambda(t) := \emptyset$ for all $t \in T_i$;
        2.2. **for** $t \in T_i, A_j \in \mathcal{A}$ **do**

2.2.1. let $S_{t,j}$ be the set of those direct prerequisites of task t that have been assigned to agent A_j;

2.2.2. for every $S_{t,j} \neq \emptyset$, send **request**$(i, j, (t, S_{t,j}))$ to agent A_j;

2.3. **for** each **request**$(j, i, (t, S))$ received from agent A_j **do**

2.3.1. $\mathcal{R}_i := \mathcal{R}_i \cup \{(j, t, S)\}$;

2.3.2. for each task $t' \in S$ without prerequisites in $T - $ **done**, send **inform**$(i, j, (t; t'))$ to agent A_j;

2.4. **for** each **inform**$(j, i, (t; t'))$ received from agent A_j **do**

2.4.1. **if** $\exists t'' \in T_i$ s.t. $t' \in \lambda(t'')$ % t'' and t' belong to the same chain **then**

add t'' in the set **todo**$_i$;

2.4.2. **else**

$\lambda(t) := \lambda(t) \cup \{t'\}$;

for $(k, t'', S) \in \mathcal{R}_i$ s.t. $t \in S$ **do**

send **inform**$(i, k, (t''; t'))$ to agent A_k;

2.5. $T_{i,k_i} := \{t \in T_i \mid \forall t' \notin T_i[t' \prec t \Rightarrow t' \in$ **done**$]\}$;

2.6. **if todo**$_i \subseteq T_{i,k_i}$ **then**

2.6.1. $T_i := T_i \setminus T_{i,k_i}$;

2.6.2. $update($**done**$, T_{i,k_i})$;

2.6.3. $\tilde{\prec}_i := \tilde{\prec}_i \cup (T_{i,k_i-1}, T_{i,k_i})$ if $k_i > 1$;

2.6.4. $k_i := k_i + 1$;

end

In Steps 2.2 and 2.3, the agents are informed which other agents are dependent on their tasks. In Step 2.3.2, the minimal elements of the task chains are determined and each minimal element is given a unique identifier that is used to identify the chain of primitive tasks. In Step 2.4, the identifiers are propagated along the task chains to determine which tasks in T_i belong to the same chain. Based on this information, a set of primitive tasks (**todo**$_i$) is determined and the agent waits (Step 2.6) until all prerequisites of **todo**$_i$ are in **done**.

The following result shows that the approximation ratio of this algorithm, in general, is much better than the previous algorithm[2].

Theorem 2. *Algorithm 4.2 is a* $\max\{2, k\}$*-approximation algorithm to compute a global plan P for a task $(T, \prec)$, where k is the maximum over all agents A_i and over all chains c in $\prec_{\text{inter}}$ of the number of times a task of the agent A_i occurs in c, i.e., $k = \max_i \{\max_c \{\mid T_{A_i} \cap c \mid\}\}$.*

5   Conclusions

We presented simple plan coordination methods to obtain a global plan for multi-agent systems based on independent plans for subtasks assigned to agents. These methods can be used as approximation algorithms for constructing (nearly) optimal plans for distributed agent systems. For example, the first algorithm creating

---

[2] The proof is omitted due to lack of space.

plans whose costs heavily depend on the depth of the task, is preferable whenever the task consists of several partially ordered subtasks each having constant depth c. The second algorithm is preferred whenever the depth of tasks is substantial or increases with the size of the task. In particular, the second algorithm is useful if the number of nonconsecutive occurrences of an agent in a chain of primitive tasks is limited. For example, in multimodal transportation systems, agents are usually situated in a specific geographic region and, therefore, occupy one consecutive part of the logistic chains. In such a situation, the worst-case performance ratio equals two.

Future research will focus on (i) different kinds of time constraints and optimization criteria such as time windows in combination with precedence constraints and time optimization and (ii) since the efficiency of coalition formation and task allocation methods depends on the way tasks are scheduled, the combination of methods for coalition formation and task allocation with plan coordination methods also needs attention.

References

1. R.J. Aumann. Survey of repeated games. In *Essays in Game Theory and Mathematical Economics in Honor of Oskar Morgenstern*, pages 11–42. Zurich, 1981.
2. R.J. Aumann and S. Hart, editors. *Handbook of Game Theory with Economic Applications*, volume 1. North-Holland, Amsterdam, 1992. Volume 2 appeared in 1994.
3. Tuomas Sandholm, Kate Larson, Martin Andersson, Onn Shehory, and Fernando Tohmé. Coalition structure generation with worst case guarantees. *Artificial Intelligence*, 111(1–2):209–238, 1999.
4. Tuomas W. Sandholm and Victor R. Lesser. Coalitions among computationally bounded agents. *Artificial Intelligence*, 94:99–137, 1997.
5. Onn Shehory and Sarit Kraus. Methods for task allocation via agent coalition formation. *Artificial Intelligence*, 101(1–2):165–200, 1998.
6. J.M. Valk, C. Witteveen, and J. Zutt. Approximation results for multi-agent planning systems. In *Proceedings of the Pacific Rim International Workshop on Multi-Agents (PRIMA)*, 2001.
7. J. von Neumann and O. Morgenstern. *Theory of Games and Economic Behavior*. Princeton University Press, Princeton, 1944.
8. Gilad Zlotkin and Jeffrey S. Rosenschein. Mechanisms for coalition formation in task oriented domains. In *Proceedings of the Twelfth National Conference on Artificial Intelligence*, 1994.

A Multi-agent Based Approach to the Inventory Routing Problem

Yizhi Lao and Hon Wai Leong

School of Computing,
National University of Singapore,
Singapore 117543,
Republic of Singapore
leonghw@comp.nus.edu.sg

Abstract. We propose a multi-agent framework for modeling and solving a complex logistic optimization problems called the Inventory Routing Problem (IRP). We use agents to represent the entities (customers, routes, deliveries) in the IRP. While each agent is driven by its own local objective functions and operations (actions), they also interact with each other. Thus, they cooperate and, at the same time, compete with each other for resources. In this way, our multi-agent framework allows us to capture the coopetitive (cooperation and competition) nature of the global optimization in the IRP. Our experimental results show that this approach is competitive against well-known methods on published benchmarks for the IRP.

1   Introduction

For the past decades, combinatorial optimisation techniques have been the subject of researchers in operations research (OR), algorithms design and analysis, and artificial intelligence (AI). The dominant view point has been that of a *central intelligence*, aware of all relevant parameters, attempting to find a global solution to a problem. However, for optimisation problems that occur in distributed systems, such a *global view* may be unrealistic. In these problems, the decision making may be performed by several agents, none of whom may have an up-to-date picture of the entire state of the system. These agents also compete for resources in optimizing multiple competing objective functions.

We propose a multi-agent approach for solving the *Inventory Routing Problem (IRP)* ([4], [5], [10]) described as follows: The *Inventory Routing Problem* deals with a system where there is a single supplier supplying a certain good (eg: petrol) to multiple customers using the *vendor managed inventory* replenishment policy. In such system, supplier has an *unlimited stock* of the goods, and each customer keeps a *local storage* of such goods which is constantly being *consumed* at some consumption rate. The supplier constantly monitors the inventory level of all customers and make centralized *replenishment decisions* – namely, *when* to deliver, *how much* to deliver and what *routes* to take.

M. Ishizuka and A. Sattar (Eds.): PRICAI 2002, LNAI 2417, pp. 345–354, 2002.

In applying the Multi-Agent approach to the IRP, we view the optimization problem as a coopetitive (co-operative and competitive) process of multiple entities with different interest [11]. For the IRP, the entities in an IRP *solution configuration* are the vehicle drivers (for routes), customers and the individual deliveries. Each entity is represented by a corresponding *software agent.* The agents have defined *operations (or actions)* that allow then to explore better solutions (from its local perspective). Through a carefully designed *control and coordination scheme*, the agents are able to *cooperate* and *compete* with each other while aiming for global optimization. We have implemented our Multi-Agent approach for the IRP and compared the results obtained with those of well-known methods on the CFS benchmarks problems ([5]). The results show that our multi-agent approach is slightly better than that of [5].

In the remainder of the paper, we present the definition of the Inventory Routing Problem in Section 2; then in Sections 3 and 4, we introduce our multi-agent based solution to the IRP. Section 5 presents experimental results and benchmark comparison. In Section 6, we give concluding remarks and possible future directions.

2   The Inventory Routing Problem

We give a concise formulation of the Inventory Routing Problem (IRP) and refer the reader to [4] and [5] for a more comprehensive description. In the IRP that we are solving, we are given a *central depot* and N *customers*, together with their locations (given as (x, y) coordinates). From this, we can compute the *distance matrix* $\Delta = [\delta_{ij}]$, where δ_{ij} is the *distance* from customer i to customer j.

Each customer has a a local *storage capacity* of C_i and a constant *demand/consumption rate* d_i. We are given a *fleet of vehicles*, each with uniform *capacity* b. We are also given a *planning period* $[0..T]$ meaning that we need to plan the replenishment to the custumers over this period. to deliver stock to all the customers over the planning period. Each *delivery route* or simply *route* is formed by a sequence of *delivery visits* (or *service points*) to different customers, starting out from the depot and returning to the depot. There are several constraints on the solutions to the IRP: (1) total delivery quantity on each route is no greater than b, (2) there is stock-out of any customer through out the planning period, and (3i) for each customer, the maximum number of visits per day is bounded by f.

A *solution to the IRP is a set of delivery routes* Figure 1 shows the space/time model of an IRP solution with two routes. Each route consists of a sequence of visits spread over different times as illustrated by the vertical time axis. Note that, in general, each customer would be visited multiple times by different routes, and its inventory level will fluctuate.

The *optimization criteria* for the IRP is a weighted combination of three cost factors: (i) the *total distance traveled*, measured at c_δ per unit distance and probably sum of total time spent on trip (measured at c_τ per unit time), (ii) the

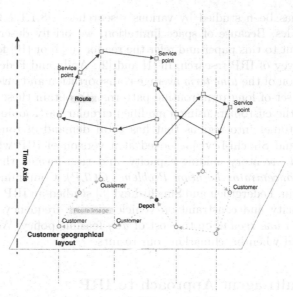

Fig. 1. Illustration of a 3-Dimensional IRP model. Horizonal plane represents geographical layout, and vertical axis represents *time* dimension. Routes are illustrated in a "spiral" shape, depicting the range of time they occupy, while their geographical image (projected in gray) forms 2-D tours.

total route setup cost, measured at c^r for each delivery route, and (iii) the *total inventory holding cost* for all customers.

The *inventory holding cost* for each customer is dependent on amount of local storage and duration they need to be kept. In a constant demand inventory model, the *customer inventory level*, $g_i(t)$, for customer i is given by $g_i(t) = \sum_{p \in S_{it}} q_{ip} - d_i t$, with $S_{it} = \{p | t_{ip} \le t\}$, where q_{ip} is the delivery quantity of the pth visit to customer i, and t_{ip} is the time of pth visit to customer i. The *inventory holding cost* for customer i is then given by $c^h \cdot \int_0^T g_i(t)dt$, where c^h is the inventory holding cost per unit time per unit stock. Figure 2 shows an example of the *inventory model* showing the customer inventory level over time.

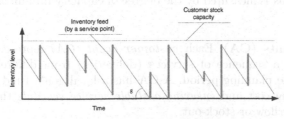

Fig. 2. Customer Inventory model. The total inventory cost for the customer is the c^h times the "area under the curve".

The IRP has been studied by various researchers ([8,1,1,2,3,5,4]) over the past two decades. Because of space limitation, we briefly describe only those that are relevant to this paper and refer the reader to [4] or [10] for a more comprehensive survey of IRP research. In [1] and [2], Anily and Federgruen studied the minimization of the *long term* average transportation and inventory costs by determining a set of long term routing patterns. To obtain these patterns, they first partition the customers using a modified circular partitioning scheme, then divide the customer into regions that has total demand of roughly one truck load. Bramel and Simchi-Levi [3] looked at a version of IRP where customers have *unlimited* inventory holding capacity, and transformed the problem into *Capacitated Concentrator Location Problem (CCLP)*. Combining the result of [1] and [3], Chan, Federgruen and Simchi-Levi [5] studied an IRP with unlimited customer capacity and constraint on vehicle visiting frequency for customers, and also gives a *lowerbound* on the cost of *any* feasible policy. We shall also use this lowerbound when benchmarking our results.

3   Our Multi-agent Approach to IRP

Multi-agent systems have traditionally been used in the development of a range of complex, typically distributed computer systems (See [9] or [12] for more details). Multi-agent systems have already been developed for many different application domains, especially industrial control systems [7].

In applying the Multi-Agent approach to the IRP, we view the optimization problem as a coopetitive (co-operative and competitive) process of multiple entities with different interest [11]. An IRP solution configuration consists of a set of routes, with each route consisting of a sequence of services (deliveries) to different customers along the route. Equivalently, an IRP configuration can be viewed as a set of *customer service plans*, one for each customer. Each plan consists of a sequence of services to the customer, which are served by different routes over time. Thus, for the IRP, the entities are the vehicle drivers (for routes), customers and the services. We therefore have the following agent classes:

Route agents (RA): Each *route agent (RA)* represents a route and consists of a sequence of services to different customer. An RA has the *local goal* of fully utilizing its delivery capacity (subject to capacity constraint b) and its *satisfaction status* is measured by the degree of capacity fulfillment and capacity violation.

Customer agents (CA): Each *customer agent (CA)* represents a customer and it contains a sequence of services (deliveries) from different routes that serves it over the planning period. A CA has a local goal of reducing the total inventory holding cost and *ensuring a stable service schedule* that reduces the risk of stock-overflow or stock-out.

Service agents (SA): Each *service agent (SA)* represents a service (delivery). Therefore, each RA will have access to its set of child SA's. And a CA will have access to its corresponding set of SA's. SA has limited operations, but they are important to the system. The local objective of a SA is to help to *reduce marginal costs* (decrease in the cost) that results from its actions.

The RA's and CA's represents the coarse-grain control (and deal with optimizing of routes and services), whereas the SA represents gives our approach the fine-grain decision making that is also important for solution space exploration.

Each agent has its own set of operations (actions) that these agents can perform in trying to optimize their local goals. In our current system, we also allow operations that improves local objectives but may violate one or more problem constraints. This allows the system more freedom to search the solution space, but introduces the problem of violation removal so as to move back to a feasible solution. In our system, we allow limited violations to occur as describe later.

Operations for Route Agents:

- *Catch Operation:* A catch operation looks for a suitable "nearby " (in a spacial and temporal neighborhood) SA from other routes to be included into this RA. The SA will be detached from its original route and included into this RA at a suitable position. This will increase its local capacity utilization and (globally) reduce route distance. Route capacity violation is allowed and this can be amended by other operations.
- *Split Operation:* A split operation looks for a suitable split point in its service sequence and breaks the route into two new routes. The original RA is reduced in size and a new RA is spawned. A split operation helps to amend routes with capacity violation.

Operations for Customer Agents:

- *Redistribute Operation:* A CA examines the delivery quantity of each service it received along the time period (by checking all its child SA's status), and move some delivery quantity from one service (agent) to another service (agent) to reducing the inventory holding cost.
- *Spawn Operation:* A CA spawns a new SA at the stock-out point to resolve the stock-out. This stock-out condition may occur when the delivery quantity for earlier SA is reduced. The newly spawned SA is assigned a new route (thus spawning also a new RA).

Operations for Service Agents:

- *Insert Operation:* Insert operation is similar to catch operation (for RA), except it is initialized by an SA. A SA surveys route in a local neighborhood, and remove itself from the current parent RA to join a new route agent which results in a reduced marginal cost.

- *Merge Operation:* It is also possible for an SA to remove itself completely, by postponing all its delivery quantity to the next service for the same customer or advancing it to the previous service. This would result two service agents to be "merged" into one.
- *Inventory Shift Operation:* This is similar to the redistribution operation of CA. However this operation only shifts inventory between the SA and its predecessor or successor (on the same customer). SA's may gain limited ability to amend route capacity violation through this operation.

The key for *central coordination* is the use of a *global cost function* to evaluate and select operations. For any operation Op, the global cost function is given by $E(Op) = C(Op) + P(Op)$, where $C(Op)$ is the marginal gain, and $P(Op)$ is the penalty cost. $C(Op)$ is defined to be the *estimated* global gain (reduction) in the objective function (incorporating total distance, time, route setup cost, and inventory holding cost). These are only "estimated" values since the *actual* gain obtained when the operation Op is deployed might propagate through many neighboring agents, and such evaluation would be outside the agents local scope. The *penalty* cost $P(Op)$ measures the "degree" of constraint violation. Thus, $P(Op)$ penalizes increase in violation and rewards decrease violation that is introduced by operation Op. The evaluation of $P(Op)$ relies on penalty coefficient of each constraint violation, and these are dynamically adjusted during the solution process. Detail of such adjustment is presented in next section.

4   Agent Coordination and Control

We introduced a sequential coordination scheme that simulates parallel agent execution. In this scheme, the agents post requests to express their preferred operations (actions). These requests are prioritized according to agent status, using a range value computed by the agent. All the requests are stored in a request-pool, while a random selector iteratively selects a request from the request-pool to process. The probability of an request being selected is proportional to its range. The schematic of this agent coordination algorithm is shown in Figure 3. Table 1 shows the agent request range computation.

```
setup: for each agent A
    post a request event
while (terminating condition not met)
    {   randomly select a request from the event pool
        inform corresponding agent to perform an operation
        adjust agent event range and repost a new event
        check for terminating condition
    }
```

Fig. 3. Request based agent coordination algorithm

Table 1. Agent request range computation

Agent	Request Range
Route Agent	$\left(\dfrac{\text{Delivery-amount}-b}{b}\right)^2 + \text{Modifier}$
Customer Agent	$\dfrac{S_i}{T \times f} + \text{Modifier}$
Service Agent	1

A periodical control scheme was also designed to adjust global environment during the solution process. This is similar to the type of the control mechanisms used in simulated annealing. Early in the solution process, we are more likely to allow agents to perform operations that violate constraints to allow for a wider solution space exploration. As search proceeds, this likelihood will be reduced to ensure that the final solution would be violation free. This control is implemented by adjusting the coefficients of the penalty function P. When the violation increases, the penalty coefficients also increases. causing operations that produce violations to be evaluated more costly, meanwhile encouraging violation amending operations. When violation decrease, we maintain or reduce the coefficients, allowing system sufficient iterations to perform more optimizing operations. (Refer to [10] for details.)

5   Experiment Results

We have implemented our multi-agent algorithm (we call it MAA) for the IRP. The system is implemented in Java. To benchmark its performance, we use the benchmarks provided by Chan, Federgruen and Simchi-Levi [5] (which we call the *CFS datasets*) as it is closest to our variant of the IRP. They also proved that the *long term average cost per unit time* of any feasible policy is at least B^* ([5]), where

$$B^* = \sum_{i=1}^{N} \left[\frac{d_i(2\delta_{0i}c^\delta + c^r)}{b} + \frac{c^h d_i/f}{2} \right].$$

However, the original CFS datasets was not available to us, and so we used the *same specification* ([5]) to generate a set of 80 CFS datasets for our experimentation. The CFS datasets consists of 80 randomly generated problem instances, based on 8 different sets of customer data and 10 different parameter settings for each set. The 8 sets of customer data contains 30, 50, 80, 100, 120, 150, 180 and 200 customers respectively. For each set, the locations of the customer are independent, and uniformly distributed over a square of size [100,100]. For each customer dataset, we use 10 different parameter settings for the route setup cost c^r, inventory holding cost c^h, and a "base" demand rate d, as shown in Table 2. The 10 parameter sets are also divided into three categories. Category I is meant to study the effect of route setup cost, Category II for inventory holding cost, and Category III the number of services per day.

Table 2. CFS dataset parameter groups

Parameter Set	Category	q	f	b	c^r	c^h	d
[1]	I	5	2	74	2	6	10
[2]	I	5	2	74	10	6	10
[3]	I	5	2	74	100	6	10
[4]	II	5	2	74	2	1	10
[5]	II	5	2	74	2	10	10
[6]	II	5	2	74	2	100	10
[7]	III	5	1	74	2	6	5
[8]	III	5	4	74	2	6	20
[9]	III	5	10	74	2	6	50
[10]	III	5	20	74	2	6	100

The 80 instances of the CFS datasets are then used to test our new algorithm. We benchmarked our solution quality against the solution quality obtained by the *CFS algorithm* ([5]), and the lower bound B^*. Table 3-4 show results for CFS, MAA and the comparison between them. In each table, we show the gap (expressed as a percentage) where $gap = (\frac{C}{B^*} - 1) \cdot 100\%$ measures the gap between the solution C obtained and the lower bound B^*.

From the tables, we can see that both the CFS and the MAA perform very well with respect to the lowerbound B^*. We also note the following:

- MAA has slightly better performance, with an overall average quality ratio of 1.078 compared to 1.09 for CFS. From table 5, we see that MAA out-performs CFS in 45 out of 80 instances.
- For the small dataset (30 customer), MAA performs much better than CFS.
- The results for Category I instances (param. set 1-3) show that both MAA and CFS performs better as the route setup cost c^r is increased, and MAA is generally slightly better than CFS.
- For Category II instances (param. set 4-6), both MAA and CFS performs better as the inventory holding cost cost c^h is increased. However, CFS is slightly better than MAA.
- For Category III instances (param. set 7-10), as the base demand is increased, the performance of CFS seem to be worse, while the MAA performs better. Here, MAA clearly out-performs CFS, and the difference increases as the base demand is increased.

It has been noted that CFS in [10] that the CFS algorithm gives priority to the inventory allocation sub-goal in its optimization algorithm which accounts for its good performance for Category II instances. However, when priority is given to other criteria (as in Categories I and III), CFS is not as effective. In contrast, the MAA is robust across all the three categories of CFS instances. This can be attributed to the distributed decision making inherent in our multi-agent approach. The system can flexibly shift tradeoffs between the various criteria as their importance changes. (We refer the interested reader to [10] for more experimental results.)

Table 3. Solutions quality of CFS on CFS datasets, measured as percentage exceeding lowerbound B^*. Source [5]

Param set	30	50	80	100	120	150	180	200	Avg
1	14.0	11.1	11.0	10.0	9.6	9.4	8.6	9.0	10.3
2	13.7	9.8	10.9	9.9	9.6	9.4	8.5	8.9	10.1
3	10.3	8.9	8.6	7.9	7.9	7.6	6.7	7.0	8.1
4	15.3	11.1	11.5	12.0	10.5	10.0	9.0	9.3	11.1
5	11.2	8.9	8.8	8.0	7.8	7.5	7.0	7.2	8.3
6	1.7	1.3	1.3	1.2	1.1	1.1	1.0	1.0	1.2
7	10.0	8.0	7.8	7.1	6.9	6.7	6.2	6.4	7.4
8	15.0	11.2	11.8	11.4	10.6	10.3	9.2	9.6	11.1
9	15.3	11.2	11.6	11.9	10.5	10.0	9.1	9.3	11.1
10	15.4	10.4	11.1	12.2	10.1	9.6	8.8	8.9	10.8
Avg	12.2	9.2	9.4	9.2	8.5	8.2	7.4	7.7	9.0

Table 4. Solution quality of our MAA on CFS Datasets, measured as percentage exceeding lowerbound B^*.

Param set	30	50	80	100	120	150	180	200	Avg
1	9.9	9.4	10.6	10.5	9.2	8.4	10.2	8.7	9.6
2	10.5	9.4	10.2	10.3	9.4	9.0	10.1	8.2	9.6
3	7.5	7.4	9.1	8.6	8.1	6.8	8.0	7.5	7.9
4	10.7	9.0	11.6	12.1	10.5	8.2	11.0	8.5	10.2
5	9.3	8.2	9.1	8.3	8.1	8.2	8.8	7.7	8.5
6	3.9	3.5	2.5	1.2	1.9	2.7	2.5	2.2	2.6
7	10.5	7.9	8.6	8.1	7.1	7.9	8.3	7.4	8.2
8	9.3	9.7	10.9	11.3	10.1	8.4	10.5	8.8	9.9
9	7.8	6.8	7.4	9.4	8.0	6.6	8.2	6.7	7.6
10	6.3	4.2	3.7	4.4	4.5	2.8	4.4	3.9	4.3
Avg	8.6	7.6	8.4	8.4	7.7	6.9	8.2	7.0	7.8

Table 5. Comparison of MAA and CFS on CFS Datasets. Each entry is obtained by subtracting the each entry in Table 3 from the corresponding entry in Table 4. The highlighted negative entries indicate where MAA out-performs CFS.

Param set	30	50	80	100	120	150	180	200	Avg
1	-4.1	-1.7	-0.4	0.5	-0.4	-1.0	1.6	-0.3	-0.7
2	-3.2	-0.4	-0.7	0.4	-0.2	-0.4	1.6	-0.7	-0.5
3	-2.8	-1.5	0.5	0.7	0.2	-0.8	1.3	0.5	-0.2
4	-4.6	-2.1	0.1	0.1	0.0	-1.8	2.0	-0.8	-0.9
5	-1.9	-0.7	0.3	0.3	0.3	0.7	1.8	0.5	0.2
6	2.2	2.2	1.2	0.0	0.8	1.6	1.5	1.2	1.3
7	0.5	-0.1	0.8	1.0	0.2	1.2	2.1	1.0	0.8
8	-5.7	-1.5	-0.9	-0.1	-0.5	-1.9	1.3	-0.8	-1.3
9	-7.5	-4.4	-4.2	-2.5	-2.5	-3.4	-0.9	-2.6	-3.5
10	-9.1	-6.2	-7.4	-7.8	-5.6	-6.8	-4.4	-5.0	-6.5
Avg	-3.6	-1.6	-1.1	-0.7	-0.8	-1.3	0.8	-0.7	-1.1

6   Conclusion

In this paper we presented a novel multi-agent based solution approach to the IRP problem. Our approach is effective in capturing the distributed nature and also the coopetitive nature of the entities in the problem and the solution. Entities are modelled as agents implemented in software and agents have local operations (or actions). In this way, we are able to map the solution space exploration into a series of actions of local agents. We also devised a coordination scheme which make the agents cooperate and compete n the search for a good global solution. Experimental results with the CFS datasets suggest that our new approach gives competitive results. We are currently studying several issues related to our multi-agent approach in order to improve its performance and to gain a better understanding of the approach. We are also extending our approach to tackle related problems such as the *multi-depot IRP*, and *IRP with mixed inventory types*.

References

1. Anily, S. and Ecdergruen, A. "One Warehouse Multiple retailer Systems with Vehicle Routing Costs", Management Science, Vol. 36, No. 1, January 1990.
2. Anily, S. and Federgruen, A. "two-echelon Distribution System with Vehicle Routing Costs and Central Inventories", Operations Research, Vol. 41, No. 1, January-February 1993.
3. Bramel, J and Simchi-Levi, D. "A Location Based Heuristic for General Routing Problems", Operations Research, Vol. 43, No. 4, July-August, 1995.
4. Campbell, A. M., Clarke, L. W., Kleywegt, A. J. and Savelsbergh, M. W. P. "The Inventory Routing Problem", Fleet Management and Logistics, Kluwer Academic Publishers, 1998, 95-113.
5. Chan, L. M. A., Federgruen, A. and Simchi-Levi, D. "Probabilistic Analysis and Practical Algorithms for Inventory-Routing Models", Operations Research, vol. 46, No. 1, January-February, 1998.
6. Durfee, E. H., "Distributed Problem Solving and Planning", Luch, M. et al.(Eds.) ACAI 2001, LNAI 2086, pp. 118-149, 2001.
7. Ferber, J., "Multi-agent Systems: An Introduction to Distributed Artificial Intelligence", Harlow:Addison-Wesley, 1998.
8. Federgruen, A. and Zipkin, P. "A Combined Vehicle Routing and Inventory Allocation Problem", Operations Research, Vol. 32(1984), 1019-1036.
9. Franklin, S. and Graesser, A., "Is it an Agent, or just a Program?: A Taxonomy for Autonomous Agents", Proceedings of the Third International Workshop on Agent Theories, Architectures, and Languages, Springer-Verlag, 1996.
10. Lao, Y. Z., "A Multi-Agent Based Framework for the Inventory Routing Problem", MSc Thesis, School of Computing, National University of Singapore, 2002.
11. Nievergelt, J., Rolim, J. and Widmayer, P., "Transport Network Management: Cooperative and Competitive Decisions in Distributed Combinatorial Optimization", Research Project under Swiss Science Foundation, ETH-Zurich, 1995-2000.
12. Russell, S. and Norvig, P., "Intelligent Agents", *in* Artificial Intelligence: A Modern Approach, Prentice-Hall, Inc., 1995.

An Agent-Based Hybrid Intelligent System for Financial Investment Planning

Zili Zhang[1]* and Chengqi Zhang[2]

[1] School of Computing and Mathematics
Deakin University, Geelong Victoria 3217, Australia
zzhang@deakin.edu.au
[2] Faculty of Information Technology, University of Technology, Sydney
PO Box 123 Broadway, NSW 2007 Australia

Abstract. Many complex problems including financial investment planning require hybrid intelligent systems that integrate many intelligent techniques including expert systems, fuzzy logic, neural networks, and genetic algorithms. However, hybrid intelligent systems are difficult to develop due to complicated interactions and technique incompatibilities. This paper describes a hybrid intelligent system for financial investment planning that was built from agent points of view. This system currently consists of 13 different agents. The experimental results show that all agents in the system can work cooperatively to provide reasonable investment advice. The system is very flexible and robust. The success of the system indicates that agent technologies can significantly facilitate the construction of hybrid intelligent systems.

1 Introduction

Real-world applications such as financial investment planning are almost always made up of a large number of components that interact in varying and complex ways. This leads to complex behaviour that is difficult to understand, predict and manage. Take one sub-task of financial planning – financial portfolio management – as an example. The task environment has many interesting features, including [1]: (1) the enormous amount of continually changing, and generally unorganized, information available; (2) the variety of kind of information that can and should be brought to bear on the task (market data, financial report data, technical models, analysts' reports, breaking news, etc.); and (3) the many sources of uncertainty and dynamic change in the environment.

It is obvious that financial planning is a typical complex problem. In financial investment planning many different components or sub-tasks are involved, each of which requires different types of processing. To solve such complex problems, a great diversity of techniques are required. These techniques can be divided into two categories: (1) traditional hard computing techniques including operations

---

* The author's address in China: Computer Science Department, Southwest China Normal University, Chongqing 400715.

M. Ishizuka and A. Sattar (Eds.): PRICAI 2002, LNAI 2417, pp. 355–364, 2002.

research, system science/engineering, expert systems, and (2) soft computing techniques including fuzzy logic (FL), neural networks (NN), and genetic algorithms (GA). In this paper, the techniques in both categories are called *intelligent techniques*. These techniques are complementary rather than competitive and thus must be used in combination and not exclusively [2]. This results in systems called *hybrid intelligent systems*.

Hybrid intelligent systems are computational systems that integrate different intelligent techniques in these two categories. These systems are now being used to support complex problem solving and decision making in a wide variety of tasks. Hybrid intelligent systems allow the representation and manipulation of different types and forms of data and knowledge which may come from various sources. Refined system knowledge is used during reasoning and decision making processes producing more effective results.

However, the design and development of *hybrid intelligent systems* is difficult because they have a large number of parts or components that have many interactions. Existing software development techniques (for example, object-oriented analysis and design) cannot manage these complex interactions efficiently as these interactions may occur at unpredictable times, for unpredictable reasons, between unpredictable components. Is there any better way to construct hybrid intelligent systems? This paper describes the attempt to build a hybrid intelligent system for financial investment planning from agent points of view.

An agent is an encapsulated computer system that is situated in some environment and that is capable of flexible, autonomous action in that environment in order to meet its design objectives [3]. A multi-agent system (MAS) can be defined as a loosely coupled network of entities that work together to make decisions or solve problems that are beyond the individual capabilities or knowledge of each entity [4]. These entities – agents – are autonomous and may be heterogeneous in nature. From a multi-agent perspective, agents in MASs are autonomous and can engage in flexible, high-level interactions. The flexible nature of interactions means that agents can make decisions about the nature and scope of interactions at run-time rather than design time. MASs are good at complex, dynamic interactions. Thus a multi-agent perspective is suitable for modeling, design, and construction of hybrid intelligent systems. The success of the agent-based hybrid intelligent system for financial investment planning provides a strong support for this claim. This paper will demonstrate how to design and implement such a system and presents some useful experimental results.

The remainder of the paper is structured as follows. Section 2 is the description of the investment planning problem and the technical models used to solve the problem. The agent architecture for investment planning is discussed in Section 3. The emphasis is on the flexibility and robustness of the system. The implementation details are described in Section 4. The experimental results are presented in Section 5. The comparison with related work and evaluation of the system is given in Section 6. Finally, Section 7 is the concluding remarks.

2   Description of the Investment Planning Problem

When a person wants to invest some money somewhere, he usually turns to the financial investment adviser for advice. The first thing the adviser needs to do is to understand the client's individual circumstances. The adviser may ask the client to provide the following information about himself: his financial position (annual income, total net-worth etc.), age, tax effectiveness, and his investment attitude (aggressive or conservative) etc. Based on the information, the adviser should evaluate the client's financial risk tolerance ability and adjust it according to the interest rate trend (falling or increasing). With the client's risk tolerance as well as his age information, the adviser is then provide advice to the client how to allocate portions of his investment across the three main asset types: savings, income, and growth (asset allocation). This should be based on some investment advisory model.

Suppose the adviser suggests the client invest the growth part of his investment in the stock market after evaluating his financial risk tolerance ability. How can one select a portfolio for the client under his constraint (risk tolerance level, return rate etc.)? The adviser should gather some information about the stock market. The information includes market data, financial report data, technical models, analysts' reports, breaking news etc. After gathering the information, the adviser then makes a portfolio selection decision based on some models (e.g., the Markowitz model, the fuzzy probability model etc.). This is a typical scenario for investment planning.

In the agent-based financial investment planning system, the following models/techniques will be integrated together: a client financial risk tolerance model and a client asset allocation model, both are based on fuzzy logic [5]; two interest rate prediction models, one based on neural networks, the other based on fuzzy logic and genetic algorithms [6]; three portfolio selection models–Markowitz's model [7], the fuzzy probability model, and the possibility distribution model [8]; and expert systems with explanation mechanisms. In addition to these models/techniques, an operations research software package called *LINDO* for solving quadratic programming problems (*http://www.lindo.com/*) and a matrix software package called *MatrixLib* for solving eigenvalues of matrices (*http://www. mathtools.com/*) will also be integrated.

3   The Agent Architecture for Investment Planning

In order to identify which components should be contained in a typical financial planning system, without loss of generality, consider a financial house providing investment advice for clients. In such a house, there are: a front counter or reception desk clerk, one or more personnel officer(s), and many financial investment experts (decision makers). The advice giving (decision making) process is initiated by a user contacting the front desk clerk with a set of requirements. The clerk asks the personnel officer to provide the experts' profile, and then delegates the task to one or more experts based on experts' profiles. The experts then work on the task and try to give their recommendations with or without external help. After the experts finish preparing a recommendation (if the task was assigned to more than one expert, the recommendations from different experts must be combined to form a final one), they pass it to the front desk clerk. Finally, the clerk sends the advice to the user. Such a typical process can help us analyze and design a multi-agent system for financial planning.

Existing software development techniques (typically, object-oriented) are inadequate for modeling agent-based systems. Extant approaches fail to adequately capture an agent's flexible, autonomous problem-solving behavior, the richness of an agent's interactions, and the complexity of an agent system's organizational structures. For these reasons, an agent-oriented methodology called *Gaia* [9] was used to analyze and design this agent-based hybrid intelligent system for financial investment planning. In Gaia, analysis and design are well-separated phases. Based on Gaia, the emphasis of the analysis and design is to identify the key *roles* in the system and document the various *agent types* that will be used in the system.

Based on the statements in the first paragraph in this section and the Gaia methodology, it is comparatively straightforward to identify the roles in the agent-based hybrid intelligent system for financial planning. The front desk clerk's behavior falls into two distinct roles: USERHANDLER acting as an interface to the user and WORKPLANNER overseeing the process inside the organization. The personnel officer's behavior falls into another two roles: CAPABILITYRECORDER keeping track of the profiles and CAPABILITYMATCHER checking the profiles. The experts' behaviors are covered by DECISIONMAKER, HELPPROVIDER, and DECISIONAGGREGATOR roles. The final role is that of the USER who requires the decision.

Based on the key *roles* identified, the agent model can be generated (Figure 1). This shows, for most cases, a one-to-one correspondence between roles and agent types. The exception is for the CAPABILITYRECORDER and CAPABILITYMATCHER roles which, because of their high degree of interdependence, are grouped into a single agent type.

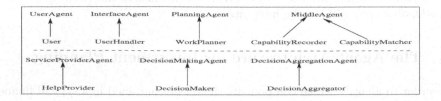

Fig. 1. The Agent Model of the System

From the above discussion, it is clear that there are seven types of agents in the hybrid intelligent system – user agent, interface agent, planning agent, middle agent, service provider agent, decision making agent, and decision aggregation agent. Now it is time to find an appropriate multi-agent architecture to put all these agents together so as to form the agent-based hybrid intelligent system for financial planning.

When incorporating intelligent techniques into multi-agent systems to form agent-based hybrid intelligent systems, one criterion that must be met, is that any agent in the system can access any of the intelligent techniques available in the system when needed. Meanwhile, the flexibility, robustness, and interoperability of the resulting system must be ensured.

With all these observations in mind, the architecture of the financial planning system is determined, which is shown in Figure 2. The behaviors of each kind of agent in the system (except the user agent) are briefly described below:

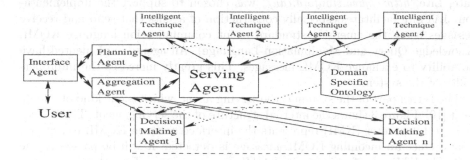

Fig. 2. Architecture of Agent-Based Hybrid Intelligent System

Interface Agent. This agent interacts with the user (or user agent). It asks the user to provide his personal information and requirements, and provides the user with a final decision or advice that best meets the user's requirements.

Planning Agent. The planning agent is in charge of the activation and synchronization of different agents. It elaborates a work plan and is in charge of ensuring that such a work plan is fulfilled. It receives the assignments from the interface agent.

Decision Making Agent. It is application-specific, i.e., it has its own knowledge base; it must have some meta-knowledge about when it needs the help of intelligent technique agents (e.g., pre or post processing some data); it can ask intelligent technique agents to accomplish some sub-tasks.

Serving Agent. The serving agent is a matchmaker – one kind of middle agent [10]. It keeps track of the names, ontologies, and capabilities of all registered intelligent technique agents in the system; it can reply to the query of a decision making agent with appropriate intelligent technique agent's name and ontology.

Service Provider Agent. Most of the service provider agents in the system are intelligent technique agents. Each intelligent technique agent can provide services for decision making agents with one or some kind of combined intelligent techniques; it can send back the processed results to decision making agents; it must advertise its capabilities to the serving agent.

Decision Aggregation Agent. When decision making agents finish the assigned tasks they return the results to the decision aggregation agent. The aggregation agent chooses one of the alternative decisions, or performs an aggregation of the different results into a final one.

The ontology is the foundation for agent communication. All agents in the system interpret the content of received messages based on the ontology.

4   Implementation of the System

The most important implementation criterion of such a system is platform independent. With this observation in mind, the JATLite (Java Agent Template, Lite, *http://java.stanford.edu/*) was chosen to support the implementation. JATLite facilitates especially construction of agents that send and receive messages using the emerging standard agent communication language KQML (Knowledge Query and Manipulation Language). All agents implemented have the ability to exchange KQML messages. This greatly increases the interoperability of the system.

The kernel part of the system is the serving agent, which is one kind of middle agent [10]. Figure 3 shows the internal structure of the serving agent. The KQML Message Interpreter (KMI) represents the interface between KQML router and agents. Once an incoming KQML message is detected, it will be passed to the KMI. The KMI transfers incoming KQML messages into a form that agents can understand. The implementation of KMI is based on JATLite KQMLLayer Templates. The service provider maintenance module in the serving agent has three functions: To add an entry that contains the intelligent technique agent's name, capability, and ontology to the database; delete an entry from the database; and retrieve the database to find out intelligent technique agents with a specific capability. The last function is usually called *matchmaking*. The introduction of middle agent in the system facilitates the flexibility and robustness. How middle agents can result in the flexibility and robustness of the system will be discussed in another paper.

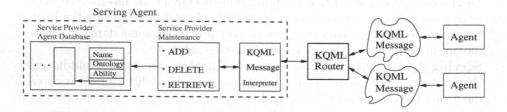

Fig. 3. Serving Agent Structure

As mentioned in Section 2, some legacy software packages are integrated in the system. This implies that these software packages must be converted into agents in some way. Generally, there are three main approaches to be taken: implementing a *transducer*, implementing a *wrapper*, and *rewriting* the original program [11]. Here the second approach – implementing a wrapper – was adopted to wrap the software packages by using Java Native Interface [12] and JATLite KQML layer templates.

Under the support of JATLite, the practical architecture of the system is depicted in Figure 4. Figure 5 shows the user interface of the system, which can start from any Internet Browser or appletviewer.

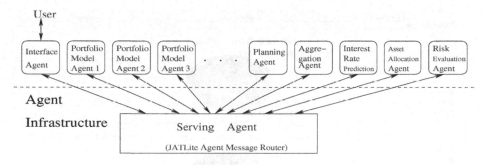

Fig. 4. Practical Architecture of the System

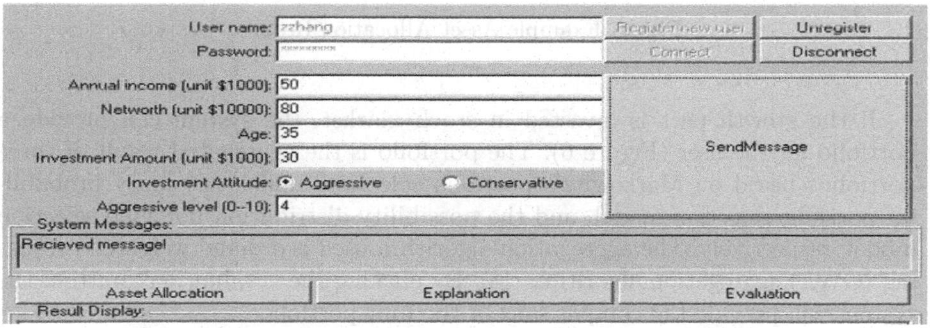

Fig. 5. User Interface of the System

To use the system, the user needs to type the user name and the password he likes in the corresponding fields and click "register new user" to register for the first time. Thereafter, just input the registered user name and password and click "connect". The user then can input his annual income, networth etc. information to the system and click "sendmessage" button. The system provides asset allocation information, explanations of how to get the results, and the evaluation of different portfolios in the "result display" window (see the next section). If the user wants to leave the system, click "unregister" and "disconnect".

5 Experimental Results

The system can provides reasonable financial investment planning information based on the user provided data and some relevant models. Figure 6 shows the asset allocation results when the annual income is $50,000, networth $800,000, age 35, investment amount $30,000, and investment attitude is aggressive (level 4). By clicking the "explanation" button, the corresponding explanation of how to get the results is displayed in the "result display" window.

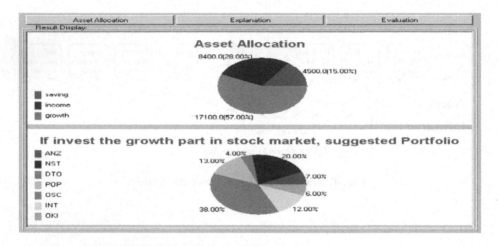

Fig. 6. Example Asset Allocation Results

If the growth part is invested in stock market, the system can provide a portfolio for the user (Figure 6). The portfolio is the aggregated result of three portfolios based on Markowitz's portfolio selection model, the fuzzy probability portfolio selection model, and the possibility distribution portfolio selection model, respectively. The aggregation algorithm used is ordered weighted averaging (OWA) aggregation algorithm [13]. By clicking the "evaluation" button, the system will provide the comparisons of the four portfolios.

6 Comparison with Related Work and Evaluations

This paper described the construction of a hybrid intelligent system from agent points of view. Thus far, there is also some other research work involved in this topic.

One of such attempts is the MIX multi-agent platform [16]. Another such attempt is the PREDICTOR system [2] (pp.153-173). In [14], Khosla and Dillon introduce a computational architecture called IMAHDA (Intelligent Multi-Agent Hybrid Distributed Architecture). A more recent attempt is the multi-agent architecture for fuzzy modeling [15]. Delgado et al. proposed a hybrid learning system that combines different fuzzy modeling techniques by means of a multi-agent architecture. In [17], Jacobsen proposed a generic architecture for hybrid intelligent systems.

Among the above agent-based hybrid frameworks or systems, the MIX, PREDICTOR, and the architecture for fuzzy modeling only integrated very limited soft computing techniques. Both the MIX and PREDICTOR systems are focused on the integration of neural networks and symbolic technologies such as expert systems. The multi-agent architecture of Delgado et al. concentrated on the integration of different fuzzy modeling techniques such as fuzzy clustering, fuzzy rule generation, and fuzzy rule tuning techniques. In MIX and PREDICTOR systems, the way for integrating intelligent techniques into multi-agent systems is to embed the intelligent techniques in each individual agent. The MIX and IMAHDA architectures are inflexible as no middle agent [10] was used. The work in [17] is focused on the micro (intra-agent) level of agents, i.e., the integration and interaction of different components within one agent. The macro (inter-agent) level integration and interaction are ignored.

Compared with the related work, the hybrid intelligent system described in this paper has the following crucial characteristics that differentiate this research from others: (1) Each decision making agent can easily access all the intelligent techniques and other techniques (service providers) available in the system whenever needed. One service provider agent can also ask other service provider agents for help; (2) The ability to add/delete service provider agents to/from the system dynamically; (3) The presence of the serving agent in this framework allows adaptive system organization; (4) Overall system robustness is facilitated through the use of the serving agent. For example, if a particular service provider (e.g., interest rate prediction agent) disappears, a requester agent (decision making agent) can find another one with the same or similar capabilities by interrogating the serving agent; (5) The agent-based hybrid intelligent systems can make decisions about the nature and scope of interactions at run-time.

From the above characteristics, one can easily see that the system is very *flexible and robust*. The *interoperability* among agents is good as all agents use the standardized agent communication language – KQML.

7   Concluding Remarks

This paper described an agent-based hybrid intelligent system for financial investment planning. This system consists of 13 different agents. Many techniques/packages including fuzzy logic, neural networks, genetic algorithms, expert systems, operations research software package, matrix operation software package, portfolio selection models based on standard probability theory, fuzzy probability theory, and possibility distribution theory were integrated under a unifying agent framework.

Based on the experiments conducted, it is evident that the system can provide reasonable financial investment advice and is flexible, robust, and interoperable.

The success of the system indicates that agent technologies can significantly facilitate the building of hybrid intelligent systems.

Acknowledgement. The authors would like to thank Mr Hong Hu's support in implementing the system.

References

1. K. Sycara, K. Decker and D. Zeng, Intelligent Agents in Portfolio Management, in: N. R. Jennings and M. J. Wooldridge (Eds.), *Agent Technology: foundations, Applications, and Markets,* Springer, Berlin, 1998, 267-281.
2. S. Goonatilake and S. Khebbal (Eds.), *Intelligent Hybrid Systems,* Wiley, 1995.
3. M. Wooldridge, Agent-Based Software engineering, *IEE Proc. Software Engineering,* Vol. 144, No. 1, 1997, 26-37.
4. G. Weiss (Ed.), *Multiagent Systems: A Modern Approach to Distributed Artificial Intelligence,* The MIT Press, 1999.
5. G. Bojadziev and M. Bojadziev, *Fuzzy Logic For Business, Finance, and Management,* World Scientific, Singapore, 1997.
6. Stephen T. Welstead, *Neural Network and Fuzzy Logic Applications in C/C++,* Wiley, New York, 1994.
7. H. Markowitz, *Portfolio Selection: Efficient Diversification of Investments (2nd ed.),* Blackwell, 1991.
8. H. Tanaka, P. Guo, and I. Turksen, Portfolio Selection Based on Fuzzy Probabilities and Possibility Distributions, *Fuzzy Sets and Systems,* Vol. 111, 2000, 387-397.
9. M. Wooldrige, N. Jennings, and D. Kinny, The Gaia Methodology for Agent-Oriented Analysis and Design, *Journal of Autonomous Agents and Multi-Agent Systems,* Vol. 3, No. 3, 2000, 285-312.
10. K. Decker, K. Sycara, and M. Williamson, Middle Agents for the Internet, *Proceedings of 15th International Joint Conference on Artificial Intelligence,* Nogoya, Japan, 1997, 578-583.
11. M. R. Genesereth and S. P. Ketchpel, Software Agents, *Communications of ACM,* Vol.37, No.7, 1994, 48-53.
12. R. Gordon, *Essential JNI: Java Native Interface,* Prentice-Hall, New Jersey, 1998.
13. Z. Zhang and C. Zhang, Result Fusion in Multi-Agent Systems Based on OWA Operator, *Proceedings of 23rd Australasian Computer Science Conference,* IEEE Computer Society Press, NJ, 2000, 234-240.
14. R. Khosla and T. Dillon, *Engineering Intelligent Hybrid Multi-Agent Systems,* Kluwer Academic Publishers, Boston, 1997.
15. M. Delgado, A. F. Gómez-Skarmeta et al., A Multi-Agent Architecture for Fuzzy Modeling, *International Journal of Intelligent Systems,* Vol. 14, 1999, 305-329.
16. C. Iglesias, J. Gonzales, and J. Velasco, MIX: A General Purpose Multiagent Architecture, in: M. Wooldridge, J. Muller, and M. Tambe (Eds.), *Intelligent Agents II (ATAL'95),* LNCS 1037, Springer, 1996, 251-266.
17. H.-A. Jacobsen, A Generic Architecture for Hybrid Intelligent Systems, in: T. Furuhashi et al. (Eds.), *Deep Fusion of Computational and Symbolic Processing,* Physica-Verlag, 2001, 145-173.

Socially Intelligent Aerial Combat Simulator

Henry Hexmoor[1,2] and Xin Zhang[1]

[1]Department of Computer Science & Computer Engineering
University of Arkansas
Fayetteville, AR 72701

[2] Center for Multisource Information Fusion
Department of Industrial Engineering
State University of New York at Buffalo
Buffalo, NY 14260
{hexmoor, xxz03}@uark.edu

Abstract. We are exploring teaming in complex and dynamic environments that requires reasoning about roles and social influences. Towards that end we describe our implemented testbed and experiments that empirically show effects of such reasoning in a team setting.

1 Introduction

We have developed a testbed to explore teamwork and explicit reasoning about roles. We are seeking methods whereby agents reason about teamwork issues such as forming, joining, and working with teammates. Beyond the model of teamwork such as Cohen and Levesque's now famous Joint Intentions theory [2], there has been some work on monitoring team effectiveness and tools for composing teams; Karma-Teamcore is an example [7]. Tambe's work describes a methodology he calls Team Oriented Programming whereby a human designer interacts with the system to determine roles and individuals and assign roles and plans to individuals. Our developments are similar but the intent is for the agents to autonomously determine when and how they work with a team, and there is no notion of an external system designer. In this paper we present our testbed and discuss preliminary results of contrasting strategies for agents who might work in a team. Elsewhere, we considered fundamental issues about the nature of teams of agents and the mental states of the agents required for the formation of a team [1]. We put forward some criteria for the existence of a team as a guide for the development of systems of artificial social agents. We posited that a "*team*" is an aggregation of agents with a common mental state that includes having a common intention, awareness of being a member of the team and the team's abilities, and a cooperative attitude. Furthermore team members must have autonomy in order to form intentions. Later we extended that work to measure team effectiveness [3]. This paper offers empirical results for effectiveness in a class of teams.

M. Ishizuka and A. Sattar (Eds.): PRICAI 2002, LNAI 2417, pp. 365-374, 2002.

In our implemented testbed three or more fighter aircraft agents have the mission to deliver a bomb over a remote designated site. There is a one to one relationship between agents and planes. Artificial agents control all the planes except one, which is controlled by a human operator. The human operator controls its plane in the field along with the other planes, and will have similar visual and auditory sensing as well as similar flight maneuvering capabilities. The system is implemented in Java.

We simulate five Surface to Air Missile sites (SAMs), which are randomly generated each time when the program starts running. Figure 1 shows the main simulator screen with two agent-controlled planes flying close together followed by a human-controlled plane. A user friendly GUI allows the user to see the base runway (lower left in Figure 1), mountains, terrain, target (beyond the screen in the upper right), and SAMs. Figure 1 shows one of the planes firing just short of a SAM site. As the agent interacts, a message window pops up to show the aircraft agent information, shown in Figure 2. The autonomous agents are allowed 10 atomic roles based on the situation. There is also several buttons in the main GUI (Figure 1) allowing users to stop or run the application at any time. Running is indicated by "play" in Figure 1.

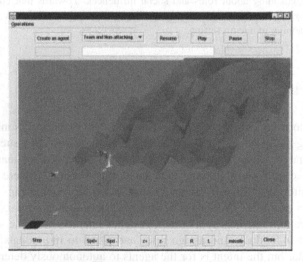

Fig. 1. Testbed and its GUI

Sensors onboard planes report locations of threats from SAMs. SAMs can be either averted or neutralized. The planes flying over the terrain with SAMs have limited sensing ability. Therefore, judicious sharing of sensed data as well as sharing fire power are important. SAM sites move small random distances. SAMs have limited capabilities for shooting the aircraft in their range modeled with probabilities, e.g. 5% when a SAM has full power. SAMs are distracted and have more difficulty when there are multiple planes, or when the agent has already been informed of the SAM position by its teammates. We model the SAM's ability to shoot by calculating the dynamic probabilities of downing planes. The agent's overall decision to act comes from consideration of the conversational and physical states, as well as the status of its social network. The agents are by and large autonomous in order to react to the environment. For example, after taking off from the base station, agents can fly toward targets while avoiding SAMs. *Roles* are used here to describe the agents' performances at different stages.

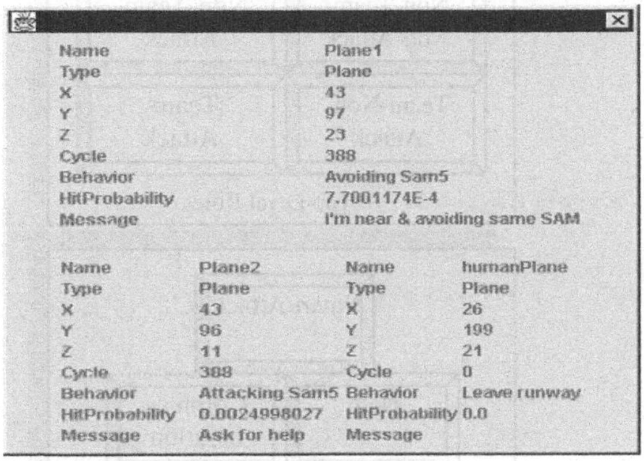

Name	Plane1		
Type	Plane		
X	43		
Y	97		
Z	23		
Cycle	388		
Behavior	Avoiding Sam5		
HitProbability	7.7001174E-4		
Message	I'm near & avoiding same SAM		
Name	Plane2	Name	humanPlane
Type	Plane	Type	Plane
X	43	X	26
Y	96	Y	199
Z	11	Z	21
Cycle	388	Cycle	0
Behavior	Attacking Sam5	Behavior	Leave runway
HitProbability	0.0024998027	HitProbability	0.0
Message	Ask for help	Message	

Fig. 2. Agent information pop up window

The agent can adopt different roles to perform a variety of functionalities according to the environment. Agents and roles don't need to follow one to one assignment. Different agents can adopt a given role simultaneously, but one agent can only adopt one role at a time.

In the remainder of this paper, we will present the team-oriented ideas in the testbed, and discuss how agents handle roles in team or non-team formation. We will then outline an experiment where we measure the time to complete the mission versus the probability of being shot down under a few strategies, which we call top level roles. We then review related work and offer concluding remarks.

2 Team Roles

2.1 Role Hierarchy

We have developed a role hierarchy based on the testbed, shown in Figure 3. The following ten atomic roles are at the lowest level: Take-off, Fly-toward-target, Avoid-sam, Avoid-airplane, Attack-sam, Go-around, Send-message, Receive-message, Respond-message and Land. The agent will assume only one of these ten atomic roles at a time. Take-off is the role that the agent adopts when it has just departed from the base station. The agent will take Fly-toward-target role at later time in order to fly over the terrain to the target. Agents take the Avoid-airplane role when two agents are too close to each other in order to avoid collision. Avoid-sam is the role that agents assume to avoid the danger posed by a SAM site after detecting the SAM. Other types of atomic roles will be explained later.

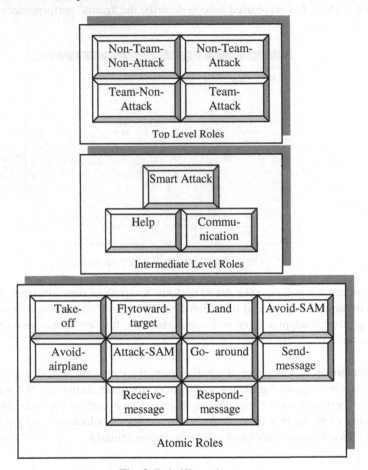

Fig. 3. Role Hierarchy

More complex roles are composed of atomic roles for more sophisticated capabilities. Help, Communication, and Smart-Attack are three intermediate roles. Help is a social action that agents in a team use to fly together and to attack a SAM site. If one agent needs help, other agents can assume Help roles to help the agent confronting a SAM in its attack on the SAM. Communicate is a speech act for agents to inform one another about their locations as well as status of help. The Communication role is composed of three atomic roles of Send-message, Receive-message, and Respond-messages. When an agent is a part of a team, Communication role is assumed by a team member to exchange information with other agents. An agent takes Smart-Attack role when the agent sees a SAM and has committed to attack. Smart-Attack Role is composed of Attack-sam role and Go-around role, which means the agent attacks the SAM while maintaining a safe distance and moving around the SAM toward the target. The Attack-sam role alone does not take self-protection and moving toward target into account.

Combining atomic and intermediate roles, we defined four complex roles at the top-most level for the testbed: Non-Team-Non-Attack, Non-Team-Attack, Team-Non-Attack, and Team-Attack as the main roles. When adopting Non-Team-Non-Attack role, each agent performs independently, and the agent does not attack the SAMs. After the agent takes off from the base, it will fly toward the target. When it sees SAMs, it will avoid the SAMs until land. Non-Team-Attack role is the same as Non-Team-Non-Attack role, except that the agents assume Smart-Attack role. When a SAM is detected within their visual range they could attack but since the distances are far, their attack will be inaccurate. In this role, agents wait until they reach closer to the SAM for more accurate attack.

When the agents take Non-Team roles (both in Attack and in Non-Attack roles), they do not communicate or consider one another in their decision making process. Under Non-Team roles, the agent is independent, and will fly without taking account of other agents.

In Team roles (both in Team-Non-Attack and Team-Attack roles), all the agents will be in one team, and are acting as team members while performing their own task. Each agent will consider the performance of other agents via Communication, or Help roles. In Team-Non-Attack role, agents will communicate with one another to stay informed of such as the location of the SAMs they have detected. Therefore, even if an agent doesn't see any SAMs on its way to the target, it might already know where SAMs are by getting the messages from other team members. Communication provides agents with broader viewing areas (since the agent can "see" what the others "see"), thus have higher chance of avoiding SAMs. Since the agents in Team-Non-Attack role doesn't have attack features, they don't need to fly near to the agent to help each other.

In Team-Attack role, agents will form a team to aid one another in attacking a SAM site within certain distance. When agents form a team, each agent can communicate with other agents, such as the agent can inform the team member of seeing a SAM, or when the agent is in danger, it can ask for help from other agents. When an agent receives a "need help" message from other agents, and is willing to go to help, it will assume the Help role. After adopting the Help role, the agent will change its flight direction from going toward the target to going near the agent who needs help, and attack the SAM with that agent. The Help role only appears in the Team-Attack role to help other agents attack the SAMs.

2.2 Role Transitions and Exchanges

An agent can adopt only a single atomic role at one time. The initial role for each agent is Take-off. Under certain situations, an agent relinquishes its role for another.

If the role change is irreversible we will call this role change a *transit*. For example, consider an agent who starts with the role of Take-off from the base station. After some time, the agent will change to the role of Fly-toward-target. After the agent decides to adopt Fly-toward-target role, it cannot go back to the Take off role. If the agent can return to the current role (i.e., reversible) we will call the role change an *exchange*. For an example, consider that the agent is under the Attack-sam role. After the agent successfully avoids the SAM or destroys the SAM, the agent can change its role back to Fly-oward-target once again.

Figure 4 shows role transition and role exchange in our testbed. For Take-off role, the agent takes off from the base station. After some time cycles, the agent will transit its role to Fly-to-target. If the agent doesn't see anything in its visual field, it will keep this role until it adopts the Land role for landing on the destination. If the agent encounters a SAM before reaching the target, it can decide to avoid it or attack it. To avoid a SAM, the agent exchanges its role to Avoid-sam role. Avoid-sam role will determine which direction the agent should turn and when it is safe enough for the agent to exchange back to Fly-to-target role. To attack a SAM, the agent exchanges its role to Attack-sam role. This role will determine how to attack the SAM, and also this role will be combined with Go-around role to find the best point to make the attack. When two agents fly too near to each other, they will adopt Avoid-airplane role, which is similar to the Avoid-sam role. When the agent is within the landing field, it will transit its role to the Land role and land in the destination. These role transitions and exchanges are pre-designed by us and not automatically inferred by the system.

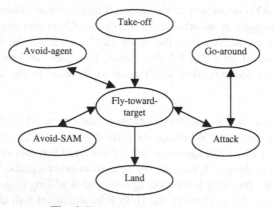

Fig. 4. Role transitions and exchanges

3 Experimental Setup and Analysis

In the testbed experiment, we are interested in measuring the effectiveness of each of the four top level roles. In the testbed, we implemented 2 autonomous agents that at any time agents are in danger of being shot down by the SAMs. The most dangerous situation is when an agent encounters a SAM for the first time. Each time the agents pass by the SAMs, they will risk being shot down by the SAMs. We can use the probability of the agent being shot down (Hit Probability) as the main value of measuring the effectiveness of the top level roles. If the probability of being shot down is very low, we can say that effectiveness of the role is high; otherwise, the effectiveness is low. In order to measure the probabilities of being destroyed, we set up several parameters to help analyze the testbed.

3.1 Experiment Parameters

We have developed a probabilistic model of planes being shot down that is based on a model of the SAM's power and accuracy rate. We do not consider partial damage, and each hit is considered fatal. Initially, each SAM's power is 100%, and its accuracy to shoot down an agent-controlled plane is 5%. When an agent attacks a SAM, the SAMs' power is decreased 2%. After the initial encounter with each subsequent encounter, the SAM's accuracy is halved in team-attack or team-non-attack roles. This is due to the fact that the agent who has met the SAM first will inform the other agents about the SAM's position by communication. We model each agent's probability of being shot down when passing by each SAM as equation (1):

*Hit Probability = (SAM's power) * (SAM's accuracy)*   (1)

The maximum probability for each agent in a fresh encounter is 5%. This probability is lower in all other cases determined by whether the agent is attacking, and the number of times the plane has encountered the SAM. In the case of Team-Attack and Team-Non-Attack roles, since team members inform one another about SAMs they encountered, fewer fresh encounters occur. The Hit Probability of each agent is accumulated when it encountered more SAMs until it reaches the target.

In our testbed we set up a timer, called *cycle*, to measure the running time for each agent from taking off from the base until reaching the target. It takes a longer time for the agent to attack SAMs than to avoid SAMs. The extra time is for communications, or helping other agents.

All of the agents in the testbed in each run must choose only one of those 4 roles and maintain it until completion. We measured the number of steps for planes to fly from beginning to end of each mission with simulation of cycles of agent's top level loop. As the agents approach SAM sites they experience probabilities of being shot down. We summed and averaged these probabilities per mission, per agent, per SAM. This average probability is termed "Average Hit Probability". Since for each run the position of SAMs are not fixed, the number of SAMs that the agents will encounter in each run is not fixed.

3.2 Result Analysis

In Figure 5, each position represents one run of the testbed, where the horizontal axis shows the time in cycles for this run, and the vertical axis shows the Average Hit Probability of the agents in a single run. No plane is considered shot down in the run and every plane gets to the other side. However, each plane gathers cumulative measures of being destroyed as they fly near SAMs. We ran the simulation for 20 runs for each of the four top level role types for a total of 80 runs corresponding to 80 data points in Figure 5. From the figure we can see that by and large agents with Team roles have lower Hit Probability than agents with Non-Team roles. Team-Attack is the best role among the four roles for the lowest threat of being shotdown. Team-Non-Attack is the second, Non-Team-Attack is the third, and Non-Team-Non-Attack is the least effective role. In the Team roles, the Average Hit Probability is lowered roughly 5.6 times by attacking from Non-Attack (about 0.025) to Attack (about 0.0045). If the objective is to minimize Hit Probability, attack is clearly preferred.

When considering the cycles to complete each mission, on the average Non-Team-Non-Attack takes the shortest time, Team-Non-Attack is the second, Non-Team-Attack is the third, and Team-Attack takes the longest time. By not attacking, agents take a shorter time to complete the mission. If the objective is to minimize time, not attack roles are preferred. The Average Hit probability is halved with not attack from Non-Team (about 0.048) to Team roles (about 0.024). But if we had taken the possibility of communication interceptions into account, the advantage might not be as good.

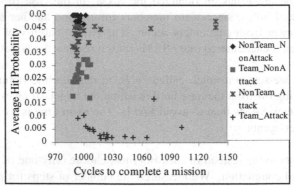

Fig. 5. Mission Cycles versus Average Hit Probability

4   Related Work

Sycara's work ([4] and [6]) is closely related to our approach to teamwork, as is [5]. However, Sycara intends to provide a general level of cohesion for heterogeneous agents and a toolkit for assembling teams. She is considering large open agent groups on the Internet. Much like public services of a town, Sycara's middle agents mediate transactions between agents.

Recent developments from Milind tambe's group include a monitor for distributed teams that minimizes the amount of required communication through having the monitor infer the progress of team plans by observing the actions of member agents [7]. Tambe's Overseer is an example of an agent assistant. Inferring agent states from team actions suffers from uncertainty and from growth of computational complexity that is exponential in the number of agents being monitored. By modeling the group as a whole, rather than modeling the individual agents constituting the group, Overseer is able to effectively predict team responses during normal and failed plan execution in linear time. The gain is accomplished through restricting attention to coherent monitoring hypotheses. The trade off is that the team is not accurately modeled in some failure modes because an inaccurate, but efficient, temporal model is used. Knowledge bases containing the plan hierarchy, and containing the group hierarchy enable *socially attentive* monitoring. Tambe's approach blends reasoning about teamwork and reasoning about uncertainty.

5   Conclusion and Future Work

This paper presented an empirical investigation of roles and social influences in a testbed we have implemented. Our preliminary results demonstrate that responding to team members in need of help improves the team's overall effectiveness. While "team-attack" has the minimum hit probability, the length of operation is assumed to be within acceptable tolerance degree. This extends our earlier treatment of teams and measurement of team effectiveness along the dimensions of cohesion. We plan to use our testbed for further quantifications of team effectiveness along many other dimensions.

A particular focus of our ongoing work is the human operator and interactions of agents with the human operator. The human interpretation of social action "help" is quite varied. Human usage of "help" and reactions to it are not as deterministic as actions of agents in the simulator. Since there are also differences between people and even between two different runs we will automatically record these interactions for further analysis and richer models of "help" within a team.

Acknowledgement. We appreciate contributions of Babar Asif, Muhammad Arrabi, Ciprian Caleau, Srinivas Battula, and Dr. Gordon Beavers. This work is supported by AFOSR grant F49620-00-1-0302 and a subcontract from State University of New York at Buffalo' Center for Multisource Information Fusion.

References

1. G. Beavers and H. Hexmoor, 2001. Teams of Agents, In the Proceedings of IEEE SMC, Arizona.
2. P. Cohen, H. Levesque, I. Smith, 1997. On Team Formation, In J. Hintika and R. Tuomela, *Contemporary Action Theory*, Synthese.
3. H. Hexmoor, and G. Beavers, 2002. Measuring Team Effectiveness, In proceedings of 20th IASTED International Multiconfernce: Applied Informatics (AI 2002), Innsbruck, Austria.
4. T. Lenox, R. Payne, S. Hahn, M. Lewis, K. Sycara, 1999. MokSAF, How should we support teamwork in human-agent teams? *CMU-RI-TR-99-31, The Robotics Institute, Carnegie Mellon Universit..*
5. E. Salas, C. Bowers, and E. Edens (Eds), *Improving Teamwork in Organizations* Lawrence Earlbaum Pubs, 2001.
6. K. Sycara, Brokering and Matchmaking for Coordination of Agent Societies: A Survey. In *Coordination of Internet Agents*, A. Omicini et al. (eds.), Springer., 2001.
7. M. Tambe, D. Pynadeth, and N. Chauvat, 2000. Building Dynamic Agent Organizations in Cyberspace, *IEEE Internet Computing*, March-April issue.

Construction of Large-Scale Bayesian Networks by Local to Global Search

Kyu-Baek Hwang[1], Jae Won Lee[2], Seung-Woo Chung[1], and
Byoung-Tak Zhang[1]

[1] School of Computer Science and Engineering, Seoul National University,
Seoul 151-742, Korea
{kbhwang, swchung, btzhang}@bi.snu.ac.kr
[2] School of Computer Science and Engineering, Sungshin Women's University,
Seoul 136-742, Korea
jwlee@cs.sungshin.ac.kr

Abstract. Most existing algorithms for structural learning of Bayesian networks are suitable for constructing small-sized networks which consist of several tens of nodes. In this paper, we present a novel approach to the efficient and relatively-precise induction of large-scale Bayesian networks with up to several hundreds of nodes. The approach is based on the concept of *Markov blanket* and makes use of the divide-and-conquer principle. The proposed method has been evaluated on two benchmark datasets and a real-life DNA microarray data, demonstrating the ability to learn the large-scale Bayesian network structure efficiently.

1 Introduction

Bayesian networks [7] are useful tools for classification and data mining. They are particulary helpful because of their ability to give an insight into the underlying nature of the domain that generates the data. Accordingly, Bayesian networks have been applied to many data mining tasks, such as medical diagnosis [9] and microarray data analysis [5]. However, there are some obstacles that prevent the prevalent use of Bayesian networks as data mining tools for real-world problems. One is the scalability of structural learning algorithms. Most existing algorithms are inappropriate to learning large-scale Bayesian networks with hundreds of nodes because of their time and space complexities. In this paper, an efficient structural learning algorithm for such Bayesian networks is suggested.

There have been two kinds of approaches to learning Bayesian networks from data. The first is based on dependency analysis among variables. In this approach, the underlying network structure that produces the data is discovered by some conditional independence tests on variables [12]. The other approach solves the structural learning problem in the viewpoint of optimization [3]. Here, the learning algorithm searches for the network structure which best matches the data. The fitness of a structure is measured by some scoring metrics (e.g. the minimum description length (MDL) score and the Bayesian Dirichlet (BD) score). The search strategy is the core of the second approach. The search space

M. Ishizuka and A. Sattar (Eds.): PRICAI 2002, LNAI 2417, pp. 375–384, 2002.

is super-exponential in the number of variables of the Bayesian network and the problem of finding the best structure is known to be NP-hard [1]. So, heuristic methods such as greedy hill-climbing are used in a general way. The greedy search algorithm [3] is not guaranteed to find the best solution but only a local maximum. Nevertheless, the greedy search algorithm has proven to be quite effective in practice.

Each approach has its own drawbacks. In the former, the conditional independence test may produce the incorrect results and mislead the structural learning process. The latter approach has a tendency to find a dense network structure which may represent the improper causal relationships among variables without careful tuning of the scoring metrics (e.g. the proper assignment of prior probabilities for the BD score or the proper representation of the penalizing term for the MDL score). The exponential time complexity is the problem of both approaches especially in the case of dealing with hundreds of variables.

The recent work in the approach based on dependency analysis is best described in [8]. With the benefit of the concept of *Markov blanket*, unnecessary dependency tests are avoided here. The algorithm described in [8] is very effective for the precise construction of the network structure in polynomial time with restrictions on the maximum size of the Markov blanket. In addition, its randomized variant shows an acceptable performance for more general cases. In the framework of score-based approach, [4] suggested the "sparse candidate" algorithm. This algorithm reduces the size of search space by restricting the possible parents of each node before performing the greedy search and makes it possible to learn the Bayesian network structure with hundreds of variables efficiently. For finding the optimal Bayesian network structure from data, [13] suggested an efficient algorithm using the branch and bound technique.

The proposed algorithm in this paper ("local to global search" algorithm) belongs to the second approach (score-based search). To reduce the global search space, the local structure around each node is constructed before performing the greedy search algorithm. Thus, the proposed algorithm is based on the divide-and-conquer principle. The boundary of the local structure of each node is based on the concept of Markov blanket.

The paper is organized as follows. In Section 2, the concept of the Markov blanket structure as local structural boundary is described. The "local to global search" algorithm is explained in Section 3. We evaluate the proposed algorithm in comparisons with other structural learning algorithms in Section 4. Finally, concluding remarks are given in Section 5.

2   The Markov Blanket Structure

In this section, the Markov blanket and the concept of the *Markov blanket structure* are described. In the following, $\mathbf{X} = \{X_1, ..., X_n\}$ denotes the set of all the variables of interest. The Markov blanket [10] of X_i, $\mathbf{MB}(X_i)$ is the subset of $\mathbf{X} - X_i$ which satisfies the following equation.

$$P(X_i|\mathbf{X} - X_i) = P(X_i|\mathbf{MB}(X_i)). \tag{1}$$

In other words, $\mathbf{MB}(X_i)$ isolates X_i from all the other variables in $\mathbf{X} - X_i$. More than one Markov blanket for a variable could exist. The minimal Markov blanket is called Markov boundary. In this paper, Markov blanket denotes Markov boundary. In the Bayesian network structure G, $\mathbf{MB}_G(X_i)$ is composed of all the parents of X_i, all the children of X_i, and all the parents of each child of X_i excluding X_i itself. We designate the subgraph structure consisting of X_i and $\mathbf{MB}_G(X_i)$ in G as the Markov blanket structure of X_i. Fig. 1 shows an example Markov blanket structure of a node in the Bayesian network.

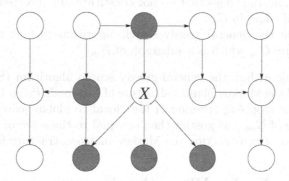

Fig. 1. An example Bayesian network structure. The shaded nodes correspond to the members of $\mathbf{MB}(X)$. The subgraph consisting of X and all the shaded nodes is the Markov blanket structure of X.

3   The "Local to Global Search" Algorithm

Before giving an explanation of the "local to global search" algorithm, we briefly describe the general greedy search algorithm for structural learning of the Bayesian network. The general greedy search algorithm proceeds as follows.

- Generate the initial Bayesian network structure G_0 (an empty structure or a randomly generated structure).
- For $m = 1, 2, 3, ...$, until convergence.
  - Among all the possible local changes (insertion of an edge, reversal of an edge, and deletion of an edge) in G_{m-1}, the one that leads to the largest improvement in the score is performed. The resulting graph is G_m.

The stopping criterion is when the score of G_{m-1} is equal to the score of G_m. At each iteration of the greedy search algorithm when learning the Bayesian network with n nodes, about $O(n^2)$ local changes should be evaluated to select the best one. In the case of hundreds of variables, the cost for these evaluations becomes very expensive.

The key idea of the "local to global search" algorithm is to reduce the search space considered in the general greedy search algorithm by constructing the

Markov blanket structure of each node in advance. The "local to global search" algorithm proceeds as follows.

- Generate the initial Bayesian network structure G_0 (an empty graph).
- Loop for $m = 1, 2, 3, \ldots$ until convergence.
  1. Construct the Markov blanket structure of each node based on G_{m-1} and the data D.
  2. Merge all the Markov blanket structures into a graph H_m (H_m could have directed cycles).
  3. In H_m, all the edges that do not constitute any directed cycle are fixed as valid edges in G_m.
  4. Perform the general greedy search algorithm to find a good network structure G_m which is a subgraph of H_m.

In the above algorithm, the general greedy search algorithm (Step 4) and the construction of the Markov blanket structure of each node (Step 1) are performed alternately. The stopping criterion of the "local to global search" algorithm is when the score of G_{m-1} is greater than or equal to the score of G_m.

The method of constructing the Markov blanket structure for X_i in Step 1 is as follows.

- For all $X_j \subset \mathbf{X} - X_i - \mathbf{MB}_{G_{m-1}}(X_i)$, the *conditional mutual information*, $I(X_i; X_j | \mathbf{MB}_{G_{m-1}}(X_i))$ is calculated to select the candidate members for the Markov blanket of X_i.
- The general greedy search algorithm is performed on the selected candidate members and X_i to construct the Markov blanket structure of X_i. When performing the general greedy search algorithm, the Markov blanket structure of each node in G_{m-1} is preserved.

The conditional mutual information [2] measures the dependency between X_i and X_j given the value of $\mathbf{MB}_{G_{m-1}}(X_i)$ and is calculated as follows:

$$
\begin{aligned}
&I(X_i; X_j | \mathbf{MB}_{G_{m-1}}(X_i)) \\
&= I(X_i; X_j, \mathbf{MB}_{G_{m-1}}(X_i)) - I(X_i; \mathbf{MB}_{G_{m-1}}(X_i)).
\end{aligned} \tag{2}
$$

In (2), $I(X_i; \mathbf{MB}_{G_{m-1}}(X_i))$ is unnecessary because it does not depend on X_j and the only necessary term to select the candidate members is calculated as

$$
\begin{aligned}
I(X_i; X_j, \mathbf{MB}_{G_{m-1}}(X_i)) &= \sum \hat{p}(X_i, X_j, \mathbf{MB}_{G_{m-1}}(X_i)) \\
&\cdot \log \frac{\hat{p}(X_i, X_j, \mathbf{MB}_{G_{m-1}}(X_i))}{\hat{p}(X_i)\hat{p}(X_j, \mathbf{MB}_{G_{m-1}}(X_i))}.
\end{aligned} \tag{3}
$$

Here, $\hat{p}(\cdot)$ denotes the empirical probability calculated from the data. The selection of candidate members may be guided by some threshold on the conditional mutual information value or by some restrictions on the size of the Markov blanket. Once the candidate members for the Markov blanket are selected, the general greedy search algorithm searches for the good Markov blanket structure.

The key point of the "local to global search" algorithm lies in Step 2 and 3. Merging all the Markov blanket structures and fixing the edges that do not form any directed cycle reduce the great amount of the evaluation cost of the greedy search algorithm in Step 4. However, fixing the edges found in Step 1 can also lead to the deterioration of the score. And the above algorithm is not guaranteed to find even the local maxia. The reason is as follows. The greedy search algorithm usually employs the decomposable scoring metric such as the BD (Bayesian Dirichlet) score [6] and the MDL (minimum description length) score [3]. The decomposable score has the property such that,

$$Score(G, D) = \Sigma_i Score(X_i | \mathbf{Pa}_G(X_i), D), \tag{4}$$

where G is the Bayesian network structure, D is the data, and $\mathbf{Pa}_G(X_i)$ is the parents of X_i in G. Because the score of the network can be decomposed into the score of each node, the increase in the score of each node also increases the score of the network. In the "local to global search" algorithm, the score of each node can be degraded through merging the Markov blanket structures into the global network structure H_m because of the possible changes of its parents. This is the trade-off between speed and accuracy. However, in many domains, the initial Bayesian network structure is an empty graph due to the lack of the domain knowledge and a small number of iterations of the "local to global search" algorithm could find the appropriate Bayesian network structure rapidly.

Time Complexity

We now describe the time complexity of the "local to global search" algorithm. In Step 1, in order to determine the candidate members for the Markov blanket of X_i, the conditional mutual information test is done for all other nodes. This takes time of $O(n \cdot (M \cdot |X_i| \cdot |X_j| \cdot |\mathbf{MB}_{G_{m-1}}(X_i)|))$. Here, M is the number of instances in the data D, and $|\cdot|$ denotes the cardinality of a variable or the set of variables. $|X_i| \cdot |X_j| \cdot |\mathbf{MB}_{G_{m-1}}(X_i)|$ can be regarded as a constant with the appropriate restrictions on the maximum size of the Markov blanket, k. And the selection of candidate members for the Markov blanket is done for all the nodes $\{X_1, ..., X_n\}$. Therefore, the selection of candidate members for the Markov blanket takes time of $O(n^2 M)$. The next is the greedy search procedure to determine the Markov blanket structure of a node. At each iteration of the greedy search algorithm, the number of possible local changes is bounded by $O(k^2)$. With the assumption of the moderate maximum size of the Markov blanket ($k \leq 20$), the greedy search procedure takes not so much time.

Step 2 and 3 merges all the Markov blanket structures into a global network and the time bound is $O(n)$.

In Step 4, the greedy search algorithm evaluates $O(n^2)$ local changes at each iteration. For large n (e.g. $n \geq 800$), the conventional greedy search algorithm takes very much time to search for the good network structure. In the "local to global search" algorithm, this step takes not so much time because of the greatly reduced search space through Step 1, 2, and 3.

4   Experimental Evaluation

To evaluate the performance of the "local to global search" algorithm, two kinds of artificial datasets and a real-life microarray data were used. In the experiments, we compared the "local to global search" algorithm with the general greedy search algorithm and the "sparse candidate" algorithm [4] in the respect of the learning speed and the accuracy of the learned results. As the scoring metric, the BD (Bayesian Dirichlet) metric with uninformative prior [6] was adopted. To ensure fairness in the comparison, the same basic module for the greedy search procedure was used in all three algorithms. The experiments were performed on a PentiumIII 1GHz machine with 256MB RAM. In the "local to global search" algorithm, the maximum size of the Markov blanket was restricted by a constant k.

Artificial Datasets

Table 1 shows the characteristics of two Bayesian networks that produced artificial datasets. Although these networks have only tens of nodes, the experiments on the artificial datasets make it possible to compare the accuracy of the algorithms in the respect of reconstructing the precise network structure. Five artificial datasets of 10000 instances were generated from each of these Bayesian networks.

Table 2 compares three structural learning algorithms in the respect of the learning speed. The "sparse candidate" algorithm is much faster than other two algorithms. The "local to global search" algorithm with $k = 5$ is faster than the general greedy search algorithm. However, the "local to global search" algorithm with $k = 10$ is not so much faster than the general greedy search algorithm and even slower on the Hailfinder datasets. This is due to the conditional mutual information test for the selection of the candidate Markov blanket members in the "local to global search" algorithm. Most variables in the Hailfinder network have more categorical values than the variables in the ALARM network. The Hailfinder network even has a variable which has 11 categorical values. Accordingly, the conditional mutual information tests on the Hailfinder datasets take extremely long time.

Table 3 compares three structural learning algorithms in the respect of the accuracy of the learned results (in the likelihood score). The general greedy

Table 1. The characteristics of two Bayesian networks used to generate artificial datasets. These networks are generally used as benchmarks to test the performance of structural learning algorithm for Bayesian networks.

Network	# of nodes	# of edges
ALARM network	37	46
Hailfinder network	56	66

Table 2. The comparison of the learning speed (in seconds) of three structural learning algorithms. The left (right) table represents the results on the five datasets generated from the ALARM (Hailfinder) network. (**GG** = general greedy search algorithm, **SC**k = "sparse candidate" algorithm with maximum candidate parents size of k, **LG**k = "local to global search" algorithm with Markov blanket size of k)

	GG	SC5	SC10	LG5	LG10			GG	SC5	SC10	LG5	LG10
A1	143	26	39	42	134	**H1**		352	55	89	191	959
A2	146	30	41	37	172	**H2**		351	56	89	196	1625
A3	129	27	39	46	128	**H3**		370	56	90	276	2015
A4	150	26	41	45	118	**H4**		366	59	88	278	1663
A5	136	27	40	41	133	**H5**		362	57	90	290	1450
Avg.	140.8	27.2	40.0	42.2	137.0	**Avg.**		360.2	56.6	89.2	246.2	1542.4

Table 3. The comparison of the accuracy (in the likelihood score of the learned networks) of three structural learning algorithms. The left (right) table represents the results on the five datasets generated from the ALARM (Hailfinder) network. (**GG** = general greedy search algorithm, **SC**k = "sparse candidate" algorithm with maximum candidate parents size of k, **LG**k = "local to global search" algorithm with Markov blanket size of k)

	GG	SC5	SC10	LG5	LG10			GG	SC5	SC10	LG5	LG10
A1	-9.483	-9.764	-9.577	-9.686	-9.577	**H1**		-49.685	-49.762	-49.714	-49.772	-49.813
A2	-9.524	-9.847	-9.597	-9.610	-9.765	**H2**		-49.707	-49.790	-49.742	-49.805	-49.788
A3	-9.536	-9.847	-9.609	-9.750	-9.630	**H3**		-49.695	-49.777	-49.724	-49.764	-49.847
A4	-9.466	-9.790	-9.546	-9.519	-9.597	**H4**		-49.677	-49.751	-49.721	-49.861	-49.789
A5	-9.541	-9.815	-9.589	-9.639	-9.614	**H5**		-49.748	-49.829	40.779	-19.819	-49.845

search algorithm shows the best accuracy in the respect of the likelihood score of the learned Bayesian networks. The "sparse candidate" algorithm and the "local to global search" algorithm are slightly worse than the general greedy search algorithm. Fig. 2 compares the accuracy of each algorithm in the respect of the ability of reconstructing the correct network structure. In every case, the general greedy search algorithm finds the more accurate structures than other two algorithms. On the ALARM datasets, the performances of the "sparse candidate" algorithm and the "local to global search" algorithm are comparable. On the Hailfinder datasets, the "sparse candidate" algorithm shows a slightly better performance than the "local to global search" algorithm.

DNA Microarray Data

To test the ability of the "local to global search" algorithm for the construction of large-scale Bayesian networks, the NCI60 dataset [11] was used. The NCI60 dataset consists of 60 human cancer cell lines from 9 kinds of cancers, that is, colorectal, renal, ovarian, breast, prostate, lung, and central nervous system

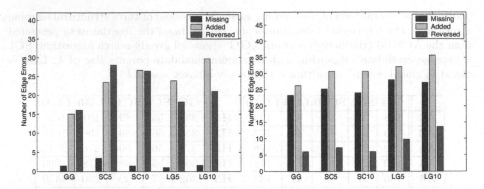

Fig. 2. The average edge errors for the ALARM network datasets (left) and the Hailfinder network datasets (right). In every case, the general greedy search algorithm finds the better structures than other two algorithms. On the ALARM datasets, the performances of the "sparse candidate" algorithm and the "local to global search" algorithm are comparable. In the case of the Hailfinder datasets, the "sparse candidate" algorithm shows a slightly better performance than the "local to global search" algorithm. (**GG** = general greedy search algorithm, **SC**k = "sparse candidate" algorithm with maximum candidate parents size of k, **LG**k = "local to global search" algorithm with Markov blanket size of k)

origin cancers, as well as leukaemias and melanomas. On each cell line, the gene expression pattern is measured by cDNA microarray of 9703 genes including ESTs. And 1400 chemical compounds were tested on the 60 cell lines. From these attributes, genes and drugs (chemical compounds) that have more than 3 missing values across 60 samples as well as unknown ESTs were eliminated for robust analysis. Consequently, the analyzed NCI60 dataset includes 60 samples with 890 attributes (805 gene expression levels, 84 drug activities, and one additional variable for the kind of cancer). Hence, the task is to learn the structure of Bayesian network with 890 nodes. All the attribute values are continuous and discretized into three categorical values (low, normal, and high) according to their mean values and the standard deviations across 60 data samples. With varying threshold values for discretization, three datasets (NCI1, NCI2, and NCI3) were made.

Table 4 shows the comparison of the "sparse candidate" algorithm and the "local to global search" algorithm on these datasets. The general greedy search algorithm was inapplicable to the NCI60 dataset because of its time and space complexity. The "local to global search" algorithm with $k = 5$ is the fastest. In the respect of the accuracy, the "local to global search" algorithm with $k = 8$ shows a slightly better performance than others.

5   Conclusion

We presented a novel method for structural learning of large-scale Bayesian networks. It is used as a component learning algorithm in the framework of

Table 4. The comparison of the learning speed (in seconds) and the accuracy (in the likelihood score of the learned results) of the "sparse candidate" algorithm and the "local to global search" algorithm on the NCI60 dataset. The left (right) table represents the learning time (the likelihood score). (**SC**k = "sparse candidate" algorithm with maximum candidate parents size of k, **LG**k = "local to global search" algorithm with Markov blanket size of k)

	SC5	SC8	LG5	LG8			SC5	SC8	LG5	LG8
NCI1	7568	8678	7123	10987	**NCI1**		-777.35	-777.01	-779.08	-773.12
NCI2	7542	8443	7089	10223	**NCI2**		-768.54	-768.34	-769.76	-768.23
NCI3	7345	8789	7343	11092	**NCI3**		-787.35	-788.01	-787.20	-787.10

greedy hill-climbing, and avoids many unnecessary computations by constructing the Markov blanket structure of each node in advance. Since most of the network structure is learned through economic local search procedures, the space and time complexities of global search is greatly reduced.

Comparative analysis shows that the proposed method significantly outperforms the conventional greedy search algorithm in terms of the learning speed. The accuracy of the learned results in terms of the likelihood score or the ability of reconstructing the original structure is not so much degraded compared to the general greedy search algorithm. One disadvantage of the "local to global search" algorithm is that the performance is severely degraded when dealing with the dataset which has variables of large cardinalities. In comparisons with the state-of-the-art techniques for learning large-scale Bayesian networks (e.g. the "sparse candidate" algorithm [4]), the proposed method shows a slightly better performance in the accuracy and the learning speed although the experiments are confined on one real-life dataset. The choice of the parameter k of the "local to global search" algorithm does not seem to affect much the accuracy of the learned results.

As a conclusion, the proposed method is suitable for learning the large-scale Bayesian network with hundreds of variables efficiently from the data which has variables with moderate cardinalities ($2 \sim 4$).

Acknowledgements. This work was supported by the Korean Ministry of Education and the Ministry of Science and Technology under the BK21-IT, BrainTech, and IMT-2000 Programs.

References

1. Chickering, D.M.: Learning Bayesian networks is NP-complete. In: Fisher, D., Lenz, H.-J. (eds.): Learning from Data: Artificial Intelligence and Statistics V. Springer-Verlag, Berlin Heidelberg New York (1996) 121-130
2. Cover, T.M., Thomas, J.A.: Elements of Information Theory. John Wiley & Sons, New York (1991)

3. Friedman, N., Goldszmidt, M.: Learning Bayesian networks with local structure. In: Jordan, M.I. (ed.): Learning in Graphical Models. MIT Press, Cambridge (1999) 421-459
4. Friedman, N., Nachman, I., Pe'er, D.: Learning Bayesian network structure from massive datasets: the "sparse candidate" algorithm. Proceedings of the Fifteenth Conference on Uncertainty in Artificial Intelligence (UAI) (1999) 206-215
5. Friedman, N., Linial, M., Nachman, I., Pe'er, D.: Using Bayesian networks to analyze expression data. Proceedings of the Fourth Annual International Conference on Computational Biology (RECOMB) (2000) 127-135
6. Heckerman, D., Geiger, D., Chickering, D.M.: Learning Bayesian networks: the combination of knowledge and statistical data. Machine Learning **20**(3) (1995) 197-243
7. Heckerman, D.: A tutorial on learning with Bayesian networks. In: Jordan, M.I. (ed.): Learning in Graphical Models. MIT Press, Cambridge (1999) 301-354
8. Margaritis, D., Thrun, S.: Bayesian network induction via local neighborhoods. Advances in Neural Information Processing Systems 12 (2000) 505-511
9. Nikovski, D.: Constructing Bayesian networks for medical diagnosis from incomplete and partially correct statistics. IEEE Transactions on Knowledge and Data Engineering **12**(4) (2000) 509-516
10. Pearl, J: Probabilistic Reasoning in Intelligent Systems: Networks of Plausible Inference. Morgan Kaufmann, San Francisco (1988)
11. Scherf, U. et al.: A gene expression database for the molecular pharmacology of cancer. Nature Genetics **24** (2000) 236-244
12. Spirtes, P., Glymour, C., Scheines, R.: Causation, Prediction, and Search. 2nd edn. MIT Press, Cambridge (2000)
13. Suzuki, J.: Learning Bayesian belief networks based on the minimum description length principle: an efficient algorithm using the B & B technique. Proceedings of the Thirteenth International Conference on Machine Learning (ICML) (1996) 462-470

Using Bayesian Networks with Hidden Nodes to Recognise Neural Cell Morphology

Jung-Wook Bang and Duncan Gillies

Department of Computing, Imperial College
London, United Kingdom
{jwb3, dfg}@doc.ic.ac.uk

Abstract. Bayesian decision trees are based on a formal assumption that the unconnected nodes are conditionally independent given the states of their parent nodes. This assumption does not necessarily hold in practice and may lead to loss of accuracy. We propose a methodology whereby naïve Bayesian networks are adapted by the addition of hidden nodes to model the data dependencies more accurately. We examined the methodology in a computer vision application to classify and count the neural cell automatically. Our results show that a modified network with two hidden nodes achieved significantly better performance with an average prediction accuracy of 83.9% compared to 59.31% achieved by the original network.

1 Introduction

Bayesian Networks utilise both probabilistic reasoning and graphical modelling for describing the relationships of variables in a given domain based on the assumption of conditional independence [1]. However, in practical cases the variables may contain a certain degree of dependence. Parameters of a network imply a statistical relationship between any two linked nodes. However, if there is conditional dependence between nodes not joined by arcs, the validity of a network can be questioned.

Pearl proposed a star-structure methodology to handle the dependency problem by adding a hidden node whenever any two nodes have strong conditional dependency given a common parent [2][3]. Pearl's idea was to simulate the common cause between two nodes by introducing a hidden node, though he did not provide a mechanism for determining the parameters of a discrete node. In general, there are two ways to add a hidden node into a network. Firstly, a domain expert can subjectively add a hidden node by identifying the common cause. The subjective approach, however, faces difficulty because in many cases there will not be sufficient information about the common cause. The alternative is to use a systematic objective approach to add a hidden node in a network and estimate the number of states and the link matrices statistically. In neural networks, hidden nodes have been widely used to discover sym

M. Ishizuka and A. Sattar (Eds.): PRICAI 2002, LNAI 2417, pp. 385–394, 2002.

metries or replicated structures. In particular, Boltzmann machine learning and backward propagation training have been proposed to determine hidden nodes. [4]

Kwoh and Gillies [5] proposed a method of introducing discrete hidden nodes in Bayesian networks. The basic idea was to use gradient descent to update the conditional probabilities of the matrices linking a hidden node to its parent and children. The method was inspired by previous research in machine learning, particularly Boltzmann machine learning [6][7] and the Expectation-Maximisation (EM) method [8]. Friedman proposed a technique called the Model Selection Expectation-Maximization (MS-EM) to update a network with hidden nodes. This approach, however, required the predefined size of the hidden node prior to certain processes being carried out [9]. Bang and Gillies [10] extended Kwoh and Gillies' idea by proposing a diagonal propagation method which created a symmetric scheme for computing the error function thus compensating the weakness of forward propagation in the gradient descent process.

In this paper, we will examine the possible deployment of hidden nodes in naïve Bayesian networks that perform a decision-making, and illustrate the method by applying it to a computer vision system for classifying neural cell types.

2   Hidden Node Methodology

Hidden nodes are added to a network by first identifying a triple (A, B, C in Fig. 2.1) where the child nodes have high conditional dependency given some states of the parent node. Once the hidden node is introduced into the network, its states and conditional probabilities are set to make B and C conditionally independent given H. This requires the use of a representative data set with values for A, B and C.

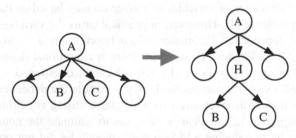

Fig. 2.1. Adding hidden nodes

Kwoh and Gillies [5] utilised gradient descent to determine the conditional probability matrices. They worked with an error function that compares the true value at a node, with the computed value derived by propagating data from the other nodes through the hidden node. The conditional probabilities were adjusted to minimise this error. They used both backward and forward propagation. In backward propagation the child nodes are instantiated and the error is computed at the root node. In forward propagation the root node is instantiated, and the error is computed at the child nodes. This is illustrated in Fig. 2.2.

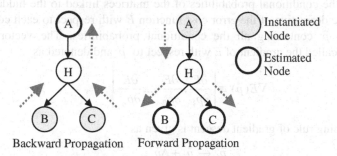

Backward Propagation   Forward Propagation

Fig. 2.2 P ropagation for hidden node

Bang and Gillies [10] proposed an extension of the previous method by utilising diagonal propagation. Fig. 2.3 illustrates this new propagation method. Notice that in both cases we are instantiating two nodes, and making an error estimate at the third. This in practice may result in a more stable convergence scheme.

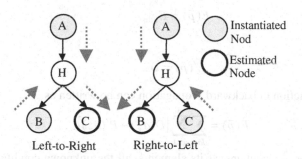

Left-to-Right   Right-to-Left

Fig. 2.3. Diagonal propagation

If comparing the case of forward propagation with diagonal propagation, we find that, in the former case, the posterior probability of the estimated node B is solely influenced by node A. In contrast, the posterior probability of the estimated node B for the right-to-left case of diagonal propagation is computed using evidence from both nodes A and C. For that reason, we hypothesise that a diagonal propagation method may improve the overall performance of estimating hidden nodes in Bayesian networks.

3   Formalisation of Hidden Node Methodology

To update the conditional probabilities of the matrices linked to the hidden node, we compute the derivative of the error cost function E with respect to each component of the vector $\vec{p}$ containing all the conditional probabilities. The vector derivative, $\nabla E(\vec{p})$, is called the gradient of E with respect to $\vec{p}$ and denoted as

$$\nabla E(\vec{p}) \equiv \left[\frac{\partial E}{\partial p_1}, \frac{\partial E}{\partial p_2}, \dots \frac{\partial E}{\partial p_n} \right]. \tag{1}$$

The training rule of gradient descent is given as

$$\vec{p}_i \leftarrow \vec{p}_i + \Delta \vec{p}_i. \tag{2}$$

where $\Delta \vec{p}_i$ is $-\mu \nabla E$. μ is a positive constant called the step size (or a learning rate) that determines how fast the process converges. The step size typically lies in the range of 0.01 to 0.1. For individual probabilities the rule is written as

$$p_i \leftarrow p_i - \mu \left[\frac{\partial E}{\partial p_i} \right]. \tag{3}$$

The objective of gradient descent is the determine iteratively the minimum error:

$$E(\vec{p}) = E_{\min} \tag{4}$$

or equivalently

$$E'(\vec{p}) = 0. \tag{5}$$

The error function in backward propagation can be written as

$$E(\vec{p}) = \sum_{data} \sum_{x=1}^{|A|} [D(a_x) - P'(a_x)]^2. \tag{6}$$

where the vector $\vec{p}$ contains, as its elements, all the unknown conditional probabilities in the link matrices. $P'(a_x)$ is the posterior probability of parent node A that is calculated by instantiating the children and propagating these values through the hidden node. $D(a_x)$ is the desired value of the parent node taken originally from the data.

Exact gradient descent solutions are only available in the linear cases. We, therefore, need to expand the equations to derive discrete operating equations. The operating equations for gradient descent are derived using the chain rule to differentiate the error function. In backward propagation, for example, we instantiate child nodes B and C simultaneously. Then the information from the instantiated nodes propagates through hidden node H until it reaches node A. The derivative of the error cost function $E(p)$ with respect to the three link matrix elements is as follows.

$$\frac{\partial E(p)}{\partial P(h_t \mid a_i)} = \sum_{data} \sum_{x=1}^{|A|} \left[\frac{\partial E(p)}{\partial P'(a_x)} \frac{\partial P'(a_x)}{\partial \lambda(a_i)} \frac{\partial \lambda(a_i)}{\partial P(h_t \mid a_i)} \right] \tag{7}$$

$$= \sum_{data} \left\{ \sum_{x=1}^{|A|} -2[D(a_x) - P'(a_x)] \cdot \alpha\pi(a_i)[\delta(i, x) - P'(a_x)] \cdot \lambda(h_t) \right\} \tag{8}$$

where λ and π are information passing (up and downward within a network, respectively), where $\delta(i, x) = 1$ for $j = y$, 0 otherwise. The normalisation factor α is

$$\frac{1}{\sum_{x=1}^{|A|} \pi(a_x)} . \tag{9}$$

The denominator of α implies sum over the state of target node A.

$$\frac{\partial E(p)}{\partial P(b_j \mid h_t)} = \sum_{data} \sum_{x=1}^{|A|} \left[\frac{\partial E(p)}{\partial P'(a_x)} \frac{\partial P'(a_x)}{\partial \lambda(a_x)} \frac{\partial \lambda(a_x)}{\partial \lambda(h_t)} \frac{\partial \lambda(h_t)}{\partial P(b_j \mid h_t)} \right] \tag{10}$$

$$= \sum_{data} \left\{ \sum_{x=1}^{|A|} -2[D(a_x) - P'(a_x)] \cdot \alpha\pi(a_x)[1 - P'(a_x)] \cdot P(h_t \mid a_x) \cdot P'(c_z) \cdot \sum_{z=1}^{|C|} P(c_z \mid h_t) P'(b_j) \right\} . \tag{11}$$

$$\frac{\partial E(p)}{\partial P(c_k \mid h_t)} = \sum_{data} \sum_{x=1}^{|A|} \left[\frac{\partial E(p)}{\partial P'(a_x)} \frac{\partial P'(a_x)}{\partial \lambda(a_x)} \frac{\partial \lambda(a_x)}{\partial \lambda(h_t)} \frac{\partial \lambda(h_t)}{\partial P(c_k \mid h_t)} \right] \tag{12}$$

$$= \sum_{data} \left\{ \sum_{x=1}^{|A|} -2[D(a_x) - P'(a_x)] \cdot \alpha\pi(a_x)[1 - P'(a_x)] \cdot P(h_t \mid a_x) \cdot P'(b_y) \cdot \sum_{y=1}^{|B|} P(b_y \mid h_t) P'(c_k) \right\} . \tag{13}$$

Updating of the conditional probabilities of the matrices is achieved by substituting equations 8, 11 and 13 into 3. Further details can be found in Kwoh and Gillies [5] and Bang and Gillies [10].

4 Applications to the Morphological Classification of Neural Cells

Developmental biologists are frequently interested in classifying the development of cells in culture. In this way they can determine the effects of pollutants (or other reagents) on growth. Oligodendrocytes are a class of cell that is frequently studied. They provide the myelin sheath needed for nervous impulse conduction. Failure of these cells to develop leads to the disease multiple sclerosis. In studies, biologists view culture dishes under a microscope and attempt to count the cells using a small number of classes, for example, progenitors, immature type 1, immature type 2 and differentiated. This is a difficult, inaccurate and subjective method that could be greatly improved by using computer vision.

Our data was taken from studies in which the cultures were photographed using a Photonic Science microscope camera. Biologists classified the cells in the pictures into four developmental classes. One data set had 12 progenitor cells, 24 immature type 1, 15 immature type 2 and 9 fully differentiated cells. The images were then processed to extract several features, of which five proved to have good discriminant properties [11]. These were called the Scholl coefficient [12], the fractal dimension [13], the 2nd moment [14], the total length and the profile count.

We conducted a series of tests using the cell class as a hypothesis node, and the five measured features as variables. In particular, we were interested in the possibility of improving the prediction accuracy of the networks with the help of hidden nodes.

4.1 Naïve Bayesian Networks

A naïve Bayesian network was constructed using a randomly selected training data set and then evaluated with a randomly selected test data set. The process was repeated 1000 times for each test. Fig. 4.1.1 shows the naïve Bayesian network with five variables connected to a root node, *neuron type*.

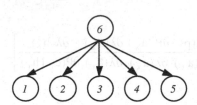

1: Sholl Coefficient
2: Fractal Dimension
3: Profile Count
4: Total Length
5: 2nd Moment
6. Neuron Type

Fig. 4.1.1. A naïve Bayesian network in the morphometric analysis of neural cells

The prediction accuracy of the network was measured in terms of the success ratio (%) of finding the correct answer by comparing the calculated posterior probability of the network with the desired posterior probability in the data. Fig. 4.1.2 illustrates the initial study to decide the ratio of the training data to the test set data. Even though 90/10 performed well, we used 70/30 and 80/20 through out the experiment since 90/10 could yield a biased outcome due to the small number in the test set. After we conducted our series of experiments based on these two ratios, we averaged them to generate the final results. The initial naïve network produced an average prediction accuracy of 59.31%.

Fig. 4.1.2.
The prediction accuracy of
the data in determining the
training/test set size ratio

4.2 Training Hidden Node(s)

Based on the results of the conditional dependency measure derived from the mutual information formulae proposed by Chow and Liu [15], we found that the *Sholl Coefficient* and *2nd Moment* showed the strongest conditional dependency (0.731) as shown in Table 4.2.1. Other node pairs also showed considerable conditional dependencies.

Table 4.2.1. Conditional dependency given *neuron type*

	Fractal Dimension	*Profile Count*	*Total Length*	*2nd Moment*
Sholl Coefficient	0.584309 (3)	0.38721 (8)	0.515724 (4)	0.731219 (1)
Fractal Dimension		0.500339 (6)	0.609505 (2)	0.506806 (5)
Profile Count			0.4171 (7)	0.301292 (10)
Total Length				0.341497 (9)

We investigated the effect on performance of adding hidden nodes between the different pairs of variables in the network. The places where each hidden node was added are indicated by the node numbers of Fig. 4.1.1. In our experiments we used two different propagation methods for the gradient descent (backwards and forwards (BF), and backwards and diagonals (BLR)). In all cases the performance was found to improve, and though there was a trend to finding better improvement when placing hidden nodes between the higher correlated variables. It was, therefore, found that measuring the conditional dependence of two nodes given their parents provided an effective way of deciding where to place the hidden node as shown in Fig. 4.2.1.

When examining the correlation between conditional dependency and improvement ratio of BF and BLR and, we obtained 0.69 and 0.74, respectively.

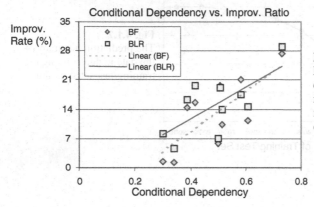

Fig. 4.2.1. Relation between conditional dependency and improvement ratio in morphological classification of neural cells.

After investigating the single hidden node cases, we tried using a number of structures using two hidden nodes. These were placed at sites where the conditional dependency was high. Examples of the modified network structures are shown in Fig. 4.2.2. The best performance could be achieved by the introduction of two hidden nodes. The overall improvement in the decision capability of the network is shown in Fig. 4.2.3. The addition of two hidden nodes improved the performance to above 83.9% in contrast to the original 59.31%.

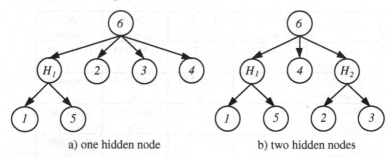

a) one hidden node   b) two hidden nodes

Fig. 4.2.2. Examples of the structure variations of a naïve Bayesian network with up to two hidden node(s)

5 Summary and Discussion

This study demonstrated that hidden nodes are effective in improving the performance of Bayesian networks, and confirms our earlier results [5][10]. The improvement in performance is due to the reduction of conditional dependence. Generally it was found that measuring the conditional dependence of two nodes given their parents provided an effective way of deciding where to place the hidden node. The data set that we used did contain a high degree of correlation between the variables allowing for potential improvement through the use of hidden nodes.

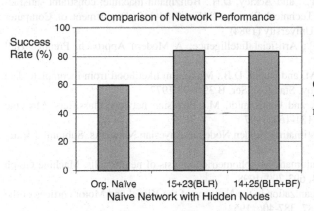

Comparison of Network Performance

Fig. 4.2.3.
Overall performance of two variants of the original network with hidden node(s)

The methodology has the advantage of starting from a naïve structure where causal information is as simple as possible, and there is great potential for identifying variables that are related through a common cause or hidden variable. This allows great flexibility in identifying structural changes to the network. The methodology has two further advantages. Firstly the resulting classifier is always tree structured, and therefore fast and efficient to use in practice. Secondly, the performance is guaranteed to be equal or better than the original network, since the three new link matrices, associated with the hidden node, can encode all the information of the original link matrix joining the two children to the parent.

Computationally there are problems associated with the gradient descent method. For large data sets it will be slow, and it runs the risk of becoming trapped in a local minimum. Heuristic methods, such as simulated annealing can reduce the effects of the latter problem. However, these drawbacks are small compared to the benefits of improved performance.

Acknowledgements. The authors would like to thank Jon Williamson and Donald Gillies of the Philosophy and Artificial Intelligence Group in the Department of Philosophy at King's College London, and Peter Lucas of the Department of Computing Science at Aberdeen University, for their help and advice on this work.

References

1. Pearl, J.: Probabilistic Reasoning in Intelligent Systems: Networks of Plausible Inference. Morgan Kaufman, San Mateo, California (1988)
2. Pearl, J.: Fusion, propagation, and structuring in belief networks. Artificial Intelligence, 29:241-288, 1986
3. Verma, T.S. and Pearl J.: Equivalence and Synthesis of Causal Models. Uncertainty in Artificial Intelligence, 6, Cambridge, MA, Elsevier Science Publishers, 220-22, 1991

4.   Ackley, D.H., Hinton, G.E., and Sejnowski, T.J.: A learning algorithm for Boltzmann machines. Cognitive Science, 9;147-169, 1985
5.   Kwoh C-K. and Gillies, D.: Using hidden nodes in Bayesian networks. Artificial Intelligence, 88:1-38, 1996
6.   Hinton, G.E. Sejnowski, T.J. and Ackley, D.H.: Boltzmann machine: constraint satisfaction networks that learn, Technical Report, CMU-CS-84-119, Department of Computer Science, Carnegie Mellon University (1984)
7.   Russell, S. and Norvig, P.: Artificial Intelligence: A Modern Approach. Prentice Hall (1995)
8.   Dempster, A.P., Laird, N.M. and Rubin, D.B.: Maximum likelihood from incomplete data via the EM algorithm. J. Roy. Stat. Soc. Ser. B 39:1-38 1977
9.   Friedman, N., Geiger, D., and Goldszmidt, M.: Bayesian network classifiers, Machine Learning, vol. 29, no. 2-3, 131-163, 1997
10. Bang, J. and Gillies, D.: Estimating Hidden Nodes in Bayesian Networks. Submitted & accepted to ICMLAI 2002
11. Kim, J. and Gillies, D.: Automatic Morphometric analysis of neural cells. Machine Graphics & Vision, Vol. 7, No. 4, 693-709, 1998
12. Sholl, D. A.: Dendritic Organization in the Neurons of the Visual and Motor cortices of the Cat. Journal of Anatomy, 87, 387-406, 1953
13. Flook, A. G.: The use of Dilation Logic on the Quantimet to Achieve Fractal Dimension Characterisation of Textured and Structured Profiles. Powder Technology, 21, 195-198, 1978
14. Wechsler, H.: Computational Vision. Academic Press Inc (1990)
15. Chow, C.K. and Liu, C.N.: Approximation discrete probability distributions with dependence trees. IEEE Trans. Inform. Theory 14:462-467, 1968

Recognizing 100 Speakers Using Homologous Naive Bayes

Hung-Ju Huang[1] and Chun-Nan Hsu[2]

[1] Department of Computer and Information Science,
National Chiao-Tung University,
Hsinchu City 300, Taiwan
hungju@cis.nctu.edu.tw

[2] Institute of Information Science, Academia Sinica,
Nankang 115, Taipei City, Taiwan
chunnan@iis.sinica.edu.tw

Abstract. This paper presents an extension of the naive Bayesian classifier, called *"homologous naive Bayes (HNB),"* which is applied to the problem of text-independent, close-set speaker recognition. Unlike the standard naive Bayes, HNB can take advantage of the prior information that a sequence of input feature vectors belongs to the same unknown class. We refer to such a sequence a *homologous set*, which is naturally available in speaker recognition. We empirically compare HNB with the Gaussian mixture model (GMM), the most widely used approach to speaker recognition. Results show that, in spite of its simplicity, HNB can achieve comparable classification accuracies for up to a hundred speakers while taking much less resources in terms of time and code size for both training and classification.

1 Introduction

The naive Bayesian classifier is a simple yet robust technique that generally performs well in a wide variety of application domains. This paper presents a variant of the naive Bayesian classifier, called *"homologous naive Bayes (HNB),"* which is applied to the problem of text-independent, close-set speaker recognition. The key difference between HNB and the standard naive Bayes is that HNB can take advantage of the prior information that a sequence of input feature vectors belongs to the same unknown class. We refer to such a sequence a *homologous set*, which is naturally available in speaker recognition. HNB classifies one homologous set at a time while the standard naive Bayes classifies one feature vector at a time. Derived from the Bayes rule and independence assumptions, HNB is designed to deliberately take advantage of homologous sets in test data. We compare HNB with some other straightforward extensions of the standard naive Bayes such as majority vote to classify homologous sets. Results show that HNB outperforms these extension methods and requires much less query vectors in the input homologous sets to significantly improve the classification accuracies.

We also empirically compare HNB with the Gaussian mixture model (GMM), the most widely used approach to speaker recognition. Results show that HNB

M. Ishizuka and A. Sattar (Eds.): PRICAI 2002, LNAI 2417, pp. 395–403, 2002.

can achieve comparable classification accuracies for up to a hundred speakers while taking much less resources in terms of time and code size for both training and classification. A remarkable point is that in our experiments, we discretize the input continuous features into ten bins in both training and classification. In our previous work [1], we give an explanation on why discretization works better than parameter estimation for the naive Bayes with continuous inputs. The results here provide additional evidence to our point.

2   Naive Bayesian Classifiers

A naive Bayesian classifier classifies a query vector $\mathbf{x}$ by selecting class c that maximizes the posterior probability

$$p(c|\mathbf{x}) \propto p(c) \prod_{x \in \mathbf{x}} p(x|c), \tag{1}$$

where x is a variable in $\mathbf{x}$, $p(x|c)$ is the *class-conditional density* of x, given class c. If x is a continuous variable, a conventional approach is to assume that $p(x|c) = N(x; \mu_c, \sigma_c^2)$, where $N(x; \mu_c, \sigma_c^2)$ is the probability distribution function of a normal distribution. In this case, training involves learning the parameters μ_c and σ_c from the training data [2]. This approach has been shown to be less effective than discretization when $p(x|c)$ is not normal, and discretization is often used. Generally, discretization involves partitioning the domain of x into k intervals as a pre-processing step. Subsequently, we can treat x as a discrete variable with k possible values.

In our previous work [1], we had explained why well-known discretization methods, such as entropy-based [3], bin-log$l$ and ten-bin, work well for naive Bayesian classifiers with continuous variables, regardless of their complexities. In addition, we identified conditions when discretization may hurt the classification performance. In summary, to avoid performance degradation, a discretization method should partition the domain of a continuous variable into intervals such that their cut points are close to decision boundaries to minimize the distortion due to the discretization, and their width should be large enough to cover sufficient examples. Since a naive Bayes takes all variables into account simultaneously, the impact of a "wrong" discretization for one variable can be absorbed by other variables under zero-one loss performance measure. Also, due to the way that a naive Bayes learns, correct classification of a given example depends only on the interval containing the values of that example, and is completely independent of how other regions are discretized. As a result, a wide variety of discretization methods can have similar performance in general.

3   Classifying a Homologous Set

We start by showing that a classifier must deliberately take advantage of the knowledge that all data have the same unknown class label; otherwise the knowledge will not improve the expected accuracy, and this is the case in general.

Consider a classifier which classifies one query vector into one of the n classes with accuracy σ. Suppose m query vectors were classified individually with this classifier. The expected value of the accuracy to classify these m query vectors is still σ. This can be derived by the expectation formula [4] as follows.

$$E_1 = \sum_{i=0}^{m-1} \frac{m-i}{m} \frac{m!}{(m-i)!i!} \sigma^{m-i}(1-\sigma)^i = \sigma. \tag{2}$$

On the other hand, suppose we have the information that the m vectors actually belong to the same class and classify them together (taking them as one object) using the same classifier. The expected value of the accuracy is:

$$E_2 = \frac{m}{m}\binom{1}{1}\sigma(1-\sigma)^0 + \frac{0}{m}\binom{1}{0}\sigma^0(1-\sigma) = \sigma. \tag{3}$$

The expected values of the above two cases are the same. This implies that the prior information that the query vectors come from the same class does not automatically improve the accuracy.

Let $\mathbf{X} = \{\mathbf{x}_1, \ldots, \mathbf{x}_n\}$ be a homologous set of query vectors with the same unknown class label c and each query vector $\mathbf{x}_t$ in $\mathbf{X}$ has r features $(x_{t1}, \ldots, x_{tr})$. We assume that $\mathbf{x}_1, \ldots, \mathbf{x}_n$ are drawn independently, and the symbol O denotes the prior information that all members in the homologous set have the same unknown class label. According to the Bayesian decision theory, we should classify this homologous set by selecting the class c that maximize $p(c|\mathbf{X}, O)$, the probability of c given $\mathbf{X}$ and O. We can derive three straightforward "extension" methods to estimate $p(c|\mathbf{X}, O)$ for classifying the query vectors in a homologous set. One method is by voting, which uses naive Bayes to classify each member in the homologous set and selects the class label predicted most often. Another is "Avg" method, which estimates $p(c|\mathbf{x}_t)$ for each $\mathbf{x}_t \in \mathbf{X}$ and averages the results to obtain $p(c|\mathbf{X}, O)$. The "Max" method estimates $p(c|\mathbf{x}_t)$ for each $\mathbf{x}_t \in \mathbf{X}$ and selects the maximum probability as $p(c|\mathbf{X}, O)$. The classification rule of the above methods is to pick the class c that maximizes $p(c|\mathbf{X}, O)$. The above methods are based on the idea that we can combine the estimation of $p(c|\mathbf{x}_t)$ to obtain $p(c|\mathbf{X}, O)$, by averaging or by selecting the maximum values. In fact, we can derive a method purely from the Bayes rule and independence assumptions as follows:

$$p(c|\mathbf{X}, O) = p(c|\mathbf{x}_1, \mathbf{x}_2, \ldots, \mathbf{x}_n, O) \tag{4}$$

$$= \frac{p(c)p(\mathbf{x}_1, \mathbf{x}_2, \ldots, \mathbf{x}_n, O|c)}{p(\mathbf{x}_1, \mathbf{x}_2, \ldots, \mathbf{x}_n, O)} \tag{5}$$

$$\propto p(c)p(\mathbf{x}_1, \mathbf{x}_2, \ldots, \mathbf{x}_n, O|c) \tag{6}$$

$$= p(c)p(\mathbf{x}_1|c)p(\mathbf{x}_2|c, \mathbf{x}_1)p(\mathbf{x}_3|c, \mathbf{x}_1, \mathbf{x}_2)\cdots$$
$$p(\mathbf{x}_n|c, \mathbf{x}_1, \mathbf{x}_2, \ldots, \mathbf{x}_{n-2}, \mathbf{x}_{n-1})p(O|c, \mathbf{x}_1, \mathbf{x}_2, \ldots, \mathbf{x}_{n-1}, \mathbf{x}_n) \tag{7}$$

$$= p(c)p(\mathbf{x}_1|c)p(\mathbf{x}_2|c)\cdots$$
$$p(\mathbf{x}_{n-1}|c)p(\mathbf{x}_n|c)p(O|c, \mathbf{x}_1, \mathbf{x}_2, \ldots, \mathbf{x}_{n-1}, \mathbf{x}_n) \tag{8}$$

$$= p(c)p(\mathbf{x}_1|c)p(\mathbf{x}_2|c)\dots p(\mathbf{x}_{n-1}|c)p(\mathbf{x}_n|c) \qquad (9)$$

$$= p(c)p_c(\mathbf{x}_1)p_c(\mathbf{x}_2)\dots p_c(\mathbf{x}_{n-1})p_c(\mathbf{x}_n). \qquad (10)$$

We can simplify (7) to (8) because of the assumption that all members in $\mathbf{X}$ are drawn independently[1]. Since O is logically implied by the event that $\mathbf{x}_1, \dots, \mathbf{x}_n$ are of class c, $p(O|c, \mathbf{x}_1, \mathbf{x}_2, \dots, \mathbf{x}_{n-1}, \mathbf{x}_n) = 1$ and we can reduce (8) to (9). For the sake of being concise, we transit (9) to (10). Finally, since the naive Bayes assumes that all features are independent given class c, Equation (10) can be decomposed by the following equations:

$$(10) = p(c)p_c(x_{11}, x_{12}, \dots, x_{1r})p_c(x_{21}, x_{22}, \dots, x_{2r})\dots$$
$$p_c(x_{n1}, x_{n2}, \dots, x_{nr}) \qquad (11)$$

$$= p(c)p_c(x_{11})p_c(x_{12})\dots p_c(x_{1r})p_c(x_{21})\dots p_c(x_{n(r-1)})p_c(x_{nr}) \qquad (12)$$

$$= p(c) \prod_{t=1}^{n} \prod_{l=1}^{r} p_c(x_{tl}). \qquad (13)$$

Therefore, the classification rule is to pick class c that maximizes (13) . We call this method "HNB" (Homologous Naive Bayes). Note that the training procedure of the above methods remains unchanged as the standard naive Bayes.

To evaluate the methods described above, we select fifteen real data sets from UCI ML repository [5] for our experiments. In the first experiment, we investigate the performance of the methods when there are three elements in a homologous set. We reported the average of the accuracies after running five-fold cross-validation on each data set. Table 1 gives the result. The result in Table 1 reveals that HBN significantly outperforms all other methods in all the data sets.

A large homologous set increases the chance that a naive Bayes correctly classifies a majority of the query vectors, thus ameliorating the performance of voting. In order to compare the performance of HNB and voting with different sizes of homologous sets, we selected a large data set ("Waveform", size = 5000) and repeated the same procedure as in the first experiment for different sizes of homologous sets (from one to 100). Note that when the size of homologous sets is one, both HNB and voting are reduced to a standard naive Bayes. This case serves as the base line for performance evaluation. Figure 1 plot the resulting curves, which show that the performance of voting improves as the size of homologous sets increases, but the curves of HNB grow faster. We repeat the same experiment for several other standard data sets from UCI repository and obtain similar results.

4   Application in Speaker Recognition

Speaker recognition is particularly relevant to our case because a large number of query vectors can be extracted from a short speech sentence, and obviously

---

[1] A feature vector may depend on other feature vectors in real situations if they come from the same class.

Table 1. Average accuracies of the naive Bayes using different extension methods when the size of a homologous set is three.

DATA SET	HNB	VOTING	AVG	MAX
AUSTRALIAN	**97.16**	94.40	93.88	78.58
BREAST	**99.27**	98.42	98.36	93.27
CHESS	**94.19**	93.09	90.38	85.05
CRX	**95.00**	92.61	92.75	91.16
GERMAN	**86.02**	81.88	76.22	71.79
GLASS	**80.71**	68.29	70.00	65.41
HEART	**95.00**	93.03	89.09	85.61
HEPATITIS	**95.00**	86.33	94.00	91.00
IRIS	**100.0**	100.0	100.0	100.0
LETTER	**96.85**	86.42	91.24	88.03
PIMA	**88.39**	85.74	78.99	74.32
SONAR	**93.95**	82.89	91.05	75.52
VEHICLE	**73.44**	66.75	71.25	60.12
WAVEFORM	**94.61**	77.71	87.45	79.42
WINE	**100.0**	98.63	99.09	98.63
AVERAGE	92.64	87.07	88.25	85.53
BEST	15	1	1	1

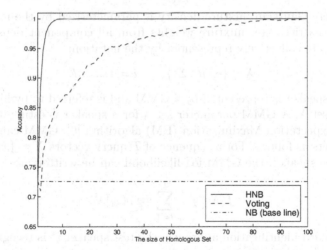

Fig. 1. Accuracies for classifying homologous sets with different sizes for the data set "Waveform".

those vectors must come from the same speaker. A speaker recognition system should take advantage of this information.

In recent speaker recognition evaluations carried out by the National Institute of Standards and Technology (NIST) [6], the best GMM [7] based systems have outperformed the HMM [8] based systems. In this section, we will briefly review the Gaussian mixture model approach to speaker recognition and report our preliminary results on the empirical comparison between HNB and GMM in a text-independent, close-set speaker recognition task.

4.1 Gaussian Mixture Model

A Gaussian mixture density is a weighted sum of M component densities and is given by the form [7]:

$$p(w|\lambda) = \sum_{i=1}^{M} c_i b_i(w), \tag{14}$$

where w is a d-dimensional random vector, $b_i(w)$, $i = 1, ..., M$ is the component density and c_i, $i = 1, ..., M$ is the mixture weight. Each component density is a d-variate Gaussian function of the form:

$$b_i(w) = \frac{1}{(2\pi)^{\frac{d}{2}} |\Sigma_i|^{\frac{1}{2}}} exp\{-\frac{1}{2}(w - \mu_i)' \Sigma_i^{-1}(w - \mu_i)\}. \tag{15}$$

with mean vector μ_i and covariance matrix Σ_i. The mixture weights must satisfy the constraint that:

$$\sum_{i=1}^{M} c_i = 1. \tag{16}$$

The complete Gaussian mixture density is parameterized by the mean vectors, covariance matrices and mixture weights from all component densities. These parameters are collectively represented by the notation:

$$\lambda = \{c_i, \mu_i, \Sigma_i\}, \quad i = 1, ..., M. \tag{17}$$

Then each speaker is represented by a GMM and is referred to by his/her model parameter set λ. A GMM parameter set λ for a speaker is estimated using the standard Expectation Maximization (EM) algorithm [9]. GMM can classify homologous sets as follows. For a sequence of T query vectors $X = \{x_1, x_2, ..., x_T\}$ for the same speaker, the GMM log-likelihood can be written as:

$$f(X|\lambda) = \sum_{t=1}^{T} \log p(x_t|\lambda). \tag{18}$$

In the standard identification approach, the test speaker i^* is recognized from a set of S speakers by:

$$i^* = \arg\max_{i=1}^{S} f(X|\lambda_i). \tag{19}$$

Several system parameters must be tuned for training a Gaussian mixture speaker model, but a good theoretical guide for setting the initial values of those parameters has not been found. The most critical parameter is the order M of the mixture. Choosing too few mixture components can produce a speaker model that cannot accurately model the distinguishing characteristics of a speaker's distribution. Choosing too many components reduces performance when there are a large number of model parameters relative to the available training data [7].

4.2   Experiments

The database of the experiments reported in this paper is a subset of the TCC-300, Mandarin Chinese maintained by many research institutes in Taiwan. We used the speech data recorded at the National Chiao-Tung University. All speech signals were digitally-recorded in a laboratory using a personal computer with a 16-bit sound blaster card and a head-set microphone. The sampling rate was 16 kHz. A 30-ms Hamming window was applied to the speech every 10 ms, allowing us to obtain one hundred feature vectors from one second speech data. For each speech frame, both a 12th-order linear predictive analysis and a log energy analysis were performed. Firstly we filtered the feature vectors whose log energy value was lower than 30. This can be viewed as a silence removing process. A feature vector for training or testing contains the twelve linear predictive parameters. More than ten sentences are recorded from each subject speaker, and from each sentence, more than four thousand feature vectors are extracted. The evaluating procedure is described as follows: We randomly select five sentences for each speaker, one for testing and the others for training. Then we randomly select one thousand feature vectors from each sentence. Hence, for each speaker there are four thousand feature vectors for training and one thousand feature vectors for testing. There are several parameters must to be tuned for training a Gaussian mixture speaker model. $M = 32$ for GMM is used in our experiments, this setting is suggested in [7] and works well in our data sets. In contrast, no parameter tuning is necessary for HNB.

We run a five-fold cross-validation on different numbers of speakers and different homologous set sizes. One hundred query vectors represent one second speech data. We report the average accuracies, the average CPU time for training and classification in CPU timer ticks. Table 2 gives the results, which show that GMM uses smaller sizes of test vectors than HNB to reach a high accuracy. However, HNB takes much less resources in terms of time and code size for both training and classification.

More precisely, the average training speed of HNB surpasses GMM by about 329 times, and the average classification speed by about 15.73. It take about 0.5 seconds of additional test data on average for HNB than GMM to reach high accuracies ($> 99\%$). Since one more additional second of speech may not incur too much a handle to the speakers, this seems to be a tolerable or even favorable trade-off we can take in favor of HNB.

5   Conclusions and Future Work

HNB appears to be a promising approach to speaker recognition according to our preliminary study. We plan to purchase standard speaker recognition benchmark data sets from LDC and NIST to perform a thorough evaluation of our approach.

Acknowledgements. The speech data set was the courtesy of the Speech Processing Laboratory, Department of Communication Engineering, National Chiao Tung University, Taiwan.

Table 2. Results of the application in speaker recognition

SIZE OF A HOMOLOGOUS SET	AVERAGE CLASSIFICATION ACCURACY (IN %) NUMBER OF SPEAKERS					
	16		30		100	
	HNB	GMM	HNB	GMM	HNB	GMM
1	31.43	52.31	24.31	44.23	12.30	30.57
20	92.90	99.42	94.43	99.68	86.74	99.54
50	97.93	100.0	98.93	99.93	96.85	99.94
100	99.13	100.0	99.53	100.0	98.42	99.98
200	99.50	100.0	99.60	100.0	98.88	100.0
300	99.58	100.0	99.78	100.0	99.13	100.0
400	100.0	100.0	99.85	100.0	99.20	100.0
500 (5 SEC)	100.0	100.0	100.0	100.0	99.40	100.0

NUMBER OF SPEAKERS	AVERAGE TRAINING TIME (IN CPU TICKS)		
	HNB	GMM	SPEEDUP
16	382.22	128056.44	335.03
30	716.22	240300.22	335.51
100	2446.85	776147.26	317.20
AVERAGE	–	–	329.19

SIZE OF A HOMOLOGOUS SET	AVERAGE CLASSIFICATION TIME (IN CPU TICKS) NUMBER OF SPEAKERS					
	16		30		100	
	HNB	GMM	HNB	GMM	HNB	GMM
1	0.19	3.88	0.38	5.867	6.55	101.59
20	3.57	50.92	6.84	103.96	115.94	1767.48
50	8.71	122.95	16.40	251.15	280.40	4109.76
100	16.90	242.50	31.70	500.31	542.16	8375.25
200	32.80	485.12	61.53	992.09	1049.73	16764.13
300	48.54	728.04	90.91	1490.00	1543.33	23206.66
400	64.50	967.39	120.66	1983.46	2043.27	30950.51
500 (5 SEC)	80.00	1223.64	149.93	2484.63	2534.53	38834.37

The research reported here was supported in part by the National Science Council of ROC under Grant No. NSC 89-2213-E-001-031.

References

1. Hsu, C.N., Huang, H.J., Wong, T.T.: Why discretization works for naive bayesian classifiers. In: Machine Learning: Proceedings of the 17th International Conference (ML 2000), San Francisco, CA (2000)

2. John, G., Langley, P.: Estimating continuous distributions in Bayesian classifiers. In: In Proceedings of the Eleventh Annual Conference on Uncertainty in Artificial Intelligence (UAI '95). (1995) 338–345
3. Fayyad, U.M., Irani, K.B.: Multi-interval discretization of continuous valued attributes for classification learning. In: Proceedings of the Thirteenth International Joint Conference on Artificial Intelligence (IJCAI '93), Chambery, France (1993) 1022–1027
4. Ross, S.: A First Course in Probability. Prentice Hall (1998)
5. Blake, C., Merz, C.: UCI repository of machine learning databases (1998)
6. Przybocki, M.A., Martin, A.F.: NIST speaker recognition evaluation. In: Workshop on Speaker Recognition and its Commercial and Forensic Applications (RLA2C), Avignon, France (1998)
7. Reynolds, D.A., Rose, R.C.: Robust text-independent speaker identification using gaussian mixture speaker models. IEEE Transactions on Speech and Audio Processing **3** (1995) 72–83
8. de Veth, J., Bourlard, H.: Comparison of hidden markov model techniques for automatic speaker verification in real-world conditions. Speech Communication **17** (1995) 81–90
9. Dempster, A.P., Laird, N.M., Rubin, D.B.: Maximum likelihood from incomplete data via the EM algorithm. Journal of the Royal Statistical Society **Series, B (39)** (1977) 1–38

An Approach to Microscopic Clustering of Terms and Documents

Akiko Aizawa

National Institute of Informatics, Japan,
akiko@nii.ac.jp

Abstract. In this paper, we present an approach to clustering in text-based information retrieval systems. The proposed method generates overlapping clusters, each of which is composed of subsets of associated terms and documents with normalized significance weights. In the paper, we first briefly introduce the probabilistic formulation of our clustering scheme and then show the procedure for cluster generation. We also report some experimental results, where the generated clusters are investigated in the framework of automatic text categorization.

1 Introduction

In the field of information retrieval the document-clustering problem has been extensively studied, and numbers of traditional statistical clustering methods, such as hierarchical agglomerative clustering [1] or partitional K-means [2] have been applied to different retrieval applications. In recent years, several studies have pointed out the advantage of using simultaneous clustering of terms and documents, examples of which include the Information Bottleneck Method [3][4], and co-clustering using Bipartite Spectral Graph Partitioning [5]. It has been reported that by focusing on only limited subsets of terms and documents, those simultaneous clustering methods reduce the noise caused by the existence of irrelevant terms (in the case of documents clustering) or documents (in the case of terms clustering) [3].

Most of the previous approaches to clustering, including simultaneous clustering, construct either a partition or a hierarchy of target documents, where the generated clusters are either exclusive or nested. In addition, in most cases, the number of generated clusters is pre-determined, typically a relatively small number, in order to reduce the cost of the clustering execution to a reasonable level. Although such strategies are reasonable in the context of unsupervised document classification, they cannot be applied directly when the purpose of the clustering is to generate conceptual or linguistic categories. These categories are frequently used as indices of requests from users in text-based retrieval systems and they overlap arbitrarily in nature.

Based on the background, this paper presents a framework of clustering where documents, terms, and other related attributes are locally and simultaneously analyzed to generate small sizes of clusters that overlap each other. Individual

M. Ishizuka and A. Sattar (Eds.): PRICAI 2002, LNAI 2417, pp. 404–413, 2002.

clusters, referred to as *micro-clusters* in this paper, contain multiple subsets of associated elements, such as documents or terms. Our major motivation in considering such clusters is that the universal properties of text-based information spaces, namely, the large scale, the sparseness, and the local redundancy [6], may better be manipulated by focusing on only limited sub-regions of the space, relaxing the hard constraint of exclusiveness of the clusters. We expect such a clustering scheme becomes indispensable when dealing with large-scale information spaces, where conventional matrix decomposition-based methods, such as Latent Semantic Indexing, become computationally impractical.

The rest of the paper is organized as follows. In Section 2, the mathematical definition of a 'micro-cluster' is shown, together with the entropy-based criteria for its evaluation. In Section 3, a procedure for generating the micro-clusters is given, where an initiating cluster is formulated using relevance feedback from an arbitrarily selected element, and then the generated cluster is improved using the proposed evaluation criteria. Section 4 presents the results of preliminary experiments. Section 5 is the conclusion. For simplicity of explanation, we focus on the co-occurrences between 'documents' and 'terms' in Sections 2 and 3, but in our experiments in Section 4, the results presented are shown to be applicable to more general cases, with more than two attributes.

2   Mathematical Development

The proposed probabilistic formulation has the following two major features. First, clustering is generally defined as an operation of agglomerating a group of cells in the contingency table. Such an interpretation is unique because existing probabilistic approaches, including those with a duality view, agglomerate the entire rows or columns of the contingency table simultaneously. Second, the estimation of the occurrence probability is discounted for low frequency terms. The discounting scheme enables us to trade-off: (i) the loss of averaging probabilities in the agglomerated clusters, and (ii) the improvement of probability estimation accuracy by using the larger samples obtained by the agglomeration.

2.1   Definition of Micro-Clusters

Let $D = \{d_1, \cdots, d_N\}$ be a collection of N target documents, and S_D be a subset of documents such that $S_D \subset D$. Similarly, let $T = \{t_1, \cdots, t_M\}$ be a set of M distinct terms that appear in the target document collection, and S_T be a subset of terms such that $S_T \subset T$. A *cluster*, denoted as c, is defined as a combination of S_T and S_D:

$$c = (S_T, S_D). \tag{1}$$

The co-occurrences of terms and documents can be expressed as a matrix of size $M \times N$, whose (i, j)-th cell represents the existence of t_i ($\in T$) in d_j ($\in D$). Although we primarily assume the value is either '1' (exist) or '0' (not exist) in this paper, our formulation can be easily extended to the cases where the value represents the actual number of occurrences of t_i in d_j.

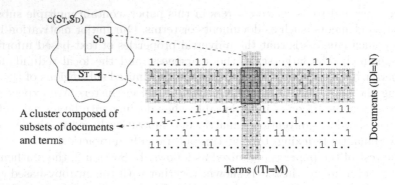

Fig. 1. Example of a cluster defined on a co-occurrence matrix.

2.2 Entropy-Based Criteria for Cluster Evaluation

In probabilistic information retrieval, it is common practice to consider t_i and d_j as independently observed events. Then, a cluster $c = (S_T, S_D)$ is defined as a single co-occurrence event of observing one of $t_i \in S_T$ in either of $d_j \in S_D$. Let $\mathcal{T}$ and $\mathcal{D}$ be two random variables corresponding to an event of observing a term and a document, respectively. Denote their occurrence probabilities as $P(\mathcal{T})$ and $P(\mathcal{D})$, and their co-occurrence probability as a joint distribution $P(\mathcal{T}, \mathcal{D})$. By definition, from traditional information theory, the mutual information (entropy) between the two random variables, denoted as $\mathcal{I}(\mathcal{T}, \mathcal{D})$, is calculated as:

$$\mathcal{I}(\mathcal{T}, \mathcal{D}) = \sum_{t_i \in T} \sum_{d_j \in D} P(t_i, d_j) log \frac{P(t_i, d_j)}{P(t_i)P(d_j)}. \tag{2}$$

Next, the mutual information after agglomerating S_T and S_D into a single cluster is calculated as:

$$\mathcal{I}'(\mathcal{T}, \mathcal{D}) = \sum_{t_i \notin S_T} \sum_{d_j \notin S_D} P(t_i, d_j) log \frac{P(t_i, d_j)}{P(t_i)P(d_j)} + P(S_T, S_D) log \frac{P(S_T, S_D)}{P(S_T)P(S_D)}. \tag{3}$$

The fitness of a cluster, denoted as $\delta\mathcal{I}(S_T, S_D)$, is defined as the difference of the two information values [8]:

$$\delta\mathcal{I}(S_T, S_D) = \mathcal{I}'(\mathcal{T}, \mathcal{D}) - \mathcal{I}(\mathcal{T}, \mathcal{D})$$

$$= P(S_T, S_D) log \frac{P(S_T, S_D)}{P(S_T)P(S_D)} - \sum_{t_i \in S_T} \sum_{d_j \in S_D} P(t_i, d_j) log \frac{P(t_i, d_j)}{P(t_i)P(d_j)}. \tag{4}$$

We define the significance of t_i in $c = (S_T, S_D)$ as the contribution of t_i to the entire entropy calculation given by Eq. (2):

$$\delta\mathcal{I}(t_i, S_D) = \sum_{d_j \in S_D} P(t_i, d_j) log \frac{P(t_i, d_j)}{P(t_i)P(d_j)}. \tag{5}$$

Similarly, the significance of d_j in (S_T, S_D) is calculated as:

$$\delta\mathcal{I}(S_T, d_j) = \sum_{t_i \in S_T} P(t_i, d_j) log \frac{P(t_i, d_j)}{P(t_i)P(d_j)}. \tag{6}$$

In other words, all the terms and documents in a cluster are ordered according to their significance weights, as given by Eqs. (5) and (6).

The probability of each event is estimated using a simple discounting method similar to the absolute discounting in probabilistic language modeling studies [7]. The method subtracts a constant value δ, called a discounting coefficient, from all the observed term frequencies and estimates the probability of t_i. Note that the discounting effect is stronger for low frequency terms. Without discounting, the value of $\delta\mathcal{I}(S_T, S_D)$ in Eq. (4) is always negative or zero. However, with discounting, the value becomes positive for uniformly dense clusters, because the frequencies of individual cells are always smaller than their agglomerated values.

So far, we have restricted our focus on one-to-one correspondences between terms and documents. However, the proposed framework can easily be extended to more general cases with $k(\geq 2)$ attributes. For example, given k random variables $X_1, \cdots, X_k$, Eq. (4) can be extended as:

$$\delta\mathcal{I}(S_{X_1}, \cdots, S_{X_k}) = P(S_{X_1}, \cdots, S_{X_k}) log \frac{P(S_{X_1}, \cdots, S_{X_k})}{P(S_{X_1}) \cdots P(S_{X_k})}$$

$$- \sum_{x_1 \in S_{X_1}} \cdots \sum_{x_k \in S_{X_k}} P(x_1, \cdots, x_k) log \frac{P(x_1, \cdots, x_k)}{P(x_1) \cdots P(x_k)}. \tag{7}$$

3   Strategy for Cluster Generation

The proposed procedure is composed of repeated cycles of generation and testing. In each cycle, an initial cluster is formulated using a term or a document randomly selected from either of the specified spaces. Then, non-significant terms and documents are sequentially eliminated from the initiated cluster. Finally, the newly generated cluster is tested for duplication with other existing clusters. The proposed clustering procedure can also be formulated in the framework of evolutionary computation as an online optimization process of maintaining a population of micro-clusters [9].

3.1   Cluster Initiation

Given a co-occurrence matrix, we can extract a bipartite graph expression of the co-occurrences by representing terms and documents as nodes, and non-zero elements of the co-occurrence matrix as links (Figure 2). The purpose of cluster initiation is to collect neighboring terms and documents on the graphical representation. In our present implementation, the following naive method shown in (Figure 2) is used:

Procedure for cluster initiation:

(1) Select a term t_i ($\in T$) randomly to initiate a cluster.
(2) Select all the documents that contain the given term and let the set be S_D.
(3) Select all the terms that are contained in at least one document in S_D, and let the set be S_T.
(4) An initial cluster is given as $c = (S_T, S_D)$.

The same procedure is also applicable when starting from a document.

On the graphical representation, the process can be viewed as a two-step expansion, starting from a selected term or document node. Here, the number of expansions is determined heuristically depending on the nature of the target data. Other graph-based methods, such as the minimum-cut detection algorithm, can be also applied to cluster initiation.

3.2   Local Improvement and Testing

After the cluster initiation, significance weights of all the terms and documents in the cluster are calculated using Eqs. (5) and (6) derived above. Based on the values, the sizes of S_T and S_D are first limited to a fixed number k_{max}, so that only the top k_{max} ranked terms and documents are used in the succeeding local improvement step. The main purpose of limiting S_T and S_D is to avoid the explosion of computation caused by terms of exceptionally high frequency.

Next, the terms and the documents in the cluster are examined for elimination in increasing order of their significance values. Note that the probabilistic interpretation of the significance weights is common for both terms and documents; that is, the contribution of the corresponding term or document to the whole entropy of the cluster is given by Eq. (2). Based on this, we do not distinguish terms and documents in the sequential elimination step, but consider a single unified sorted list of the two. That is, the elimination is complementary for terms and documents without any explicit control. The only restriction is that when all but one member of either the term or the document subsets are removed from the unified list, the elimination process is automatically terminated.

The local improvement step in our current implementation is formulated as:

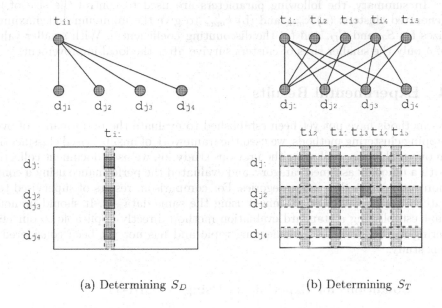

(a) Determining S_D (b) Determining S_T

Fig. 2. Cluster initiation by collecting neighboring nodes on the bipartite graph.

Procedure for local improvement:

(1) Sort all the terms and documents in $c = (S_T, S_D)$ according to their evaluation values given by Eqs. (5) and (6).

(2) Select the term or document that has not been examined before and has the worst remaining fitness value.

(3) Remove the element from the cluster and let the new cluster be $c = (S_T', S_D')$, where either $S_T' = S_T$ or $S_D' = S_D$.

(4) Calculate the fitness of the new cluster. If $\delta\mathcal{I}(S_T', S_D') \geq \delta\mathcal{I}(S_T, S_D)$, keep $c(S_T', S_D')$. Otherwise, keep $c(S_T, S_D)$. Go to (1).

(5) If the procedure has tested all the elements in the cluster, or, either $|S_D| = 1$ or $|S_T| = 1$, end.

Note that the resulting cluster is only locally optimized, because the improvement depends on the order of examining terms and documents in the cluster.

The newly generated cluster is tested if (i) the evaluation value given by Eq. (4) is positive, and also if (ii) the sizes of subsets S_T and S_D are both equal or greater than a pre-determined number k_{min}. We use $k_{min} \geq 2$ to exclude trivial cases where only a single document or a single term is contained in a cluster. Clusters that do not satisfy either of the conditions are discarded. Finally, the generated cluster is checked for duplication. If there exists a cluster that contains either a term or a document subset identical to the one of the newly generated cluster, then, the evaluation values of the two clusters are compared, and the inferior one is discarded.

In summary, the following parameters are used to control the size of the generated clusters: (a) k_{min} and (b) k_{max} to give the minimum and maximum sizes for S_T and S_D, and (c) the discounting coefficient δ. With smaller values of δ only the smaller sizes of clusters survive after the local improvement.

4   Experimental Results

As methods have not yet been established to evaluate the performance of overlapping clustering methods, we used the framework of unsupervised classification in our evaluation. Following the previous study [6], we used document collection with a uniquely assigned category, and evaluated the performance using a confusion ratio across different categories. For comparison, results of supervised text categorization were also examined using the same data set. It should be noted that establishing a standard evaluation method directly applicable to our clustering method itself is a challenging topic and has not yet been considered in our study.

4.1   Conditions for Experiments Using NTCIR-J1

The test collection used in our experiments was the NTCIR-J1 [10], a Japanese text collection specifically constructed for retrieval tasks. NTCIR-J1 is composed of abstracts of academic conference papers presented at national conferences organized by Japanese academic societies. From the more than 60 academic societies whose abstracts are registered in NTCIR-J1, we focused on the following three societies: The Japanese Society for Artificial Intelligence (JSAI), the Information Processing Society of Japan (IPSJ) and the Japan Society of Civil Engineering (JSCE).

In preparing the data for the clustering experiments, the fields of title, keywords, abstract, and authors of each paper were first extracted together with the academic society in which the paper was presented. The first three fields were analyzed by the morphological analyzer ChaSen Version 2.02 [11], and nouns and compound nouns were then extracted, based on the patterns of the Part-Of-Speech tags. Finally, the co-occurrence information between: (i) the documents, (ii) the authors, and (iii) the identified terms, was gathered to formulate an information space of the triple 'documents-terms-authors' attribute set. The academic society field was used for evaluation in text categorization experiments. The numbers of documents, authors, and the extracted terms for each society are shown in Table 1.

4.2   Clustering Results

In the experiment, documents from three different societies, JSAI, IPSJ, and JSCE, were first mixed, and then the proposed clustering method was applied. The values of parameters were $\delta = 0.9$, $k_{min} = 3$, and $k_{max} = 50$. The resulting clusters totaled 68,891, with the average cluster containing 9.4 documents, 49.1 terms, and 19.8 authors. This means that the average numbers of clusters

Table 1. Data used in the experiments.

	JSAI	IPSJ	JSCE	mixed
Number of documents	2,014	26,497	20,482	48,993
Number of authors	2,354	24,109	23,194	47,645
Number of terms	35,184	325,320	257,282	578,131

assigned to each element was: 13.2 for a document, 5.9 for a term, and 2.4 for an author. The generated clusters were first examined to determine whether the members came from a single or from multiple societies. The single society ratio was approximately 92%.

Next, 100 documents were chosen from each society as test examples. Assuming the originating societies of the remaining documents are known, a total of 300 test documents were categorized into either one of the three societies, based on the membership of other members of the micro-clusters to which they belonged. The result is shown in Table 2-(a). For example, the table shows that 73 JSAI documents were categorized correctly into their original society, while 25 were categorized mistakenly as IPSJ, etc. Of the 300 documents tested, only three were 'isolated', that is, did not belong in any cluster.

Table 2. Clustering abstracts from two different societies.

(a) *Micro-clustering results*

	judgment		
	JSAI	IPSJ	JSCE
JSAI	73	25	0
IPSJ	18	80	1
JSCE	17	5	78

(b) *Text categorization results*

	judgment		
	JSAI	IPSJ	JSCE
JSAI	35	65	0
IPSJ	0	100	0
JSCE	0	15	85

Although the clustering parameters were still heuristically adjusted, the result seems to be adequate as an unsupervised categorization method. For comparison, the performance of a supervised text categorization method for the same training and test documents is shown in Table 2-(b). The adopted supervised method, which uses the same entropy-based criteria for categorization, showed better performance than a naive Bayes classifier with the multi-class categorization task described in our previous study [12].

We have also checked manually the 22 misclassified JSCE documents and noted the subject of each abstract. It transpired that all the documents were somewhat connected to topics in computer science: there are nine documents related to *education*, eight to *expert systems*, three to *modeling*, and two to *databases*. On the other hand, the IPSJ document misclassified as JSCE was irrelevant to civil engineering. Because JSAI and IPSJ both deal with computer science studies, human judgment was not possible.

In the above experiments, we have formulated the categorization task so that the category size distribution of the training documents is totally different to that of the tested documents, in order to examine the performance for minority classes. We have also compared the performance using a test set with a proportionally assigned society ratio, and have observed comparable performance, that is, 0.94 accuracy for the micro-clustering method and 0.95 accuracy for the supervised method. Comparing the proposed micro-clustering method with existing text categorization methods, the distinctive feature of the former is that the documents on borders are readily viewed and examined. This property of micro-clustering is particularly important when human intervention is required in classifying documents. The resulting clusters seem to be consistently good; however, the details are left for future investigation.

5 Future Issues

In this paper, we report a method of generating overlapping micro-clusters in which documents, terms, and other related elements of text-based information are grouped together. Although our investigation is still in its initial stages, based on the results of the experiments, we expect that the proposed method can be a powerful tool for exploring huge information spaces.

Our discussion in this paper is based on document clustering, but it is also possible to view the cluster generation process as a variation of term indexing. Traditional matrix transformation-based indexing methods, such as Latent Semantic Indexing (LSI) [13], generate concept vectors as the principal components of an optimally reduced feature space. The proposed method, instead of dealing with concept vectors that are globally optimized and with many non-zero weights, tries to generate small sub-vectors of terms and documents that are only optimized locally. In [14], the exclusively generated term clusters using k-means were reported to be quite close to the term vectors obtained by LSI.

Also related to our study is the detection of strongly connected sub-structures of the bipartite graph extracted from a co-occurrence matrix. The problem has become popular in recent studies of information extraction, the examples of which include discovery of Web communities using reference links [15], and matrix clustering for Customer Relationship Management in data mining [16]. Our strategy can be viewed as a variation of such graph structure extraction methods and is characterized by its probabilistic formulation, which allows us to extend the scope beyond simple bipartite graphs.

Future issues include: (1) enhancing the probabilistic models considering other discounting techniques in linguistic studies; (2) developing a strategy for initiating clusters combining different attribute sets, such as documents or authors; and also (3) establishing a method of evaluating overlapping clusters. We are also looking into the possibility of applying the proposed framework to Web document clustering problems.

References

1. El-Hamdouchi, A., Willet, P.: Comparison of hierarchic agglomerative clustering methods for document retrieval. The Computer Journal, **32(3)** (1989)
2. Cutting, D.R., Karger, D.R., Pedersen, J.O., Tukey, J.W.: Scatter/Gather: a cluster-based approach to browsing large document collections. Proceedings of the 15th Annual International ACM SIGIR Conference on Research and Development in Information Retrieval (SIGIR 1992) (1992) 318–329
3. Slonim, N., Tishby, N.: Document clustering using word clusters via the information bottleneck method. Proceedings of the 23rd Annual International ACM SIGIR Conference on Research and Development in Information Retrieval (SIGIR 2000) (2000) 2008–2015
4. Tishby, N., Pereira, F.C., Bialek, W.: The information bottleneck method. Proceedings of the 37th Annual Allerton Conference on Communication, Control and Computing (1999) 368–377
5. Dhillon, I.S.: Co-clustering documents and words using bipartite spectral graph partitioning. Proceedings of the Seventh ACM SIGKDD International Conference on Knowledge Discovery and Data Mining (2001) 269–274
6. Joachims, T.: A statistical learning model of text classification for support vector machines. Proceedings of the 24th Annual International ACM SIGIR Conference on Research and Development in Information Retrieval (SIGIR 2001) (2001) 128–136
7. Kita, K.: Probabilistic language models. University of Tokyo Press (1999)
8. Aizawa, A.: A method of cluster-based indexing of textual data. Proceedings of the 19th International Conference on Computational Linguistics (COLING 2002) (2002) (accepted)
9. Aizawa, A.: A co-evolutionary framework of clustering in information retrieval systems. Proceedings of IEEE Congress on Evolutionary Computation 2002 (2002) 1787–1792
10. Kando, N., Kuriyama, K., Nozue, T., Eguchi, K., Kato, H., Hidaka, S.: Overview of IR tasks. Proceedings of the 1st NTCIR Workshop on Research in Japanese Text Retrieval and Term Recognition (NTCIR Workshop 1) (1999) 11–44
11. Matsumoto, Y., Kitauchi, A., Yamashita, T., Hirano, Y., Matsuda, K., Asahara, M.: Morphological analysis system ChaSen 2.0.2 users manual. NAIST Technical Report, NAIST-IS-TR99012, Nara Institute of Science and Technology (1999)
12. Aizawa, A.: Linguistic techniques to improve the performance of automatic text categorization. Proceedings of the Sixth Natural Language Processing Pacific Rim Symposium (NLPRS 2001) (2001) 307–314
13. Deerwester, S., Dumais, S.T., Furnas, G.W., Landauer, T.K., Harshman, R.: Indexing by latent semantic analysis. Journal of American Society of Information Science **41** (1990) 391–407
14. Dhillon, I.S., Modha, D.S.: Concept decomposition for large sparse text data using clustering. Machine Learning, **42:1** (2001) 143–175
15. Murata, T.: Discovery of Web communities based on the co-occurrence of references. Proceedings of Discovery Science 2000, Lecture Notes in Artificial Intelligence, **1967** (2000) 65–75
16. Oyanagi, S., Kubota, K., Nakase, A.: Matrix clustering: a new data mining algorithm for CRM. Journal of Information Processing Society of Japan, **42(8)** (2001) 2156–2166 (in Japanese)

Effective Methods for Improving Naive Bayes Text Classifiers

Sang-Bum Kim[1], Hae-Chang Rim[1], DongSuk Yook[1], and Heui-Seok Lim[2]

[1] Dept. of CSE, Korea University
Anam-dong 5 ka, SungPuk-gu
SEOUL, 136-701, KOREA
[2] Dept. of Info&Comm, Chonan University
Anseo-Dong, Chonan
ChungChong-NamDo, 330-180, Korea

Abstract. Though naive Bayes text classifiers are widely used because of its simplicity, the techniques for improving performances of these classifiers have been rarely studied. In this paper, we propose and evaluate some general and effective techniques for improving performance of the naive Bayes text classifier. We suggest document model based parameter estimation and document length normalization to alleviate the problems in the traditional multinomial approach for text classification. In addition, Mutual-Information-weighted naive Bayes text classifier is proposed to increase the effect of highly informative words. Our techniques are evaluated on the Reuters21578 and 20 Newsgroups collections, and significant improvements are obtained over the existing multinomial naive Bayes approach.

1 Introduction

Text categorization is the problem of assigning predefined categories to free text documents. There are several similar tasks such as text filtering and routing. All of these tasks require text classifiers that decide which class is more relevant to a given document or which document is more relevant to a fixed user interest. Thus, text classifiers should be able to rank categories given a document and rank documents given a class. A growing number of statistical learning methods have been applied to these problems in recent years, including nearest neighbor classifiers[7], naive Bayes classifiers[5], and support vector machines[3], etc. Among these methods, naive Bayes text classifiers have been widely used because of its simplicity although they have been reported as one of poor-performing classfiers in text categorization task[8,2]. Since several studies show that naive Bayes performs surprisingly well in many other domains[1], it is worth of clarifying the reason that naive Bayes fails in the text classification tasks and improving them. This paper describes the problems in traditional naive Bayes text classification approach and suggests some effective techniques for improving them.

M. Ishizuka and A. Sattar (Eds.): PRICAI 2002, LNAI 2417, pp. 414–423, 2002.

2   Multinomial Naive Bayes for Text Classifier

For text categorization task, a naive Bayes is used to calculate probabilities of a class given a document. Similar to the traditional probabilistic information retrieval model, what we are concerned about is not the probability itself calculated by the naive Bayes formula but the ability to give higher scores to more relevant documents given a class or to more relevant classes given a document. For this reason, one can use the log-odds ratio as relevance score rather than the probability itself. Thus, the relevance score of document d_i for class c_j is calculated with Bayes' rule as follows:

$$Relevance(d_i, c_j) = log\frac{P(c_j|d_i)}{P(\bar{c}_j|d_i)} = log\frac{P(d_i|c_j)}{P(d_i|\bar{c}_j)} + log\frac{P(c_j)}{P(\bar{c}_j)} \qquad (1)$$

and, we can estimate the priors as follows:

$$P(c_j) = \frac{\text{number of documents belong to } c_j}{\text{total number of documents}}$$

Now, the only parameters we should estimate are $P(d_i|c_j)$ and $P(d_i|\bar{c}_j)$.

There have been two approaches to estimate them; multivariate approach and multinomial approach. In the multivariate approach, a document is considered as a $|V|$-dimensional vector $D = (w_1, w_2, \cdots w_{|V|})$ which is the result of $|V|$ independent Bernoulli trials, where $|V|$ is the vocabulary size and w_k is a binary variable representing the occurrence or non-occurrence of the k-th word in the vocabulary. The most serious problem in this approach is that there is no way to reflect the information about term frequencies. This weak point of the multivariate approach was experimentally surveyed by [5].

On the other hand, the multinomial approach specifies that a document is represented by the set of word occurrences from the document. The order of the words is lost, but the number of occurrences of each word in the document is captured. When calculating the probability of a document, one multiplies the probability of the words that occur. In the multinomial approach, the first part of formula (1) is calculated as follows:

$$log\frac{P_n(d_i|c_j)}{P_n(d_i|\bar{c}_j)} = log\frac{P(|d_i|)|d_i|! \prod_{k=1}^{|V|}\frac{P_n(w_k|c_j)^{TF_{ik}}}{TF_{ik}!}}{P(|d_i|)|d_i|! \prod_{k=1}^{|V|}\frac{P_n(w_k|\bar{c}_j)^{TF_{ik}}}{TF_{ik}!}}$$

$$= \sum_{k=1, w_k \in d_i}^{|V|} TF_{ik} \cdot log\frac{P_n(w_k|c_j)}{P_n(w_k|\bar{c}_j)} \qquad (2)$$

In formula (2), TF_{ik} represents the number of w_k in the document d_i. The parameters $P_n(w_k|c_j)$ and $P_n(w_k|\bar{c}_j)$ are estimated as follows:

$$P_n(w_k|c_j) = \frac{\theta + \sum_{i=1}^{|\mathcal{D}|} TF_{ik}P(y_i = c_j|d_i)}{\theta \cdot |V| + \sum_{s=1}^{|V|}\sum_{i=1}^{|\mathcal{D}|} TF_{is}P(y_i = c_j|d_i)} \qquad (3)$$

$$P_n(w_k|\bar{c}_j) = \frac{\theta + \sum_{i=1}^{|\mathcal{D}|} TF_{ik}P(y_i \neq c_j|d_i)}{\theta \cdot |V| + \sum_{s=1}^{|V|}\sum_{i=1}^{|\mathcal{D}|} TF_{is}P(y_i \neq c_j|d_i)} \qquad (4)$$

The laplacean prior is used to avoid probabilities of zero or one. For our experiment, parameter θ is set to 1. This estimation technique has been generally used to implement naive Bayes classifiers in most studies[8,2,5].

There are, however, some issues in estimating parameters and calculating scores. The parameter estimation according to formula (3) regards all of documents belong to c_j as one huge document. In other words, this estimation method does not take into account the fact that there may be important differences among term occurrences from documents with different lengths. The other problem is that the score of a document increases according to TF_{ik} linearly as one can find in formula (2). [4] pointed out that this model assigns extreme poterior log-odds to long documents, and may not be suitable for the purpose of ranking documents given a class, although this problem is somewhat less serious for classification tasks without comparisons across documents. In section 3, we propose two techniques including document model based estimation and document length normalization to alleviate the problems caused by traditional multinomial naive Bayes text classifiers. In addition, we suggest weighted naive Bayes classifier to avoid feature selecting operation and increase the effect of highly informative words.

3   Our Approach

3.1   Document Model Based Parameter Estimation

Our first hypothesis is that the occurrence of term w_k in short document should be treated as more weighted event than that in long document. For example, in Fig. 1, it is our intuition that w2 is more likely term in class c_j than w1, because short documents usually have only the important terms and w2 appears twice in the short document. In addition, log-odds ratio of terms should increase according to the number of documents which belog to c_j and have the term. From this point of view, w3 should be low-weighted.

We suggest a document model based parameter estimation(DMBE), which calculates class model parameters by expanding it with document model parameters. DMBE estimates class model parameters as follows:

$$P_d(w_k|c_j) = \sum_{i=1}^{|\mathcal{D}|} P(w_k|d_i)P(d_i|c_j) = \sum_{i=1,d_i \in C_j}^{|\mathcal{D}|} LH_{ki} \cdot \frac{1}{\sum_{i=1}^{|\mathcal{D}|} P(y_i = c_j|d_i)} \quad (5)$$

$$P_d(w_k|\bar{c}_j) = \sum_{i=1}^{|\mathcal{D}|} P(w_k|d_i)P(d_i|\bar{c}_j) = \sum_{i=1,d_i \notin C_j}^{|\mathcal{D}|} LH_{ki} \cdot \frac{1}{\sum_{i=1}^{|\mathcal{D}|} P(y_i \neq c_j|d_i)} \quad (6)$$

In formula (5), LH_{ki} means likelihood of w_k in d_i and $P(d_i|c_j)$ is considered as a uniform distribution. However, it may also reflect the importance of specific training documents if one use different $P(d_i|c_j)$ for each training document. Document model parameter LH_{ki} may be estimated with maximum likelihood

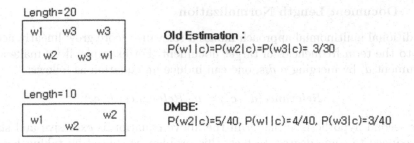

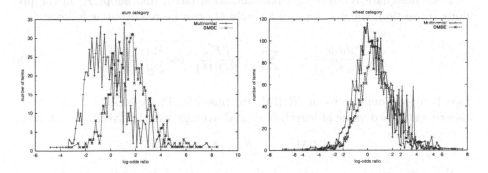

Fig. 1. Examples of parameter estimation : DMBE weights more to the terms occuring in short documents.

Fig. 2. Number of terms in each interval of log-odds ratio with traditional estimation(Multinomial) and document-model based estimation(DMBE)

estimation(MLE). For the same purpose with the traditional multinomial naive Bayes, we estimate these likelihoods as follows rather than MLE:

$$
LH_{ki} = \begin{cases} \frac{\theta + TF_{ik}}{\theta \cdot |V| + dl_i} & \text{if } w_k \in d_i \\ \frac{\theta}{\theta \cdot |V| + \text{avdl}} & \text{otherwise} \end{cases} \tag{7}
$$

where, dl_i and avdl means document length of d_i and average document length over the collection, respectively.

DMBE has two distinctive features. First, this estimation method makes a distinction between term occurrences in short documents and those in long documents. Second, it gives default weights for missing terms in each document, and finally tend to have higher log-odds ratio than the traditional estimation. As shown in Fig. 2, log-odds ratio values by DMBE is a little higher than those by the conventional estimation, and it makes the scores of the long documents more higher than that of the short documents. Another difference between two curves is that DMBE curve is more close to the normal distribution than Multinomial curve. In other words, DMBE makes more smooth distribution.

3.2 Document Length Normalization

Traditional multinomial approach makes a relevance score grow linearly according to the term frequencies of target document. For example, if we make a new document d_i' by merging n d_is, one can induce an equation as follows:

$$Relevance(d_i', c_j) = n \cdot Relevance(d_i, c_j)$$

Our second hypothesis is that n in the above equation is excessive and should be reduced to some degree. In fact, this problem is caused by taking log-odds ratio as relevance score to remove the length-related factors such as $P(|d_i|)$ and $|d_i|!$. Since it is difficult to estimate $P(|d_i|)$, we suggest a document length normalization without giving up the strategy of taking log-odds ratio.

If we designate $NORM$ as a normalization factor and adopt P_d in the previous subsection, the first term of formula (1) can be rewritten as follows:

$$log \frac{P_d(d_i|c_j)}{P_d(d_i|\bar{c}_j)} = \sum_{k=1, w_k \in d_i}^{|V|} \frac{TF_{ik}}{NORM} \cdot log \frac{P_d(w_k|c_j)}{P_d(w_k|\bar{c}_j)} \tag{8}$$

Two heuristic definitions of NORM are possible. First, NORM is defined as linearly combined value of length of d_i and average length(LNORM) as follows:

$$NORM_l = \alpha \cdot dl_i + (1 - \alpha) \cdot avdl$$

Second method is to combine document length of d_i with average document length exponentially(ENORM) as follows:

$$NORM_e = dl_i{}^\alpha \cdot avdl^{1-\alpha}$$

In both cases, α range from 0 to 1, and if α is 0, it means no normalization, α is 1, perfect normalization using only the document length.

LNORM as a normalization factor has been widely used in traditional ad-hoc retrieval systems [6], and improved their performances considerably. ENORM technique is our novel technique. One distinctive feature of this technique is that $avdl^{1-\alpha}$ can be dropped because it is a constant dividing relevance score, that is, $NORM_e = dl_i{}^\alpha$. With this simplified normalization factor, length normalization effect by ENORM can be easily understood. For example, ENORM replaces n in the previous d_i' example with $n^{(1-\alpha)}$.

Document length normalization makes it possible to give appropriate scores to the target documents given a class. However, this technique doesn't have any effect to the category-ranking tasks where the parameters related to a given document are fixed.

3.3 MI-Weighted Naive Bayes Classifier

Feature selection is generally carried out as a preprocessing step, and text classifiers are trained with various machine learning algorithms in the feature space.

This scenario is very inefficient in case that new additional training documents are provided continuously because the feature set should be redefined according to the modified term statistics in the new training document set, and classifiers should be trained again with this new feature set. With the weighted naive Bayes framework, one can construct multinomial naive Bayes text classifier as follows ,which defines feature set dynamically and does not need to be retrained:

$$
log\frac{P(d_i|c_j)}{P(d_i|\bar{c}_j)} = log\frac{P(|d_i|)|d_i|!\prod_{k=1}^{|V|}\frac{\left(P(w_k|c_j)^{f_{kj}}\right)^{TF_{ik}}}{TF_{ik}!}}{P(|d_i|)|d_i|!\prod_{k-1}^{|V|}\frac{\left(P(w_k|\bar{c}_j)^{f_{kj}}\right)^{TF_{ik}}}{TF_{ik}!}}
$$

$$
= \sum_{k=1,w_k\in d_i}^{|V|} TF_{ik} \cdot f_{kj} \cdot log\frac{P(w_k|c_j)}{P(w_k|\bar{c}_j)} \qquad (9)
$$

Function f_{kj} returns the weight of feature word w_k for class c_j with various feature selection strategies. For example, one can use every term as feature by defining f_{kj} as a constant function that always returns 1. Or, f_{kj} may be implemented as one of the statistical measures like mutual information or chi-square statistic to use subset of vocabulary as feature words. In this case, f_{kj} is executed with stored information at the point of time when the new text is classified. Actually, existing multinomial text classifiers that use only the subset of total vocabulary as features can be refered to as a *binary-weighted naive Bayes classifier* where f_{kj} returns 1 if w_k is a feature word for category c_j, and 0, otherwise.

There have been no vigorous efforts to the weighted naive Bayes text classifier. We tried to adopt this framework by defining f_{kj} as a function that returns mutual information between w_k and c_j, *MI-weighted naive Bayes classifier*, as follows:

$$
f_{kj} = \left|log\frac{P(w_t,c_j)}{P(w_t)P(c_j)}\right| = \left|log\frac{\left(\sum_{j=1}^{|V|}\sum_{i=1}^{|\mathcal{D}|}TF_{ij}\right)\left(\sum_{i=1}^{|\mathcal{D}|}TF_{ik}P(c_j|d_i)\right)}{\left(\sum_{i=1}^{|\mathcal{D}|}TF_{ik}\right)\left(\sum_{j=1}^{|V|}\sum_{i=1}^{|\mathcal{D}|}TF_{ij}P(c_j|d_i)\right)}\right|
$$

We use absolute value because the terms with negative mutual information are also informative. *MI-weighted naive Bayes classifier* increases the effect of highly informative terms, However, the degree of influence for those terms may be difficult to guess, and we investigate this method empirically in Section 4.

4   Experimental Results

We have conducted experiments on the two commonly used corpora in text categorization task; Reuters21578[1] and 20 Newsgroups[2]. For the experiments, documents were seperated according to the "ModApte" split that consists of 9,603 training documents and 3,299 test documents. 20 Newsgroups consists of

[1] http://www.research.att.com/~lewis
[2] http://www-2.cs.cmu.edu/afs/cs/project/theo-3/www/

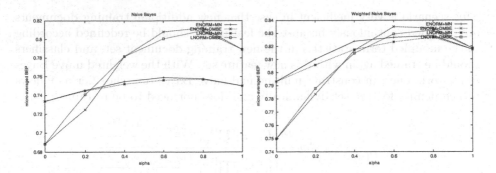

Fig. 3. BEP Performaces of naive Bayes classifiers on Reuters21578 collection according to normalization parameter α

19,997 Usenet articles collected from 20 different newsgroups. We use 2/3 of documents for training and 1/3 for testing. Stopword removal and stemming are applied to these two collections. Two different measures are used to evaluate various text classifiers for our experiments. First, we use Break even point(BEP) to evaluate the performances on Reuters21578 collection. BEP, which is the point where precision and recall are equal, is a standard information retrieval measure for binary classification. In addition, they are micro-averaged over all categories, which is general method to evaluate classifiers where the distribution of classes is skewed. For the experiments on 20 Newsgroups collection, the performances are reported using accuracy measure.

Results of the break even performaces over the Reuters21578 collection as a function of the normalization parameter α are shown in Fig. 3. In these figures, it is obvious that the document length normalization is effective, especially where α is 0.6 or 0.8. Our novel ENORM competes well with traditional normalization heuristic LNORM. ENORM slightly outperforms LNORM in all cases, but not significant. In addition, the two clear observations from these figures are possible. The first is that DMBE considerably drops the performances if the score of document is not normalized by its length, in other words, α is 0. The second is that normalization technique is less effective to the traditional multinomial classifier, compared to DMBE. Fig. 4, which describes score distribution of **wheat** category for DMBE and traditional multinomial classifier(MN) according to document length, shows the reason. As is mentioned in Section 3, DMBE generates higher log-odds ratio than that by MN. Consequently, DMBE tends to give positive log-odds ratio to many terms, while MN gives negative log-odds ratio. This characteristic makes DMBE give the many long documents relatively high scores. As one can see in this figure, most long documents with DMBE have high positive scores, especially if the documents are extreamly long. On the contrary, MN generates many negative relevance scores. Based on these considerations, one can understand that long documents is extremely prefered if their scores by DMBE are not normalized. Similarily, normalization technique

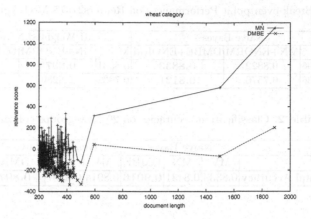

Fig. 4. Score distributions of traditional multinomial classifier and DMBE

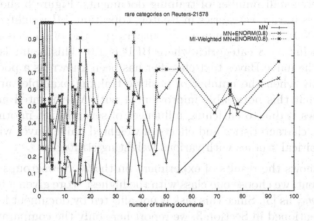

Fig. 5. Performances on the rare categories in Reuters21578

is less effective in case of traditional multinomial as one can find in Figure 3. It is because that many long documents already take some degree of penalties due to the many terms that have negative log-odds ratio in the document.

Table 1 shows micro-averaged BEP performances over 10 large categories and 90 all categories of Reuters21578 collection. In this result, ENORM is used with α being 0.8. The baseline performance of 0.7336 for all 90 categories with traditional multinomial naive Bayes classifier is similar to other reported performances of multinomial naive Bayes text classifier[3,2]. Our text classifiers without adopting weighted naive Bayes significantly outperform the baseline. Although it is not a focus of this paper to compare naive Bayes with other learning methods, micro-averaged BEP of 0.8121 where both DMBE and ENORM are applied is enough to compete against other learning methods. Moreover,

Table 1. Break even point Performances on Reuters21578 Mod-Apte collection.

	Naive Bayes			MI-Weighted Naive Bayes		
	MN	MN+ENORM	DMBE+ENORM	MN	MN+ENORM	DMBE+ENORM
10 cat.	0.8496	0.8822	**0.8833**	0.8531	**0.8973**	0.8962
90 cat.	0.7336	0.7576	**0.8121**	0.7932	0.8280	**0.8339**

Table 2. Classification accuracies on 20 Newsgroups collection.

	Naive Bayes			MI-Weighted Naive Bayes		
	MV	MN	DMBE	MV	MN	DMBE
Total Accuracy	0.8333	0.8431	**0.9016**	0.8914	0.8707	**0.8972**

we are able to attain the highest BEP 0.8339 with the weighted naive Bayes. Our MI-weighted naive Bayes works very well especially in the categories which have relatively small number of training documents. Figure 5 shows the result of performaces in rare categories in Reuters collection. MI-weighted naive Bayes with MN+ENORM(0.8) significantly outperforms the other classifiers in most categories including 8 categories where BEP is 1.0. This result is quite mean-ingful since the naive Bayes text classifier has been known as a poor-performing one, especially when the number of positive training examples are very small. We believe that this noticeable improvement with MI-wieghted naive Bayes in rare categories is due to enriching influences of several high informative words. However, the characteristics and effects of weighted naive Bayes will be clarified by more empirical studies with various weighting strategies.

Table 2 shows the results of experiment on the 20 Newsgroups collection. In this experiment, we choose one class with the highest score given a test document in the same way as [5]. Since this task is not affected by document length normal-ization as mentioned in Section 3, we report here only the comparative results of multivariate, multinomial, and multinomial with DMBE classifiers in both the cases of naive Bayes and MI-weighted naive Bayes. The baseline performance is 84.31% with multinomial naive Bayes classifier. DMBE achieves 90.16% accuracy and there is 6.9% points improvement. It outperforms the traditional multino-mial naive Bayes in all of classes except for the class `talk.politics.mideast` with the naive Bayes. MI-weighted naive Bayes improves the performances of multivariate and multinomial classifiers, but the performace of DMBE is a slightly decreased. Actually, it is inappropriate to use weighted naive Bayes clas-sifier since the weights of features for each class are different from one another, and thus cross-category comparison of scores might be unfair. Nevertheless, the improved accuracies of multivariate and multinomial classfiers suggest that it is very helpful to emphasize the influences of highly informative terms on total score.

5 Conclusion and Future Work

We proposed and evaluated some general and effective techniques for improving performance of the naive Bayes text classifier. Our new multinomial classifier use document model based estimation(DMBE) and the score is normalized by the novel normalization factor(ENORM). In empirical results on two standard benchmark collections, above techniques significantly improved the performace of traditional multinomial text classifiers. In addition, we have mentioned that the existing naive Bayes text classifier using a subset of the vocabulary can be interpreted as binary-weighted naive Bayes. We evaluated the more general version of binary-weighted naive Bayes, MI-weighted naive Bayes text classifiers. Although we can get better performace compared to non-weighted naive Bayes, more theoretical justification and empirical analysis should be required. In future, we would like to build a formal model of weighted naive Bayes text classifier with proposed techniques and develop a novel thresholding strategy suitable for probablisitic text classification model.

References

1. P. Domingos and M. J. Pazzani. On the optimality of the simple bayesian classifier under zero-one loss. *Machine Learning*, 29(2/3):103–130, 1997.
2. S. Dumais, J. Plat, D. Heckerman, and M. Sahami. Inductive learning algorithms and representation for text categorization. In *Proceedings of CIKM-98, 7th ACM International Conference on Information and Knowledge Management*, pages 148–155, 1998.
3. T. Joachims. Text categorization with support vector machines: learning with many relevant features. In *Proceedings of ECML-98, 10th European Conference on Machine Learning*, pages 137–142, 1998.
4. D. D. Lewis. Naive (Bayes) at forty: The independence assumption in information retrieval. In *Proceedings of ECML-98, 10th European Conference on Machine Learning*, number 1398, pages 4–15, 1998.
5. A. K. McCallum and K. Nigam. A comparison of event models for naive bayes text classification. In *Proceedings of AAAI-98 Workshop on Learning for Text Categorization*, pages 137–142, 1998.
6. A. Singhal, C. Buckley, and M. Mitra. Pivoted document length normalization. In *Proceedings of SIGIR-96, 19th ACM International Conference on Research and Development in Information Retrieval*, pages 21–29, 1996.
7. Y. Yang and C. G. Chute. An example-based mapping method for text categorization and retrieval. *ACM Transactions on Information Systems*, 12(3):252–277, 1994.
8. Y. Yang and X. Liu. A re-examination of text categorization methods. In *Proceedings of SIGIR-99, 22nd ACM International Conference on Research and Development in Information Retrieval*, pages 42–49, 1999.

Efficiently Clustering Documents with Committees

Patrick Pantel and Dekang Lin

Department of Computing Science
University of Alberta
Edmonton, Alberta T6H 2E1 Canada
{ppantel, lindek}@cs.ualberta.ca

Abstract. The general goal of clustering is to group data elements such that the intra-group similarities are high and the inter-group similarities are low. We present a clustering algorithm called CBC (Clustering By Committee) that is shown to produce higher quality clusters in document clustering tasks as compared to several well known clustering algorithms. It initially discovers a set of tight clusters (high intra-group similarity), called committees, that are well scattered in the similarity space (low inter-group similarity). The union of the committees is but a subset of all elements. The algorithm proceeds by assigning elements to their most similar committee. Evaluating cluster quality has always been a difficult task. We present a new evaluation methodology based on the editing distance between output clusters and manually constructed classes (the answer key). This evaluation measure is more intuitive and easier to interpret than previous evaluation measures.

1   Introduction

Document clustering was initially proposed for improving the precision and recall of information retrieval systems [14]. Because clustering is often too slow for large corpora and has indifferent performance [7], document clustering has been used more recently in document browsing [3], to improve the organization and viewing of retrieval results [5], to accelerate nearest-neighbor search [1] and to generate Yahoo-like hierarchies [10].

In this paper, we propose a clustering algorithm, CBC (Clustering By Committee), which produces higher quality clusters in document clustering tasks as compared to several well known clustering algorithms. Many clustering algorithms represent a cluster by the centroid of all of its members (e.g., K-means) [11] or by a representative element (e.g., K-medoids) [9]. When averaging over all elements in a cluster, the centroid of a cluster may be unduly influenced by elements that only marginally belong to the cluster or by elements that also belong to other clusters. Using a single representative from a cluster may be problematic too because each individual element has its own idiosyncrasies that may not be shared by other members of the cluster.

CBC constructs the centroid of a cluster by averaging the feature vectors of a subset of the cluster members. The subset is viewed as a committee that determines which other elements belong to the cluster. By carefully choosing committee mem-

M. Ishizuka and A. Sattar (Eds.): PRICAI 2002, LNAI 2417, pp. 424–433, 2002.
© Springer-Verlag Berlin Heidelberg 2002

bers, the features of the centroid tend to be the more typical features of the target class.

We introduce a new evaluation methodology that is based on the editing distance between clustering results and manually constructed classes (the answer key).

2   Related Work

Generally, clustering algorithms can be categorized as hierarchical and partitional. In hierarchical agglomerative algorithms, clusters are constructed by iteratively merging the most similar clusters. These algorithms differ in how they compute cluster similarity. In single-link clustering, the similarity between two clusters is the similarity between their most similar members while complete-link clustering uses the similarity between their least similar members. Average-link clustering computes this similarity as the average similarity between all pairs of elements across clusters. The complexity of these algorithms is $O(n^2\log n)$, where n is the number of elements to be clustered [6]. These algorithms are too inefficient for document clustering tasks that deal with large numbers of documents. In our experiments, one of the corpora we used is small enough (2745 documents) to allow us to compare CBC with these hierarchical algorithms.

Chameleon is a hierarchical algorithm that employs dynamic modeling to improve clustering quality [8]. When merging two clusters, one might consider the sum of the similarities between pairs of elements across the clusters (e.g. average-link clustering). A drawback of this approach is that the existence of a single pair of very similar elements might unduly cause the merger of two clusters. An alternative considers the number of pairs of elements whose similarity exceeds a certain threshold [4]. However, this may cause undesirable mergers when there are a large number of pairs whose similarities barely exceed the threshold. Chameleon clustering combines the two approaches.

Most often, document clustering employs K-means clustering since its complexity is linear in n, the number of elements to be clustered. K-means is a family of partitional clustering algorithms that iteratively assigns each element to one of K clusters according to the centroid closest to it and recomputes the centroid of each cluster as the average of the cluster's elements. Because the initial centroids are randomly selected, the resulting clusters vary in quality. Some sets of initial centroids lead to poor convergence rates or poor cluster quality.

Bisecting K-means [13], a variation of K-means, begins with a set containing one large cluster consisting of every element and iteratively picks the largest cluster in the set, splits it into two clusters and replaces it by the split clusters. Splitting a cluster consists of applying the basic K-means algorithm α times with $K=2$ and keeping the split that has the highest average element-centroid similarity.

Hybrid clustering algorithms combine hierarchical and partitional algorithms in an attempt to have the high quality of hierarchical algorithms with the efficiency of partitional algorithms. Buckshot [3] addresses the problem of randomly selecting initial centroids in K-means by combining it with average-link clustering. Cutting et al. claim its clusters are comparable in quality to hierarchical algorithms but with a lower complexity. Buckshot first applies average-link to a random sample of $\sqrt{n}$ elements to generate K clusters. It then uses the centroids of the clusters as the initial K centroids of K-means clustering. The complexity of Buckshot is $O(K \times T \times n + n \log n)$. The parameters K and T are usually considered to be small numbers. Since we are dealing with a large number of clusters, Buckshot and K-means become inefficient in practice. Furthermore, Buckshot is not always suitable. If one wishes to cluster 100,000 documents into 1000 newsgroup topics, Buckshot could generate only 316 initial centroids.

3   Representation

CBC represents elements as feature vectors. The features of a document are the terms (usually stemmed words) that occur within it and the value of a feature is a statistic of the term. For example, the statistic can simply be the term's frequency, tf, within the document. In order to discount terms with low discriminating power, tf is usually combined with the term's inverse document frequency, idf, which is the inverse of the percentage of documents in which the term occurs. This measure is referred to as tf-idf [12]:

$$tf\text{-}idf = tf \times \log idf$$

We use the mutual information [2] between an element and its features.

In our algorithm, for each element e, we construct a **frequency count vector** $C(e) = (c_{e1}, c_{e2}, \ldots, c_{em})$, where m is the total number of features and c_{ef} is the frequency count of feature f occurring in element e. In document clustering, e is a document and c_{ef} is the term frequency of f in e. We construct a **mutual information vector** $MI(e) = (mi_{e1}, mi_{e2}, \ldots, mi_{em})$, where mi_{ef} is the mutual information between element e and feature f, which is defined as:

$$mi_{ef} = log \frac{\frac{c_{ef}}{N}}{\frac{\sum_i c_{if}}{N} \times \frac{\sum_j c_{ej}}{N}}$$

where $N = \sum_i \sum_j c_{ij}$ is the total frequency count of all features of all elements.

We compute the similarity between two elements e_i and e_j using the *cosine coefficient* [12] of their mutual information vectors:

$$sim(e_i, e_j) = \frac{\sum_f mi_{e_i,f} \times mi_{e_j,f}}{\sqrt{\sum_f mi_{e_i,f}^2 \times \sum_f mi_{e_j,f}^2}}$$

4   Algorithm

CBC consists of three phases. In Phase I, we compute each element's top-k similar elements. In our experiments, we used $k = 20$. In Phase II, we construct a collection of tight clusters, where the elements of each cluster form a **committee**. The algorithm tries to form as many committees as possible on the condition that each newly formed committee is not very similar to any existing committee. If the condition is violated, the committee is simply discarded. In the final phase of the algorithm, each element is assigned to its most similar cluster.

Input:	A list of elements E to be clustered, a similarity database S from Phase I, thresholds θ_1 and θ_2.
Step 1:	For each element $e \in E$
	Cluster the top similar elements of e from S using average-link clustering.
	For each cluster discovered c compute the following score: $|c| \times$ avgsim(c), where $|c|$ is the number of elements in c and avgsim(c) is the average pairwise similarity between elements in c.
	Store the highest-scoring cluster in a list L.
Step 2:	Sort the clusters in L in descending order of their scores.
Step 3:	Let C be a list of committees, initially empty.
	For each cluster $c \in L$ in sorted order
	Compute the centroid of c by averaging the frequency vectors of its elements and computing the mutual information vector of the centroid in the same way as we did for individual elements.
	If c's similarity to the centroid of each committee previously added to C is below a threshold θ_1, add c to C.
Step 4:	If C is empty, we are done and return C.
Step 5:	For each element $e \in E$
	If e's similarity to every committee in C is below threshold θ_2, add e to a list of residues R.
Step 6:	If R is empty, we are done and return C.
	Otherwise, return the union of C and the output of a recursive call to Phase II using the same input except replacing E with R.
Output:	a list of committees.

Fig. 1. Phase II of CBC.

4.1   Phase I: Find Top-Similar Elements

Computing the complete similarity matrix between pairs of elements is obviously quadratic. However, one can dramatically reduce the running time by taking advantage of the fact that the feature vector is sparse. By indexing the features, one can retrieve the set of elements that have a given feature. To compute the top similar elements of an element e, we first sort the mutual information vector $MI(e)$ and then only consider a subset of the features with highest mutual information. Finally, we compute the pairwise similarity between e and the elements that share a feature from this subset. Since high mutual information features tend not to occur in many elements, we only need to compute a fraction of the possible pairwise combinations. With 18,828 elements, Phase I completes in 38 minutes. Using this heuristic, similar words that share only low mutual information features will be missed by our algorithm. However, in our experiments, this had no visible impact on cluster quality.

4.2   Phase II: Find Committees

The second phase of the clustering algorithm recursively finds tight clusters scattered in the similarity space. In each recursive step, the algorithm finds a set of tight clusters, called committees, and identifies residue elements that are not covered by any committee. We say a committee **covers** an element if the element's similarity to the centroid of the committee exceeds some high similarity threshold. The algorithm then recursively attempts to find more committees among the residue elements. The output of the algorithm is the union of all committees found in each recursive step. The details of Phase II are presented in Figure 1.

In Step 1, the score reflects a preference for bigger and tighter clusters. Step 2 gives preference to higher quality clusters in Step 3, where a cluster is only kept if its similarity to all previously kept clusters is below a fixed threshold. In our experiments, we set $\theta_1 = 0.35$. Step 4 terminates the recursion if no committee is found in the previous step. The residue elements are identified in Step 5 and if no residues are found, the algorithm terminates; otherwise, we recursively apply the algorithm to the residue elements. Each committee that is discovered in this phase defines one of the final output clusters of the algorithm.

4.3   Phase III: Assign elements to Clusters

In Phase III, every element is assigned to the cluster containing the committee to which it is most similar. This phase resembles K-means in that every element is assigned to its closest centroid. Unlike K-means, the number of clusters is not fixed and the centroids do not change (i.e. when an element is added to a cluster, it is not added to the committee of the cluster).

5   Evaluation Methodology

Many cluster evaluation schemes have been proposed. They generally fall under two categories:

- comparing cluster outputs with manually generated answer keys (hereon referred to as **classes**); and
- embedding the clusters in an application (e.g. information retrieval) and using its evaluation measure.

One approach considers the average entropy of the clusters, which measures the purity of the clusters [13]. However, maximum purity is trivially achieved when each element forms its own cluster.

Given a partitioned set of n elements, there are $n \times (n - 1) / 2$ pairs of elements that are either in the same partition or not. The partition implies $n \times (n - 1) / 2$ decisions. Another way to evaluate clusters is to compute the percentage of the decisions that are in agreement between the clusters and the classes [15]. This measure sometimes gives unintuitive results. Suppose the answer key consists of 20 equally sized classes with 1000 elements in each. Treating each element as its own cluster gets a misleadingly high score of 95%.

The evaluation of document clustering algorithms in information retrieval often uses the embedded approach [5]. Suppose we cluster the documents returned by a search engine. Assuming the user is able to pick the most relevant cluster, the performance of the clustering algorithm can be measured by the average precision of the chosen cluster. Under this scheme, only the best cluster matters.

The entropy and pairwise decision schemes each measure a specific property of clusters. However, these properties are not directly related to application-level goals of clustering. The information retrieval scheme is goal-oriented, however it measures only the quality of the best cluster. We propose an evaluation methodology that strikes a balance between generality and goal-orientation.

Like the entropy and pairwise decision schemes, we assume that there is an answer key that defines how the elements are supposed to be clustered. Let C be a set of clusters and A be the answer key. We define the editing distance, $dist(C, A)$, as the number of operations required to transform C into A. We allow three editing operations:

- merge two clusters;
- move an element from one cluster to another; and
- copy an element from one cluster to another.

Let B be the baseline clustering where each element is its own cluster. We define the quality of cluster C as follows:

$$1 - \frac{dist(C, A)}{dist(B, A)}$$

This measure can be interpreted as the percentage of savings from using the clustering result to construct the answer key versus constructing it from scratch (i.e. the baseline).

We make the assumption that each element belongs to exactly one cluster. The transformation procedure is as follows:

1. Suppose there are m classes in the answer key. We start with a list of m empty sets, each of which is labeled with a class in the answer key.
2. For each cluster, merge it with the set whose class has the largest number of elements in the cluster (a tie is broken arbitrarily).
3. If an element is in a set whose class is not the same as one of the element's classes, move the element to a set where it belongs.

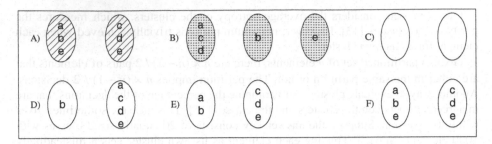

Fig. 2. An example of applying the transformation rules to three clusters. A) The classes in the answer key; B) the clusters to be transformed; C) the sets used to reconstruct the classes (Rule 1); D) the sets after three merge operations (Step 2); E) the sets after one move operation (Step 3); F) the sets after one copy operation (Step 4).

Table 1. The number of classes in each test data set and the number of elements in their largest and smallest classes.

DATA SET	TOTAL DOCS	TOTAL CLASSES	LARGEST CLASS	SMALLEST CLASS
Reuters	2745	92	1045	1
20-news	18828	20	999	628

4. If an element belongs to more than one target class, copy the element to all sets corresponding to the target classes (except the one to which it already belongs).

$dist(C, A)$ is the number of operations performed using the above transformation rules on C.

Figure 2 shows an example. In D) the cluster containing e could have been merged with either set (we arbitrarily chose the second). The total number of operations is 5.

6   Experimental Results

6.1   Test Data

We conducted document-clustering experiments with two data sets: Reuters-21578 V1.2[1] and 20news-18828[2] (see Table 1). For the Reuters corpus, we selected documents that:

1. are assigned one or more topics;
2. have the attribute LEWISSPLIT="TEST"; and
3. have <BODY> and </BODY> tags.

---

[1] http://www.research.att.com/~lewis/reuters21578.html
[2] http://www.ai.mit.edu/people/jrennie/20_newsgroups/

Table 2. Cluster quality (%) of several algorithms on the Reuters and 20-news data sets.

	REUTERS	*20-NEWS*
CBC	65.00	74.18
K-means	62.38	70.04
Buckshot	62.03	65.96
Bisecting *K*-means	60.80	58.52
Chameleon	58.67	n/a
Average-link	63.00	70.43
Complete-link	46.22	64.23
Single-link	31.53	5.30

There are 2745 such documents. The 20news-18828 data set contains 18828 news-group articles partitioned (nearly) evenly across 20 different newsgroups.

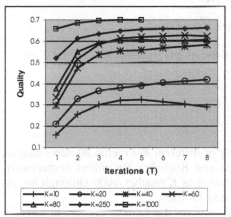

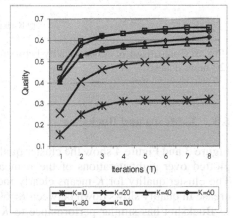

Fig. 3. *K*-means cluster quality on the 20-news data set for different values of *K* plotted of over eight iterations.

Fig. 4. Buckshot cluster quality on the 20-news data set for different values of *K* plotted of over eight iterations.

6.2 Cluster Evaluation

We clustered the data sets using CBC and the clustering algorithms of Section 2 and applied the evaluation methodology from the previous section. Table 2 shows the results. The columns are our editing distance based evaluation measure. CBC outperforms *K*-means with *K*=1000 by 4.14%. On the 20-news data set, our implementation of Chameleon was unable to complete in reasonable time. For the 20-news corpus, CBC spends the vast majority of the time finding the top similar documents (38 minutes) and computing the similarity between documents and committee centroids (119 minutes). The rest of the computation, which includes clustering the top-20 similar documents for every one of the 18828 documents and sorting the clusters, took less than 5 minutes. We used a Pentium III 750MHz processor and 1GB of memory.

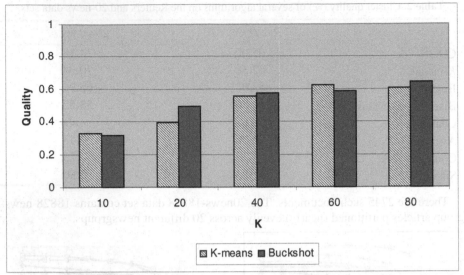

Fig. 5. Comparison of cluster quality between K-means and Buckshot for different K on the 20-news data set.

6.3 K-Means and Buckshot

Figure 3 and Figure 4 show the cluster quality of different K's on the 20-news data set plotted over eight iterations of the K-means and Buckshot algorithms respectively. The cluster quality for K-means clearly increases as K reaches 1000 although the increase in quality slows down between K=60 and K=1000.

Buckshot has similar performance to K-means on the Reuters corpus; however it performs much worse on the 20-news corpus. This is because K-means performs well on this data set when K is large (e.g. K=1000) whereas Buckshot cannot have K higher than $\sqrt{18828} = 137$. On the Reuters corpus, the best clusters for K-means were obtained with $K = 50$, and Buckshot can have K as large as $\sqrt{2745} = 52$. However, as K approaches 52, Buckshot degenerates to the K-means algorithm, which explains why Buckshot has similar performance to K-means. Figure 5 compares the cluster quality between K-means and Buckshot for different values of K on the 20-news data set.

7   Conclusion

Document clustering is an important tool in information retrieval. We presented a clustering algorithm, CBC, which can handle a large number of documents, a large number of output clusters, and a large sparse feature space. It discovers clusters using well-scattered tight clusters called committees. In our experiments on document clustering, we showed that CBC outperforms several well-known hierarchical, partitional, and hybrid clustering algorithms in cluster quality. For example, in one experiment, CBC outperforms K-means by 4.14%.

Evaluating cluster quality has always been a difficult task. We presented a new evaluation methodology that is based on the editing distance between output clusters and manually constructed classes (the answer key). This evaluation measure is more intuitive and easier to interpret than previous evaluation measures.

Acknowledgements. The authors wish to thank the reviewers for their helpful comments. This research was partly supported by Natural Sciences and Engineering Research Council of Canada grant OGP121338 and scholarship PGSB207797.

References

1. Buckley, C. and Lewit, A. F. 1985. Optimization of inverted vector searches. In *Proceedings of SIGIR 85*. pp. 97–110.
2. Church, K. and Hanks, P. 1989. Word association norms, mutual information, and lexicography. In *Proceedings of ACL-89*. pp. 76–83. Vancouver, Canada.
3. Cutting, D. R.; Karger, D.; Pedersen, J.; and Tukey, J. W. 1992. Scatter/Gather: A cluster-based approach to browsing large document collections. In *Proceedings of SIGIR-92*. pp. 318–329. Copenhagen, Denmark.
4. Guha, S.; Rastogi, R.; and Kyuseok, S. 1999. ROCK: A robust clustering algorithm for categorical attributes. In *Proceedings of ICDE'99*. pp. 512–521. Sydney, Australia.
5. Hearst, M. A. and Pedersen, J. O. 1996. Reexamining the cluster hypothesis: Scatter/Gather on retrieval results. In *Proceedings of SIGIR-96*. pp. 76–84. Zurich, Switzerland.
6. Jain, A.K.; Murty, M.N.; and Flynn, P.J. 1999. Data Clustering: A Review. *ACM Computing Surveys* 31(3):264–323.
7. Jardine, N. and van Rijsbergen, C. J. 1971. The use of hierarchical clustering in information retrieval. *Information Storage and Retreival*, 7:217–240.
8. Karypis, G.; Han, E.-H.; and Kumar, V. 1999. Chameleon: A hierarchical clustering algorithm using dynamic modeling. *IEEE Computer: Special Issue on Data Analysis and Mining* 32(8):68–75.
9. Kaufmann, L. and Rousseeuw, P. J. 1987. Clustering by means of medoids. In Dodge, Y. (Ed.) *Statistical Data Analysis based on the L1 Norm*. pp. 405–416. Elsevier/North Holland, Amsterdam.
10. Koller, D. and Sahami, M. 1997. Hierarchically classifying documents using very few words. In *Proceedings of ICML-97*. pp. 170–176. Nashville, TN.
11. McQueen, J. 1967. Some methods for classification and analysis of multivariate observations. In *Proceedings of 5th Berkeley Symposium on Mathematics, Statistics and Probability*, 1:281-298.
12. Salton, G. and McGill, M. J. 1983. *Introduction to Modern Information Retrieval*. McGraw Hill.
13. Steinbach, M.; Karypis, G.; and Kumar, V. 2000. *A comparison of document clustering techniques*. Technical Report #00-034. Department of Computer Science and Engineering, University of Minnesota.
14. van Rijsbergen, C. J. 1979. *Information Retrieval*, second edition. London: Buttersworth. Available at: http://www.dcs.gla.ac.uk/Keith/Preface.html
15. Wagstaff, K. and Cardie, C. 2000. Clustering with instance-level constraints. In *Proceedings of ICML-2000*. pp. 1103–1110. Palo Alto, CA.

Topic Extraction from Text Documents Using Multiple-Cause Networks

Jeong-Ho Chang[1], Jae Won Lee[2], Yuseop Kim[3], and Byoung-Tak Zhang[1]

[1] School of Computer Science and Engineering, Seoul National University,
Seoul, Korea, 151-742
{jhchang, btzhang}@bi.snu.ac.kr
[2] School of Computer Science and Engineering, Sungshin Women's University,
Seoul, Korea, 136-742
jwlee@cs.sungshin.ac.kr
[3] Ewha Institute of Science and Technology, Ewha Woman's University,
Seoul, Korea, 120-750
yskim01@ewha.ac.kr

Abstract. This paper presents an approach to the topic extraction from text documents using probabilistic graphical models. Multiple-cause networks with latent variables are used and the Helmholtz machines are utilized to ease the learning and inference. The learning in this model is conducted in a purely data-driven way and does not require prespecified categories of the given documents. Topic words extraction experiments on the TDT-2 collection are presented. Especially, document clustering results on a subset of TREC-8 ad-hoc task data show the substantial reduction of the inference time without significant deterioration of performance.

1 Introduction

Due to the popularity of the Internet and the advance in digital library, we have seen an exponential increase in the amount of on-line text and digitized documents. But the abundance of large databases itself does not lead us to easy acquisition of relevant information, since it can be a tiresome and time-consuming work to look over and organize all documents about various topics. As a result, the demand for automatic text analysis – such as clustering, classification, summarization – is more increasing than ever before.

Recently, there have been much research in automatic topic extraction and semantic analysis, as a tool for data-driven text analysis, such as Latent Semantic Analysis (LSA) [3] using singular value decomposition. Similar approaches based on probabilistic generative models have been also proposed. These includes the Probabilistic Latent Semantic Analysis (PLSA) [7] and the Non-negative Matrix Factorization (NMF) [8], where documents are modelled by multinomial distribution and Poisson distribution, respectively. It has been shown that these approaches can enhance performance in such applications as language modelling, text categorization, and information retrieval.

M. Ishizuka and A. Sattar (Eds.): PRICAI 2002, LNAI 2417, pp. 434–443, 2002.

In this paper, we present an effective probabilistic approach based on the multiple-cause models [2][5][10] for topic extraction from unstructured text documents. A topic is represented by a set of its relevant or related words, and a document is assumed to be the result of a combination of one or more topics. If a specific topic is activated, it causes its related words more likely to appear and others less likely in a document. In the case that more than one topic are activated simultaneously, a document is generated by the cooperation of these topics.

To ease the learning and inference in the model, we adopt an approximation method based on the Helmholtz machine [1] and use an on-line stochastic algorithm for the model fitting, unlike the works in [9] where a deterministic gradient ascent method is used in the application of their multiple-cause mixture model to the text categorization. Additionally, we introduce some heuristics for incorporating the word frequency information in the binary-valued Helmholtz machines.

2   The Multiple-Cause Model

In the multiple-cause model, it is postulated that a data naturally arises from the consequences of a set of hidden causes [5]. Formally, the model can be represented by multiple-cause networks, and we describe these networks in terms of the analysis of text documents.

2.1   Multiple-Cause Networks

Figure 1 shows the typical form of the multiple-cause network [5]. Topics are represented by latent nodes and words in the vocabulary are by input nodes. Each topic z_k is a binary variable indicating its presence or absence, and is described as a set of independent *Bernoulli* distributions, one distribution for each term. When it is given a document collection $D = \{d_1, d_2, \ldots, d_N\}$ of which each d_n $(1 \leq n \leq N)$ is independent and identically distributed, the log probability of D under this model is given by

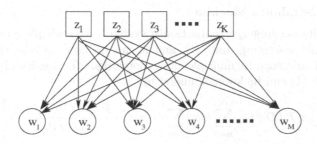

Fig. 1. The multiple-cause networks

$$\log P(D|\theta) = \sum_{n=1}^{N} \log P(d_n|\theta)$$

$$= \sum_{n=1}^{N} \log \left[\sum_{\mathbf{z}} P(\mathbf{z}|\theta) P(d_n|\mathbf{z}, \theta) \right], \tag{1}$$

where θ is the parameter set of the model, and $\mathbf{z}$ is one of all the possible combinations of topics, for example $\mathbf{z} = (1, 0, 1, \ldots, 0)$. Considering the network structure and dependency separation [5] in Figure 1, it is assumed that individual words in a document are conditionally independent given a specific topic configuration. That is,

$$P(d_n|\mathbf{z}, \theta) = \prod_{m=1}^{M} P(w_m|\mathbf{z}, \theta). \tag{2}$$

If we encode documents using binary word vectors considering only the presence or absence of words in documents, the variable w_m is a binary variable. There are several alternatives for calculating the probability $P(w_m|\mathbf{z})$, including sigmoid function [1][5], noisy-OR function [10], and competitive function [2]. For the present work, we adopt the competitive function for the activation function. This function is given by

$$P(w_m = 1|\mathbf{z}) = 1 - \frac{1}{1 + \sum_k \theta_{km} z_k}, \tag{3}$$

where θ_{km} is non-negative and interpreted as the contribution to the odds that if z_k is 1 then w_m is 1. And $P(w_m = 0|\mathbf{z})$ is $1 - P(w_m = 1|\mathbf{z})$. Details about the derivation of this function are referred to [2].

In the above settings, however, each document can be generated in exponentially many ways with the number of possible latent topics. The computational costs considering all of these explanations can make standard maximum likelihood approaches such as EM algorithm intractable [1][5]. With 20 possible topics, for example, we must consider 2^{20} ($> 1,000,000$) configurations for each document. Therefore generally some approximations have been used, and we choose the *Helmholtz machine* [1] for this.

2.2   The Helmholtz Machines

The Helmholtz machine is a connectionist system with multiple layers of neuron-like stochastic processing units [1], and it can be used to ease the process of learning and inference in multiple-cause networks. The log-likelihood given in the Equation (1) can be lower-bounded by

$$\log P(D|\theta) = \sum_{n=1}^{N} \log \left[\sum_{\mathbf{z}} Q(\mathbf{z}|d_n) \frac{P(\mathbf{z}|\theta) P(d_n|\mathbf{z}, \theta)}{Q(\mathbf{z}|d_n)} \right]$$

$$\geq \sum_{n=1}^{N} \sum_{\mathbf{z}} Q(\mathbf{z}|d_n) \log \frac{P(\mathbf{z}|\theta) P(d_n|\mathbf{z}, \theta)}{Q(\mathbf{z}|d_n)}, \tag{4}$$

where $Q(\mathbf{z}|d_n)$ is an approximation to the true posterior probability $P(\mathbf{z}|d_n, \theta)$. If this lower bound is maximized, the true log likelihood can be approximately maximized [1].

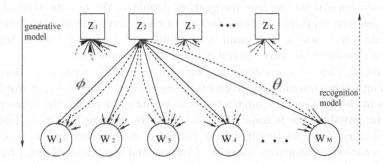

Fig. 2. A two-layer Helmholtz machine. The solid lines represent the top-down generative connections and the dotted lines represent the bottom-up recognition connections

The Helmholtz machine introduces a recognition network to estimate the distribution $Q(\mathbf{z}|d_n)$. So the machine is composed of a pair of networks. Figure 2 shows a simple Helmholtz machine with one input layer and one hidden layer.

The newly introduced recognition network is implemented by bottom-up connections ϕ, and the $Q(\mathbf{z}|d_n)$ is estimated by a parametric form $Q(\mathbf{z}|d_n, \phi)$. Since individual latent nodes in the recognition network are conditionally independent given all the values of input nodes, the probability is represented simply by

$$Q(\mathbf{z}|d_n, \phi) = \prod_{k=1}^{K} Q(z_k|d_n, \phi). \tag{5}$$

And the probability $Q(z_k|d_n, \phi)$ is calculated by

$$Q(z_k|d_n, \phi) = \frac{1}{1 + \exp\left(-\sum_{m=0}^{M} \phi_{mk} w_m\right)}. \tag{6}$$

where w_0 is 1, and ϕ_{0k} is a recognition bias to z_k. Using this approximation, we can simplify and accelerate the procedure of estimating posterior probabilities for documents.

3   Applying to Text Documents

The Helmholtz machine is basically a binary-valued Bayesian network, so it needs some modifications to handle the document of which each element is the number of occurrence of the corresponding word. In the work of [4], they have modelled the observed units as discrete Poisson random variables, by which they have tried to automatically discover stochastic firing patterns in large ensembles of neurons. In our experiments for text documents, however, it didn't work well compared with the original binary Helmholtz machines. Rather, We utilize the idea of the *replica* in [11] where the restricted Boltzmann machines with replicas have been applied to the face recognition problem. We assume that the input nodes can have multiple *replicas* and all of them have the identical weights to and from latent nodes. The number of replicas of an input node is set to the frequency count of the corresponding word in a document.

In recognition of a document d, activities of latent topics are determined according to the probabilities given by the Equation (6). If the mth word occurs l times in the document, l binary replicas are introduced for the corresponding node. In practice this is implemented simply by setting $w_m = l$. The model is fitted using a stochastic algorithm, the *wake-sleep* algorithm [1][6]. Learning in the wake-sleep algorithm consists of interleaved iterations of two phases, the *wake* phase and the *sleep* phase. In relation to the generalized EM algorithm, the wake phase plays the role corresponding to the generalized M-step and the sleep phase corresponding to the generalized E-step [5].

Table 1 describes the learning algorithm of the Helmholtz machine when applied to text documents. This algorithm proceeds in the same way as described in [6] except for two differences. First, the activation probabilities of the latent nodes are estimated considering the frequency information of words. In this way, in estimating the latent topics, words which appear many times in a document are distinguished from those with just one occurrence. Second, activation probabilities of input nodes in the generative network are given by *competitive rule* as indicated in Section 2.1. Especially if the word count is greater than 1, this rule is applied to its binary-valued replica. So in the update rule for the generative weight θ_{km} from the kth latent node to mth input node, s_m is a binary value, that is 0 or 1.

4   Experiments

4.1   Topic Words Extraction

We have performed some experiments on topic extraction with a subset of TDT-2 collection. The subset contains topics which have relatively many relevant documents , resulting in 10,685 documents in total. Stop words in a standard stop word list have been eliminated, and words which occur in at least 10 documents have been selected. For the ease of interpretation of results, no stemming or further preprocessing has been performed. Finally, the resulting vocabulary size is 12,467.

We have trained Helmholtz machines with varying number of latent nodes. Table 2 shows 9 latent factors extracted with 32 latent factors. For each topic z, all the words are sorted according to their probabilities $P(w|z)$, and the top 15 words are shown. It can be seen that words in the same factor are semantically related or, in a weak sense, refer to the same topic.

Table 1. The learning procedure based on the wake-sleep algorithm

---

INPUT: (D, ϕ, θ, η, N, M, K)
D is the set of text documents. Each document $d_n = (w_1, w_2, \cdots, w_M)$ is represented by a numeric vector, where w_m is the frequency of the word in the document.
η is the learning rate.
ϕ is the set of parameters in the recognition model, and θ is the set of parameters in the generative model.
N and M are the number of documents and the vocabulary size, respectively, and K is the number of latent topics.

Iterate the two phases until the algorithm converges.

Wake phase

1. A document d is clamped on the input nodes. Using the recognition model, the latent topics are sampled from their conditional probabilities calculated by the Equation (6).
2. θ is updated to make the latent topics picked above more likely for d.

$$\theta_{km} = \theta_{km} + \eta\frac{1 - p_m}{p_m}(s_m - p_m)s_k \qquad (1 \leq k \leq K, \quad 1 \leq m \leq M)$$

$$\theta_{0k} = \theta_{0k} + \eta(s_k - p_k) \qquad \text{(biases to the latents)} \qquad (1 \leq k \leq K)$$

where p_k and p_m are the activation probabilities for the latent topics and words, respectively, on the generative model. s_k and s_m are the actual values of 0 or 1.

Sleep phase

1. In the generative model, the latent topics are randomly selected according to the following probabilities.

$$p_k = \frac{1}{1 + \exp(-\theta_{0k})}$$

From this, a *"fantasy"* document is generated in input layer.
2. ϕ is updated to make this fantasy case more likely.

$$\phi_{mk} = \phi_{mk} + \eta s_m(s_k - p_k) \qquad (1 \leq k \leq K, \quad 1 \leq m \leq M)$$

where p_k is the activation probability for kth latent topics on the recognition model. s_k and s_m are the actual value of 0 or 1.

Table 3 shows three latent factors extracted with 64 latent factors. With this increased factors, it is shown that the topic on *"winter Olympics"*, the fourth in Table 2, is represented by three more specific latent factors. This shows the properties of multiple-cause models on text documents where several semantic factors can be combined to represent documents. In examining the results in

Table 2. Topic word sets from TDT-2 corpus. 15 most probable words are shown for each topic word set in decreasing order

15 most probable words for each latent generator
tobacco, smoking, gingrich, newt, trent, republicans, congressional, republicans, attorney, smokers, lawsuit, senate, cigarette, morris, nicotine
iraq, weapons, united, saddam, military, iraqi, inspectors, hussein, security, baghdad, nations, inspections, gulf, destruction, war
lewinsky, monica, president, starr, clinton, house, white, counsel, independent, jury, investigation, sexual, kenneth, grand, relationship
olympics, olympic, games, nagano, winter, gold, medal, men, team, skating, women, athletes, ice, ski
israeli, minister, israel, peace, prime, bank, netanyahu, palestinian, west, secretary, talks, arafat, benjamin, united, albright
india, pakistan, pakistani, delhi, hindu, vajpayee, nuclear, tests, atal, kashmir, indian, janata, bharatiya, islamabad, bihari
suharto, habibie, demonstrators, riots, indonesians, demonstrations, soeharto, resignation, jakarta, rioting, electoral, rallies, wiranto, unrest, megawati
market, stock, prices, percent, points, asia, asian, fell, index, investors, rose, stocks, financial, markets, analysts
pope, cuba, visit, paul, john, caban, castro, fidel, havana, communist, cubans, church, human, catholic, pontiff

Table 3. Topics on the winter Olympics : "ice hockey", "skating", "general & ski"

"ICE HOCKEY"	team, hockey, ice, canada, game, olympic, players, goal, tournament, league, scored, goalie, coach, round, victory, national, czech, period, nhl, $\cdots$, puck, stick, $\cdots$
"SKATING"	skating, figure, program, olympic, world, champion, skate, short, competition, lipinski, judges, medal, tara, triple, ice, kwan, jumps, skater, michelle, performance, $\cdots$
"GENERAL & SKI"	won, olympics, winter, games, nagano, world, race, medal, gold, silver, team, $\cdots$, ski, finish, event, final, slalom, snow, $\cdots$

detail, we have found some interesting facts. In Table 4, the first two columns represent the different contexts where the word 'race' is used: arms race and race in sports like ski. And the last two columns represent the different usages of another word 'court': court related with law and court related with sports like basketball. In this way, the different meanings or usages of the same word can be differentiated. Similar experimental results and interpretation for text documents with PLSA and NMF are presented in [7][8], respectively.

Table 4. Four selected topics from 64 latent factors for the subset of TDT-2 Corpus

"nuclear race"	"winter Olympics"	"legal affair"	"basketball"
india	won	case	jordan
nuclear	olympics	*COURT*	bulls
tests	winter	judge	jazz
pakistan	games	law	nba
weapons	nagano	federal	finals
hindu	world	attorney	basketball
arms	*RACE*	legal	*COURT*
RACE	medal	justice	pippen
sanction	gold	lawyers	points
security	silver	supreme	phil
delhi	team	evidence	teams
nationalist	lillehammer	trial	game

4.2   Document Clustering

We also experimented for the document clustering by the learning of Helmholtz machines. This might provide, though indirect, some quantitative view on the performance besides the qualitative results of the previous section. The dataset contains 1,069 documents of 4 topics from TREC-8 ad-hoc task data, including *'Foreign minorities, Germany'*(ID 401), *'Estonia, economy'* (ID 434), *'inventions, scientific discoveries'* (ID 439), and *'King Husayn, peace'* (ID 450). Stop words have been removed and the words with at least 5 document frequency have been selected, which result in 8,828 words. The number of latent nodes were set to four and the algorithm was run ten times with random initializations.

The clustering is performed by two methods of estimating posterior probabilities, one is by $Q(z|d)$ and the other by $P(z|d)$. Given a document d, $Q(z|d)$ is estimated simply using the recognition network, and $P(z|d)$ is by the conjugate

Table 5. Confusion matrix for a subset of *TREC* ad-hoc task data. Each document d is assigned to the most active cluster according to $Q(z|d)$ and $P(z|d)$. The bottommost row shows the average error rates across the runs where the 4 topics were relatively well separated, and the numbers of such "successful" runs are shown in the parentheses

| | HM with frequency | | | | | | | | HM with binary | | | | | | | |
| | $Q(z|d)$ | | | | $P(z|d)$ | | | | $Q(z|d)$ | | | | $P(z|d)$ | | | |
Topic ID	401	434	439	450	401	434	439	450	401	434	439	450	401	434	439	450
401	**297**	2	0	1	**297**	3	0	0	**284**	12	2	2	**285**	12	3	0
434	2	**343**	2	0	0	**346**	1	0	0	**338**	7	2	0	**333**	13	1
439	1	4	**124**	0	0	1	**128**	0	8	19	**101**	1	0	31	**98**	0
450	2	1	0	**290**	0	4	1	**288**	0	3	5	**285**	1	2	2	**288**
Error rates	1.85 ± 0.45% (8)				1.68 ± 0.49% (8)				6.92 ± 0.97% (5)				6.95 ± 0.85% (5)			

gradient method using the generative network as in [9][10]. The predicted topic $\hat{t}$ of the document d is that with the highest $Q(z_k|d)$ or $P(z_k|d)$, that is,

$$\hat{t} = \text{argmax}_k Q(z_k|d) \quad \text{or} \quad \text{argmax}_k P(z_k|d). \tag{7}$$

Table 5 shows the confusion matrix for the case with the best clustering result and the average performances across the runs where the topics are relatively well separated. As can be seen in the results, there are no significant differences between $Q(z|d)$ and $P(z|d)$ in the clustering performance. In terms of inference for a given document, however, the estimation of $Q(z|d)$ required much less computational costs than $P(z|d)$ in CPU time, *0.02 sec/doc* and *0.98 sec/doc* on a Linux system with AMD Athlon 1 GHz CPU, respectively. So, the approximation of multiple-cause networks by the architecture of Helmholtz machines could provide fast inference for newly presented documents, especially for those with high dimensionality.

The right part in Table 5 shows the clustering result when documents are represented by the binary encoding which considers only whether a word occurs in a document or not. In this case the performance is poor compared to the result using word frequency information, especially for ID 439 about scientific discoveries. From this, we argue that, though it is not utilized directly in the parameter estimation of the model but only in estimating active latent factors, the word frequency information helps produce better topic decomposition.

5   Conclusions

In this paper, we have presented a multiple-cause network based approach for topic decomposition of text documents. To ease the learning and inference in the network, we utilized the approximation given by Helmholtz machines. The competitive function has been used as the activation function for input nodes in the generative network, and the word frequency information was incorporated into the recognition network when estimating likely latent topics for each document.

In the experiments on TDT-2 collection, we have presented the topic decomposition results with varying number of latent topics and have shown the characteristics of the multiple-cause model for text documents. In the document clustering experiment, we estimated likely latent topics both on the recognition network and on the generative network. The former has provided much faster inference than the latter, without significant deterioration of the performance. And though confined to estimating latent topics for given documents, the incorporation of the word frequency has been experimentally shown to be helpful for the analysis of text documents.

Acknowledgments. This work was supported by the Korean Ministry of Science and Technology under the BrainTech Project and by the Korean Ministry of Education under the BK21-IT Program. Yuseop Kim is supported by Brain Korea 21 project performed by Ewha Institute of Science and Technology.

References

1. Dayan, P., Hinton, G.E., Neal, R. M., Zemel, R. S.: The Helmholtz machine. Neural Computation **7** (1995) 889–904
2. Dayan, P., Zemel, R.S.: Competition and multiple cause models. Neural Computation **7** (1995) 565-579
3. Deerwester, S., Dumais, S.T., Furnas, G.W., Landauer, T.K., Harshman, R.: Indexing by latent semantic analysis. Journal of the American Society for Information Science. **41** (1990) 391–407
4. deSa, V.R., deCharms, R.C., Merzenich, M.M.: Using Helmholtz machines to analyze multi-channel neuronal recordings. Advances in Neural Information Processing Systems 10 (1998) 131–137
5. Frey, B.J.: Graphical Models for Machine Learning and Digital Communication. The MIT Press (1998)
6. Hinton, G.E., Dayan, P., Frey, B.J., Neal, R.M.: The wake-sleep algorithm for unsupervised neural networks. Science **268** (1995) 1158–1161.
7. Hofmann, T.: Probabilistic latent semantic indexing. Proceedings of the 22th International Conference on Research and Development in Information Retrieval (SIGIR) (1999) 50-57
8. Lee, D.D., Seung, H.S.: Learning the parts of objects by non-negative matrix factorization. Nature **401** (1999) 788-791
9. Sahami, M., Hearst, M., Saund, E.: Applying the multiple cause mixture model to Text Categorization. Proceedings of the 13th International Conference on Machine Learning (1996) 435–443
10. Saund, E.: A multiple cause mixture model for unsupervised learning. Neural Computation **7** (1995) 51–71
11. Tch, Y.W., Hinton, G.E.: Rate-coded restricted Boltzmann machines for face recognition. Advances in Neural Information Processing Systems 13 (2001) 908–914

A Comparative Study on Statistical Machine Learning Algorithms and Thresholding Strategies for Automatic Text Categorization

Kang Hyuk Lee[1], Judy Kay[1], Byeong Ho Kang[2], and Uwe Rosebrock[2]

[1] School of Information Technologies, University of Sydney, NSW 2006, Australia
{kangl, judy}@it.usyd.edu.au
[2] School of Computing, University of Tasmania, Hobart, Tasmania 7001, Australia
{bhkang, uwer}@utas.edu.au

Abstract. Two main research areas in statistical text categorization are similarity-based learning algorithms and associated thresholding strategies. The combination of these techniques significantly influences the overall performance of text categorization. After investigating two similarity-based classifiers (k-NN and Rocchio) and three common thresholding techniques (RCut, PCut, and SCut), we describe a new learning algorithm known as the keyword association network (KAN) and a new thresholding strategy (RinSCut) to improve performance over existing techniques. Extensive experiments have been conducted on the Reuters-21578 and 20-Newsgroups data sets. The experimental results show that our new approaches give better results for both micro-averaged F_1 and macro-averaged F_1 scores.

1 Introduction

The goal of text categorization is to learn a classification scheme that can be used for the problem of automatically assigning arbitrary documents to predefined categories (or classes). Text categorization has many applications in which this plays a vital role, such as document routing, document management, and document dissemination. Traditionally, experts who are knowledgeable about the categories conduct text categorization manually. This requires substantial human resources. Given that the amount of online textual information is growing rapidly, the need for reliable automatic text categorization has been increasing.

There has been a wide range of statistical learning algorithms applied to this automatic text categorization task. They include the Rocchio relevance feedback algorithm [2, 4, 7], k-Nearest Neighbor (k-NN) classification [15, 19], naive Bayes probabilistic classification [4, 6, 8], support vector machines [5], and neural networks [14]. After two preprocessing steps (representation and feature selection), answering the questions of how to discriminate informative words in the reduced vector space and how to give them more weight than other non-informative words is the main task of classifiers. After exploring two representatives of the similarity-based classifiers, namely Rocchio

M. Ishizuka and A. Sattar (Eds.): PRICAI 2002, LNAI 2417, pp. 444-453, 2002.
© Springer-Verlag Berlin Heidelberg 2002

and k-NN, this paper describes the keyword association network (KAN), a new representation and learning algorithm, designed to effectively address these open questions.

The last step, to obtain a mapping from a new document to relevant categories, is achieved with thresholding techniques applied to the similarity score for each document-category pair. Existing common techniques are rank-based thresholding (RCut), proportion-based assignment (PCut), and score-based optimization (SCut). These techniques have been extensively evaluated on various corpora in [16, 17]. The choice of thresholding strategy has a significant impact on the performance of classifiers. This choice is also influenced by the characteristics of dataset. This means that finding the optimal thresholding strategy for any given classifier and data set is difficult and combining the strengths of the existing thresholding strategies is a challenge in text categorization [17]. This paper presents a new thresholding technique (RinSCut) that combines the strengths of RCut and SCut to overcome the weaknesses of two thresholding strategies. The empirical results on the Reuters-21578 and 20-Newsgroups data sets show that our new approaches outperform existing techniques.

2   Reviews on Common Techniques

2.1   Representation and Feature Selection

The common representation adopted by most statistical learning algorithms is the "bag-of-words" representation. In this representation, each document D is transformed to have the form of a vector $d = (v_1, v_2, \ldots, v_n)$. Here, each v_i is the weighting value of the ith feature (term or word) and n is the total number of features in D. The weights are calculated as a combination of two common weighting schemes, $TF(i,D)$ and $IDF(i)$. The term frequency $TF(i,D)$ is the number of times the ith feature occurs in document D and the inverse document frequency, $IDF(i)$, is $log\{|N| / DF(i)\}$, where $DF(i)$ is the number of documents in which the ith feature occurs at least once and $|N|$ is the total number of documents in the training set. Because the document lengths may vary widely, a length normalization factor is applied to the term weighting function. The weighting equation that is used [3] in this experiment is given as:

$$v_i(d) = \frac{[\, logTF(i, D) + 1.0\,] \times IDF(i)}{\sqrt{\sum_{i=1,n} \{[logTF(i, D) + 1.0] \times IDF(i)\}^2}} \tag{1}$$

Typically, this vector space is very high dimensional and this makes it computationally intractable to apply most statistical learning algorithms. So, it is critical to reduce this huge vector space before applying statistical algorithms. This dimension reduction, known as feture selection, can be achieved by using the following techniques: document frequency, term frequency, mutual information, information gain, and OddsRatio etc. [9, 18]. Then, the main task of learning algorithms is to find informative features for the resulting reduced vector space.

2.2 Statistical Learning Algorithms: Rocchio and k-NN

The Rocchio classifier is based on a relevance feedback algorithm [11]. Because of its various heuristic components, there have been several similar algorithms corresponding to the particular choice of heuristics. In this algorithm, each category C has a vector of the form $c = (x_1, x_2, \dots , x_n)$. This prototype vector c is prepared by summing the vectors of the positive documents as well as of the negative documents and, then by calculating a weighted difference for each.

$$c = [\alpha \times |C|^{-1} \times \Sigma_{d \in C} d] - [\beta \times (|N| - |C|)^{-1} \times \Sigma_{d \notin C} d] \qquad (2)$$

where α and β are adjustment parameters for positive and negative examples, d is the vector of document, and $|C|$ is the number of documents in the category C. The similarity value between a category and a new document is obtained as the inner product between corresponding feature vectors. The problem in this classifier is that some relevant features in a rare category will have small weights if they appear equally in the negative document set. It is also very sensitive to the number of irrelevant words, since all features participate equally in the similarity calculation. As a result, if the set of discriminating features of a category is only a small subset of the overall vector space, the category will very likely have low performance.

K-nearest neighbor. The k-Nearest Neighbor (k-NN) classifier is an instance-based learning algorithm. The main idea of this algorithm is that a document itself has more representative power than the generalized category feature vector. For a new document, it computes the similarity to all the training documents using the cosine metric used in [15]. The similarity scores are then sorted in descending order. The final score for a category is the summation of the similarity scores of the documents of that category in the k top-ranking documents. One drawback of this algorithm is that noisy examples have direct impact on the quality of the ranking. Furthermore, the time taken for the similarity calculation increases in proportion to the size of the training data set. Like Rocchio, the k-NN classifier does not cope effectively with irrelevant features that cause overfitting.

2.3 Common Thresholding Strategies

A thresholding strategy is used in the last step of the similarity-based classifiers to obtain binary assignments of categories to arbitrary documents. Rank-based Thresholding (RCut) sorts the similarity scores of categories for each document and assigns a "YES" decision to the t top-ranking categories. Using a validation set or a training set, the threshold, t, is predefined automatically by optimizing the global performance, not the local performance of each category. RCut will give the best performance when all the test documents belong to the same number of categories. However, when documents have a variable number of categories this strategy may result in a low macro-averaged performance.

Given a ranking list of each category (c_i), Proportion-based Assignment (PCut) assigns a "YES" decision to k_i top-ranking test documents. The threshold, k_i, is $n \times P(c_i) \times \omega$ where n is the number of documents in a validation set or a training set, $P(c_i)$ is the probability of the ith category, and ω is the real-valued parameter given by the user or predetermined automatically in the same way as t for RCut. While performing well in the text categorization experiments [16], PCut cannot be used for on-line categorization.

Score-based Optimization (SCut) learns the optimal threshold for each category. The optimal threshold is the similarity score that optimizes the performance measure of each category. If documents belong to a variable number of categories and the local performance of each category is the primary concern, this strategy may be a better choice than RCut. However, it is not trivial to find an optimal threshold, and this problem becomes more apparent with the small set of training data. As a result, SCut has a potential weakness in overfitting to the training set.

3 Keyword Association Network (KAN)

3.1 Need for New Learning Algorithm

We noticed that a crucial question in statistical text categorization is how to cope with irrelevant features effectively. The answer to this question could be considered at the level of feature and category. With respect to the feature level, we have focused on how to find semantics and to assess the importance of a feature in a given document. And, with respect to the level of category, we focused on how to establish the discriminating features in each category and how to represent these features using a suitable representation.

To give a feature an appropriate weight according to both its relevant meaning and its importance, our main focus lies on the collocating features in a given document. As an example of capturing the correct meaning, consider the word, "apple", that conveys different meanings in a category and a document. Suppose the feature "apple" in the document is in the context Farm and, in the category it is in the context Computer. By looking at other words in the document, a human can differentiate between the semantics of "apple" in the document and the same word in the category. This approach can be applied to measuring the importance of words in a given document. Because current farming uses computer technology, this document in the context Farm might contain several words overlapping with the Computer category, and those overlapping words should have minor importance in the document. If we adopt the statistical approaches already described, the similarity measure between the document and the category may be high and, as a result, this document may be incorrectly considered as being Computer-related. As a result, the similarity measurement without considering the features in the context of the document will lead to an incorrect classification.

The important aspect at the level of category is that the most critical feature set size is different for different categories and it is relatively small. Some categories have one or two discriminating words. Identifying the existence of those words in the documents is enough for a categorization. Using the same feature set size across all the categories could be a major cause of low system performance. It suggests that using a different representative feature set size for different categories would lead to higher performance for a classifier, if the proper size can be determined and a suitable representation method can be found.

3.2 New Representation and Learning Algorithm: KAN

Previous work showed that it is possible to automatically find words that are semantically similar to a given word based on the collocation of words [12, 13]. Our goal was to use this type of statistical information to determine the importance and semantic meaning of a word in a given document. KAN is constructed by means of a network representation based on statistical information. The degree of relationship between two features is represented by a confidence value. This measure was used in finding association rules [1] that have been identified as an important tool for knowledge discovery in huge transactional databases. In KAN, the confidence value is used for measuring how the presence of one word in a given document may influence the presence of another. When the category C has a set of k unique features $\{W = (w_1, w_2, ... , w_k)\}$, the construction and utilization of KAN for the text categorization is based on the following statistical information: the support, the confidence, and the discriminative power functions. They are defined as follows.

Definition 1. For the feature w_i, the positive support, $SUP_p(w_i)$, is the number of documents in a category for the training set that contain w_i and the total support, $SUP_T(w_i)$, is the number of documents that contain w_i in the complete training set.

Definition 2. The confidence value of w_i to w_j in a category, $CONF(w_i, w_j)$, is the proportion of positive documents which contain w_i and also have w_j, i.e., $SUP_p(w_i, w_j)$ / $SUP_p(w_i)$.

High confidence w_i to w_j can be interpreted as indication that the meaning and importance of w_j is associated with the existence of w_i. In each category, the discriminative features are identified automatically using two discriminative power functions $DPF1$ and $DPF2$ which are defined as follows.

Definition 3. Two discriminative power functions $DPF1(w_i)$ and $DPF2(w_i)$ for feature w_i are:

$$DPF1(w_i) = SUP_p(w_i) / SUP_T(w_i) \tag{3}$$

$$DPF2(w_i) = SUP_p(w_i) / |C| \tag{4}$$

where $|C|$ is the number of documents in category C.

According to above discriminative power functions, the ideal discriminating feature for a category will appear in all the documents in the category and the number of documents in this category will be same with the number of documents which contains the feature in the training set. In KAN, if two function values of a feature satisfy the user specified minimum values, this feature is considered as a representative feature and plays an important role in the similarity calculation. Figure 1 shows an example of KAN for a particular category in Reuters-21578 when the minimum values for $DPF1$ and $DPF2$ are 0.5 and 0.2 respectively. In this example, the nodes "agriculture", "grain", and "wheat" are presented as the discriminating features satisfying two minimum values. These will provide most of the overall similarity score. An important factor in achieving high performance in text categorization is to remove the influence of the large number of irrelevant features that occur evenly across the categories. KAN is designed to distinguish them from the discriminating features in a category and use them by adding more weight to the small number of discriminating features.

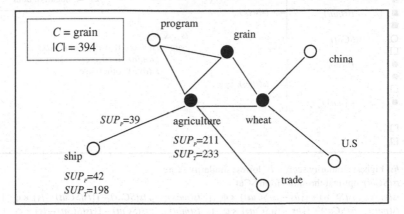

Fig. 1. An example of KAN for the grain category in Reuters-21578 dataset.

For a category C which has the unique feature set $\{W = (w_1, w_2, \ldots , w_k)\}$, the vector having the form $c = (x_1, x_2, \ldots , x_k)$ is prepared as follows: $c = \sum_{d \in C} d \times |C|^{-1}$ where d is the vector of a document calculated using the equation (1) and $|C|$ is the number of documents in the category C. The similarity score between the category C and a test document D which is represented by the vector of the form $(v_1, v_2, \ldots , v_k)$ is computed using the following function:

$$\text{Similarity}(D, C) = \sum_{i=1,k} [(x_i \times v_i) + \delta] \tag{5}$$
$$\delta \text{ is } \quad \sum_{j=1,k\&j\neq i} [x_i \times CONF(w_j,w_i) \times v_i] \text{ if } w_i \in R$$
$$\qquad 0 \text{ otherwise}$$

where R is the set of discriminative features in the category C.

4   New Thresholding Strategy: RinSCut

RinSCut is designed to overcome weaknesses in both SCut and RCut. For each category, it computes the two threshold scores, ts_{top} and ts_{bottom}, as shown in Figure 2 and the range of above two threshold values is considered as the ambiguous zone. For the new documents that have the similarity scores belonging to this zone, the rank threshold, t, is used to make the final decision. The threshold, t, is predefined by optimizing the local performance of each category. As a result, unlike in RCut, each category may have different t in RinSCut. For a test document D having the similarity score, Similarity(D, C), it assigns a "YES" decision if Similarity$(D, C) \geq ts_{top}$ and a "NO" decision if Similarity$(D, C) < ts_{bottom}$. If Similarity(D, C) is between ts_{top} and ts_{bottom}, the assignment decision depends on the rank-based threshold t.

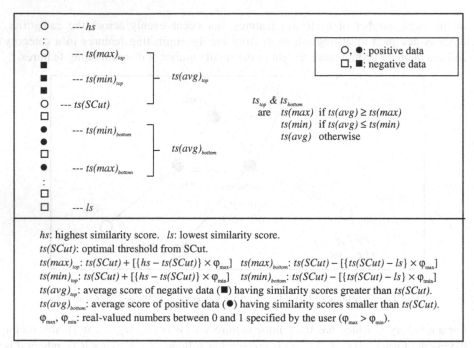

hs: highest similarity score. ls: lowest similarity score.
ts(SCut): optimal threshold from SCut.
$ts(max)_{top}$: $ts(SCut) + [\{hs - ts(SCut)\} \times \varphi_{max}]$ $ts(max)_{bottom}$: $ts(SCut) - [\{ts(SCut) - ls\} \times \varphi_{max}]$
$ts(min)_{top}$: $ts(SCut) + [\{hs - ts(SCut)\} \times \varphi_{min}]$ $ts(min)_{bottom}$: $ts(SCut) - [\{ts(SCut) - ls\} \times \varphi_{tmin}]$
$ts(avg)_{top}$: average score of negative data (■) having similarity scores greater than $ts(SCut)$.
$ts(avg)_{bottom}$: average score of positive data (●) having similarity scores smaller than $ts(SCut)$.
φ_{max}, φ_{min}: real-valued numbers between 0 and 1 specified by the user ($\varphi_{max} > \varphi_{min}$).

Fig. 2. Example showing how to calculate ts_{top} and ts_{bottom} in RinSCut.

5 Experiments

5.1 Data Sets

The 20-Newsgroups[1] collected by Ken Lang consists of 20,017 articles posted to 20 different Usenet discussion groups. Because each article belongs to exactly one newsgroup, RCut seems to be the optimal thresholding strategy in this data set. So, the performance of each classifier will be measured using the RCut. For the test set, 30% of the articles were randomly selected. The Reuters-21578[2] consists of 21,578 articles appeared on the Reuters newswire. We split the articles into training and test sets according to the Modified Lewis Split. Instead of analyzing all 135 categories, we choose the categories having at least 10 articles in both training and test sets. The number of selected categories is 53. This results in a corpus of 6,984 training data and 3,265 test data. In this data set, the SCut and RinSCut will be applied to each classifier, because many articles have the variable number of categories.

5.2 Experimental Setup

For the preprocessing steps, we applied a stop-list and Porter's stemming algorithm [10] to the articles. We used information gain for the feature selection and took the same number of features, 50 in these experiments, for all categories in both data sets.

---

[1] http://www.ai.mit.edu/people/jrennie/20_newsgroups
[2] http://www.research.att.com/~lewis/reuters21578.html

We have implemented three classifiers - Rocchio, k-NN, and KAN - with three thresholding strategies - RCut, SCut, and RinSCut. The performance was measured using the standard F_1 measure that is designed to balance recall and precision by giving them equal weight [16].

$$F_1 = 2 \times \text{Recall} \times \text{Precision} / (\text{Recall} + \text{Precision}) \tag{6}$$

We computed the macro-averaged F_1 as well as the micro-averaged F_1 in order to analyze the performance on individual categories. We conducted the experiments by increasing the size of the training data to construct learning curves for the classifiers. Table 1 shows the amount of training data in each round. The training set for each round is a superset of the one for the previous round. For KAN, we use 0.5 as the minimum value for *DPF1* and 0.2 for *DPF2* to define the representative features in the categories. To compute the vectors of categories for the Rocchio algorithm, we use $\alpha = 16$ and $\beta = 4$ as suggested in [2]. The value k used in these experiments for the k-NN is 10, 30, and 50. Then, we chose the value with the best result in each round. For RinSCut, 0.3 and 0.1 are assigned to φ_{max} and φ_{min} respectively.

Table 1. Number of unique training data in each round.

Round Data set	1	2	3	4	5	6	7	8	9	10
Reuters	106	212	371	689	1272	2409	3696	5136	6202	6984
Newsgroups	80	160	300	580	1140	2260	3520	4920	5980	13998

5.3 Results

Figure 3 shows the micro-averaged and macro-averaged F_1 performance of each classifier with the RCut on 20-Newsgroups data set. Each classifier achieves the similar performance on both measures and it is due to the fact that articles in trainging and test sets are divided almost evenly among 20 groups. KAN gives better performance than the other classifiers although the difference is minor with the large number of training data. In Figure 4 and 5, the performance of each classifier on the Reuters-21578 data set is shown. With the SCut in Figure 4, KAN performs significantly better than k-NN and Rocchio in both micro-averaged and macro-averaged F_1. Note here on the macro-

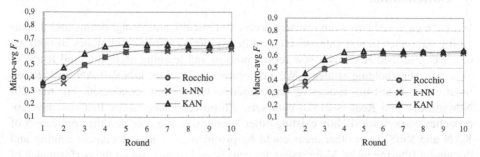

Fig. 3. Micro-averaged F_1 and Macro-averaged F_1 performance with the RCut on the 20-Newsgroups data set.

averaged measure that KAN outperforms Rocchio and k-NN after round 3. This result demonstrates that our effort to capture the characteristics of each category using a discriminative feature set is achieved, and these discriminative features in each category increase the overall macro-averaged performance. In Figure 5, RinSCut gives similar learning curves to SCut for three classifiers. On both measures, RinSCut gives better performance than SCut across all the rounds for each classifier. On the basis of the data in Figure 4-5, it seems that the best choice across techniques for the Reuters-21578 data set would be KAN with RinSCut.

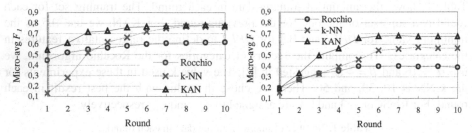

Fig. 4. Micro-averaged F_1 and Macro-averaged F_1 performance with the SCut on the Reuters-21578 data set.

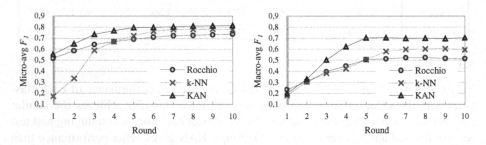

Fig. 5. Micro-averaged F_1 and Macro-averaged F_1 performance with the RinSCut on the Reuters-21578 data set.

6 Conclusions

We have explored two main research areas, statistical learning algorithms and thresholding strategies to text categorization. After outlining current techniques in both areas, we described KAN as a new representation and learning algorithm and RinSCut as a new thresholding strategy. We implemented Rocchio, k-NN, KAN with RCut, SCut, and RinSCut. Extensive experiments have been conducted on the 20-Newsgroups and Reuters-21578 data sets. Empirical results show that our new approaches outperform slightly existing other techniques. We note that the application of KAN and RinSCut in other areas could be promising, such as document routing and document filtering tasks. More research is envisaged to investigate the performance of our new approaches in these application areas.

References

1. Agrawal, A., Mannila, H., Srikant, R., Toivonen, H., Verkamo, A.I.: Fast Discovery of Association Rules. In: U. M. Fayyad, G. Piatetsky-Shapiro, P. Smith, R. Uthurusamy (eds). Advances in Knowledge Discovery and Data Mining, AAAI/MIT Press (1996) 307-328
2. Buckley, C., Salton, G., Allan, J.: The Effect of Adding Relevance Information in a Relevance Feedback Environment. International ACM SIGIR Conference (1994) 292-300
3. Buckley, C., Salton, G., Allan, J., Singhal, A.: Automatic Query Expansion Using SMART: TREC 3. The Third Text Retrieval Conference (TREC-3), National Institute of Standards and Technology Special Publication 500-207, Gaithersburg, MD (1995)
4. Joachims, T.: A Probabilistic Analysis of the Rocchio Algorithm with TFIDF for Text Categorization. In Proceedings of the 14th International Conference on Machine Learning ICML'97 (1997) 143-151
5. Joachims, T.: Text Categorization with Support Vector Machines: Learning with Many Relevant Features. In European Conference on Machine Learning (ECML-98) (1998)
6. Lewis, D.D., Ringuette, M.: Comparison of Two Learning Algorithms for Text Categorization. In Proceedings of the Third Annual Symposium on Document Analysis and Information Retrieval (SDAIR'94), Nevada, Las Vegas (1994)
7. Lewis, D.D., Schapire, R.E., Callan, J.P., Papka, R.: Training Algorithms for Linear Text Classifiers. In Proceedings of the 19th Annual International ACM SIGIR Conference on Research and Development in Information Retrieval (1996) 298-306
8. McCallum, A., Nigam, K.: A Comparison of Event Models for Naive Bayes Text Classifiers. In AAAI-98 Workshop on Learning for Text Categorization (1998)
9. Mladenic, D., Grobelnik, M.: Feature Selection for Unbalanced Class Distribution and Naive Bayes. In Proceedings of the 16th International Conference on Machine Learning (ICML-99) (1999)
10. Porter, M.F.: An Algorithm for Suffix Stripping. Program, Vol. 14. No. 3. (1980) 130-137
11. Rocchio, J.: Relevance Feedback in Information Retrieval. In G. Salton (ed): The SMART Retrieval System: Experiments in Automatic Document Processing, Prentice-Hall (1971)
12. Ruge, G.: Experiments on Linguistically Based Term Associations. Information Processing & Management, Vol. 28. No. 3. (1992) 317-332
13. Sekine, S., Carroll, J., Ananiadou, A., Tsujii, J.: Automatic Learning for Semantic Collocation. Proceedings of the Third Conference on Applied Natural Language Processing, ACL (1992) 104-110
14. Wiener, E., Pedersen, J.O., Weigend, A.S.: A Neural Network Approach to Topic Spotting. In Proceedings of the Fourth Annual Symposium on Document Analysis and Information Retrieval (SDAIR'95) (1995)
15. Yang, Y.: Expert Network: Effective and Efficient Learning from Human Decisions in Text Categorization and Retrieval. In Proceedings of the 17th International ACM SIGIR Conference on Research and Development in Information Retrieval (1994) 13-22
16. Yang, Y.: An Evaluation of Statistical Approaches to Text Categorization. Journal of Information Retrieval, Vol. 1. No. 1/2. (1999) 67-88
17. Yang, Y.: A Study on Thresholding Strategies for Text Categorization. In Proceedings of the 24th Annual International ACM SIGIR Conference on Research and Development in Information Retrieval (SIGIR'01) (2001)
18. Yang, Y., Pedersen, J.O.: Feature Selection in Statistical Learning of Text Categorization. In 14th International Conference on Machine Learning (1997) 412-420
19. Yavuz, T., Guvenir, A.: Application of k-Nearest Neighbor on Feature Projections Classifier to Text Categorization. In Proceedings of the 13th International Symposium on Computer and Information Sciences – ISCIS'98, U. Gudukbay, T. Dayar, A. Gursoy, E. Gelenbe (eds), Antalya, Turkey (1998) 135-142

PATI: An Approach for Identifying and Resolving Ambiguities

Jae Won Lee[1] and Sung-Dong Kim[2]

[1] School of Computer Science and Engineering, Sungshin Women's University,
Seoul, Korea 136-742
jwlee@cs.sungshin.ac.kr
[2] Department of Computer Engineering, Hansung University,
Seoul, Korea 136-792
sdkim@hansung.ac.kr

Abstract. This paper describes the rule-based approach for ambiguity resolution used by English sentence parser in E-TRAN 2001, an English to Korean machine translation system. Parser's Ambiguity Type Information (PATI) is used to automatically identify the types of ambiguities observed in competing candidate trees produced by the parser and summarizes the types into a formal representation. PATI provides an efficient way of encoding knowledge into grammar rules and calculating rule preference scores from a relatively small training corpus. We compare the enhanced grammar with the initial one in view of the amount of ambiguity. The experimental results show that the rule preference scores could significantly increase the accuracy of ambiguity resolution.

1 Introduction

E-TRAN 2000 [1] is an English to Korean machine translation system developed for domain-independent translation that requires both broad-coverage and high accuracy. Increasing coverage usually also increases the number of parse trees for sentences previously covered, with lowering accuracy for these sentences. We address two problems to provide a solution to the problem of increasing both parsing coverage and accuracy. One is the problem of reducing ambiguity by managing grammar rules in a more efficient way or improving parsing technology. The other is to employ rational preference functions that produce a score for sorting candidate trees in a preference order.

In [2], ambiguity is reduced using constraint functions that prevent a structure from being built for a given syntactic context. But it is not clear which kinds of structures can be prevented without any loss of coverage. Some studies about 'local ambiguity packing' [3][4] also try to reduce the number of analyses. They are mainly concerned in temporal or spatial performance problems and rarely address the coverage problem. Given a fixed amount of ambiguity, the accuracy of ambiguity resolution ultimately depends on the preference functions, which are based on *preference semantics* [5], for ranking competing candidate trees

M. Ishizuka and A. Sattar (Eds.): PRICAI 2002, LNAI 2417, pp. 454–462, 2002.

produced by a parser. But, when applied to a large scale application, they usually fail to offer satisfactory performance because it is quite difficult to acquire and manage reasonable preference functions. Wang [6] tried to associate the syntactic preference function first described in [7] with the semantic preference functions. It seems to fail to reach to practical performance for open domain applications [8][9]. One remarkable study by Alshwai et al. on integration of various preference functions [10] encourages the development of a more practical analysis system. Especially, the notion of 'mean distance' for the evaluation of lexical collocation preference functions, which considers frequencies in badly parsed trees, was proved to be very effective.

With an extension of the mean distance method to a syntactic preference function, we propose PATI (Parser's Ambiguity Type Information) as a new way of coping with ambiguity in rule-based natural language analysis. PATI is a weighted, directed graph that represents the differences of applied grammar rules among candidate trees. In PATI, the directions of edges represent priority relations among rule sets and the weights represent frequencies of those relations. It can identify the target of disambiguation more definitely and provide helpful information for designing and implementing the strategy for disambiguation. E-TRAN 2001 uses a general chart parser with a grammar formalism based on Generalized Phrase Structure Grammar [11]. PATI is automatically constructed using information extracted from candidate trees one of which is marked as a correct one with its constituent structure. PATI guides the hand-tuning of the initial grammar for the purpose of reducing ambiguities. The tuning could considerably save the human efforts in providing clues about the essential knowledge to be encoded into the rules. PATI is then used to calculate the rule preference scores that are based on the frequency information of the rules. The function is different from those in previous works in that all the candidate trees produced by the system, not only the best tree, are taken into account. Experimental results show that PATI is useful to develop large scale grammar and to identify various kinds of ambiguity types. It is also shown that the PATI keeps the accuracy of ambiguity resolution.

In Section 2, PATI is defined with some preliminary definitions. Grammar tuning process is described in Section 3. Rule preference function is explained in Section 4 with the overall scoring scheme for ambiguity resolution. Experimental results are shown in Section 5 and Section 6 concludes the paper and gives some future works.

2   Definition of PATI

We start by preliminary definitions for comparing candidate trees of a sentence.

Definition 1. Let t_1, t_2, ..., t_n be n candidate trees produced by analyzing a sentence s, R_k be a set of rules applied for building $t_k(1 \leq k \leq n)$ and $t_c(1 \leq c \leq n)$ be the correctly parsed tree. *Rule set difference D_i^c* is defined as $D_i^c = (R_c - R_i)$ and *priority pair P_i^c* is defined as $P_i^c = (D_c^i, D_i^c)$, where $c \neq i$, and $1 \leq i \leq n$. Finally *priority pair set* of s, $PS(s)$, is defined as the set of $n-1$ priority pairs and *difference set* $DS(s)$ as the set of $2(n-1)$ rule set differences.

Definition 2. Suppose we analyze a corpus $\mathcal{C}$ using a rule set $\mathcal{R}$. *Priority relation graph* is a directed, weighted graph $G = (V, E)$, where $V = \bigcup_{s \in \mathcal{C}} DS(s)$, $E = \bigcup_{s \in \mathcal{C}} PS(s)$, and the weight w of an edge is the frequency that the edge appears in the analysis of $\mathcal{C}$.

Though a priority relation graph can represent types of ambiguity, it includes some redundant information. In Fig. 1, four priority pairs from (a) to (d) result from the analysis of the sentences from (1) to (4). The difference sets of priority pairs in (a) ~ (c) also appear in (d). The priority pair (d) can be regarded as the combination of the three priority pairs (a) ~ (c). To get a more compact representation of ambiguity types, it is desirable to remove edges and vertices like (d). For this, we give some more definitions.

(1) I know that you are happy.
(2) He sees sleeping babies.
(3) I ate a fish with bones.
(4) They know that it contains operating systems for their PC.

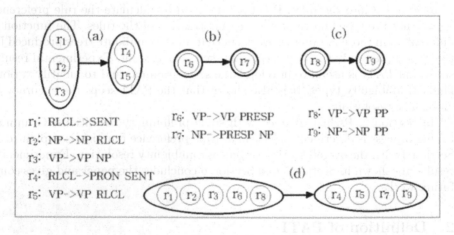

Fig. 1. Examples of priority pairs

Definition 3. Let $e_i = (v_1^i, v_2^i)$, $e_j = (v_1^j, v_2^j)$ are two distinct edges of a priority relation graph. If $v_1^i \subseteq v_1^j$ and $v_2^i \subseteq v_2^j$, then e_i is defined to *subsume* e_j and we denote this as $e_i \sqsupseteq e_j$.

Definition 4. For an edge $e = (v_1, v_2) \in E$, if there is no $e' \in E$ such that $e' \sqsupseteq e$, then e is a *minimal edge* and v_1, v_2 are *minimal vertices*.

Finally, the definition of PATI is as follows.

Definition 5. Given a priority relation graph $G = (V, E)$, PATI is $\hat{G} = (\hat{V}, \hat{E})$, where

$$\hat{V} = \{v | v \in V \text{ and } v \text{ is a minimal vertex}\},$$

$$\hat{E} = \{e | e \in E \text{ and } e \text{ is a minimal edge}\},$$

$$\hat{w}(e) = w(e) + \sum_{e' \sqsubseteq e, e' \in E} w(e'),$$

and *ambiguity type* is a pair of vertices connected with at least one edge.

3   Grammar Tuning

The appropriateness of linguistic knowledge encoded into grammar rules is a major factor affecting performance of the rule-based approach for ambiguity resolution. But it is quite difficult to determine what is the essential knowledge to be encoded for a grammar under development. Frequency information of PATI provides efficient methods for refining grammar rules. We present two representative methods, *constraint strengthening* and *rule splitting*.

The purpose of constraint strengthening is to reduce the occurrences of ungrammatical candidate trees. Consider the following example.

[**sent** [**pp** Out of the subjects she is taking at] [**sent** [**np** school], [**sent** two are required and three are elective].]

This analysis can be produced by the rule $SENT^1 \rightarrow NP^2 \, PUNC^3 \, SENT$ and $SENT \rightarrow PP^4 \, SENT$. The former rule is for analyzing sentences that contain vocatives. Putting a constraint to the latter rule, the rule is modified as $SENT \rightarrow NP \, PUNC \, SENT[-VOCAT]$ and the above ungrammatical analysis can be prevented. We automatically collect such candidates using *frequency ratio of two vertices*, FR, which is defined as:

$$FR(v_i, v_j) = \begin{cases} \frac{min(\hat{w}(v_j, v_i), \hat{w}(v_i, v_j))}{max(\hat{w}(v_j, v_i), \hat{w}(v_i, v_j))} & \text{if } (v_j, v_i) \in \hat{E} \text{ and } (v_i, v_j) \in \hat{E}, \\ 0 & \text{otherwise.} \end{cases}$$

We extract ambiguity types with FR value of 0 and investigate the sentences related with those types.

---

[1] SENT is a non-terminal symbol representing a sentence.
[2] NP is a non-terminal symbol representing a noun phrase.
[3] PUNC is a non-terminal symbol representing a punctuation mark.
[4] PP is a non-terminal symbol representing a prepositional phrase.

If FR of two vertices is not 0, there exist two edges between the two vertices. FR near to 1 implies that the corresponding ambiguity type cannot be effectively resolved by any kinds of syntactic preference functions. For example, prepositional phrase attachment problem is represented by the following two vertices, in view of PATI.

$$v_1 = \{NP \to NP\,PP\}$$

$$v_2 = \{VP^5 \to VP\,PP\}.$$

Intuitively we can guess that $FR(v_1, v_2)$ may be near to 1 and that other kinds of preference functions such as lexical collocation functions are needed to resolve this ambiguity type. In the rest of this paper, we refer this kind of ambiguity type as *high FR (HFR) type*. Contrarily FR value near 0 means that syntactic information can play an important role in resolving that ambiguity type. Rule preference functions may be very effective for disambiguation in this case. Constraint strengthening is a more active method in the sense that it can prevent ungrammatical trees from being produced.

Rule splitting can make grammar rules more suitable for efficient ambiguity resolution by reducing the overall portion of HFR types in $PATI$. As explained above, if HFR types are reduced, syntactic preference function can works better in integration with other kinds of preference functions. Let's consider again the PP attachment problem mentioned above. The rule in v_2 attaches PP to VP[6]. By adding subcategorization information of the predicate of VP into the constraints of the rule, we can expect HR decreases for ambiguity types related with PP attachment. More generally, for a current rule (a) shown below, a new constraint c_{i+1} is considered in addition for splitting and the resulted rule (b) and (c) will have c_{i+1} and $\neg c_{i+1}$ respectively as their new constraints. Ambiguity types with HR which is greater than a certain threshold can be extracted from PATI and rule splitting is considered.

(a) $r_0[c_0, c_1, \ldots, c_i]$
(b) $r_1[c_0, c_1, \ldots, c_i, c_{i+1}]$
(c) $r_2[c_0, c_1, \ldots, c_i, \neg c_{i+1}]$

4   Rule Preference Function and Overall Scoring Scheme

In large scale rule based analysis systems, it is general to choose various kinds of preference functions and combine them to produce a score for selecting the best parsed candidate tree. Some functions are based on lexical or semantic collocations, and others are based on syntactic information.

In this paper, we focus on the latter though we also have functions based on lexical probabilities or collocations. Syntactic preference functions may simply

---

[5] VP is a non-terminal symbol representing a verbal phrase.
[6] Here the current content of constraints on the non-terminals is not presented for simplicity.

count particular constructs such as adjunct and attachment, or estimate probabilities of rules. Assuming that various aspects of syntactic structures are already reflected in PATI, this paper adopts a syntactic preference function that is only based on the rule preference function, $RP(r)$, defined as follows:

$$RP(r) = \log f_h(r) - \log f_l(r),$$

$$f_h(r) = \sum_{r \in v_i,\, (v_j, v_i) \in \hat{E}} \hat{w}((v_j, v_i)),$$

$$f_l(r) = \sum_{r \in v_i,\, (v_i, v_j) \in \hat{E}} \hat{w}((v_i, v_j)),$$

where r is a rule, $f_h(r)$ is the sum of weights of incoming edges into the vertices containing r, and $f_h(r)$ is the sum of weights of outgoing edges.

The syntactic preference function is defined as follows:

$$SP(t) = \sum_{r \in PR(t)} RP(r),$$

where t is a candidate tree and $PR(t)$ is a set of rules participating in building the tree. The syntactic preference function is combined with other preference functions to produce evaluating scores for candidate trees. We use a lexical preference function that is based on part-of-speech probabilities and a semantic collocation function [12][13]. All the preference functions are combined by the method proposed in [10].

5   Experiments

In this section, we present two types of experimental results. One supports the usefulness of PATI for grammar development in large scale rule based natural language analysis system. The other shows that PATI could increase the accuracy of ambiguity resolution.

Table 1. Corpus for constructing PATI

Sentence Length	Area-1	Area-2	Area-3	Total
1 ~ 10	542	411	340	1,293
11 ~ 20	410	457	417	1,284
21 ~ 30	248	282	393	923
Total	1,200	1,150	1,150	3,500

Area-1: High School English Textbook.
Area-2: IBM Manual 'SQL/DS Concepts and Facilities'.
Area-3: USA Today.

We developed a general purpose parser implemented by C language in a Unix machine. The overall success rate[7] of the parse was 97.1%. For broad coverage of the analysis, initial grammar rules were constructed with minimal constraints. PATI was constructed from the information extracted from the initial grammar and a corpus in Table 1.

Table 2 shows the statistics of the initial PATI. In the table, "Sum of Frequencies" represents the sum of weights of edges corresponding to an ambiguity type. The *ambiguity complexity (AC)* represents the amount of ambiguity in sentence analysis and is defined as follows:

$$AC = \frac{\text{sum of frequencies in a corpus}}{\text{\# of sentences in a corpus}}.$$

Table 2. Statistics of ambiguity types from the initial grammar

Area	$FR \leq 0.2$		$FR > 0.2$		Total		AC
	Number of Types	Sum of Frequencies	Number of Types	Sum of Frequencies	Number of Types	Sum of Frequencies	
Area-1	38	4,203	95	11,820	133	16,023	13.35
Area-2	43	4,808	90	13,028	133	17,836	15.51
Area-3	41	5,560	88	15,893	133	21,453	18.65

Using an initial PATI, grammar is tuned in a way described in Section 3. A new PATI is constructed by constraint strengthening and rule splitting. The statistics of the PATI is given in Table 3.

Table 3. Statistics of ambiguity types from the tuned grammar

Sentence Area	$FR \leq 0.2$		$FR > 0.2$		Total		AC
	Number of Types	Sum of Frequencies	Number of Types	Sum of Frequencies	Number of Types	Sum of Frequencies	
Area-1	114	3,478	177	5,745	291	9,223	7.69
Area-2	108	3,810	173	6,317	291	10,127	8.81
Area-3	119	4,011	172	7,091	291	11,102	9.65

The increase of the number of ambiguity types is due to that of the number of rules by rule splitting process. But the ratio of ambiguity types with FR values under 0.2 becomes larger. This implies that more portion of an entire ambiguity types could be effectively resolved by syntactic preference function. The table also shows that sum of frequencies in a corpus decreases though the number of ambiguity types increases. This is important because it contributes to reducing the amount of ambiguity.

---

[7] The success rate is defined as the ratio of the number of correctly parsed sentences and the number of total sentences.

Test corpus is also constructed using sentences from three areas used in constructing PATI. Table 4 shows the statistics of the test corpus.

Table 4. Test corpus

Sentence Length	Area-1	Area-2	Area-3	Total
1 ~ 10	134	120	148	402
11 ~ 20	181	185	245	611
21 ~ 30	180	194	213	487

Table 5 shows the accuracy of ambiguity resolution using overall scoring scheme in Section 4. In the comparison of the performance of ambiguity resolution of rule probability (*Rule Prob.*) with that of syntactic preference function (*SP*) based on PATI, the latter shows better performance. The rule probability is the number of occurrences of a rule leading to correct parse trees divided by the number of occurrences of all rules leading to the same trees. The occurrences are counted only from the correct candidate trees. On the contrary, PATI contains information from all the candidate trees. This may give rise to better performance of *SP*.

Table 5. Performance comparison of preference functions

Sentence Length	Number of Sentences	Average Number of Candidates	Accuracy (%) Rule Prob.	SP	Combine
1 ~ 10	402	3.71	52.42	86.72	92.25
11 ~ 20	611	5.33	33.70	74.50	89.68
21 ~ 30	487	8.02	19.81	59.94	82.83
Total	1,500	5.77	34.21	73.05	88.14

6 Conclusion

We proposed PATI as an efficient way of developing grammar rules for large scale application and providing a syntactic preference function for ambiguity resolution. An initial PATI was constructed from an initial grammar and a parsed corpus. The grammar was enhanced with the help of the PATI and a new PATI was again constructed to get a syntactic preference function. The PATI contains information about more ambiguity types with reducing ambiguity complexity of the analysis. We could achieve a very high accuracy of ambiguity resolution for an open domain test corpus. We also verified that the syntactic preference function based on the PATI contributes significantly to this problem.

All kinds of ambiguous situations, not only the well known cases, such as PP attachment problem, but also the cases that have never been treated with formal linguistic description could be identified by PATI. Furthermore, PATI could be obtained directly from a comparatively small parsed corpus and at a low cost of human effort.

As the future work, we present two kinds of studies. We will develop tools supporting grammar tuning to reduce human effort. Machine learning techniques will be adopted for more effective integration of the syntactic preference function with other kinds preference functions. This is expected to improve the accuracy of ambiguity resolution.

Acknowledgement. This research was financially supported by Hansung University in the year of 2001.

References

1. http://www.easytran.com.
2. Baker, K.L., Franz, A.M., Jordan,P.W.: Coping with Ambiguity in a Large-Scale Machine Translation System. Proceedings of COLING-94 (1994)
3. Oepen, S., Carroll, J.: Ambiguity Packing in Constraint-based Parsing – Practical Results. Proceedings of the 1st Conference of the North American Chapter of the Association for Computational Linguistics (NAACL'00), Seattle, WA (2000)
4. Lavie, A., Rose, C.: Optimal ambiguity packing in context-free parsers with interleaved unification. Proceedings of the 6th International Workshop on Parsing Technologies, Trento, Italy (2000) 147–158
5. Fass, D., Wilks, Y.: Preference Semantics, Ill-Formedness, and Metaphor. American Journal of Computational Linguistics, vol.9(3-4) (1983) 178–187
6. Wang, J.: Syntactic Preferences for Robust Parsing with Semantic Preferences. Proceedings of COLING-92, Nantes (1992) 239–245
7. Kimball, J.: Seven Principles of Surface Structure Parsing in Natural Language. Cognition, vol. 2 (1973) 15–47
8. Dyer, M.G.: Symbolic NeuroEngineering and natural language processing: a multi-level research approach. Advances in Connectionist and Neural Computation Theory, Vol. 1, Ablex Publishing Corp., Norwood, N.J. (1991) 32–68
9. Waltz, D.L., Pollack, J.B.: Massive Parallel Parsing: A Strongly Interactive Model of Natural Language Interpretation. Cognitive Science, Vol. 9 (1985) 51–74
10. Alshawi, H., Carter, D.: Training and Scaling Preference Functions for Disambiguation. Computational Linguistics, 20(4) (1994) 635–648
11. Gazdar, G., Klein, E., Pullum, G., Sag, I.: Generalized Phrase Structure Grammar, Blackwell (1985)
12. Shim, K.S.: Structural Disambiguation of to-infinitives using Augmented Collocations. Ph.D. thesis, Department of Computer Engineering, Seoul National University (1994)
13. Chun, S.J.: A Study on Prepositional Phrase Attachment and the Transfer of the Preposition using Semantic Hierarchy. Master thesis, Department of Computer Engineering, Seoul National University (1994)

Extracting User Profiles from E-mails Using the Set-Oriented Classifier

Sebon Ku[1], Bogju Lee[2], and Eunyong Ha[3]

[1]School of Engineering, Information and Communications University (ICU), Korea
prodo@icu.ac.kr
[2] Dept. of Computer Engineering, Dankook University, Korea
blee@dankook.ac.kr
[3] Dept. of Computer Science, Anyang University, Korea
eyha@aycc.anyang.ac.kr

Abstract. More and more people rely on e-mails rather than postal letters to communicate to each other. Although e-mails are more convenient, letters still have many positive features. The ability to handle "anonymous recipient" is one of them. This paper proposes a software agent that performs the routing task as human beings for the anonymous recipient e-mails. The software agent named "TWIMC (To Whom It May Concern)" receives anonymous recipient e-mails, analyze it, and then routes the e-mail to the mostly qualified person (i.e., e-mail account) inside the organization. The agent employs the Set-oriented Classifier System (SCS) that is a genetic algorithm classifier that uses set representation internally. The comparison of SCS with the Support Vector Machine (SVM) shows that the SCS outperforms SVM under noisy environment.

1 Introduction

As the Internet and computers become commodities in our daily lives, electronic communications such as e-mails are rapidly substituting traditional postal mails. Compared with e-mails, however, postal mails still have many positive features. Among them is an ability to handle "anonymous recipients". People used to send anonymous recipients a letter by designating "To Whom It May Concern" inside the letters. For example, a secretary receives a letter and reads its content and routes to a qualified person. Of course, the secretary should know well of the member's personal interest, job function, and business role in her/his organization. If an organization provides a special and universally accepted e-mail account such as "TWIMC (To Whom It May Concern)" (e.g., twimc@acompany.com), people will be able to send e-mails to anonymous recipients as in postal mails. Another example is the handling of a representative e-mail account in the call centers. Customers' queries and orders are usually sent to a representative e-mail account (e.g., info@acompany.com). The company has to spend considerable effort to find proper persons and route the received mails. We call this an "automatic e-mail routing (AER)" problem. The AER problem can be defined as follows.

M. Ishizuka and A. Sattar (Eds.): PRICAI 2002, LNAI 2417, pp. 463-471, 2002.

X: a set of e-mail instances

x: an e-mail instance, $x \in X$

e: an instance of e-mail account (including an anonymous account)

C_e: the target concept for e, that is, $C_e: X \rightarrow \{0, 1\}$

D: the positive and negative training data for the target concept

$D = \{<x, C(x)>\}$

H: the hypothesis of an approximated target concept by using D

The goal of the AER problem: Find $H_e(X) = C_e(X)$ for all e

In this paper, we propose an autonomous software agent that performs the routing task. We name the software agent "TWIMC", that is, "To Whom It May Concern". The TWIMC receives an anonymous recipient e-mail, analyzes it, and then routes it to the most qualified person (i.e., e-mail account) inside the organization. The AER also has the characteristics similar to the automatic text categorization (ATC) problem. However, AER also has a different characteristic with ATC, due to a large amount of noise. We propose a novel algorithm that generates a robust and efficient classifier, named Set-oriented Classifier System (SCS). It uses set representation for the chromosome in the genetic algorithm-based classifier. We also use a new fitness evaluation technique, which drastically decreases the computation time of fitness function evaluation. We evaluate the accuracy and robustness of the SCS with the real e-mail data and compare the performance with that of the Support Vector Machine (SVM). The result shows that the SCS outperforms SVM under noisy environment. Without noise data, recall of SCS is higher than SVM by 2.1%, however, with noise data, the difference of recall becomes up to 12%. This experiment shows that TWIMC could be used in the real situation.

The rest of the paper is organized as follows. We present related work in Section 2. The SCS is explained in Section 3. The section 4 presents the evaluation of the SCS including the comparison with the SVM. Finally, the conclusion follows in Section 5.

2 Related Works

Some companies like Calypso Message Center (http://www.calypsomessagecenter.com) and White Pajama (http://www.whitepajama.com) have tried to handle the AER problem in their call center systems. The system integrates the solution that uses routing rules based on keywords. This approach, however, has a significant defect in that defining and maintaining the rules is a cumbersome work.

The automatic text categorization (ATC) is a problem of assigning category labels to new documents based on the likelihood suggested by a training set of labeled documents [15]. This problem is very similar to the AER problem: both use text data, and training data are well provided. Many algorithms have been proposed or adopted to solve the ATC problem. Examples include Naïve Bayes [2, 6], Decision Tree [4], Neural-Network [3], RIPPER [13], and k-Nearest Neighbor algorithms [1, 14]. The Support Vector Machine (SVM) is one of these algorithms that showed high performance [8, 11]

Some Artificial Intelligence researchers proposed genetic algorithms (GA) to solve the problems. The Learning Classifier Systems (LCS), a GA-based classifier system, is used in many problem domains like pattern classification and reinforcement learning [10, 12]. LCS has various representation schemes like if-then rules, fuzzy logic rules, or tree structures [5, 7].

3 SCS (Set-Oriented Classifier System)

Before explaining the SCS, we should mention the Set-Oriented Genetic Algorithm (SGA), our earlier work [16]. The SGA uses set-oriented variable length chromosome. The crossover and mutation were denoted by the combination of set operations like union and intersection. The approaches used in the SGA crossover operators are: (i) Mix the genes of parents (ii) The lengths of children could be shorter or longer than those of parents. First all of the genes from the two parents are mixed, and then divided and distributed to the two children randomly. Then the duplicated genes are removed from the resulting children. Suppose A and B are the two sets representing the parents. Also let A' and B' be the resultant sets representing the two children. If $A+B$ represents a union set of the sets A and B that allows the duplicated elements, the children sets A' and B' are represented by

$$A' = C \text{ where } C \subset (A + B)$$
$$B' = (A + B) - C$$

For example, suppose the parents are denoted by two sets $\{1, 2, 3, 5, 8, 10\}$ and $\{3, 5, 11, 14, 17\}$. Then A+B is $\{1, 2, 3, 5, 8, 10, 3, 5, 11, 14, 17\}$. The resulting children could be $\{2, 3, 5, 10, 11\}$ and $\{1, 5, 8, 14, 17\}$.

The "gene-flipping" mutation operation in the canonical GA is done in a different way in SGA. A gene to be mutated is changed by other randomly chosen element. In other words, if A' is a resultant set that is mutated from A, then $A' = A - \{a\} \cup \{b\}$ where $a \in A$ and $b \in U$. U is the set of all elements in the problem. Note that multiple mutations might take place in a chromosome. We have showed that the proposed algorithm is efficient and fast in solving the knapsack problem [16].

Many researchers have pointed out that the one of the positive characteristics of genetic algorithms is the robustness to noisy data and huge hypothesis space. The SCS is a novel genetic algorithm classifier system that uses set-oriented chromosome representation and fast fitness evaluation scheme. Our motivation is to exploit the robustness of GA in noisy data environment like the AER. An individual in the SCS is basically a rule and it is represented by a set-oriented chromosome. After the SCS terminates, the population contains a certain number of useful rules. A rule in the system has the form: *if the document contains all the words in the include-set A and does not contains any of the words in the exclude-set B then the document is classified as the category C.* The set-oriented chromosome is denoted $<A, B>$. Note that the category C is not encoded in the chromosome. The dominant class that is explained later is used as the category C. For example, an individual with $<\{3,4\}, \{6,9,10\}>$ represents the rule that *if the document contains the words 3 and 4 and does not contain any of the words 6, 9, or 10, the document is classified as some category C.* The stochastic universal sampling selection with elitist model is used as the selection scheme. Crossover operator of the SCS is similar with that of SGA. Firstly, all of the genes from the two parents are mixed, and then divided and distributed to the two children randomly. The duplicated genes are removed from the resulting children. Only difference is that the chromosomes of the SCS have two sets. Therefore, we need to deal with these two sets separately. When parents are chosen randomly, either include-set or exclude-set is chosen and crossover occurs. Mutation operator is also same with SGA. A gene to be mutated is changed by another randomly chosen attributes. However, a biased mutation operator is used in which the mutation is more likely to occur in the exclude-set.

3.1 The Algorithm

The outline of the SCS is as follows. It consists of two loops: inner and outer loops.

```
 1. Initialize rule set
 2. Repeat
 3.      Initialize population
 4.      Evaluation
 5.      Repeat
 6.          Selection
 7.          Crossover
 8.          Mutation
 9.          Evaluation
10.          Extract rules
11.      Until GA termination condition
12. Until enough rules are found
```

3.2 Fitness Function

In SCS, the two word sets in each individual define a covered subset of the training data. The covered subset consists of similar documents that share certain property. Of course, training data in the same covered subset can belong to different classes. We use two factors in designing the fitness function. One is the size of covered set and the other is variety of classes in the set. Desired rules that we want to find are the ones that have high coverage and high monotony. The higher the coverage of a rule, the larger the training data is in the covered set. The higher the monotony, the less is the number of distinct classes in the covered set. The coverage can be easily calculated by counting the size of covered set. We calculate the degree of monotony as follows. Basically the entropy is employed as the measure of monotony. The entropy of a covered set s of training data is defined by the formula below.

s = a covered set explained by an individual

Ns = the size of set s

Ni = the number of documents, which belong to class i in the set s

DCs = the dominant class of set s, i.e., the class that has maximum training data

Mi = the number of found rules in the previous iteration, which belong to class i

$$Entropy\ (s) = \sum_{i=1}^{c} - \frac{Ni}{Ns} \log_2 \frac{Ni}{Ns}$$

$$Fitness(s) = Ns * (1 - Entropy(s)) / (1 + Mi)$$

Each set s has a dominant class, which is the class of the largest subset that is composed of the same class in set s. For example, suppose a covered set s is composed of documents {3, 4, 8, 19}. The class of documents 3, 4, and 8 is 1, and the class of documents 19 is 2. In this case, dominant class of set s is 1. If we find a rule with a dominant class i, this rule is regarded as a classifier that predicts whether a new instance belongs to class i or not. On the other hand, from the class point of view, each class has a number of individuals. Here, Mi denotes the number of individuals that belongs to class i. The denominator term in the fitness function formula is added for the fitness sharing. Without this term, most of the found rules would be from only a few classes, which occupy a large portion of the training data.

4 Experiments and Results

For the experiment, we utilized real e-mail data. Our assumption on the data set is that there is a small portion of useful e-mails to help find an adequate business role of an e-mail user. This reflects the real situation better than assuming large volumes of pure significant e-mails.

Table 1. E-mail corpus that is used in the experiment

E-mail Address	Test	Train	Noise 1	Noise 2	Noise 3	Noise 4	Noise sum
Address1	35	70	68	69	64	52	253
Address2	50	104	98	90	93	89	370
Address3	55	112	95	98	97	88	378
Address4	30	60	58	52	59	57	226
Address5	7	14	14	14	14	14	56
Address6	3	7	7	7	7	6	27
Address7	6	14	14	14	12	14	54
Address8	7	14	13	14	14	8	49
Address9	4	8	8	8	8	8	32
Address10	11	23	18	19	20	18	75
Sum	208	426	393	385	388	354	1520

From each collected e-mail account, we choose 3~20 e-mails as the test data. Then the training data are chosen as twice as test data. We started from 208 test data and 426 training data (leftmost two columns). The training data at this stage are all significant e-mails. Then we added the noisy data from 393 up to 1520. The noise data sets could be junk e-mails, personal e-mails, or news mail, which do not reflect the unique business role of the user. Therefore, the noise e-mails are not helpful to build a model for the user. The intention the experiment is to reveal how robust the SVM and the SCS are with noisy data. We also vary the size of the test and training data between classes: among the ten classes four have relatively large data and the other six classes have small data. The figure 1 below shows the entropy of total corpus. As expected, the entropy of corpus to increase as the noisy data increase. At the beginning, total entropy of corpus was about 0.3, but the entropy increased up to 0.6 at the end. The final training data included four times noisy data of original training data. The higher the entropy, the harder to find accurate rules. From the figure below, we can conclude that the noise of corpus is increased as the noise data are added.

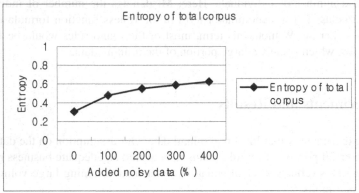

Fig. 1. The entropy of used corpus

The configuration of SCS running parameters was as follows. The inner loop iteration was limited to 70. The outer loop iteration was limited to 400. Population size was 100. The figure 2 shows the result of the address 1 only. The x-axis represents the size of training data that includes noise. The y-axis represents the micro-averaging recall on the test data set. The graph shows the decreasing of accuracy as noise data are added. When there are no noisy data, the recall of SCS is 100% and SVM is about 95%. The training data at this phase are all significant e-mails. In this experiment, we purposely limited the size of training data relatively small. Under these conditions, SCS outperforms SVM in every experiment.

Fig. 3 shows the performance result of SVM and SCS in average. The x-axis represents the size of training data and y-axis represents the micro-averaging recall on the test data set. As expected, the accuracy is decreased as noise data are added. When there is no noise, SCS performs a little bit (2.1%) better than the SVM. As we add noise data, the SCS starts to outperform the SVM. The decrease rate of accuracy of

SCS is smaller than that of SVM. When we have maximum noise data, difference was 12%. This supports our assumption that SCS is robust to noisy data.

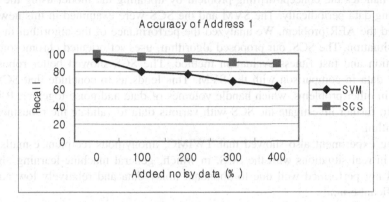

Fig. 2. The result of recall comparison between SVM and SCS on the address 1

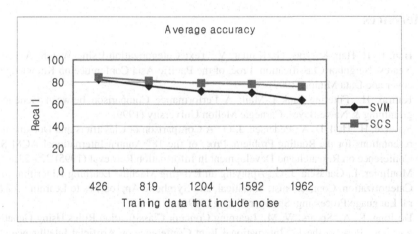

Fig. 3. The result of accuracy comparison between SVM and SCS

5 Conclusion

We propose a new method that automatically routes e-mails to the best-qualified recipient by using a machine-learning algorithm. This has potential applications areas in anonymous recipient e-mails and e-mail call centers. In this method, everyday (incoming) e-mail collections are used as training data to "learn" the business role of each e-mail account. In fact, e-mails are a very valuable resource in which the business roles and job functionality can be extracted. From the machine learning point of view, each e-mail address is one class. This differs from previous work regarding e-mail mining, which applied text categorization techniques to filter out spam mails or automatically organize personal e-mail directories. The new method also automatically handles the concept-drifting problem by updating the model using the "recent" training data periodically. The SVM and the SCS were examined in this new domain named the AER problem. We analyzed the performance of the algorithm in virtually real situation. The SCS, our proposed algorithm, uses set-oriented chromosome representation and fast fitness evaluation method. The SCS showed better robustness to noisy data in comparison with the SVM. This leads us to conclude that SCS can be used in other problems, which handle volumes of data and noise together. It is necessary to further investigate the SCS with various data to validate the robustness of the algorithm.

The experiment also showed that TWIMC, anonymous recipient e-mails, can be used in real situations with the SCS, in which, general machine-learning algorithms could not performed well due to abundant noisy data and relatively low number of significant e-mails.

References

1. Han, E.-H. Han, Karypis, G., Kumar, V.: Text Categorization Using Weight Adjusted k-Nearest Neighbor Classification. Proc. of the Pacific-Asia Conference on Knowledge Discover and Data Mining (1999)
2. Katirai, H.: Filtering Junk E-Mail: A Performance Comparison between Genetic Programming & Naïve Bayes. Carnegie Mellon University (1999)
3. Schutze, H., Hull, D. A., Pedersen, J. O.: A Comparison of Classifiers and Document Representations for the Routing Problem. Proc. of the 18th Annual International ACM SIGIR Conference on Research and Development in Information Retrieval (1995) 229-237
4. Moulinier, I., Ganascia, J.-G.: Applying an Existing Machine Learning Algorithm to Text Categorization. Connectionist, Statistical, and Symbolic Approaches to Learning for Natural Language Processing, Springer-Verlag (1996)
5. De Jong, K. A., Spears, W. M.: Learning Concept Classification Rules Using Genetic Algorithms. Proc. of the 12th International Joint Conference on Artificial Intelligence (1991) 651-656
6. Grobelnik, M., Mladenic, D.: Efficient text categorization. Proc. of the 10th European Conference on Machine Learning Workshop on Text Mining (1998)
7. Rendon, M. V.: Reinforcement Learning in the Fuzzy Classifier System. Proc. 1st International Conference on Learning Classifier Systems (1992)
8. Cristianini, N., Shawe-Taylor, J.: An Introduction to Support Vector Machines and Other Kernel-Based Learning Methods, Cambridge University Press (2000)
9. Klinkerberg, R., Joachims, T.: Detecting Concept Drift with Support Vector Machines. Proc. of the 17th International Conference on Machine Learning (2000)
10. Saxon, S., Barry, A.: XCS and the Monk's Problems. Proc. of the 2nd International Workshop on Learning Classifier Systems (1999)
11. Joachims, T.: Text Categorization with Support Vector Machines - Learning with Many Relevant Features. Proc. of the European Conference on Machine Learning (1998) 137-142,
12. Mitchell, T. M.: Machine Learning, McGraw-Hill T. M. (1997)

13. Cohen, W. W.: Learning Rules that Classify E-Mail. Proc. of the AAAI Spring Symposium on Machine Learning and Information Access (1996)
14. Yang, Y.: An Evaluation of Statistical Approaches to Text Categorization. Journal of Information Retrieval, Vol. 1 (1999) 67-88
15. Yang, Y., Liu, X.: A Re-examination of Text Categorization Methods. Proc. of the ACM SIGIR Conference on Research and Development in Information Retrieval (1999)
16. Ku, S., Lee, B.: A Set-Oriented Genetic Algorithm and the Knapsack Problem. Proc. of the Congress on Evolutionary Computation (2001)

Wrapper Generation by Using XML-Based Domain Knowledge for Intelligent Information Extraction

Jaeyoung Yang, Jungsun Kim, Kyoung-Goo Doh, and Joongmin Choi

Dept. of Computer Science and Engineering, Hanyang University
1271 Sa-1 Dong, Ansan-Si, Kyunggi-Do 425-791, Korea
{jyyang,jskim,doh,jmchoi}@cse.hanyang.ac.kr

Abstract. This paper discusses some of the issues in Web information extraction, focusing on automatic extraction methods that exploit wrapper induction. In particular, we point out the limitations of traditional heuristic-based wrapper generation systems, and as a solution, emphasize the importance of the domain knowledge in the process of wrapper generation.

We demonstrate the effectiveness of domain knowledge by presenting our scheme of knowledge-based wrapper generation for semi-structured and labeled documents. Our agent-oriented information extraction system, XTROS, represents both the domain knowledge and the wrappers by XML documents to increase modularity, flexibility, and interoperability. XTROS shows good performance on several Web sites in the domain of real estate, and it is expected to be easily adaptable to different domains by plugging in appropriate XML-based domain knowledge.

1 Introduction

Information extraction is the task of recognizing and extracting the specific fragments of a document that constitute its core semantic content[7]. As an example, Fig. 1 shows three *Home-for-Sale* Web pages and their possible extraction results. In general, the process of information extraction relies on a set of extraction rules, called *a wrapper*, tailored to a particular information source. A wrapper is a rule or a procedure that understands information provided by a specific source and translates it into a regular form that can be used to extract particular attribute values, or *features*. A wrapper is specialized to a single information source, and since a semi-structured Web source normally presents its contents to the browser in a uniform way, a single wrapper is enough for each Web site. However, different Web sources employ different formats of interface and output presentation, so we have to build a new wrapper for each different site. Obviously, the three sites introduced in Fig. 1 should employ different wrappers.

Depending on the automaticity of the wrapper generation process and the degree of the domain knowledge utilization, the techniques of wrapper generation can be classified into three categories: manual wrapper generation, heuristic wrapper induction, and knowledge-based wrapper induction.

M. Ishizuka and A. Sattar (Eds.): PRICAI 2002, LNAI 2417, pp. 472–481, 2002.

Fig. 1. Information extraction from three Web sites about *Home-for-Sale*

In the *manual wrapper generation* method, the extraction rules are written by humans through careful examinations on a herd of sample pages. ARANEUS[2] and TSIMMIS[5] are the example systems that adopt the manual approach. Despite its highly precise performance, this manual wrapper construction is not preferred for intelligent Web information management mainly because it is not scalable. Namely, the human developer must describe a new extraction rule for each different information source that is newly created or structurally changed. Also, the user is limited to obtain comparable information only from the known information sources.

To overcome these drawbacks, the concept of wrapper induction[6], that automatically builds a wrapper through learning from a set of resource's sample pages, has been suggested. This method uses the wrapper technology to extract specific information from heterogeneous information sources. Automatic wrapper induction can be based on either heuristics or domain knowledge. *Heuristic wrapper induction* has been adopted by most traditional systems such as ARIADNE[1], SHOPBOT[4], STALKER [9], WHISK[12], and MORPHEUS[13]. An example heuristic that has been very useful in most systems is that *a text fragment with a dollar sign followed by a number (e.g., $250) can be regarded as the price information*. Some of comparison shopping agents have shown reasonable performance even with only a few heuristics. However, this approach is not effective since the heuristics are mostly simple and naive. In Fig. 1, we may extract the price information using the heuristics only, but cannot extract the information about the number of bedrooms since the system has no idea about the meaning of **BR**, **Beds**, or **Bedrooms**. As a result, the systems can extract only a limited number of apparent features such as the price or the ISBN number.

Knowledge-based wrapper induction tries to solve these problems by defining and applying the domain knowledge during wrapper generation. Acquiring and representing the domain knowledge are done manually, but the wrapper generator uses this knowledge to build a more powerful wrapper automatically. The knowledge-based approach is expected to extract more features from the document than the heuristic approach. For example, we can extract the number of bedrooms in Fig. 1 by describing the meaning and the usage styles of BR, Beds, and Bedrooms in the domain knowledge for real estate.

This paper proposes a scheme of knowledge-based wrapper generation for semi-structured and labeled documents. The implementation of an agent-oriented information extraction system, XTROS, is described. XTROS automatically generates a wrapper for each information source and extracts the specific parts of information by applying this wrapper to the corresponding source. The wrapper generation algorithm recognizes the meaning of logical lines of a sample document by using the domain knowledge, and then finds the most frequent pattern from the sequence of logical lines. Eventually, the wrapper is constructed based on the position and the structure of this pattern.

In XTROS, both the domain knowledge and the wrappers are represented by XML documents. The XML representation increases modularity and flexibility by providing more formal ways of representing extraction rules, and facilitates simpler implementation by employing XML parsers and interpreters. Furthermore, the interoperability inherent in XML is fully exploited to make the XML-based wrapper portable and sharable among multiple parties in a distributed environment. XWRAP[8] also adopts an XML-based approach by building a hierarchical tree from an HTML document. In XWRAP, however, the user has to provide the meaning of tree components, and only those HTML documents which are hierarchically decomposable can be processed. In contrast, XTROS excludes user involvement during wrapper learning with the help of the domain knowledge, and is able to process any labeled HTML documents.

We demonstrate the effectiveness of this knowledge-based approach by adapting XTROS for use in learning extraction rules for a domain consisting of real estate pages sampled from the Web. XTROS is expected to be easily adaptable to different domains by simply plugging in new domain knowledge.

This paper is organized as follows. Section 2 specifies the kinds of documents XTROS can handle and presents the XML representation of the domain knowledge. Section 3 explains the wrapper generation algorithm. Section 4 describes the implementation and evaluates the system with some experimental results. Finally, Section 5 concludes with the summary and future direction.

2   Domain Knowledge

XTROS is designed to handle semi-structured documents, especially *labeled* documents[3]. A semi-structured document contains both structured and unstructured components. The unstructured part includes menus, headers, advertisements, or addresses, that should be ignored during the extraction process. The structured part typically consists of several item descriptions that are obtained from a database search, and thus all displayed in the same format. An example is a number of house descriptions displayed in a real estate site for a user query. In a labeled document, each portion of data that needs to be extracted is expressed by a *label-value* pair, where *label* denotes the meaning of its

```
<KNOWLEDGE>
  <OBJECTS>
    <OBJECT>PRICE</OBJECT>                    <BATH>
    <OBJECT>BED</OBJECT>                        <ONTOLOGY>
    <OBJECT>BATH</OBJECT>                         <TERM>BATHROOMS</TERM>
    <OBJECT>CITY</OBJECT>                         <TERM>BATHROOM</TERM>
    <OBJECT>MLS</OBJECT>                          <TERM>BATHS</TERM>
    <OBJECT>DETAIL</OBJECT>                       <TERM>BATH</TERM>
    <OBJECT>IMG</OBJECT>                          <TERM>BA</TERM>
  </OBJECTS>                                    </ONTOLOGY>
  <PRICE>                                       <FORMAT>
    <ONTOLOGY>                                    <FORM>DIGITS [ONTOLOGY]</FORM>
      <TERM>PRICE</TERM>                          <FORM>[ONTOLOGY] DIGITS</FORM>
      <TERM>$</TERM>                            </FORMAT>
    </ONTOLOGY>                                </BATH>
    <FORMAT>                                    <MLS>
      <FORM>[ONTOLOGY] DIGITS</FORM>            <ONTOLOGY>
      <FORM>DIGITS [ONTOLOGY]</FORM>              <TERM>MLS ID#</TERM>
    </FORMAT>                                     <TERM>MLS ID</TERM>
  </PRICE>                                       <TERM>MLS#</TERM>
  <BED>                                        </ONTOLOGY>
    <ONTOLOGY>                                  <FORMAT>
      <TERM>BEDROOMS</TERM>                       <FORM>[ONTOLOGY] DIGITS</FORM>
      <TERM>BEDROOM</TERM>                      </FORMAT>
      <TERM>BEDS</TERM>                       </MLS>
      <TERM>BED</TERM>                         <DETAIL>
      <TERM>BR</TERM>                            -- omiitted ----
      <TERM>BD</TERM>                          </DETAIL>
    </ONTOLOGY>                                 <IMG>
    <FORMAT>                                      -- omiitted ----
      <FORM>DIGITS [ONTOLOGY]</FORM>          </IMG>
      <FORM>[ONTOLOGY] DIGITS</FORM>        </KNOWLEDGE>
    </FORMAT>
  </BED>
```

Fig. 2. An XML-based domain knowledge for the real estate domain

value counterpart. In the domain of real estate, the description of each house contains a number of label-value pairs such as $3195000, 5BR, `Baths:3`, and so on. Here, `$`, `BR`, and `Baths` can be recognized as the labels that denote a dollar amount, the number of bedrooms, and the number of bathrooms, respectively, and 3195000, 5, and 3 are the values. Note that a label can appear before or after its value.

Domain knowledge usually describes terms, concepts, and relationships widely used for a particular application domain. It makes up for the weaknesses revealed in lexicon-oriented analysis[10,11], and plays a crucial role in recognizing the semantic fragments of a document in a given domain. This paper proposes an XML-based scheme for representing the domain knowledge, and an example is shown in Fig. 2 for the domain of real estate.

In our representation, the knowledge for a single domain is represented within the `<KNOWLEDGE>..</KNOWLEDGE>` structure. The `<KNOWLEDGE>` construct contains the `<OBJECTS>..</OBJECTS>` structure that lists the features (called *objects*) whose values are to be extracted. The objects for the real estate domain we have chosen include PRICE(the price of a house), BED(the number of bedrooms), BATH(the number of bathrooms), CITY(the address), MLS(Multiple

Listings Service number, specifying a unique ID number), DETAIL(a hyperlink to detailed information), and IMG(a picture of the house).

An XML construct is maintained for each object. For example, `<PRICE>` .. `</PRICE>` corresponds to the PRICE object, `<BED>` .. `</BED>` corresponds to the BED object, and so on. Each XML construct for an object consists of two elements, `<ONTOLOGY>` and `<FORMAT>`. `<ONTOLOGY>` lists the terms that are used to recognize the existence of an object. The PRICE object has `PRICE` and `$` as its `<ONTOLOGY>` terms so that a fragment can be recognized as PRICE if it contains the string `"PRICE"` or the symbol `$`. `<FORMAT>` describes the data type of the object value and the positional relationship between the ontological terms and the values. For example, the `<FORMAT>` of PRICE tells that its data type is the digit, and the price value can appear before or after the ontological term.

Domain knowledge is obtained manually by examining a number of test sites for the same domain. The `<ONTOLOGY>` of an object lists all possible labels gathered from the test pages as its `<TERM>` elements. For example, the `<ONTOLOGY>` of the `<BED>` construct includes both `BR` and `BEDS` so that it can recognize both sites shown in Fig. 1. Similarly, the `<FORMAT>` of an object lists all possible orderings as its `<FORM>` elements. Domain knowledge can be expanded easily by simply adding missing `<TERM>`s and `<FORM>`s in the XML representation. This flexibility makes it possible for this XML-based representation to be easily applicable to different domains.

3   Wrapper Generation

One key function of the wrapper generator for the real estate domain is to learn the format of house descriptions from successful search result pages. Our wrapper generation is divided into three phases, i.e., converting HTML sources into logical lines, determining the meaning of logical lines, and finding the most frequent pattern.

In the first phase, the HTML source of the search result page is broken down into a sequence of logical lines. A *logical line* is conceptually similar to a line that the user sees in the browser, and the learner identifies it by detecting some HTML delimiter tags such as `<br>`, `<p>`, `<li>`, `<td>`, and `<tr>`. All the HTML tags except `<a href=..>` and `<img src=..>` are considered unnecessary and hence removed.

The second phase of the algorithm is to determine the meaning of each logical line by checking the existence of any object in the domain knowledge. A given logical line is recognized as a certain object if it contains any `<TERM>` in its `<ONTOLOGY>` specification, and also conforms to any `<FORM>` in its `<FORMAT>` definition. When a logical line contains more than one object, the original line is divided into several subparts before applying this module.

Once its meaning is determined, each logical line is represented by a predefined data structure. This frame-like data structure has 5 slots: `object`, `line`, `cat`, `type`, and `format`. Here, `object` describes the meaning of the line, `line` contains the original line with the recognition marks for the ontology and the

Table 1. Resulting data structure from logical lines

No.	object	line	cat	type	format
1	IMG	`<A HREF="..">` `{[<IMG[{ALT=".."}]>]}`	6	IMGURL	[ONTOLOGY] IMGURL
2	PRICE	`{[[{$}]3195000]}`	0	DIGITS	[ONTOLOGY] DIGITS
3	BED	`{[5[{BR}]]}`	1	DIGITS	DIGITS [ONTOLOGY]
4	BATH	`{[5[{BA}]]}`	2	DIGITS	DIGITS [ONTOLOGY]
5	MLS	`{[[{MLS ID:#}]  P209731]}`	4	DIGITS	[ONTOLOGY] DIGITS
6	DETAIL	`{[<A HREF=".."> [{View` `Property}]]}`	5	URL	URL [ONTOLOGY]

format, `cat` is a category number assigned to the corresponding object, `type` is the data type of the object value, and `format` defines the positional relationship between the ontology and the value. For readability and faster pattern matching, each object is assigned a category number. In XTROS, 0 is assigned for PRICE, 1 for BED, 2 for BATH, 3 for CITY, 4 for MLS, 5 for DETAIL, 6 for IMG, and 9 for any general text which cannot be recognized as one of the above 7 cases. For example, the resulting data structure after analyzing the sequence of logical lines for the house description in Fig. 1(a) is shown in Table 1. Note that the resulting pattern string for this house is 601245 which is a sequence of the `cat` column values in the table.

After the categorization phase, the entire page can be expressed by a sequence of category numbers. The third phase of our algorithm finds the most frequent pattern in this sequence that proceeds as follows.

Step1 Find all candidate patterns(substrings). A candidate pattern should not contain duplicate attributes. Hence, 6012456 cannot be a candidate pattern since there are two 6s.

Step2 Obtain the frequency of a candidate pattern p, defined as F_p. This indicates how many times p occurs in the sequence.

Step3 Obtain the number of attributes in p, defined as NA_p.

Step4 Calculate the total frequency of attributes of p in the sequence, defined as TNA_p. Note that $TNA_p = NA_p \times F_p$.

Step5 Select the pattern p with the maximum TNA_p value.

Step6 If there are more than one pattern with the same maximum value, select the longer one.

For example, consider the following sequence that is obtained from a HOMES search result page containing 6 house descriptions. Note that each house description has the sequence of 601245, except for the third one whose sequence is 60125 because of missing MLS number.

$$601245 \ 601245 \ 60125 \ 601245 \ 601245 \ 601245$$

Eventually, 601245 is selected as the pattern for this site, since it has the maximum TNA value. This pattern implies that this site describes each house

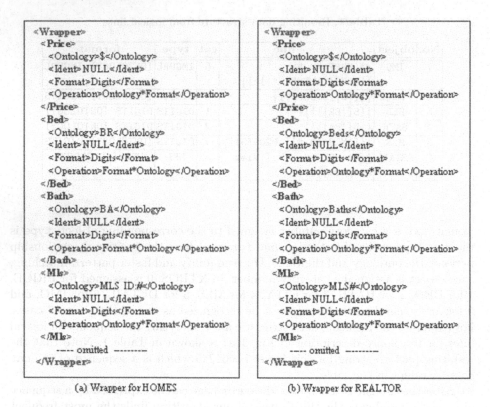

(a) Wrapper for HOMES   (b) Wrapper for REALTOR

Fig. 3. XML-based wrappers for two real estate site

by presenting the information in the order of a picture of the house, its price, the number of bedrooms, the number of bathrooms, the MLS ID number, and a hyperlink for the details. An XML-based wrapper is built based on the most frequent pattern. Fig. 3(a) shows the wrapper for the HOMES site shown earlier in Fig. 1(a).

A wrapper is represented by the `<Wrapper>` .. `</Wrapper>` structure that describes the pattern obtained from the previous pattern search module. Note that a single XML construct is built for each object found in the sample page. Each construct consists of `<Ontology>`, `<Ident>`, `<Format>`, and `<Operation>` elements. Here, `<Ontology>` specifies a term that is examined first to determine the existence of the object, `<Ident>` denotes a delimiter that discriminate one object from the other, `<Format>` specifies the data type of the value to be extracted, and `<Operation>` indicates whether the ontological term appears before or after the object value. For example, the `<Bed>` construct in Fig. 3(a) indicates that the interpreter must look for the token BR to get the number of bedrooms in a page of the HOMES site. Also, the `<Operation>` specification tells that the value occurs before the BR token. Note that this wrapper is applicable only to the HOMES site, so a different wrapper must be generated for a different

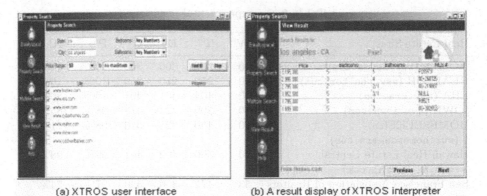

(a) XTROS user interface   (b) A result display of XTROS interpreter

Fig. 4. XTROS execution screen shots

site. For example, the wrapper for the REALTOR site shown in Fig. 1(b) must have `Beds` as the `<Ontology>` value of the `<Bed>` construct. The wrapper for the REALTOR site is shown in Fig. 3(b).

4   Implementation and Evaluation

The interface, the learner, and the interpreter of XTROS are all implemented in Java. Fig. 4 shows the user interface and a screen shot that displays the result of the XTROS interpreter. Currently, the interpreter extracts the price, the number of bedrooms, the number of bathrooms, and the MLS number.

For performance evaluation, XTROS was run on the collection of Web pages that are obtained from the search results for some test queries in the real estate domain. XTROS does not require many training instances for learning, so one or two Web pages are used for the wrapper induction.

We have done an extensive analysis by examining the precision and recall measures for 9 real estate sites. For each site, we collected approximately 50 Web pages, each of which contains 5 to 10 house descriptions. Table 2 shows the result of this experiment with the URLs of the sites that were tested. This table includes the data for the total number of items(i.e., house descriptions) that are tested(T), the number of items extracted(E), the number of items correctly extracted(C), the precision measure(P), and the recall measure(R). The precision is calculated by the formula $P = \frac{C}{E}$, and the recall is calculated by $R = \frac{E}{T}$.

As revealed in the table, XTROS worked perfectly for 4 sites including HOMES and REALTOR. The precision measures are almost perfect for all sites. However, it achieved low recall ratios for some sites, including 71% for HOME-SEEKERS. This resulted from the fact that the HOMESEEKERS site has two different styles of displaying the information about the number of bathrooms. For example, the value for the label `Baths` can be `6(full) 1(half)` whose format is quite different from the ordinary digit type. Other low-recall sites have

Table 2. An experimental result

Real Estate Sites	W[a]	T[b]	E[c]	C[d]	P[e]	R[f]
HOMES (www.homes.com)	50	300	300	300	100%	100%
REALTOR (www.realtor.com)	50	250	250	250	100%	100%
ERA (www.era.com)	50	464	401	401	100%	86%
IOWN (www.iown.com)	50	500	424	418	98%	85%
HOMESEEKERS (www.homeseekers.com)	50	450	321	316	98%	71%
Hawaii Real Estate Central (www.hicentral.com)	50	500	492	491	99%	98%
San Francisco Association of Realtors (www.sfrealtors.com)	53	472	350	340	97%	74%
San Antonio Board of Realtors (www.sahomesearch.com)	50	500	500	500	100%	100%
Northwest MLS (www.nwrealestate.com)	50	250	250	250	100%	100%

[a] no. of Web pages tested
[b] no. of items tested
[c] no. of items extracted by XTROS
[d] no. of items correctly extracted by XTROS
[e] precision measure (P = C/E)
[f] recall measure (R = E/T)

similar peculiarities. We are currently working on some of these difficulties, and other than that, we can claim that XTROS behaves very well for most of the semi-structured and labeled documents.

5   Conclusion

We have presented an intelligent Web information extraction system XTROS that represents the domain knowledge and the wrapper by XML documents, and automatically generates wrappers from semi-structured labeled documents. XTROS shows good performance on several Web sites in the domain of real estate, and it is expected to be adaptable to different domains with easy modification of the XML-based domain knowledge.

One of XTROS's current limitations is that it only works for the labeled documents, not functioning with non-labeled ones such as table-type descriptions. We need to work out for resolving this problem, and we are tackling it by investigating a method of building hierarchical trees for the table-type documents and recognize the meaning of table elements by referring their parent nodes. Eventually, we are aiming at building a customized wrapper learning agent that can be applied to a multi-domain environment.

References

1. Ambite, J., Ashish, N., Barish, G., Knoblock, C., Minton, S., Modi, P., Muslea, I., Philpot, A., Tejada, S.: ARIADNE: A system for constructing mediators for Internet sources. Proceedings of the ACM SIGMOD International Conference on Management of Data. (1998) 561–563
2. Atzeni, P., Mecca, G., Merialdo, P.: Semi-structured and structured data in the web: Going back and forth. Proceedings of the ACM SIGMOD Workshop on Management of Semi-structured Data. (1997) 1–9
3. Blum, A., Mitchell, T.: Combining labeled and unlabeled data with co-training. Proceedings of the Conference on Computational Learning Theory. (1998)
4. Doorenbos, R., Etzioni, O., Weld, D.: A scalable comparison-shopping agent for the world wide web. Proceedings of the First International Conference on Autonomous Agents. (1997) 39–48
5. Hammer, J., Garcia-Molina, H., Nestorov, S., Yerneni, R., Breunig, M., Vassalos, V.: Template-based wrappers in the TSIMMIS system. Proceedings of the ACM SIGMOD International Conference on Management of Data. (1997) 532–535
6. Kushmerick, N., Weld, D., Doorenbos, R.: Wrapper induction for information extraction. Proceedings of the International Joint Conference on Artificial Intelligence. (1997) 729–735
7. Kushmerick, N.: Gleaning the web. IEEE Intelligent Systems. **14** (1999) 20–22
8. Liu, L., Pu, C., Han, W.: XWRAP: An XML-based wrapper construction system for web information sources. Proceedings of the Sixteenth International Conference on Data Engineering. (2000)
9. Muslea, I., Minton, S., Knoblock, C.: A hierarchical approach to wrapper induction. Proceedings of the Third International Conference on Autonomous Agents. (1999) 190–197
10. Riloff, E.: Automatically constructing a dictionary for information extraction tasks. Proceedings of the Eleventh Annual Conference on Artificial Intelligence. (1993) 811–816
11. Soderland, S., Fisher, D., Aseltine, J., Lehnert, W.: CRYSTAL: Inducing a conceptual dictionary. Proceedings of the 15th International Conference on Artificial Intelligence. (1995) 1314–1321
12. Soderland, S.: Learning information extraction rules for semi-structured and free text. Machine Learning. **34** (1999) 233–272
13. Yang, J., Lee, E., Choi, J.: A shopping agent that automatically constructs wrappers for semi-structured online vendors. Lecture Notes in Computer Science. **1983** (2000) 368–373

Modified PrefixSpan Method for Motif Discovery in Sequence Databases

Hajime Kitakami[1], Tomoki Kanbara[1], Yasuma Mori[1],
Susumu Kuroki[1], and Yukiko Yamazaki[2]

[1] Hiroshima City University
3-4-1 Ozuka-Higashi, Asa-Minami-Ku,
Hiroshima 731-3194, JAPAN
{kitakami,mori,kuroki}@its.hiroshima-cu.ac.jp
[2] Center for Genetic Resource Information
National Institute of Genetics
1111 Yata, Mishima-Shi, Shizuoka-Ken 411, JAPAN
yyamazak@lab.nig.ac.jp

Abstract. We propose a motif discovery system that uses a modified PrefixSpan method to extract frequent patterns from an annotated sequence database that has such attributes as a sequence identifier (sequence-id), a sequence, and a set of items. The annotations are represented as the set of items in the database. Frequent sequence patterns and frequent item patterns are extracted from the annotated sequence database. Frequent sequence patterns are located in both identical and non-identical positions among those sequences. In general, the existing PrefixSpan method can extract a large number of identical patterns from the sequence databases. However, the method does not include a function to extract frequent patterns together with gaps or wild character symbols. This new method allows the incorporation of gap characters. Moreover, the method allows effective handling of the annotated sequence database that consists of a set of tuples including a sequence together with a set of items. Furthermore, the prototype has been applied to the evaluation of three sets of sequences that include the Zinc Finger, Cytochrome C, and Kringle motifs.

1 Introduction

Extracting frequent sequence patterns in a sequence database provides the answer to many problems and has many applications, such as the analysis of customer purchase behavior, Web access patterns, scientific experiments, disease treatments, natural disasters, and DNA or amino acid sequences [1,2,3,4]. An annotated sequence database is usually stored with a set of sequences together with their domain features. The annotations are represented as their domain features in the database. The domain features of each tuple in the database correspond to a set of items in the field of data mining.

We focus on a problem that mainly appears in the field of molecular biology. Molecular biologists generally consider that a motif represents a specific amino

M. Ishizuka and A. Sattar (Eds.): PRICAI 2002, LNAI 2417, pp. 482–491, 2002.
© Springer-Verlag Berlin Heidelberg 2002

acid sequence pattern in a database and that motifs relate to protein functions that have been conserved during molecular evolution. There are two approaches to extract frequent sequence patterns in the database. The first uses multiple alignment [5,6]. There are several methods, such as pair-wise alignment and optimization. Pair-wise alignment is applied to ordered pairs in a dendrogram, which is constructed from a set of sequences. While optimization is a kind of refinement to find a more optimal solution, it is achieved by applying simulated annealing to an approximate solution, which is computed by multiple alignment. However, no method can process a part of the set of items, including the biological features, in annotated sequence databases. Moreover, this is not useful for users, since the result of the multiple alignment, which requires a large amount of time, is only one solution for any set of sequences. The approach does not permit users to select a useful pattern.

In order to solve the problems mentioned above, the following solutions could be used. One approach is to use a previously developed sequential pattern mining method [1,2,3,4,7] that follows the Apriori method. The PrefixSpan method [4] based on Apriori performs better than other methods [1,2,3]. However, PrefixSpan does not include a function to extract frequent patterns together with gaps or wild characters. Moreover, PrefixSpan operates indifferently to the number of frequent patterns that are extracted from the annotated sequence databases.

We propose a motif discovery system that uses a modified PrefixSpan method [8] to extract frequent patterns from the annotated sequence database that consist of biological features and different amino acid sequences. Frequent patterns are located in both identical and non-identical positions among those sequences. In general, the existing PrefixSpan method extracts a large number of frequent patterns from the sequence databases. Few of the frequent sequence patterns extracted by this method are useful to biologists, since the sequence patterns do not make allowances for gaps or wild characters. Our new method allows the incorporation of gap characters. Furthermore, we have applied our prototype to the evaluation of three sets of sequences that include the Zinc Finger, Cytochrome C, and Kringle motifs.

2   Problem Definition and PrefixSpan Method

We first define the problem of sequential pattern mining and then, using an example, illustrate the existing PrefixSpan method.

The running database is the annotated sequence database in Table 1. The annotated sequence database consists of three attributes, namely, a sequence-identifier (sequence-id), a sequence, and a set of items. Any sequence in the database is an ordered list of character sets, but any set of items is a non-ordered list of items. Many sequence patterns and item patterns frequently repeat themselves in the annotated sequence database. Each sequence pattern is represented as a sub-sequence if it has more than one character. The term "frequent sequence pattern" refers to a sub-sequence that appears frequently in a sequence of the annotated sequence database. On the other hand, the term "frequent item pattern" refers to a subset of items that appears frequently in a set of items of the annotated sequence database.

Table 1. Annotated sequence database

Sequence-id	Sequence	Set of items
1	FKYAKUL	f, a, c, d, g, i
2	SFVKA	a, b, c, f, l, o
3	ALR	b, f, n, j, o
4	MSKPL	b, c, k, s
5	FSKFLMAU	a, f, c, e, l, n

Table 2. Sequence database

Sequence-id	Sequence
100	MFKALRTIPVILNMNKDSKLCPN
200	MSPNPTNIHTGKTLR

The number of elements in a set of tuples including a pattern is defined as the support count [9] of the pattern. For example, let us consider the item pattern, "a" and "f", in Table 1, which stores 5 tuples. Since the item pattern appears in 3 tuples of the table, the support count of the pattern is a value of 3 or the support value is 60 percent. Similarly, considering the sequence pattern, F**A, where * marks one wild card symbol called a gap in the field of molecular biology, since the sequence pattern appears in 3 tuples of the table, the support count of the pattern has a value of 3 or the support value is 60 percent. In this paper, a pattern that exceeds the support count or value is considered to be a frequent pattern. To extract frequent patterns from an annotated sequence database, a user must define the minimum support count or value, which will be called the mini-support threshold hereafter.

Table 2 contains an example in which frequent sequence patterns can be found in a sequence database with only two sequences. The minimum support count is assigned a value of 2 in this example. In general, an n-length pattern is a sequence pattern with length n, in which the length of a sequence pattern is the number of characters in the sequence.

The existing PrefixSpan method [4] uses an algorithm that recursively generates $(k + 1)$-length sequence patterns from k-length sequence patterns in the sequence database, where $1 \leq k$. Initially, the program scans the database to find all of the frequent items in the sequences. Each of these frequent items is a 1-length sequence pattern. These include: <M>: 2; <K>: 2; <L>: 2; <R>: 2; <T>: 2; <I>: 2; <P>:2; <N>: 2; <S>: 2; and <P>: 2, where $< pattern >: count$ represents the pattern and its associated support count. The method then generates 2-length patterns from 1-length patterns in the database. For example, when 2-length patterns are generated from a 1-length pattern, <M>: 2, which appears in two sequences, the character M is located in the following positions: Therefore, the method can be used to extract 2-length

100	M**F**KALRT**I**PVILNMN**K**DSKLCPN
200	M**S**PNPTN**I**HTG**K**TLR

frequent patterns with the prefix M as <MI>:2, <MK>:2, <ML>:2, <MN>:2, <MP>:2, and <MT>:2, as shown in Figure 1. It does not distinguish the pattern <M*K> included in the first sequence from the pattern <M**********K> included in the second sequence. Both patterns are represented as <MK>:2 in the method. A set of the postfix-sub-sequences for character M is called a projected database. The character **I** in the <MI> pattern is found from a projected database consisting of two postfix-sub-sequences for **M**; namely, it appears for a second time in the database. Therefore, the 2-length pattern <**MI**> satisfies the minimum support count. Three-length frequent patterns with the prefix MI are extracted as both <MIK>:2 and <MIL>:2, satisfying the minimum support count. The last character of <MIK>, **K**, is found from the projected database that is created as a set of the postfix-sub-sequences for the characters MI. Similarly, frequent patterns with the prefixes <MK>, <ML>, and others can be found by constructing projected databases with postfix-sub-sequences for <MK>, <ML>, and others.

The existing PrefixSpan method creates projected databases with long postfix-sub-sequences. Therefore, large numbers of meaningless patterns can be extracted from the projected database, which is a problem.

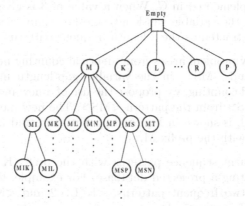

Fig. 1. Mining tree constructed by existing PrefixSpan method

3 New Method

We first propose the modified PrefixSpan method to solve the problem clarified in section 2 and then illustrate one of the methods to extract both frequent sequence patterns and frequent item patterns from the annotated sequence database using the two examples in Tables 1 and 2.

3.1 Modified PrefixSpan Method

In order to solve the problem in section 2, the range of each postfix-sub-sequence is restricted in the modified PrefixSpan method [8]; in other words, the user provides the number of gaps needed to extract meaningful frequent patterns. If a user does not provide the number of gaps, he implicitly allows an infinite number of gaps. The modified PrefixSpan method that provides the maximum number of gaps is called a variable gap-length method. The variable gap-length method required to handle the finite number of gaps becomes the same as the existing PrefixSpan method.

When generating 2-length patterns from a 1-length pattern, <M>:2, which is included in two sequences, using the example in Table 2, where max-gap=3, the candidate characters included in the 2-length pattern are located in the following positions:

100	M FKAL RTIPVILN M NKDS KLCPN
200	M SPNP TNIHTG K TLR

The underlined sub-sequence (above) is designated as the projected database of the modified PrefixSpan method. The starting position of each tuple in the projected database is stored in Table 3. Each tuple in the table is represented as a linear list implemented in C. When a value of 3 is given as the maximum number of gaps in the variable gap-length method, only two patterns shown in Figure 2 can be extracted as the 2-length frequent patterns with the prefix M.

However, a new problem arises from identical counting between the two patterns, <M**S> and <MS>, in the variable gap-length method. In order to avoid this identical counting, we propose the use of a new method to distinguish the pattern <M**S> from the pattern <MS>. The new method, called a fixed gap-length method, is shown in Figure 3, and it can avoid finding any 2-length frequent patterns with the prefix M.

Similarly, frequent sequence patterns with the prefix K and others can be found by constructing a projected database. For example, the fixed-gap length method can find two frequent patterns, <K*L>:2 and <K*LR>:2, with the prefixes K and K*L, respectively.

The frequent-pattern database constructed from this method would be useful to discover biological motifs.

Table 3. Starting position of each tuple

	Support count	Sequence-id = 100			Sequence-id = 200			
A	1	5						
C	1	22						
:	:	:			:			
L	2	6	13	21	15			
M	2	2	15		2			
:	:	:			:			
V	1	11						

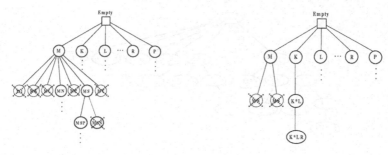

Fig. 2. Pruned mining tree constructed by variable gap-length method

Fig. 3. Pruned mining tree constructed by fixed-gap method

3.2 Extracting Frequent Patterns

In this section, we will illustrate the method to extract item patterns together with sequence patterns from the annotated sequence database shown in Table 1, where the minimum support count and maximum number of gaps are a value of 3. The pattern extract is addressed with a four-step approach. First, the fixed gap-length method proposed in section 3.1 is applied to a part of the sequence in Table 1. The result would be the extraction of such frequently occurring sequence patterns as <A>:4, <F>:3, <F**A>:3, <K>:4, <K*L>:3, <L>:4, <S>:3. We eliminate meaningless patterns that are such 1-length patterns as <A>:4, <F>:3, <K>:4, <L>:4, and <S>:3, in the field of molecular biology. Second, after combining the frequent sequence patterns and Table 1, a new table, shown in Table 4, is created, in which the sequence attribute in Table 1 is discarded. Both attributes, the set of items and the set of frequent sequence patterns, are integrated in Table 4 into one attribute, since the set of frequent sequence patterns is a non-ordered list of patterns that has the same form as the set of items in Table 4. The integration generates another new table constructed from a sequence-id and the one attribute stated previously. Third, frequent patterns can be extracted from the other new table using a FP-growth algorithm [10,11]. As a result, such frequent patterns as <f,c,F**A>:3, <f,c,F**A>:3, <f,a,F**A>:3, <c,a,F**A>:3, <c,K*L>:3, and others can be obtained. The extracted frequent patterns are represented as a Trie structure [11] to reduce the size of storage and are shown in Figure 4. Finally, we select frequent patterns including both an item and a sequence pattern

Table 4. Set of items and sequence patterns

Sequence-id	Set of items	Set of Sequence patterns
1	f, a, c, d, g, i	F**A, K*L
2	a, b, c, f, l, o	F**A
3	b, f, n, j, o	
4	b, c, k, s	K*L
5	a, f, c, e, l, n	K*L, F**A

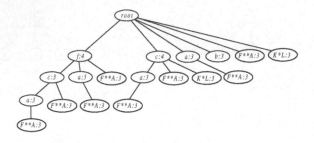

Fig. 4. Mining results represented as Trie structure

from the Trie structure. In this example, we can obtain the meaningful frequent patterns such as <f,c,a,F**A>:3, <f,c,F**A>:3, <f,a,F**A>:3, <f,F**A>:3, <c,a,F**A>:3, <c.F**A>:3, and <a,F**A>:3. We eliminate the residual patterns such as <f>:4, <f,c>:3, <f,c,a>:3, <F**A>:3, and others, generated by combinations on the Trie structure, since they are meaningless patterns without relationship the item and the sequence pattern. After obtaining the meaningful frequent patterns, we can easily construct association rules from the frequent patterns.

4   Experimental Results

Figure 5 is a data-flow diagram of the process used to identify motifs. The figure includes two subsystems that are surrounded by a dotted rectangle. The left subsystem in the dotted rectangle outlines a procedure for generating a large number of frequent patterns, which require a database query interface that can be used on the Internet. The right subsystem in the rectangle outlines a procedure for retrieving useful motifs from the frequent-pattern database using the query interface. The prototype system incorporates both of these subsystems and is implemented in C, SQL [12], and CGI (common gateway interface).

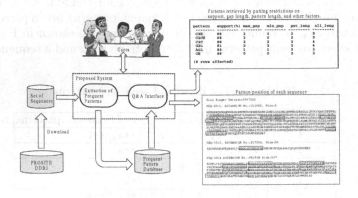

Fig. 5. System configuration

Table 5. Examples of patterns extracted from each of three data sets

Set of sequences	Number of sequences	Max. length (Byte)	Min length (Byte)	Extracted pattern	Supp. Count (%)	CPU time (sec)
Full text search (Zinc Finger)	467	4036	34	H3H7C2C	69	96
PS00190 (Cytochrome C)	783	4196	25	C2CH	98	64
PS00280 (Kringle)	70	3176	53	F3GC6F5C	94	60

4.1 Performance Evaluation

We have reported on the performance of the modified PrefixSpan method and compared it with the variable and fixed gap-length methods using the prototype system. Moreover, we have shown the website interface of the question and answer system. All of the experiments were performed on a 500-MHz Pentium III PC computer with 256 megabytes of main memory.

Table 5 is an example of the frequent sequence patterns that were extracted from three sequence sets. The three sets included such motifs as Zinc Finger, Cytochrome C, and Kringle. We compared the variable and the fixed gap-length methods for a set of sequences that included Zinc Finger motifs. Full-text searching for the keyword "zinc finger" in DDBJ [13] revealed one set of 476 sequences. Moreover, we extracted two sets that included the Cytochrome C and Kringle motifs from PROSITE [14]. The Cytochrome C and Kringle sets were assembled from PROSITE sequences with accession numbers PS00190 and PS00280, respectively.

Figure 6 is a graph that compares the two methods when a mini-support threshold = 80%. The fixed gap-length method produced about 30 times fewer patterns than the variable gap-length method, with respect to 8 gaps. The fixed gap-length method was computed about 5 times faster than the variable gap-length method, with respect to 8 gaps.

After applying the fixed gap-length method to each of the three sets, the extracted pattern was obtained, along with the associated support count and CPU time, where the max-gap = 10 and the mini-support threshold = 60%.

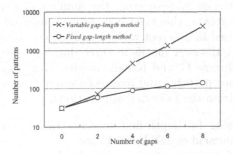

Fig. 6. Number of patterns generated by system

4.2   Question and Answering Interface

A Web-based question and answer interface was implemented for the frequent-pattern database shown in Figure 5. The Web page interface allows a user to input parameters, such as a set of frequent patterns, a minimum support threshold, and the number of gaps. When the user clicks the submit button to select parameters, the interface accesses frequent-pattern databases and outputs the results to a screen. The screen in Figure 7 shows the results of querying the frequent-pattern database extracted from the Cytochrome C sequence set. Fortunately, the frequency of the motif 'C2CH' was found to be highly ranked, where a value of 2 means the number of gaps. Moreover, the interface shown in Figure 8 allows a user to visualize the pattern positions. The mark '^' in the figure shows the starting position of the 'C2CH' motif in the sequence set.

Fig. 7. Output page of search results

Fig. 8. Page to output the position of a pattern given by user

5   Conclusion

A new system has been proposed for extracting frequent patterns from an annotated sequence database. The system is based on the modified PrefixSpan method. The system reduces the required computational time to extract frequent sequence patterns by restricting the number of gaps or wild characters in each pattern. Moreover, this system provides a user interface that permits a database to be queried in different ways. Finally, we evaluated the ability of our prototype system to discover motifs in three database sets, which included the Zinc Finger, Cytochrome C, and Kringle motifs. More experiments for extracting frequent sequence patterns and frequent item patterns will be scheduled for the future. We envision the following applications:

1. Parallel processing for depth-first searches that extract frequent patterns from large amino acid or DNA databases.
2. Development of a visual interface that displays the extracted patterns together with the sequences in a Web browser.

3. Extensions for managing such mutations as insertions, deletions, and others, in addition to handling gap characters or wildcard symbols.

Acknowledgments. We thank the staff of the international DNA data banks for their help in obtaining the biological databases. This work was supported in part by a Grant-in-Aid for Scientific Research (C) (2) from the Japanese Society for the Promotion of Science and a Hiroshima City University Grant for Special Academic Research.

References

1. Agrawal, R., Srikant, R.: Mining Sequential Patterns. In: Proc. 1995 International Conference on Data engineering (ICDE'95). (1995) 3–14
2. Sirikant, R., Agrawal, R.: Mining Sequential Patterns: Generation and Performance Improvements. In: Proc. 5th International Conference on Extending Database Technology (EDB'96). (1996) 3–17
3. Han, J., Pei, J., Mortazavi-Asl, B., Chen, Q., Dayal, U., Hsu, M.V.: Free Span: Frequent Pattern-Projected Sequential Pattern Mining. In: Proc. of International Conference on Knowledge Discovery and Data Mining (KDD 2000). (2000) 355–359
4. Pei, J., Han, J., Mortazavi-Asl, B., Pinto, H.: PrefixSpan: Mining Sequential Patterns Efficiently by Prefix-Projected Pattern Growth. In: Proc. of 7th International Conference on Data Engineering (ICDE2001), IEEE Computer Society Press (2001) 215–224
5. Waterman, M.S., Smith, T.F., Beyer, W.A.: Some Biological Sequence Metrics. Adv. Math **20** (1976) 367–387
6. Gusfield, D.: Algorithms on Strings, Trees, and Sequences. Cambridge University Press (1997)
7. Eskin, E., Pevzner, P.: Finding Composite Regulatory Patterns in DNA Sequences. In: Proceedings of the Tenth International Conference on Intelligent Systems for Molecular Biology (ISMB-2002). (2002)
8. Kanbara, T., Mori, Y., Kitakami, H., Kuroki, S., Yamazaki, Y.: Discovering Motifs in Amino Acid Sequences using a Modified PrefixSpan Method. Currents in Computational Molecular Biology 2002, Washington DC (2002) 96–97
9. Fayyard, U.M., et al., eds.: Advances in Knowledge Discovery and Data Mining. AAAI Press / MIT Press (1996)
10. Han, J., Pei, J., Yin, Y.: Mining Frequent Pattern without Candidate Generation. In: Proc. ACM SIGMOD. (2000) 1–12
11. Ryu, H., Kitakami, H., Mori, Y., Kuroki, S.: Applying Set of Answers collected from Questionnaire to Generation of Association Rules using Trie Structure. In: Proceedings of 2nd Data Mining Workshop (in Japanese). Number 16, ISSN 1341-870X, Japan Society for Software Science and Technology (2001) 11–19
12. SYBASE: Transact-SQL Users Guide, Sybase Inc. (1989).
13. DDBJ: http://www.ddbj.nig.ac.jp/Welcome.html.
14. PROSITE: http://au.expasy.org/prosite/.

A Multi-agent Bioinformatics Integration System with Adjustable Autonomy

Konstantinos Karasavvas[1], Albert Burger[2], and Richard Baldock[2]

[1] Heriot-Watt University, Edinburgh EH14 4AS, UK,
ceekk@cee.hw.ac.uk
[2] MRC Human Genetics Unit, Edinburgh EH4 2XU, UK,
{A.Burger, R.Baldock}@hgu.mrc.ac.uk

Abstract. In this paper we describe a Multi-Agent Bioinformatics Integration System that aims at helping users make the most of the available integration facilities while also increasing their trust in the system. To this end, an explanation facility that helps the users to better understand how the system has arrived at a particular answer is provided. This is especially useful when non-expert users want to take control of critical-decisions, i.e. adjust the system's autonomy. This is accomplished by interacting with users and asking for their intervention in decisions, according to their own preferences.

A prototype for the proposed approach has been developed for the Mouse Atlas database at the Medical Research Council in Edinburgh, Scotland, integrating 3D mouse anatomy, in-situ gene expression data and gene sequence data.

1 Introduction

Over the last ten years the bioinformatics community has witnessed an impressive growth of bioinformatics tools and databases available on the Internet. For some time, biologists have had a great variety of resources to choose from, but they also had to manually query each resource separately, then possibly use these results to make further queries to other resources and so on. The need for integration systems became quickly evident.

Several such systems have been developed (1)(2) their main objective being to *federate* biological resources by providing a unified interface. Then, when a query is submitted, the integration system decomposes it to sub-queries, sends these to the appropriate resources and then processes the results to compile the final answer to be presented to the user. Such transparency—to the users—is generally beneficial but, as is argued in (3) and later in this section, there are cases where it can be a disadvantage and thus needs to be controlled.

Recently, *agent technology* has become popular in bioinformatics systems (4)(5)(6). While there is no consensus on a definition for agents, it is widely accepted that one of the main characteristics of agency is *autonomy*. By autonomous agents we mean agents that have overall control of their behaviour. Although such control is usually helpful—because it indicates automation—users find it

M. Ishizuka and A. Sattar (Eds.): PRICAI 2002, LNAI 2417, pp. 492–501, 2002.

difficult to completely trust autonomous agents (7) because they can loose some of the control over the system and be restricted in the choices they can make, e.g. a user might prefer a specific method for solving a task but the autonomous agent chooses another.

In addition to the above, bioinformatics integration systems raise another issue of trust. As was demonstrated in (3), identical queries can result in different answers, if there are alternative ways of solving a problem. Choices made may be due to 1) users wanting to experiment with different options, such as use of different databases or algorithms, or 2) dynamic system factors, such as availability and efficiency of systems resources, or protocols used (e.g. in the contract net protocol a request is sent to a number of agents and a contract is made with one of them when both participants agree to the task; consequently the choice does not only depend on the initiator of the request, but also on which agent agrees to the contract terms).

While this dynamism is not uncommon in general, it makes an important difference in the biological domain because there are often multiple sources of similar but not identical data — due to natural, experimental and interpretation variation. Such potential differentiation makes it important to have more control over the internal reasoning of the system.

In order to remedy this lack of trust and to increase user control, some systems provide support for *adjustable autonomy* (8). In our system, autonomy is adjusted by allowing the user—according to his/her preferences—to take control when a *critical-decision*[1] is reached. A potential problem here lies in the need for the user to know a lot about the integration logic, which is not desirable or else only expert users would be able to use the system. For this reason we provide an explanation facility—to help the user in the decision-making—and a way to calculate just how critical a decision is (section 3).

To demonstrate the approach proposed in this paper, we have implemented a prototype multi-agent bioinformatics system which integrates *Mouse Gene Expression Information Resource (MGEIR)* (9) and BLAST[2] —an Internet bioinformatics sequence search tool. MGEIR is a collection of databases that document gene-expression information for the mouse embryo. Three of the main data sources of the MGEIR are the *Edinburgh Mouse Atlas (EMA)* (10) for the anatomy data, the *MGI Gene Expression Database* (formerly GXD) (11) and the *MRC Graphical Gene Expression Database (GGED)* (12). When describing the prototype system and the protocols that govern agent interactions, we use the following query: *determine if one of the genes that match a specific protein sequence is expressed in a specific region (a region selected from the 3D EMA model) of the mouse embryo.*

The remainder of this paper is organized as follows. The next section introduces the architecture of our multi-agent system, the decision modes and an

---

[1] A critical-decision is a decision where the choice could possibly differentiate the results.

[2] http://www.ncbi.nlm.nih.gov/BLAST/

sample execution of our prototype. Section 3 gives an analysis of how criticality is measured in a decision and in section 4 we examine explanation. Finally, in section 5 we provide a conclusion.

2   Architecture

2.1   Overview

Our system is a *purely communicative* MAS: there is no external environmental influence and the agents communicate only by means of messages. The system is based on the FIPA specifications, and a FIPA-compliant development tool, JADE, is used for implementation purposes. Messages exchanged between agents are formed in a high-level language, FIPA Agent Communication Language (ACL), and the ACL content language is SL0—a subset of the FIPA suggested Semantic Language (SL). In turn, the SL0 content conforms to specified ontologies (see subsection 2.6).

The general architecture in terms of the agents of the system can be seen in figure 1. A brief description of the different types of agents is given below:

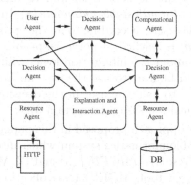

Fig. 1. General Architecture

User Agent (UA). This is the entry point of a request. Users interact with this type of agent to formulate queries, get explanations and/or critical-decision choices and view final results. A UA knows how to translate an interface query to a message (ACL) and send it, and how to display a received message.

Computational Agent (CA). This type of agent accepts requests for specific tasks. Each CA specializes in solving a number of computational problems. Estimating criticality of decision agents—and storing the results—takes place in a special purpose CA, called Comparison Agent (CoA).

Decision Agent (DA). This type of agent has mediating capabilities. It accepts a task, it decomposes it to sub-tasks as necessary, sends them to other agents and then integrates the results before returning them. Additionally it can be customized to either make a critical-decision or forward it to EIA.

Resource Agent (RA). This type of agent has all the required knowledge to access a specific information resource. It knows how to translate a request it receives in FIPA ACL to the appropriate resource query language and how to construct the resource's answer back to a proper ACL message—to send back to the requesting agent.

Explanation and Interaction Agent (EIA). This type of agent has the important role of providing the user with either an explanation of why a choice was made or with the available choices—together with argumentation on the benefits of each—to allow the user to decide. Upon initialization DAs notify EIA of their critical-decisions, which the latter uses to build a table containing the DAs, their critical-decisions and the possible choices for each of these decisions. During execution it also receives partial execution plans from DAs, so that in the end a complete execution trace can be compiled to be used in the explanation.

2.2   Decision Modes

The user is able to configure the system and the execution of his request through the UA. The UA queries the EIA for the set of available critical decision types that may occur and it will then present them to the user. Currently there are three different operational modes from which the user has to select one for each type of critical-decision:

Automatic/Interactive. The default mode of execution is automatic. During automatic mode critical-decisions are handled by the appropriate DA without consulting the user. In contrast, if interactive mode is chosen and DAs reach this type of decision they will ask the user to decide.

Comparative. When comparative mode is set the DA behaves according to the automatic/interactive settings but in addition it 'silently' executes a number of possible choices of the critical-decision in question. If the possible choices are too many only a pre-specified number of them will be followed. Furthermore, requests for executing a task for comparison have a lower priority (compared with normal task execution) thus enabling agents to ignore them—maybe temporarily—if overloaded. When all results are back the DA sends them to the CoA, which analyses their differences.

Explanation. Setting explanation mode for a critical decision provides a description (to the user) of the possible decision choices available and why the one chosen was selected by the system.

The choice of decision mode is communicated to agents during execution together with the requests concerning the actual application domain tasks. An extra slot (UserDefinedSlot) was defined in the ACL messages—according to FIPA specifications—to contain the configuration, so as to keep the two completely independent.

2.3 Prototype

We have implemented a MAS, based on the architecture presented in 2.1, that integrates mouse gene-expression resources—currently MGEIR and BLAST. In this section we will briefly describe the agents that have been implemented for our prototype MAS. Note that critical decisions that can be handled by the system are mentioned in the description of the appropriate DAs.

UserAgent is of UA type. A simple interface has been implemented to formulate a limited number of test queries.

ComparisonAgent is of CA type. It is responsible for estimating criticality of decisions (see section 3) and storing the results. It also informs other agents of these results upon request.

EIAgent is of EIA type.

MGEIRAgent is of DA type. It accepts high-level requests concerning mouse gene-expression information and decomposes them to sub-requests (see introduction for an example). It then checks with the DF for agents able to accept these sub-requests and forwards them.

MouseGeneSequenceAgent is of DA type. It expects requests containing a sequence (DNA or protein) and its task is to find which genes correspond to that sequence. It is responsible for selecting which database/tool to use and which parameters to apply to the database's algorithm (if applicable). It requests available RAs, e.g. BLASTAgent, from the DF.

BLASTAgent is of RA type. It knows how to convert a request from SL0—from the content of an ACL message—to an appropriate format understood by BLAST and connect (to BLAST) via a socket connection. Then, it converts the reply to SL0 again and sends an ACL message back to the requesting agent.

MouseExpressedGeneAgent is of DA type. It accepts a request containing a set of genes and certain image coordinates based on the EMA. It then checks if the given genes are expressed in the image region. The agent decides if a domain (textual) or spatial (image) match will be applied.

MouseAtlasAgent is of RA type. It converts the SL0 content of an ACL message to the appropriate CORBA request(s)—supported by EMA—and then converts the reply to SL0, which is sent back to the requester.

The execution of a sample query by this system is given below.

2.4   System Initialization

During start-up, all agents that offer services have to register these services with the DF. When a service is needed, agents communicate with the DF—centralized brokering—to get back a set of agents able to provide the required service. Additionally, all DAs that can deal with critical decisions have to register with the EIA. The registration message should contain the type of decision (3) and the possible choices and comments (benefits/drawbacks) on each choice.

2.5   Protocols

To achieve the kind of functionality mentioned in the introduction our agents have to follow certain protocols. On the lower-level, for purposes of agent communication, the FIPA interaction protocols are used—like *FIPA-Request*. The FIPA-Request interaction protocol specifies a conversation between two agents, where the first can request a task from the second. The latter can then refuse or accept by sending an acknowledgment back followed finally with the result of the task or a reason of failure.

While this could be sufficient for requesting a task, it cannot specify the overall cooperation needed to achieve user intervention—adjustable autonomy— and/or how an explanation is constructed for planning and decision-making. For that purpose we developed a higher-level protocol, one that coordinates interactions between the DAs, the EIA and the CoA. We called this protocol *Explanation and Interaction Protocol (EIP)*.

The EIP is initiated when a DA gets a request from a UA. It can be described in stages:

1. The first DA, *root* DA, constructs a solution plan. It then checks the user preferences to see if the plan contains critical-decisions that:
   - the user wants to take control of, in which case it sends a request to the EIA, and/or
   - the user wishes to measure criticality on, in which case a number of possible choices are followed/executed and when the results come back they are forwarded to the CoA to measure their similarity[3].

   It then notifies the EIA of the (partial) plan and executes it. The plan contains requests to other DAs and/or requests to RAs.
2. Non-root DAs will also act according to the previous stage. On the bottom of the DAs-tree, the *leaf* DAs, will send requests only to RAs.
3. Upon request for user interaction, the EIA will forward the critical-decision to the UA together with comments on the possible effects that this decision could have on the result. The user will make his choice through the UA and the latter will then inform EIA of the decision taken, which in turn will inform the DA.
4. Answers will be integrated—when appropriate—in DAs and send back to the requesters. Finally, the root DA will construct a final answer and it will ask EIA for an explanation.
5. The EIA will compile the plan notifications to a complete trace of the execution. Using that trace, it will construct an explanation and it will send it back to root DA.
6. Finally, in the last stage, the root DA will forward the answer, together with the explanation back to the UA.

In figure 2 we use an AUML collaboration diagram that illustrates the interactions of a sample execution from our prototype system, according to EIP. This example is based on the sample query given in the introduction. In order

---

[3] The more similar the results are, the less critical the decision is.

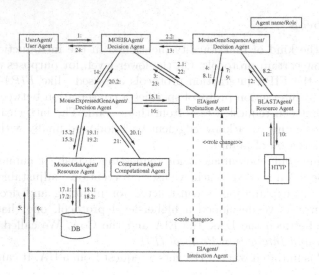

Fig. 2. AUML collaboration diagram showing agent interactions

to demonstrate all types of critical-decision modes (see subsection 2.6), each of the DAs operates in a different mode. MGEIRAgent operates in automatic mode. It decomposes the initial request it receives (1:) into two sub-tasks—we assume that the second sub-task requires information from the first and thus they cannot run concurrently. MGEIRAgent makes all necessary decisions automatically and notifies EIA of the partial plan (2.1:). At the same time it asks the MouseGeneSequenceAgent to deal with one of the sub-tasks (2.2:). The latter operates in interactive mode; we can see that it first requests user intervention from EIA (4:)—which in turn contacts the UserAgent (5:)—before finalizing its plan and notifying EIA (8.1:). Finally, after MGEIRAgent gets the results from the first sub-task (13:) it submits the second sub-task to MouseExpressedGeneAgent (14:), which operates in comparative mode. That means that it has to execute more than one decision choice. By default it also operates automatically so it notifies the EIA of the partial plan (15.1) and then sends a request for each choice—two choices for the purposes of the example—to MouseAtlasAgent (15.2: and 15.3). After receiving the results (19.1: and 19.2:), MouseExpressed-GeneAgent sends them for comparison (20.1:) while sending a reply back to MGEIRAgent (20.2:). The final result is integrated in the MGEIRAgent and then send to EIA (22:) to add appropriate explanations (if the user requested so) before returning the results to the UserAgent (24:). Note that the requests to the RAs are not part of the EIP but are included for completeness.

2.6 Ontologies

Ontologies are needed to ensure that our agents share a common understanding of the meaning of information exchanged. Again, FIPA specifications provide an ontology of communication, defining the FIPA interaction protocols. In our system we needed to define two additional ontologies. One to define the EIP—called Explanation-Interaction-Ontology (EIO)—and one to define the domain of application (developmental genetics)—called MGEIR-Ontology.

These ontologies help separate domain knowledge from system knowledge. New agents that want to communicate with our system need only to understand the MGEIR-Ontology ontology. If they want to take part in the EIP, they also have to understand the EIO ontology.

3   Decision Criticality

When assessing the criticality of a decision, the Comparison Agent (CoA), receives k sets $(k > 1)$, where k is the number of possible choices that the critical decision has. Each set corresponds to the result obtained from a choice. Our aim is to compare all the sets and calculate their differentiation—or similarity—as a percentage.

We first start by comparing only two sets, A_1 and A_2. Their similarity s_{12} is the fraction of the cardinality of common elements over the mean cardinality of both sets, and thus (1).

$$s_{12} = \frac{|A_1 \cap A_2|}{\frac{|A_1|+|A_2|}{2}} = 2 \cdot \frac{|A_1 \cap A_2|}{|A_1| + |A_2|} \quad (1) \qquad \overline{s_k} = \frac{1}{n}\left(\sum_{i=1}^{k-1}\sum_{j=i+1}^{k} s_{ij}\right) \quad (2)$$

In the case of more than two sets we need to make all possible comparisons in pairs. A result of k sets consists of $n = k(k-1)/2$ pairs, and thus will make that many comparisons. Then, (2) calculates the mean similarity of k sets.

Now we also have the mean differentiation of the k sets, $\overline{d_k} = 1 - \overline{s_k}$. Finally, we can express both similarity and differentiation means as percentages with $\overline{S_k} = \overline{s_k} \cdot 100$ and $\overline{D_k} = \overline{d_k} \cdot 100$ respectively.

As an example consider the three sets, $A_1 = \{a, b, c\}$, $A_2 = \{a, b\}$ and $A_3 = \{a, b, d\}$. First, we find all possible pairs: $n = 3(3-1)/2 = 3$. Then we apply equation (2) and we get: $\overline{s_k} = 1/n(s_{12} + s_{13} + s_{23}) =$

$$= \frac{1}{n}\left(\frac{2 \cdot |A_1 \cap A_2|}{|A_1| + |A_2|} + \frac{2 \cdot |A_1 \cap A_3|}{|A_1| + |A_3|} + \frac{2 \cdot |A_2 \cap A_3|}{|A_2| + |A_3|}\right) = 0.75$$

Thus, sets A_1, A_2 and A_3 differ by 25% ($\overline{D_k} = (1 - \overline{s_k}) \cdot 100$).

Of course $\overline{D_k}$ reflects the differentiation of a critical-decision over only one query. While this is useful for analyzing the possible fluctuation on a specific query, we would also like to have a general differentiation measure for a critical-decision over the history of all queries. We call this criticality of a decision d, and it is simply the mean:

$$\overline{C_d} = \frac{1}{h} \sum_{i=1}^{h} \overline{D_k^i} \tag{3}$$

where h is the history—number of queries—on that critical-decision.

We should note here that the method used to calculate criticality was based on an intuitive argument. Further work and testing is needed to acquire the necessary empirical data in order to justify our approach or not—in which case alternatives need to be studied.

4 Explanation

Our system aims to help users understand the choices that have to be made—automatically or interactively—during execution. Each choice in a critical-decision is associated with an annotation. Currently, the annotation is a string which provides the benefits and/or drawbacks of each choice. In automatic mode the system will use the annotations to explain its choice to the user and in interactive mode these annotations will be presented to help the user decide.

We should mention here important work on *data provenance* (13). Its investigators argue that information, before its arrival at the form in which we see it has been changed, possibly several times, and thus it is not reliable. In order to deal with that problem they suggested adding annotations each time a change occurs to the data. These annotations, if available, could be used to complement our decision-choices' annotations.

A complete execution trace is also important because it provides the overall picture. It shows how the task was decomposed, which agents participated, and so on. This information is very useful for providing statistics for the execution (e.g. how often an agent is selected for certain queries, how many DAs are needed to solve a certain task, etc.). Additionally, a complete trace describes the process of execution which could be helpful because it enables us to use reconstructive explanation (14). The planning process, however, is distributed among the DAs. We have to unify the partial plans, which is why the EIP requires each DA to notify the EIA of its partial plan. In the end of the execution the EIA will be able to construct the complete trace.

5 Conclusion

Our biologist co-workers are very positive about the new prospects that open up with this system. On one hand it offers the flexibility that agent technology provides—dynamically adding new DAs, RAs, etc.—while on the other hand a framework has been developed that manages agent autonomy based on decision criticality. The paper described a possible multi-agent architecture together with a higher-level agent interaction protocol for such a system. A prototype implementation of the system demonstrates its basic technical feasibility. A thorough evaluation of the system by biologists is currently being prepared.

References

[1] Baker, P.G., Brass, A., Bechhofer, S., Goble, C., Paton, N., Stevens, R.: Tambis—a transparent access to multiple bioinformatics information sources. Proceedings of the Sixth International Conference on Intelligent Systems for Molecular Biology (1998) 25–34

[2] Letovsky, S.I., ed.: 17. In: BIOINFORMATICS Databases and Systems. Kluwer Academic Publishers (1999)

[3] Karasavvas, K., Baldock, R., Burger, A.: Managing transparency in distributed bioinformatics systems. European Media Lab Workshop on Management and Integration of Biochemical Data (2000)

[4] Bryson, K., Luck, M., Joy, M., Jones, D.: Applying agents to bioinformatics in geneweaver. Proceedings of the Fourth International Workshop on Collaborative Information Agents (2000)

[5] Decker, K., Zheng, X., Schmidt, C.: A multi-agent system for automated genomic annotation. Proceedings of the Fifth International Conference on Autonomous Agents (2001) 433–440

[6] Imai, T., et al.: Implementing an integrated system for heterogeneous molecular biology databases with intelligent agents. IEEE Pacific Rim Conference on Communications, Computers and Signal Processing 2 (1997) 807–810

[7] Cesta, A., D'Aloisi, D., Collia, M.: Adjusting autonomy of agent systems. AAAI Spring Symposium on Agents with Adjustable Autonomy (1999) 17–24

[8] American Association for Artificial Intelligence: AAAI Spring Symposium on Agents with Adjustable Autonomy, American Association for Artificial Intelligence (1999)

[9] Bard, J., Kaufman, M., Dubreuil, C., Brune, R., Burger, A., Baldock, R., Davidson, D.: An internet-accessible database of mouse development anatomy based on a systematic nomenclature. Elsevier Science **Mechanisms of Development 74** (1998) 111–120

[10] Letovsky, S.I., ed.: The Edinburgh Mouse Atlas: Basic structure and informatics. In: Bioinformatics Databases and Systems. Kluwer Academic Publishers (1999) 102–115

[11] Ringwald, R., Davis, G., Smith, A., Trepanier, L., Begley, D., Richardson, J., Eppig, J.: The mouse gene-expression database GXD. Seminars in Cell and Developmental Biology **8** (1997) 489–497

[12] Davidson, D., et al.: The mouse atlas and graphical gene-expression database. Seminars in Cell and Developmental Biology **8** (1997) 509–517

[13] "http://db.cis.upenn.edu/Research/provenance.html".

[14] Wick, M.R., Thompson, W.B.: Reconstructive expert system explanation. Artificial Intelligence **54** (1992) 33–70

Using Case-Based Reasoning Approach in Planning Instructional Activities

Rhodora L. Reyes and Raymund C. Sison

College of Computer Studies, De La Salle University, Manila
{rhoda, raymund}@ccs.dlsu.edu.ph

Abstract. Case-Based Reasoning (CBR) is a methodology in artificial intelligence that uses specific previous experiences as basis for reasoning about new similar situations. In providing individualized instruction, tutors learn from their experiences and use these experiences as foundations for identifying the appropriate instructional activities. Most of the approaches used in designing tutoring systems that adapts to its learners use the rule-based approach. If rules were used, a lot of work will be done chaining rules only to find out that it is not useful [Jona, 1998]. Cases can quickly recognize whether a teaching strategy is relevant to apply in a given situation. This paper presents how CBR model can be used to enable the tutor model to use previously successful instructional strategies to the present learning scenario.

1. Introduction

People often solve problem based on specific previous experiences. An artificial intelligence methodology that uses previously experienced specific situations as basis for reasoning about a new similar situation is called Case-Based Reasoning (CBR). CBR can mean adapting old solutions to meet new demands, using old cases to critique new solutions or reasoning from precedents to interpret a new situation or create an equitable solution to a new problem. (Kolodner, 1993).

An example task where this kind of problem solving can be seen is in tutoring. Human tutors identify appropriate teaching strategies based on their experiences with similar situations. Situations can be in the form of having similar types of students, lessons being taught or instructional scenario. Tutors also considers remembers which experience were successful or not and which factor probably caused the success or failure of the instructional plan. The same approach can be used in the tutor module of an Intelligent Tutoring System (ITS). The tutor module must be able to recognize the similarity and differences of the new situation from its past experiences especially in the type of learners that it has.

Different learners have different needs. The task becomes more important when dealing with students on the web. Therefore, Internet-based tutoring systems must be able to reference to past experience in order for it to know which approach will be appropriate given a situation (or case). However, no past situation is ever exactly the

M. Ishizuka and A. Sattar (Eds.): PRICAI 2002, LNAI 2417, pp. 502-511, 2002.

same as a new one and oftentimes domain knowledge for instructional strategies is incomplete, thus making the tutor model incapable of using the instructional method appropriate to the learner. It is therefore necessary to create a tutor model that has the capability to understand new situations in terms of old experiences and adapt an old solution to fit a new situation. (Reyes& Sison 2000, Reyes & Sison 2001a). Most of the approaches used in designing tutoring systems that adapts to its learners use the rule-based approach. If rules were used, a lot of work will be done chaining rules only to find out that it is not useful (Jona, 1998). Cases can quickly recognize whether a teaching strategy is relevant to apply in a given situation.

This paper presents how CBR approach is used in a tutoring system called CBR-Tutor[1]. CBR-TUTOR is an Internet agent-based tutoring system that uses the CBR approach in providing adaptive instruction to its learners (Reyes and Sison 2000). It is composed of four types of agents. These are the System Agent (SA), Case Facilitator Agent (CFA), Case-Based Information Agent (CIA) and Case-Based Tutor Agent (CTA). The CTAs interact directly with the learner. It has a set of local cases, which are commonly used. If the local cases are not useful for the new situation, the CTA will request retrieval from the global set of cases. The CIAs are responsible for storing and retrieving cases from the global case libraries. These cases contain situations experienced by the CTAs in the system.

This paper presents how CBR model can be used to enable the tutor model to use previously successful instructional strategies to the present learning scenario. The succeeding sections will focus on the discussion on how each phase of the CBR is designed in CBR-Tutor. Section 2 discusses the representation and organization of cases. In section 3, we describe the retrieval and adaptation of cases. Section 4 presents the evaluation and learning of cases. We conclude in Section 5 with a the summary and discussion of the cases and ongoing research.

2. Representation and Organization of Cases

A case-based reasoner is heavily dependent on the structure and content of its collection of cases. Cases in CBR-Tutor are stored in the Case-Based Library (CBL). There are two types of case libraries in CBR Tutor, the *global case-based libraries* (GCBLs) and the *local case-based library* (LCBL). The GCBLs is the repository of all cases that are being shared by different Case-Based Tutor Agents (CTAs) while LCBLs are local to each CTAs. LCBLs contain the most recent and commonly used cases by the CTA. This section discusses how cases are represented, indexed and organized in CBR-Tutor. [2]

---

[1] Detailed discussion can be found in (Reyes and Sison, 2001a).
[2] Detailed discussion can be found in (Reyes and Sison, 2001b).

2.1 Case Representation and Indexing

The cases are represented using the frame *structure* (Figure 2). Predicate notation is used to describe the slots in the frame. This representation is used because it is functional. Each case in the case-based libraries has three major parts: *situation description, solution* and *outcome* (Figure 1). The *situation description* describes the goal (or set of goals), constraints on the goals, and other features of the problem situation. The *solution* part of the case contains the steps used to derive the solution (i.e., tutoring plan of action) and the justifications for decisions that were made. Finally, the *outcome* part of the case contains information about the success or failure of the solution and the repair strategy used when the case is adapted to a new situation.

The case representation in CBR-Tutor are specified as collections of abstract frames and their role bindings. Given, the representation it is easy to see the correspondences between bindings in the situation description and solutions frames. The case were represented in this way to make adaptation of cases simple.

CBR-Tutor Case
Situation Description
• Goal, event, topic, learner goal learning style, student level learner error , topics taken
Solution
• set_of_objects - presentation materials and description • activities - main and optional activities
Outcome
• Result of applying the activity • Feature that caused failure • New value for the failed feature • How the case was modified

Fig. 1. The structure of a CBR-Tutor Case.

Indexing is the process of assigning labels to cases to direct a search and specify under what conditions each case can be useful. The *functional methodology* was used in choosing the indexing vocabulary for the CBR-Tutor. This methodology focuses on the purposes of indexes: to designate situations in which some lesson a case can teach might be relevant (Kolodner, 1993). A set of cases was derived and then a vocabulary that covers the set was obtained. Three steps were undertaken in identifying the indexes:

• A set of cases that represents the problem that arise in the domain are collected. For each of the sample case, the problem goals were identified; the situation (context) in which the problem arises was described in detail; the solution chosen was described including the outcome of the solution.
• For each of the case, the lessons it can teach were identified.
• Given situations identified in step 2, the indexes that will make each case retrievable were identified and represented.

2.2 Case Organization

The cases in CBR-Tutor are organized by modifying Robert Schank's *dynamic memory model* (Aamodt, 1994) as shown in Figure 3. The organizational structure is composed of the Generalized Episode (GE), which contains the common features among the cases being organized, and it also contains organizational structure that indexes those cases. Thus, CBR-Tutor's organizational structure has three different types of objects: *common features, indexes* and *cases.* An index is composed of an *index name* and *an index value.* The index may point to a more specific organizational structure (or GE). The difference of the CBR-Tutor's organization of cases from the dynamic memory model is that indexing in CBR-Tutor is redundant and prioritized. The structure is said to be a *prioritized redundant discrimination network.*

In this structure, a node can either be a GE that contains common features among cases, an index name, index value or a case. As shown in Figure 2, the cases are classified in different ways (or discriminated) based on the index. The triangle in the diagram represents that the cases are being classified using different indexes. The boxes with a line contains the common features among most of the cases (GE) while the simple boxes represents the *index name* (classification) while the labels in the arcs represent *index values.* The node containing the *index values* can hold as its sub-node a case or a GE. In Figure 3, the node containing the *index value topic 1* holds as its sub-node a GE while the *index value review* has the sub-node *Case 1.*

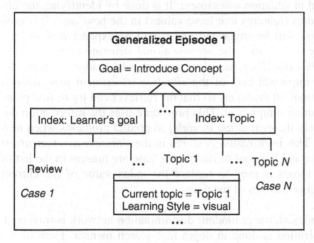

This case organization introduces redundancy in the network. The redundancy in the network assures that at least one of the networks will find a matching case since parallel search will be done in this structure. To keep the redundancy under control, the common features are eliminated from consideration as further classification is done. For example, if a feature (and feature value) of the case that is being added in the network is found out to be common to other cases, that particular

Fig. 2. Redundant Organizational Structure of cases in CBR-Tutor

feature will not be included in the prioritize list of indexes. The prioritized list of indexes contains the list of features of a case based on its priorities. Priorities are based on the weights assigned to the features. The feature with the highest priority is inserted first in the organizational network.

3. Retrieval and Adaptation

The first process in a CBR-cycle is the retrieval of useful and similar cases. The previous sections discussed how a case is indexed and organized, which are important factors in the retrieval process. This section focuses on the discussion on how cases are retrieved and adapted in CBR-Tutor.

3.1 Case Retrieval

Case retrieval does not only focus on the similarity among cases, it must be able to find useful cases that are similar to the new problem that will help the reasoner (i.e., CTA) perform its given tasks. Before retrieving, a reasoner must be able to anticipate problems so that the reasoner can retrieve cases that avoid them (Reisbeck, 1989).

In CBR-Tutor, the CIAs are mainly responsible for retrieving useful cases. However, CTAs can also retrieve from its local case-based library and only requests for retrieval of cases to the CFA if it doesn't have an appropriate case. As all other case retrievals, case retrieval in CBR-Tutor has a combination of searching and matching.

The first step in case retrieval is situation assessment. Situation assessment is used both for retrieving and learning a new case. It is the process of analyzing and elaborating the current case (or situation) for retrieval and organizing cases for learning. The purpose of the situation assessment is to identify what possible indexes will be used. Elaboration is used in situation assessment. It is done by identifying the observable and predictive features (features that have values) in the new case. It is possible that several elaborations will be suggested and it will be expensive if all suggested elaboration would be done. Since the organizational structure of the cases is designed as *prioritized redundant discrimination network*, elaboration is generally suggested by priority. One important task of the *situation assessment procedure* is that it tells the retriever of *potential problems* so that the retriever can try to find plans that avoid these problems during *adaptation*. This procedure uses the information determined by CTA (particularly the *evaluation module*) to predict problems when new goals or situations come in. This information is stored in the *situation assessment list of anticipators*. If the indexes and the goal of the current case are present in the list of anticipators, the suggested values is used to replace the index value of the current case. This will be the new set of indexes of the case.

After the new case is indexed, the redundant discrimination network is traversed. Traversal of the case organization is done in depth-first search manner. Each of the indexes identified during the situation assessment procedure is compared to the first level indexes of the network (or tree). For every first level node that corresponds to the indexes of the new case, a depth-first search is done. The degree of similarity and match is computed until a case is found. The aggregate match score of the old case to the new case is computed.

Matching and ranking is a procedure in case retrieval that selects which cases are appropriate among the cases in the case library. The nearest-neighbor matching approach is used. Since the numeric evaluation function can only rank cases but cannot recognize cases that are not useful, an exclusion step is included to look for difference between cases that are known to predict if the cases are not useful (i.e., different in reasoning goal). Since only cases having the same goal as the new case are matched against the new case, cases that are not useful are automatically eliminated. This is based on the belief that the teaching goal is an important factor in deciding what instructional strategy to use. This belief is also shown in the result of the survey among teachers regarding the factors that they use in planning for instructional activities. Figure 3 shows the algorithm for checking correspondences and computing the degree of similarity.

In the presented retrieval method, whenever a candidate set or partial matches have been collected and better matching cases need to be extracted from the set, aggregate matching is required. Aggregate match is computed using the numeric evaluation function that combines that degree of match along each dimension with a value representing the importance of the dimension. After all the related cases with their aggregate match score are retrieved, the cases are ranked from highest to lowest. If more than one case have the highest rank, then all of those cases are returned. Otherwise, only the highest case is given to the requesting tutor agent (or CTA).

---

1.   Index correspond to each other if:
    1.1.   Values fill the same attribute
    1.2.   Values fill the same role in two predicate clauses
2.   The degree of similarity of corresponding features are computed by distance on a qualitative and quantitative scale
3.   The degree of match is computed the following function:

$$\frac{\sum_{i=1}^{n} w_i (sim\ (f_i^{\,l}, f_i^{\,r})}{\sum_{i-1}^{n} w_i}$$

Where,
w_i = the weight of the importance of dimension i, values ranging from 0-1
sim = the similarity function for primitives, values ranging from 0-1, and
$f_i^{\,l}\ and f_i^{\,r}$ = Values for the feature f_i in the input and retrieved cases, respectively

    3.1.   Add the results for all features to derive an *aggregate match score*.
    3.2.   Rank cases from highest to lowest

Fig. 3. Algorithm for checking correspondence and computing the degree of similarity and match

The next step in adaptation after reinstantiation is choosing what gets adapted. In CBR-Tutor, one major issue considered before choosing what to adapt is the connectedness of an item to other component parts. The connectedness is explicitly specified through the bindings in the case representation.

Critics were used to choose both what to adapt and the adaptation method that will be applied. Critics are special-purpose heuristics that are controlled through the use of rules. Whenever the topic, learning style, student level, learner errors and topics taken of a new case is different from the old case, the substitution method is used to adapt the solution part of the retrieved (old) case to the new case. Reinstantiation is used as the substitution method, which was discussed previously. The transformation method is used when the event, learning goal, learner errors and topics taken of the old case is different from the new case. The critics use *commonsense transforma-*

tion[3] and *case-based adaptation*[4]. These critics transforms the old case to fit the new case by deleting or inserting an activity in the solution part, by deleting or inserting an element in the set of objects, adjusting the number of examples or exercise that should be given. The other adaptation method used is case-based adaptation. In this method, a case is used to guide adaptation.

4. Case Evaluation, Repair, and Learning

Evaluation and Repair of the solution case[5] is done by the CTA after it has executed the solution case. It is difficult for a tutoring system to evaluate the correctness or appropriateness of the tutoring plans it presents. Unlike other case-based systems (e.g., designing a bridge, creating a recipe) where they evaluate their solutions by simulating them, CBR-Tutor evaluates its proposed solution case based on the student feedback and/or student's performance.

Evaluation of the solution can be done while tutoring activities are being executed or after the tutoring activities have been executed. There are two types of feedback that the CBR-Tutor considers for evaluation, the *students feedback* and *student's performance*. The student feedback triggers evaluation to be done while tutoring activities are being executed while the student's performance helps evaluate the solution case after the execution of tutoring activities.

In cases where the student interrupted the tutor while the teaching activities in the solution case is being executed, it is considered as a *student's feedback*. Student feedback can take the form of student's request. It may have the following values: *new topic, new example, new exercise, review, and end session*. Whenever a student interrupts the current session and makes a request, evaluation is done to determine if the current plan needs to be modified. Modification of cases is called *repair*. To repair the current case, the adaptation methods discussed in the previous section are applied.

The process of evaluating the current solution case when the student makes a request while the tutoring activities are being executed involves recording the current activity and the activities executed before evaluating and repairing the current solution. This is done so that after the solution case has been repaired, the tutoring activities will not start from the top and repeat the activities that had been done before. Normally, if the student makes a request, the tutoring strategies that answer the request are appended to the current set of teaching strategies. In such cases, the recorded activities are used as tags to prompt the tutor where to start using the repaired

---

[3] "Commonsense transformation uses a small set of heuristics that use knowledge about the relative importance of different components on an item to determine whether deletions or substitutions should be done ." (Kolodner, 1993)

[4] Case-based adaptation uses cases to tell how adaptation is done in the old solution.

[5] Solution case is the result of applying adaptation to the old case to meet the requirements of the new situation.

solution case. However, if the effect of *repairing* the current solution case is to totally change the set of teaching strategies then the recorded list of activities are not used.

As an effect of repairing the current solution plan, the values in the *outcome part* of the case are modified. The repair strategies that are used are recorded in the *repair-strategy attribute* while the features that caused the need for repair are recorded in the *feedback attribute* stating that the plan has been modified. The list of these features is used as failure predictors by the case retrieval algorithm. This list will be included in the list of failure predictors along with the reasoning goals of the current solution case. This process is done during the case learning process.

If during the execution of the tutoring activities there is no interruption then evaluation is done at the end of execution. The plan is considered successful. However, the student's performance is checked using the student database. If the student's performance is low then it will be recorded in the case, and it will be stated in the repair-strategy that a new case is retrieved. A new case is then retrieved using the new situation. The new situation will now consider changes made in the student database (e.g., topics taken, learner errors, and performance level) and these changes will now be used as indexes in retrieving similar cases. At the end of the session, all recorded cases are forwarded to the case-learning module. The learning of cases is done only at the end of the session so as not to make the system slower

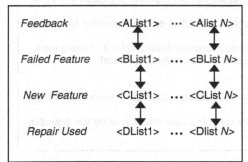

Fig. 4. Correspondence between the Values of the Outcome Part Attributes

It is possible to have many repairs that have been applied to a case. In this case, the list of feature at the feedback attribute will correspond to the list of repair strategies in the *repair strategy attribute (i.e., feedback value 1* corresponds to *list value 1 of failed feature, new feature and repair used)*. Figure 4 shows the correspondence. The figure shows that the values of *<Alist 1>* in the *feedback attribute* caused the values of *<&list1>* in the *failed feature new feature value*
and repair *strategy attributes*. This correspondence will be used in the future for determining possible adaptations that will be done. This will also be used in identifying *anticipators*[6].

4.1. Case Learning

Learning in all case-based reasoning systems occurs as a natural consequence of reasoning (Kolodner, 1993). In CBR-Tutor, the CTA is responsible for identifying cases to be learned through its evaluator component. CBR-Tutor achieves its learning in

---

[6] Anticipators are sets of features and values with the corresponding reasoning goal that helps the case retriever anticipate and avoid potential problems.

several ways, re-indexing, and creation of new generalizations and the acquisition of new cases. Because case-based planner (like CBR-Tutor that plans instructional strategies) makes use of existing plans to create new ones, the most natural thing for it to be learning is new plans so that it can adapt them for later use.

In all case-based planners, the most important issue in learning plans is indexing since it does it function (i.e., plan) by finding the best match between new goals and old plans (Riesbeck and Schank, 1989). Therefore, a case-based planner must learn new plans, features to predict a problem and learn specific fixes that can be applied to repair the plan it has to use. Re-indexing in CBR-Tutor occurs when a case is re-trieved and evaluated to be inappropriate so that the case will not be retrieved as is in situations such as the new situation (where it was proven to be inappropriate). This is done by checking the *outcome* of executing the solution case. The solution case (if modified) is re-indexed based on the value of the *feedback* and *failed_feature attributes*. At the same time, *anticipators* are added to the *list of anticipators*. The algorithm for re-indexing adopts the algorithm for constructing the hierarchy of cases. Figure 5 shows the re-indexing algorithm.

When the case fails:
1. If the value of *feedback* attribute contains *fail* then re-index the case by:
    1.1. Add *failed_features* and the corresponding *goal* to the *list of anticipators*
    1.2. Deleting the case from the current hierarchy
    1.3. Removing the list of values of *failed_feature* from the *prioritized feature list* in the hierarchy
    1.4. Updating the value of *feedback* to *failed* or *plan-modified* before re-indexing
    1.5. Insert the case (with the modified *prioritized feature list* in 1.2) using the algorithm in constructing the redundant discrimination network.

When the case succeeds:
2. If the value of the end of the list in the *feedback attribute* is *successful* or *plan-modified* or *plan-extended* then
    2.1. Add the case into the memory using the new situation using the algorithm for organizing/adding cases

---

Fig. 5. Algorithm for Re-indexing and Adding a Case.

5. Summary and Conclusion

This paper presented how CBR is used in the design of CBR-Tutor. All the phases of CBR applied to planning instructional activities in CBR-Tutor were discussed. In CBR-Tutor, planning is done per topic and the strategies are modified as interaction is being done with the learner (real time). The cases in CBR-Tutor are organized as re-dundant discrimination network. This affects how cases are retrieved and re-indexed (or learned). Currently, more cases are being collected to be able to test and analyze the results of the application of CBR approach in a tutoring system. Also, the system is currently evaluated to empirically show that the use of CBR in designing a tutoring system overcomes the rule-based system's shortcomings.

References

1. Aamodt, A., Plaza, E. (1994). Case-Based Reasoning: Foundational Issues, Methodological Variations, and System Approaches. *AI Communications*. IOS Press, Vol. 7:1, pp. 39-59

2. Jona, Menachem (1998). Representing and Applying Teaching Strategies in Computer-Based Learning-by-Doing Tutors. In Schank, R. (Ed). *Inside Multi-Media Case-Based Instruction*. Lawrence Erlbaum Associates, Publishers. Mahwah, New Jersey.

3. Kolodner, J. (1993). *Case-Based Reasoning*. Morgan Kaufmann Publishers, Inc.

4. Reisbeck, C. and Schank, R. (1989). *Inside Case-based Reasoning*. Hillsdale, New Jersey: Lawrence Erlbaum Associates, Publishers.

5. Reyes, R. and Sison, R.(2000). CBR-Tutor: A Case-Based Reasoning Approach to an Internet Agent-Based Tutoring System. *International Conference on Computers In Education/ International Conference on Computer–Assisted Instruction 2000*. Taipei, Taiwan. November 21-24, 2000

6. Reyes,R. and Sison R. (2001) . Using Case-Based Reasoning in an Internet-based Tutoring Systems. *International Conference in Artificial Intelligence in Education 2001 (AIED 2001)*. San Antonio, Texas. May 2001.

7. Reyes, R. and Sison, R. (2001b). Representing and Organizing Cases in CBR-Tutor. *International Conference on Computers In Education/ International Conference on Computer –Assisted Instruction 2000*. South Korea. November 2001

8. Sison, R . (2000). Multistrategy Discovery and Detection of Novice Programmer Errors. Machine Learning, 38, 157-180. Kluwer Academic Publishers, Netherlands.

Feature Construction for Student Group Forming Based on Their Browsing Behaviors in an E-learning System

Tiffany Y. Tang[*][1] and Keith C. Chan[2]

[1]Dept. of Computer Science, Univ. of Saskatchewan, Saskatoon, SK S7N 5A9, Canada
yat751@mail.usask.ca

[2]Dept. of Computing, the Hong Kong Polytechnic University, Hung Hom, Hong Kong
cskcchan@comp.polyu.edu.hk

Abstract. Group learning is an effective and efficient way to promote greater academic success. However, almost all group-learning systems stress collaborative learning activity itself, with few focused on how groups should be formed. In this paper, we present a novel group forming technique based on students' browsing behaviors with the help of a curriculum knowledge base. To achieve this, a data clustering technique was adopted. Before clustering, new features are constructed based on an arithmetic-composition-based feature construction technique. Preliminary results have shown that the new features can well represent the problem space and thus make the group forming outcomes more convincing.

1. Introduction

Group learning has been explored extensively in various education systems [e.g. 1, 11, 16] since it is deemed as an effective way to promote greater academic achievement. However, most of the existing systems only stress collaborative learning activities inside that group (e.g. collaborative learning, competitive learning etc.), and little attention is put on the formation of that group. In our ongoing research, we investigate group-forming based upon students' browsing behaviors[1] in either web-based or non-web-based learning environments where tutors are spatially and physically separated from students [15]. It is believed that students' browsing activities are a reliable indicator of their knowledge skills, interests, and learning progress. Therefore, by monitoring their browsing activities, we could place together students with similar learning

---

[*] The work was conducted while the author was still with Department of Computing, Hong Kong Polytechnic University, Hong Kong.

[1] Generally, students' browsing behaviors can be seen as sequences of their activities: chapter by chapter order in non-web-based learning environments or page by page URL order in web-based learning environments. In the context of this paper, students' browsing behaviors refer to the later.

M. Ishizuka and A. Sattar (Eds.): PRICAI 2002, LNAI 2417, pp. 512-521, 2002.
© Springer-Verlag Berlin Heidelberg 2002

characteristics, and then various actions can be taken accordingly. The group-forming in our discussion here is based on an observation of students' learning activities, i.e. in the absence of any questionnaires or examinations. The difficulty in this group-forming is in determining or constructing the right features/variables for clustering process, because the available data is very limited and may contain severe noises. Our work here attempts to construct new features and analyzes them using simulated data with the help of *curriculum knowledge,* which would be described later. We also show that some extracted features may not be able to represent well the actual features in the existence of severe noises and/or an inherently deficient structure. Before we proceed, a brief overview of related works and some basic concepts are given here. It has been observed in [6] that to some extent, *users' (or customers') browsing behaviors* are related to their degree of interest towards a page or topic. And the findings have already been applied to personalized newspaper-browsing [7], information filtering [8], etc. In the context of learning environments, however, the students' browsing behaviors have rarely been extensively used to aid tutoring/learning. There are a few exceptions of research conducted that mainly made use of the "footprints" students left while browsing to aid learning [4, 9, 14]. For example, in [9], the JUPITIER system is capable of recording students' browsed documents, and recommending relevant *kanji* words to them. In another distance learning environment, tutors can construct a personalized-e-articles-reading tree based on the predetermined keyword(s), while the e-articles are mandatory reading materials [14]. From another perspective, these two methods are much like text or keywords driven information retrieving, because no students' learning characteristics are considered. Ha etc. [4], however, takes these into consideration. They presented a prototype to mine aggregate paths for learners engaged in a distance education environment based on the information of learners' educational levels. But they only considered the analysis of path traversal pattern of learners and did not consider the *curriculum knowledge,* which is the key factor here.

Curriculum knowledge is a meta-level knowledge that contains the goal structure of the course, organizing methods of the contents and in which order how the course contents should be delivered to students [2]. One of the few tutoring systems equipped with a curriculum knowledge base is the SQL-Tutor developed by Gang and his colleagues [2]. Yet, the entire curriculum knowledge base is constructed solely based on instructors' understanding of the course materials. However, in our view, students' browsing behaviors and the curriculum knowledge should not be separated. "The domain of learning", the "type of instructional material", and a learner's characteristics had long been identified as factors which can jointly contribute to the success of a distance learning environment [3]. But very few of current ITSs (Intelligent Tutoring Systems) address these factors together. In our ongoing research, we intend to take a more comprehensive way of facilitating learning by combining learners' browsing behaviors and curriculum knowledge together. Part of the curriculum knowledge are constructed based on tutors' understanding and experiences with the course contents, while the rest of it will be generated based on the clustered student groups. In this paper, we will show how to use curriculum knowledge and learners' browsing behavior to extract learners' relevant skills.

The organization of the rest of this paper is as follows: in the next section we will describe the pre-stored curriculum knowledge base, followed by a discussion on data generation process. Then feature construction technique will be illustrated. The experiments to test the technique and an analysis will also be described. Finally, we will present the clustering process and its result with the constructed features and some original ones. We conclude this paper by a brief analysis of the feature construction and the clustering algorithm.

2. Curriculum Knowledge in Our Domain

Figure 1 below shows part of the pre-stored curriculum knowledge base of the course contents in our system. Each node represents a chapter, and each directed-edge denotes the prerequisite relationship between two chapters. We assume that there is one topic in each chapter. Table 1 lists three main properties which describe the difficulty of learning that chapter, i.e., W: writing level, T: technical level, and P: presentation level. $W, T, P \in \{0,1,...,10\}$. The *writing level* of a topic includes page/sentences length, number of conceptual definition, verbal usage and writing organization. *Technical level* includes mathematical/symbolic formulation, algorithms, proof of theorems, etc. *Presentation level* contains graphical presentation, say, system architecture or flow diagram, examples, case study, etc. The levels of them are determined subjectively by authors based on their experiences, where higher value represents higher difficulty. Each topic/sub-topic is literally an URL in a web-based instruction environment or a real chapter in a computer-based instruction environment. Without loss of generality, in the rest of this paper we will use the term chapter to indicate each topic/sub-topic. Moreover, in order to learn each chapter smoothly, the learner should understand some important part of its prerequisite chapters. The fractions (%) of prerequisite knowledge for each chapter are shown in the round bracket in table 1. For example, in order to learn chapter 2, learner should understand at least 50% of the important part of chapter 1. Of course, if a learner has learned 50% of the important part of chapter 1, it does not mean that she can learn chapter 2 smoothly, because those 50% knowledge does not exactly match those needed in understanding chapter 2.

In addition, we assume that the course is *mandatory* for all students; during the course of study, they will not be interrupted by any *external* factors such as answering phone calls, talking, making notes etc, but they might be affected by *internal* learning factors such as memory retention; students might have some prior knowledge. For most ITSs, it is assumed that students do not have any prior knowledge. The fact that they started with a prior knowledge of the subject content would cause noises to learning speed and outcomes. However, we would relax this assumption by allowing students to have prior knowledge in six of the 14 chapters. But, we will test both cases, either with or without prior knowledge. Moreover, in most research on web learning, it is assumed that students will move on to learn a new topic only after they have understood current one(s) [13]. However in our framework, they are allowed to proceed as long as they are prepared in terms of their *expectancy* towards current topic.

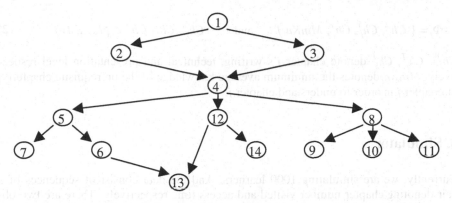

Fig. 1. A directed tree structure of the course content

Table 1.

Node/ Chapter <W, T, P> and (prerequisite chapter: min. % of knowledge)	
1. <7, 1, 1>	8. <4, 6, 4> (Ch4: 30%)
2. <5, 4, 1> (Ch1: 50%)	9. <4, 8, 8> (Ch8: 60%)
3. <7, 6, 3> (Ch1: 60%)	10. <5, 8, 8> (Ch8: 60%)
4. <2, 1, 1> (Ch2: 50%), (Ch3: 50%)	11. <4, 8, 8> (Ch8: 60%)
5. <5, 6, 4> (Ch4: 30%)	12 <5, 8, 5> (Ch4: 30%)
6. <3, 3, 4> (Ch5: 50%)	13. <5, 8, 6> (Ch6: 70%), (Ch12: 90%)
7. <4, 4, 4> (Ch5: 80%)	14 <6, 8, 6> (Ch12: 90%)

And the time spent on each page is always considered as her effective learning time (In most web-based research, pages accessed for a time less than a threshold are denoted as navigation usage type [12]. In this paper, we assume that time spent on every page by students is larger than the threshold). For each learner i, we have L^i denoting his/her overall learning characteristics, where

$$L^i = \{R, T, A, B, Ex\} \quad \text{and} \quad B \in \{b_1, b_2, b_3, b_4, b_5, b_8, b_{12}\} \tag{1}$$

R, denotes the overall reading skill of each learner. T, or *TechnicalKnowledge* denotes learners' previous knowledge, which might help them understand any chapter's technical aspects. A, or *AnalyticalSkill* represents learners' ability in understanding diagrams, flowcharts, etc. Some students may possess relevant knowledge to some extent, denoted as their B or *BasicKnowledge*, which can facilitate their learning speed and overall learning outcomes. Ex specifies a learner's *subjective* attitude and expectancy towards the knowledge to be acquired. It can also be seen as how much knowledge the learner should earn before she moves on. If the expectancy is not earned enough, backward learning is necessary. It is one of the major features of our system. We also assume that for learner i, L^i is stable throughout his/her studies. It is reasonable in that a learner's overall learning skills will not be largely affected through the learning of only one course. For chapter/topic j, we have Φ_j, denoting *content complexity*, where

$$\Phi_j = \{ Ch_j^W, Ch_j^T, Ch_j^P, MinKn_j \} \quad \text{and} \quad Ch_j^W, Ch_j^T, Ch_j^P \in \{1, ..., 10\} \tag{2}$$

Ch_j^W, Ch_j^T, Ch_j^P denote chapter j's writing, technical and presentation level respectively; $MinKn_j$ denotes the minimum average knowledge of the prerequisite chapter(s) of chapter j in order to understand chapter j.

3. Simulator

Currently, we are simulating 1000 learners. And the data consist of sequences of a pair denoting chapter number visited and access time respectively. There are two objects: *Learner* and *Chapter*. For learner i and chapter j (Ch_j):

Kn_j^i : learner i's knowledge of Ch_j, $Kn_j^i \in \{0, 1, ..., 1000\}$, note here that it is incremental as the learner continues to learn

Ex_j^i : learner i's expectancy for Ch_j, $Ex_j^i \in \{0, 1, ..., 1000\}$

$_{pre}j$: the prerequisite chapter(s) of Ch_j

Kn_{prej}^i : learner i's knowledge of the prerequisite chapter(s) of Ch_j

R^i : learner i's *ReadingSkill*, $R^i \in [50, 100]$

T^i : learner i's *TechnicalKnowledge*, $T^i \in [50, 100]$

A^i : learner i's AnalyticalSkill, $A^i \in [50, 100]$

```
1.   FUNCTION Process_Chapter(j)
2.       WHILE Knⱼⁱ < Exⱼⁱ
3.           Increase the time spent on chapter j by
                  Chⱼᵂ / Rⁱ + Chⱼᴾ / Aⁱ + Chⱼᵀ / Tⁱ
4.           Knⱼⁱ = Knⱼⁱ + 1
5.           FOR each pre-requisite of chapter j, ₚᵣₑj:
6.               IF Knₚᵣₑⱼⁱ < 1000 AND
                     Knₚᵣₑⱼⁱ / MinKnⱼ < Random_value ∈ [0.4, 1.4] THEN
7.                   {    Record the time spent on chapter j
8.                       Exₚᵣₑⱼⁱ = Exₚᵣₑⱼⁱ + Random_value∈ [0, 100]
9.                       IF Exₚᵣₑⱼⁱ > 1000 THEN Exₚᵣₑⱼⁱ = 1000 END IF
10.                      RECURSIVE CALL FUNCTION Process_Chapter(ₚᵣₑj)
11.                  } END IF
12.          LOOP FOR
13.      LOOP WHILE
14.      Record Knⱼⁱ
15.      Record the rest time spent on chapter j
16.  END FUNCTION
```

Fig. 2. The learner i's learning activities

4. Feature Construction

In feature construction, new features are generated from given features and added to help clustering the data set [5]. In our domain, how to select chapter(s) that can be used to well represent a learner's abilities is the key to uncover the relationships between a learner's abilities and access time.

4.1. A Formal Description of Feature Construction

Formally, given observed browsing behavior of learners as $S = [S^1 S^2 ... S^i]$, a priori known content complexity as $\Phi = [\Phi_1 \Phi_2 ... \Phi_j]$, actual learners' characteristics as $L = [L^1 L^2 ... L^i]$, and estimated learners' characteristics as $L_e = [L^1_e L^2_e ... L^i_e]$. Where L_e is an estimation derived based on feature construction function $F(S, \Phi)$. Then the problem of feature construction is defined as finding

$$\underset{Le}{Min}\left[L_e \perp L\right] = \underset{F}{Min}\left[F(S,\Phi) \perp L\right] \tag{3}$$

Where $\perp$ is a binary operator to measure the accuracy of L_e in estimating L such as a simple correlation operator or distance measure. For learner i, we have sequence

$$S^i = (Ch_1, Time^i_1)(Ch_2, Time^i_2) .... (Ch_j, Time^i_j) \tag{4}$$

Since the learner may visit the same chapter more than once, then, we performed a simple computation on the generated sequences by counting the total number of visits and the total time spent in reading each chapter. Then, the data become:

$$(Frequency(ch_j), TotalTime(ch_j)), \forall ch_j \in \{1, 2, ..., 14\} \tag{5}$$

We divide the chapters into three categories, i.e. chapters without branch, chapters with branches but not crucial in learning their subsequent chapters and chapters with many branches and very important in learning their subsequent chapters. Only chapters in the last categories may cause higher frequency of visits. But, if the learner has higher expectancy to study those chapters, then she will well understand them in the first visits and therefore make less return to them in the future. Consequently, by comparing the frequency of visits to those chapters across all learners, we could derive the expectancy of them toward those chapters. In our simulated data, we use independent distribution in generating expectancy. Since we assume that the total time spent on each chapter is linearly dependent on learner's abilities, a direct method for feature construction is by linear regression. However, there are two main reasons for not adopting linear regression here:
1. A varying expectancy and requirement over chapters cause the regression based on the total time spent on those chapters to be less powerful.
2. The learner might forget, so she needs to go back. Therefore, some noises might be observed. In our simulation, the number of data is only 14 (i.e., the number of chapter), which is too small to neglect those noises.

Next we will describe a data manipulation approach, i e. arithmetic-composition-based feature construction.

4.2. An Arithmetic-Composition-Based Feature Construction

In order to find a representative of learners' reading skill, we choose the total time spent on chapter 1 only. Because from table 1, the difficulty of chapter 1 is <7, 1, 1>, which its writing level equals to 7 while its technical level and analytical level equal to 1. This extremely contrast pattern may help the magnification of total time due to reading process only. Therefore, the total time spent on this chapter will well represent learners' reading skills. Problem arises when there is no contrasting pattern in the curriculum knowledge. A small arithmetic manipulation is used here. Formally, the problem becomes finding the maximum contrast of element $x \in \{W, T, P\}$ using arithmetic-composition function $G(<W, T, P>_j)$.

5. Experimentation

Totally, there are 50 sets of data generated using the algorithm described before, where each 10 sets of data represents different initial conditions, therefore there are 5 initial conditions. The differences among the 10 data sets lie in the initial distribution of learners' properties, i.e., their expectancies and prior knowledge. For the first set of data, we assume that learners have a wider range of both expectancies and prior knowledge, called Free Learning (FL). As for the second set, we assume that learners have a narrower range of both expectancies and prior knowledge, called Less Free Learning (LFL). In the third set, we assume that learners have narrower range of expectancies and without any prior knowledge, called No Prior Knowledge Learning (NPKL). In the forth set, we assume that learners have very narrow range of expectancies but with wider range of prior knowledge, called Mandatory Learning (ML). For the last set of data, we assume that learners have very narrow range of expectancies and without any prior knowledge, called No Prior Knowledge and Mandatory Learning (NPKML).

5.1. Verifications

We attempt to find whether the constructed features (i.e. which chapter or combined chapters) can be reliably used to represent learners' real abilities. If so, then these constructed features are added for clustering. We have two ways to accomplish this. Firstly, a comparison of the correlation between constructed features with that of real abilities is taken into consideration. Secondly, we compare clusters generated from constructed features and clusters generated from the real abilities of students.

From the first experiment, we get the correlation between constructed features with that of real abilities. From the first set of data, the correlation between total time spent on chapter 1 and reading skills is -0.43, which means a moderate inverse relationship. Moreover, we conclude that: Chapter 1 has higher correlation to the reading ability in all treatment, i.e. -0.43 to -0.96. Chapters 6, 8, and 12 have relatively stable and high correlation to all abilities in all treatments, i.e., their average correlation and standard deviation are -0.43 and 0.15 respectively. Chapters 2 and 5 have relatively high correlation to all abilities in the absence of prior knowledge (NPKL and NPKML), i.e., $-0,52$. Chapter 4 has relatively high correlation to reading ability in mandatory treatment (ML and NPKML). Chapters 9, 10 and 11 have relatively high correlation to technical and analytical abilities in mandatory treatment (ML and NPKML).

In order to compare the effectiveness of the feature construction approach, we extract the coefficients of the least squares regression. Then we compute the correlation between those parameters with the real abilities. The averages of their correlation are shown in the left column of table 2 below. As a comparison, we choose (chapter 1; <7, 1, 1>) and two arithmetic composition, i.e., (chapter 8 + chapter 12; <9, 14, 9>) as described earlier, and (2 x chapter 6 - chapter 2; <1, 2, 7>), to represent reading skills, technical knowledge, and analytical knowledge, respectively. The averages of correlation are shown in the right column of table 2.

Table 2. Average correlation to real abilities

	Linear Regression			Arithmetic composition		
	Reading	Technical	Analytical	Reading	Technical	Analytical
FL	-0.33	-0.25	0.14	-0.43	-0.47	-0.26
LFL	-0.56	-0.33	-0.16	-0.81	-0.68	-0.31
NPKL	-0.60	-0.39	-0.17	-0.91	-0.73	-0.28
ML	-0.49	-0.19	-0.46	-0.54	-0.46	-0.64
NPKML	-0.85	-0.59	-0.71	-0.96	-0.74	-0.83

We conclude that constructed feature from (chapter 1; <7, 1, 1>), (chapter 8 + chapter 12; <9, 14, 9>), and (2 x chapter 6 - chapter 2; <1, 2, 7>) can better represent real abilities of reading skills, technical knowledge, and analytical skills respectively.

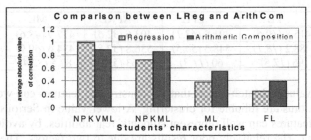

Fig. 3. The correlation between actual and constructed students' characteristics using linear regression and arithmetic selection

Figure 3 above shows that when learners do not have previous knowledge and are serious on learning, then linear regression technique can predict the actual value very precisely (correlation > .98). Otherwise arithmetic selection outperforms linear regression. All the evaluations we made are based on the *correlation* between constructed features and learners' real abilities. That correlation can only represent the reliability of each constructed feature, which would be used in clustering for group formation.

5.2. A Weighted-Euclidean-Distance-Based Data Clustering

A simple distance-based clustering is used to test our constructed features. In this experiment, we only choose the three constructed features described above. We adopt the *weighted Euclidean distance*, in which the weight is the inverse value of the total sum of the difficulty level,

$$w_x = [G_j(W) + G_j(T) + G_j(P)]^{-1} \tag{6}$$

where G_j is the arithmetic-composition function specifically for contrasting $x \in \{W, T, P\}$. And the *weighted Euclidean distance* between two points, m and n, is

$$d_{mn} = [\Sigma \ w_x(x_m - x_n)^2]^{0.5} \tag{7}$$

The distance-based clustering will partition all the data into an element of cluster set C according to the nearest distance between the data and the center of clusters. The number of cluster is set to 3, representing low, medium and high ability. And we choose the minimum, average, and maximum values as their initial centers. Then the cluster results are compared to the clusters obtained from learners' real abilities. We use the same clustering method for learners' real abilities, except without weighting the distance measure. Those two sets of clusters are analyzed by using error measurement. We categorize the result by three simple criteria, i.e., match, erroneous, and seriously erroneous label. The results for each treatment are shown in table 3 below. The italic value in parentheses represents its standard deviations.

Table 3. Clustering result

	FL	LFL	NPKL	ML	NPKML
Match	415.8 *(19.6)*	391.5 *(63.1)*	403.6 *(32.6)*	477.9 *(43.6)*	580 *(52.5)*
Error	488.2 *(18.1)*	548.5 *(56.5)*	536.8 *(32.8)*	434.6 *(69.9)*	402 *(39.4)*
Serious	96 *(17.5)*	60 *(11.3)*	59.63 *(5.29)*	87.5 *(32.4)*	18 *(23.8)*

A higher value in Match means that the constructed features can well represent the real abilities, thus are reliable for clustering. A lower value in Serious means that the constructed features can well represent students' real abilities, by avoiding serious error in labeling. The relatively poor results are due to two factors. The first is that the algorithm can not always find an optimal result, e.g. if we sort the data, the result may be better. The second is that the number of experiment is relatively small (10 experiments for each treatment). However, we have shown the right way in constructing representative features in clustering.

6. Conclusions and Future Work

In general, we have observed:
1. Under some assumptions, the passive observation of browsing behavior can be used in extracting learner's properties/abilities.
2. In free learning, terminal chapters cannot accurately represent real properties. But in mandatory treatment, some of them can accurately represent real properties.

3. A sharp/contrasting pattern of the level of difficulty could represent real properties very well, which is shown by the performance of chapter 1 in our simulation.

4. An arithmetic composition of learners' learning time on each chapter with some information about the curriculum knowledge could increase the accuracy of the constructed features.

In this paper, we only focus on how to construct features for the clustering algorithm. Yet, later on, we shall attempt to design a representative or model-based clustering which would be better comparing to the simple clustering algorithm we adopted.

References

[1] Dorneich, M.C. and Jones, P.M. The design and implementation of a learning collaboratory. *Proc. of 2000 IEEE Int'l Conf. on Systems, Man, and Cybernetics*, vol. 2, 146-1151.

[2] Gang, Z, Wang, J.T.L and Ng, P.A. Curriculum knowledge representation and manipulation in knowledge-based tutoring systems. *IEEE Trans. of Knowledge and Data Engineering*, 8(5), 679-689.

[3] Girishwar, M. Development of learning skills in the context of distance education. *Indian Journal of Psychometry and Education, vol. 24(1):1-6*, Jan.1993.

[4] Ha, S.H., Bae, S.M. and Park, S.C. Web mining for distance education. *Proc. of the 2000 IEEE Int'l Conf. on Management of Innovation and Technology*, vol.2, 715-219, 2000.

[5] Han, J. and Kamber, M. *Data mining: concepts and techniques*. Morgan Kaufmann Publishers.2000.

[6] Hijikata,Y. Estimating a user's degree of interest in a page during Web browsing. *Proc. of 1999 IEEE Int'l Conf. Systems, Man, and Cybernetics, SMC'99*, vol.4, 105-110.

[7] Kamba, T., Sakagami, H. and Koseki, Y. Anatagonomy: a personalized Newspaper on the World Wide Web. *Int'l J. Human Computer Studies, Vol.46, No.6*, June 1997, 789-803.

[8] Lang, K. News Weeder: learning to filter Netnews. *Proc. of the 12th Int'l Conf. on Machine Learning, ICML'95*, Morgan Kaufmann, San Francisco, 1995, 331-339.

[9] Ochi,Y.; Yano,Y.; Hayashi,T. and Wakita,R. JUPITER: a kanji learning environment focusing on a learner's browsing. *Proc. of the 3rd Asia Pacific Conf. on Computer Human Interaction, 446-451*, 1998.

[10] Saxe, G.B., Gearhart, M. and Seltzer, M. Relations between classroom practices and student learning in the domain of fractions. *Cognition and Instruction, vol 17(1):1-24*, 1999: Lawrence Erlbaum Assoc. Publishers.

[11] Shaw, M.J., Harrow, B. and Herman, S. Distributed artificial intelligence for multi-agent problem solving and group learning. *Proc. of the 24th Annual Hawaii Int'l Conf. on System Sciences*, 1991, vol. 4, 13-26.

[12] Srivastava, J. Mining web data for E-commerce (Powerpoint file). An invited tutorial talk in *PKDD'2001*, HK.

[13] Stern, Mia. K and Woolf, B.P. Curriculum sequencing in a web-based tutor. *Proc. of the Int'l Conf. on Intelligent Tutoring Systems (ITS'98)*.

[14] Tang, C, Lau, R.W.H., Li, Q., Yin, H., Li, T. and Kilis, D. Personalized courseware construction based on web data mining. *Proc. of the 1st Int'l Conf. on Web Information Systems Engineering*, vol.2, 204-211, 2000.

[15] Tang, T.Y., Chan, K.C., Winoto, P., and Wu, A. Forming student clusters based on their browsing behaviors. *Proc. of the 9th Int'l Conf. on Computers in Education*, Korea, Nov 12-15, 2001, vol. 3, 1229-1235.

[16] Wooten, E. C. Cooperative learning: introduced in three different levels of electrical engineering courses at a military institution. *Proc. of the 28th Int'l Conf. on Frontiers in Education*, vol.3, 1179-1184.

Web-Based Tutoring System for Computer Security

Chong-woo Woo and Jin-woo Choi

Dept. of Computer Science, Kookmin University
861-1 Chongnung-Dong, Sungbuk-ku, Seoul, Korea
cwwoo@kookmin.ac.kr

Abstract. The recent development of the computer network technology has brought us many benefits including the electronic business. But also, one serious side effect is the explosive increase of the unauthorized computer access, and it becomes a big social problem. Of course, there are many security solutions in the market, but they cannot stop such intrusions or reduce the damages resulting from such accident. Besides, the protection of the system requires significant amount of the budget. Therefore, we need to think of minimizing damages or avoiding from the intrusions. One possible solution might be providing a training system to the system managers who are in charge of maintaining and protecting the servers. In this paper, we are suggesting a simulated security training system in the virtual learning environment. The system is being built based on the ITS structure primarily, and mainly focused on providing the simulated security exercises adaptively. For instance, since the system maintains the solution paths, the student's problem solving steps are monitored and being interrupted with advising messages when necessary. It is designed as a client/server environment, so the student needs only the web browser to access the system. And the student can execute the selected task in the Java applet-based virtual OS environment according to the learning scenario.

1 Introduction

The recent development of the computer network technology has brought us many benefits, including the electronic business. But also, a serious side effect is the explosive increase of the unauthorized computer access, and it becomes a big social problem. Of course, there are many security solutions, such as the firewall or Intrusion Detection System (IDS), which are being studied in various directions [1][5][6]. And some of them become successful commercial products. But until now, they cannot stop the attacker and the damages are sharply increasing. Besides, such protection requires a significant amount of the budget. One possible solution about this side effect might be training the system manager who is in charge of maintaining and protecting the computer system. Of course the managers are running into many kinds of security educations, but most of them are lectures, which does not really help them to keep up with the existing field experiences. Therefore, there is a strong need of exercising on the computer security education, especially development of a simulation program to train the system managers.

M. Ishizuka and A. Sattar (Eds.): PRICAI 2002, LNAI 2417, pp. 522-531, 2002.
© Springer-Verlag Berlin Heidelberg 2002

The recent research on the security education for the system manager is the ID-Tutor [9]. This system creates an audit file using the AI planning method, and the student can simulate the system, and being tutored based on the tutoring rules. The system provides a good framework for the security education, since the simulation could give more comprehensive insights for understanding the mechanism of the system. Other than the ID-Tutor, we do not have any particular security training system yet, which means we need to study on this topic urgently.

In this paper, we are describing a security tutoring system aiming for training the system managers to combat for the computer intrusions. On building the system, we have several implementation goals. First, as we explained in the above, the security training system will give significant educational effect for the system managers, and also it may contribute for reducing the overall cost on the protection of the computer systems. Second, the system can be extended easily without re-building the system. So that, we developed the system on the UNIX security problem, with one specific issue on the 'vulnerability' and later, we are extending the system with different topic successfully. Third, the system must provide the student a virtual learning environment without effect anything on the system. This virtual environment can be explained fully in the next section. Fourth, the system must be intelligent enough to support each individual user adaptively. With the ITS capability, the system maintains each student's history as a student model and could support the student in various ways including the hint, and help messages. Finally, the architecture is being built based on a client/server. Therefore, the student needs only the web browser to access and manipulate the tasks within the virtual OS environment according to the well-designed learning scenario.

2   System Design

The test domain of the system is the UNIX security problem. Since the UNIX security topics are too diverse to implement within a single tutoring system, we have limited the scope of the system only within the 'vulnerability' issue first. We selected this issue because the 'vulnerability' is one of the most important tasks that the system manager needs to check in everyday situation, and also needs to learn the step-by-step procedure carefully [4]. From the successful implementation of the initial version of this topic, we extended the system with another topic. That is, the attacker tracing system, which follows the attacker with some evidences in the system-generated log files [10]. This topic is also important, because the computer intrusion become too serious, we need to learn more active response mechanism. We are developing a training system with these security topics.

The system begins with a set of topics (a curriculum), which is generated from the knowledge base dynamically. The selected topic (a goal) by the student is to be expanded into several tasks (sub-goals) by the instructional planner, and the each generated task can be achieved by asking the student to simulate the situation. The main focus lies on the development of virtual learning environment and creation of web-based Intelligent Tutoring System (ITS)[2][8]. For the simulation exercise, we are providing a virtual learning environment, which does not need to modify any file structure in the system. This environment looks like a real OS environment, so that the student could feel the real situation. In order to build the main architecture of the system, we have adapted a typical ITS structure [see figure 1], including the expert module, the tutor module, the student module, and the user interface module. The detailed structure of each module is explained in the next subsection.

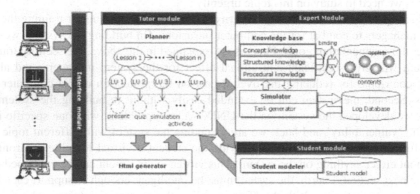

Fig. 1. The main architecture of the System

2.1 The Learning Environment

We first have implemented a virtual learning environment in Java applet. Within this virtual UNIX Operating System, the student can practice the security exercises. The advantages of the system is on the following few facts.

User Interface: The user interface for the system is the command-driven, since the simulation exercise requires students to be familiar with a series of the specific UNIX commands in sequence. The commands are executable virtually, and the student can find out the results. For example, if the student's command is 'mkdir temp', then 'temp' directory is actually created in the given environment.

Knowledge-Structure: The knowledge base is created with the S-expression, which is similar to LISP-like structure. This S-expression can be easily extended or manipulated. We do not actually create any physical directory rather we could have the same effect by just extending the knowledge structure. In addition, we need the LISP-like interpreter to allow this S-expression. Also, we need to prepare the LISP-like templates to provide the environment the student. For instance, in the [Figure 3], the root directory is created in the beginning, and the $username is ready to bind with user login ID.

Virtual OS: In fact, the virtual OS is expressed as a string, and it does not need to be executed in the Server-side. Therefore, the simulation does not affect the actual file system. For example, the real 'telnet' application uses the network resource and the memory space, but this virtual OS does not use any memory space. Also, the student's command does not need to execute any actual system process. This would be another advantage.

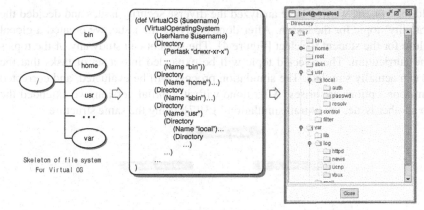

Fig. 3. The Structure for the virtual OS

2.2 ITS Structure

The system has adapted the ITS structure, but it is being developed with only the essential part in this version with emphasizing on the security contents, leaving the rest for the next update.

The expert module consists of a 'domain knowledge base', 'problem solver', and 'task generator'. The domain knowledge base is designed with the concept of object-oriented structure, and includes several different types of knowledges; the concept knowledge to explain upon request from the student, procedural knowledge to check the student's progress and give hints when necessary, and some other objects, such as, images objects and applet objects to combine with the text knowledge. The 'task generator' collects the necessary objects, such as the applets and other related knowledge, and combines them together to generate a simulation exercise. The problem solver provides an appropriate feedback after analyzing the student's performance during the simulation.

The tutor is basically in charge of planning the entire lesson contents. In this system, the tutor provides a curriculum first. And then from the selected topic, it generates a lesson plan, such as, concept explanation, step-by-step practice, and simulation. The concepts are about basic security definitions, usage of UNIX commands, and etc. After going through reading the concepts, the system will ask the student to solve the simulation exercise. The control for system is basically mixed-initiative: at the beginning of the lesson, the student can select the scenario on the given menu, or the student can ask for the system to suggest the topic. In both cases, the tutor can plan a lesson for the selected topic dynamically.

The student model represents the student's learning progress. In this system, we have implemented in minimal, so that we could only check correct or incorrect answers. This will be updated with more diverse strategy for the next version of the system.

3 The Virtual Simulation

To build the system, we first have analyzed the diverse security issues and decided the 'vulnerability' topic for the lesson. After done studying the issue, we created a global curriculum for the student to select [Figure 4]. The student can study any of the topics from the curriculum. The selected topic will be expanded into a set of tasks that the student can actually simulate. The simulation process will be evaluated, and corrected if any misconceptions are arises. After done with it's initial version, we extended the topic to another issue, 'audit trail simulation ' [3][7], using the same structure.

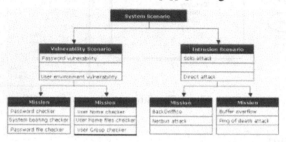

Fig. 4. Curriculum for the Simulation System

3.1 Task Generation

After the virtual OS is created, the next step is to generate a complete task environment for the student to exercise. For example, if the student selects a topic, then all the necessary information is collected from the knowledge base and forms an applet. The detailed process is as follows.

①   Select a task from the menu.
②   Retrieves the related knowledge structure from the knowledge base
③   Loads the required objects into the structure
④   Collects the procedural knowledge, and binds them all into the structure
⑤   Makes S-expression structure

This procedure works for other security topics. For instance, if the selected topic is the 'buffer overflow attack'. Then the 'log' knowledge structure is created first retrieving from the knowledge base, and the log data table is constructed as S-expression. The rest of the processes are the same as before. The student gets this generated task as an applet in the student's viewer.

3.2 Procedural Event

The system has another type of knowledge, which is 'event knowledge'. The event knowledge provides diversity for the student's performance. The same task can be performed differently based on the dynamic event knowledge. For example, the 'password checker' task can have 'newmail' event or 'nomail' event, based on the event knowledge. Besides, this event knowledge does not depend on the control from the server rather it works within the simulation environment by the event controller.

3.3 Evaluation

The system evaluates the student with the following procedure. When the task is selected, the system generates the correct answer as a sequence of UNIX commands. Then student modeler evaluates the student's answer by comparing with the correct answer. Then, the tutor receives the final result from the modeler, and reply to the student with appropriate acknowledgements.

In the 'audit trail simulation', the student supposed to check the log data table to make an answer, since the attacker leaves some evidences in the log files. The modeler needs to examine whether the student have solved the problem in correct steps or intuitively. This requires very careful analysis of judging the student's problem solving behavior. We have approached with a 'check-box' strategy, which needs to be checked for each line in the log data tables if suspicious. The log data is designed as in the [Figure 5], each of which has a different table structure. The evaluation procedure for this example works as follows.

① The student click answers into 'check-box'. This action is recorded in the studentmodel.

② Upon completion, the student's answer sheet is sent to the system, and being compared with the correct answer database.

③ If incorrectly matched line is detected, then the 'color' field is filled in with weighted value depends on the importance level.

④ The value for this field is used as the feedback, so that the designated log item is colored in different color in the student's viewer, which gives the student a warning [see figure 7].

This process repeats until the system receives all the correct response, and the number of repeated process and the number of corrected lines will be recorded. This record will be maintained as a student model, and used as a basis for analyzing the student's weakness on the specific topic

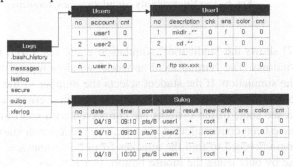

Fig. 5. Log Database

4 Implementation

We have developed the system using the JDK 1.3. We used MS Access for building the database and Microsoft NT4.0 for the server. The [Figure 6] shows a snapshot from the 'vulnerability' simulation exercise, and the [Figure 7] shows the 'audit trail' simulation exercises.

In the [Figure 6], we made sub-menus, 'directory, task, view, window, and help'. The 'Directory' menu shows the virtual OS in tree structure. The 'Task' menu shows brief explanations about the task to perform, which shows in the middle window. The student can enter UNIX commands directly in this window, and get immediate response. When the lesson is done, the student can push the 'done' button. The 'View' menu displays the information regarding the currently opened windows. The 'Window' menu orders the opened windows in vertical or horizontal locations. The 'Help' menu gives help messages about the simulation procedure. We have made this 'help message' to be appear in another pop-up window, since we do not want to interfere the student's problem solving. In order to make another browser for the help messages, we inserted the links in the knowledge base, so that we can consult the on-line man pages anytime we want.

Fig. 6. The Vulnerability Simulation Environment

The [Figure 7] shows the 'audit trail' simulation exercises. From the figure, we can see several windows. The 'virtual local network' window represents the virtual local network for the simulation. If the student selects the number of the system, for example, the number '7', then it will make the network with 7 computer systems. On the figure, we can see some of the systems are connected with solid line, which explains the systems have been communicated already. The student can start from the 'system 0', and can begin proceed to find the attacker from this computer. The student works in this exercise by only using the mouse button. For instance, if the student clicks the right mouse button in the figure, then the pop-up menu appears and provides information about the previous attacked system. On the upper-right side of the window, we can find several log data, which we can select from the taps on the top. The same information appears in the bottom-right side of the window, as a tree structure. If we select any one of them, the detailed information appears as a structured table in this window. From this, the student can check the suspicious line for the intrusion. Also, if the student does not know what the each column stands for, then the systems provides some help messages on the right-middle window. For example, we can see the help message about 'Result' field of the 'Sulog' from the figure.

When the student identifies the location of the previous attacked system, and then clicks the 'Intrusion' field from the pop-up menu, which will make the attacked path as dotted line, from the current system to the previous one. When the student finishes finding all the necessary connections to the previous attacked systems, then click on the 'Done' button, which sends the final answer to the server. The server compares the information about the student's problem solving with the correct answer from the database. If the student has made any mistake, then the system will provide a feedback asking the student to do the same task.

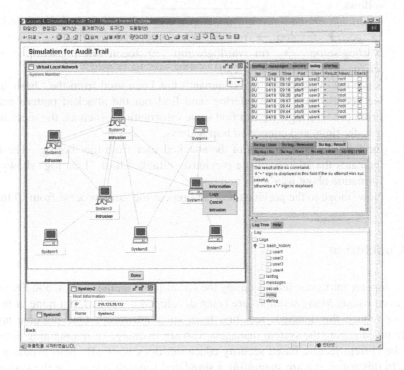

Fig. 7. The Audit Trail Simulation Environment

4.1 Sample Tracing Scenario

The real attack situation differs from case to case, so that we have created a scenario as the most general case. Here, we have one possible intrusion scenario, for example, 'buffer overflow attack'. The student's task is summarized as the follows.

① Examine the 'message log' from the attacked server, and find the evidence for the 'buffer overflow' attack. The buffer overflow attack leaves different log data than the others.

② Search the users who were logged in during the 'buffer overflow' attack has happened, from the 'last log' of the attacked server,

③ Search the log file, '.bash_history', for each individual logged in user
   The .bash_history file lists the entered commands for each user, but it does not record the time period.

④ Search the commands that could be used for possible attack, from the '.bash_history' file, for the each user. For example, the sequence might be as follows.
   mkdir." " → cd ." " → ⟶| ftp xxx.xxx.xx.x |→ tar –xvfz *.tar → cd exploit → gcc → ./exploit → rm /var/log/messages → rm /var/log/secure → rm /var/log/sulog → rm /var/log/wtmp → touch /var/log/wtmp → pico /etc/passwd → reboot → exit

⑤ Since the evidence of 'ftp' commands has been used from the '.bash_history', we need to search the 'xferlog' and find out the attacked pattern and time. From the 'xferlog', we can find some informations, such as, the username, file transfer time, and connected host address.

⑥ Find out the host address of the attacked user from the 'lastlog'. The address indicates the address of the previously attacked host. 'Last log' shows the information about user's ID, and time.

⑦ Now, move to the previous host, and repeat the same process from ① to ⑥.

5 Conclusion

The computer intrusions are becoming the social problem these days, and the situation gets even worse. Many solutions are being developed or studied, but none of them can stop or reduce the damages resulting from such intrusions. One possible approach might be educating the system managers who are in charge of maintaining the system. But the current lecture-based security education does not really help avoiding the attack. In this paper, we are suggesting a simulated training system for the system manager, which could be another solution for minimizing the damages from the attacker. The security topics are too diverse that we limited the scope of the system on the UNIX security topics.

The significance of the system can be described as follows. First, this simulated virtual training system could provide the system managers a real working environment. And working with this system, they can have hands-on practice. Second, this system might give another defending solution against the intrusion. Because after spending large amount of budgets for the system protection, still the damages are increasing rapidly. Third, the recent increase of the intrusion changes the security policy more actively, and this system could work for a framework for the active response system by tracing the attacker. Fourth, the recent IDS is trying to expand its functionality including the attacker tracing mechanism. Therefore, this system can be plugged in to the previous IDS as a training or educational function. Fifth, the system maintains the solution paths, which is used to monitor the student's problem solving steps and can be a basis for providing a hint when it is needed. Finally, the system is designed as a client/server, so the student needs only the web browser to access the system. And the student can manipulate the tasks in the Java applet-based virtual OS environment according to the learning scenario. We are in the middle of developing the system, so that we are not done any evaluation yet.

References

1. Anderson, D., Frivold, T., and Valdes, A.: Next-generation intrusion-detection expert system(NIDES). Technical Report SRI-CSL-95-07, Computer Science Laboratory, SRI International, Menlo Park, CA (1995).
2. Alpert, S., Singley, K., and Fairweather, P.: Porting a Standalone Intelligent Tutoring System on the Web. Proceedings of ITS'2000 workshop (2000) 1-11.
3. CERT Advisory CA-1991-18 Active Internet ftp Attacks, http://www.cert.org/advisories/CA-1991-18.html
4. Farmer, D., and Spafford, E. H.: The COPS Security Checker System. Proceedings of the Summer USENIX Conference (1990) 165-170.
5. Garvey, T., and Lunt, T.: Model based intrusion detection, Proceedings of the 18th National Information Security Conference. (1995) 372-385.
6. Kumar, S.: Classification and Detection of Computer Intrusions. PhD thesis, Purdue University (1995)
7. Lunt, T.: Automated Audit Trail Analysis and Intrusion Detection: A Survey. Proceedings of the 11th National Computer Security Conference (1988) 74-81.
8. Nakabayashi, K., Maruyama, M., Koike, Y., Kato, Y., Touhei, H., and Fukuhara, Y.: Architecture of an Intelligent Tutoring System on the WWW, Proceedings of AI-ED'97. (1997) 39-46.
9. Rowe, N. C. and Schiavo, S.: An Intelligent Tutor for Intrusion Detection on Computer Systems. Computers and Education (1998) 395-404.
10. Understanding system log files on a Solaris 2.x operating system, http://www.cert.org/security-improvement/implementations/i041.12.html

A Simple Illumination Normalization Algorithm for Face Recognition

Jaepil Ko, Eunju Kim, and Hyeran Byun

Dept. of Computer Science, Yonsei University
134, Shinchon-dong Sudaemoon-ku, Seoul, 120-749, Korea
{nonezero, outframe, hrbyun}@csai.yonsei.c.kr

Abstract. Most of the FR (face recognition) systems suffer from sensitivity to variations in illumination. For better performance the FR system needs more training samples acquired under variable lightings but it is not practical in real world. We introduce a novel pre-processing method, which makes illumination-normalized face image for face recognition. The proposed method, ICR (Illumination Compensation based on Multiple Regression Model), is to find the plane that best fits the intensity distribution of the face image using the multiple regression model, then use this plane to normalize the face image. The advantages of our method are simple and practical. The planar approximation of a face image is mathematically defined by the simple linear model. We provide experimental results to demonstrate the performance of the proposed ICR method on public face databases and our database. The experiments show a significant improvement of the recognition rate.

1 Introduction

The visual recognition system suffers from the different appearances of objects according to the illumination conditions [1]. Especially face images are highly sensitive to the variations in illumination conditions so small change in illumination produces large changes in appearance of face [2]. That makes face recognition/verification problem more difficult to handle. The FERRET test report shows that the performance significantly drops in the case of the illumination changes [3,4]. Until now many face recognition methods have been proposed and there are several methods for dealing with illumination problem. For details, reader should consult recent survey paper [5].
The first approach to handle the face effects results from illumination changes is constructing illumination model from several images acquired under different illumination condition [6]. The representative method, the illumination cone model that can deal shadow and multiple lighting sources, is introduced by [7,8]. This approach is not practical in smart card application, which can just memorize one or two prototypes of a person and to construct the cone model for a person it needs well-controlled image capturing circumstances. The standard answer for the problem with variable lightings, the second approach, is to extract illumination invariant features, such as edges, cor-

M. Ishizuka and A. Sattar (Eds.): PRICAI 2002, LNAI 2417, pp. 532-541, 2002.

ner, and contour, which is often considered as the basic image representation but these are insufficient to contain useful information for recognition. Furthermore, edges are susceptible to the illumination conditions for complex object and when the image has cluttered background. Instead of edge-based description, image-based description is preferred in face recognition system. The method use low-dimensional representation of image by subspace technique such as eighenfaces and fisherfaces [9]. In the above case, with the assumption that the first few principal components are strongly involved in illumination effects, discarding the first three principal components improves recognition performance under illumination changes [10]. However, the performance is not improved on images captured under normal illumination. Because in the case of normal lighted images discarding the first three components could also eliminate important information for recognition. Another eigenspace method was developed by [11]. The major idea was to incorporate a set of gradient based filter banks into the eigenspace recognition framework. It might strongly depend on gradient operator being charge of illumination variations. Generally, to enhance the performance of the appearance-based face recognition system we needs more training samples, but it is usually infeasible. To obtain illumination normalized prototype face image assuming just one image is available the symmetric shape-from-shading algorithm was proposed by [12] which is strongly depends on symmetry property of a face image for solving ill-posed problem.

In this paper, we assume that we do not have enough training images like [12] and storage for keeping prototype face images, and also assume that there is one ambient light which can give rise to cast-shadow on the face image. In this paper, we describe a novel pre-processing method to get illumination-normalized face image for alleviating illumination effects. The method is to find the plane that best fits the intensity distribution of the face image using the multiple regression model, then use this plane to normalize the face image.

This paper is organized as follows. In the next section, we overview multiple regression model in brief. Section 3, we describe our illumination normalization algorithm, ICR (Illumination Compensation based on the multiple Regression model), for face images to get normalized face image. The significantly improved performance of PCA face recognition system by applying our proposed method in preprocessing step is shown in section 4. Finally, in section 5 conclusions are drawn.

2   Multiple Regression Model

In this section, we will give a brief overview of MRM (multiple regression model) well known technique in statistics. For details of MRM see the book [13]. MRM is the linear regression model for multivariate case. The multiple regression model can be written as

$$\mathbf{Y} = \mathbf{X}\boldsymbol{\beta} + \mathbf{e} \tag{1}$$

where $\mathbf{Y}$ is an $n \times 1$ response vector, $\mathbf{X}$ is an $n \times (k+1)$ matrix for an k input variables and n samples, and $\mathbf{e}$ is an $n \times 1$ random error vector that we shall assume is normally distributed with mean 0 and variance σ^2.

The parameters $\boldsymbol{\beta}$ and σ^2 must be estimated from the samples. If we let $\mathbf{B}^T = [B_0 B_1 \cdots B_k]$ of the least square estimator of the $\boldsymbol{\beta}$. Then the least square estimator $\mathbf{B}$ are given by

$$\mathbf{B} = (\mathbf{X}^T \mathbf{X})^{-1} \mathbf{X}^T \mathbf{Y} \tag{2}$$

After estimating parameter $\boldsymbol{\beta}$ and σ^2, we can get the plane, $\mathbf{Y}$ that best fits the distribution of input samples.

3 Illumination Compensation Based on the Multiple Regression Model (ICR)

3.1 Background

The cast-shadow due to the illuminant direction changes seriously the appearance of a face image that degrades the performance of the face recognition systems. To cope with the problem, we focused on a method that just needs the input face image itself to make the same appearance of the face image with regardless of the illumination direction without any complex illumination model. In this section, we describe a simple algorithm for normalizing the face images. The idea is to find the plane that best fits the intensity distribution of the input face image then, use this plane to normalize the face image. To find the best-fit intensity plane of the face image, we use the multiple regression model as follow. In finding the best-fit intensity plane of a face image, input variable is the coordinate of each pixel and response is the intensity value of the location and the number of samples are number of pixels of a face image. After estimating parameters, we can get a new intensity value of the location for each pixel, then we construct the best-fit intensity plane by them. Now, we can use the intensity plane as a reference to normalize the face image.

3.2. ICR Algorithm

We start with a face image whose dimension is q from $n \times m$ face image pixels.

$$\mathbf{x} = \left[x_0, x_1, \cdots, x_{q-1} \right]^T \tag{3}$$

then, we generate q samples for the regression model.

$$\mathbf{z}_k = [i, j, x_k]^T, \ k = i \times m + j, \ (\ i = 0,1,\cdots,n-1, j = 0,1,\cdots,m-1\ ) \tag{4}$$

where the *i* and *j* are input values and x_k is response value for the regression model. After applying samples $\mathbf{z}_k$ to the regression, we can get the best-fit intensity plane:

$$\mathbf{y} = [y_0, y_1, \cdots, y_{q-1}]^T \tag{5}$$

The center value in the best-fit intensity plane $y_c = [\max(y_i) - \min(y_j)] / 2$, $i<j<q$, is computed. The next step is that we reverse the intensity plane against its center value:

$$\mathbf{y'} = [y_c - y_0, y_c - y_1, \cdots, y_c - y_{q-1}]^T \tag{6}$$

Finally, we can get the illumination-normalized face image by adding the original input image **x** and the adjusted intensity image **y'**.

The Fig. 1 shows the steps of the above algorithm by figures. It shows an original input image, the best-fit intensity plane, adjusted intensity plane, and illumination- normalized face image by applying our method respectively. The final image appears a little bit uniform intensity preserving its relative intensity.

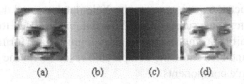

(a)   (b)   (c)   (d)

Fig. 1. (a) input image, (b) the best-fit intensity plane, (c) adjusted intensity plane, (d) final result from adding (a) and (c)

3.3 ICR Results

To compare the existing preprocessing technique, HE (histogram equalization), is shown in the Fig. 2. The HE is widely used for preprocessing step in the face recognition systems with the expectation to increase the recognition performance. However, The original function of the HE is just to enhance the contrast of an input image. The HE processed image shows the higher contrast than the original image. This property of the HE strengthens difference between the original input image and the processed output image. It can degrade the performance of the face recognition systems. As you can see in Fig. 2, there is a slight difference between the left part and right part of the original face image. The result image with histogram equalization shows strong contrast between both sides. If the histogram equalized face images only are used to prototype images for the face recognition systems, the new test images acquired under other illumination conditions will be strange to the prototype images. The result image with ICR removes the cast-shadow appeared in the original image. We expect that this effect will improve recognition performance. The result image from the composite processing shows the fine contrast with week cast-shadow.

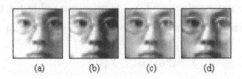

Fig. 2. (a) Original image, (b) histogram equalized image, (c) ICR processed image, (d) histogram equalization followed by ICR

4 Experimental Results

In this section, we demonstrate that performance of ICR in preprocessing point of view by comparing the histogram equalization widely used for normalizing illumination effect in the face recognition systems. We also compare the standard technique that drops the first three components in PCA for removing the illumination effects [10]. We have conducted experiments on the Yale database and the ORL database, and our database. In the test on a subset of the Yale database related to the light conditions, we demonstrate significant improvements in recognition performance with PCA face recognition system and also show the comparable results with the technique discarding a few leading principle components.

4.1 Geometric Normalization

All the face images are preprocessed to normalize geometry and to remove background. The preprocessing procedure is that we first manually locate the centers of the eyes for translation, rotation and scaling of the face images then, apply the histogram equalization, ICR or composite method. The next step is to scale facial pixels to have zero mean and unit variance that is required for PCA inputs. In the last step, we mask the face images to remove the background and hair.

4.2 Test Database

The subset of the Yale database only consists of face images that were captured under normal, right, and left lighting. We collected 45 face images from 15 persons. We have constructed our database by scanning 200 face images containing one image per person from the picture that was taken under the same condition. The most of the face images in our database have a slight cast-shadow on right part of the face. The ORL database consists of 400 face images of 40 persons, 10 images per individual. The sample images are shown in Fig. 3.

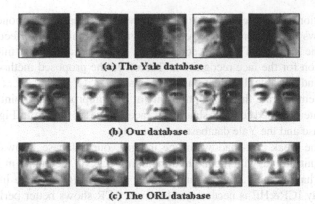

(a) The Yale database

(b) Our database

(c) The ORL database

Fig. 3. Some example face images used in our experiments. (a) severe cast-showed images, (b) light cast-shadowed images, (c) images acquired under almost frontal lightings

4.3 Results

To demonstrate that out proposed method works well on the face images with cast-shadow, we tested on the Yale database and our database. Instead of including illumination specific face images, the ORL database used on the test of the general face images. On the Yale database, we constructed the eigenspace with just frontal lighting face images and then used those images as a gallery set. Both right and left cast-shadowed face images were used as a probe set. On our database, we constructed the eigenspace with all the images in the database and then used those images as a gallery set, and then made a probe set by flipping the face image against the vertical-center line. On the ORL database, we constructed the eigenspace with 200 face images among the database and then used those images as a gallery set and the other 200 face images were used as a probe set. We compared recognition rate by preprocessing methods as follows.

> ORG : no processing.
> HE : histogram equalization
> ICR : proposed our method
> ICR&HE : composite method of histogram equalization and ICR.

Fist, we show the comparable result with the method of discarding leading components in eigenspace. The results on the Yale database are shown in Fig. 4. The peak recognition rates of the ORG and HE that do not include ICR technique are reached at the point using PCA without first 2 components and first 3 components respectively. However, in case that the face images are acquired under simple frontal illumination condition, it is difficult for us to expect the same results because discarding leading components in eigenspace can loose important information for recognition instead of removing illumination effects. When we apply our proposed method to the image, the peak recognition rate is reached at the point with all leading components. This experiment shows that the proposed method alleviates illumination effect regardless of considering the number of leading components to be discarded that might be important information for the face recognition. Therefore the proposed method can be used both normal and variable illumination conditions.

Second, we demonstrate the recognition rate at the preprocessing point of view. The recognition rate obtained for cast-shadowed face images is shown in Fig. 5 and Fig. 6 for our database and the Yale database respectively.

The test on the weak cast-shadowed face images, our database, shows the improvement of recognition rate with the method including ICR on the rank 1 in Fig. 5. ICR itself does not handle the variations of intensity among different face images. That is the reason why ICR&HE is necessary. However, ICR shows better performance than ICR&HE in Fig.5, because our database images were acquired under the same intensity circumstance. The similar results are shown in Fig. 6. On the test of the Yale database consisted of severe cast-shadowed face images, the methods applying ICR show the significant improvement of the recognition rate.

In case that the database is composed of the face images acquired variable situations but not strongly specified to the illumination conditions, the test on the ORL database, we could not achieve the significant improvement, but the methods applying ICR continuously record better performance than ORG and HE over all ranks (see Fig. 7). Moreover, we still have used all the leading principle components under all the situations without degrading the recognition performance with the proposed method. In other word, we do not need consider whether the leading components are involved with the illumination effects. According to the experiments above, our proposed method can have better performance in the face recognition system if the cast-shadow is more severe, and it can't degrade the performance on the test of the face images acquired under various conditions.

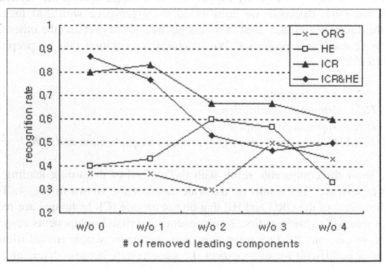

Fig. 4. The rank 1 recognition rate by discarding leading components on the Yale Database

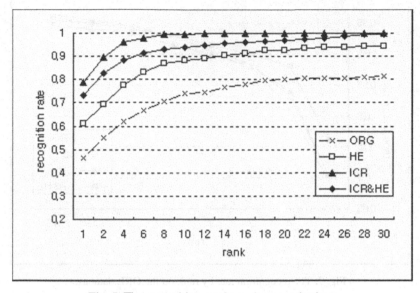

Fig. 5. The recognition rate by rank on our database

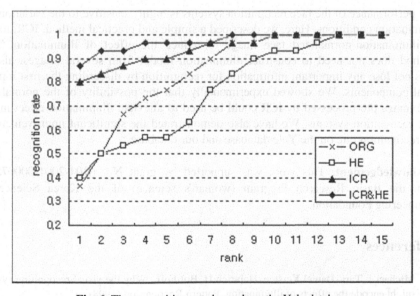

Fig. 6. The recognition rate by rank on the Yale database

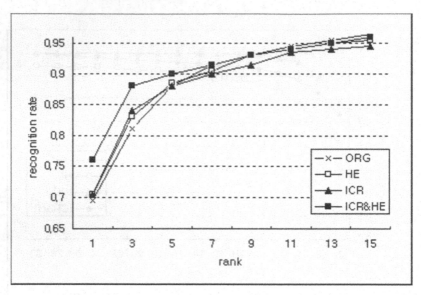

Fig. 7. The recognition rate by rank on the ORL database

5 Conclusions

The performance of the face recognition systems is highly sensitive to the variations in illumination conditions. Here, we described a simple and practical method, ICR, to get an illumination-normalized face image to reduce the effect of illumination. This method does not need to construct illumination model from several images, also it does not lose any important information for recognition by discarding the first n principal components. We showed experimentally that the possibility of the normalized face image pre-processed by ICR could be used to alleviate illumination effect in the face recognition systems. We have also demonstrated the significant improvement of the recognition rate on the Yale database and our database.

Acknowledgement. This work was supported by grant No. (R04-2001-000075-0) from the Basic Research Program (woman's science) of the Korea Science & Engineering Foundation.

References

1.   Michael J. Tarr, Daniel Kersten, Heinrich H. Bulthoff. Why the visual recognition system might encode the effects of illumination, Pattern Recognition (1998)
2.   Yael Adini, Yael Moses, and Shimon Ullman. Face Reconition: The problem of Compensating for Changes in Illumination Direction, IEEE Trans. on PAMI Vol. 19, No. 7 (1997) 721-732

3. P. J. Phillips, H. Moon, P. Rauss, and S. A. Rizvi. The FERET Evaluation Methodology for Face-Recognition Algorithms. IEEE Conference on CVPR, Puerto Rico (1997) 137-143

4. S. Rizvi, P. Phillips, and H. Moon. The FERET verication testing protocol for face recognition algorithms. IEEE Conference on Automatic Face- and Gesture-Recognition (1998) 48-53

5. R. Chellappa and W. Zhao. Face Recognition: A Literature Survey. ACM Journal of Computing Surveys (2000)

6. A. Yuille, D. Snow, R. Epstein, P. Belhumeur. Determining Generative Models of Objects Under Varying Illumination: Shape and Albedo from Multiple Images Using SVD and Integrability, International Journal of Computer Vision, 35 (3)(1999) 203-222

7. P. N. Belhumeur and D. J. Kriegman. What is the set of images of an object under all possible lighting conditions?, IEEE Conference on CVPR (1996)

8. Athinodoros S. Georghiades, David J. Kriegman, Peter N. Belhumeur. Illumination Cones for Recognition Under Variable Lighting: Faces, IEEE Conference on CVPR (1998) 52-58.

9. M.Turk and A. Pentland. Eigenfaces for recognition. Journal of Cognitive Neuroscience,Vol 3 (1991)

10. V. Belhumeur, J. Hespanha, and D. Kriegman. Eigenfaces vs. fisherfaces: Recognition using class specific linear projection. IEEE Trans. on PAMI (1997) 711-720

11. Bischof, H.; Wildenauer, H.; Leonardis, A. Illumination insensitive eigenspaces, IEEE Conference on Computer Vision, Vol. 1 (2001) 233-238

12. Wen Yi Zhao; Chellappa, R. Illumination-Insensitive Face Recognition Using Symmetric Shape-from-Shading, IEEE Conference on CVPR, Vol. 1, (2000) 286-293

13. S. M. Ross. Introduction to Probability and Statistics for Engineers and Scientists, Wiley, New York (1987)

A Self-Adaptive Architecture and Its Application to Robust Face Identification

Paul Robertson and Robert Laddaga

Massachusetts Institute of Technology
Artificial Intelligence Laboratory
{paulr,rladdaga}@ai.mit.edu

Abstract. Conventional approaches to most image understanding problems suffer from fragility when applied to natural environments. This is especially true of face recognition programs. The GRAVA architecture provides support for self awareness and situational awareness that allows robust recognition to occur. We describe the architecture and explain how it achieves robustness. GRAVA is a reflective architecture that supports self-adaptation that has been successfully applied to a number of visual interpretation domains. This paper describes the protocols and the main interpreter for GRAVA, as well as the application of the architecture to face recognition.

Keywords: Self-Adaptive Architecture, Face Recognition, Image Understanding, Information Fusion.

1 Introduction

Image understanding programs have tended to be very brittle and perform poorly in situations where the environment cannot be carefully constrained. Natural vision systems in humans and other animals are remarkably robust. The applications for robust vision are myriad. Robust vision is essential for many applications such as mobile robots, where the environment changes continually as the robots moves, and robustness is essential for safe and reliable operation of the robot.

There are by now many face recognition systems that work spectacularly well in constrained situations, but in natural environments, where lighting and pose can vary widely, they perform poorly.

In this paper we give an overview of a robust face identification program and describe the architecture (GRAVA) that supports it. GRAVA has already been successfully applied to satellite image interpretation [5,6] and is now being used to identify faces in video images with unconstrained pose and lighting. The face identification system has many useful applications that include intelligent spaces and security.

For an image understanding system to interpret an image it is necessary for it to deal with the complexity in the image. Where we have been most successful in building vision systems has been in applications where the complexity and

M. Ishizuka and A. Sattar (Eds.): PRICAI 2002, LNAI 2417, pp. 542–551, 2002.
© Springer-Verlag Berlin Heidelberg 2002

variation of the image content can be carefully managed. Examples of such situations include factory inspection applications and face recognition applications in which the face is deliberately positioned into a canonical location. Natural environments contain rich variety. It is very hard to build a single algorithm that can deal with the natural range of possibilities, but two aspects of the world provide a means of meeting the challenge: 1) any particular situation only has to deal with a subset of that variety at any time; and 2) the subsets are not random but tend to occur in clusters or contexts.

The GRAVA architecture is *aware* of the context in which it is operating, as determined by the images being processed. GRAVA supports diversity by constructing a network of agents that can interpret the current context, and by rebuilding the network of agents as the context changes. In this way, the running system of agents is always well matched with the image being interpreted.

In addition to knowledge of faces that the agents themselves use to recognize faces, GRAVA brings to bear two other kinds of knowledge. One of these is knowledge of the contexts that can be presented by the environment (contextual awareness), and the other is self-awareness, or meta-knowledge about the state of the program and the agents.

Self awareness provides the knowledge necessary for the program to make changes to itself. Contextual awareness provides the knowledge necessary to know when it is necessary to change and what it is necessary to change to.

2   The Face Recognition Problem

Most face identification and recognition systems work by measuring a small number of facial features given a canonical pose and matching them against a database of known faces. Frequently however in practical applications few frames show a full frontal face. Furthermore lighting may vary significantly. These factors frustrate attempts to identify a face. Many applications have much more relaxed recognition goals. If the task is to track people as they move throughout a monitored space the task may be to identify the individual from a relatively small set of people. For face profiles different models involving ear, eye, and nose may prove successful. By building a face recognizer that can seamlessly switch between different contexts such as pose and lighting we can construct a recognizer that is robust to normal changes in the natural environment. This permits a much wider application of face recognition technology.

Our application involves recognizing people as they move about an intelligent space [1] in an unconstrained way. To better understand contexts consider the face "pose" contexts:

Figure 1 shows four pose contexts: "profile", "oblique", "off-center", and "frontal". The profile view is supported by agents that measure points along the profile of the face, the corner of the eye, and the lips. The oblique view with ear supports measurements of the ear and measurements of the position of the ear, eye, and nose. The triangle formed by the eye, ear, and nose help to determine the angle of the face to the camera which allows measurements to be normalized

Fig. 1. Four Pose Contexts

before recognition. The off-center view permits measurements of points on the eyes, nose, and mouth. The shape of the nose can be measured but the width of the base of the nose cannot be measured due to self-occlusion. The frontal view allows nose width to be measured but the nose shape cannot be measured. There are other contexts that include/exclude ears. The different contexts control, among other things, what models can be used for matching, what features can be detected and what transformations must be made to normalize the measurements prior to matching. This example shows contexts for pose but there are also contexts for lighting, race, gender, and age.

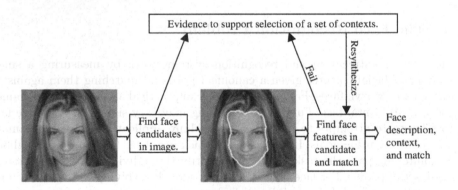

Fig. 2. Recognizer Schematic

The recognizer supports a collection of face candidate finders, face models, feature finders, and normalization algorithms implemented as agents. The face recognition process is shown schematically in Figure 2. Face candidate finder agents look for face like shapes in the image and generate evidence that supports the selection of a set of contexts based on the shape and shading of the face candidate. Agents appropriate to the context are selected to make a special purpose face recognizer. If the recognizer doesn't succeed in finding appropriate features where they are expected to be the system self-adapts by using available evidence to select a more appropriate context, constructing a new recognizer, and trying again. The system iterates in this manner until appropriate lighting, race, age, gender, and pose contexts have been chosen and the best match has been achieved. Convergence on the right set of contexts is rapid because evidence in support of a context is collected each time an agent runs.

What is unique about the recognizer outlined above is that it has multiple ways of recognizing faces, it divides up a complex space of lighting, age, race, sex, and pose into contexts that can be composed in a huge number of ways and self-adapts the recognizer at runtime. In the following section we describe the self-adaptive architecture that supports this capability.

3   An Overview of the GRAVA Architecture

The purpose of the reflective architecture is to allow the image interpretation program to be aware of its own computational state and to make changes to it as necessary in order to achieve its goal. The steps below provide a schematic introduction to the GRAVA architecture.

1. The desired *behavior* is specified in the form of statistical models by constructing a corpus.
2. The behavior, which covers several different imaging scenarios, is broken down into contexts. Contexts exist for different levels of the interpretation problem. Each context defines an expectation for the computational stage that it covers. Contexts are like frames and schemas; but because the contexts are gathered from the data automatically it is not necessary to define them by hand.
3. Given a context a program to interpret the image can be generated from that context. This is done by *compiling* the context into a program by selecting the appropriate agents.
4. The program that results from compiling a context can easily know the following things:
   a) What part of the specification gave rise to its components.
   b) Which agents were involved in the creation of its components.
   c) Which models were applied by those agents in creating its components.
   d) How well suited the current program is to dealing with the current input.
5. The division of knowledge into agents that perform basic image interpretation tasks and agents that construct programs from specifications is represented by different reflective levels.

3.1   Reflective Interpreter for Self-Adaptation

The problem of self-adaptive software is to respond to changing situations by re-synthesizing the program that is running. To do this we reify the software development process, and provide it reflectively in the running program.

The techniques for implementing reflection [7,4] described above have become common in modern languages and architectures. Unlike traditional implementations, which have largely been supportive of human programmer adaptation of languages and architectures, we use reflection as a way of supporting self-adaptation of the program *by itself.* There are two principal differences in our use of reflection:

1. We open up the program to itself so that by knowing what it knows it can use what it knows to alter itself in order to respond to changes in the real world.
2. We do not wish to change the semantics of the program/language, we wish to change the program itself.

A reflective layer is an object that contains one or more "interpreter". Reflective layers are stacked up such that each layer is the meta-level computation of the layer beneath it. In particular each layer is generated by the layer above it. The face identification application described in this paper uses two layers.

Each layer can reflect up to the layer above it in order to self-adapt. The prototype GRAVA implementation is written in Yolambda [3] a dialect of Scheme [2]

```
(defineClass ReflectiveLayer
  ((description) ;; the (input) description for this layer
   (interpreter) ;; the interpreter for this layers description
   (knowledge)   ;; a representation of world knowledge
   (higherlayer) ;; the meta-level above this
   (lowerlayer)));; the subordinate layer
```

A reflective layer is an object that contains the following objects.

1. *description:* the description that is to be interpreted.
2. *interpreter:* a system consisting of one or more cascaded interpreters that can interpret the description.
3. *knowledge:* a problem dependent representation of what is known about the world as it pertains to the interpretation of the subordinate layer. For the face identification application knowledge consists of evidence accumulated from agents supporting each of the contexts (age, race, sex, lighting, and pose).
4. *higherlayer:* the superior layer. The layer that produced the interpreter for this layer.
5. *lowerlayer:* the subordinate layer.

The semantics for a layer are determined by the *interpret, elaborate, adapt* and *execute* methods which we describe in turn below.

Figure 3 shows the relationship between reflective layers of the GRAVA architecture.

Reflective Layer "n" contains a description that is to be interpreted as the description for layer "n+1". A program has been synthesized either by the layer "n-1" or by hand if it is the top layer. The program is the interpreter for the description. The result of running the interpreter is the most probable interpretation of the description—which forms the new description of the layer "n+1".

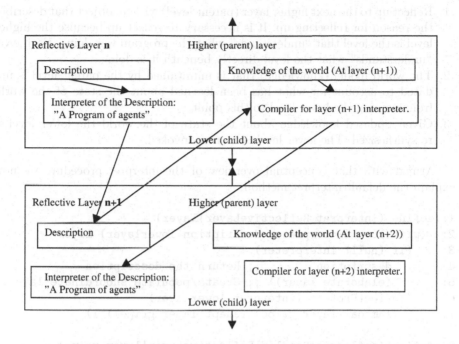

Fig. 3. Meta-Knowledge and Compilation

All the layers (including "n") also contain a compiler. Unless the layer definition is overridden by specialization, the compiler in each layer is identical and provides the implementation with a theorem prover that compiles an interpreter from a description. The compiler runs at the meta level in layer "n" and uses the knowledge of the world at layer "n+1" which resides in level "n". It compiles the description from level "n+1" taking in to account what is known at the time about level "n+1" in the *knowledge* part of layer "n". The compilation of the description is a new interpreter at layer "n+1".

Below we describe the meta-interpreter for layers in GRAVA.

The interpret method is the primary driver of computation in the reflective architecture. The reflective levels are determined by the program designer. In order for the self-adaptive program to "understand" its own computational structure, each layer describes the layer beneath it. In self-adapting, the architecture essentially searches a tree of meta-levels. This is best understood by working through the details of the architecture.

In the simplest of situations the top level application of "interpret" to the top layer results in the recursive descent of "interpret" through the reflective layers finally yielding a result in the form of an interpretation. Along the way however unexpected situations may arise that cause the program to need to adapt. Adaptation is handled by taking the following steps:

1. Reflect up to the next higher layer (parent level) with an object that describes the reason for reflecting up. It is necessary to reflect up because the higher level is the level that "understands" what the program was doing. Each level "understands" what the level directly beneath it is doing.
2. The world model (knowledge) that is maintained by the parent level is updated to account for what has been learned about the state of the world from running the lower level to this point.
3. Given updated knowledge about the state of the world the lower level is re-synthesized. The lower level is then re-invoked.

Armed with that conceptual overview of the interpret procedure we now explain the default interpret method.

```
1:(define (interpret ReflectiveLayer|layer)
2:  (withSlots (interpreter description lowerlayer) layer
3:    (if (null? interpreter)
4:        description           ;; Return the description
5:        (elaborate layer)) ;; Create/populate subordinate layer.
6:    (reflectProtect (interpret lowerlayer)
7:      (lambda (layer gripe) (adapt layer gripe))))))

8:(define (reflectionHandler ReflectiveLayer|layer gripe)
9:  (adapt layer gripe))
```

Line 3 checks to see if the layer contains an interpreter. If it does not the result of evaluation is simply the description which is returned in line 4. This occurs when the lowest level has been reached.

If there is an interpreter, the elaborate method is invoked (line 5). "elaborate" (described below) constructs the next lower reflective layer.

"reflectProtect" in line 6 is a macro that hides some of the mechanism involved with handling reflection operations.

(reflectProtect *form handler*) evaluates *form* and returns the result of that evaluation. If during the evaluation of *form* a reflection operation occurs the *handler* is applied to the layer and the gripe object provided by the call to reflectUp. If the handler is not specified in the reflectProtect macro the generic procedure reflectionHandler is used. The invocation of the reflection handler is not within the scope of the reflectProtect so if it calls (reflectUp ...) the reflection operation will be caught at the next higher level. If reflectUp is called and there is no extant reflectProtect the debugger is entered. Therefore if the top layer invokes reflectUp the program lands in the debugger.

When the reflection handler has been evaluated the reflectProtect re-evaluates the *form* thereby making a loop. Line 7 is included here to aid in description. It is omitted in the real code allowing the reflectionHandler method to be invoked. The handler takes care of updating the world model based on the information in *gripe* and then adapts the lower layer. The handler therefore attempts to self adapt to accommodate the new knowledge about the state of the world until success is achieved. If the attempt to adapt is finally unable to produce a viable lower level interpreter it invokes reflectUp and causes the meta level interpretation level to attend to the situation.

```
1:(define (elaborate ReflectiveLayer|layer)
2:  (withSlots (lowerlayer) layer
3:    (let ((interpretation (execute layer))
4:          (llint (compile layer interpretation)))
5:      (set! lowerlayer ((newLayerConstructor layer)
6:                        higherlayer: layer
7:                        description: interpretation
8:                        interpreter: llint)))))
```

The purpose of the elaborate layer is to build the initial version of the subordinate layer. It does this in three steps:

1. Evaluate the interpreter of the layer in order to "interpret" the layer's description. The interpretation of $layer_n$ is the description of $layer_{n+1}$.
   Line 3 invokes the interpreter for *layer* with *(execute layer)*. This simply runs the MDL agent interpreter function defined for this layer. The result of executing the interpreter is an interpretation in the form of a description.
2. Compile the layer. This involves the collection of appropriate agents to interpret the description of the lower layer.
   Line 4 compiles the new layer's interpreter. Layer n contains knowledge of the agents that can be used to interpret the description of layer $n + 1$. The description generated in line 3 is compiled into an interpreter program using knowledge of agents that can interpret that description.
3. A new layer object is instantiated with the interpretation resulting from (1) as the description and the interpreter resulting from *compile* in step (2) as the interpreter. The new layer is wired in to the structure with the bi-directional pointers (lowerlayer and higherlayer).
   In line 5, (newLayerConstructor layer) returns the constructor procedure for the subordinate layer.

The adapt method updates the world state knowledge and then recompiles the interpreter for the lower layer.

```
1:(define (adapt ReflectiveLayer|layer gripe)
2:  (withSlots (updateKnowledge) gripe
3:     (updateKnowledge layer))   ;; update the belief state.
4:  (withSlots (lowerlayer) layer
5:     (withSlots (interpreter) lowerlayer
6:       (set! interpreter (compile layer)))))
```

The representation of world state is problem dependent and is not governed by the reflective architecture. In each layer the world state at the corresponding meta level is maintained in the variable "knowledge". When an interpreter causes adaptation with a reflectUp operation an update procedure is loaded into the "gripe" object. Line 3 invokes the update procedure on the layer to cause the world state representation to be updated.

Line 6 recompiles the interpreter for the lower layer. Because the world state has changed the affected interpreter should be compiled differently than when the interpreter was first elaborated.

```
1:(define (execute ReflectiveLayer|layer)
2:   (withSlots (description interpreter knowledge) layer
3:    (run interpreter description knowledge)))
```

3.2   Protocol for Interpreters

An interpreter is a special kind of computational agent that contains agents which it sequences. To support those activities the interpreters support a protocol for meta-information shown in Figure 4(left).

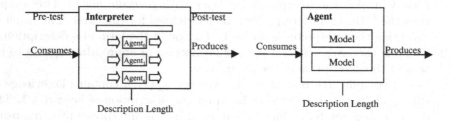

Fig. 4. Protocols for Interpreter and Agent Meta-Information

1. *(pretest anInterpreter anInput)* – Returns *true* if the input is suitable for the interpreter and *false* otherwise.
2. *(posttest anInterpreter anOutput)* – Returns *true* if the output is acceptable and *false* otherwise.
3. *(descriptionLength anInterpreter anInput)* – Returns the description length of the interpreter. The description length is $-log_2(P(success))$ where $P(success)$ is the probability that the interpreter will successfully interpret the scene.

3.3   Protocol for Agents

In order for agents to be selected and connected together by the theorem prover/ compiler they must advertise their semantics. The purpose of the compiler is to select appropriate agents and connect them together to form a program. To support those activities the agents support a protocol for meta-information shown in Figure 4(right).

1. *(consumes anAgent)* – Returns a list of types that the interpreter expects as input.
2. *(produces anAgent)* – Returns a list of types that the interpreter produces as output.
3. *(descriptionLength anAgent)* – Returns the description length of the agent. The description length is $-log_2(P(correct))$ where $P(correct)$ is the probability that the agent will diagnose the feature in the same way as the specification.

4 Conclusions

Most papers on face recognition describe a single way of modeling a face and an algorithm that fits the model to images of faces in a canonical pose and compares those models to known faces in a database. In our system there are many models for faces and many agents for locating each of the features that may be used by each model. Our models are similar to those that are in widespread use involving measurements of key points on the face and using principle component analysis to produce a face model from a corpus of training faces. Rather than trying to use one model to cover all cases however, we first divide the complex space up into multiple contexts and then provide multiple methods for modeling and matching faces. The self-adaptive architecture described in this paper is the key to the robustness of the system.

Although there are many more feature recognizers than on most face identification programs only a small subset are configured into the interpretation program at any point in time so the system performance is not degraded by the multiplicity of approaches.

Little is known about the stability of systems built this way and there are as yet no known guidelines for building systems that are intended to be stable. More work remains to be done in this area.

References

1. R. A. Brooks et al. The intelligent room project. In *Proceedings of the Second International Cognitive Technology Conference (CT'97), Aizu, Japan*, 1997.
2. IEEE. Ieee standard for the scheme programming language. IEEE Standard 1178-1990, IEEE Pisscaataway, 1991.
3. R. Laddaga and P. Robertson. *Yolambda Reference Manual*. Dynamic Object Language Labs, Inc., 1996.
4. P. Maes and D. Nardi. *Meta-Level Architectures and Reflection*. North-Holland, 1988.
5. P. Robertson. A corpus based approach to the interpretation of aerial images. In *Proceedings IEE IPA99*. IEE, 1999. Manchester.
6. P. Robertson. *A Self-Adaptive Architecture for Image Understanding*. PhD thesis, University of Oxford, 2001.
7. B.C. Smith. Reflection and semantics in lisp. In *Proceedings 11th Annual ACM Symposium on Principles of Programming Languages, Salt Lake City, Utah*, pages 23–35, January 1984.

Realizing Audio-Visually Triggered ELIZA-Like Non-verbal Behaviors

Hiroshi G. Okuno[1,2], Kazuhiro Nakadai[2], and Hiroaki Kitano[2,3]

[1] Graduate School of Informatics, Kyoto University, Kyoto 606-8501, Japan
okuno@nue.org   http://winnie.kuis.kyoto-u.ac.jp/~okuno/
[2] Kitano Symbiotic Systems Project, ERATO, Japan Science and Technolog Corp.
Mansion 31 Suite 6A, 6-31-15 Jingumae, Shibuya, Tokyo 150-0001 Japan
nakadai@symbio.jst.go.jp   http://www.symbio.jst.go.jp/~nakadai/
[3] Sony Computer Science Laboratories, Inc., Shinagawa, Tokyo 141-0022
kitano@csl.sony.co.jp   http://www.symbio.jst.go.jp/~kitano/

Abstract. We are studying how to create social physical agents, i.e., humanoids, that perform actions empowered by real-time audio-visual tracking of multiple talkers. Social skills require complex perceptual and motor capabilities as well as communicating ones. It is critical to identify primary features in designing building blocks for social skills, because performance of social interaction is usually evaluated as a whole system but not as each component. We investigate the minimum functionalities for social interaction, supposed that a humanoid is equipped with auditory and visual perception and simple motor control but not with sound output. Real-time audio-visual multiple-talker tracking system is implemented on the humanoid, *SIG*, by using sound source localization, stereo vision, face recognition, and motor control. It extracts either auditory or visual streams and associates audio and visual streams by the proximity in localization. Socially-oriented attention control makes the best use of personality variations classified by the Interpersonal Theory of psychology. It also provides task-oriented funcitons with decaying factor of belief for each stream. We demonstrate that the resulting behavior of *SIG* invites the users' participation in interaction and encourages the users to explore *SIG*'s behaviors. These demonstrations show that *SIG* behaves like a physical non-verbal Eliza.

1 Introduction

Social interaction is essential for humanoid robots, because they are getting more common in social and home environments, such as a pet robot in a living room, a service robot at office, or a robot serving people at a party [4]. Social skills of such robots require robust complex perceptual abilities; for example, it identifies people in the room, pays attention to their voice and looks at them to identify, and associates voice and visual images. Intelligent behavior of social interaction should emerge from rich channels of input sensors; vision, audition, tactile, and others.

Perception of various kinds of sensory inputs should be *active* in the sense that we hear and see things and events that are important to us as individuals, not sound waves or light rays [7]. In other words, selective attention of sensors represented as looking versus seeing or listening versus hearing plays an important role in social interaction.

M. Ishizuka and A. Sattar (Eds.): PRICAI 2002, LNAI 2417, pp. 552–562, 2002.
© Springer-Verlag Berlin Heidelberg 2002

Other important factors in social interaction are recognition and synthesis of emotion in face expression and voice tones [3,2].

Selectivity and *capacity limitation* are two main factors in attention control [19]. A humanoid does some perception intentionally based on selectivity [23]. It also has some limitation in the number of sensors or processing capabilities, and thus only a limited number of sensory information is processed. Since selectivity and capacity limitation are the flip side of the same coin, only selectivity is argued in this paper. Selective attention of auditory processing called the *cocktail party effect* was reported by Cherry in 1953 [6]. At a crowded party, one can attend to one conversation and then change to another one. But the questions are to what one pays one's attention and how one changes one's attention.

Personality in selective attention consists in answers of these questions. Reeves and Nass uses the *Five-Factor Model* in analyzing the personality of media including software agents [20]. The *big five* dimensions of personality are *Dominance/Submissiveness*, *Friendliness*, *Conscientiousness*, *Emotional Stability*, and *Openness*. Although these five dimensions generally define an agent's basic personality, they are not appropriate to define humanoid's one, because the latter three dimensions cannot be applied to current capabilities of humanoids.

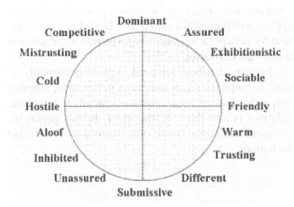

Fig. 1. Interpersonal Circumplex: variation of personality

Fig. 2. *SIG* the Humanoid

We use the *Interpersonal Theory* instead for defining personality in selective attention. It deals with people's characteristic interaction patterns, as is shown in Figure 1, varying along the *Dominance/Submissiveness* and *Friendness/Hostility*. The variation is represented by the *interpersonal circumplex*, which is a circular model of the interpersonal domain of personality [11].

Physically embodied agents, or humanoid robots have no explicit personality as far as we know. Usually personality is emphasized in language generation, whether verbal or textual. Although the most important human communication means is language, non-verbal sensori-motor based behavior is non-the-less important. In this paper, we use personality to define attention control and report some observations of non-verbal interactions between humanoid and human.

1.1 Related Work

Personality for software agents are studied extensively. Bates and his group propose *believable agents* that can express emotion clearly in appropriately timed manner [1]. Loyall and Bates built engaging characters that allow the viewer to suspend disbelief long enough to interact in interesting ways with the character, or to be engaged by the character's interactions with another computer character [12]. Their system uses language, verbal or in text form. Cassell developed conversational agents that integrate face and gesture [5]. She also argues that implementation of conversational agents should be based on actual study of human-human interaction. Hayes-Roth organizes the Virtual Theater project, which studies the creation of intelligent, automated characters that can act either in well-defined stories or in improvisational environments [8].

Personality for robots are also investigated to widen communication channels in human-robot interaction, although most work do not mention personality explicitly. Ono *et al.* use the robot called *Robovie* to make common attention between human and robot by using gestures [18]. Breazeal incorporates the capabilities of recognition and synthesis of emotion in face expression and voice tones into the robot called *Kismet* [3,2]. Waldherr *et al.* makes the robot called *AMELLA* that can recognize pose and motion gestures [21]. Matsusaka *et al.* built the robot called *Hadaly* that can localize the talker as well as recognize speeches by speech-recognition system so that it can interact with multiple people [13]. Nakadai *et al* developed *real-time* auditory and visual multiple-tracking system for the upper-torso humanoid called *SIG* [14]. They extended the system to attain in-face interaction by incorporating *auditory fovea* that is the azimuth dependency in resolution of sound source localization [17].

Physically embodied agents, or humanoid robots have no explicit personality as far as we know. Usually personality is emphasized in language generation, whether verbal or not. Although the most important human communication means is language, non-verbal sensori-motor based behavior is non-the-less important. In this paper, we use personality to define attention control and report some observations of non-verbal interactions between humanoid and human.

2 Humanoid Hardware

As a testbed of integration of perceptual information to control motor of high degree of freedom (DOF), we designed a humanoid robot (hereafter, referred as *SIG*) with the following components:

- 4 DOFs of body driven by 4 DC motors — Each DC motor has a potentiometer to measure the direction.
- A pair of CCD cameras of Sony EVI-G20 for stereo vision input.
- Two pairs of omni-directional microphones (Sony ECM-77S). One pair of microphones are installed at the ear position of the head to collect sounds from the external world. Each microphone is shielded by the cover to prevent from capturing internal noises. The other pair of microphones is to collect sounds within a cover.
- A cover of the body (Figure 2) reduces sounds to be emitted to external environments, which is expected to reduce the complexity of sound processing.
  This cover, made of FRP, is designed by our professional designer for making human robot interaction smoother as well [16].

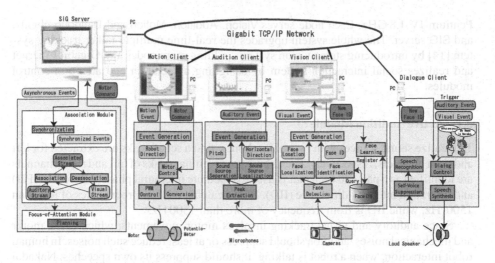

Fig. 3. Hierarchical architecture of real-time audio and visual tracking system

3   Perceptual Systems in Real-Time Multiple-Talker Tracking

The real-time multiple-talker tracking system is designed based on the client/server model (Figure 3). Each server or client executes the following logical modules:

1. Audition client extracts auditory events by pitch extraction, sound source separation and localization, and sends those events to Association.
2. Vision client uses a pair of cameras, extracts visual events by face extraction, identification and localization, and then sends visual events to Association.
3. Motor client generates PWM (Pulse Width Modulation) signals to DC motors and sends motor events to Association.
4. Association module groups various events into a stream and maintains association and deassociation between streams.
5. Attention module selects some stream on which it should focus its attention and makes a plan of motor control.
6. Dialog client communicates with people according to its attention by speech synthesis and speech recognition. We use "Julian" automatic speech recognition system [10].

The status of each modules is displayed on each node. SIG server displays the radar chart of objects and the stream chart. Motion client displays the radar chart of the body direction. Audition client displays the spectrogram of input sound and pitch (frequency) vs sound source direction chart. Vision client displays the image of the camera and the status of face identification and tracking.

To attain real-time tracking, the above modules are physically distributed to five Linux nodes connected by TCP/IP over Gigabit Ethernet TCP/IP network and run asynchronously. The system is implemented by distributed processing of five nodes with

Pentium-IV 1.8 GHz. Each node serves Vision, Audition, Motion and Dialogue clients, and SIG server. The whole system upgrades the real-time multiple-talker tracking system [14] by introducing stereo vision systems, adding more nodes and Gigabit Ethernet and realizes social interaction system by designing association and attention control modules.

3.1 Active Audition Module

To localize sound sources with two microphones, first a set of peaks are extracted for left and right channels, respectively. Then, the same or similar peaks of left and right channels are identified as a pair and each pair is used to calculate interaural phase difference (IPD) and interaural intensity difference (IID). IPD is calculated from frequencies of less than 1500 Hz, while IID is from frequency of more than 1500 Hz.

Since auditory and visual tracking involves motor movements, which cause motor and mechanical noises, audition should suppress or at least reduce such noises. In human robot interaction, when a robot is talking, it should suppress its own speeches. Nakadai *et al* presented the *active audition* for humanoids to improve sound source tracking by integrating audition, vision, and motor controls [15]. We also use their heuristics to reduce internal burst noises caused by motor movements.

From IPD and IID, the epipolar geometry is used to obtain the direction of sound source [15]. The key ideas of their real-time active audition system are twofold; one is to exploit the property of the harmonic structure (fundamental frequency, $F0$, and its overtones) to find a more accurate pair of peaks in left and right channels. The other is to search the sound source direction by combining the belief factors of IPD and IID based on Dempster-Shafer theory.

Finally, audition module sends an auditory event consisting of pitch ($F0$) and a list of 20-best direction (θ) with reliability for each harmonics.

3.2 Face Recognition and Identification Module

Vision extracts lengthwise objects such as persons from a disparity map to localize them by using a pair of cameras. First a disparity map is generated by an intensity based area-correlation technique. This is processed in real-time on a PC by a recursive correlation technique and optimization peculiar to Intel architecture [9].

In addition, left and right images are calibrated by affine transformation in advance. An object is extracted from a 2-D disparity map by assuming that a human body is lengthwise. A 2-D disparity map is defined by

$$DM_{2D} = \{D(i,j)|i = 1, 2, \cdots W, j = 1, 2, \cdots H\} \tag{1}$$

where W and H are width and height, respectively and D is a disparity value.

As a first step to extract lengthwise objects, the median of DM_{2D} along the direction of height shown as Eq. (2) is extracted.

$$D_l(i) = Median(D(i,j)). \tag{2}$$

A 1-D disparity map DM_{1D} as a sequence of $D_l(i)$ is created.

$$DM_{1D} = \{D_l(i)|i = 1, 2, \cdots W\} \tag{3}$$

Next, a lengthwise object such as a human body is extracted by segmentation of a region with similar disparity in DM_{1D}. This achieves robust body extraction so that only the torso can be extracted when the human extends his arm. Then, for object localization, epipolar geometry is applied to the center of gravity of the extracted region. Finally, vision module sends a visual event consisting of a list of 5-best Face ID (Name) with its reliability and position (distance r, azimuth θ and elevation ϕ) for each face.

3.3 Stream Formation and Association

Association synchronizes the results (events) given by other modules. It forms an auditory, visual or associated stream by their proximity. Events are stored in the short-term memory only for 2 seconds. Synchronization process runs with the delay of 200 msec, which is the largest delay of the system, that is, vision module.

An auditory event is connected to the nearest auditory stream within $\pm 10°$ and with common or harmonic pitch. A visual event is connected to the nearest visual stream within 40 cm and with common face ID. In either case, if there are plural candidates, the most reliable one is selected. If any appropriate stream is found, such an event becomes a new stream. In case that no event is connected to an existing stream, such a stream remains alive for up to 500 msec. After 500 msec of keep-alive state, the stream terminates.

An auditory and a visual streams are associated if their direction difference is within $\pm 10°$ and this situation continues for more than 50% of the 1 sec period. If either auditory or visual event has not been found for more than 3 sec, such an associated stream is deassociated and only existing auditory or visual stream remains. If the auditory and visual direction difference has been more than $30°$ for 3 sec, such an associated stream is deassociated to two separate streams.

4 Attention System

Attention control focuses on one of auditory, visual, or associated streams. It has two modes; socially-oriented and task-oriented. Selective attention is performed according to personality. To define personality, the interpersonal circumplex of the Interpersonal Theory is used. With two mutually independent axes, dormant and friendly, variations of personality are *Dominant, Assured, Exhibitionistic, Sociable, Friendly, Warm, Trusting, Different, Submissive, Unassured, Inhibited, Aloof, Hostile, Cold, Mistrusting*, and *Competitive* (Figure 1) [11].

Since these variations are represented as a circle (circumplex), each variation of personality is represented as a point, (r, θ), inside the interpersonal circumplex, where $0 \leq r \leq 1$ and $0 \leq \theta \leq 2\pi$. Therefore, the value of *Friendly/Hostile* axis and that of *Dominant/Submissive* axis are represented as $r \cos \theta$ and $r \sin \theta$, respectively. Each variation occupies a pie of $\pi/8$. For example, *Friendly* is specified as a pie section of $-\frac{\pi}{16} \sim \frac{\pi}{16}$, and *Dominant* as that of $\frac{3\pi}{16} \sim \frac{5\pi}{16}$.

4.1 Socially-Oriented Attention Control

In this paper, we focus on *passive immediate sensorial attention* in the sense that the stimulus is a sense-impression and no derived ways is considered. We believe that passive attention control with non-verbal interaction is complementary to verbal interaction.

To what the system attend is called "*interested*". The total amount of interest in the system keeps the same and a newly focused stream takes all the amount of *interest* in winner-take-all competition between streams. attention control module selects the stream of the largest *interest*. Three mental factors are defined based on personality.

1. *interest* in a new stream — When a new stream is generated, other streams lose *interest* multiplied by the value of r. Then the new stream gets the total amount of lost *interest*. This means that a robot of large r changes its focus to a new stream. When an auditory stream and a visual one are associated, the sum of *interest* of each stream is given to the associated one.
2. decay of *interest* — The *interest* of a focused stream is reduced at the rate of e^{-kT} every minute, where k is {1.5 - "the value of *Dominant/Submissive*"}/3. The lost *interest* is distributed to other streams.
3. decay of belief — Disappeared stream still remains in the system, because a un-seen talker resumes to talk after a short time of silence. If disappeared stream is deleted immediately, the continuity of stream is difficult to maintain. The value of *Friendly/Hostile* is used as the decay factor of belief.

As an example of socially-oriented control, we implement a companion robot. It should pay attention to a new auditory or visual event, the precedence of streams selected by focus-of-attention control is specified from higher to lower as follows:

auditory stream ≻ *associated stream* ≻ *visual stream.*

4.2   Task-Oriented Attention Control

Task-oriented attention control forces Attention to behave according to a specific script. In this paper, we implement a simple receptionist robot. It should focus on the user, the precedence of streams selected by focus-of-attention control is specified from higher to lower as follows:

associated stream ≻ *auditory stream* ≻ *visual stream.*

One scenario to evaluate the above control is specified as follows: (1) A known participant comes to the receptionist robot. His face has been registered in the face database. (2) He says Hello to *SIG*. (3) *SIG* replies "Hello. You are XXX-san, aren't you?" (4) He says "yes". (5) *SIG* says "XXX-san, welcome to the party. Please enter the room.".

5   Experiments and Observation

Experiments was done with a small room in a normal residential apartment. The width, length and height of the room of experiment is about 3 m, 3 m, and 2 m, respectively. The room has 6 down-lights embedded on the ceiling.

5.1 Task-Oriented Interaction: *SIG* as a Receptionist Robot

Figure 4 depicts two snapshots of this script. Figure 4 a) shows the initial state. The loud speaker on the stand is the mouth of *SIG*'s. When a participant comes to the receptionist, but *SIG* has not noticed him yet, because he is out of *SIG*'s sight. When he speaks to *SIG*, Audition generates an auditory event with sound source direction, and sends it to Association, which creates an auditory stream. This stream triggers Attention to make a plan that *SIG* should turn to him, and *SIG* does it (Figure 4 b)).

This experiment demonstrates *SIG*'s two interesting behaviors. One is voice-triggered tracking, and the other is that *SIG* does not pay attention to its own speech. As a receptionist robot, once an association is established, *SIG* keeps its face fixed to the direction of the talker of the associated stream. Therefore, even when *SIG* utters via a loud speaker on the left, *SIG* does not pay an attention to the sound source, that is, its own speech.

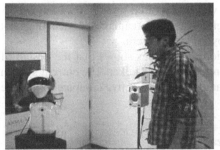

a) When a participant comes and says "Hello", *SIG* turns toward him.

b) *SIG* asks his name and he introduces himself to it.

Fig. 4. Temporal sequence of snapshots of *SIG*'s interaction as a receptionist robot

a) The leftmost man says "Hello" and SIG is tracking him.

b) The second right man says "Hello" and SIG turns toward him.

Fig. 5. Temporal sequence of snapshots for a companion robot: scene (upper-left), radar and sequence chart (upper-right), spectrogram and pitch-vs-direction chart (lower-left), and face-tracking chart (lower-right).

5.2 Socially-Oriented Interaction: *SIG* as a Companion Robot

When four talkers actually talks spontaneously in attendance of *SIG*, *SIG* tracks some talker and then changes focus-of-attention to others. The observed behavior is evaluated by checking the internal states of *SIG*; that is, auditory and visual localization shown in the radar chart, auditory, visual, and associated streams shown in the stream chart, and peak extraction as shown in Figure 5 a)∼b).

The top-right image consists of the radar chart (left) and the stream chart (right) updated in real-time. The former shows the environment recognized by *SIG* at the moment of the snapshot. A pink sector indicates a visual field of *SIG*. Because of using the absolute coordinate, the pink sector rotates as *SIG* turns. A green point with a label is the direction and the face ID of a visual stream. A blue sector is the direction of an auditory stream. Green, blue and red lines indicate the direction of visual, auditory and associated stream, respectively. Blue and green *thin* lines indicate auditory and visual streams, respectively. Blue, green and red *thick* lines indicate associated streams with only auditory, only visual, and both information, respectively.

The bottom-left image shows the auditory viewer consisting of the power spectrum and auditory event viewer. The latter shows an auditory event as a filled circle with its pitch in X axis and its direction in Y axis.

The bottom-right image shows the visual viewer captured by the *SIG*'s left eye. A detected face is displayed with a red rectangle. The top-left image in each snapshot shows the scene of this experiment recorded by a video camera.

The temporal sequence of *SIG*'s recognition and actions shows that the design of companion robot works well and pays its attention to a new talker. The current system has attained a passive companion. To design and develop an active companion may be important future work.

5.3 Observation: *SIG* as a Non-verbal Eliza

As socially-oriented attention control, interesting human behaviors are observed. The mechanism of associating auditory and visual streams and that of socially-oriented attention control are explained in advance to the user.

1. Some people walk around talking with their hand convering *SIG*'s eyes in order to confirm the performance of auditory tracking.
2. Some people creep on the floor with talking in order to confirm the performacne of auditory tracking.
3. Some people play hide-and-seek games with *SIG*.
4. Some people play sounds from a pair of loud speakers with changing the balance control of pre-amplifier in order to confirm the performance of auditory tracking.
5. Whe one person reads loud a book and then another person starts to read loud a book, *SIG* with *Dominant* personality turns its head to the second talker for a short time and then is back to the first talker and keeps its attention on him/her. On the contrary, *SIG* with *Submissive* personality often turns its head to each talker. In either case, the value of r is set to 1.

Above observations remind us of Eliza [22], although *SIG* does not say anything except a receptionist robot. When the user says something to *SIG*, it turns to him/her, which invites the participation of the user into interaction. *SIG* also invites exploration of the principles of its functioning, that is, the user is drawn in to see how *SIG* will respond to variations in behavior. Since *SIG* takes only passive behaviors, it does not arouse higher expectations of verisimilitude that it can deliver on.

Needless to say, there are lots of work remaining to validate the proposed approach for personality of artifacts. We are currently working to incorporate active social interaction by developing the capability of listneing to simultaneous speeches.

6   Conclusions

In this paper, we demonstrate that auditory and visual multiple-talker tracking subsystem can improve social aspects of human robot interaction. Although a simple scheme of behavior is implemented, human robot interaction is drastically improved by realtime multiple-talker tracking system. We can pleasantly spend an hour with *SIG* as a companion robot even if its behavior is quite passive.

Since the Interpersonal Theory research community provides software for analysing circumplex correlation matrices, we have plan to gather the data of user interaction to evaluate whether the presented architecture of selective attention based on personality realizes the target variation of personality. In this persuit may lead to a general theory of personality for software agents and humanoid robots.

Acknowledgments. We thank our colleagues of Symbiotic Intelligence Group, Kitano Symbiotic Systems Project, in particular, Kenichi Hidai (currently with Sony DCL), for their discussions. We also thank Prof. Tatsuya Kawahara of Kyoto University for his supports in using "Julius" automatic speech recognition system.

References

1. BATES, J. The role of emotion in believable agents. *Communications of the ACM 37*, 7 (1994), 122–125.
2. BREAZEAL, C. Emotive qualities in robot speech. In *Proceedings of IEEE/RSJ International Conference on Intelligent Robots and Systems (IROS-2001)* (2001), IEEE, pp. 1389–1394.
3. BREAZEAL, C., AND SCASSELLATI, B. A context-dependent attention system for a social robot. In *Proceedints of 16th International Joint Conference on Atificial Intelligence (IJCAI-99)* (1999), pp. 1146–1151.
4. BROOKS, R. A., BREAZEAL, C., IRIE, R., KEMP, C. C., MARJANOVIC, M., SCASSELLATI, B., AND WILLIAMSON, M. M. Alternative essences of intelligence. In *Proceedings of 15th National Conference on Artificial Intelligence (AAAI-98)* (1998), AAAI, pp. 961–968.
5. CASSELL, J. More than just another pretty face: Embodied conversational interface agents. *Communications of the ACM 43*, 4 (2000), 70–78.
6. CHERRY, E. C. Some experiments on the recognition of speech, with one and with two ears. *Journal of Acoustic Society of America 25* (1953), 975–979.
7. HANDEL, S. *Listening*. The MIT Press, MA., 1989.
8. HAYES-ROTH, B., BALL, G., LISETTI, C., PICARD, R., AND STERN, A. Affect and emotion in the user interface. In *Proceedings of 1998 International Conference on Intelligent User Interfaces* (1998), ACM, pp. 91–96.

9. KAGAMI, S., OKADA, K., INABA, M., AND INOUE, H. Real-time 3d optical flow generation system. In *Proc. of International Conference on Multisensor Fusion and Integration for Intelligent Systems (MFI'99)* (1999), pp. 237–242.

10. KAWAHARA, T., LEE, A., KOBAYASHI, T., TAKEDA, K., MINEMATSU, N., ITOU, K., ITO, A., YAMAMOTO, M., YAMADA, A., UTSURO, T., AND SHIKANO, K. Japanese dictation toolkit – 1997 version –. *Journal of Acoustic Society Japan (E) 20*, 3 (1999), 233–239.

11. KIESLER, D. The 1982 interpersonal circle: A taxonomy for complementarity in human transactions. *Psychological Review 90* (1993), 185–214.

12. LOYALL, A. B., AND BATES, J. Personality-rich believable agents that use language. In *Proceedings of the First International Conference on Autonomous Agents* (1997), pp. 106–113.

13. MATSUSAKA, Y., TOJO, T., KUOTA, S., FURUKAWA, K., TAMIYA, D., HAYATA, K., NAKANO, Y., AND KOBAYASHI, T. Multi-person conversation via multi-modal interface — a robot who communicates with multi-user. In *Proceedings of 6th European Conference on Speech Communication Technology (EUROSPEECH-99)* (1999), ESCA, pp. 1723–1726.

14. NAKADAI, K., HIDAI, K., MIZOGUCHI, H., OKUNO, H. G., AND KITANO, H. Real-time auditory and visual multiple-object tracking for robots. In *Proceedings of 17th International Joint Conference on Artificial Intelligence (IJCAI-01)* (2001), vol. II, IJCAI, pp. 1425–1432.

15. NAKADAI, K., LOURENS, T., OKUNO, H. G., AND KITANO, H. Active audition for humanoid. In *Proceedings of 17th National Conference on Artificial Intelligence (AAAI-2000)* (2000), AAAI, pp. 832–839.

16. NAKADAI, K., MATSUI, T., OKUNO, H. G., AND KITANO, H. Active audition system and humanoid exterior design. In *Proceedings of IEEE/RAS International Conference on Intelligent Robots and Systems (IROS 2000)* (2000), IEEE, pp. 1453–1461.

17. NAKADAI, K., OKUNO, H. G., AND KITANO, H. Exploiting auditory fovea in humanoid-human interaction. In *Proceedings of 18th National Conference on Artificial Intelligence (AAAI-2002)* (2002), AAAI, *(in print)*.

18. ONO, T., IMAI, M., AND ISHIGURO, H. A model of embodied communications with gestures between humans and robots. In *Proceedings of 23rd Annual Meeting of the Cognitive Science Society (CogSci2001)* (2000), AAAI, pp. 732–737.

19. PASHLER, H. *The Psychology of Attention*. The MIT Press, MA., 1997.

20. REEVES, B., AND NASS, C. *The Media Equation: How People Treat Computers, Television, and New Media Like Real People and Places*. Cambridge University Press, Cambridge, UK, 1996.

21. WALDHERR, S., THRUN, S., ROMERO, R., AND MARGARITIS, D. Template-based recoginition of pose and motion gestures on a mobile robot. In *Proceedings of 15th National Conference on Artificial Intelligence (AAAI-98)* (1998), AAAI, pp. 977–982.

22. WEIZENBAUM, J. Eliza – a computer program for the study of natural language communication between man and machine. *Communications of the ACM 9*, 1 (1966), 36–45.

23. WOLFE, J., CAVE, K. R., AND FRANZEL, S. Guided search: An alternative to the feature integration model for visual search. *Journal of Experimental Psychology: Human Perception and Performance 15*, 3 (1989), 419–433.

Audio-to-Visual Conversion Using Hidden Markov Models

Soonkyu Lee and DongSuk Yook

Speech Information Processing Laboratory
Department of Computer Science and Engineering, Korea University
Sungbookgoo Anamdong 5-1, Seoul, Korea 136-701
http://voice.korea.ac.kr
{mudwall,yook}@voice.korea.ac.kr

Abstract. We describe audio-to-visual conversion techniques for efficient multimedia communications. The audio signals are automatically converted to visual images of mouth shape. The visual speech can be represented as a sequence of visemes, which are the generic face images corresponding to particular sounds. Visual images synchronized with audio signals can provide user-friendly interface for man machine interactions. Also, it can be used to help the people with impaired-hearing. We use HMMs (hidden Markov models) to convert audio signals to a sequence of visemes. In this paper, we compare two approaches in using HMMs. In the first approach, an HMM is trained for each viseme, and the audio signals are directly recognized as a sequence of visemes. In the second approach, each phoneme is modeled with an HMM, and a general phoneme recognizer is utilized to produce a phoneme sequence from the audio signals. The phoneme sequence is then converted to a viseme sequence. We implemented the two approaches and tested them on the TIMIT speech corpus. The viseme recognizer shows 33.9% error rate, and the phoneme-based approach exhibits 29.7% viseme recognition error rate. When similar viseme classes are merged, we have found that the error rates can be reduced to 20.5% and 13.9%, respectably.

1. Introduction

With the recent advances in computer and multimedia technologies, audio-to-visual conversion becomes an important area for efficient multimedia communications. In multimedia environments, using both sounds and images is a natural and efficient way to communicate between men and machines. Images synchronized with sounds can transfer information more reliably than sounds alone. Audio-to-visual conversion techniques can help to create speaking facial images from speech data. The speech data is converted to a sequence of visemes, which are the visual equivalent of phonemes. From the viseme sequence, its corresponding facial images can be synthesized. The audio-to-visual conversion techniques can be applied to many areas such as human-computer interaction, videophone, and character animation. In this paper, we will focus on the viseme recognition from audio data.

Several methods have been proposed to handle the audio-to-visual conversion. In VQ (vector quantization) based methods, a codebook that represents entire acoustic space

M. Ishizuka and A. Sattar (Eds.): PRICAI 2002, LNAI 2417, pp. 563-570, 2002.

of speech feature vectors is created during training process. A testing speech feature vector is classified as one of the codewords in the codebook, and the images corresponding to the codeword are selected for the visual image synthesis [4]. This method is simple to implement and easy to train. However, the error in quantization can cause extra classification errors. Another approach uses artificial neural networks[1]. Some neural networks such as TDNN (time-delay neural network) [11] can make use of contextual information and learn very complex classification functions. In some experiments for speech processing [9][11], neural networks show very high classification accuracy and robustness to noises. However, the training process is computationally too expensive especially for a large amount of training data. The third approach uses HMM (hidden Markov models) [7]. It assumes that the speech signal can be modeled by the Markov process. The parameters of HMMs are estimated during training process from a large amount of training corpus. The testing speech is scored against the HMMs and the most likely model sequence is selected for the given speech signals [6]. The most likely phoneme sequence can be computed in the same way, and it can be easily converted to the corresponding viseme sequence. The HMM-based speech recognition is one of the popular methods because of its relatively high recognition accuracy and trainability using a large amount of data. In this paper, we compare two approaches in building viseme recognizers using HMMs. The first approach uses an HMM for each viseme, while a general phoneme recognizer is utilized in the second approach.

The rest of this paper is organized as follows. In Section 2, we review the visual speech unit called viseme. In Section 3, the audio-to-visual conversion systems using HMMs are described. Some experimental results of the systems are analyzed in Section 4. Section 5 concludes the paper with some suggestions to the future works.

2. Visemes

A *viseme* is a unit of visual speech. A generic facial image or lip shape is associated with a viseme in order to represent a particular sound. Fisher [2] introduced the word viseme, which is a compound word of "visual" and "phoneme". A viseme can be used to describe a set of phonemes visually. It can help to increase speech recognition accuracy for both human and machines by visually recognizing the shape of speakers' lip movements [3][8]. There are many-to-one mappings from phonemes to visemes. Table 1 shows the typical 41 phonemes used in English language including silence. The viseme mapping is shown in the last column of the table. We named each viseme after one of the phoneme that belongs to the viseme. For example, phonemes /p/, /b/, and /m/ belong to viseme /p/. According to the shape of mouth and placement of tongue, we grouped the 41 phonemes into 14 visemes.

The lip shapes of 6 consonant visemes and 7 vowel visemes are shown in Figures 1 and 2, respactably. The viseme names are shown above the lip images, and the phonemes are shown below the images.

Table 1. Phonemes and visemes in English language.

	Phone classes	Phonemes	Example words	Visemes
Consonants	Stops	b	bee	p
		d	day	t
		g	gay	k
		p	pea	p
		t	tea	t
		k	key	k
	Affricates	jh	joke	ch
		ch	choke	ch
	Fricatives	s	sea	t
		sh	she	ch
		z	zone	t
		zh	azure	ch
		f	fin	f
		th	thin	t
		v	van	f
		dh	then	t
	Nasals	m	mom	p
		n	noon	k
		ng	sing	k
	Glides	l	lay	k
		r	ray	w
		w	way	w
		y	yacht	k
		hh	hay	k
Vowels		iy	beet	iy
		ih	bit	iy
		eh	bet	eh
		ey	bait	eh,iy
		ae	bat	eh
		aa	bott	aa
		aw	bout	aa,uh
		ay	bite	aa,iy
		ah	but	ah
		ao	bought	ao
		oy	boy	ao,iy
		ow	boat	ao,uh
		uh	book	uh
		uw	boot	uh
		er	bird	er
Others		pau	pause	#
		h#	silence	#

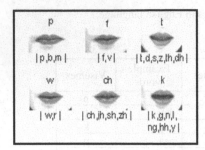

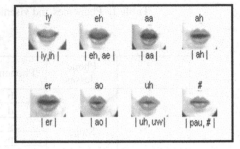

Fig. 1. The 6 consonant visemes.   **Fig. 2.** The 7 vowel visemes and 1 silence viseme.

3. Viseme Recognition

An HMM is a stochastic model, into which some temporal restrictions can be incorporated. It can be used to capture the acoustic characteristic of speech sound. An HMM can be considered as a special case of the *Bayesian* classifier, where the most probable utterance $\hat{U}$ for given speech X is selected among all possible utterances $U*$ as follows;

$$\hat{U} = \arg \max_{U \in U*} P(U|X) \tag{1}$$

One of the distinguishing characteristics of speech is that it is dynamic. Even within a small segment such as a phoneme, the speech sound changes gradually. The previous phones affect the beginning of a phone, the middle portion of the phone is relatively stable, and the following phones affect the end of the phone. The temporal information of speech feature vectors plays an important role in recognition process. In order to capture the dynamic characteristics of speech within the framework of the Bayesian classifier, certain temporal restrictions should be imposed. A 3-state left-to-right HMM is typically used for this purpose. Figure 3 shows an example of such an HMM, where $a_{i,j}$ is the transition probability from the state i to the state j, and $b_i(x)$ is the observation probability of the speech feature vector x in the state i.

The observation probability may be modeled as a set of Gaussian distribution functions. The likelihood of a viseme for a given segment of speech can be approximately computed using a Viterbi path score [10]. The most likely sequence of visemes for the audio signals can also be found using the Viterbi algorithm. Figure 4 shows the diagram of a viseme recognizer, where each viseme is modeled using an HMM with multiple Gaussian distribution functions per state.

Another way of using HMMs for viseme recognition is utilizing a phoneme recognizer. A general phoneme recognizer can be trained in the similar way as the viseme recognizer. The difference is that each phoneme is modeled using an HMM. In this approach, the audio signals are first converted to a sequence of phonemes. Then, the phoneme sequence is mapped to a viseme sequence using Table 1. The schematic diagram of this approach is shown in Figure 5.

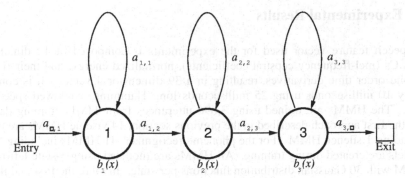

Fig. 3. 3-state left-to-right HMM

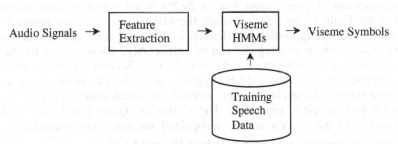

Fig. 4. A viseme recognition system using viseme HMMs.

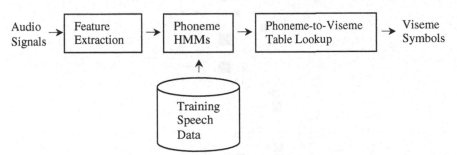

Fig. 5. A viseme recognition system using phoneme HMMs.

In the next section, we show some experimental results of these approaches in applying HMMs to viseme recognition.

4. Experimental Results

A speech feature vector used for the experiments is composed of 12 dimensional MFCCs (mel-frequency cepstral coefficients), normalized energy, and their first and second order time derivatives, resulting in a 39 dimensional vector. It is computed every 10 milliseconds using 25 milliseconds long Hamming windowed speech signals. The HMMs are trained using 3,696 utterances from TIMIT training data [5]. For the first approach described in the previous section, 14 viseme HMMs are created including 1 silence HMM. For the phoneme recognizer, 41 HMMs including silence models are created during training. All HMMs are modeled using 3-state left-to-right HMM with 30 Gaussian distribution functions per state. In total, the first and the second systems have 1,260 and 3,630 Gaussian distributions, respectably. In both cases, 1,344 utterances from the testing portion of TIMIT are used for the evaluation.

The baseline viseme recognition system shows 33.9% viseme recognition error rate. The baseline phoneme recognizer shows 37.1% phoneme recognition error rate, which corresponds to viseme error rate of 29.7% when converted into viseme sequences using Table 1. In order to reduce the viseme error rate, we merge similar viseme classes according to their mouth shapes. First, we split /er/ into /ah/ and /r/, and merge them with the existing /ah/ and /r/, respectably. By doing this for the phoneme-based system, the error rate is reduced to 28.9%. Second, we group visemes /t/ and /ch/ together, and /iy/, /eh/, and /ah/ together. The error rate is reduced to 24.5%. Not only the shape of mouth but also the confusion matrices shown in Figures 6 and 7 motives this and the rest of groupings. The x axes in Figures 6 and 7 are the reference visemes and the y axes are the recognized visemes. For example, a lot of viseme /k/'s are classified as viseme /p/ in both Figures 6 and 7.

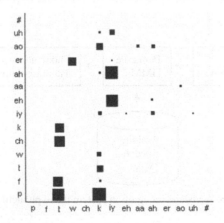

Fig. 6. Confusion matrix of the viseme-based system.

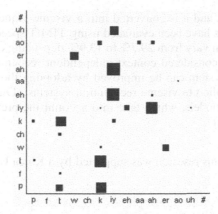

Fig. 7. Confusion matrix of the phoneme-based system.

We keep merging the viseme classes until there are only 3 classes left; consonants, vowels, and silence. That is, /t/ and /k/ are merged, and /iy/ and /uh/ are merged, resulting in 21.4% error rate. Further error reduction is obtained by merging /p/ and /t/, /p/ and /w/, and /p/ and /f/ and /iy/ and /aa/, successively. The error rates are reduced to 19.6%, 17.3%, and 13.9%, respectably. The comparison of the viseme-based and the phoneme-based systems in this experiment is summarized in Table 2.

Table 2. Comparison between the viseme-based and the phoneme-based systems with varying viseme sets.

Merge	Viseme	Viseme-based		Phoneme-based	
		Error (%)	Reduction Rate	Error (%)	Reduction Rate
Baseline	14	33.9		29.7	
er → ah+r	13	33.7	0.50	28.9	2.60
t+ch, iy+eh+ah	10	30.2	10.9	24.5	17.5
t+k, iy+uh	8	29.7	12.3	21.4	27.9
p+t	7	26.9	20.6	19.6	34.0
p+w	5	27.0	20.3	17.3	41.7
p+f, iy+aa	3	20.5	39.5	13.9	53.1

5. Conclusions

The audio-to-visual conversion is becoming an important area of interests as the multimedia communication environments become popular. Automatic conversion of audio signals to the visual speech units can help to create natural dynamic images of speaking faces. In this paper, we studied the viseme recognizers, which produce a sequence of viseme symbols from speech waveforms. We compared two approaches in using HMMs for the audio-to-visual conversion. The first approach is based on the viseme recognizer, where each viseme is model with a single HMM. The second approach uses a general phoneme recognizer. The audio signals are recognized as a sequence of phonemes, and it is converted into a viseme sequence. The performances of the two approaches have been evaluated using TIMIT speech data. We have found that the error rates can vary from 29.7% to 13.9% depending on the viseme sets used.

In this paper, we considered context-independent recognition units. Typically, a speech recognition system can be improved by adopting the contextual information. The same can be applied to viseme recognition systems. One of our next steps is to consider tri-viseme models, which take into account the previous and the following visemes in the context.

Acknowledgment. This research was supported by a Korea University Grant.

References

[1] K. Choi, and J. Hwang, "Baum-Welch HMM inversion for audio-to-visual conversion", *IEEE International Workshop on Multimedia Signal Processing*, pp. 175-180, 1999.
[2] C. Fisher, "Confusions among visually perceived consonants", *Journal on Speech and Hearing Research*, vol. 11, pp. 796-804, 1968.
[3] K. Grant, B. Walden, and P. Seitz, "Auditory-visual speech recognition by hearing-impaired subjects: consonant recognition, sentence recognition, and auditory-visual integration", *Journal of Acoustic Society of America*, vol. 103, pp. 2677-2690, 1998.
[4] S. Morishima and H. Harashima, "A media conversion from speech to facial image for intelligent man-machine interface", *IEEE Journal on selected areas in communications*, vol. 9, no. 4, pp. 594-600, 1991.
[5] Nist Speech Disc 1-1.1, TIMIT Acoustic-phonetic continuous speech corpus, October 1990.
[6] L. Rabiner, "A tutorial on hidden Markov models and selected applications in speech recognition", *Proceedings of the IEEE*, vol. 77, no.2, pp. 257-286, 1989.
[7] R. Rao, T. Chen and R. Mersereau, "Audio-to-visual conversion for multimedia communication", *IEEE Transaction on Industrial Electronics*, vol. 45, no. 1, pp. 15-22, 1998.
[8] A. Rogozan and P. Delelise, "Adaptive fusion of acoustic and visual sources for automatic speech recognition", *Speech Communication*, vol. 26, pp. 149-161, 1998.
[9] S. Tamura and A. Waibel, "Noise reduction using connectionist models", *IEEE International Conference on Acoustics, Speech, and Signal Processing*, pp. 553-556, 1988.
[10] A. Viterbi, "Error bounds of convolutional codes and an asymmetrically optimum decoding algorithm", *IEEE Transactions on Information Theory*, IT-13, pp. 260-267, 1967.
[11] A. Waibel, T. Hanazawa, G. Hinton, K. Shikano, and K. Lang, "Phoneme recognition using time-delay neural networks", *IEEE Transactions on Acoustics, Speech, and Signal Processing*, vol. 37, no. 3, pp. 328-339, 1989.

Scripting the Bodies and Minds of Life-Like Characters

Helmut Prendinger, Sylvain Descamps, and Mitsuru Ishizuka

Department of Information and Communication Engineering
Graduate School of Information Science and Technology
University of Tokyo
7-3-1 Hongo, Bunkyo-ku, Tokyo 113-8656, Japan
{helmut,descamps,ishizuka}@miv.t.u-tokyo.ac.jp

Abstract. In this paper, two systems will be described. First, we present an architecture for emotion-based agents, called SCREAM, that allows to encode affect-related processes for an animate character. Content authors may design the mental make-up of the agent by declaring a variety of parameters relevant to affective communication and obtain quantified emotional reactions. Second, we report on MPML, an XML-style markup language that facilitates the control and coordination of animated characters in web-based environments. Both systems are integrated such that the 'bodies' and 'minds' of life-like characters can be easily controlled.

1 Introduction

Artificial Intelligence (AI) is traditionally concerned with agents' intellectual skills that can optimize their efficiency or accuracy in completing certain tasks, such as planning, learning, or natural language understanding [17]. On the other hand, Hayes-Roth and Doyle's [7] work on 'animate characters' aims to make agents *life-like* or *believable* as well as more 'broad' in their competence, rather than efficient or accurate. Research in this direction has attracted significant interest recently, and life-like agents have already been developed for a wide variety of tasks, including tutor agents in interactive learning environments [9], presenter agents on the web [1,8], and virtual actors for entertainment [16].

However, the success of many of those systems relies on the expertise of their designers, who are typically programmers. We believe that the growing popularity of animated agent systems will increase the demand for tools that allow content experts rather than programmers to script interactive behavior.

In this paper, we will describe two tools that may significantly facilitate the design of life-like characters: SCREAM and MPML. While the SCREAM system is intended to *animate* an agent, e.g., by giving it goals and attitudes (an individual persona), the MPML tool allows to control the agent's visual appearance as an *animated* character. We take 'life-likeness' as an umbrella term for agents that are both animate and animated.

M. Ishizuka and A. Sattar (Eds.): PRICAI 2002, LNAI 2417, pp. 571–580, 2002.

SCREAM (**SCR**ipting **E**motion-based **A**gent **M**inds) is a system for scripting a character's 'mind'. The system allows to specify a character's mental makeup and endow it with emotion and personality which are considered as key features for the life-likeness of characters. A character's mental state can be scripted at many levels of detail, from driven purely by (personality) traits to having full awareness of the social interaction situation, including character-specific beliefs and beliefs attributed to interacting characters or even the user. MPML (**M**ultimodal **P**resentation **M**arkup **L**anguage) is a system that is responsible for scripting a character's 'body'. It facilitates the control and synchronization of the embodied behavior of characters.

The rest of the paper is organized as follows. The next section provides a step-by-step introduction to the core components of the SCREAM system architecture. Each of the modules is explained in terms of its role in the generation of an agent's affective behavior, together with details about its implementation. Section 3 briefly reports on MPML, a markup language for character control, by describing some of its tagging schemes. Section 4 demonstrates how our system works. In Section 5, we conclude the paper.

2   The SCREAM System

The SCREAM system allows authors to control interactive emotional reactions of multiple characters in a natural way. While the system is written in Java for portability, a Java based Prolog system called Jinni [2] is used to support high-level scripting of an agent's mind components: Emotion Generation, Emotion Regulation, Emotion Expression, and the Agent Model. SCREAM can be easily extended by adding or modifying rules that encode the character's cognitive processes. An overview of the system architecture is given in Fig. 1. Each of its components will be discussed in the following sections.

2.1   Emotion Generation

A core activity of an emotion-based agent mind is the generation and management of emotions, which is dealt with by three modules, the *appraisal* module, the *emotion resolution* module, and the *emotion maintenance* module. They will be described in the following. We start with a brief description of the input to the emotion generation component.

Input to an Agent's Mind. Input consists of communicative acts of the form

com_act(S,H,Concept,Modalities,Sit)

where S is the speaker, H the addressee, *Concept* the information conveyed by S to H in situation *Sit*, and *Modalities* is the set of communicative channels used by S, such as specific facial displays, acoustical correlates of (expressed) emotions, linguistic style, gestures, and posture.

Appraisal Module. Reasoning about emotion models an agent's *appraisal process*, where events are evaluated as to their emotional significance for the agent

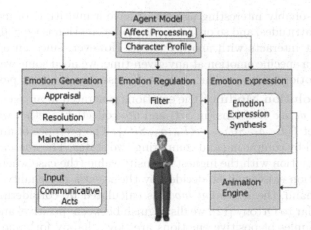

Fig. 1. SCREAM System Architecture.

[13]. The significance is determined by so-called 'emotion-eliciting conditions', which comprise an agent's relation to four types of abstract mental concepts: (i) *beliefs*, i.e., state of affairs that the agent has evidence to hold in the (virtual) world; (ii) *goals*, i.e., states of affairs that are (un)desirable for the agent, what the agent wants (does not want) to obtain; (iii) *standards*, i.e., the agent's beliefs about what ought (not) to be the case, events the agent considers as praiseworthy or blameworthy; and (iv) *attitudes*, i.e., the agent's dispositions to like or dislike other agents or objects, what the agent considers (not) appealing.

Following the emotion model of Ortony, Clore, and Collins [13] (the OCC model), we conceive emotion types as classes of eliciting conditions, each of which is labelled with an emotion word or phrase. In total, twenty-two classes of eliciting conditions are identified: *joy, distress, happy for, sorry for, resent, angry at*, and so on. Consider the emotion specification for fortunes-of-others emotion *resent* (being distressed about another agent's joy). The following rule is written in Prolog-style form close to the actual code:

$$\text{resent}(L1,L2,F,\delta,Sit) \text{ if directed\_to}(L1,L2,Sit) \text{ and } \text{dislikes}(L1,L2,\delta_{NApp(F)},Sit)$$
$$\text{and } \text{joy}(L2,L1,F,\delta_{Des(F)},Sit)$$

The rule reads as follows. The (locutor-)agent $L1$ resents agent $L2$ about state of affairs F in situation Sit with intensity degree δ if $L2$ is the addressee in Sit, $L1$ dislikes $L2$ with 'non-appealingness' degree δ_{NApp}, and believes that $L2$ is joyful about F with 'desirability' degree δ_{Des}. Whether this belief is true or not is entirely in the content author's control, and typically specified in the communicative act description. We assume intensities $\delta_i \in \{0, \ldots, 5\}$ such that zero is the lower threshold, i.e., the mental concept is not active, and five is the maximum value. By default, intensities δ_i are combined to an overall intensity δ by logarithmic combination $\delta = \log_2\left(\sum_i 2^{\delta_i}\right)$. Although this way to combine intensities seems plausible, content authors might wish to employ a different combination rule (e.g., additive), and edit the combination rule in question.

Since a reasonably interesting agent will have a multitude of mental states (beliefs, goals, attitudes, and so on), more than one emotion is typically triggered when the agent interacts with another agent. However, since an agent should clearly express a specific emotion at any given time, we need some way to resolve the agent's emotions. This problem will be discussed in the next paragraph.

Emotion Resolution Module. The emotions generated in an agent at a given time are called *active* emotions (in Sit) and are collected together with their intensities in a set $\{\langle E_1, \delta_1, Sit \rangle, \ldots, \langle E_n, \delta_n, Sit \rangle\}$. The presence of multiple emotions is resolved by computing and comparing two states. The *dominant emotion* is simply the emotion with the highest intensity value (the case where no unique dominant emotion exists will be decided by the agent's personality, see below). On the other hand, the *dominant mood* is calculated by considering all active emotions. Similar to Ortony [12], we distinguish between 'positive' and 'negative' emotions. Examples of positive emotions are 'joy', 'happy for', and 'sorry for', whereas 'resent' and 'angry at' are negative emotions. Then the dominant mood results by comparing the overall intensity value associated with the positive and negative emotion sets, which is obtained by logarithmic combination. The *winning emotional state* is decided by comparing the intensities for dominant emotion and dominant mood. Thereby, we can account for situations where an agent has a joyful experience, but is still more influenced by its overall negative emotions (mood) for another agent. In situations where equal intensities (of active emotions, moods, etc.) result, we consider the agreeableness dimension of an agent's personality. The agreeableness dimension is numerically quantified, with a value $\gamma_A \in \{-5, \ldots, 5\}$. Consequently, an agent with disagreeable personality (e.g., $\gamma_A = -3$) would favor a winning negative emotional state to a (winning) positive emotion if both have the same intensity level.

Emotion Maintenance Module. This module handles the decay process of emotions. Depending on their type and intensity, emotions may remain active in the agent's memory for a certain time during the interaction [15]. A decay function decreases the intensity levels of the active emotions each 'beat' by n levels until the intensity is equal of smaller than zero. A beat is defined as a single action-reaction pair between two agents. The actual decay rate is determined by the emotion type and the agent's personality such that with agreeable agents, negative emotions decay faster than positive ones.

2.2   Emotion Regulation

In their seminal work on non-verbal behavior, Ekman and Friesen [6] argue that the expression of emotional states (e.g., as facial expression) is governed by social and cultural norms, so-called *display rules*, that have a significant impact on the intensity of emotion expression. We will treat emotion regulation as a process that decides whether an emotion is expressed or suppressed. Moreover, a value is calculated that indicates to what extent an emotion is suppressed. An agent's emotion regulation is depending on a multitude of parameters [14,5]. We broadly categorize them into parameters that constitute a social threat for the agent, and parameters that refer to the agent's capability of (self-)control. Although this distinction is somewhat arbitrary, we found that it allows authors to state regulation parameters in a simple and intuitive way.

Communication is always embedded into a social context where participants take social roles with associated communicative conventions. Following Brown and Levinson [3], we take *social power* θ_P and *social distance* θ_D as the most important social variables $(\theta_P, \theta_D \in \{0, \ldots, 5\})$. We assume that roles are ordered according to a power scale, where *social_power(L2,L1,θ_P,Sit)* means that agent $L2$ is θ_P ranks higher than agent $L1$. Social distance refers to the familiarity or 'closeness' between agents, and can be stated as *social_distance(L1,L2,θ_D,Sit)*. Based on θ_P and θ_D, the *social threat* θ for $L1$ from $L2$ is computed as $\theta = \log_2 \left(2^{\theta_P} + 2^{\theta_D}\right)$. If θ_P and θ_D are both zero, θ is set to zero. Note that the social variables are not meant to reflect 'objective' ratings of power or distance, but the modelled agent's assumed assessment of the ratings.

The following set of parameters describe the agent's *self-control* each of which takes a value $\gamma_i \in \{-5, \ldots, 5\}$. Greater positive values indicate that the agent is capable and willing to suppress negative emotions whereas greater negative values indicate that the agent tends to also express negative emotions. Besides the agent's agreeableness, we also consider the *extroversion dimension of personality*. Extrovert agents typically express their emotions independent of their impact on another agent whereas introvert agents tend to refrain from doing so. For artistic reasons, we discourage authors from using the zero value, since agents with 'neutral' personality might fail to express their emotions succinctly. Moreover, if the agent assumes that the *interlocutor's personality* is unfriendly (disagreeable), it will rather not express a negative emotion. An interesting phenomenon in interactions among humans are *reciprocal feedback loops* where one agent's linguistic friendliness results in the interlocutor agent's adaption of its otherwise unfriendly behavior.

The overall control value γ is computed as $\gamma = \frac{\sum_i \gamma_i}{N}$ where the denominator N scales the result according to the number of considered control parameters. Basically, the equation captures the intuition that different control parameters may defeat each other. Thus, the control of an agent that is very extrovert but deals with a very unfriendly interlocutor might be neutralized to some degree.

The **(Social) Filter Module** operates on the winning emotional state, the social threat, and the overall control value. It outputs an *external emotion* with a certain intensity $\epsilon \in \{0, \ldots, 5\}$, i.e., the *type* of emotion that will be displayed by the agent. The Filter module consists of only two rules, one for positive and one for negative emotions. The general form of a social filter rule is as follows.

external_emotion(L1,L2,E,ϵ,Sit) **if** social_threat(L1,L2,θ,Sit) **and**
control(L1,L2,γ,Sit) **and**
winning_emotional_state(L1,L2,E,δ,Sit)

The most difficult problem here is to adequately combine the intensity values associated with the social threat experienced by the agent, the agent's control capability, and the emotional state. The default combination function for negative emotions is $\epsilon = \delta - (\theta + \gamma)$. Intuitively, the function balances the social threat against the agent's control, whereby high values for threat may neutralize the lacking self-control of the agent to a certain extent. The filter rule for positive emotions is syntactically identical but uses a different combination function: $\epsilon = \delta - (\theta - \gamma)$. Here, it is the agent's low control that dominates the expression of emotions. Alternatively, we provide a decision network to determine whether and to what extent an agent expresses its emotional state, based on its check for negative consequences of emotion expression.

2.3 Emotion Expression

External emotions must eventually be described in terms of the agent's reactions and behaviors. We use a simplified version of Ortony's categorization of emotion response tendencies [12], and distinguish between expressive and information-processing responses. *Expressive responses* include somatic responses (flushing), behavioral responses (fist-clenching, throwing objects), and two types of communicative responses, verbal and non-verbal (e.g., frowning). *Information-processing responses* concern the agent's diversion of attention and evaluations (which we handle in the Affect Processing module). The Animation Engine currently used only allows for rather crude forms of combining verbal and non-verbal behavior [10]. Body movements (including gestures) may precede, overlap, or occur subsequently to verbal utterances. An interesting alternative is the BEAT system [4] that autonomously suggests appropriate gestures for given speech.

2.4 Affect Processing

The Agent Model describes an agent's mental state. We distinguish *static* and *dynamic* features of an agent's mind state, such that the agent's personality and standards are considered as static whereas goals, beliefs, attitudes and social variables are considered as dynamic. Here, we are mainly concerned with change of attitude as a result of social interaction.

Ortony [11] suggests the notion of *(signed) summary record* to capture our attitude toward or dispositional (dis)liking of another person. This record stores the sign of emotions (i.e., positive or negative) that were induced in the agent L by an interlocutor I together with emotions' associated intensities. In order to compute the current intensity of an agent's (dis)liking, we simply compare the (scaled) sum of intensities of elicited positive and negative emotions (δ^{σ}, $\sigma \in \{+, -\}$), starting in situation $Sit_0^{L,I}$, the situation when the interaction starts. We will only consider the intensity of the winning emotional state δ_w. If no emotion of one sign is elicited in a situation, it is set to zero.

$$\delta^{\sigma}(Sit_n^{L,I}) = \frac{\sum_{i=0}^{n} \delta_w^{\sigma}(Sit_i^{L,I})}{n+1}$$

Positive values for the difference $\delta^+ - \delta^-$ indicate an agent's liking of an interlocutor and negative ones indicate disliking. The more interesting case where an interlocutor the agent likes as a consequence of consistent reinforcement (suddenly) induces a high-intensity emotion of the opposite sign, e.g., by making the agent very angry, is captured by the following update rule.

$$\delta(Sit_n^{L,I}) = \delta^\sigma(Sit_{n-1}^{L,I}) \times \omega_h \mp \delta_w^{\overline{\sigma}}(Sit_n^{L,I}) \times \omega_r$$

The weights ω_h and ω_r denote the weights we apply to historical and recent information, respectively. ω_h and ω_r take values from the interval $[0, 1]$ and $\omega_h + \omega_r = 1$. A greater weight of recent information is reflected by using a greater value for ω_r. As to the question how the obtained (dis)liking value affects future interactions with the interlocutor, two interpretations are considered. While *momentary (dis)liking* means that the new value is active for the current situation and then enters the summary record, *essential (dis)liking* results in the new value replacing the summary record.

3   MPML: A Markup Language for Character Control

We currently use the Microsoft Agent package [10] as our Animation Engine, which allows to embed animated characters into a web page based JavaScript interface. The package comes ready with controls for animating 2D cartoon-style characters, speech recognition and a Text-to-Speech (TTS) engine. In order to facilitate the process of scripting more complex scenarios, including, e.g., sequential and parallel activity of multiple characters, we have developed an XML-style markup language called MPML (Ishizuka *et al.* [8]).

Basic tagging schemes for a character's behavior and multi-character coordination are `<act/>` where a character performs a pre-defined animation sequence ("alert", "blink", "decline", "explain", "greet", "sad", "suggest", etc.); `<speak>...</speak>` where a character speaks a pre-defined sentence which is also displayed in a balloon; `<listen>...</listen>` where the character is prepared to recognize pre-defined user utterances; `<seq>...</seq>` for sequential behavior of multiple characters, and `<par>...</par>` for parallel behavior of multiple characters.

In short, MPML is a powerful and easy-to-use markup language that allows content authors to script rich web-based scenarios featuring animated characters. Typically, MPML is used to design characters with scripted behaviors, i.e., the author has full control over a character's verbal and non-verbal behavior. However, the restriction to scripted behavior can be relaxed by interfacing MPML with SCREAM's reasoning module that supports autonomous control of a character's affective behavior. Communication between MPML and the Java applet (driving SCREAM by Java-to-Jinni and Jinni-to-Java method calls) is realized by special tagging schemes. The `<execute/>` tag may call a Java method, e.g., to assert a communicative act of another agent to the character's knowledge base. The `<consult>...</consult>` tagging scheme together with the child tagging scheme `<test>...</test>` is used to retrieve the character's reaction from SCREAM. Depending on the value of the `test` element, the character will perform a sequence of verbal and non-verbal behaviors.

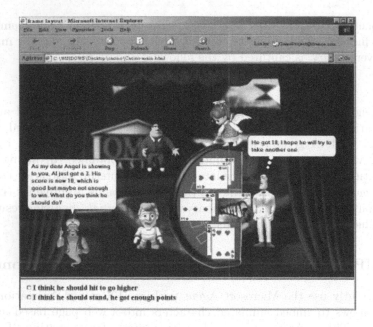

Fig. 2. Casino Scenario.

4   Illustrative Example

In this section we will illustrate how our system works. As an interaction setting, we choose a casino scenario where a user and other characters can play the "Black Jack" game. Fig. 2 shows the situation where the character "Genie" practices Black Jack with the user by commenting the game of character "Al" (Genie is the character at the bottom-left of the Internet Explorer window, and Al is the male character to the right of the dealer).

We will now watch the user playing five games of Black Jack and thereby demonstrate how Genie's mental make-up as well as the (affective) interaction history determine his behavior. For expository reasons, we let the user *never* follow Genie's advice, and we use a very sparse Agent Model. Among others, Genie is assumed as rather agreeable and extrovert, he is socially close to the user and also (initially) slightly likes the user. His goals are that the user wins (with low intensity), and that the user follows his advice (with high intensity). Note that the outcome of the the game, i.e., whether the user wins or looses, is independent of her or him following Genie's advice.

- In the **first game** (user looses) Genie's winning emotional state is *distress* with intensity 4, because the user did not follow his advice. However, he displays *distress* with low intensity as his agreeable personality effects a decrease in the intensity of negative emotion expression.
- In the **second game** (user looses) Genie is sorry for the user with intensity 4, since positive ('sorry for' the user's lost game) emotions decay slowly

and sum up, which leads to an increase in Genie's liking of the user. His personality traits let him express the emotion with even higher intensity.

- In the **third game** (user looses) Genie gloats over the user's lost game, because at that point, the negative emotions dominate the positive ones as a consequence of the user's repeated refusal to follow Genie's advice. Hence Genie's attitude changes to slightly disliking the user which lets him experience *joy* over the user's *distress* (*gloat* with intensity 5). Again, Genie's friendly personality decreases the intensity of the external emotion.

- In the **fourth game** (user wins) Genie's emotional state is *bad mood* with intensity 5, slightly more than his *happy for* emotion (as the user wins the game this time). Here an overall, unspecific affective state (mood) is expressed with low intensity, rather than a specific emotion.

- In the **fifth game** (user wins) Genie's dominant emotional state is *resent* with intensity 4, because he slightly dislikes the user and consequently is distressed that the user won although she or he ignored his advice. Genie expresses his emotion with reduced intensity.

An exhaustive exploration of all possible interaction patterns in the described game scenario reveals that Genie's reactions are conform at the beginning games and show more variety in the subsequent games. This can be explained by the evolution of Genie's attitude toward the user, depending on whether the user follows or refuses to follow Genie's advice. In effect, Genie's attitude decides, e.g., whether he is *sorry for* or *resents* the user's lost game. However, in accordance with Genie's agreeableness, his emotional reactions are mostly positive.

5   Conclusion

Recent years have witnessed a growing interest in life-like, believable characters, as they might be a crucial component of enhanced learning and presentation systems. Although it is widely recognized that emotion and personality are key factors for characters' believability, tools that facilitate the autonomous generation of affective behavior are still rare. Notable exceptions are [15,1,14,5].

In this paper, we discuss models and tools for scripting and coordinating affective interactions with and among animated believable characters. While MPML is a powerful tool for controlling and coordinating the visual behavior of characters (their 'body'), the SCREAM system constitutes a practical technology for scripting the mental processes underlying a character's affective behavior (its 'mind'). Most importantly, it is more flexible than systems with a similar aim [15,1,5] as the author may decide on the level of detail at which the character is scripted (the 'granularity' feature). If many levels of indirection of the agent's behavior are desirable, the author may define all of the available parameters and also control the influence of each parameter by editing the combination functions. In certain settings, however, only a subset of the parameters might be of interest, e.g., when the author wants to script a (interactive) presentation agent that is only driven by goals and personality. The system will manage the elicited emotions and produce an output that reflects the provided influences.

Acknowledgments. This research is supported by the Research Grant (1999-2003) for the Future Program from the Japanese Society for the Promotion of Science (JSPS).

References

1. E. André, T. Rist, S. van Mulken, M. Klesen, and S. Baldes. The automated design of believable dialogue for animated presentation teams. In J. Cassell, S. Prevost, J. Sullivan, and E. Churchill, editors, *Embodied Conversational Agents*, pages 220-255. The MIT Press, 2000.
2. BinNet Corp. *Jinni 2000: A high performance Java based Prolog for agent scripting, client-server and internet programming*, 2000. URL: www.binnetcorp.com.
3. P. Brown and S. C. Levinson. *Politeness. Some Universals in Language Usage.* Cambridge University Press, 1987.
4. J. Cassell, H. Vilhjálmsson, and T. Bickmore. BEAT: the Behavior Expression Animation Toolkit. In *Proceedings of SIGGRAPH-01*, pages 477-486, 2001.
5. B. de Carolis, C. Pelachaud, I. Poggi, and F. de Rosis. Behavior planning for a reflexive agent. In *Proceedings 17th International Conference on Artificial Intelligence (IJCAI-01)*, 2001.
6. P. Ekman and W. V. Friesen. The repertoire of nonverbal behavior: Categories, origins, usage, and coding. *Semiotica*, 1:49-98, 1969.
7. B. Hayes-Roth and P. Doyle. Animate characters. *Autonomous Agents and Multi-Agent Systems*, 1(2):195-230, 1998.
8. M. Ishizuka, T. Tsutsui, S. Saeyor, H. Dohi, Y. Zong, and H. Prendinger. MPML: A multimodal presentation markup language with character control functions. In *Proceedings Agents'2000 Workshop on Achieving Human-like Behavior in Interactive Animated Agents*, pages 50-54, 2000.
9. W. L. Johnson, J. W. Rickel, and J. C. Lester. Animated pedagogical agents: Face-to-face interaction in interactive learning environments. *International Journal of Artificial Intelligence in Education*, 11:47-78, 2000.
10. Microsoft. *Developing for Microsoft Agent.* Microsoft Press, 1998.
11. A. Ortony. Value and emotion. In W. Kessen, A. Ortony, and F. Craik, editors, *Memories, thoughts, and emotions: Essays in the honor of George Mandler*, pages 337-353. Hillsdale, NJ: Erlbaum, 1991.
12. A. Ortony. On making believable emotional agents believable. In R. Trappl, P. Petta, and S. Payr, editors, *Emotions in Humans and Artifacts*. The MIT Press, 2001.
13. A. Ortony, G. L. Clore, and A. Collins. *The Cognitive Structure of Emotions.* Cambridge University Press, 1988.
14. H. Prendinger and M. Ishizuka. Social role awareness in animated agents. In *Proceedings 5th International Conference on Autonomous Agents (Agents-01)*, pages 270-277, 2001.
15. W. S. N. Reilly. *Believable Social and Emotional Agents.* PhD thesis, Carnegie Mellon University, 1996. CMU-CS-96-138.
16. D. Rousseau and B. Hayes-Roth. A social-psychological model for synthetic actors. In *Proceedings 2nd International Conference on Autonomous Agents (Agents-98)*, pages 165-172, 1998.
17. S. J. Russell and P. Norvig. *Artificial Intelligence. A Modern Approach.* Prentice Hall, Inc., Upper Saddle River, New Jersey, 1995.

An Affective Decision Making Agent Architecture Using Emotion Appraisals

Penny Baillie[1] and Dickson Lukose[2]

[1] Department of Mathematics and Computing, University of Southern Queensland,
Toowoomba, Qld., 4350, Australia
penny.baillie@usq.edu.au
http://www.sci.usq.edu.au/staff/bailliep
[2] Mindbox Inc., STE 25, 180 Glenbrook Road, Stamford, Connecticut, 06902, USA.
dickson.lukose@mindbox.com

Abstract. Interacting intelligently within a temporally dynamic environment calls for adaptive performances from artificial beings. One mechanism currently being explored to produce an intuitive-like behaviour in AI applications is that of emotion. Several popular psychological theories of emotion have been the basis for a number of agent models that are capable of synthesizing emotions. However, while these models have demonstrated limited success, they lack the dynamic scalability to form complex emotional dimensions that are necessary for producing adaptive behaviour. This paper examines how an affective appraisal made with discrete evaluations of an event can overcomes contemporary limitations. An artificial agent that has had this theory integrated into its architecture is demonstrated. A formal model of the agent's Ontology and its Multidimensional Affective Decision Making process is outlined, with examples demonstrating an affective decision making process.

1 Introduction

As modes of entertainment move from the theatres and books into personal computers, user's are demanding more from computerised characters. The need for quality autonomous artificial agents capable of behaving intelligently and adapting to their ever-changing virtual environment is paramount. To this end, we have developed the Emotionally Motivated Artificial Intelligence (EMAI) architecture. The domains of interactive fiction, computer games and virtual reality demands that a computerised character be able to suspend a user's disbelief [1] that their interaction with the agent is anything but unreal. In order to achieve this, we have focused on the knowledge representation and the synthesis and generation of emotions in our EMAI architecture. The purpose being to produce an autonomous computerised character that uses emotions to adapt to its environment through quantitative atomic appraisals of events and to generate behaviour using affective decision making. In short, an EMAI agent can change its behaviour based on its emotional state generated from interactions with its environment. The agent uses this emotional feedback for predicting future emotional states and

M. Ishizuka and A. Sattar (Eds.): PRICAI 2002, LNAI 2417, pp. 581–590, 2002.
© Springer-Verlag Berlin Heidelberg 2002

deciding how to behave. In this paper, we initially present a brief overview of the EMAI architecture, continue with a description of its ontology and follow with an in-depth formalisation of the architecture's affective decision making process and conclude with a summary of experimentation performed with an EMAI agent.

2   The EMAI Architecture

The EMAI architecture consists of several major processing and knowledge representation areas [2]. Each of these areas works together in a complex network of information gathering, manipulating and updating. As shown in Figure 1, any agent implemented using the EMAI architecture receives *external sensory data* from its environment. It also processes *internal sensory data* from the Motivational Drive Generator in the Knowledge Area. Internal State Registers simulate low level biological mechanisms. The Sensory Processor and the Affective Space integrate both types of sensory data into the agent's belief system via an emotional filtering process. Sensory input (both internal and external) received by the

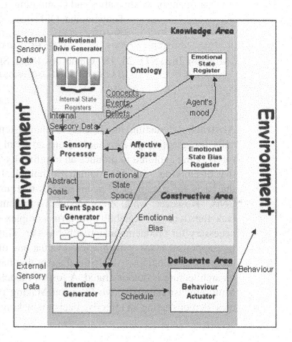

Fig. 1. The EMAI Architecture

Sensory Processor may activate goals in the agent. The goals are processed by the agent's Constructive Area where plans are chosen that will satisfy these goals. These plans are generated by the Event Space Generator, which generates a series of events that could be performed by the agent to satisfy its goals. Each *event* represents a self-contained independent activity that the agent can perform and can be defined by a set of *elements*, namely actions, objects, a time and a context. Before the agent schedules the events for execution in the Deliberate Area, each event is ordered by the Intention Generator in collaboration with the Affective Space (via appraisal based decision making) and sorted from most *liked* to least *liked*. Once the agent has the list of events sorted by emotional affect, the Behaviour Actuator begins executing them in order. The events being executed by the Behaviour Actuator at any moment in time become the EMAI agent's outward behaviour.

To facilitate the use of appraisal based decision making in the Affective Space, the six dimensional appraisal model proposed by Smith and Ellsworth [3] is used[1]. This model identifies 6 orthogonal dimensions: *pleasantness, anticipated effort, certainty, attentional activity, responsibility* and *control*, across 15 emotions: *happiness, sadness, anger, boredom, challenge, hope, fear, interest, contempt, disgust, frustration, surprise, pride, shame* and *guilt*. The in-depth examination of the analytical and information handling processes in each of the areas of the architecture is not possible within the spatial constraints of this paper. Instead, we focus on the ontology and the formalisation of the affective appraisals performed by an EMAI agent in association with the architecture's affective space and how they are used in decision making.

3 EMAI Ontology

The EMAI Ontology organises elements from the agent's realm, using conceptual graph theory [4],[5] and the formalisation of new concepts: the Goal Hierarchy [6], Event Graphs and Activity Digraphs. Event Graphs and Activity Digraphs are new abstractions defined in this paper for representing events and plans. The Ontology presents the knowledge that an EMAI agent possesses about its environment.

3.1   Goal Hierarchy

The Goal Hierarchy contains the entire set of goals that are used to generate tasks within the agent. For example, if the agent were to represent an animal, then it would be programmed with a Goal Hierarchy suitable for simulating the behaviour of a goal-orientated animal. This Goal Hierarchy may look similar to Figure 2. The more this Goal Hierarchy is decomposed into primitive goals the closer it

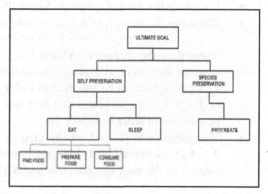

Fig. 2. A Simple Goal Hierarchy

comes to representing specific events. At the most primitive level of the Goal Hierarchy there exists a partially ordered set of goals that are synonymous with the events and plans that can be performed to satisfy a goal. For example, the goal EAT decomposed into three partial subgoals; FIND FOOD, PREPARE FOOD and CONSUME FOOD. The goals in the Goal Hierarchy are either abstract or primitive. An abstract goal can be broken down into subgoals (of which some will be abstract, while others may be primitive). Subgoals are either AND-ed or OR-ed. A set of AND-ed subgoals indicates that all of the subgoals need to be successfully achieved to satisfy the supergoal. A set of OR-ed subgoals indicates that at least one of the sub-goals needs to be

---

[1] The design of the Affective Space is such that any quantitative appraisal theory could be implemented. Smith and Ellsworth's model was chosen as the discrete values for the appraisal dimensions had been gather through human experimentation and were readily available. For further appraisal theories see [7].

successfully achieved to satisfy the supergoal. The definition of Goal Hierarchy can be stated as follows:

Definition: A Goal Hierarchy is a partially ordered set G whose elements are called *goals*. Each goal in G is specified as *abstract* or *primitive*. Considering that the symbol '•' indicates ordering and g and h are goals, G is such that:

- If $g • h$, then g is called the *subgoal* of h; and h is called the supergoal of g, written $h • g$.
- The Goal Hierarchy G contains one ultimate goal, called the *ultimate goal (U)*, and two *subultimate* goals called *self-preservation (U_1)* and *species-preservation (U_2)*.
- The partial ordering over G is determined by the *subgoal* relation, represented by the characters "•" for *subgoal*, "<" for *proper subgoal*, "•" for *supergoal*, and ">" for *proper supergoal*. If g is any goal, $U • g$ and $g • U$.
- For any goal g where $g • U$, $g • U_1$ and $g • U_2$ then g will be a proper subgoal of U_1 and/or U_2.
- If a goal g has a set of subgoals S such that $S = \{\phi\}$, g is said to be *primitive*.
- The subgoals, $\{s_1..s_n\}$, of the set of subgoals, S, for a goal, g, can be arranged in sentences of propositional logic where the logical connective AND is represented by the character "Λ" and OR is presented by the character "V". A sentence such as $(s_1 \Lambda s_2 \Lambda s_3) \Rightarrow g$ indicates that of all the subgoal in S, only s_1, s_2 and s_3 need to be satisfied in order to satisfy the g. A sentence such as $(s_1 V s_2 V s_3) \Rightarrow g$ indicates that only one of the subgoals (s_1,s_2 or s_3) need to be satisfied in order to satisfy the g.
- The subgoals $S=\{s_1...s_n\}$, of the goal, g, can be arranged into subsets of S, $A_1...A_m$, such that all goals in A_i are joined in a sentence of propositional logic using Λ as the logical connective and $A_1 V A_2 V...V A_n$.

3.2   Event and Plan Definitions

Each goal in the Goal Hierarchy has an associated event (with the same name) that can be performed by the agent to satisfy or partially satisfy the goal. An event is represented in the agent's knowledge base as a conceptual graph in the form dictated by the Theory of Reasoned Action [8]. This theory defines a behavioural event as having four elements; *action, object, time* and *context*. A generic event is represented

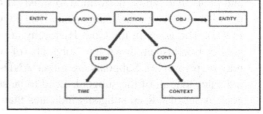

Fig. 3. A Conceptual Graph Representation of an Abstract Event

by the conceptual graph shown in Figure 3. Associated with this graph are three sets of conceptual graphs that represent the precondition, postcondition and delete graphs that are used during event reasoning. In other words, a goal a in the Goal Hierarchy G, at any level of abstract, n, written as $G_{a,n}$ is represented by a conceptual graph abstraction called the Event Graph. Each Event Graph has associated with it a set of graphs that represent the precondition, postcondition and delete list[2]. An Event Graph can be defined as:

Definition: An *Event Graph* is an *n-adic* abstraction, $v_{1..n}$, $w_{1..m}$, $x_{1..o}$ u, where u is the conceptual graphs (i.e., body) representing the Event Graph, $v_{1..n}$ *represents* a set of n conceptual graphs that represents the pre-condition that must be satisfied before this event can be executed, $w_{1..m}$ represents a set of m conceptual graphs that represents the post-conditions that will result from executing this event, and $x_{1..o}$ represents a set of o conceptual graphs that will be removed from the memory, after execution of this event. In other words, the preconditions denote the knowledge that must exist before the event is executed, the postconditions denote the knowledge that is created as a result of executing the event and the delete list represents knowledge that is no longer needed after the event has been executed. For example, the Event Graph for the FIND-FOOD could be represented as:

```
[FIND] -
        (OBJ)  -> [FOOD]
        (AGNT)-> [AGENT: EMAI]
        (TIM)  -> [NOW]
        (LOC)  -> [BACKYARD]
```

where the corresponding precondition, postcondition and delete sets of conceptual graphs are as shown below:

```
Precondition:  {[AGENT: EMAI]<-(AGNT)<-[ACCESS]->(OBJ)->[FOOD]}
Postcondition: {[AGENT: EMAI]<-(POSS)->[FOOD]}
Delete list:   {[AGENT: EMAI]<-(AGNT)<-[ACCESS]->(OBJ)->[FOOD]}
```

To facilitate knowledge passing during the graph execution process, it is essential that the graph processor utilises *co-reference links* within a graph, and *line of identity* between graphs. Definitions of these concepts are given in [4]. Consider the following Event Graph, that is made up of conceptual graphs g_1, g_2, g_3, and g_4:

```
g1:    [FIND] -
              (OBJ)  -> [FOOD:*a]
              (AGNT) -> [AGENT: *b] -> (LOC) -> [SHOP:*c]
              (TIM)  -> [NOW]
              (LOC)  -> [SHOP:*c]
g2:    [AGENT: *b]<-(AGNT)<-[ACCESS]->(OBJ)->[FOOD:*a]
g3:    [AGENT: *b]<-(POSS)->[FOOD:*a]
g4:    [AGENT: b]<-(AGNT)<-[ACCESS]->(OBJ)->[FOOD:*a]
```

In the above Event Graph, the concept SHOP in g_1 is a co-reference (indicated by the variable *c. There exists a line of identity between all four graphs via the concepts

---

[2] Conceptual graphs that must be removed from the knowledge base after execution.

FOOD and AGENT. So, during graph processing, if the generic concept [AGENT: *b] in g_1 is specialized to [AGENT: EMAI], the graph processor will automatically follow the coreference links and line of identity to specialize g_2, g_3 and g_4 as follows:

g_2:   [AGENT: EMAI]<-(AGNT)<-[ACCESS]->(OBJ)->[FOOD:*a]

g_3:   [AGENT: EMAI]<-(POSS)->[FOOD:*a]

g_4:   [AGENT: EMAI]<-(AGNT)<-[ACCESS]->(OBJ)->[FOOD:*a]

The Goal Hierarchy by itself does not include any plans that show how the subgoals interact to satisfy the parent goal. To this end, the Goal Hierarchy is accompanied by a set of Activity Digraphs that explain how goals combine to form plans. Activity Digraphs can be formed at various

Fig. 4. Activity Digraph for EAT

levels of abstraction. For example, at level 3, the Activity Digraph accompanying the Goal Hierarchy of Figure 2 might look like that in Figure 4. In an Activity Digraph (not to be confused with a conceptual graph) the vertices correspond to the events (represented by Event Graphs) that must be performed and an edge is drawn from vertex i to vertex j if event i must precede event j. The plans in the Activity Digraphs need not be as simplistic as simple sequencing They can represent any degree of complexity and can easily represent all the major control structures (i.e., FOR, WHILE, REPEAT, CASE, etc.). Each event in the plan will have a set of pre-conditions, co-conditions and post-conditions that need to be analysed by the agent before, during and after execution. To construct a conceptual graph representation of an Activity Digraph, two temporal relation types are used to specify the temporal ordering of the Event Graphs: *FINISH_BEFORE_START (FBS)* and *START_WHEN_START (SWS)* [9],[10]. An Activity Digraph can be defined as follows:

Definition: An *Activity Digraph* labeled *t* is defined as a *n*-adic abstraction $v_1,..,v_n$ $w_1,...,w_m$ *u*, where *u* is the conceptual graph (i.e., body) representing the *activity diagraph*, $v_1,..,v_n$ which is in turn the set of conceptual graphs representing the initial state, while $w_1,...,w_m$ is the set of graphs representing the final state.

The Activity Digraph in Figure 4 can be represented as:

[FIND-FOOD]->(FBS)->[PREPARE-FOOD]->(FBS)->[CONSUME-FOOD]

4   Affective Space

EMAI uses an emotional prioritising procedure to select behaviours by scheduling its events for execution. However, before the prioritising can begin, an event must be assigned an emotion. Emotion is identified in an Affective Space. The affective space, Φ, is defined as a six dimensional space bounded by the 6 appraisals from Smith and Ellsworth's model (the dimensions are Pleasantness, Responsibility, Effort, Attention, Control, and Certainty). The Affective Space is occupied by points that ascertain an EMAI agent's current emotional state and the pure emotion points of *happiness, sadness, anger, boredom, challenge, hope, fear, interest, contempt, disgust, frustration, surprise, pride, shame* and *guilt*[3]. Each emotional state is a point, Ω, in that space defined by a six point coordinate based on the value of the six cognitive appraisals toward an event. Ω can be defined as:

$$\Omega = \{P, E, C, A, R, O\} \tag{1}$$

where *P, E, C, A, R* and *O* are the six appraisal dimensions of pleasantness, effort, certainty, attention, responsibility and control, respectively. Each of these values is determined by the analyses given earlier in this paper. The formalisation of these dimensions is presented in [11].

5   Event Appraisal

The emotion assigned to the event is calculated by considering the agent's emotional responses to each of the elements involved in the event. Interaction during an event or behaviour can be viewed as consisting of four atomic elements (Petty and Cacioppo 1996). They are 1) the action being performed; 2) the target or targets that are the object of the action; 3) the context of the action, for example, where it is being performed; and, 4) the temporal alignment of the action, for example, the time of day or month. An event *E* is made up of a set of actions *a*, a set of objects *o*, occurs at a time *t*, and has context *c*, written as in Expression (8):

$$E = \{a, o, c, t\} \tag{8}$$

For each element *e*, in an event *E*, the *valence*, Ω_e is defined as:

$$\Omega_e = \{P_e, E_e, C_e, A_e, R_e, O_e\} \tag{9}$$

Based on the outcome of event *E*, the agent will assign a weighting *w*, to the valence for each of the elements, *e*. As the weighting of an element and resulting emotion with respect to an event are dynamic, the time, *t*, at which the valence is being calculated must also be taken into consideration. Therefore, the valence resulting from an event E, written as $\Omega_{E,t}$ is calculated as:

$$\Omega_{E,t} = \sum_{e=1}^{n} w_{e,t} \Omega_{e,t} \tag{10}$$

where *n* is the number of elements associated with event *E*, and

$$0 \le w_{e,t} \le 1$$

and

$$\sum_{e=1}^{n} w_{e,t} = 1$$

The agent attributes a change in its emotional state to be the result of the event and therefore updates the valence of the event accordingly. The change in the valence of an event is:

---

[3] The location of each emotion within the affective space is taken from the values specified by Smith and Ellsworth [3].

$$\Delta_{\Omega_E} = \Omega_{O,t+1} - \Omega_{E,t} \tag{11}$$

After this has been calculated the emotional states for each element in the event set can be updated as:

$$\Omega_{e,t+1} = \Omega_{e,t} + w_{e,t+1}\Delta_{\Omega_E} \tag{12}$$

Instead of the element taking on the final valence of the event, the previous valence of the element is taken into account along with the weighting of affect that the element had in the resulting valence for the event. If the event's resulting valence is the same as its initial state and $w_{e,t} = w_{e,t+1}$ then the emotional state for the element will not change. A worked example of this process can be found in [12].

6   Affective Decision Making

EMAI's decision-making procedure is twofold. Firstly, the agent prioritises its behaviours by ordering events in the deliberate area based on the number of times an event has been triggered by a goal and thus representing the urgency of an event. Secondly, the agent further orders the events by calculating the resulting emotional effect that performing the event will have on the agent's emotional state. The agent's emotional state Ω_{EMAI}[4] is the result of weighing the importance of an event w_E and summating the m number of resultant valences for all episodes of all events performed by the agent *EMAI*, thus:

$$\Omega_{EMAI,t} = \sum_{E=1}^{m} w_{E,t}\Omega_{E,t} \tag{13}$$

where $\quad 0 \le w_{E,t} \le 1$

and $\quad \sum_{E=1}^{m} w_{E,t} = 1$

In Figure 6 the agent's emotional state is not at the exact location of any of the pure emotions, but it is closest to happiness, therefore the agent is said to be in a happy state. Figure 6 also shows the valence of two events (Ω_{E1} and Ω_{E2}) plotted as an emotional point in the Affective Space. If these events have been given the same priority for execution, the agent needs to make an emotional decision about which event to execute. One event is closest to the emotion challenge and the other is closest to anger.

The agent assesses each of the events by calculating how the execution of the event will affect the agent's current emotional state using Expression 14.

$$\Omega_{EMAI,t+1} = \Omega_{EMAI,t} + w_{E,t+1}\Delta_{\Omega,EMAI} \tag{14}$$

---

[4] This formulae is the scaled up version of Expression 10. Expression 10 dealt with one event and multiple elements. Expression 13 deals with one agent and multiple events.

where $w_{E,t+1}$ is the weighted affected that an event has on the agent's current emotional state and $\Delta_{\Omega,EMAI}$ is the different between the agents current emotional state and the valence of the event E.

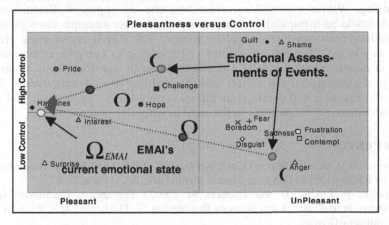

Fig 6. Resultant Emotional States Generated by Combining the Agent's Current Emotional State (Ω_{EMAI}) and Two Events' States (Ω_{F1}, Ω_{F2}).

7 Results of Experimentation with an EMAI Agent

To evaluate the use of the EMAI architecture for the production of believable computerised characters, the EMAI architecture was used to simulate the computerised character of a pet dog. 17 evaluators spent two hours interacting (training, feeding, disciplining etc.) with the EMAI dog and a randomly acting dog. Further details can be found in [12]. A large amount of data was collected from each evaluator focusing on the believability of each dog. Table 1 summarises the results obtained from the participants. They show a statistical significance in favour of the behaviour produced by the EMAI dog when rated on a 7 point scale with 1 being unreasonable and 7 being reasonable.

Table 1. Mean Responsibility Rating

Trait	EMAI	Random	t	P
Learning Skills	6.61	2.44	10.93	<0.0005
Behaviour	6.56	3.9	12.41	<0.0005
Emotional State	6.06	2.56	6.51	<0.0005
Goal Setting	5.78	2.00	11.48	<0.0005

8 Conclusions and Further Work

We believe that this atomic quantitative dimensional approach to synthesizing emotions in artificial beings is a powerful concept. In our EMAI experiment, we have demonstrated the integration of a model proposed by Smith and Ellsworth [3] with our existing agent architecture. For preliminary experimentation [6] we have chosen to simulate a simple pet dog as most people can identify with and have expectations on how a dog will behave and the behaviours and goals of a dog are much simpler than a person. Our initial testing with this agent has been promising. While it is still not clear how the six appraisal dimensions of the model should be manipulated during a simulation, our attempts show promise and do produce reasonable emotional responses. The EMAI architecture still has a long way to go. We need to address issues such as complex emotional states, how an emotional state affects a decision, how an emotional state should affect the agent's perception and beliefs and the building of elaborate events. To these ends, our research will continue its efforts on the EMAI architecture and advance the understanding of emotions in the field of affective computing.

References

1. Stern, A. (1999). "AI Beyond Computer Games". 1999 AAAI Spring Symposium, Artificial Intelligence and Computer Games, Menlo Park, AAAI Press 77-80.
2. Baillie, P., Lukose, D. and Toleman, M. (2002). Engineering Emotionally Intelligent Agents, in Intelligent Agent Software Engineering, V. Plekhanova & S. Wermter eds, Idea Publishing Group.
3. Smith, C. A. and P. C. Ellsworth (1985). "Attitudes and Social Cognition." Journal of Personality and Social Psychology 48 (4): 813-838.
4. Sowa, J. F. (1984). *Conceptual Structures: Information Processing in Mind and Machine*, Addison-Wesley, Reading.
5. Sowa, J. F. (2001). *Knowledge Representation: Logical, Philosophical, and Computational Foundations*, Brooks Cole Publishing Co., Pacific Grove.
6. Baillie, P., Lukose, D. and Toleman, M. (2000). How to Give an Agent An Attitude. in *Proceedings of Agents in Simulation Workshop I, Passau, Germany,* University of Passau, Passau pp. 7-12.
7. Picard, R. (1997). "Affective Computing". The MIT Press, London.
8. Petty, R. E. and J. T. Cacioppo (1996). "Attitudes and Persuasion: Classic and Contemporary Approaches", Westview Press.Boulder, Colorado
9. Lukose, D., (1992). Goal Interpretation as a Knowledge Acquisition Mechanism, PhD Thesis, Department of Computing and Mathematics, Deakin University, Geelong, Victoria, 3217, Australia.
10. Lukose, D. (1996). *MODEL-ECS: Executable Conceptual Modeling Language*, in Gaines, B. and Musen, M. (Eds.), Proceedings of the 10 th Knowledge Acquisition for Knowledge Based Systems Workshop (KAW'96), Voyager Inn, Banff, Alberta, Canada, November 9-14, 1996.
11. Baillie, P. & Lukose, D. (2002), Multidimensional Affect Appraisals for Artificial Intelligences, in Proceedings of ACE 2002, Vienna, Austria, University of Vienna, Vienna, pp. 745-750.
12. Baillie, P. (2002), 'An Agent with a Passion for Decision Making', in Proceedings of Agents in Simulation 2002, Passau, Germany, University of Passau, Passau, pp. 7-12.

Logic Programming for Agents

Hisashi Hayashi, Kenta Cho, and Akihiko Ohsuga

Computer and Network Systems Laboratory
Corporate Research and Development Center, TOSHIBA Corporation
1 Komukai, Toshiba-cho, Saiwai-ku, Kawasaki-shi, 212-8582, Japan
{hisashi3.hayashi, kenta.cho, akihiko.ohsuga}@toshiba.co.jp

Prolog is one of the best-known logic programming languages and suitable for implementing an inference engine for agents. However, Prolog does not take into account the dynamic nature of agents such as knowledge acquisition and action execution. This poses a problem because the agent might work in a dynamic environment where unexpected things can happen. In order to use a Prolog-like procedure as an inference engine of an agent, the procedure should be able to modify the computation, if necessary, after updating the program or executing an action. We introduce a new Prolog-like procedure which integrates planning, action execution, program updates, and plan modifications. Our new procedure computes plans by abduction. During or after a computation, it can update a program by adding a rule to the program or deleting a rule from the program. After updating the program, it modifies the computation, cuts invalid plans, and adds new valid plans. We use the technique of Dynamic SLDNF (DSLDNF) [1] [2] to modify computation after updating a program. It is also possible to execute an action during or after planning. We can use three types of actions: an action without a side effect; an action with a side effect which can be undone; an action with a side effect which cannot be undone. Following the result of action execution, the procedure modifies the computation: invalid plans are erased; some actions are undone; some redundant actions are erased. Even if a plan becomes invalid, it is possible to switch to another plan without loss of correctness.

References

1. H. Hayashi. Replanning in Robotics by Dynamic SLDNF. IJCAI Workshop "Scheduling and Planning Meet Real-Time Monitoring in a Dynamic and Uncertain World", 1999.
2. H. Hayashi. Computing with Changing Logic Programs. PhD thesis, Imperial College of Science, Technology and Medicine, University of London, 2001.

M. Ishizuka and A. Sattar (Eds.): PRICAI 2002, LNAI 2417, p. 591, 2002.
© Springer-Verlag Berlin Heidelberg 2002

Evolutionary Multi-agents System
for Prediction of Social Behavior in Large Cities

Marie Piron, Alain Cardon, and Christophe Cambier

GEODES-IRD – Institut de recherche pour le développement, 32 rue H Varagnat,
93143 Bondy - FRANCE
Marie.Piron@bondy.ird.fr,
{Alain.Cardon, Christophe.Cambier}@lip6.fr

We deal with complex software architectures based on agents. More precisely, we are interested with systems involving a very large amount of software weak agents. For instance, such a system can be the sub-system of representation of the world for an autonomous robot walking and acting in its environment. Another example is provided by the system of interpretation of behavior of social organization. In both cases, the systems are build with an intelligent control of its inner information stream. They are composed of a lot of no fixed parts, evolving in run according to the external information. All the inner parts are expressed with variable groups of agents.

The structure of the system is built using ontology. Thus, by expressing the knowledge in the domain, and all the concepts and their relationships, we deduce the elements of action, knowledge, functionality that are expressed with some kind of agents. Each one of these agents is simple, weak like, rational, and strongly bound up with altogether. Using a specific agentification method, we obtain a massive multi-agent system. And, meanwhile the system is running, some agents are created again, increasing the complexity of the organization. We are in the case where the organization of agents is a like a very complex and dynamic system, where the basic elements are active and pro-active, as always agents are. And such an organization can be distributed on networks.

The behavior of the agent organization is made of actions, communication, transformation of agents, and also creation and death for some agents. Then, the main problems are the representation of the behavior of such a large dynamic organization, and also its control. Then, we can express the global state of the organization. At last, such a system provides a way for the real time evaluation of all massive multi-agent systems. We propose a model based on specific multi-agent architecture, grasping the initial agent organization, supplying a geometrical representation of the current state of the agents of the organization. Such a system expressing its self current state can situate its organization in the evolution of groups of agents, can appreciate the state of the distributed organizations in the case of a distributed system and, like that, can modifies in real-time its behavior. Such a system is self-adaptive in its behavior, like the social behavior in large cities.

We apply such a system for the analysis of the discourses of the decision-makers in management of crisis situations. The task at hand was trying to build an understanding of a dynamic of the complex urban migrations in large city. To reach this difficult goal, we have proposed an original architecture of the Representation System based on the morphology of the behavior of a very large and distributed

M. Ishizuka and A. Sattar (Eds.): PRICAI 2002, LNAI 2417, pp. 592-593, 2002.
© Springer-Verlag Berlin Heidelberg 2002

aspectual agent organization, evaluated with an analysis organization upon a morphologic organization. In the urban application, the identification of model of preferential attribution of the residences to the households and the inhabitants to their habitat is in the heart of "problems of society".

Agent-Based Cooperative Distributed Tutoring Systems

Elhadi Shakshuki[1] and Trang Dang[2]

[1] Computer Science Department
Acadia University
Wolfville, Canada, B0P 1X0
Elhadi.Shakshuki@acadiau.ca
[2] Clarica Life Insurance
Waterloo, Canada N2J 4C5
Trang.Dang@clarica.ca

Abstract. The growth of online computer-based tutoring systems requires a new design paradigm for effective training and learning. In this environment, the number and the distribution of the tutoring systems make it difficult to support users for effective training and learning based on their own time and pace. Toward this end, this work proposes a multi-agent system architecture for cooperative distributed tutoring systems. The architecture consists of several interface agents. The agents act as mediators between the learners and the tutoring system. The interface agents interact with the learners and tutoring system to provide them with the set of materials that match their performance from distributed tutoring systems. The agents have a problem solving capability to make changes to the tutoring material schedule. A prototype of this system is implemented using IBM Agent Building and Learning Environment.

The advance in computer technology, allowed more and more computer-based tutoring systems to offer varies training and learning materials electronically. This makes it possible for us ers to have more freedom to take a course in their own time and pace. However, users might not be able to stay on schedule with the course materials because of their skills. To this end, there is a need to provide the user with a schedule of a specific topic and keep track of his/her performance.

This work proposes an agent that can act as an assistant to help the learner through a learning program. It has the abilities (1) to proactively assist a learner through the learning process, (2) to be responsive to his/her needs, (3) to be competent in adapting the interface to the learner's preferences and level, (4) to collaborate with other agents to jointly satisfy the users' need.

The scheduling problem of the proposed system has the ability to solve problems in domains where the actual time to finish a sub-task may deviate from the allotted one with soft and hard real-time deadlines. In addition, multiple solution methods make tradeoffs in solution quality and timelines.

M. Ishizuka and A. Sattar (Eds.): PRICAI 2002, LNAI 2417, p. 594, 2002.
© Springer-Verlag Berlin Heidelberg 2002

A Computational Model of Reasoning as Socially-Constructed Process

Ruediger Oehlmann

Kingston University, School of Computing and Information Systems,
Penrhyn Road, Kingston upon Thames, KT1 2EE, UK
R.Oehlmann@kingston.ac.uk

Social-constructionists argue that people understand the world by constructing their view of the world in the sense that any observation can only become meaningful in social interchanges. This aspect of reasoning has been investigated in psychological and AI studies by focussing on the reasoning strategy of perspective taking. Perspectives are viewed as mental representations that describe partial knowledge of a task domain, including causal links between knowledge components, (domain perspective) and as representations about other participants (social perspectives) including knowledge about how these participants might see the world.

Verbal protocols of participants were recorded who changed their perspective when they tried to understand a mechanical device. While in an individual task setting, most participants changed the perspective about the device and demonstrated improved reasoning after changing the perspective, this result could not be replicated in a setting of collaborating pairs of participants. The failure to change the perspective could be attributed to a cognitive overload caused by reasoning about the task domain and the social context at the same time. This is supported by the result of a third experiment, where collaborating participants externalized their perspectives by generating graphical presentations.

Based on these results, a software architecture, referred to as COLLABORATOR, has been developed that simulates the social-constructionist reasoning and its constraints. The system has two procedurally identical sub-systems that utilize case-based planning[1]. Each system is capable of generating verbal statements representing domain and social perspectives[2], as well as external models of these perspectives.

In addition to the "cognitive overload" hypothesis, which is supported by the verbal protocols, tests with the COLLABORATOR system suggest that each sub-system needs to assess the contribution of its partner system. This requires a social model of the partner system. Therefore perspective changes on the domain level and on the social level are interleaved and externalisation helps to minimize the dependencies between processes.

References

1. Hammond, K Case-Based Planning Academic Press, New York (1989)
2. Oehlmann, R.: Metacognitive Attention: Reasoning about strategy selection. In J. Moore and J. Lehman(eds.), Proc. 17th Annual Conference of the Cognitive Science Society, (Pittsburgh 1995), Lawrence Erlbaum Assoc., Hillsdale, NJ (1995) 66–71

M. Ishizuka and A. Sattar (Eds.): PRICAI 2002, LNAI 2417, p. 595, 2002.
© Springer-Verlag Berlin Heidelberg 2002

Managing Information Complexity of Supply Chains via Agent-Based Genetic Programming

Ken Taniguchi, Setsuya Kurahashi, and Takao Terano

Graduate School of Systems Management, University of Tsukuba,
3-29-1 Otsuka, Bunkyo-ku, Tokyo 112-0012, Japan
{taniguti, kurahasi, terano}@gssm.otsuka.tsukuba.ac.jp

Abstract. This paper proposes agent-based formulation of a Supply Chain Management (SCM) system for manufacturing firms. We model each firm as an intelligent agent, which communicates each other through the blackboard architecture in distributed artificial intelligence. To cope with the issues of conventional SCM systems, we employ the concept of information entropy, which represents the complexity of the purchase, sales, and inventory activities of each firm. Based on the idea, we implement an agent-based simulator to learn 'good' decisions via genetic programming in a logic programming environment. From intensive experiments, our simulator have shown good performance against the dynamic environmental changes.

The model proposed on this paper is different from the conventional centralized SCM. In this model, agents are assigned to distributed sites and autonomously adjust the purchase plan. The basic purchase plan is based on MRP(Material Requirements Planning) or DRP(Distribution Resource Planning) in order to achieve more realistic SCM. Each process looks up Web News in this model to keep track of the situation of the other processes and to adjust the own purchase plan based this information. For example, when the production in a factory has been delayed, it is reflected to its result on the Web News and the other processes can recognize it. The adjustment shall be autonomously made only by the processes which requires the adjustment in response to the changes on other processes or the changes on connections of processes.

References

1. S.Sivadasan, J.Efstathiou, R.Shirazi, J.Alves, G.Frizelle, A.Calinescu: Information Complexity as a Determining Factor in the Evolution of Supply Chains, *International Workshop on Emergent Synthesis - IWES'99*, pp.237–242, 1999.
2. Ken Taniguchi, Setsuya Kurahashi and Takao Terano: Managing Information Complexity in a Supply Chain Model by Agent-Based Genetic Programming, *Proceedings of the Genetic and Evolutionary Computation Conference (GECCO-2001) Late Breaking Papers*, pp.413-420, 2001.

M. Ishizuka and A. Sattar (Eds.): PRICAI 2002, LNAI 2417, p. 596, 2002.
© Springer-Verlag Berlin Heidelberg 2002

Semantic Integration of E-business Models Based on Multi-layered Repository

Noriaki Izumi[1] and Takahira Yamaguchi[2]

[1] Cyber Assist Research Center, National Institute of Advanced Industrial Science and Technology 2–41–6 Aomi Koto-ku Tokyo 135–0064 JAPAN,
niz@ni.aist.go.jp,
[2] Shizuoka University, 3–5–1 Johoku Hamamatsu Shizuoka 432–8011, JAPAN,
yamagutii@cs.inf.shizuoka.ac.jp,

Abstract. In order to realize business application according to new business idea, this paper proposes a semantic integration of e-business models for the business applications development. Our method rebuilds required heterogeneous repositories into a multi-layered repository based on ontologies. The proposed repository consists of component libraries and their use patterns from a level on enterprise activities to a level of software.

1 Overview

In order to achieve the unified support in the construction of business models and applications, we have dealt with the following heterogeneity as the research issues:

1. Conceptual diversity of business know-how required such as business strategies, experimental practices, software development skills, and so on,
2. Expressive variety of repositories available to access and share by the project members such as various online documents, enterprise data stocks, software library resources, and so on.

In this work, in order to provide the unified support of e-commerce application construction on both business model level and software architecture level, we have proposed the framework of the extraction of the required information based on ontologies with reusable repositories such as e-business process handbook, Common KADS and J2EE libraries.

We have implemented the prototype system by JAVA[1] and confirmed that it supports us in various phases of business application development including business model manifestation, detailed business model definition and an implementation of business software applications.

References

1. N.Izumi, T.Yamaguchi: " Development Support of E-Commerce Applications By Integrating Heterogeneous Repositories Based on Ontologies" Electronic Commerce Research and Applications, Elsevier (*to appear*)(*2002*).

M. Ishizuka and A. Sattar (Eds.): PRICAI 2002, LNAI 2417, p. 597, 2002.

Randomization and Uncertain Inference*

Henry E. Kyburg[1,2] and Choh Man Teng[2]

[1] Computer Science & Philosophy, Univ. of Rochester, Rochester NY 14627, USA
[2] Inst. for Human & Machine Cognition, 40 S. Alcaniz St., Pensacola FL 32501, USA

In many experiments *randomization* is an important part of the protocol, yet precisely the same data could be produced by an experiment in which randomization played no part. From a Bayesian point of view, randomization plays at most a small role. From a classical point of view, randomization is central to ensuring that the long run error rates are controlled as they are claimed to be.

Take for example the testing of the lady who claimed to be able to tell whether milk or tea was put into a cup first [1]. We cannot demand the cups to be exactly alike, but if we randomize, in the long run these differences will "cancel out". However, once the test has been administered, we need to take into account what we do indeed know. Suppose all red cups were made with milk first. This assignment can occur even with a perfectly randomized experiment, but such knowledge should cast doubt on the validity of the conclusions.

Kadane and Seidenfeld examined a number of arguments for randomization from a Bayesian perspective, but found none of them compelling [2]. For example, it can be said that a randomized test is more efficient as we do not have to explicitly balance all the covariates. However, the details to be omitted should be those that are suppressible, *not* those that might matter, as seems to be what randomization is called to achieve. Once we know the actual experimental conditions, the different prior opinions about "nuisance factors" can give rise to different interpretations of the results.

We propose the use of evidential probability [3], an interval valued framework that makes use of three principles to resolve reference class issues. (1) *Richness*. Statistics obtained by conditioning on prior probabilities should preside over differing statistics of the marginalization of the distribution. (2) *Specificity*. Statistics about a more specific class should preside over differing statistics about a more general class. (3) *Precision*. An interval that includes the union of all other intervals can be ignored. Evidential probability makes it possible to retain the the frequency bounds on error, while taking into account the ancillary statistics.

References

1. Fisher, R.A.: The Design of Experiments. Hafner, New York (1971)
2. Kadane, J., Seidenfeld, T.: Randomization in a Bayesian perspective. Journal of Statistical Planning and Inference **25** (1990) 329–345
3. Kyburg, Jr., H.E., Teng, C.M.: Uncertain Inference. Cambridge University Press, New York (2001)

* This work has been supported in part by the National Science Foundation STS-9906128 and ITS-0082928, and NASA NCC2-1239.

M. Ishizuka and A. Sattar (Eds.): PRICAI 2002, LNAI 2417, p. 598, 2002.
© Springer-Verlag Berlin Heidelberg 2002

Checkers Strategy Evolution with Speciated Neural Networks*

Kyung-Joong Kim and Sung-Bae Cho

Dept. of Computer Science, Yonsei University
134 Shinchon-dong, Sudaemoon-ku, Seoul 120-749, Korea
uribyul@candy.yonsei.ac.kr, sbcho@cs.yonsei.ac.kr

Checkers is a very simple game and easy to learn. Unlike chess, it is simple to move and needs a few rules. With respect to checkers, the evolutionary algorithm can discover a neural network that can be used to play at a near-expert level without injecting expert knowledge about how to play the game. Evolutionary approach does not need any prior knowledge to develop machine player but can develop high-level player. However, conventional evolutionary algorithms have a property of genetic drift that only one solution often dominates at the last generation. Because of genetic drift, it is difficult to discover diverse checkers players that have different properties in search space with simple evolutionary algorithm. Combining diverse solutions can make better performance than single dominating solution by complementing each other.

Game tree is used to find optimal move in checkers with min-max search strategy. Simple evolutionary algorithm with speciation technique is used to find optimal neural network structure that evaluates leaf nodes of game tree (Fig. 1.). In this research, crowding algorithm is adopted to speciated population. In first step, population of neural networks is initialized with random manner and genetic operations change chromosomes that represent weights and biases of neural network. In second step, each of the two children competes with one of the two parents, according to similarity. The similarity between two neural networks is based on the Euclidean distance of weights and biases of them. Fitness level is determined relatively by the information of competition result with parents. In third step, representative individuals are extracted from each species that is identified by clustering the last generation population and combined. Representative player is the winner of tournament competition among all individuals in a cluster. Combination of representative player is based on the mixture of evaluation values about leaf nodes in a game tree with the method of average, maximum, and minimum.

Simple EA and speciated EA have a population of 100 individuals and are evolved in 50 generations. There are 68 games in 1:1 match because the number of speciated players is 68. In this match, simple EA is a bit better than speciated EA (defeat rate of speciated EA: 47%). Meanwhile, average, max, and min combining of speciated players can defeat simple EA player with the rate 63.6%, 50% and 40% respectively. In this experiments, average combination method performs better than other methods.

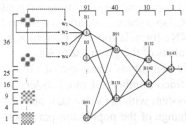

Fig. 1. Neural network architecture for evaluating leaf node of a game tree.

---

* This research was supported by Brain Science and Engineering Research Program sponsored by Korean Ministry of Science and Technology.

M. Ishizuka and A. Sattar (Eds.): PRICAI 2002, LNAI 2417, p. 599, 2002.
© Springer-Verlag Berlin Heidelberg 2002

Generation and Optimization of Fuzzy Neural Network Structure

Zbigniew Świątnicki[1] and Vladimír Olej[2]

[1] Department of Logistic Management, Logistics Institute
Military University of Technology
Kaliskiego 2, 00-908 Warsaw, Poland
zswiat@wat.waw.pl

[2] Department of Information Systems, School of Finance
Matej Bel University
Tajovského 10, 974 01 Banská Bystrica, Slovak Republic
olej@financ.umb.sk

The paper presents a possibility of exploitation of distributed genetic algorithms (DGAs) for optimization of the neural networks (NNs) and fuzzy neural networks (FNNs) structure and its application to pattern recognition. Generally, there can be several approaches to generation structure of NNs based on genetic algorithms (GAs). Two of them are used most frequently. In the first approach, NNs are only generated from a genotype while in the second approach two genotypes are used. These methods make use of GAs to determine: synapse weights NNs, where their structure is known in advance; NNs structure and synapse weights. This proposal belongs to the second group of methods. These make use of GAs to determine structure and synapse weights NNs (FNNs).

A genetic method to generate a FNNs, which has both structure and synapse weights adequate for a given task is proposed. Genetic algorithms are robust adaptive optimization methods based on biological principles. They represent an efficient technique of learning based on the dynamics of the evolution. Fuzzy neural networks employing basic fuzzy logic operations. In the learning process (by DGAs), they afford for shortening the time of method convergence towards the global maximum. Crisp numbers express input and output values of FNNs. Input values in the FNNs formulation can be realized as fuzzy sets, outputs as membership function values of the given fuzzy set.

Distributed genetic algorithms make use of GAs. Their task is to divide the population between defined numbers of independent GAs. All independent GAs works in a distributed system with the same task and with their own population. A DGA provides the exchange of the population parts between individual GAs. The conditions of this exchange (the number of individuals, the method of choice of individuals, etc.) are predetermined by the user. The fitness η is evaluated at every GA independently of the other GAs. It affords for decreasing the time consumption of the convergence towards the global maximum.

M. Ishizuka and A. Sattar (Eds.): PRICAI 2002, LNAI 2417, p. 600, 2002.
© Springer-Verlag Berlin Heidelberg 2002

FuzzyDrive: A Fuzzy Rule-Based Auto Pilot System

W.L. Tung and C. Quek

Intelligent Systems Laboratory, Nanyang Technological University,
School of Computer Engineering, Blk N4 #2A-32, Nanyang Avenue, Singapore 639798
ashcquek@ntu.edu.sg

The proposed fully automated pilot system for *Intelligent Vehicles* (IV) consists of the *Generic Self-organising Fuzzy Neural Network* (GenSoFNN) coupled with a driving simulator as shown in Fig. 1.

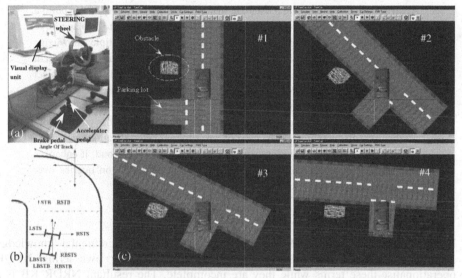

Fig. 1. (a) Hardware setup of simulator (b) Sensors used in the simulator car and (c) A 4-steps left-in reverse parking sequence performed by the GenSoFNN based auto pilot system

The firing frequency of the fuzzy rules derived by the GenSoFNN for the *steering control* (SA), *throttle position* (TPS) and *brake position* (BTS) sub-control systems of the simulator car for the left-in reverse parking simulation is shown as Fig. 2.

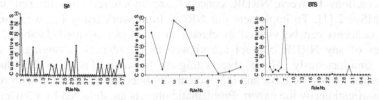

Fig. 2. Rule firing frequency of the three sub-control systems (SA, TPS and BTS)

The extracted fuzzy rule no. 3 from the TPS subsystem is – If *vehicle speed* is *slow* then apply *half throttle*. This fuzzy rule is intuitive to the human cognitive process.

M. Ishizuka and A. Sattar (Eds.): PRICAI 2002, LNAI 2417, p. 601, 2002.
© Springer-Verlag Berlin Heidelberg 2002

Implementing NRDR Using OO Database Management System (OODBMS)

Ghassan Beydoun and Lina Al-Jadir

Department of Mathematics and Computer Science
American University of Beirut
P.O. Box 11-0236, Beirut, Lebanon
Phone: (961-1) 350.000, fax: (961-1) 744.461
{ghassan.beydoun, lina.al-jadir}@aub.edu.lb

Abstract. Motives for using a database management system (DBMS) to build a knowledge base system (KBS), include KBS's lack of ability to manage large sets of rules, to control concurrent access and to manage multiple knowledge bases simultaneously. In work, we build a KBS using a database management system DBMS for its schema evolution ability. We use this ability of an Object Oriented DBMS (OODBMS) to manage the consistency of an incrementally built knowledge base (KB).

The significance of this work is two folds: first, it provides an efficient mechanism maintaining consistency of an evolving classification hierarchy, using built-in schema evolution features of an OODBMS. Second, it enhances the interface of an OODBMS, to allow intelligent classification queries over stored objects.

1 Implementing NRDR Using F2

In PRICAI98, we introduced Nested RDR (NRDR), an incremental knowledge acquisition approach which allows experts to introduce their own terms. NRDR operationalise these terms while they are incomplete. The resultant NRDR KB is a conceptual hierarchy, where a concept (term) introduced by an expert is defined by a set of rules. To modify a concept definition, exception rules are added only, they are never deleted or modified. This greatly eases maintenance and development of a concept definition, but interactions between NRDR concepts may cause inconsistencies to occur in the KB. In this work, we use an OODBMS technology to manage the effort to deal with inconsistencies.

Interactions between NRDR concepts are monitored and tracked using an OODBMS, F2 [1]. To implement our NRDR framework using F2, we observe that NRDR concepts can be viewed as classes in an object-oriented database. In turn, instances of any NRDR concept are viewed as F2 objects belonging to different classes simultaneously. These objects migrate between classes in F2 (during the development of NRDR KB), and they potentially become inconsistent with respect to past classifications by the expert. Problematic objects are detected by F2 triggers, and existing NRDR development policies [2] are then applied. Addition of any new classes is handled by schema evolution features of F2.

The F2/NRDR interface developed in this work is currently being used to develop a medium sized KB to classify the suitability of air-conditioning systems.

M. Ishizuka and A. Sattar (Eds.): PRICAI 2002, LNAI 2417, pp. 602-603, 2002.
© Springer-Verlag Berlin Heidelberg 2002

References

1.   Al-Jadir, L., T. Estier, G. Falquet, and M. Leonard. *Evolution Features of the F2 OODBMS*. in *4th International Conference on Database Systems for Advanced Applications (DASFAA95)*. 1995. Singapore: World Scientific.
2.   Beydoun, G. and A. Hoffmann, *Theoretical Basis of Hierarchical Incremental Acquisition*. International Journal of Human Computer Interactions, Academic Press, 2001. **54**(3): p. 407-452.

Using Ripple Down Rules for Actions and Planning

Rex B.H. Kwok

School of Computer Science and Engineering, The University of New South Wales,
UNSW SYDNEY NSW, Australia 2052
rkwok@cse.unsw.edu.au

Much of the research into reasoning about actions is driven by a set of small benchmark problems. For such problems, specifying action behaviours within any particular logic of action is a simple task. In more complex domains this may not be the case. A simple and proven method for eliciting knowledge from experts – called Ripple Down Rules (RDR) – can be adapted for representing action descriptions and plans.

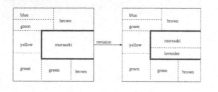

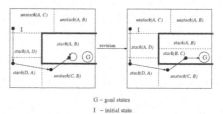

G – goal states
I – initial state

Fig. 1. A pictorial representation of RDR classification and revision behaviour.

Fig. 2. Planning with RDR.

The behaviour of an RDR rule base can be viewed pictorially in Figure 1. RDR divides a state space into a number of disjoint regions. Attached to each region is a particular conclusion. Any particular point will lie within a single region and will be classed as the conclusion attached to that region. When an RDR tree is revised, a region is split in two. One part remains attached to the old conclusion while the other is attached to the conclusion given by the expert. The dividing line for this split is determined by conditions chosen by the expert.

RDR is adapted for learning action behaviours by mapping a point to a representation of initial conditions and the conclusion to the action result. With STRIPS, the RDR conclusion would be expressed as two sets of literals: an *add list* and a *delete list*. In revision, conditions are generated from differences in initial conditions.

Planning involves transforming an initial state description via actions to a state description satisfying a goal condition. To implement this in RDR, the conclusion is identified with an action. With the action specification RDR (defined above) specifying how an action behaves in different states, this *planning* RDR will return different actions depending on the current state description. A plan is generated by repeatedly passing a state description through the RDR rule base. At each step an action is suggested. The way that action changes the state description can be obtained from the action specification RDR. Goals represent a region in the state space and the task of the planning RDR is to attach actions to regions and direct the initial state to some goal state. Incorrect steps in the plan can be modified by splitting one region into two. A graphic representation of this procedure can be seen in Figure 2. Given a finite state space and a default action, this iteration policy will either reach a state description satisfying the goal or enter a behavioural loop. Looping behaviour is used to trigger RDR revision.

M. Ishizuka and A. Sattar (Eds.): PRICAI 2002, LNAI 2417, p. 604, 2002.

A Generative Dependency Grammar

Stefan Diaconescu

SOFTWIN, Technical Director,
Str. Fabrica de Glucoza Nr. 5, Sect.2, 72246 Bucharest, Romania

Abstract. We propose a new kind of grammar: the Generative Dependency Grammar (GDG) based on dependency trees (DT) and a generative process. By generating a surface text using these GDG, the DT of the text is obtained too. GDG formalism is starting to be used for Romanian language.

In this paper we merge the Dependency Grammars and the Generative Grammars (GG) ideas in order to obtain a new kind of grammar: Generative Dependency Grammar. DG (Tesnière (1959)) tries to express the relations between words. They use dependency trees (DT) that contains usually words as nodes and relations (oriented links between words) . Consequently, DG contains dependency relations and dependency rules (or constraints). On the other hand GG (Chomsky (1988)) try to express a process to obtain phrases starting from a root simbol and using some generative rules.

We propose a new kind of DT that uses many types of nodes. The DT will be generated using a process based on generative rules. The DT and the rules will constitute a GDG[1]. GDG will eliminate some issues of DG (by example the missing of phrasal categories) and GG (the problem of discontinuous structures) and will merge the advantages of the two types of grammar (GG - the representation of phrasal categories; GDG - the handling of discontinuous structures as gaps and non projective constructions). In fact, the basic idea is: when a GDG generates a text, it builds the DT of the text too. We appreciate that GDG is adequate to represent word dependency *especially when these grammars are used in machine translation purpose and data retrieval.*

References

1. Chomsky, Noam (1988) *Generative Grammar: Its Basis, Development and Prospects.* Studies in English Linguistics and Literature, Special Issue, Kyoto University of Foreign Studies, 1988.
2. Kahane, Sylvain and others (1998). *Pseudo-projectivity: A polynomially parsable nonprojective dependency grammar.* In Proc. of ACL '98, Montreal, Canada
3. Tesnière, L. (1959) *Éléments de syntaxe structurelle*, Paris, Klincksieck

---

[1] The name GDG but with completely different structures, formalism and purpose is present also in (Kahane 1998).

M. Ishizuka and A. Sattar (Eds.): PRICAI 2002, LNAI 2417, p. 605, 2002.

Indonesian Morphological Parser with Minimum Connectivity Cost to Solve Ambiguities

Mohammad Teduh Uliniansyah, Shun Ishizaki, and Kiyoko Uchiyama

Graduate School of Media and Governance, Keio University
252-8520 Kanagawa-ken Fujisawa-shi, Endou 5322, Japan
{teduh, ishizaki, kiyoko}@sfc.keio.ac.jp

Surprisingly, there was only a few research on Indonesian Natural Language Processing. There were two international projects on machine translation systems involving Bahasa Indonesia[1] (MMTS and UNL projects). Although both projects did Indonesian morphological analysis also, only a part of prefix and suffix was taken into consideration since the number of affixes were too many to handle[1][2]. Chasen, a popular Japanese morphological analysis program uses connectivity costs to analysis japanese words and to solve ambiguous words[3][4].

Because Bahasa Indonesia has so many affixes to form words, recording all derivation words into a word dictionary is impossible because it will make the size of the word dictionary huge and the processing time much longer. Since there are many combinations of affixes and stems in Bahasa Indonesia to create words, they are often creating ambiguities. By using a part-of-speech (POS) tagged corpus, a word dictionary consisted of root words only, an affix rule table and costs for each adjacent part-of-speech (POS) of words [3][4], the ambiguities were solved. Connectivity cost values were calculated using following equation: $Cost(p1,p2) = log(N/n(p1,p2))$, where n(p1,p2) is the number of adjacent p1 and p2, and N is the total number of pairs of POS in a training corpus. We trained two training corpus five times to get best connectivity costs for pairs of POS. Using costs values acquired from training process, we analyzed two test corpus. A good analysis result (99.6%) was achieved.

Experimental results showed that training a corpus for two times was enough to get a near-best cost values of POS pairs. We also concluded that the bigger the number of sentences in a training corpus is, the better the analysis accuracy would be.

References

1. Agency for the Assessment and Application of Technology: Indonesian Enconverter System. BPPT, Jakarta (March 1999)
2. Center of the International Cooperation for Computerization: Indonesian Analysis Rules, Technical Report 6-CICC-MT44. CICC, Japan (March 1995)
3. Matsumoto, Y: Introduction to Computational Linguistics. Lecture notes. Nara Insitute of Science and Technology (2000)
4. Matsumoto, Y. et.al.: Morphological Analysis System Chasen version 2.2.6 Manual. Nara Institute of Science and Technology (2001)

---

[1] "Bahasa Indonesia" is the name of Indonesian Language

M. Ishizuka and A. Sattar (Eds.): PRICAI 2002, LNAI 2417, p. 606, 2002.
© Springer-Verlag Berlin Heidelberg 2002

Target Word Selection Using WordNet and Data-Driven Models in Machine Translation

Yuseop Kim[1], Jeong-Ho Chang[2], and Byoung-Tak Zhang[2]

[1] Ewha Institute of Science and Technology, Ewha Woman's University,
Seoul, Korea 120-750
{yskim01}@ewha.ac.kr[***]
[2] School of Computer Science and Engineering, Seoul National University,
Seoul, Korea 151-744
{jhchang, btzhang}@bi.snu.ac.kr [†]

Collocation information plays an important role in target word selection of machine translation. However, a collocation dictionary fulfills only a limited portion of selection operation because of data sparseness. To resolve the sparseness problem, we proposed a new methodology that selects target words after determining an appropriate collocation class by using a inter-word semantic similarity. We estimate the similarity by computing semantic distance of two synsets in WordNet and term-to-term similarity in data-driven models. In WordNet, semantic similarity between two word can be calculated by adapting a reciprocal of the Semantic Distance (SD). For the calculation of the SD, each synset in WordNet is assigned an M-value. The M-value is computed as follows: M-value $= \frac{radix}{sf^p}$, where $radix$ is an initial M-value, sf is a scale factor, and p is the number of edges from the root to the synset. As the data-driven models, we utilize Latent Semantic Analysis (LSA) and Probabilistic Latent Semantic Analysis(PLSA), a probabilistic application of LSA. LSA applies singular value decomposition (SVD) to the matrix. SVD is a form of factor analysis and is defined as $A = U\Sigma V^T$,where Σ is a diagonal matrix composed of nonzero eigen values of AA^T or $A^T A$, and U and V are the orthogonal eigenvectors associated with the r nonzero eigenvalues of AA^T and $A^T A$, respectively. The term-to-term similarity is based on the inner products between two row vectors of A, $AA^T = U\Sigma^2 U^T$. And To compute the similarity of w_1 and w_2 in PLSA, $P(z|w_1)P(z|w_2)$ should be approximately computed with being derived from $P(z|w) = \frac{P(z)P(w|z)}{\sum_z P(z)P(w|z)}$, where z represents contexts. For experiments, we implemented three similarity measurements applying to WordNet, LSA and PLSA and we used TREC data(AP news in 1988). We could obtain up to 18% accuracy improvement from suggested approaches, comparing to direct matching to a collocation dictionary.

[***] He is supported by Brain Korea 21 project performed by Ewha Institute of Science and Technology
[†] They are supported by Brain Tech. project from Korean Ministry of Science and Technology

A Study on Using Natural Language as a Computer Communication Protocol

Ichiro Kobayashi[1,2], Michiaki Iwazume[2], Shino Iwashita[2],
Toru Sugimoto[2], and Michio Sugeno[2]

[1] Hosei University, Faculty of Economics,
4342 Aihara-machi, Machida-shi, Tokyo 194-0298,Japan
koba@mt.tama.hosei.ac.jp
[2] Brain Science Institute, RIKEN
2-1 Hirosawa, Wako-shi, Saitama 351-0198, JAPAN
{iwazume, iwas, sugimoto}@brain.riken.go.jp

This paper proposes a new computer communication protocol based on natural language called 'language protocol', a new communication method based on the protocol, and an interface, called 'LAPI (Language Application Programming Interface)', which can connect any communicaiton standard via natural language as a medium of the standards. With the proposed methods, we show the possibility of providing flexible communication environment for any communication object which achieves communication barrier-free in which all communication objects can communicate with natural language, and propose a new concept of 'meaning processing' against information processing of the conventional computing. An overview of language protocol communication environment is illustrated in Fig. 1.

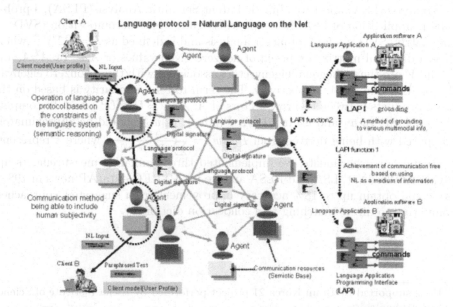

Fig. 1. Overview of Language Protocol Communication Environment

M. Ishizuka and A. Sattar (Eds.): PRICAI 2002, LNAI 2417, p. 608, 2002.
© Springer-Verlag Berlin Heidelberg 2002

Automatic Indexing Based on Term Activities

Naohiro Matsumura[1,3], Yukio Ohsawa[2,3], and Mitsuru Ishizuka[1]

[1] Graduate School of Engineering, University of Tokyo,
7-3-1 Hongo, Bunkyo-ku, Tokyo, 113–8656 Japan
{matumura, ishizuka}@miv.t.u-tokyo.ac.jp
[2] Graduate School of Business Science, University of Tsukuba,
3-29-1 Otsuka, Bunkyo-ku, Tokyo, 112–0012 Japan
osawa@gssm.otsuka.tsukuba.ac.jp
[3] PRESTO, Japan Science and Technology Corporation,
2-2-11 Tsutsujigaoka, Miyagino-ku, Sendai, Miyagi, 983–0852 Japan

Abstract. This paper proposes an automatic indexing method named PAI (Priming Activation Indexing) that extracts keywords expressing the author's main point from a document. The basic idea is that since the author writes a document emphasizing his/her main point, impressive terms born in the mind of the reader could represent the asserted keywords. Our approach employs a spreading activation model.

The human mind can be modeled as a network where concepts are connected to a number of other concepts and the states of concepts are expressed by the activities. If a concept is activated, its adjacent concepts are in turn activated. Thus, activities spread through the network. Many experiments indicate that the speed of associating a concept is in proportion to the level of activity. This kind of phenomenon is known as *priming effect* [1].

The priming effect is considered to be closely related to the process of understanding/interpreting a document in the reader's mind. Usually, an author emphasizes his/her main point in the document content, and we go on understanding/interpreting by activating related concepts as we read the content.

The mechanism of priming effect at understanding/interpreting a document, has been formalized as *Spreading Activation Model* based on the empirical experiments in cognitive science [2]. In this paper, we regard highly activated terms as strongly memorized terms in the reader's mind, and extract them as keywords representing the author's main point.

References

1. R.F. Lorch: Priming and Searching Processes in Semantic Memory: A Test of Three Models of Spreading Activation, *Journal of Verbal Learning and Verbal Behavior*, Vol. 21, pp. 468–492, 1982.
2. A.M. Collins and E.F. Loftus: A Spreading-Activation Theory of Semantic Processing, *Psychological Review*, Vol. 82, pp. 407–428, 1975.

M. Ishizuka and A. Sattar (Eds.): PRICAI 2002, LNAI 2417, p. 609, 2002.
© Springer-Verlag Berlin Heidelberg 2002

Answer Extraction by Flexible Matching, Filtering, and Interpretation

Kyung-Soon Lee[1], Jae-Ho Kim[2], and Key-Sun Choi[2]

[1] NII (National Institute of Informatics)
kslee@nii.ac.jp
[2] KAIST (Korea Advanced Institute of Science and Technology)
{jjaeh,kschoi}@world.kaist.ac.kr

This paper describes a Korean Question Answering (KorQuA) system. In our observation, QA systems need to consider these things to be more confident and intelligent: Terms in a text should be classified as the characteristics of matching. For example, range expression doesn't need exact matching and proper noun such as book title needs exact term matching. To support an answer for a question, the answer should not have negative or uncertain contexts. And date expression has a tendency to be represented as a relative expression in a news article such as last month and 2 years ago. Our KorQuA system takes a natural language question as an input and produces a list of answers ranked, which consists of three components: question interpretation, flexible passage retrieval, and answer extraction. For flexible text retrieval, terms in a question are represented as five data types: date, range, core, keyword, and expected answer type. Similarity of a passage is calculated by matching terms according to these data types. Answer extraction involves three procedures: entity extraction, answer filtering and answer interpretation. To extract candidate answers corresponding to the expected answer type, we identify named entities such as person, organization, location, date, quantities, durations, and linear measures, and semantic categories. We filtered candidate answers modified by negative context, uncertain context or uncertain background domain of a document. For date type question, we interpret a relative expression as a new answer which is not represented in a text by calculating an absolute date from a relative date expression based on the written date of a document.

We also built a Korean Question Answering Test Collection (KorQATeC-I)[1], which include derived answers as answers and exclude answers that show the inconsistency or uncertainty for fact in total stream of a document in judging answers. The document set consists of 207067 articles of three newspapers, from January of 1992 to May of 1995. The number of question is 100 which are taken from Quiz database (17461 questions) on internet and the document collection to be retrieved. The 10 questions are variant questions for 90 questions. We selected documents to be judged using various document retrieval techniques. Ten human assessors judged answers.

The performance of KorQuA system on KorQATeC-I by mean reciprocal answer rank showed 0.270, 0.476 and 0.526 for answer, 50 bytes and 250 bytes answer for the top five answers, respectively. Through component analysis, we showed that terms need to be matched flexibly according to their characteristics, answer filtering and answer interpretation make a QA system more reliable and intelligent.

---

[1] The work of KAIST was supported by Korean Ministry of Science and Technology.

M. Ishizuka and A. Sattar (Eds.): PRICAI 2002, LNAI 2417, p. 610, 2002.
© Springer-Verlag Berlin Heidelberg 2002

A Statistical Identification and Verification Method for Biometrics*

Kwanyong Lee[1] and Hyeyoung Park[2]

[1] Dept. of Computer, Information and Communication
Korea Cyber University, Seoul, Korea
kylee@mail.kcu.or.kr

[2] Lab. for Mathematical Neuroscience, RIKEN Brain Science Institute
2-1 Hirosawa, Wako, Saitama, 351-0198, Japan
hypark@brain.riken.go.jp

A biometrics system is to find out the identity of a person by measuring physical and physiological features which can distinguish the corresponding person from others. When applying the conventional machine learning methods to design a biometrics system, one first runs into the difficulty of collecting sufficient data for each person to be registered to the system. In addition, there can be almost infinite number of variations of non-registered data. Therefore, it is very difficult to analyze and predict the distributional properties of data that are essential for the system to process real data in practical applications. These difficulties require a new framework of identification and verification, which is appropriate and efficient for the special situations of biometrics systems. As a preliminary solution, the present paper proposes a simple but theoretically well-defined method based on the statistical test theory.

The purpose of biometrics systems is to classify new observed data x into two classes; authentic class A and imposter class I. The conventional approaches estimate $p(A|x)$ and $p(I|x)$, and classify the data x using them. Because the data x is given from very various sources(individuals) and the number of data from each source is small, it is difficult to estimate $p(A|x)$ and $p(I|x)$ robustly. To solve this problem, we introduce a new random variable $y = x - x'$, where x and x' are from same individual. Since y does not depend on individual classes and we can obtain more larger number of samples for y than for x, we can expect to obtain $p(A|y)$ more accurately than $p(A|x)$.

Though various machine learning techniques can be used for estimating $p(A|y)$, we apply a simple but general statistical method in this paper, as a preliminary stage. Under the assumption that y is subject to Gaussian distribution, we estimate its mean and variance. Using these statistics, we propose a similarity measure for identification, and a formula for determining threshold according to the desirable rejection rate of the system. Computational experiments on real human iris data show that the proposed measure(98.95%) is superior to the standard methods such as the simplified Mahalanovis distance(83.65%) for the identification test. Also, we can confirm the possibility that the proposed method can be applied the practical verification systems from the results of FAR and FRR on some different thresholds.

* This work is supported by the Korea Research Foundation (2001-003-E00234)

M. Ishizuka and A. Sattar (Eds.): PRICAI 2002, LNAI 2417, p. 611, 2002.
© Springer-Verlag Berlin Heidelberg 2002

Proposal of a Multimodal Dialogue Description Language

Masahiro Araki, Kiyoshi Ueda, Masashi Akita,
Takuya Nishimoto, and Yasuhisa Niimi

Kyoto Institute of Technology,
Matsugasaki Sakyo-ku Kyoto 606-8585 Japan
araki@dj.kit.ac.jp,
http://www-vox.dj.kit.ac.jp/araki/

We propose a multimodal dialogue description language by extending VoiceXML, which is a spoken dialogue description language for voice user interface. We added the specification that can output a text, image, 3D image, life-like communication agent, and multimedia clip.

Some research groups try to establish an original specification for multimodal interaction description language. However, it is a burden for contents provider or system designer to learn an utterly new language. Therefore, we selected an extension approach which modify existing markup languages.

We propose an extension of VoiceXML which can handle multimodal dialogue (Table. 1). As a design principle, we decided to maintain simple I/O handling of original VoiceXML, although some kinds of multimodal I/O, such as speech input with pointing on the image, require complex event sequence handling. Our extension does not deal with such complex event sequences.

Table 1. Extended tag of our multimodal dialogue description language

I/O	tag	mode
Output	text	assistance of speech output
	image	additional info. of speech output
	agent	emotional information and highlighting
	vrml, smil	3D image, multimedia clip
Input	image	clickable figure

The one reason of this decision is that the event sequence handling requires a detailed device dependent control. It seems to be against the basic VoiceXML standpoint that VoiceXML writer does not need the knowledge of I/O device.

The other reason of this decision is that attractive mixed modal output can be done with SMIL description. Therefore, the interactive part of dialogue proceeds on by simple output, and the information delivering dialogue uses rich SMIL output.

We have implemented interpreter for proposed multimodal VoiceXML and evaluated three kinds of tasks which have various kind of information flow: slot-filling (information flows from user to system), explanation (system to user) and database search (both directions).

M. Ishizuka and A. Sattar (Eds.): PRICAI 2002, LNAI 2417, p. 612, 2002.
© Springer-Verlag Berlin Heidelberg 2002

Image Classification by Web Images

Keiji Yanai

Department of Computer Science,
The University of Electro-Communications
1-5-1 Chofugaoka, Chofu-shi, Tokyo 182-8585, JAPAN,
yanai@cs.uec.ac.jp

While main targets of conventional Web mining are numerical and textual data, we propose Web mining for image data. Thanks to the recent rapid spread of digital imaging devices, demand for generic image classification of various kinds of real world images becomes greater. Then, we propose generic image classification using a large number of images automatically gathered from the Web as learning images. As classification methods, we use image-feature-based search exploited in content-based image retrieval(CBIR), which do not restrict target images unlike conventional image recognition methods.

The processing consists of three steps: image-gathering, learning and classification. In the gathering stage, the system gathers images related to the given keywords from the Web automatically[1]. In the learning stage, the system extracts image features and associates them with each class. Here, each class corresponds to each keyword used in the gathering stage. In the classification stage, the system classifies test images into classes using the association between image features of learning images and classes based on k-NN(nearest neighbor) search. In the learning and classification stage, we used three methods: color histogram[2], Earth Mover's Distance(EMD)[3], Integrated Region Matching(IRM)[4].

We made classification experiments for 5694 images(20 classes) gathered from the Web(Table 1), 3485 Web images with only correct ones (selecting by hand), 500 Corel images(10 classes)(Table 1), 500 Corel images by 4477 Web images(10 classes), and 500 Corel images by 3052 Web images including no incorrect ones. We used a five-fold cross-validation in the first three experiments. Table 2 shows F-measure values that represent the harmonic mean of the recall and the precision of five experimental results in three methods. Though these results were not sufficient yet, we are pursuing this project toward generic image recognition.

Table 1. 20 and 10 classes(keywords)

20: apple, bear, bike, Lake Biwa, car, cat, entrance ceremony, house, Ichiro, ferris wheel, Kinkaku Temple, lion, Moai, note PC, bullet train, park, penguin, noodle, wedding, Mt.Yari
10: dog, elephant, fish, sheep, tiger, whale + 4__

Table 2. Classification results(%)

method	Web	corel	Web-corel
histogram	28.9 (33.4)	46.8	14.9 (21.7)
EMD	37.2 (43.3)	61.4	18.2 (24.8)
IRM	33.0 (38.9)	66.3	19.5 (23.0)

M. Ishizuka and A. Sattar (Eds.): PRICAI 2002, LNAI 2417, pp. 613–614, 2002.

References

1. Yanai, K., Shindo, M., Noshita, K.: A fast image-gathering system on WWW using a PC cluster. In: Inter. Conf. on Web Intelligence (LNAI 2198). (2001) 324–334
2. Swain, M.J., Ballard, D.H.: Color indexing. International Journal of Computer Vision **7** (1991) 11–32
3. Rubner, Y., Tomasi, C., Guibas, L.J.: The earth mover's distance as a metric for image retrieval. International Journal of Computer Vision **40** (2000) 99–121
4. Wang, J.Z., Li, J., Wiederhold, G.: SIMPLIcity: semantics-sensitive integrated matching for picture libraries. IEEE Trans. on PAMI **23** (2001) 947–963

Real-Time Face Detection and Tracking Using PCA and NN

Chang-Woo Lee[1], Yeon-Chul Lee[1], Sang-Yong Bak[2], and Hang-Joon Kim[1]

[1]Dept. of computer engineering, Kyungpook National University, 702-701,
1370, Sangyuk-dong, Buk-gu, Daegu, Korea
{cwlee, yclee, kimhj}@ailab.knu.ac.kr
[2]LG Electronics Inc., 730-702, 229, Gongdan-dong, Gumi, Korea.
baksang@lge.com

Abstract. This paper proposes a real-time face detection and tracking method using principal component analysis (PCA) and neural network (NN). To improve the accuracy of the face detection, multiple methods are combined. For tracking a face, the PCA technique is used. The analysis of a set of images captured during the experiment revealed that the correct rate of face verification was an average 94.5%.

1   The Proposed Method

As shown in Fig. 1, the proposed method operates in two main steps: face detection and face tracking. In the first step, the skin color model and motion information are used to detect candidate face regions after the lighting condition is compensated. To verify the candidate face region is indeed the face image, the regions are projected into the trained eigenspace. This feature vector is directly fed into the NN. Finally we can determine the candidate face region is indeed the face or not. For tracking a face, the distance measure in the eigenspace between previously tracked face and candidate face regions newly detected is used. Camera control for the face tracking is done in such a way that the detected face region is kept on the center of the screen by controlling the pan/tilt platform.

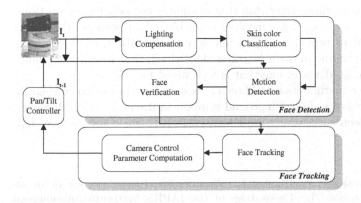

Fig. 1. Block diagram of the proposed method

M. Ishizuka and A. Sattar (Eds.): PRICAI 2002, LNAI 2417, p. 615, 2002.
© Springer-Verlag Berlin Heidelberg 2002

A Wrapper-Based Approach to Robot Learning Concepts from Images

Nicolas Bredeche[1,2], Jean-Daniel Zucker[1], and Yann Chevaleyre[1]

[1] LIP6-CNRS, UPMC, Paris, France
[2] LIMSI-CNRS, AMI, University Paris XI, Orsay, France
{nicolas.bredeche, jean-daniel.zucker, yann.chevaleyre}@lip6.fr

This work is about the building of a lexicon of shared symbols between a PI-ONEER2DX mobile robot and its human interlocutors. This lexicon contains words corresponding to objects seen in the environment. The difficulty relies in grounding these symbols with the actual data provided by the camera of the robot with respect to the learning scenario shown in figure 1.

| taking snapshots | asking a supervisor to label the snapshots | anchoring process | naming objects |

Fig. 1. Toward lexicon anchoring

In order to find a good representation of the perceptions so that grounding symbols is possible, we have built a system called PLIC that acts as a wrapper in order to automatically reformulate the data from the video camera along with a supervised machine learning algorithm that evaluates the new representations. The abstraction operators used are inspired from biological perceptual learning techniques that tend to provide a significant way to describe the environment. This approach is in the line of meta-learning algorithms, that iteratively change representations so as to discover one that is well fitted for the task.

Results from the experiments have shown that such an adaptation can significantly increase the robot's ability to ground symbols in the real world. Moreover, this approach has been successfully implemented in real world robots (see [1]).

References

1. Bredeche, N., Chevaleyre, Y., Hugues, L.: Wrapper for object detection in an autonomous mobile robot. In: Proceedings of the IAPR's Sixteenth International Conference on Pattern Recognition (ICPR2002), Quebec City, Canada. (2002)

M. Ishizuka and A. Sattar (Eds.): PRICAI 2002, LNAI 2417, p. 616, 2002.
© Springer-Verlag Berlin Heidelberg 2002

An Effective HMM-Based Intrusion Detection System with Privilege Change Event Modeling*

Hyuk-Jang Park and Sung-Bae Cho

Department of Computer Science, Yonsei University

Seoul 120-749, Korea

{twinkler, sbcho}@candy.yonsei.ac.kr

Abstract. Anomaly detection techniques have been devised to address the limitations of misuse detection approach for intrusion detection. They can abstract information about the normal behaviors of a system and detect attacks regardless of whether or not the system has observed them before. However, they have an inherent difficulty to deal with large volume of audit data to model the normal behaviors. Calculations for each trace in each pass through the training data take $O(TS^2)$, where T is the length of the trace in system calls, and S is the number of state in hidden Markov model.

In this paper, we propose an effective intrusion detection system (IDS) that improves the modeling time and performance with only considering the events of privilege flows based on the domain knowledge of attacks. Proposed privilege change model is evaluated with fixed sequences from BSM data on the situation where transitions between UID and EUID occur. A detailed analysis of the attacks reveals that acquiring root privilege can happen not only with user's change but also with group's change. To address both cases, the system exploits privilege flows of both user and group.

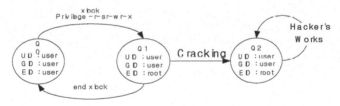

Fig. 1. An example of privilege change by buffer overflow attack

In this experiment, the performance is evaluated with 19 times u2r intrusions. Using privilege change data is approximately 250 times faster and produces 132 times decrease in quantity of sequences than using all data. Also, modeling privilege change data has less error than conventional modeling. With sufficiently large number of training data, it might show better performance and reduce computational costs. Table 1 shows the intrusion detection rate and false-positive error rate for each model.

---

* This work is supported in part by the Ministry of Information & Communication of Korea.

M. Ishizuka and A. Sattar (Eds.): PRICAI 2002, LNAI 2417, pp. 617-618, 2002.

Table 1. The anomaly detection rate for each modeling method

Modeling	State/sequence	Threshold	Sequence	Timestamp	Detection rate	F-P error
All data	5/20	-92.4	767218	5 h 7m	100%	4.234%
	15/30	-118.3	767208	6h 29m	100%	12.426%
Privilege	5/20	-53.8	5950	26.3 sec	100%	6.707%
flows data	10/30	-81.2	5792	57.5 sec	100%	0.602%

A Method on Improving of Enrolling Speed for the MLP-Based Speaker Verification System through Reducing Learning Data

Tae-Seung Lee[1], Ho-Jin Choi[2], Seung-Hoe Choi[3], and Byong-Won Hwang[1]

[1] School of Electronics, Telecommunication and Computer Engineering, Hankuk Aviation University, Seoul, Korea
[2] School of Engineering, Information and Communications University, Taejon, Korea
[3] General Studies, Hankuk Aviation University, Seoul, Korea
thestaff@hitel.net, hjchoi@icu.ac.kr,
{shchoi,bwhwang}@mail.hangkong.ac.kr,

The MLP-based speaker verification system can have to provide fast speaker enrollment process as well as high speaker recognition rate and quick speaker verification process. The multilayer perceptron (MLP) presents higher pattern recognition rate without assuming underlying density distribution against the existing parametric pattern recognition methods, and enables rapid operation by sharing internal parameters between various models. Among a variety of pattern recognition problems, speaker verification is the area to utilize effectively such advantages of the MLP. The learning of the MLP based on the error backpropagation (EBP), however, needs relatively long learning time. This shortcoming leads possibility to prolong unduly the speaker enrollment that is conducted in online in the speaker verification system based on the MLP. This paper proposes a method that reduces the background speakers indispensable for enrolling a speaker in order to shorten the speaker enrollment time affecting the usability of the speaker verification system based on the MLP. This method adopts the cohort speakers method [1] proposed in the existing parametric methods into MLP learning. The cohort speakers method selects the limited background speakers phonetically similar to an enrolling speaker on speaker enrollment process and reduces the data required to process speaker verification so that it can cut speaker verification time. On the other hand, the proposed method focuses on the data reduction for learning the MLP through the same approach. This paper calls the method as discriminative cohort speakers (DCS). To measure the performance of the DCS, an experiment is conducted that uses a MLP-based speaker verification system and Korean continuously spoken four digits database. The system evaluates speaker identity by the continuant phonemes. The whole number of background speakers is 29. In the result of the experiment, the minimum number of the speakers in cohort with no error rate increasing is 26 and the number with 0.19% increasing is 14. The time to enroll speakers is down by 4.5% and 35.4%, respectively for the above cases. As a result, this paper concludes that the DCS can enhance efficiently the speaker enrolling speed of the MLP-based speaker verification system by restricting background speakers and decreasing data to learn the MLP.

References

1. Higgins, A. L. et al.: Speaker Verification Using Randomized Phrase Prompting. Digital Signal Processing. 1 (1991) 89-106

M. Ishizuka and A. Sattar (Eds.): PRICAI 2002, LNAI 2417, p. 619, 2002.
© Springer-Verlag Berlin Heidelberg 2002

Syntactic Representations of Semantic Merging Operations

Thomas Meyer[1], Aditya Ghose[2], and Samir Chopra[3]

[1] Department of Computer Science, University of Pretoria,
Pretoria 0002, South Africa
tmeyer@cs.up.ac.za
[2] Decision Systems Laboratory
School of Information Technology and Computer Science
University of Wollongong, Wollongong, NSW 2522, Australia
aditya@uow.edu.au
[3] Knowledge Systems Group, School of Computer Science and Engineering
University of New South Wales, Sydney, NSW 2052, Australia
schopra@cse.unsw.edu.au

Recent research suggests the usefulness of conducting information merging on the level of epistemic states as an alternative to the usual approach of knowledge base merging [1,2]. We take an epistemic state to be an assignment of natural numbers to the classical valuations of the finite propositional logic under consideration. In this paper we investigate various syntactic representations of epistemic states and show how these can be employed to represent merging operations syntactically. These include *ranked knowledge bases* and their normals forms, as well as different versions of structures referred to as *partitions*. We show that there are efficient methods for transformaing any ranked knowledge base into an equivalent partition, and vice versa. We provide a uniform method for obtaining syntactic representations, in terms of partitions, of a large class of semantic merging operations. This method is linear in n times the product of the sizes of the n partitions used to represent the epistemic states to be merged. For the class of *lexicographic* merging operations, it can be proved that this method represents the best we can do in terms of computational complexity. We also show that the structure of some semantic merging operations can be exploited to obtain syntactic representations for them which can be determined much more efficiently than the uniform method provided. To be able to use these efficient methods, it is necessary to use ranked knowledge bases as the syntactic representational form.

References

1. Salem Benferhat, Didier Dubois, Souhila Kaci, and Henri Prade. Encoding information in possibilistic logic: A general framework for rational syntactic merging. In Werner Horn, editor, *ECAI 2000. 14th European Conference on Artificial Intelligence*, Amsterdam, 2000. IOS Press.
2. Thomas Meyer. On the semantics of combination operations. *Journal of Applied Non-Classical Logics*, 11(1-2):59–84, 2001.

M. Ishizuka and A. Sattar (Eds.): PRICAI 2002, LNAI 2417, p. 620, 2002.
© Springer-Verlag Berlin Heidelberg 2002

Author Index

Aizawa, Akiko 404
Akita, Masashi 612
Al-Jadir, Lina 602
Allison, Lloyd 244
Araki, Masahiro 612
Arif, M. 295

Baillie, Penny 581
Bak, Sang-Yong 615
Baldock, Richard 492
Bang, Jung-Wook 385
Beydoun, Ghassan 602
Bredeche, Nicolas 616
Buller, Andrzej 90
Burger, Albert 492
Byun, Hyeran 532

Cambier, Christophe 592
Cardon, Alain 592
Chan, Keith C. 512
Chang, Jeong-Ho 434, 607
Chao, Yuyan 29
Cheng, Jingde 39
Cheoi, Kyungjoo 315
Chevaleyre, Yann 616
Cho, Kenta 591
Cho, Sung-Bae 599, 617
Choi, Ho-Jin 275, 619
Choi, Jin-woo 522
Choi, Joongmin 472
Choi, Key-Sun 610
Choi, Seung-Hoe 619
Chopra, Samir 70, 620
Chung, Seung-Woo 375

Dang, Trang 594
Dean, Thomas 80
Descamps, Sylvain 571
Diaconescu, Stefan 605
Doh, Kyoung-Goo 472
Dowe, David L. 244

Endo, Ken 325

Fitzgibbon, Leigh J. 244
Foo, Norman Y. 7, 49, 60, 70
Fujiwara, Keisei 228

Ghédira, Khaled 97
Ghose, Aditya 620
Gillies, Duncan 385

Ha, Eunyong 463
Hassine, Ahlem Ben 97
Hayashi, Hisashi 591
He, Lifeng 29
Hexmoor, Henry 365
Hori, Koichi 305
Hovy, Eduard 6
Hsu, Chun-Nan 395
Huang, Hung-Ju 395
Huang, Zhuo 108
Hwang, Byong-Won 275, 619
Hwang, Kyu-Baek 375

Inooka, H. 295
Inoue, Hirotaka 285
Ishihara, T. 295
Ishizaki, Shun 606
Ishizuka, Mitsuru 118, 571, 609
Ito, Akira 188
Itoh, Hidenori 29
Itsuki, Noda 128
Iwashita, Shino 608
Iwazume, Michiaki 608
Izumi, Noriaki 597

Kanbara, Tomoki 482
Kang, Byeong Ho 444
Karasavvas, Konstantinos 492
Kawana, Norimitsu 29
Kay, Judy 444
Kijsirikul, Boonserm 158
Kim, Eunju 532
Kim, Hang-Joon 615
Kim, Jae-Ho 610
Kim, Jungsun 472
Kim, Kee-Eung 80
Kim, Kyung-Joong 599
Kim, Sang-Bum 414
Kim, Sung-Dong 454
Kim, Yuseop 434, 607

Kitakami, Hajime 482
Kitano, Hiroaki 325, 552
Ko, Jaepil 532
Kobayashi, Ichiro 608
Konda, Taro 198, 208
Ku, Sebon 463
Kurahashi, Setsuya 596
Kuroki, Susumu 482
Kwag, Young-Kil 275
Kwok, Rex B.H. 604
Kyburg, Henry E. 598

Laddaga, Robert 542
Lao, Yizhi 345
Lee, Bogju 463
Lee, Chang-Woo 615
Lee, Hyunjin 169
Lee, Jae Won 375, 434, 454
Lee, Kang Hyuk 444
Lee, Kwanyong 611
Lee, Kyung-Soon 610
Lee, Soonkyu 563
Lee, Tae-Seung 275, 619
Lee, Yeon-Chul 615
Lee, Yillbyung 169, 315
Leong, Hon Wai 345
Lim, Heui-Seok 414
Lin, Dekang 424
Lukose, Dickson 581

Maeno, Takashi 325
Matsuda, Takashi 255
Matsumura, Naohiro 609
Matsuo, Yutaka 118
Meknavin, Surapant 158
Meyer, Thomas 620
Mohd, Noor Md Sap 238
Mori, Yasuma 482
Motoda, Hiroshi 218, 228, 255

Nakadai, Kazuhiro 552
Nakamura, Tsuyoshi 29
Nakatsu, Ryohei 19
Narihisa, Hiroyuki 285
Niimi, Yasuhisa 612
Nishimoto, Takuya 612

Oehlmann, Ruediger 595
Ohsawa, Yukio 609
Ohsuga, Akihiko 591

Okuno, Hiroshi G. 552
Olej, Vladimír 600

Pantel, Patrick 424
Park, Hyeyoung 169, 611
Park, Hyuk-Jang 617
Pazzani, Michael J. 1
Piron, Marie 592
Prendinger, Helmut 571

Quek, C. 178, 265, 601

Reyes, Rhodora L. 502
Rim, Hae-Chang 414
Rist, Thomas 9
Robertson, Paul 542
Rosebrock, Uwe 444

Sarjon, Defit 238
Shakshuki, Elhadi 594
Sison, Raymund C. 502
Sugeno, Michio 608
Sugimoto, Toru 608
Świątnicki, Zbigniew 600

Tagawa, Takahiro 39
Tang, Tiffany Y. 512
Taniguchi, Ken 596
Teng, Choh Man 598
Tensyo, Shinjiro 208
Terano, Takao 596
Togami, Masahito 305
Tung, W.L. 178, 265, 601

Uchiyama, Kiyoko 606
Ueda, Kiyoshi 612
Uliniansyah, Mohammad Teduh 606
Ussivakul, Nitiwut 158

Valk, Jeroen 335
Vo, Quoc Bao 49

Wada, Takuya 218
Washio, Takashi 218, 228, 255
Winoto, Pinata 148
Witteveen, Cees 335
Wobcke, Wayne 138
Woo, Chong-woo 522

Yairi, Takehisa 305
Yamaguchi, Takahira 597

Yamaguchi, Tomohiro   198, 208
Yamasaki, Funinori   325
Yamazaki, Yukiko   482
Yanai, Keiji   613
Yang, Jaeyoung   472
Yook, DongSuk   414, 563
Yoshida, Tetsuya   218, 228, 255

Zhang, Byoung-Tak   375, 434, 607

Zhang, Chengqi   355
Zhang, Dongmo   70
Zhang, Jian   108
Zhang, Wenhui   108
Zhang, Xin   365
Zhang, Yan   60
Zhang, Zili   355
Zucker, Jean-Daniel   616

Lecture Notes in Artificial Intelligence (LNAI)

Vol. 2258: P. Brazdil, A. Jorge (Eds.), Progress in Artificial Intelligence. Proceedings, 2001. XII, 418 pages. 2001.

Vol. 2275: N.R. Pal, M. Sugeno (Eds.), Advances in Soft Computing – AFSS 2002. Proceedings, 2002. XVI, 536 pages. 2002.

Vol. 2281: S. Arikawa, A. Shinohara (Eds.), Progress in Discovery Science. XIV, 684 pages. 2002.

Vol. 2293: J. Renz, Qualitative Spatial Reasoning with Topological Information. XVI, 207 pages. 2002.

Vol. 2296: B. Dunin-Kęplicz, E. Nawarecki (Eds.), From Theory to Practice in Multi-Agent Systems. Proceedings, 2001. IX, 341 pages. 2002.

Vol. 2298: I. Wachsmuth, T. Sowa (Eds.), Gesture and Language in Human-Computer Interaction. Proceedings, 2001. XI, 323 pages.

Vol. 2302: C. Schulte, Programming Constraint Services. XII, 176 pages. 2002.

Vol. 2307: C. Zhang, S. Zhang, Association Rule Mining. XII, 238 pages. 2002.

Vol. 2308: I.P. Vlahavas, C.D. Spyropoulos (Eds.), Methods and Applications of Artificial Intelligence. Proceedings, 2002. XIV, 514 pages. 2002.

Vol. 2309: A. Armando (Ed.), Frontiers of Combining Systems. Proceedings, 2002. VIII, 255 pages. 2002.

Vol. 2313: C.A. Coello Coello, A. de Albornoz, L.E. Sucar, O.Cairó Battistutti (Eds.), MICAI 2002: Advances in Artificial Intelligence. Proceedings, 2002. XIII, 548 pages. 2002.

Vol. 2317: M. Hegarty, B. Meyer, N. Hari Narayanan (Eds.), Diagrammatic Representation and Inference. Proceedings, 2002. XIV, 362 pages. 2002.

Vol. 2321: P.L. Lanzi, W. Stolzmann, S.W. Wilson (Eds.), Advances in Learning Classifier Systems. Proceedings, 2002. VIII, 231 pages. 2002.

Vol. 2322: V. Mařík, O. Štěpánková, H. Krautwurmová, M. Luck (Eds.), Multi-Agent Systems and Applications II. Proceedings, 2001. XII, 377 pages. 2002.

Vol. 2333: J.-J.Ch. Meyer, M. Tambe (Eds.), Intelligent Agents VIII. Revised Papers, 2001. XI, 461 pages. 2001.

Vol. 2336: M.-S. Chen, P.S. Yu, B. Liu (Eds.), Advances in Knowledge Discovery and Data Mining. Proceedings, 2002. XIII, 568 pages. 2002.

Vol. 2338: R. Cohen, B. Spencer (Eds.), Advances in Artificial Intelligence. Proceedings, 2002. XII, 373 pages. 2002.

Vol. 2356: R. Kohavi, B.M. Masand, M. Spiliopoulou, J. Srivastava (Eds.), WEBKDD 2002 – Mining Web Log Data Across All Customers Touch Points. Proceedings, 2002. XI, 167 pages. 2002.

Vol. 2358: T. Hendtlass, M. Ali (Eds.), Developments in Applied Artificial Intelligence. Proceedings, 2002 XIII, 833 pages. 2002.

Vol. 2366: M.-S. Hacid, Z.W. Raś, D.A. Zighed, Y. Kodratoff (Eds.), Foundations of Intelligent Systems. Proceedings, 2002. XII, 614 pages. 2002.

Vol. 2371: S. Koenig, R.C. Holte (Eds.), Abstraction, Reformulation, and Approximation. Proceedings, 2002. XI, 349 pages. 2002.

Vol. 2375: J. Kivinen, R.H. Sloan (Eds.), Computational Learning Theory. Proceedings, 2002. XI, 397 pages. 2002.

Vol. 2377: A. Birk, S. Coradeschi, T. Satoshi (Eds.), RoboCup 2001: Robot Soccer World Cup V. XIX, 763 pages. 2002.

Vol. 2381: U. Egly, C.G. Fermüller (Eds.), Automated Reasoning with Analytic Tableaux and Related Methods. Proceedings, 2002. X, 341 pages. 2002 .

Vol. 2385: J. Calmet, B. Benhamou, O. Caprotti, L. Henocque, V. Sorge (Eds.), Artificial Intelligence, Automated Reasoning, and Symbolic Computation. Proceedings, 2002. XI, 343 pages. 2002.

Vol. 2389: E. Ranchhod, N.J. Mamede (Eds.), Advances in Natural Language Processing. Proceedings, 2002. XII, 275 pages. 2002.

Vol. 2392: A. Voronkov (Ed.), Automated Deduction – CADE-18. Proceedings, 2002. XII, 534 pages. 2002.

Vol. 2393: U. Priss, D. Corbett, G. Angelova (Eds.), Conceptual Structures: Integration and Interfaces. Proceedings, 2002. XI, 397 pages. 2002.

Vol. 2403: Mark d'Inverno, M. Luck, M. Fisher, C. Preist (Eds.), Foundations and Applications of Multi-Agent Systems. Proceedings, 1996-2000. X, 261 pages. 2002.

Vol. 2407: A.C. Kakas, F. Sadri (Eds.), Computational Logic: Logic Programming and Beyond. Part I. XII, 678 pages. 2002.

Vol. 2408: A.C. Kakas, F. Sadri (Eds.), Computational Logic: Logic Programming and Beyond. Part II. XII, 628 pages. 2002.

Vol. 2413: K. Kuwabara, J. Lee (Eds.), Intelligent Agents and Multi-Agent Systems. Proceedings, 2002. X, 221 pages. 2002.

Vol. 2417: M. Ishizuka, A. Sattar (Eds.), PRICAI 2002: Trends in Artificial Intelligence. Proceedings, 2002. XX, 623 pages. 2002.

Vol. 2430: T. Elomaa, H. Mannila, H. Toivonen (Eds.), Machine Learning: ECML 2002. Proceedings, 2002. XIII, 532 pages. 2002.

Vol. 2431: T. Elomaa, H. Mannila, H. Toivonen (Eds.), Principles of Data Mining and Knowledge Discovery. Proceedings, 2002. XIV, 514 pages. 2002.

Lecture Notes in Computer Science

Vol. 2389: E. Ranchhod, N.J. Mamede (Eds.), Advances in Natural Language Processing. Proceedings, 2002. XII, 275 pages. 2002. (Subseries LNAI).

Vol. 2391: L.-H. Eriksson, P.A. Lindsay (Eds.), FME 2002: Formal Methods – Getting IT Right. Proceedings, 2002. XI, 625 pages. 2002.

Vol. 2392: A. Voronkov (Ed.), Automated Deduction – CADE-18. Proceedings, 2002. XII, 534 pages. 2002. (Subseries LNAI).

Vol. 2393: U. Priss, D. Corbett, G. Angelova (Eds.), Conceptual Structures: Integration and Interfaces. Proceedings, 2002. XI, 397 pages. 2002. (Subseries LNAI).

Vol. 2395: G. Barthe, P. Dybjer, L. Pinto, J. Saraiva (Eds.), Applied Semantics. IX, 537 pages. 2002.

Vol. 2396: T. Caelli, A. Amin, R.P.W. Duin, M. Kamel, D. de Ridder (Eds.), Structural, Syntactic, and Statistical Pattern Recognition. Proceedings, 2002. XVI, 863 pages. 2002.

Vol. 2398: K. Miesenberger, J. Klaus, W. Zagler (Eds.), Computers Helping People with Special Needs. Proceedings, 2002. XXII, 794 pages. 2002.

Vol. 2399: H. Hermanns, R. Segala (Eds.), Process Algebra and Probabilistic Methods. Proceedings, 2002. X, 215 pages. 2002.

Vol. 2401: P.J. Stuckey (Ed.), Logic Programming. Proceedings, 2002. XI, 486 pages. 2002.

Vol. 2402: W. Chang (Ed.), Advanced Internet Services and Applications. Proceedings, 2002. XI, 307 pages. 2002.

Vol. 2403: Mark d'Inverno, M. Luck, M. Fisher, C. Preist (Eds.), Foundations and Applications of Multi-Agent Systems. Proceedings, 1996-2000. X, 261 pages. 2002. (Subseries LNAI).

Vol. 2404: E. Brinksma, K.G. Larsen (Eds.), Computer Aided Verification. Proceedings, 2002. XIII, 626 pages. 2002.

Vol. 2405: B. Eaglestone, S. North, A. Poulovassilis (Eds.), Advances in Databases. Proceedings, 2002. XII, 199 pages. 2002.

Vol. 2406: C.A. Peters, M. Braschler, J. Gonzalo, M. Kluck (Eds.), Evaluation of Cross-Language Information Retrieval Systems. Proceedings, 2001. X, 601 pages. 2002.

Vol. 2407: A.C. Kakas, F. Sadri (Eds.), Computational Logic: Logic Programming and Beyond. Part I. XII, 678 pages. 2002. (Subseries LNAI).

Vol. 2408: A.C. Kakas, F. Sadri (Eds.), Computational Logic: Logic Programming and Beyond. Part II. XII, 628 pages. 2002. (Subseries LNAI).

Vol. 2409: D.M. Mount, C. Stein (Eds.), Algorithm Engineering and Experiments. Proceedings, 2002. VIII, 207 pages. 2002.

Vol. 2410: V.A. Carreño, C. Muñoz, S. Tahar (Eds.), Theorem Proving in Higher Order Logics. Proceedings, 2002. X, 349 pages. 2002.

Vol. 2412: H. Yin, N. Allinson, R. Freeman, J. Keane, S. Hubbard (Eds.), Intelligent Data Engineering and Automated Learning – IDEAL 2002. Proceedings, 2002. XV, 597 pages. 2002.

Vol. 2413: K. Kuwabara, J. Lee (Eds.), Intelligent Agents and Multi-Agent Systems. Proceedings, 2002. X, 221 pages. 2002. (Subseries LNAI).

Vol. 2414: F. Mattern, M. Naghshineh (Eds.), Pervasive Computing. Proceedings, 2002. XI, 298 pages. 2002.

Vol. 2415: J. Dorronsoro (Ed.), Artificial Neural Networks – ICANN 2002. Proceedings, 2002. XXVIII, 1382 pages. 2002.

Vol. 2417: M. Ishizuka, A. Sattar (Eds.), PRICAI 2002: Trends in Artificial Intelligence. Proceedings, 2002. XX, 623 pages. 2002. (Subseries LNAI).

Vol. 2418: D. Wells, L. Williams (Eds.), Extreme Programming and Agile Methods – XP/Agile Universe 2002. Proceedings, 2002. XII, 292 pages. 2002.

Vol. 2419: X. Meng, J. Su, Y. Wang (Eds.), Advances in Web-Age Information Management. Proceedings, 2002. XV, 446 pages. 2002.

Vol. 2420: K. Diks, W. Rytter (Eds.), Mathematical Foundations of Computer Science 2002. Proceedings, 2002. XII, 652 pages. 2002.

Vol. 2421: L. Brim, P. Jančar, M. Křetínský, A. Kučera (Eds.), CONCUR 2002 – Concurrency Theory. Proceedings, 2002. XII, 611 pages. 2002.

Vol. 2423: D. Lopresti, J. Hu, R. Kashi (Eds.), Document Analysis Systems V. Proceedings, 2002. XIII, 570 pages. 2002.

Vol. 2430: T. Elomaa, H. Mannila, H. Toivonen (Eds.), Machine Learning: ECML 2002. Proceedings, 2002. XIII, 532 pages. 2002. (Subseries LNAI).

Vol. 2431: T. Elomaa, H. Mannila, H. Toivonen (Eds.), Principles of Data Mining and Knowledge Discovery. Proceedings, 2002. XIV, 514 pages. 2002. (Subseries LNAI).

Vol. 2436: J. Fong, R.C.T. Cheung, H.V. Leong, Q. Li (Eds.), Advances in Web-Based Learning. Proceedings, 2002. XIII, 434 pages. 2002.

Vol. 2440: J.M. Haake, J.A. Pino (Eds.), Groupware – CRIWG 2002. Proceedings, 2002. XII, 285 pages. 2002.

Vol. 2442: M. Yung (Ed.), Advances in Cryptology – CRYPTO 2002. Proceedings, 2002. XIV, 627 pages. 2002.

Vol. 2444: A. Buchmann, F. Casati, L. Fiege, M.-C. Hsu, M.-C. Shan (Eds.), Technologies for E-Services. Proceedings, 2002. X, 171 pages. 2002.